ECONOMIC GROWTH A...
BALANCE-OF-PAYMENT...

Also by A. P. Thirlwall

BALANCE-OF-PAYMENTS THEORY AND THE UNITED
   KINGDOM EXPERIENCE (*with Heather Gibson*)
DEINDUSTRIALISATION (*with S. Bazen*)
EUROPEAN FACTOR MOBILITY (*editor with Ian Gordon*)
FINANCING ECONOMIC DEVELOPMENT
GROWTH AND DEVELOPMENT
INFLATION, SAVING AND GROWTH IN
   DEVELOPING ECONOMIES
KEYNES AND ECONOMIC DEVELOPMENT (*editor*)
KEYNES AND INTERNATIONAL MONETARY RELATIONS
   (*editor*)
KEYNES AND *LAISSEZ-FAIRE* (*editor*)
KEYNES AND THE BLOOMSBURY GROUP
   (*editor with Derek Crabtree*)
KEYNES AND THE ROLE OF THE STATE
   (*editor with Derek Crabtree*)
KEYNES AS A POLICY ADVISER (*editor*)
REGIONAL GROWTH AND UNEMPLOYMENT IN THE UK
   (*with R. Dixon*)
THE PERFORMANCE OF THE PACIFIC ISLAND ECONOMIES

Economic Growth and the Balance-of-Payments Constraint

J. S. L. McCombie
*Fellow of Downing
College, Cambridge*

and

A. P. Thirlwall
*Professor of Applied Economics
University of Kent at Canterbury*

M
St. Martin's Press

First published in Great Britain 1994 by
THE MACMILLAN PRESS LTD
Houndmills, Basingstoke, Hampshire RG21 2XS
and London
Companies and representatives
throughout the world

A catalogue record for this book is available
from the British Library.

ISBN 0–333–48424–X hardcover
ISBN 0–333–60112–2 paperback

Printed in Great Britain by
Mackays of Chatham PLC
Chatham, Kent

First published in the United States of America 1994 by
Scholarly and Reference Division,
ST. MARTIN'S PRESS, INC.,
175 Fifth Avenue,
New York, N.Y. 10010

ISBN 0–312–10183–X

Library of Congress Cataloging-in-Publication Data
McCombie, J. S. L.
Economic growth and the balance-of-payments constraint / J. S. L.
McCombie and A. P. Thirlwall.
p.   cm.
ISBN 0–312–10183–X
1. Balance of payments.   2. Economic development.   I. Thirlwall,
A. P.   II. Title.
HG3882.M396   1994
338.9—dc20   93–1788
                                                    CIP

To
Jean, and Ian and Margaret McCombie
and to
Elizabeth

To
Sean, and Ian and Margaret McCombie
and to
Elizabeth

Contents

Contents

Acknowledgements

The authors and publishers wish to thank the following editors of journals for permission to use previously published material in: *Oxford Economic Papers*, *Regional Studies*, *Applied Economics*, *Journal of Post Keynesian Economics*, *Urban Studies* and *Banca Nazionale del Lavoro Quarterly Review*. The authors would also like to thank the many economists who have taken an interest in their work over the years, and particularly the stimulus and inspiration of the late Lord Kaldor, Professor Charles Kennedy and Dr Robert Dixon.

J.S.L.M.
A.P.T.

Introduction

This book is about how the balance of payments of a country (or region) affects its growth performance, both directly and indirectly. The current account of the balance of payments matters for three main reasons. First, if balance-of-payments weakness is caused by adverse long-run trends in the performance of exports and imports, this will have implications for real output and employment in the particular sectors of the economy affected. An obvious example is import penetration from abroad which will worsen the balance of payments and take custom away from domestic activities at the same time. In this sense the balance of payments has implications for the functioning of the real economy. Secondly, at the aggregate level, it can be stated as a truism that no country can grow faster in the long run than that rate consistent with balance-of-payments equilibrium on current account unless it can finance ever growing deficits. If this rate of output growth consistent with balance-of-payments equilibrium is below the rate achievable given the availability of domestic resources in the form of labour and the accumulation of capital, then the real economy will be depressed. In the short term, growing current account deficits may be financed by high interest rates, but this leads to the third reason why current account deficits matter. High interest rates favour the accumulation of monetary assets and discourage investment in productive assets such as plant and machinery and other physical capital on which the growth of output ultimately depends. In other words, the state of the current account balance is not simply a private matter among consenting agents concerning the intertemporal allocation of resources for consumption, but may have negative externalities on society at large.

The elementary theory behind the importance of exports and imports (or the balance of payments) for income determination analysis, can be stated as follows: A full employment equilibrium level of income and a full employment growth rate in an open economy with government activity requires that all planned leakages from the circular flow of income at full employment should be matched by an equivalent amount of expenditure. In the simple Keynesian model, planned investment must equal planned saving. In the more complex economy, there are the additional leakages of income into imports and taxation which must be matched. It was natural in the prevailing economic and intellectual conditions at the time Keynes was writing for Keynes to focus on the imbalance between saving and investment, particularly since the prevailing classical orthodoxy believed that savings and investment tended to equilibrium at full employment through adjustment in the rate of interest. In the open economy, however, an equally important consideration is the potential imbalance between export earnings and full employment imports, particularly since the power of governments to rectify this imbalance is in general much more limited than the power to fill a gap between investment and full employment saving. For many developed and less developed countries in the postwar period there is reason to believe that the ability to export to pay for full-employment imports has been a much more pervasive force determining the level of employment and growth experience. If exports fall short of full employment imports, either income and employment will fall automatically at a given terms of trade if other sectors of the economy are in overall balance; or if other sectors of the economy (such as the private and government sectors) are in overall deficit (with spending in excess of income), income may be forced to contract by government deflationary measures if a balance-of-payments deficit cannot be financed.

Professor Harry Johnson (1961) once said that the greatest disservice Keynes did to economics was to cast his model in a closed economy framework. He was probably right. There is a great deal of empirical evidence to suggest that it is impossible to understand the economic performance of nations without reference to their trading sector: that is, without reference to the performance of exports relative to the propensity to import. What is required is a simple model which brings to the fore the importance of the balance between exports and imports in both a static and dynamic context, in the same way that Keynesian theory, later extended by Harrod (1939), brought to the fore the importance of the balance between investment and saving for the determination of the equilibrium level and growth of income in the closed economy.

Before Harrod made Keynesian theory dynamic, he published an important book, *International Economics*, in 1933. There, Harrod puts forward the idea that the level of output of industrial countries is to be explained by the principle of the foreign trade multiplier which at the same time provides the mechanism for keeping the balance of payments in equilibrium. Kaldor (1979a) has argued that this proposition, underlying Keynes's principle of effective demand, never received the attention it deserved, although some economists working in the field of international trade theory (particularly P. Barrett Whale, 1937) recognised that Harrod's theory provided a far more convincing explanation of the workings of the nineteenth century gold standard than the classical theory which relied either on gold flows or on induced relative price changes. The Harrod trade multiplier predates the Keynesian investment multiplier and may be the more important mechanism in the real world for understanding not only the growth experience of countries, but also the structural transformation of developing economies and the ups and downs of the world economy at large. The international evidence to be presented later certainly suggests that the Harrod trade multiplier has strong explanatory power in many countries, and that differences in export performance and import behaviour are an important source of international growth rate differences. Kaldor, who was largely responsible for reviving the idea and significance of the Harrod trade multiplier, remarked (1975a): 'in some ways I think it may have been very unfortunate that the very success of Keynes's ideas in explaining unemployment in a depression – essentially a short period analysis – diverted attention from the foreign trade multiplier which over longer periods is a far more important principle for explaining the growth and rhythm of industrial development. For over longer periods, Ricardo's presumption that manufacturers and traders only save in order to invest, so that the amount and/or the proportion of savings would adapt to changes in the opportunities for, or profitability of, investment, seems to me more relevant than the Keynesian [alternative] assumption for explaining the true constraints on the growth of production and employment in the "capitalist" industrial sector.' Kaldor's discussion here relates to a model of the interaction between industry and agriculture, or between industrial production and primary production in the world economy, but the proposition is quite general that the gap between planned imports and exports at full employment may be a much more difficult and stubborn gap to fill in the long run than the gap between savings and investment, and therefore may act as a greater constraining influence on full employment output growth.[1]

---

[1] As a matter of historical interest, the Harrod (and Keynesian) multiplier was precisely anticipated by a Danish parliamentarian Julius Wulff in 1896 (see Hegeland, 1950, and Shackle, 1967), and by the Australian economist, L.F. Giblin in 1930 (see Giblin, 1930).

The UK's balance-of-payments position has worsened progress-ively since the Second World War in the sense that balance-of-payments equilibrium on current account has become increasingly incompatible with the maintenance of full employment and a reason-ably strong growth performance relative to other countries. In other words, the trade-offs between unemployment and the balance of payments and between growth and the balance of payments have worsened through time. In Table A we give the yearly figures for the balance of payments, unemployment and the growth of output at factor cost since 1950. The deteriorating trade-off between un-employment and the balance of payments is shown in Figure A.

It can be seen from the illustration that in the 1950s and 1960s, balance-of-payments equilibrium was compatible with less than 500,000 unemployed. In the 1970s, one million unemployed were required, and by the late 1980s the balance-of-payments position had deteriorated so markedly that today equilibrium requires at least three million unemployed.

As far as the economic growth/balance of payments trade-off is concerned, the relationship is shown in Figure B. In the years between 1951 and 1968, there is a fairly well defined and stable trade-off showing that the faster the rate of growth of output, the worse the balance of payments; and conversely, as growth slowed, the deficit improved and a surplus developed. The growth rate associated with balance-of-payments equilibrium in those years was approximately 3 per cent per annum (i.e., the point where the curve cuts the horizontal axis). From the observations for the years 1969 to 1971 there is some evidence that the devaluation of 1967 improved the balance of payments at a given growth rate, but only temporarily. This is in accordance with the theory that we shall outline in Chapter 3 that for the growth rate to be raised permanently, consistent with balance-of-payments equilibrium, currency depreciation needs to be continuous. Owing to the four-fold increase in the price of oil in December 1973, there was a dramatic worsening of the growth rate consistent with balance-of-payments equilibrium, followed in the early 1980s by an equally dramatic improvement in the *potential* growth rate consistent with payments equilibrium as the UK became a huge net exporter of oil.

Unfortunately, during the early 1980s, the increased growth poten-tial was not realised with the exchange rate kept high by a tight fiscal and monetary policy, so that between 1979 and 1981 investment contracted by 28 per cent and manufacturing output by 15 per cent.

Table A   The balance of payments on current account, the rate of
unemployment and the growth of GDP for the UK; 1951–91

| Year | Balance of payments on current account | | Unemployment (%) | Growth of GDP (% per annum) |
	(i) £ million current prices	(ii) As a percentage of GDP		
1951	−369	−2.94	1.2	3.6
1952	163	1.19	2.1	−0.1
1953	145	0.98	1.8	4.0
1954	117	0.75	1.5	4.3
1955	−155	−0.93	1.2	3.5
1956	208	1.15	1.3	1.0
1957	233	1.42	1.6	1.8
1958	350	1.75	2.2	0.1
1959	164	0.78	2.3	3.9
1960	−237	−1.06	1.7	5.7
1961	35	0.15	1.6	2.6
1962	143	0.57	2.1	1.2
1963	114	0.43	2.6	3.9
1964	−372	−1.30	1.7	4.6
1965	−77	−0.25	1.5	3.8
1966	128	0.40	1.6	1.6
1967	−281	−0.80	2.2	1.5
1968	−264	−0.70	2.4	3.6
1969	482	1.22	2.3	1.7
1970	821	1.90	2.2	1.8
1971	1114	2.28	3.0	1.4
1972	203	0.37	3.3	3.0
1973	−998	−1.58	2.3	5.9
1974	−3184	−4.39	3.3	−1.5
1975	−1524	−1.61	3.6	−1.9
1976	−772	−0.87	5.0	2.0
1977	−53	−0.14	5.4	2.8
1978	1123	0.63	5.2	3.4
1979	−453	−0.32	4.9	3.0
1980	2843	1.40	6.2	−2.9
1981	6748	3.06	9.4	−1.3
1982	4649	1.94	10.9	2.1
1983	3787	1.46	11.7	3.4
1984	1832	0.70	11.6	2.8
1985	2750	1.03	11.8	3.5
1986	−24	−0.01	11.8	3.0
1987	−4182	−1.01	10.5	4.7
1988	−15651	−3.74	8.4	4.7
1989	−19126	−4.37	6.3	1.2
1990	−17029	−4.24	5.9	0.5
1991	−6321	−1.80	8.1	−2.2

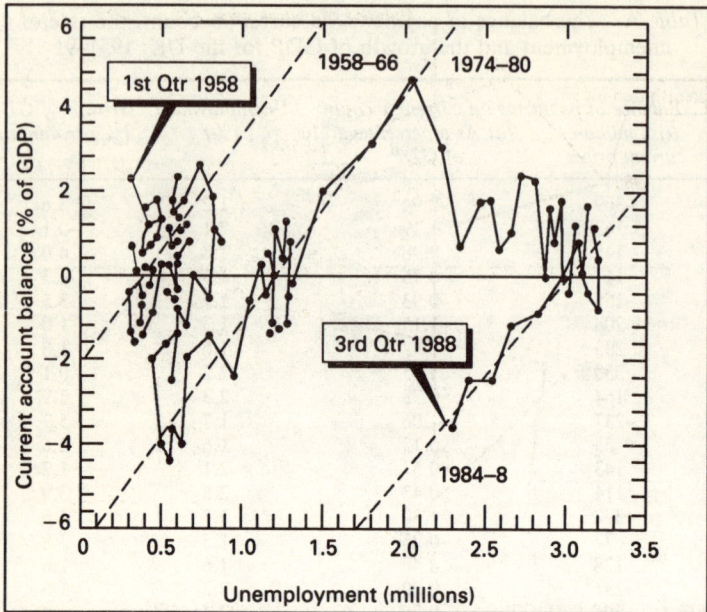

Figure A   The trade-off between unemployment and the balance of payments

Source: T. O'Shaughnessy, *Financial Times*, 1 February 1989.

The contraction in domestic demand during this period, together with the coming on-stream of the substantial oil revenues, gave the UK a substantial balance-of-payments surplus, so that there was a temptation to consider balance-of-payments problems a thing of the past. However, with the subsequent Lawson boom, a current account deficit of about one per cent of GDP re-emerged in 1987. This reached over 4 per cent in 1989 before the severe recession that commenced in 1990 began to reduce it. The UK is once again in the grip of a balance-of-payments constraint on the growth of output that plagued it throughout the 1950s, 1960s and 1970s.

We mean by the term 'balance-of-payments constraint' that a country's performance in external markets, and the response of the world financial markets to this performance, constrain the growth of the economy to a rate which is below that which internal conditions (such as the rate of unemployment and capacity utilisation) would warrant. In the 1950s and 1960s, this constraint expressed itself in the 'stop–go' policies that occurred when consumption-led booms were

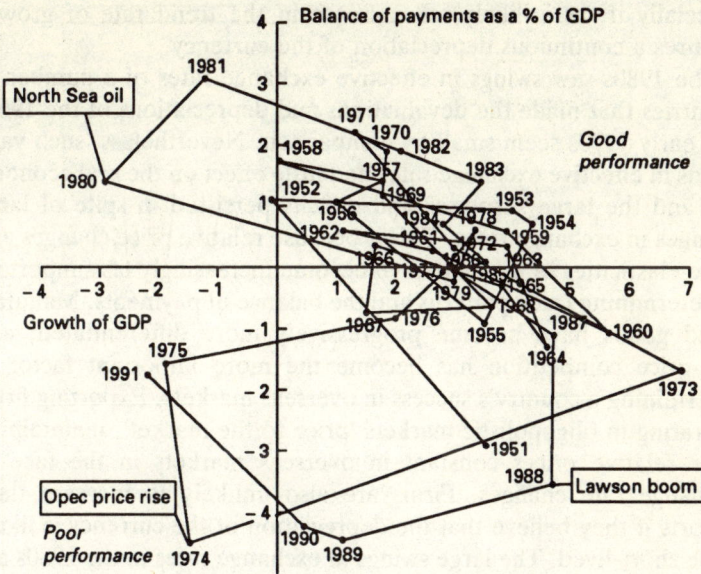

Figure B The economic growth/balance of payments trade-off 1951–91. Growth of GDP plotted against balance of payments as a percentage of GDP

brought to an abrupt end by balance-of-payments crises.

Consequently, the trend rate of growth was largely determined by the performance of exports and was arguably below the maximum growth of potential GDP. (This is not an exogenously-given datum but is partly a function of the actual growth rate. This is because a faster growth of output leads to a faster growth of productivity through the 'Verdoorn effect' which is caused by, *inter alia*, a higher rate of induced investment and of induced technical progress. See Chapter 2.)

For much of the early postwar period there was an extensive discussion as to whether or not the balance-of-payments constraint could be relieved by a flexible exchange rate. Recent experience suggests that while a devaluation can improve temporarily the balance of payments for any given growth rate, it seems ineffective in allowing the trend growth rate to increase. There are a number of reasons for this. In particular, it will be difficult for a nominal depreciation to be converted into a real depreciation if there is an inflationary feedback from higher import prices to higher domestic prices because of 'real wage resistance'. This is a distinct possibility especially if, as is likely, an increase in the trend rate of growth requires a continuous depreciation of the currency.

The 1980s saw swings in effective exchange rates of a number of countries that made the devaluations and depreciations of the 1960s and early 1970s seem small by comparison. Nevertheless, such variations in effective exchange rates had little effect on the real economies, and the large surpluses and deficits persisted in spite of large changes in exchange rates. This is because relative price changes and price elasticities of demand have become increasingly less important in determining trade patterns and the balance of payments. Manufactured goods have become progressively more differentiated, and non-price competition has become the more important factor in determining a country's success in overseas markets. Exporting firms operating in oligopolistic markets 'price to the market', maintaining their relative prices constant in overseas markets in the face of exchange rate changes. Firms are also unlikely to increase their exports if they believe that the depreciation of the currency is likely to be short-lived. The large swings in exchange rates in the 1980s are more likely to have been interpreted as the temporary consequences of short-term capital flows or speculative bubbles than were earlier smaller exchange rate changes.

David Turner (1988) of the Warwick University Macroeconomic Modelling Bureau has used the NIESR and LBS forecasting models to determine the UK's present growth rate consistent with balance-of-payments equilibrium. He found that 'on plausible assumptions, principally concerning how fast world trade is likely to expand, and on the further critical assumption that there is no change in the competitiveness of exports or imports, the LBS and NIESR models both suggest that UK growth can average no more than 1% per annum over the medium term if there is to be no further deterioration in the current account'. Turner also considered the extent to which the balance-of-payments equilibrium growth rate could be raised through a devaluation. He showed that, in order for the growth rate to be raised by approximately one percentage point to 2 per cent per annum for a five-year period, there would have to be a devaluation of sterling of between 20 and 30 per cent. (After five years, the price advantage obtained by the devaluation would have been largely eroded by the resulting domestic inflation.) A corollary to this is that for the trend growth rate to be raised above one per cent per annum, there would have to be a sustained depreciation of the exchange rate by several per cent per annum, which would be incompatible with any future membership of the Exchange Rate Mechanism of the European Monetary System.

An interesting question, not examined by Turner, is the extent to which the balance-of-payments constraint could be relaxed if there were some form of incomes policy that prevented domestic costs eventually increasing to offset the initial devaluation. We are not sanguine that this would provide a long-run solution to the UK's balance-of-payments problems. There is increasing evidence that it is non-price competition that matters in international trade, as we noted above. As Posner and Steer (1979) conclude in their survey of competition in international trade: 'Historically there is no doubt that non-price influences have dominated – the proportion of the total change they "explain" is an order of magnitude greater than the explanatory power of price competitiveness.' An improvement in price competitiveness may provide the UK with a temporary breathing space. But there is the danger that this would remove the incentive for British managers to improve non-price competitiveness and to develop the high technology products for which world demand is growing most rapidly, i.e. for those products for which there is a high world income elasticity of demand for exports. Moreover, to the extent that price elasticities are higher for the more basic homogenous commodities, a decline in the growth of relative unit labour costs may actually induce British manufacturers to trade down-market even more than at present – to produce those goods that are subject to increasing competition from the low cost newly industrialising countries.

The worsening trade-off between sustainable growth and the balance of payments is, in our view, a direct result of the policy of benign neglect towards both manufacturing industry and the state of the balance of payments. Manufacturing's crucial importance is that its output is potentially tradable, whereas a large proportion of service output is not. As we argue in this book, the UK's basic problem is that the income elasticity of demand for exports is very low, and the income elasticity of demand for manufactured imports is high. Both factors are symptoms of the same disease, *viz* weak non-price competition in terms of the characteristics of goods produced and traded: their quality, sophistication, reliability and marketing. It is a serious indictment of Mrs Thatcher's period of office that, far from an economic transformation having taken place which would allow faster growth on a sustainable basis, the sustainable growth rate has actually fallen because the balance-of-payments millstone weighs even more heavily. To improve Britain's growth prospects, which would also contribute to full employment with less inflationary pressure (at least from a lower exchange rate or higher interest rates), requires urgent attention to Britain's tradable goods sector. As the House of Lords Select Committee on Science and Technology declared recently: 'We must have a concerted campaign to promote greater esteem for manufacturing industry . . . Government must lead this campaign and proclaim the central position of manufacturing to our national prosperity . . . only a substantial increase in manufacturing output can correct the huge deficit on our balance of trade.' There is some evidence that the world income elasticity of demand for UK exports has risen since the early 1980s indicating that there may have been some improvement in the non-price competitiveness of British exports (Landesmann and Snell, 1989). If this is correct, it suggests that the UK's balance-of-payments equilibrium growth rate may have risen to about 2 per cent per annum. (Part of the increase in the income elasticity may have been due to exceptional boom conditions in the US where UK exports do particularly well.) On the other hand, Turner (1988) finds no evidence of an increase. Moreover, the balance-of-payments equilibrium growth rate will be reduced to the extent that the income elasticity of demand for imports may have also increased.

It has been argued by some commentators that there is no need to be concerned about the current account deficit since the level of overseas borrowing is now determined by the private sector on the basis of commercial calculations about the costs and benefits of such a course of action. The only difference between borrowing domestically and abroad is that a risk premium is attached to the latter because of the volatility of the exchange rate. Any excessive borrowing overseas will be self-correcting as the cost of borrowing rises with an increasing risk premium as the deficit grows. The problem with this argument is that the resulting adjustments are neither smooth nor gradual. As the overseas debt to GDP ratio increases, the world financial markets become increasingly nervous about a collapse in the exchange rate with the consequent capital losses; once the exchange rate starts to fall, speculative actions are likely to be destabilising, leading to a rapid fall in sterling with the possibility of a vicious inflationary-depreciation circle occurring. The use of high interest rates to defend sterling has an externality effect of pushing the domestic economy into recession with adverse effects on investment and employment, even when there is existing unemployment. The period of floating exchange rates from 1971 saw a number of spectacular examples of the balance of payments constraining domestic macroeconomic policies. The sterling crisis of 1976 comes readily to mind, when the Labour government's attempt to reduce unemployment in the face of excess capacity foundered on the balance-of-payments deficit and the collapse of sterling. Between early March and early June 1976, the effective value of sterling fell by a little over 12 per cent. Nevertheless, the government tried to keep interest rates low to encourage an increase in investment. As a result, sterling fell by a further 9 per cent between early-September and mid-November. The fall in the exchange rate eventually caused a *volte-face* in economic policy; the minimum lending rate was raised from 9 per cent in April to 15 per cent in November 1976 and severe cuts in the PSBR were agreed with the IMF. Other examples include the failure of the 'Mitterand experiment' in 1982 at boosting growth, and the problems of the Italian economy during 1980–1981. The 1980s have also shown that even the US is not immune from pressures engendered by a balance-of-payments deficit.

But what of the argument that if Britain were to join a European Monetary Union with a single currency, its balance-of-payments difficulties would vanish overnight? This is the view of Samuel Brittan who has argued (Economic Viewpoint, *The Financial Times*, 27 June 1991) that 'the ability to dump the balance-of-payments problem once and for all is among the greatest but least emphasised advantages of Emu'. With a single currency, it is certainly true that there can be no 'foreign' exchange problem in the normal sense and no exchange rate to defend, but there would still be imbalances between exports and imports which would not be naturally or easily compensated for by private lending and investment, or, for that matter, by inter-regional fiscal transfers in a federal political union. Those who say that balance-of-payments problems would disappear with a single currency draw the analogy with regions of a country using a single currency. Certainly, we do not talk about balance-of-payments difficulties of Sussex, Yorkshire or even of Scotland or Wales. But this does not mean that they do not exist. Any shortfall of a region's exports below its planned level of imports will manifest itself in slow growth, high unemployment and depressed economic conditions in general. In other words, it is the level of income (and the rate of growth of output) that adjusts to bring the regional, as well as the national, balance of payments back into equilibrium. This is inevitable unless the structure of industry can be altered in the depressed regions to increase the share of high technology industry for which the income elasticity of demand for exports is high; or price competitiveness is improved through subsidies or a fall in real wages; or the region receives capital inflows in the form of private sector lending or government fiscal transfers. While it is true, therefore, that the movement from a multiple currency system to a single currency does away with the outward manifestation of balance-of-payments difficulties because there is no exchange rate to defend and foreign currency reserves become irrelevant, the inward manifestation of balance-of-payments deficits remains.

In dismissing the importance of the balance of payments for the healthy functioning of the real economy, Samuel Brittan refers to the absurdity of treating trade between Sussex and Normandy entirely differently from trade between Sussex and the more distant Yorkshire when all three regions are supposed to be in a single market. But there are good reasons for treating trade between Sussex and Normandy differently from trade between Sussex and Yorkshire. This would be the case if Britain as a nation state feels a responsibility for the residents of Sussex that it does not feel for Normandy, and feels capable of dealing with disparities between Sussex and Yorkshire through its own internal fiscal system that could not be guaranteed if the viability of Sussex was being threatened by the superior competitiveness of Normandy within a monetary union using a single currency. In some circumstances, the exchange rate could be a useful, if limited, weapon for protecting the inhabitants of Sussex. (See, for example, Dow, 1986.) These issues lie at the heart of the debate over sovereignty currently preoccupying discussions over the nature of the European Community.

The issue of the balance of payments goes deeper, however, than the question of the exchange rate alone. The role of the balance of payments in accounting for inter-country growth rate differences has been ignored for too long by orthodox economic theory which in the pre-Keynesian days argued that the balance of payments, like everything else in the economic system, was self-adjusting through the price mechanism, and then in the 1950s analysed growth performance from the supply side with no reference to demand, using the concept of the aggregate production function (see Chapter 1).

The Keynesian revolution, paradoxically, did not help because Keynes's model was concerned with the short run and dealt for the most part with a closed economy. The emphasis on the imbalance between savings and investment diverted attention from the greater potential imbalance between exports and imports which in practice may be harder to rectify. A strong export performance relative to import demand is vital to the strength of aggregate demand in the system as a whole, single currency or not. Some economic sovereignty would be lost by movement to a single currency, but much more was lost when Britain joined the European Community in 1973. The ability to protect and encourage strategic industries has gone; the possibility of designing systems of managed trade to even out payments-imbalances has gone; the ability to protect against certain countries with persistent surpluses has been taken away, and differential taxes which discriminate in favour of the tradeable goods sector fall foul of the Treaty of Rome.

Britain's balance of payments is chronically weak. As we indicated earlier, high interest rates are required to finance deficits that now tend to arise when the country attempts to grow faster than only one or two per cent per annum, while further damaging the real economy.

Three centuries ago the mercantilists recognised this dilemma with great clarity, and so did Keynes in his defence of mercantilism against the classical free traders who treated the mercantilists as 'imbeciles', to use Keynes's (1936) word. As Keynes rightly recognised, the interest rate required for external balance (to finance current deficits) may be way out of line with that required for internal balance (in the sense of achieving fast growth and full employment). The problem also does not go away in a single currency area, with depressed regions (or countries) competing for investment funds.

If Britain is not to become a permanently depressed region of Europe, it needs all the monetary and fiscal instruments it can muster to break the 40-year syndrome of weak balance of payments, slow growth, depressed demand, and de-industrialisation leading to further balance-of-payments weakness. This is as true today as it was before the putative Thatcher economic miracle.

This book brings together many of the ideas that both of us have been working on over the last decade or so connected with the workings of the Harrod foreign trade multiplier and the concept of balance-of-payments constrained growth. The model and ideas to be presented provide an alternative theory of growth (and of why growth rates differ between countries) to the neoclassical theory which seeks to explain the growth process in terms of the exogenously determined and unexplained growth of factor supplies and technical progress, assuming no demand constraints. By contrast, we argue that the growth of factor supplies of labour and capital and the rate of technical progress are, within limits, endogenous to an economic system, and that a strong balance-of-payments position can set up a virtuous circle of growth working through Verdoorn's Law and the principle of circular and cumulative causation. We also contrast our ideas with some other theories that have been put forward in recent years to explain poor growth performance in the UK particularly associated with the growth of the non-market sector of the economy and various supply side weaknesses of British industry.

Chapter 1 details the growth experience of the major OECD countries since the Second World War as a prelude to a discussion of the various theories and models that have been advanced to explain growth rate differences between countries. In the applied analysis we distinguish between the long boom up to 1973 and the growth slowdown post-1973. As far as growth theory is concerned, we first focus on the neoclassical supply orientated approach to growth epitomised by the use of the aggregate production function, first employed by Abramovitz (1956) and Solow (1957) to explain the sources of economic growth, and by the subsequent growth accounting exercises pioneered by Denison (1962 and 1967). We are critical of the theory and its application on several counts, not the least being the neglect of demand and the consideration of the open economy. In this chapter we also scrutinise the Bacon and Eltis (1976) explanation of the UK's poor growth performance which originally laid emphasis on the growth of the non-market sector of the economy, depriving the marketable sector of resources and weakening the level of investment in the tradeable goods sector. Their argument unwittingly turns out to be a balance-of-payments argument. We end the chapter by considering the balance-of-payments position of various countries, and show how ineffective exchange rate adjustment has been in rectifying balance-of-payments disequilibrium. This implies income as the adjustment mechanism in the real world, which is the basis of the balance-of-payments explanation of growth rate differences between countries.

Chapter 2 considers the determinants of the growth of factor supplies in the advanced countries in the postwar period. The evidence suggests that the growth of the labour force was largely endogenous to the growth process, in contrast to the neoclassical approach, and that the labour force growth was largely determined by the growth of demand for it. Many Continental European countries were 'dual economies' in Arthur Lewis's sense of the term. Consequently, for much of the early postwar period, the growth of demand for labour, especially from the rapidly growing industrial sector, could be partially satisfied by the intersectoral transfer of labour from agriculture to industry. A number of these countries also drew heavily on immigration (the so-called 'guest workers') to offset any shortfall in the growth of the indigenous labour force. This suggests that we must look to explanations of the disparities in the growth of demand to explain differences in economic growth performance. In this chapter we also consider the Verdoorn Law which is often adduced as evidence for the existence of substantial increasing returns in manufacturing. This relationship forms an integral part of the demand orientated approach and the cumulative causation model of economic growth, which we consider in greater detail in Chapter 8.

Chapter 3 develops the concept of the Harrod foreign trade multiplier in both its static and dynamic form, and an expression is derived for a country's growth rate consistent with balance-of-payments equilibrium (also including capital flows). It is shown how closely the long-run growth experience of several countries approximates to the simple rule that growth is equal to the ratio of the growth of export volume and the income elasticity of demand for imports. The empirical regularity is strong enough, we believe, for the proposition to assume the status of a growth 'law'. We also show in this chapter that it is disparate income elasticities of demand for exports and imports that lie at the heart of 'centre–periphery' models of growth and development.

Chapter 4 discusses the importance of non-price factors in determining the pattern of trade flows between countries and the performance of exports and imports. 'New' trade theories are examined in which the role of technology and research and development is highlighted, both of which lead to a high income elasticity of demand for exports. The empirical evidence relating to the new trade theories and non-price factors in trade is also surveyed.

Chapter 5 reproduces some of the criticisms that have been levelled against the balance-of-payments constrained growth model outlined in Chapter 3, together with our response to these criticisms. These critiques have proved to be inconsequential and, in a number of cases, simply wrong. They have not led us to modify our arguments in any way.

Chapter 6 links up the idea of the Harrod trade multiplier with the Hicks super-multiplier and shows the extent to which, as exports grow faster, other components of demand can also grow faster

without balance-of-payments difficulties arising. It is this characteristic of exports that makes exports a unique component of demand:
that is, no other component of demand provides the foreign exchange
to pay for the import requirements associated with an expansion of
output.

Chapter 7 surveys some of the traditional models of export-led
growth, but is critical of them in the sense that the equilibrium
solution for output growth may generate a rate of growth of imports
in excess of the rate of growth of exports which is not sustainable. In
other words, they lack a balance-of-payments constraint. A simple
model is developed embodying such a constraint, and the equilibrium
solution is derived. A two-country model is also developed where it is
explicitly shown how the economic performance of one group of
countries may deleteriously affect the performance of another group
working through the balance-of-payments constraint.

Chapter 8 looks at export-led growth in a regional context and
develops the model into a virtuous circle model of cumulative causation based on the notion of induced productivity growth outlined in
Chapter 2. The conditions for virtuous and vicious circles are derived
both within countries and between countries. Regional problems of
slow growth and unemployment are shown to be essentially balance-
of-payments problems, even though regions within countries do not
keep balance-of-payments accounts.

Chapter 9 contains various applications of the static and dynamic
Harrod trade multiplier model. First, the model is used to analyse the
growth effects of the removal of tariff barriers within customs unions.
Secondly, in a two sector model of industry and agriculture, in which
the terms of trade are in equilibrium, it is shown that the equilibrium
level of output of the industrial sector is determined by the level of
export demand from the agricultural sector relative to the industrial
sector's propensity to import 'food'. Thirdly, it is shown how the
model can be used for policy analysis and forecasting purposes,
particularly for countries anxious to raise their growth rate consistent
with balance-of-payments equilibrium.

Chapter 10 concludes with two detailed case studies of the UK and
Australia where balance-of-payments difficulties have been particularly acute in recent years.

1 Alternative Theories of Growth Performance: I The Supply Orientated and Neoclassical Approaches

INTRODUCTION

The questions of what determine a country's growth rate (gross domestic product or GDP), and why countries grow at different rates, have always been central issues in the study of political economy. They were the major concern of Adam Smith, the 'father' of economics, in his *Inquiry into the Nature and Causes of the Wealth of Nations* (1776), and they have remained on the agenda of theoretical and empirical enquiry ever since. This is hardly surprising since it is the growth of national product that determines how fast a country's living standard grows, given the rate of population growth. A 6 per cent growth of output per head will double living standards every 10 years, whereas a 3 per cent growth of output per head will double living standards only every 25 years. Differences in country growth rates, even over a short space of time, can make a significant difference to the relative affluence of countries. After the Second World War, Britain was still among the top six richest countries in the world measured by per capita income. In the last forty years, Britain has slipped to about seventeenth in the per capita income stakes, as a result of its lamentably low growth rate relative to other countries. What accounts for this dismal performance, and the relative growth record of countries in general? This book aims at addressing these questions, focussing particularly on the relationship between the balance of payments and growth performance. A fundamental tenet of our approach is that the Keynesian notion of effective demand, when applied to the long run, can provide revealing insights into the complex question of 'why growth rates differ'. In this sense, the thesis we set out in the following chapters is avowedly Keynesian in nature.

1

In the days before the Keynesian revolution, the level of output and output per head were regarded largely as a function of a country's resource endowment and the productivity of factors of production – land, labour and capital. Countries were rich because they were exceptionally well endowed with resources, while countries were poor because they had been forsaken by nature. Output growth was viewed as supply determined. The idea that the quantity of resources used, or available, might be determined by demand was totally alien. Supply created its own demand. In the closed economy case, demand was not regarded as a constraint on output, owing to the assumption that even in a monetary economy 'saving is spending' (to use the words of Alfred Marshall, the doyen of English neoclassical economics). A failure of effective demand was regarded as impossible because all saving will find an investment outlet through variations in the rate of interest. If plans to save exceed plans to invest, the rate of interest will fall to equate the two. Income not consumed will be invested. In the open economy case, with foreign trade, the availability of foreign exchange was not regarded as a constraint on demand because, through the flexibility of traded goods' prices, the balance of payments was assumed to look after itself. Pre-Keynesian economics (both the classical and the subsequent neoclassical paradigms) presumed a world of continuous full employment with the tendency to long-run balance-of-payments equilibrium without any adjustment to output. In many ways, the modern neoclassical approach to the analysis of economic growth is still steeped in this pre-Keynesian spirit; that output is dependent on a country's resource endowment (exogenously given), and that the balance of payments is passive.

There is, of course, a trivial sense in which the neoclassical view is true; that there can be no output without the input of resources. But this basic fact hardly enhances understanding. The fundamental question is what determines the amount of resource inputs available and utilised. Land and minerals are given by nature, and in this sense land-based factors are exogenously given, but this is not true of labour inputs and capital. The strength of demand for resources, such as labour and capital, makes a difference to their supply – certainly significant enough to generate differences in output growth rates between countries. Labour supply responds to demand through migration, changes in the participation rate, and the transfer of workers from the low to high productivity sectors, especially from agriculture to industry. Capital is a *produced* means of production, and we know that investment responds to demand. Lastly, different forms of technical progress which augment the productivity of factors of production proceed more rapidly when the demand for output is strong. In other words, most of the mainsprings of economic growth are *endogenous* to an economic system. This being so, one central thesis of this book is that the neoclassical approach to the study of economic growth performance can be profoundly misleading, and that in order to understand growth rate differences between countries, the nature and extent of demand constraints must be understood, the most binding of which in an open economy is likely to be the balance of payments. The more open economies are, the greater the influence of the balance of payments is likely to be; and the longer the time period of analysis, the more factor supplies must be regarded as endogenous to an economic system (determined by the strength of demand).

While the book is not explicitly about the United Kingdom, the ideas have been developed and formulated in a country in which our theory seems to be supported in an acute form. Until the 1980s, Britain had the slowest average annual growth rate of any major industrialised country since the Second World War, and the current account of the balance of payments has been chronically weak and vulnerable. 'Stop–go' has characterised four decades of economic policy making, with periods of economic expansion brought to a grinding halt by the propensity to import that causes the growth of imports in a boom to exceed the growth of exports. The rapid increase in oil revenues together with the recession of 1979–81 meant that for the early 1980s the UK had a substantial surplus on the balance of payments. But this masked a steady deterioration in the balance of trade and by the end of the decade a familiar balance-of-payments deficit had reappeared. As Nicholas Kaldor once remarked, 'the pre-war unemployment problem [in the British economy] transmuted itself into a chronic post-war balance-of-payments problem' (Kaldor, 1971).[1]

Many competing theories have been put forward to explain the UK's growth weakness. In this chapter, we first look in general at what may be best termed the 'supply orientated' approach to economic growth, which has been largely dominated by the neoclassical paradigm. Included in the supply orientated approach is the Bacon and Eltis (1976) thesis, and other more general explanations of why productivity growth has been so slow in the UK. These explanations fundamentally stress the exogenous growth of factor supplies, together with technical progress which appears like 'manna from Heaven', as the determinants of economic growth. The alternative 'demand orientated' or Post-Keynesian approach, however, argues that even in the Golden Age of 1950–73, when most of the advanced countries are considered to have been fully employed, the growth of factor supplies was never the autonomous factor in determining economic growth. Consequently, we look in the next chapter at the evidence that has been advanced in support of this contention. If the growth disparities of the advanced countries have not been *caused* by differences in the growth of factor supplies, the answer must, by definition, lie in differences in the growth of demand. The most important component of the growth of autonomous demand for an individual country is the rate of increase of expenditure on its exports. This, acting through the balance of payments, becomes the major factor in determining the overall growth of an industrialised economy. An implication of this argument is that, in the medium to long term, there is little a country can do to increase its growth of exports through changes in the exchange rate, etc. In other words, export growth can be treated as largely exogenously determined, and a country's success or otherwise in this domain reflects the degree of its non-price competitiveness. Although the dichotomy between the supply and demand orientated approaches is useful for expository purposes, it should be remembered that, as Alfred Marshall stressed (although with respect to prices), both blades of the scissors are important. The demand orientated approach does not ignore the supply side as some critics maintain (see Chapter 5), but what is important are what may best be termed the *supply characteristics*. The success that a country has in overseas markets, and in competing with imports in its domestic markets, is primarily due to non-price competitiveness. This is reflected in such aspects as the degree of quality, delivery, servicing, and reliability of goods and services. Thus, the supply side *is* important to the extent that such factors as the skills and flexibility of the work force, the willingness of managers to innovate and the labour force to accept new techniques of production, and the more intangible concept of 'managerial dynamism', are all crucial in determining the degree of success in exporting.

We begin with a brief review of the growth experience of the major European and OECD countries in the 1970s and 1980s.

THE POSTWAR ECONOMIC PERFORMANCE OF THE ADVANCED COUNTRIES

In this section, we briefly sketch the postwar economic performance of the advanced countries. Table 1.1 presents a comparison of the levels of GDP per manhour of the various advanced countries for a number of years from 1870. The relative decline of the UK, especially since 1950, may readily be seen. Table 1.2 reports the postwar growth rates of GDP per employee and of GDP for fifteen advanced countries. It also contains the productivity and output growth rates for manufacturing.

There are a number of well-known problems with the measurement of output for much of the tertiary sector, which casts considerable doubt on the reliability of data for the growth of its productivity.[2] This is why we have also reported in Table 1.2 the growth rates of manufacturing productivity and output. These figures are also interesting in their own right, as we shall argue later that manufacturing possesses a unique role as the 'engine of growth' of the economy. Fortunately, the two sets of statistics tell very much the same story.

The postwar period falls naturally into two sub-periods, namely, 1951–73 and 1973 to the present.[3] The years from 1951 (when much of the dislocation from the Second World War had been overcome) to 1973 saw what has been termed the 'Long Boom', or 'Golden Age' to use Maddison's (1982) term. The average growth rate of GDP per annum over these twenty three years was about double that of previous eighty years. The year 1973 represented something of a watershed with all the advanced countries (with the exception of Norway) experiencing a severe recession. This ushered in a period of low growth of productivity and output for both the whole economy and manufacturing (See Table 1.2). There is still no sign of a return to the trend growth rates experienced during the Long Boom. An interesting question is, of course, whether this will ever happen. Thus, the period 1973 to the present may be aptly termed the 'Climacteric'.

THE LONG BOOM: 1951–73

The unweighted mean growth rate of the advanced countries' GDP during this period was 5.0 per cent per annum, which was over double

Table 1.1 Gross domestic product per manhour, selected years, 1870–1979 (1970 US relative prices, $)

Rank	1870		1913		1950		1979	
1	Australia	1.30	Australia	1.70	US	4.25	US	8.28
2	UK	0.80	US	1.67	Canada	3.33	Netherlands	7.48
3	Netherlands	0.74	Canada	1.45	Australia	3.05	Belgium	7.31
4	Belgium	0.74	UK	1.35	UK	2.40	France	7.11
5	US	0.70	Belgium	1.26	Sweden	2.34	Canada	7.03
6	Canada	0.61	Netherlands	1.23	Netherlands	2.27	Germany	6.93
7	Switzerland	0.55	Switzerland	1.01	Switzerland	2.21	Sweden	6.71
8	Italy	0.44	Denmark	1.00	Belgium	2.11	Norway	6.65
9	Denmark	0.44	Germany	0.95	Norway	2.03	Australia	6.48
10	Germany	0.43	Austria	0.90	France	1.85	Austria	5.89
11	Austria	0.43	France	0.90	Denmark	1.82	Italy	5.83
12	France	0.42	Sweden	0.83	Finland	1.48	UK	5.48
13	Norway	0.40	Norway	0.82	Germany	1.40	Denmark	5.27
14	Sweden	0.31	Italy	0.72	Italy	1.37	Finland	5.26
15	Finland	0.29	Finland	0.71	Austria	1.25	Switzerland	5.12
16	Japan	0.17	Japan	0.37	Japan	0.59	Japan	4.39

Source: Maddison (1982, table C10, p. 212).

Table 1.2   Growth of productivity and output (per cent per annum): selected advanced countries, 1951–89

(a) Gross Domestic Product

Country	Productivity growth[a]	GDP growth
Period 1951–73		
1 Japan	8.13	9.67
2 Austria[b]	4.87	4.76
3 Germany	4.71	5.71
4 France	4.64	5.23
5 Italy	4.62	5.00
6 Netherlands	3.94	5.05
7 Belgium	3.74	4.32
8 Norway	3.72	4.14
9 Denmark	3.42	4.72
10 Australia	2.40	4.80
11 United Kingdom	2.30	2.65
12 Canada	2.28	4.76
13 United States	2.15	3.60
Unweighted mean	3.92	4.95
Period 1973–89		
1 Japan	2.94	3.77
2 Norway	2.41	3.44
3 France	2.33	2.45
4 Belgium	2.19	2.08
5 Germany	1.90	1.98
6 Italy	1.90	2.64
7 Netherlands	1.68	1.95
8 Austria	1.67	2.32
9 United Kingdom	1.40	1.81
10 Australia	1.28	3.03
11 Denmark	1.26	1.84
12 Canada	1.21	3.43
13 United States	0.65	2.60
Unweighted mean	1.76	2.56

The slowdown: annual percentage growth rate in period 1973–89 minus that in period 1951–73

Country	Difference in productivity growth	Difference in GDP growth
1 United Kingdom	−0.90	−0.84
2 Australia	−1.12	−1.77
3 Norway	−1.31	−0.70
4 Canada	−1.07	−1.33
5 United States	−1.50	−1.00
6 Belgium	−1.55	−2.24
7 Denmark	−2.16	−2.88
8 Netherlands	−2.26	−3.10
9 France	−2.31	−2.78
10 Italy	−2.72	−2.36
11 Germany	−2.81	−3.73
12 Austria	−3.20	−2.44
13 Japan	−5.19	−5.90
Unweighted mean	−2.16	−2.39

Table 1.2   *continued*

(b) *Manufacturing*

Country	Productivity growth[b]	Output growth
Period 1951–73		
1 Japan	8.78	13.34
2 Netherlands	5.28	5.94
3 Italy	5.26	7.11
4 Germany	4.87	7.24
5 Belgium	4.85	5.28
6 France	4.75	5.88
7 Austria	4.66	5.02
8 Denmark	3.68	5.63
9 Norway	3.48	4.37
10 Australia	3.38	5.02
11 United Kingdom	3.07	3.16
12 Canada	3.03	5.16
13 United States	2.99	3.87
Unweighted mean	4.47	5.92
Period 1973–89		
1 Belgium	5.04	2.50
2 Japan	4.37	4.62
3 Italy	4.16	3.20
4 United Kingdom	3.00	0.46
5 France	2.96	1.26
6 Austria	2.95	2.36
7 Australia [d]	2.66	1.50
8 Netherlands [e]	2.63	1.39
9 United States	2.56	2.20
10 Germany	1.88	1.13
11 Denmark	1.84	1.49
12 Norway[d]	1.56	0.09
13 Canada	1.50	2.11
Unweighted mean	2.85	1.87

*The slowdown: annual percentage growth rate in period
1973–89 minus that in period 1951–73*

Country	Difference in Productivity growth	Difference in output growth
1 Belgium	+0.19	−2.78
2 United Kingdom	−0.07	−2.70
3 United States	−0.42	−1.67
4 Australia	−0.72	−3.52
5 Italy	−1.10	−3.91
6 Canada	−1.53	−3.05
7 Austria	−1.71	−2.66
8 France	−1.79	−4.62
9 Denmark	−1.84	−4.14
10 Norway	−1.92	−4.28
11 Netherlands	−2.65	−4.55
12 Germany	−2.99	−6.11
13 Japan	−4.41	−8.72
Unweighted mean	−1.61	−4.05

Notes: [a] Growth of GDP minus growth of civilian employment or all persons employed.
[b] Growth of manufacturing output minus growth of wage and salary earners or employees.
[c] Mining and quarrying is included in manufacturing.
[d] Employment is all persons employed (Australia) and civilian employment (Canada).
[e] Mining and quarrying and gas, electricity and water included in manufacturing.

Period 1951–73

Australia	1956–73	Austria	1957–73	Belgium	1951–73
Canada	1951–73	Denmark	1954–73	France	1951–73
Italy	1951–73	Japan	1953–73	Netherlands	1951–73
Norway	1951–70	Germany	1951–73	United Kingdom	1951–73
United States	1951–73				

1973–89 for all countries except the United States (1973–87) and Australia (1973–88).

Sources: *National Accounts*, OECD, Paris, (various years); *Labour Force Statistics*, OECD, Paris (various years); National Sources; Cripps and Tarling (1973).

the growth rate achieved in the period 1870–1950, which was 2.3 per cent per annum. All the advanced countries shared in this boom. Although the growth of the UK was low by international standards at 2.7 per cent per annum, this was still well above the rate of 1.6 per cent per annum achieved over the previous eighty years. Similarly, all the countries experienced growth rates of aggregate productivity that were rapid by historical standards. What is also apparent from Table 1.2 is that there were substantial differences between countries in both the growth of output and the growth of productivity. A similar picture is found when we consider manufacturing.

This sustained boom was in complete contrast to the forecast of a number of commentators writing in the 1950s. The tendency then was to attribute these exceptionally fast growth rates to a number of temporary factors such as postwar reconstruction, Marshall Aid, and trade liberalisation. It was felt that there would soon be a return of growth rates to their historic norms. The degree to which the subsequent performance of the advanced countries exceeded all expectations may perhaps be most dramatically seen by considering the detailed study by Dewhurst, Coppock and Yates entitled *Europe's Needs and Resources* and published in 1961. At that time, their book was one of the most comprehensive considerations of the economic situation of the European countries and it provided an assessment of their likely future economic performance. Table 1.3 shows just how pessimistic Dewhurst *et al.* were – the average actual growth of total output was 50 per cent higher than their forecast value, while the figure for observed productivity growth was 65 per cent higher. There was no tendency for the rapid deceleration in growth rates that they had predicted.

The Long Boom may be further subdivided into five growth cycles for most of the advanced countries (see Table 1.4). The rankings of the countries in terms of output and productivity growth over these cycles were relatively stable, with the exception of Germany whose growth rate steadily declined over the cycles of this period. The fastest growing countries, such as Japan and Italy, tended to be the same in all cycles and, conversely, the US and the UK were persistently the laggards. In other words, there was little or no tendency for the inter-country disparities in growth rates to narrow. The country with the fastest growth rate in the 1950s, Japan, was also the least developed of the industrialised countries in terms of having the lowest per capita income. On the other hand, the two countries with the highest per capita income, the US and Canada, also tended to have

Table 1.3   A comparison between the projected and actual growth rates of GNP (GDP) and aggregate productivity for the advanced countries 1955–70 (projected) and 1951–73 (actual)[a]

Country	GNP (GDP) growth % p.a.			Productivity growth % p.a.		
	Projected	Actual	Difference	Projected	Actual	Difference
Austria	2.8	4.8	−2.0	2.8	4.9	−2.1
Belgium	2.8	4.3	−1.5	2.3	3.7	−1.4
Denmark	3.0	4.7	−1.7	2.3	3.4	−1.1
France	3.4	5.2	−1.8	2.7	4.6	−1.9
Germany	2.8	5.7	−2.9	2.3	4.7	−2.4
Italy	3.8	5.0	−1.2	3.4	4.6	−1.2
Netherlands	3.5	5.1	−1.6	2.3	3.9	−1.6
Norway	3.2	4.1	−0.9	2.5	3.7	−1.2
UK	2.1	2.7	−0.6	1.8	2.3	−0.5
Unweighted mean	3.0	4.6	−1.6	2.5	4.0	−1.5

Note: [a]The exact periods for individual countries may differ from 1951 to 1973; see Table 1.1.

Sources: OECD National Accounts (various years), Dewhurst *et al.* (1961).

the slowest growth rates. There was thus a tendency towards a convergence in per capita income levels with the majority of the advanced countries tending to narrow the difference between themselves and the US. (The implications of this will be discussed later in the chapter.)

We shall be considering the reasons for the Long Boom in greater detail later. Nevertheless a few brief remarks are in order here. The proximate cause was undoubtedly the increase in both the rate of investment and in the growth of exports, compared with earlier periods (Matthews, 1968). The share of GDP invested by the advanced countries was about 50 per cent higher than in the prewar years (although there were considerable international differences in these ratios in both periods). The overwhelming econometric evidence suggests that the most important determinant of the rate of capital accumulation is the rate of growth of output itself (see Sawyer, 1982, pp. 153–4). Hence, to a certain extent, it is necessary to explain why there was such a rapid growth in the latter. But an initial boom in investment could lead to increased expectations on the part of entrepreneurs of faster growth and this through a cumulative causation process could lead to a self-fulfilling prophecy.

The rapid expansion of exports was a result of the remarkable

Table 1.4 The growth of GDP in the postwar growth cycles
(per cent per annum)

Cycle	(Approximate dates)	Japan	West Germany	Italy	France	Nether-lands	Denmark
I	1950–55	7.61	8.24	5.07	4.37	5.52	2.57
II	1955–60	10.07	5.92	5.20	4.30	3.80	5.37
III	1960–65	9.73	4.83	6.38	5.91	4.70	4.65
IV	1965–70	9.78	4.10	5.16	5.05	5.36	4.09
V	1970–73	7.69	3.86	3.85	5.44	4.36	3.43
VI	1973–79	3.76	2.38	2.56	3.06	2.46	2.04
VII	1979–86	3.59	1.39	2.74	1.57	1.12	2.15

Cycle	(Approximate dates)	Austria	Canada	Norway	Belgium	US	UK
I	1950–55	5.47	5.61	3.93	2.99	3.00	2.67
II	1955–60	4.93	4.57	3.13	4.16	3.78	2.68
III	1960–65	4.20	··	4.52	··	··	3.13
IV	1965–70	5.08	4.62	3.68	4.52	3.16	2.49
V	1970–73	5.91	5.56	4.65	4.48	3.33	3.53
VI	1973–79	2.70	3.32	4.71	2.44	2.57	1.41
VII	1979–86	1.70	2.64	3.57	1.02	2.39	1.40

Peak years

Japan	1953;	1957;	1961;	1964;	1969;	1973;	1980;	1986.
West Germany	1951;	1956;	1961;	1965;	1970;	1973;	1979;	1986.
Italy	1951;	1955;	1959;	1963;	1970;	1973;	1979;	1986.
France	1951;	1957;	1960;	1964;	1969;	1973;	1979;	1986.
Netherlands	1951;	1956;	1960;	1965;	1970;	1973;	1979;	1986.
Denmark	1954;	1957;	1962;	1965;	1969;	1973;	1979;	1986.
Austria	1951;	1957;	1961;	1966;	1970;	1974;	1979;	1986.
Canada	1951;	1956;	··	1966;	1969;	1973;	1979;	1986.
Norway	1951;	1956;	1960;	1965;	1970;	1974;	1979;	1986.
Belgium	1951;	1957;	··	1964;	1970;	1973;	1980;	1986.
US	1951;	1956;	··	1966;	1969;	1973;	1979;	1986.
UK	1951;	1956;	1960;	1965;	1970;	1973;	1979;	1986

Sources: Cripps and Tarling (1973), updated and revised using *OECD National Accounts* (various years).

liberalisation in international trade that occurred in the 1950s. The tariffs and quotas that had become prevalent in the 1930s, with the 'beggar-my-neighbour' trade policies, were rapidly dismantled under GATT. Moreover, the US quickly recognised the necessity of a prosperous Europe as a bulwark against the Warsaw Pact countries.

This resulted in the Marshall Aid programme and the development of supra-national institutions such as the IMF designed to ensure there was sufficient international liquidity to finance temporary balance-of-payments deficits to sustain the growth of world trade. Moreover, international consultations over economic policy became commonplace, in marked contrast to the interwar period when there was conflict over war reparations and little attempt to co-ordinate national economic policies (Van der Wee, 1987, part 1).

A further factor that led to buoyant demand was the increasing interventionist policies on the part of governments of all political persuasions. The Keynesian revolution had, so it was thought, given the governments an understanding of how to use macroeconomic policies to avoid recessions on the scale of the Great Depression of the 1930s. In Britain, the 1944 White Paper entitled *Employment Policy* had explicitly committed the government to ensuring full employment. Keynesian demand management policies were also adopted by the Scandinavian countries. The US was rather slower in embracing Keynesian macroeconomic policies, in spite of a commitment to full employment being enshrined in the Full Employment Act of 1946. Indeed, it was not until the Kennedy and Johnson years of the 1960s that demand management policies were actively pursued. On the Continent, the Keynesian revolution, *per se*, had much less influence. But, in these countries, there had been a much greater tradition of state intervention in industry, through, for example, the indicative planning of the French and the corporatism of the Germany economy. Japan also witnessed the pervasive influence of state planning through such agencies as the Ministry of International Trade and Industry and the Japan Development Bank.[4]

Matthews (1968), though, is sceptical about the effect of government demand management policies on economic growth, especially in the case of the UK. He attributes the rapid postwar growth to an investment boom of unusual proportions. At the end of the war, income was high, there had been a large degree of forced saving and the capital stock was at a low level. The time was thus propitious, he argues, for a large cyclical upswing in investment. The Government did play a role, but only to the extent that during the Second World War the mobilisation of resources by the Government, as a result of the hostilities, brought about a once-and-for-all increase in the level of economic activity. The investment boom was sustained for far longer than had ever occurred previously because of the backlog of investment opportunities that had accumulated during the war and by an assumed acceleration in technical progress. Also the increase in the growth of the UK's exports had a positive feedback on the rate of capital accumulation. Matthews is dismissive of the argument that macroeconomic policies were important by pointing out that, on average, the budget in the UK was in surplus. In other words, fiscal policy tended to restrict demand more often than it boosted it. Maddison (1982), on the other hand, points out that the UK was exceptional in this respect; in the other advanced countries the net effect of fiscal policy was, on the whole, expansionary.

Matthews, in addition, does not set great store by the so-called 'safety net argument'. This is the thesis that the mere fact that the British Government had given a commitment to full employment was sufficient to give entrepreneurs the confidence to invest, which, in turn, generated such a rapid growth of demand that the Government was forced to play a restraining role (largely induced by successive balance of payments crises). According to Matthews, the indicators of the expected rate of return on investment were sufficiently high over this period and in themselves are enough to explain the investment boom without recourse to the safety net argument.

The postwar period saw a rapid rise in Government expenditure. In the UK, the share of general government current expenditures on goods, services and transfers as a percentage of GDP rose from 30 per cent in 1950 to 41 per cent in 1973. For the advanced countries as a whole the figures are 22 per cent in 1950 and 40 per cent in 1977 (Maddison, 1982, p. 131). Matthews dismisses the impact of this increase in government expenditure on the grounds that it was financed by taxation, although he concedes that there would have been a limited balanced budget multiplier effect. But this overlooks the fact that the automatic stabilisers provided by social security payments etc. were quantitatively much more important in the postwar period. Moreover, government expenditure tends to be far less volatile than investment and production in the private sector, and this, in itself, would have had the effect of maintaining confidence in a high and persistent level of demand. It is difficult not to agree with Maddison (1982, pp. 130, 132) when he argues that 'Matthews dismisses too lightly the influence of the greatly increased size of government spending on goods, services and transfers in the postwar period . . . which has strengthened expectations of high and expanding demand in many ways. . . . His structuralist interpretation of the problems in the interwar period understates the role of errors in domestic and international economic policy in that period.'

We have followed the general convention in assuming that 1973 represented a marked watershed in the growth performance of the advanced countries. Matthews and Bowen (1988) differ; they argue that there is evidence of a general slowdown in the growth of GDP that began in the last cycle *prior* to 1973. This, of course, is consistent with Matthews's hypothesis that the Long Boom was the result of an abnormally large investment boom that peaked before 1973, so that there would have been a slowdown even without the dramatic events of 1973/4, although not so pronounced. On the basis of the growth rates of the largest six countries calculated over the postwar growth cycles, Matthews and Bowen conclude that Germany, Italy, the US and Japan all had lower growth rates in the cycle that ended in 1973/4 than in the previous cycle. The case of the UK, where the growth rate was in fact higher, they consider to be misleading, because the level of output in 1973 was sharply above trend. We must take issue with them, however, on this interpretation of the international data. Table 1.4 reports the growth rates for GDP for a larger sample of 12 advanced countries using Cripps and Tarling's (1973) data, which were revised and updated, and their choice of growth cycles. Of the 12 countries, growth in the cycle that terminated in 1973 was not significantly different from the growth rates achieved in the preceding periods in eight countries, namely, France, the Netherlands (although this is perhaps debatable), Denmark, Austria, Canada, Norway, Belgium, the US and the UK. There is a problem that the last cycle up to 1973 was very short and was of only either three or four years' duration, depending upon the country. While it can be argued that the level of the UK's GDP was above trend in 1973, it can equally be argued that the 1973/4 oil crisis prematurely cut short the growth cycle of a number of countries. For example, Italy had a growth rate of only 3.85 per cent per annum over the 1970–73 cycle, which was considerably below the growth rate of 5.16 per cent per annum achieved during 1965–70. But the growth rates for each individual year over the period 1970–73 were 1.62 per cent, 3.15 per cent and 6.80 per cent respectively. Another year of growth at the last rate would have considerably improved the cyclical average, making it more comparable with the preceding growth cycle. Referring to Table 1.4 again, the only case where there seems to have been a clear-cut deceleration in the rate of growth over the whole of the Long Boom is Germany. As far as the other countries are concerned, all that can be said is that overall there is no clear evidence of a slowdown prior to 1973.

Table 1.5   The growth of total gross capital stock in the postwar growth cycles (per cent per annum)

Cycle[a]	(Approximate dates)[b]	Japan	West Germany	France	Canada	Norway[c]	US	UK
II	1955–60	na	na	3.01	4.84 ⎫	na	3.14 ⎫	2.66
III	1960–65	na	5.79	4.37	⎭	na	⎭	3.52
IV	1965–70	14.07	4.88	5.11	5.11	3.73	3.50	4.01
V	1970–73	12.39	4.88	5.86	4.93	4.37	3.64	3.57
VI	1973–79	6.64	3.38	4.77	4.90	4.57	3.26	2.87
VII	1979–85	7.45	2.85	3.59	4.02	2.91	2.79	2.08

Notes: [a]The first cycle is omitted owing to lack of data.
[b]See Table 1.4 for exact periods, except that the terminal year of cycle VII is 1985.
[c]Net capital stock.

Sources: *Flows and Stocks of Fixed Capital, 1955–1980*, 1983, Paris: OECD; *Flows and Stocks of Fixed Capital, 1960–1985*, 1987, Paris: OECD.

Matthews and Bowen, using the ratio of gross fixed investment to the gross capital stock as a measure of the rate of capital accumulation, also find evidence of a long cycle in capital accumulation over the Long Boom with a peak often considerably before 1973. Table 1.5 reports the growth of the gross capital stock for six countries and, *pace* Matthews and Bowen, it is difficult to see any pronounced deceleration in the cyclical growth rates.[5,6] It would seem that, taking this evidence in conjunction with the output growth rates discussed above, there was no marked slowdown prior to 1973. As a first approximation, the Long Boom can be treated as a period of high and steady growth with no noticeable secular trend.

THE CLIMACTERIC: 1973 TO THE PRESENT

The last few months of 1973 and the beginning of 1974 saw a dramatic turnaround in the fortunes of the advanced countries. Over this short period, one of the fastest expansionary periods (from the trough of economic activity in 1970 to the peak in mid-1973) that the advanced countries had ever experienced turned into one of the deepest recessions since the 1930s.

The rapidity of what can only be termed a collapse in production caught most economic commentators by surprise. The average (un-weighted) growth of the six largest industrial countries[7] was 6.9 per cent in 1973. A year later the annual growth rate had fallen to 0.6 per cent. The various economic forecasting agencies (such as the OECD) recorded some of their worse prediction errors in their history as previously stable economic relationships broke down.

The depth of the recession may be appreciated when it is realised that in the post war period prior to 1973 a negative rate of growth had only been experienced by two countries and then only for one year each. (The United States experienced negative growth of 0.6 per cent per annum from 1969 to 1970 and the UK a growth rate of -0.1 per cent from 1951 to 1952.) Only three countries managed to escape this fate in either 1974 or 1975. The only success story was Norway which grew at 4.5 per cent over the two recessionary years of 1974 and 1975, but at the expense of a large balance-of-payments deficit. There was, however, the justifiable expectation of substantial revenues from North Sea Oil to finance the deficit.

The recession was associated with an unprecedented double digit rate of inflation in the advanced countries, initiated by the rapid growth in commodity prices, followed closely by the quadrupling of oil prices. The UN index of export prices of primary commodities, excluding petroleum, measured in terms of US dollars, doubled in the four years from 1971 to 1974. This was in marked contrast to the preceding quarter of a century when, with the exception of the brief period of the Korean War boom, the terms of trade moved against the primary producers. The cumulative deterioration was 24 per cent between 1953 and 1971, all but 3 per cent of which occurred between 1958 and 1968 (Kaldor, 1978a, p. 225). The reasons for the explosive rise in primary commodity prices are many and varied and depend upon the particular commodity in question; but what is clear is that it was a combination of both supply and demand factors.

On the demand side, continuous boom conditions were developing from 1971 onwards. It is perhaps not coincidental that five of the seven major countries had general elections in 1972.

The cause of the price rises, though, was not entirely due to de-mand. In the case of wheat, for example, the reason was partly that crop failures caused a shortfall of production of 3.4 per cent below trend consumption. But failures of this magnitude had occurred in the past without major price rises. One difference was that this time the US had run down its considerable stocks of grain reserves, since it was felt that the costs of holding these inventories were too burdensome on the American taxpayer. World reserves at the beginning of the 1972/3 marketing year were only fractionally above what they had been at the *end* of previous periods of low production in both 1967 and 1970 (Bosworth and Lawrence, 1982). This was coupled with a decision by the Russians to meet a shortfall in their domestic production of grains by imports, rather than by cutting back on domestic consumption as they had done in the past. In the case of metals, the production levels of copper, aluminum, tin and zinc were not unusual in 1973 and 1974, given the stage of the business cycle, but the processing capacity for these metals was overstretched with very high levels of capacity utilisation. It had been considered earlier that there had been over-investment in these industries in the late 1960s, especially in view of the depth of the 1970/1 recession, and so subsequent investment had been much lower, leading to a shortfall in capacity in 1973.

The balance of economic power between the OPEC producers and the seven international oil companies had been sharply moving in the former's favour since 1970. In that year, Libya, which was supplying about one quarter of Western Europe's oil needs, sharply curtailed production until the country's demands for higher posted prices and tax revenues were met. This was sufficient to send world oil prices spiralling upwards. However, it was the Middle East war in 1973 that provided the OPEC countries with the necessary political cohesion for the quadrupling of oil prices that occurred in December 1973.

These increases in primary commodity and oil prices led to a marked rise in the level of money wage settlements in the industrialised countries. The result was an unprecedented level of inflation – in the two years from 1973 to 1975 the increase in the consumer price index averaged 26 per cent for all the OECD countries, with a range (for the two-year period) of 44 per cent for the UK to 13 per cent for Germany (Kaldor, 1978a, p. 215).

The rise in primary commodity prices represented a transfer of purchasing power from the net importers of primary commodities to the net exporters (largely the less developed countries (LDCs)). The net effect of the increase in primary commodity prices (as opposed to the oil price increase) did not prove to be very deflationary because the LDCs have a high propensity to import from developed countries.

On the other hand, OPEC was unable to spend all of its increased income and initially ran a substantial surplus on current account (although by 1978 the surplus had virtually disappeared – see Table

Table 1.6   OPEC Import volume and current balance of payments

	1974	1975	1976	1977	1978
Import volume growth, %	40	36	15	14.5	4
Current balance of payments (US$ billion)	59.5	27.25	36.5	29.0	4.5

Source: Llewellyn (1983).

1.6). It was this surplus that was primarily responsible for initiating a severe recession in the rest of the world.

The oil price rise transferred to OPEC from the rest of the world an amount equivalent to about 2 per cent of the GDP of OECD countries. This gave rise to deflationary pressures which initially were partially offset by a move to a more expansionary fiscal stance by the OECD countries. Monetary policy was also accommodating, with a fall in nominal interest rates in some countries. But these policy measures were not sufficient to prevent the sharp fall in GDP in most of the advanced countries. The proximate cause of this was a 'sharp, and unpredicted, collapse in private non-residential investment and also a dramatic reduction in inventories' (Llewellyn, 1983).

There was rapid growth in 1976, mainly consumption-led as the savings ratio fell rapidly, but this was not sustained for more than a couple of years. The OECD economies were nowhere near their productive potential when the second oil price rise occurred in 1979/80. By this time, monetarism was in the ascendancy. Concern with inflation had become paramount, and governments, particularly in Germany, the UK and the US, pursued, or at least tried to pursue, non-accommodating monetary policy. Likewise, there was also concern about the state of the balance of payments, especially in those countries such as Japan and Germany that had traditionally run large current account surpluses. The monetarist counter-revolution was by now well established and expansionary fiscal policy was assumed to be self-defeating as it merely 'crowded out' the putatively more efficient private investment. Over the cycle from 1979 to 1991, the growth of GDP for the advanced countries was, if anything, less than that experienced from 1973 to 1979.

What has also given rise for concern is that, as we have noted above, the Climacteric has also been associated with a fall in the growth of productivity in both the whole economy and manufacturing to about half the rates achieved over the Long Boom.

In the early 1980s, there was much discussion about whether the Climacteric represented a return to the more historic rates of growth or was merely a temporary aberration caused by the two exceptional recessions. If the Long Boom, with its exceptionally fast growth in prosperity, had not occurred, it is doubtful if so much concern would have been expressed about the post-1973 growth rates. Morris (1983) and Prais (1983), for example, were both sceptical that the slowdown in productivity growth represented a decline in the trend rate of growth. They noted that if the severe recessions of 1974/5 and 1978/9 are removed, there is not a very noticeable slowdown in productivity growth. With the benefit of a longer period, it is now clear that this view is too sanguine; the growth rates of productivity and output over the period 1979–88 are not very different (and in some cases actually lower) than those experienced in 1973–9, and are substantially lower than those of the Long Boom (see Table 1.3).

From this brief review of postwar economic performance, the following questions arise.

(i) Why were productivity and output growth rates for the advanced countries as a whole so much faster during the Long Boom than those achieved during the previous fifty years?

(ii) Why were there such persistent disparities between the advanced countries in their productivity and output growth rates during the Long Boom? It will be noticed from Table 1.2 that those countries with a fast growth of output generally had a fast growth of productivity. Was this purely coincidental or was there some causal relationship at work?

(iii) Why did the slowdown in the trend rates of both productivity and output growth occur after 1973?

(iv) Was it the Long Boom or the Climacteric that represented an abnormal phase of economic growth? Can we expect growth rates ever to return to the values experienced over 1950–73 or must this period be simply regarded as a temporary phenomenon?

In the course of this book, we shall outline a post-Keynesian theory that attempts to supply the answers to these questions. To commence, however, we shall consider the neoclassical approach to the analysis of growth, to which our own approach will stand in contrast.

THE NEOCLASSICAL GROWTH ACCOUNTING APPROACH

At the heart of the neoclassical approach to the understanding of growth rate differences between countries is the concept of the aggregate production function. This is a technological relationship which expresses the level of output as a function of the level of inputs, such as labour, capital, and land, together with such other factors as the state of technology, the degree of managerial and labour efficiency, etc. In practice, the arguments of the production function are normally confined to just three factors, namely, labour, capital and technology. The basis of the production function is the individual production process at the plant level, and it is assumed that these micro-production functions can be aggregated to produce a well-defined relationship at the aggregate level, i.e. for the whole economy, for manufacturing or for individual industries. For the moment, we shall assume that this is correct, although, as we shall see, severe reservations have been expressed about this assumption (Walters, 1963). (For example, if the micro-production functions are of a Cobb–Douglas form, then they cannot be summed to give an aggregate production function which is itself of a Cobb–Douglas form (Blaug, 1974, chapter II).)

The production function can be expressed in a general form as:

$$Q_t = F(L_t; K_t; t) \tag{1.1}$$

where Q, L and K denote output, the labour input (normally expressed as the numbers employed or the total hours worked) and the capital input (the capital stock which, when adjusted for capacity utilisation, is assumed to be a good proxy for the flow of capital services). Time, denoted by t, is included to allow for disembodied technical change, which is assumed to shift the production function upwards over time. This is to say that the level of output is assumed to increase over time because of technical progress, even if the volume of factor inputs remains constant.

Differentiating equation (1.1) with respect to time gives:

$$\frac{dQ}{dt} = \frac{\partial F}{\partial L} \cdot \frac{\partial L}{\partial t} + \frac{\partial F}{\partial K} \cdot \frac{\partial K}{\partial t} + \frac{\partial F}{\partial t} \tag{1.2}$$

(dropping the time subscripts, for the moment, for notational ease).

Dividing equation (1.2) by Q gives:

$$\frac{1}{Q} \cdot \frac{dQ}{dt} = \frac{1}{Q} \cdot \frac{\partial F}{\partial L} \cdot \frac{\partial L}{\partial t} + \frac{1}{Q} \cdot \frac{\partial F}{\partial K} \cdot \frac{\partial K}{\partial t} + \frac{1}{Q} \cdot \frac{\partial F}{\partial t} \qquad (1.3)$$

This may be expressed as:

$$q_t = \frac{L}{Q} \cdot \frac{\partial F}{\partial L} \ell_t + \frac{K}{Q} \cdot \frac{\partial F}{\partial K} k_t + \lambda_t \qquad (1.4)$$

or:

$$q_t = \alpha_t \ell_t + \beta_t k_t + \lambda_t \qquad (1.5)$$

where the lower-case letters denote the instantaneous proportionate growth rates of the several variables. $\lambda = (1/Q)(\partial F/\partial t)$ is the rate of technical progress. $\alpha = (L/Q)(\partial F/\partial L)$ and $\beta = (K/Q)(\partial F/\partial K)$ are the output elasticities of labour and capital respectively. If constant returns to scale prevail, $\alpha + \beta = 1$.

Referring back to equation (1.3), $\partial F/\partial L$ and $\partial F/\partial K$ are the marginal products of labour and capital respectively. If we assume that competitive conditions hold then these will equal the wage rate and the rental price of capital. Consequently, equation (1.5) may be expressed as:

$$q_t = a_t \ell_t + (1 - a_t)k_t + \lambda_t \qquad (1.6)$$

where a and $(1 - a)$ are the shares of labour and capital in total output. The shares have time subscripts because they can change over time (except in the case of the Cobb–Douglas production function which has the elasticity of substitution equal to unity and therefore shares that are always constant).

Ever since the work of Cobb and Douglas in the 1920s and 1930s much ingenuity has gone into finding specific functional forms that will provide good statistical fits to the data represented by equation (1.5). For example, if the output elasticities are constant and technical progress is neutral in the Hicksian sense that it does not alter the ratio of marginal products of factors of production at a given capital to labour ratio, the Cobb–Douglas production function will give the best fit. Assuming a constant rate of technical progress,[8] this takes the multiplicative form:

$$Q_t = A_0 e^{\lambda t} L_t^\alpha K_t^{(1-\alpha)} \qquad (1.7)$$

where e represents the exponential function. Equation (1.7) may be expressed in terms of natural logarithms as:

$$\ln Q_t = \ln A_0 + \lambda t + \alpha \ln L_t + (1-\alpha)\ln K_t \qquad (1.8)$$

Many production function studies have found that, in the words of Griliches and Ringstad (1971, p. 63), 'it is very hard to improve upon the simple Cobb–Douglas form', although there are more general functional forms such as the Constant Elasticity of Substitution (CES) and Translog production functions available, if necessary. (The Cobb–Douglas is a special case of the CES which, in turn, is a special case of the Translog production function.) Moreover, it is often found that the estimates of the output elasticities are not significantly different from the values of the relevant factor shares. This has led Douglas (1976, p. 914) to conclude

A considerable body of independent work tends to corroborate the original Cobb–Douglas formula, but, more important, the approximate coincidence of the estimated coefficients with the actual shares received also strengthens the competitive theory of distribution and disproves the Marxian.

The growth accounting approach to the analysis of growth performance does not attempt to explain the growth of output by directly estimating a production function such as equation (1.8). Rather, it assumes that the neoclassical conditions are met and uses equation (1.6) to apportion any country's growth rate to the growth of labour and capital, leaving technical progress, or total factor productivity growth, as a residual.

The growth of total factor productivity (*tfp*) is thus given by:

$$tfp_t \equiv \lambda_t \equiv q_t - \{a_t \ell_t + (1-a_t)k_t\} \qquad (1.9)$$

It is the growth of output less the growth of labour and capital each weighted by its factor share.

The growth of labour productivity is defined as:

$$p_t \equiv q_t - \ell_t \qquad (1.10)$$

Comparing equation (1.9) with (1.10), it can be seen that the concept of total factor productivity growth represents an improvement over labour productivity growth in measuring the rate of technical progress, in that it explicitly makes an allowance for the growth of the capital stock. One drawback of using the growth of labour productivity as a measure of the rate of change in economic efficiency is that it is clearly only a partial index. For example, a rapid growth of labour productivity could be primarily due to a rapid increase in the amount of machinery with which each employee has to work. The growth of total factor productivity makes an explicit allowance for this. Equation (1.6) may be alternatively written in terms of labour productivity growth as:

$$p_t = \lambda_t + (1 - a_t)(k_t - \ell_t) \tag{1.11}$$

where λ is the growth of labour productivity than cannot be accounted for by the growth of capital intensity.

As an example of the growth accounting approach, let us consider the performance of the UK during the last decade of the Long Boom, i.e. from 1963 to 1973. During this period the growth of GDP was 3.18 per cent per annum, the growth of total persons employed was 0.13 per cent per annum and the growth of the gross capital stock was 3.85 per cent per annum. The share of labour shows very little annual variation, and takes an average value of 0.68.[9] It will be recalled that the growth of output may be written as:

$$q = \lambda + a\ell + (1 - a)k \tag{1.12}$$

where the lower-case letters denote the annual percentage exponential growth rates over the ten-year period, and a and $(1 - a)$ are the average values of the relevant factor shares.

Substituting the above values into equation (1.12) gives:

$$3.18\% = \lambda + 0.68(0.13\%) + 0.32(3.85\%) \tag{1.13}$$

The growth of total factor productivity (λ) equals 1.86 per cent per annum which compares with a growth of labour productivity of 3.05 per cent per annum. 58 per cent of output growth cannot be accounted for by the growth of the conventional factor inputs. Or to put this another way, from equation (1.11), 61 per cent of the growth of labour productivity is unexplained after allowance has been made for the growth in capital intensity and is therefore attributed to the effect of technical progress. Given all the problems associated with the measurement of output in the tertiary (or service) sector, some growth accounting exercises confine themselves to the private business sector or to industry rather than using GDP, as we have done.

The fact that such a large proportion of output growth cannot be explained by the growth of conventional inputs may seem to be surprising, but it is a result that has been confirmed by most, if not all, of the many empirical studies on the measurement of technical progress that treat it as exogenous and disembodied. The impetus for this approach undoubtedly came from Solow's (1957) famous article 'Technical Change and the Aggregate Production Function', together with the work of Abramovitz (1956). Making the usual neoclassical assumptions, Solow found that output per hour doubled in the US between 1909 and 1949; and of this over 80 per cent could be attributable to 'technical change in the broadest sense' while less than 20 per cent could be attributed to the growth in the capital–labour ratio. Looking back on this work, Solow (1988, p. 313) finds the result was 'startling'; 'I think I had expected to find a larger role for straightforward capital formation than I actually found'. Nevertheless, while a considerable amount of work has been done in trying to whittle down this residual over the last 35 years, it has proved to be remarkably stubborn. (A major exception to this is Scott's (1989) unorthodox *New View of Economic Growth* which is discussed in the Appendix.) Even where the conventional growth accounting approach has 'explained' the whole of the residual, the exact assumptions made have often proved to be contentious. (See, for example, the interchange between Jorgenson and Griliches (1967, 1972) and Denison (1969, 1972).) Denison shows convincingly that the claim by Jorgenson and Griliches to have explained most of the residual merely by measuring more accurately the growth of the factor inputs, especially capital, was premature.)

There would be little dispute that the seminal full-blown growth accounting study is Denison's (1967) *Why Growth Rates Differ*, which was a detailed study of the sources of growth of eight European countries and the United States over the period 1950–62. (Solow did not go beyond trying to account for the growth of output in terms of the growth of persons employed and the growth of the capital stock.) Anticipation of Denison's 1967 study can be found in his earlier work on the United States (Denison, 1962). He has further refined and developed his approach since his 1967 work and, in particular, has used it to examine the productivity slowdown since the early 1970s (Denison, 1974, 1979, 1984, 1985). The technique has also been used to examine the sources of growth for the UK in a historical context (Matthews, Feinstein and Odling-Smee, 1982). The multitude of studies that have been undertaken using this approach have been extensively surveyed by Maddison (1987).

The attempt to reduce the residual (which, after all, is nothing more than a measure of our ignorance) has been twofold. Some 'neoclassical purists' have sought only to augment the estimates of the growth of the inputs and to thereby reduce the growth of total factor productivity. This is particularly true of Jorgenson in his studies with a number of colleagues, e.g. Jorgenson and Griliches (1967) and Jorgenson, Gallop and Fraumeni (1987). Others, especially Denison himself, have adopted a far more pragmatic approach by also allowing for increasing returns, for disequilibrium factors such as the intersectoral movement of labour, for the catch-up bonus, etc. These factors are, to a large extent, incompatible with the pure neoclassical assumptions.

We may summarise the more comprehensive growth accounting approach by means of the following equation:

$$q = v(R + \rho + \Sigma \, a_i \ell_i^* + \Sigma \, (1 - a_i)k_i^* + \Sigma \, d_i) \qquad (1.14)$$

v denotes the degree of returns to scale with increasing returns implying a value of greater than unity. (Denison, in effect, imputes returns to scale to output growth rather than to the growth of the tangible factor inputs, which is the more usual procedure.) R is the residual and ρ is the rate of disembodied technical change. ℓ_i^* is the growth of the various labour inputs. k_i^* is the growth of the non-labour inputs such as equipment and machinery, structures, dwellings, inventories, non-residential land and the growth of R&D 'capital'. The * superscript denotes that these inputs may be adjusted in some way. For example, the growth of the labour input may be adjusted for changes in the age and sex composition of the labour force as well as for changes in the average hours worked. The growth of the capital input may be adjusted for changes in capacity utilisation. d_i is the contribution to economic growth of the disequilibrium factors, namely, improvements in resource allocation.

A potential source of ambiguity is what is precisely meant by the terms 'residual', the growth of total factor productivity, and by

technical progress, since the definitions differ to some degree between authors. In equation (1.14), the residual is the growth of
output that remains unaccounted for when the growth of all other
factors together with returns to scale have been allowed for. The rate
of technical progress, ρ, Denison (1967) takes to be the 'residual' in
the US, which is the most advanced country. Denison argues that
attributing some growth of output to exogenous technical progress,
or 'advances in knowledge not elsewhere classified', is a legitimate
practice. Thus by definition the 'true' residual for the US is zero. It is
then assumed that the rate of technical progress for the European
countries also takes this value of ρ. It may be argued that as there is
no explanation as to what determines the rate of technical progress
in the US, and that ρ still represents specification or measurement
errors, the dichotomy made between R and ρ is unwarranted. Nevertheless, the exact meaning of the term 'the residual' used by various
authors is usually made clear by the context in which it is used. We
shall limit the term 'the growth of total factor productivity' to the
residual that remains after an allowance has been made for the
growth of the tangible inputs under the assumption of constant returns to scale.

THE SOURCES OF GROWTH: 1950–73

Table 1.7(a) reports a summary of Denison's (1967) estimates of the
sources of growth for eleven countries during the Long Boom,
although for eight countries the terminal date is 1962.[10] Consequently, we have supplemented these figures with the results of a
study by Kendrick (1981) (Table 1.7(b)). The methodology of Kendrick follows that of Denison quite closely, although there are differences. Denison, for example, uses Net National Income while
Kendrick confines his attention to the Gross Business Product. The
reason Kendrick adopts the latter is because of the difficulties inherent in the measurement of output in the non-business sector, noted
above.

   The first point to note is that the growth of total factor productivity
explains by far the largest part of the growth of output. On the basis
of Denison's results, the growth of total factor productivity (R_1) on
average accounts for 58 per cent of the growth of output. The range is
from 74 per cent (France) to 40 per cent (Canada). A similar picture
emerges from Kendrick's results. It is worth noting in passing that the

Denison figure for the UK is very close to the 58 per cent we found in our simple example above. This is notwithstanding the various adjustments that were made to the growth of the inputs. Consequently, the net effects of these in accounting for economic growth were very small.

THE ADJUSTMENT TO THE GROWTH OF THE LABOUR INPUT

As a first approximation, we used in our example the growth of employed persons as a proxy for the growth of the labour input. But clearly this is unsatisfactory; ideally the growth of the number of persons employed should be adjusted for changes in the average number of hours worked and for changes in the age–sex composition. Denison (1962), however, argued that above 2,529 hours a year any cut in the average hours worked is fully compensated for by increased work intensity. (See Maddison, 1987, pp. 661–2 who disputes the validity of this adjustment. This also serves to emphasise the large subjective element that frequently occurs in trying to provide quantitative estimates in the growth accounting approach.) Female workers are sometimes given a weight of less than unity to reflect their lower productivity than men, at least as measured by wage rates. Maddison (1987), for example, applies a weight of 0.6 for the 1913–50 period.

A major innovation of Denison (1962) was to adjust the labour force for quality changes and this has now become standard practice in the growth accounting literature. It has long been realised that education is not merely a consumption good, but also represents investment in human capital. General schooling, while not necessarily imparting vocational skills, has the advantage of making the labour force more flexible in that it can obtain greater benefit from any subsequent apprenticeships and on the job training, as well as being more responsive to new ideas and techniques of production. Education thus tends to raise the efficiency of labour by improving its quality (Schultz, 1961).

The postwar period saw a rapid expansion in the amount of schooling received by the average worker. The amount of years spent by the representative person in the education system rose steadily, both through choice as per capita income rose and because of legislation which raised the minimum school-leaving age in a number of

Table 1.7(a) Sources of growth of net national income: selected advanced countries 1950–62 – Denison's estimates

Sources of growth	Belgium	Denmark	France	W. Germany	Italy	Netherlands	Norway	UK	US	Japan (1953–71)	US (1948–69)	Canada (1950–67)
Net National Income (NNI) (adjusted)	3.03	3.63	4.70	6.27	5.60	4.07	3.43	2.38	3.36	8.81	4.00	4.95[d]
Total Factor Input	1.17	1.55	1.24	2.78	1.66	1.91	1.04	1.11	1.95	3.95	2.09[e]	3.02
(i) Labour input[a]	0.76	0.59	0.45	1.37	0.96	0.87	0.15	0.60	1.12	1.85	1.30	1.85
(ii) Capital input	0.41	0.96	0.79	1.41	0.70	1.04	0.89	0.51	0.83	2.10	0.79	1.14
Total Factor Productivity or residual R_1 (% of NNI)	1.86 (61)	2.08 (57)	3.46 (74)	3.49 (56)	3.94 (70)	2.16 (53)	2.29 (70)	1.27 (53)	1.41 (42)	4.86 (55)	1.91 (48)	1.96 (40)

Economies of scale	0.51	0.65	1.00	1.61	1.22	0.78	0.57	0.36	0.36	1.94	0.42	0.66
Improved allocation of resources	0.51	0.68	0.95	1.01	1.42	0.63	0.92	0.12	0.29	0.95	0.64	0.64
Residual R_2 (% of NNI)	0.84 (28)	0.75 (21)	1.51 (32)	0.87 (14)	1.30 (23)	0.75 (26)	0.90 (27)	0.79 (33)	0.76 (23)	1.97 (22)	1.19 (30)	0.66 (13)
Advances in technology[b]	0.76	0.76	0.76	0.76	0.76	0.76	0.76	0.76	0.76	1.19	1.19	1.19
Residual R_3 (% of NNI)	0.08 (3)	−0.01 (n.m.)[c]	0.75 (16)	0.11 (2)	0.54 (10)	−0.01 (10)	0.14 (4)	0.03 (1)	0.0 (0)	0.78 (9)	0.0 (0)	−0.53 (n.m.)[c]

Notes: [a] Adjusted for changes in hours of work, age–sex composition, and education.
[b] Taken as the final residual of the US, the most advanced country.
[c] n.m. denotes not meaningful.
[d] May not add up due to rounding.
[e] Estimate for 1955–62 period.

Sources: Denison (1967, ch. 21), Denison and Chung (1976, table 4.8, pp. 42–3).

Table 1.7(b) Sources of growth of gross business product: selected advanced countries 1960–73 – Kendrick's estimates

Sources of growth	Belgium	Canada	France	W. Germany	Italy	Japan	Sweden	UK	US
Gross Business Product (GBP)	**5.3**	**5.8**	**5.8**	**4.6**	**5.6**	**10.8**	**4.2**	**2.9**	**4.4**
Total Factor Input	**1.3**	**3.0**	**2.1**	**1.3**	**0.8**	**4.9**	**0.7**	**1.2**	**2.6**
(i) Labour input[a]	-0.3	0.8	0.2	-0.8	-0.6	1.3	-0.9	-0.1	0.9
(ii) Capital input	1.6	2.2	1.9	2.1	1.4	3.6	1.6	1.3	1.7
Capacity utilisation	0.1	0.2	-0.1	0.0	0.0	0.0	-0.1	-0.1	0.1
Total Factor Productivity or residual R_1 (% of GBP)	**3.9** (74)	**2.6** (45)	**3.8** (66)	**3.3** (72)	**4.8** (86)	**5.9** (55)	**3.8** (86)	**1.8** (62)	**1.7** (39)
Economies of scale	0.5	0.6	0.6	0.5	0.6	1.1	0.4	0.3	0.4
Improved allocation of resources	0.4	-0.2	0.4	0.3	0.8	1.1	0.5	0.2	0.2
Residual R_2 (% of GBP)	**3.0** (57)	**2.2** (38)	**2.8** (48)	**2.5** (54)	**3.4** (61)	**3.7** (34)	**2.7** (64)	**1.3** (45)	**1.1** (25)

Advances in technology	1.6	0.9	1.6	1.2	1.4	2.3	0.6	0.7	1.2
(i) Exogenous technical progress[b]	0.5	0.5	0.5	0.5	0.5	0.5	0.5	0.5	0.5
(ii) Direct effects of R&D	0.3	0.4	0.4	0.6	0.3	0.5	0.2	0.2	0.5
(iii) Domestic technical diffusion	0.8	0.0	0.7	0.1	0.6	1.3	-0.1	0.0	0.2
Residual R_3 (% of GBP)	1.4 (26)	1.3 (22)	1.2 (21)	1.3 (28)	2.0 (36)	1.4 (13)	2.1 (50)	0.6 (21)	-0.1 (n.m.)[c]
Effect of government regulation	-0.1	-0.1	-0.1	0.0	-0.1	-0.2	-0.1	0.0	-0.1
Residual R_4 (% of GBP)	1.5 (28)	1.4 (24)	1.3 (22)	1.3 (28)	1.9 (34)	1.6 (15)	2.2 (55)	0.6 (21)	0.0 (0)

Notes: [a]Adjusted for changes in hours of work, age–sex composition, and education.
[b]Taken as the final residual of the US, the most advanced country.
[c]Denotes not meaningful.

Source: Calculated from Kendrick (1981, tables 1 and 7, pp. 128 and 141, respectively).

countries. The need arises for the construction of an index of the labour input that explicitly takes into account this increasing quality. The procedure adopted by Denison is, perhaps not surprisingly, firmly grounded in the neoclassical tradition. The rationale is based on the assumption that 'if workers with one level of education earn 50 per cent more, on the average, than *otherwise similar* individuals with less education, they will be counted . . . as 50 per cent more labour. The reason is by now familiar: average earnings of large groups of individuals are taken to be proportional to the average values of their marginal products' (Denison, 1967, p.79). The amount of education a worker received is proxied by the number of years of formal schooling that the person undertook. In order to aggregate the different amounts of schooling, we need some weighting system. As Denison (1967, p. 83) asks: 'Is a college graduate to be counted as the equivalent of $1\frac{1}{2}$, 2 or 3 elementary school graduates?' The weighting chosen by Denison (1962) in his US study was 60 per cent of the average earnings received by a person with a specific number of years of schooling. It is only 60 per cent rather than 100 per cent because of other factors unrelated to education that cause disparities in earnings such as differences in intrinsic intelligence. The effect is that if a person with eight years education accounts for one unit, someone with no formal education represents 0.70 of a unit while a college graduate will be 1.81. For example, if a college graduate receives 135 per cent more income than someone with eight years schooling, then the efficiency adjusted labour unit of the graduate is $1 + (0.6)(1.35)$ $= 1.81$. A similar weighting system was used by Denison in his 1967 study for the European countries.

The estimates of improvement in the quality of the labour force are relatively small when compared with the size of total factor productivity growth in most countries. In the case of the US, Denison estimated that it contributed 0.49 percentage points to the growth of output over 1950–62. The growth of education was not so fast in the other advanced countries over this period. For Northwest Europe, the contribution was 0.23 percentage points which only accounted for 5 per cent of the growth of national income. While the effect was to reduce the growth of total factor productivity for each country, it nevertheless resulted in an increase, rather than a reduction, in both the relative and absolute differences in the growth of total factor productivity between the other advanced countries and the US. As we have already observed, when all the adjustments to the growth of the labour force are taken into account, including the age and sex composition of the labour force and changes in the hours worked, the net effect turns out to be comparatively small.

THE CONTRIBUTION OF INCREASING RETURNS TO SCALE

Denison, unlike many other economists in the neoclassical tradition, stresses economies of scale as an important factor in accounting for output and productivity growth. The major difficulty with this assumption is that it raises the well-known problems for the neo-classical marginal productivity theory of distribution and, hence, the use of factor shares as weights. Denison is well aware of this problem, but his reconciliation of the two conflicting assumptions is not particularly convincing.[11]

While admitting that 'no pretence is made that these gains [from increasing returns to scale] can be measured precisely or without personal judgement', Denison has no doubt as to their importance. 'If the estimates developed are at all near the mark, economies of scale go a long way toward explaining why differences among countries in growth rates were as large as they were in the postwar period' (1967, p. 225). This may be readily confirmed from Table 1.8 where it may be seen that economies of scale account for between 46 per cent (West Germany) and 22 per cent (the US) of total factor productivity growth. In the case of West Germany and France, for example, economies of scale account for nearly as much of output growth as the growth of the tangible factor inputs.

The relationship between the degree of returns to scale and the contribution of increasing returns to output growth is as follows.

From equation (1.14) the growth of output under the assumption of constant returns to scale, q', is given by:

$$q' = q/v \qquad (1.15)$$

where q is the observed growth of output.

Hence, the degree of increasing returns is given by:

$$v = q/q' \qquad (1.16)$$

The percentage point contribution of increasing returns to scale to output growth is:

$$q - q' = q\,(1 - 1/v) \qquad (1.17)$$

Table 1.8 Denison's estimates of the contribution of increasing returns to scale to output growth, 1950–62

Country	(1)	(2)	(3)
Japan[a]	1.94	40	1.28
United States[b]	0.42	22	1.12
United States	0.36	28	1.12
Canada[c]	0.66	34	1.15
Belgium	0.51	27	1.20
Denmark	0.65	31	1.22
France	1.00	29	1.27
West Germany	1.61	46	1.35
Italy	1.22	31	1.28
Netherlands	0.78	36	1.24
Norway	0.57	24	1.20
United Kingdom	0.36	28	1.18

Column (1): Percentage point contribution of increasing returns to the growth of national income.

Column (2): Contribution as a percentage of total factor productivity growth.

Column (3): Implied degree of homogeneity (v).

Notes: [a]1953–71; [b]1948–69; [c]1950–67.

Source: Calculated from Table 1.7.

It may be seen from Table 1.8 that the values of v are substantial, ranging from 1.35 (West Germany) to 1.12 (United States).

Denison (1967) identifies three separate sources of returns to scale that make up the contribution to output growth reported in Table 1.8.

The first type is what is perhaps thought of as conventional economies of scale. This is the lowering of unit costs as the size of the national market increases. With the growth of sales, there are greater opportunities for both inter-industry and intra-industry specialisation, increased division of labour and larger production runs. To these must be added the significant cost savings that result from bulk buying and selling, with resulting lower transaction costs per unit. In *Why Growth Rates Differ*, the following values for this category of returns to scale are assumed to exist: 1.10 for the United States, 1.11

for the large European Countries, 1.15 for Italy and 1.12 for the small European countries (except Norway, which has a value of 1.13).

The second type of economies of scale Denison infers from the fact that the relative prices of the fastest growing products are lower when measured in US than European prices. According to Denison, this is because the US, with its higher per capita income, is able to reap the benefits of producing these high income elasticity of demand goods and services before the European countries. These benefits are passed on to the consumer in the form of lower relative prices. The contribution to growth from this type of economies of scale ranges from 0.91 percentage points in Germany (compared with 0.63 percentage points for the first type of economies of scale) to 0.11 percentage points for Belgium (compared with 0.33 percentage points).

The third and final contribution that economies of scale make is that brought about by the increase in the size of the retail markets with the rapid increase in car ownership over the postwar period. Denison attributes somewhat arbitarily an increase of 0.07 percentage points in the annual growth rate to this source, with the exception of the United Kingdom which is assigned 0.05 percentage points.

Kendrick's estimates of the contribution of increasing returns for 1960–73 is based upon a degree of homogeneity of 1.10 which is considerably less than most of the values used by Denison (Table 1.8). Others are even more sceptical about the importance of increasing returns. Jorgenson and Griliches (1967) assume constant returns to scale in their work. Maddison (1987, p. 671) argues that 'empirical evidence on economies of scale is scarce' (although see Chapter 2) and assumes that the scale bonus is only 3 per cent of GDP growth, i.e. $v = 1.03$.

THE CONTRIBUTION OF THE INTER-SECTORAL TRANSFER OF LABOUR

The postwar period has seen massive structural change in the economies of the advanced countries. In most of the countries there has been a substantial transfer of labour out of agriculture, initially into industry and then later into services. The size of the agricultural sector immediately after the Second World War was quite large in some countries. For example, agriculture accounted for 29 per cent of total employment in France in 1950. Denmark (28 per cent) and West Germany (25 per cent) were not far behind. On the other hand, the

United Kingdom had a much smaller proportion with only 5 per cent employed in agriculture. Over the postwar period, there was a large movement of workers off the land. By 1979, agriculture's share had fallen to 9 per cent in both France and Denmark and to 6 per cent in West Germany.

The cause of this decline in agricultural employment was twofold. First, the low income elasticity of demand for foodstuffs meant that the growth of agricultural output was the lowest of all the sectors of the advanced countries (Cripps and Tarling, 1973, Appendix 3). Second, mechanisation, the consolidation of farms (allowing considerable economies of scale to be reaped) and rapid technical progress all combined dramatically to reduce the labour requirements of agriculture.

A feature common to most of the advanced countries was that both wages and labour productivity in agriculture were considerably below those found in the rest of the economy. In the countries which had an especially large agricultural sector, farming was a family occupation; as much a way of life as a job. Since much of the labour was supplied by the family, the number of workers on the farm was more often dictated by social rather than economic considerations. This led to a great deal of disguised unemployment, with workers being paid nearer to their average product than their marginal product. In the extreme case, there was surplus labour in the sense that the loss of the marginal worker would not have reduced output at all.

Consequently, the transfer of workers from this low productivity sector to higher productivity sectors, especially industry, in the early part of the postwar period led to an increase in aggregate productivity (and a temporary acceleration in aggregate productivity growth) for purely arithmetical reasons. This is a picture that is perhaps more familiar in the developing countries and it was to analyse this situation that the 'dual sector' or 'dual economy' model of economic development was constructed (Lewis, 1954). A number of authorities (notably, Cornwall, 1977; Kindleberger, 1967; and Kaldor, 1978a) have argued that this approach is equally applicable to analysing the growth of the advanced countries and represents a negation of the neoclassical paradigm. We examine this approach in Chapter 2, but for the moment it is sufficient to note that there is widespread agreement that there was, in many countries, an excessive allocation of labour to agriculture in the sense that at the margin the loss of a worker reduced total agricultural output by considerably less than the wage. Denison extended this argument to that part of the service sector where there were many small businesses run by self-employed proprietors. Once again, the empirical pragmatism of Denison lies uneasily with the underlying neoclassical assumptions of the growth accounting approach.

The contribution that the inter-sectoral transfer of labour makes to output growth is calculated by making a number of assumptions, most notably that the loss in agricultural output through the transfer of factor inputs to the non-farm sector is less than the gain in output in the rest of the economy. A similar procedure is employed when considering the self-employed tertiary sector.

The impact of the transfer is quite substantial (especially in the case of the fast growers, Japan, Italy, France and West Germany as may be seen in Table 1.7, *viz* the contribution due to the 'improved allocation of resources'). In the period 1960–73, the gains in output were smaller, which reflect the progressive exhaustion of the agricultural reserve army of labour.

Another possible source of gain (or loss) is the intra-sectoral transfer of labour, or the movement of labour between the low and high productivity activities, *within* a particular sector. These intra-sectoral differences in productivity are not nearly so large as those that exist between agriculture and the rest of the economy. Consequently, it is perhaps not all that surprising to learn that the gains from, for example, the intra-industry reallocation of labour, are negligible (Beckerman, 1965).

To summarise the position so far: after allowance has been made for the growth of factor inputs, the contribution of increasing returns to scale and the progressive improvement in the intersectoral allocation of resources, there remains anything between a quarter and a third of output growth during the period 1950–62 still to be accounted for. For 1960–73, the figures are somewhat higher ranging from 28 to 52 per cent, although, as we have mentioned, the estimates for the two periods are not strictly comparable. The remaining residual, R_2, still shows a great deal of inter-country variation.

THE CONTRIBUTION OF TECHNICAL PROGRESS AND RESEARCH AND DEVELOPMENT

Perhaps one of the least understood aspects of the growth process is what determines the pace of technical change. Indeed, the very concept of technological progress is not without its difficulties. In many statistical estimations of production functions, it is assumed that technical change appears autonomously and shifts the production function over time and this is captured by a time trend. (More sophisticated approaches try to relate the rate of technical change to the degree to which it is embodied in investment; but this still does not answer the question as to where the new knowledge comes from in the first place. It is still assumed that it appears 'like manna from heaven' at an exogenously determined rate. Moreover, Denison (1964) considers that the quantitative impact of the embodiment effect is negligible.) In the growth accounting approach, as we have seen, the impact of technical progress is generally taken to be that portion of output growth that cannot be explained after account has been taken of all other factors, or, rather, of as many as can be quantified, which, of course, is not the same thing.

In his 1967 study, Denison largely circumvented the conceptual problem of how to measure the contribution of technical progress. He simply assumed that the contribution of 'advances in knowledge' was the value of the residual of the most advanced country which was the United States, and this contribution to output growth (some 0.8 percentage points per annum) was imputed to all the other countries. The residual defined as 'the unexplained growth of output' was therefore zero for the US. As we noted above, this can hardly be said to be a very satisfactory procedure.

A moments reflection should be enough to remind us that some of the most spectacular technological advances – such as those generated by the NASA space programme or the Concorde project – were not accomplished without a considerable research cost. Considerable expenditure is devoted to investment in research and development (R&D), whether it is on the salaries of designers and scientists, on their equipment or on the finance of the various prototypes. It is possible to extend the concept of the production function with these expenditures being considered as 'inputs', and the value of improvements or new products due to this new knowledge as 'output'. Obviously, such a production function would be subject to much greater stochastic influence than a conventional production function. By its very nature, production of new knowledge, *per se*, is a very risky and uncertain business and much expenditure has to be written off with very little to show for it.

Expenditure on R&D may be considered analogous to, and indeed an alternative to, purchases of more tangible capital goods. Both will, *ceteris paribus*, serve to raise the productivity of labour. Consider a simple example: it is proposed to increase the yield of corn. This could be achieved by investing in already existing technology – by applying fertiliser to the fields, for example. On the other hand, money could be spent on R&D in order to develop a new hybrid variety of corn that has a greater crop yield. In a world devoid of uncertainty and indivisibilities, the division of expenditure between these two types of investment should be such that their private rates of return are equal.

Denison (1967, p. 288), however, is very sceptical of the importance of R&D. 'The purpose of most – probably the bulk – of R&D expenditures, moreover, is such that it does not affect the growth rate no matter how successful it may be . . . . [T]here is no way of knowing whether those fruits of organized research that do affect the measured growth rate contribute 0.1, 0.7, or any intermediate amount to the total contribution of advances of knowledge. The fact that expenditures for research and development have expanded so much in the United States while estimates of the contribution of advances of knowledge have not may suggest that organized R&D is not very important to measured growth. But even this remark must be qualified by noting that we do not know how large has been the increase in R&D expenditures of the types that are relevant to measured growth.'

The problem is, of course, that not only do we live in a world of uncertainty, but also the production of new knowledge often has significant externalities attached to it. The development of a new process by a particular company may well improve the efficiency of other firms in the industry if they had access to it. There may well be 'spillovers' between different industries or from military and space programmes to civilian production methods. This presents one of the major problems in ensuring sufficient resources are devoted to R&D. From a social point of view, knowledge should be diffused as quickly and as cheaply as possible to ensure the greatest possible social benefit is obtained. On the other hand, the more entrepreneurs see the private returns to their R&D being diminished by the actions of their competitors, the less willing they will be to commit funds to this type of investment. There is thus a trade-off between the benefits of the rapid and widespread adoption of new techniques and the volume of private investment devoted to R&D. It is this that provides the rationale for the limited protection of new ideas by patent rights and the funding of basic research by the government (Arrow, 1962).

There is a good deal of evidence to suggest that there are high rates of return to R&D. Two different types of research have been pursued in an endeavour to measure this. The first is the detailed case-study approach that traces out the impact of a particular innovation. This work primarily focuses on the social rates of return and the benefits of the new development are compared with all the associated research costs – not just those that were directly involved in the successful outcome. Even so, the 'internal rates of return implied by these estimates are quite high (10 to 50 per cent per annum) even though they are usually based on conservative assumptions, and, at their lower end (such as the 12 per cent estimate for polio vaccines by Weisbrod), are at a level worth investing more if the opportunity to do so were to arise again' (Griliches, 1973, p. 60).

There are two objections that can be raised concerning the inferences that are drawn from these 'causal-historical' studies. The first is that they are unrepresentative as they tend to be concentrated on the more prominent and successful innovations. Secondly, the choice of the subject for study is largely constrained by the availability of data and does not reflect what would normally be thought of as major industrial inventions. (Apart from hybrid corn, other studies have dealt with poultry breeding research, agricultural research projects, polio vaccines and military transport aircraft.)

The second type of study which largely avoids these criticisms is the econometric estimation of the aggregate production function with the growth of an index of R&D expenditures explicitly included as an input. The production function is typically specified as:

$$Q = A_0 e^{\lambda t} L^\alpha K^\beta K_{RD}^\gamma \tag{1.18}$$

with the notation as before and where K_{RD} is an index of the stock of R&D and γ is the elasticity of output with respect to the stock of R&D.

There are, however, a number of difficulties with the calculation of the stock of R&D. As with tangible investment, allowance should be made for depreciation and obsolesence. With time, new developments make earlier knowledge redundant or, at least, severely reduce its revenue generating capacity. (After all, knowledge of the most efficient design of sailing clippers is not so useful today as it was a century ago.) There also seems to be a complicated lag structure in the relationship between R&D expenditure and its effect on output. There is some evidence that the lag takes an inverted v. The maximum benefit occurs after about five years with little return after about 10 to 16 years (Evenson, 1968, cited by Griliches, 1973).

Another problem is that a substantial proportion of R&D (often over 50 per cent) in most countries is either undertaken directly by public agencies or under contract for the government by private firms (see Table 1.9). In both cases, in the US and most other countries, the volume of 'output' measured by the statistical authorities is defined to be simply the deflated value of the inputs. Thus, there is no independent measure of output for nearly all the research in the defence industries, the space programme and medicine. Indeed, an increase in the speed and effectiveness of medical practice will actually show up as a decline in hospital efficiency (productivity) to the extent that output is measured by the number of patient days. There is also the problem of measuring the output of R&D in the private sector, especially as most of it results in the improvement of the quality of products. Price indices often do not adequately allow for changes in quality.

With these reservations in mind, we are now in a position to consider the contribution to output growth that R&D makes. Estimations of equation (1.18), or similar specifications, typically find estimates of γ of about 0.05 for US public research investments in agriculture and 0.1 for private research investments in selected US manufacturing industries (Griliches, 1973, p. 63).

Related to this econometric analysis is the growth accounting approach. Expressing equation (1.18) in growth rates we obtain:

$$q = \lambda + \alpha\ell + \beta k + \gamma k_{RD} \qquad (1.19)$$

or, rearranging:

$$tfp = \lambda + \gamma k_{RD} = q - \alpha\ell - \beta k \qquad (1.20)$$

Given the difficulties of obtaining accurate estimates for k_{RD} and γ, an alternative approach is to use the condition that:

$$\gamma = \frac{\partial Q}{\partial K_{RD}} \cdot \frac{K_{RD}}{Q} \qquad (1.21)$$

and

$$\gamma k_{RD} = \frac{\partial Q}{\partial K_{RD}} \cdot \frac{I_{RD}}{Q} = \rho \frac{I_{RD}}{Q} \qquad (1.22)$$

where ρ is the marginal product of R&D or the social rate of return and I_{RD}/Q is net investment in research expressed as a ratio to output. If it is assumed that there is little or no depreciation, the R&D intensity variable (I_{RD}/Q) can be approximated by the ratio of observed R&D expenditure to GDP. Griliches (1988a, p. 15) considers that 'the assumption that knowledge does not depreciate is not too bad if one is interested in time series comparisons within a well-defined industry or aggregate and the total stock of R&D capital is changing only slowly. Then the difference between changes in gross and net investment is unlikely to be very large.'

Following Griliches (1973, p. 65), we assume a social rate of return of 30 per cent. Let us further assume that total R&D expenditures are about 3 per cent of GDP and that about half of R&D expenditures has an effect on output, as conventionally measured. Of this figure of 1.5 per cent, let us assume that, for sake of argument, about half represents net investment. Consequently, the contribution of the growth of R&D stocks is $\gamma k_{RD} = 0.3 \times 0.75 = 0.23$ percentage points.

Table 1.9 reports the ratios of R&D expenditure and gross fixed capital formation as a proportion of GDP. It is noticeable how small R&D expenditure is compared with the more tangible forms of investment. Table 1.10 reports Kendrick's (1981) estimates of the growth rates of real R&D capital stocks and the contribution made to output growth (γk_{RD}) for 1960–73 and 1973–9. Kendrick estimated the latter using equation (1.22) and taking ρ as 50 per cent. He found that for the US the contribution to output growth was 0.5 percentage points per annum during 1960–73. Only West Germany, with 0.6 percentage points, had a higher value. Thus, while in the case of the US, γk_{RD} explains a not insignificant part of the country's relatively small growth of total factor productivity (although the contribution is greater than that obtained by other estimators, e.g. Denison, 1985), it accounts for a negligible part for the other countries.

If, in our earlier example, we had assumed, like Kendrick, that ρ was 50 per cent (rather than 30 per cent), the contribution that k_{RD} makes rises from 0.22 to just under 0.4 percentage points. This latter figure is very similar to that of Kendrick.

The relative unimportance of R&D in explaining the residual has also been demonstrated by Scott (1981). He considers Denison's estimate of the growth of output attributable to 'advances in knowledge and n.e.c.' of 1.41 per cent per annum over the period 1948–73. If this is attributable to R&D, it implies a rate of return of over 50 per cent. Furthermore, Scott considers that, since it is very difficult to

Table 1.9   The ratios of R&D to GDP and gross fixed capital formation to GDP, selected advanced countries, 1960–79

Country	% of R&D financed by government	R&D as a % of GDP			Gross fixed capital formation as a % of GDP		
	1963[a]	1960	1973	1979	1960	1973	1979
Belgium	24	n.a.	1.30	1.48	19.3	21.4	21.0
Canada	55	0.83	1.03	0.92	21.9	21.4	21.0
France	64	1.30	1.78	1.74	20.1	23.8	21.3
W. Germany	41	0.96	2.23	2.39	24.3	24.5	22.7
Italy	33	0.48	0.49	0.86	22.6	20.8	18.7
Japan	28	1.36	1.95	1.94	30.1	36.7	31.7
Sweden	48	1.45	1.68	1.80	22.1	21.8	19.5
UK	54	2.52	1.97	1.83	16.4	19.6	17.8
US	64	2.67	2.34	2.32	17.6	18.5	18.1

Note: [a]1964 for West Germany, Sweden, and the US; 1964–5 for the UK.

Sources: R&D as a % of GDP: Kendrick (1981, table 11, p. 158); Gross fixed capital formation as a % of GDP: *OECD National Accounts* (various years); % R&D financed by government: Matthews (1973, table 1.2, p. 17).

Table 1.10   Rate of growth of real R&D capital stocks, per cent per annum, (k_{RD}) and the contribution of the growth of R&D stocks to output growth, percentage points per annum (γk_{RD})

Country	1960–73		1973–79	
	k_{RD}	γk_{RD}	k_{RD}	γk_{RD}
Belgium	7.7	0.3	7.1	0.2
Canada	10.1	0.4	4.5	0.2
France	11.5	0.4	5.2	0.2
West Germany	12.7	0.6	9.2	0.4
Italy	12.0	0.3	7.2	0.1
Japan	14.3	0.5	11.6	0.3
Sweden	3.7	0.2	6.0	0.2
UK	1.6	0.2	1.0	0.1
US	4.1	0.5	1.3	0.1

Source: Kendrick (1981, tables 7, 11, 12).

distinguish applied R&D from other investment, it is more appropriate to attribute the residual to *basic* R&D. This implies a rate of return to basic R&D of some 2,300 per cent per annum. As Scott (1981, p. 214) concludes: 'it is difficult to believe that the average rate of return to R&D expenditure was 50 per cent p.a. let alone a higher figure'.

THE CONTRIBUTION OF THE DIFFUSION OF INNOVATIONS AND TECHNOLOGICAL 'CATCH-UP'

As we have already noted, Denison takes the rate of technical progress for the countries in his sample as the value of the residual of the United States after an allowance has been made for changes in the quality of the inputs, increasing returns to scale and gains due to the improved allocation of resources (R_2 in Table 1.7a and b). This value represents output growth resulting from R&D and exogenous technical progress, although it also reflects measurement errors associated with the estimates of the other sources of growth in the United States. Denison is thus left with a final unexplained residual for all the countries other than the United States (R_4).

Kendrick attempts to go further than this and calculates directly the contribution of R&D, as well as trying to estimate the contribution of the domestic diffusion of innovations, by examining changes in the average age of the fixed capital stock. The final residual he attributes primarily to a 'catch-up' phenomenon which is due to the international diffusion of technology from the technological leader to those less technically developed. (We have not followed this procedure when reporting his results in Tables 1.7a and b and 1.13. For reasons that will become apparent below, we have preferred to follow Denison's procedure.)

The technological catch-up hypothesis assumes that the United States is the country at the technological frontier while the other advanced countries lag behind, to a greater or lesser extent. As a result, Europe and Japan have been able to benefit in terms of a temporary acceleration in their rate of technical progress by acquiring this more advanced technology. The United States is, by definition, not able to benefit from the international diffusion of technology and has to rely on its own R&D expenditure to promote technical change. It also has the burden of having to meet many of the development costs of inventions etc., from which other countries can subsequently benefit. Consequently, we should expect the United States to have the slowest growth rate of total factor productivity and labour productivity of all the advanced countries, which indeed proves to be the case. Over time, the rate of technical progress of the other countries will diminish and converge with that of the US as the technological gap shrinks. This implies that the levels of productivity and per capita income of the various countries should also progressively tend to converge, for which there is evidence (Dowrick and Nguyen, 1989). An implicit assumption underlying this hypothesis is that there exist techniques of production in the US which, if they had been known in the other advanced countries, would have been immediately adopted. It is important to note that the existence of convergence, *per se*, does not necessarily mean that the international diffusion of innovations is important; there are other factors that could be responsible for the convergence and we return to this below.

The technological catch-up thesis has been found plausible by a number of researchers, including Gomulka (1971, 1979), Cornwall (1976, 1977), Singer and Reynolds (1975), Marris (1982), Maddison (1982, chapter 5), Lindbeck, (1983), Giersch and Wolter (1983) and Baumol (1986). It is typically assumed that disparities in the state of technology are reflected in differences in the levels of productivity, or per capita income, between countries. Thus, the growth of productivity due to the catch-up is often postulated to be a function of the level of productivity (or the per capita income) of a particular country relative to that of the leading country, the United States.

A rationale for this argument is as follows. Let us assume that the economy of a country, denoted by the subscript i, is described by a Cobb–Douglas production function, subject to constant returns to scale:

$$Q_i = A_i L_i^{\alpha} K_i^{(1-\alpha)} \tag{1.23}$$

The level of productivity is given by:

$$P_i = A_i^{\frac{1}{\alpha}} \left[\frac{K_i}{Q_i} \right]^{\frac{(1-\alpha)}{\alpha}} \tag{1.24}$$

If it is assumed as a 'stylised fact' that there is very little difference in the capital–output ratios of the various advanced countries for the postwar period (although this may be misleading, especially for earlier periods), the ratio of the level of technology of the United

States to the country concerned will be given by (assuming no difference between the countries in the output elasticities):

$$\frac{P_{US}}{P_i} = \left[\frac{A_{US}}{A_i}\right]^{\frac{1}{\alpha}} \qquad (1.25)$$

Consequently, under these circumstances, the ratio of the productivity of the most advanced country (the United States) to the other countries (or the logarithmic transformation of this ratio) may prove to be a suitable proxy for the technological gap. Since there is a close correspondence between GDP per worker and per capita income, the latter is sometimes used in constructing the proxy. However, the ratio of productivities will not be a good proxy for the technological gap to the extent that the capital–output ratios differ between countries or there are increasing returns to scale.

Baumol (1986) used data from Maddison (1982) for 16 industrial countries and found that there was a strong inverse relationship between their growth rates of GDP over the period from 1870 to 1979 and the logarithm of their 1870 productivity levels. He interpreted this as strong evidence for the convergence hypothesis. In other words, as the relatively less advanced countries progressively took advantage of the stock of advanced technology of the leading country (or countries), there was a steady convergence of per capita incomes. However, De Long (1988) has convincingly demonstrated that this result is largely due to a combination of sample bias and to likely measurement errors in the 1870 income levels. The 'ex post' sample of countries that Maddison and Baumol use are those that were the most successful. For example, if the level of income of the second poorest country in 1870 is taken as the cut-off point for inclusion in the sample, then Argentina, Chile, East Germany, New Zealand, Portugal and Spain should be added, giving a 'once rich' sample of 22 countries. (If the income level of the poorest country in 1870, namely Japan, was used as the cut-off point, the sample would have to include half the countries of the world.) When the sample of 22 countries was used, together with an appropriate econometric technique to take account of the likely measurement errors, De Long (1988 p. 1148) came to the conclusion that: 'The long-run data do not show convergence on any but the most optimistic reading. They do not support the claim that those nations that should have been able to rapidly assimilate industrial technology have all converged.' (See also the reply by Baumol and Wolff, 1988.)

Giersch and Wolter (1983, table 3, p. 40) also found that there was a statistically significant relationship between the growth of GDP per employee and the gap variable for the period 1964 to 1973, but this broke down from 1973 to 1979. This led them to conclude that part of the post-1973 slowdown may have been due to the exhaustion of catch-up opportunities.

Other attempts to test the diffusion and convergence hypotheses include estimating the following alternative equations using cross-country data, generally for the advanced countries for the postwar years:

$$tfp = a_1 + b_1\,GAP + \varepsilon_1 \qquad\qquad (1.26a)$$

$$p = a_2 + b_2\,(k - \ell) + b_3\,GAP + \varepsilon_2 \qquad\qquad (1.26b)$$

$$q = a_3 + b_4\ell + b_5 k + b_6\,GAP + \varepsilon_3 \qquad\qquad (1.26c)$$

where *GAP* and *tfp* denote the proxy for the technological gap and the growth of total factor productivity. ε is the error term. The other variables have their customary meaning.

The equations are best interpreted as specifications of a Cobb–Douglas aggregate production function. Equations (1.26a) and (1.26b) impose the constraint that there are constant returns to scale, although this is not true of equation (1.26c), where the coefficients are freely estimated. Both specifications explicitly take into account the effect of the growth of factor inputs on the growth of productivity and output, unlike Baumol's (1986) analysis.

Equation (1.26a) has been estimated, for example, by Lindbeck (1983, TA:5, pp. 32–3). He found that the coefficient of the technological gap was statistically significant and took the expected sign. This was interpreted as confirming the importance of technological catch-up, in that the greater the technological gap, the greater the growth of total factor productivity that results from the international diffusion of innovations. However, the estimation of equation (1.26b) did not give a statistically significant coefficient of the gap variable at the 95 per cent confidence level. This led him to conclude that, in this case, it was not possible to separate the effects of capital accumulation and the diffusion of innovations.

Equation (1.26c) forms the basis for the analysis of Dowrick and Nguyen (1989) using data for the OECD countries from 1950 to 1985. However, they use the gross investment–output ratio as a proxy for the growth of capital. (It should be noted that in their specification the coefficients b_4 and b_5, because of the inclusion of the gap variable, are not simply the estimates of the output elasticities of labour and the investment–output ratio.) They found that the gap (the logarithm of per capita GDP relative to that of US) was statistically significant and that 'the principal findings are that, although the convergence of income levels has been weak since 1973, and the evidence of systematic income convergence since 1950 is critically dependent on the sample selection criteria, TFP catch-up stands out as a dominant and stable trend' (Dowrick and Nguyen, 1989, p. 1028).

Another test is due to Cornwall (1976 and 1977) and consists of estimating the following equation:

$$q = a_4 + b_7(I/Q) + b_8\ POP + b_9\ x + b_{10}\ GAP + \varepsilon_4 \qquad (1.27)$$

where I/Q is the investment–output ratio, POP is the growth of population, and x is the growth of manufactured exports. Equation (1.27) is estimated by Cornwall for the manufacturing sector and is essentially a demand function. Cornwall does not believe that the growth of the advanced countries has been determined by the exogenous growth of the factor inputs, as is implicit in the specification of equations (1.26a, b, and c) (see Chapter 2). The I/Q variable was included because 'the higher is $[I/Q]$ the greater should be demand pressures and the lower will be the "macro risks" of investment. In addition, the higher the investment ratio, the greater should be the proportion of a country's capital stock that embodies the latest techniques' (Cornwall, 1976, p. 311, omitting a footnote). Population growth was included to capture the effects of the growth of the size of the market and, hence, economies of scale. It always proved to be insignificant. Export growth was included since it determines the growth of manufacturing output through a multiplier effect (see Chapter 3). The results proved sensitive to whether or not Japan was included in the sample. Excluding Japan, the coefficient on I/Q was found to be statistically insignificant.

Marris (1982) adopts a similar specification except that he also includes the growth of exports and the rate of inflation as other explanatory factors and takes as his regressand the growth of GDP per capita. Again, in both cases, the coefficient of the technological gap variable turns out to be statistically significant.

However, not everyone is convinced by such arguments and evidence that the diffusion of technology is an important factor in explaining the economic growth disparities. Kaldor (1966b, p. 13), for example, asks how can the progress of knowledge account for the fact that, for example, in the period 1954–1960 productivity in the German motor-car industry increased at 7 per cent per year and in Britain only 2.7 per cent a year? Since large segments of the car industry in both countries were controlled by the same American firms, they must have had the same access to improvements in knowledge and know-how.

In a later paper (Kaldor, 1975a), he further questions how the diffusion argument can explain the fact that by the early 1970s Japan had overtaken the United States in many high technology industries. The theory also has difficulty in explaining how the lead changes between countries and why, for example, the United Kingdom, which was the technological leader in the 19th century, has now slipped so far behind the United States.

Cripps and Tarling (1973, p. 3) likewise find it plausible to assume that 'all [the advanced countries] have access to the same body of technical knowledge'.

There is little doubt that much of Japan's rapid productivity growth in the 1950s and 1960s was due to the import of advanced production processes and technology from abroad. The Japanese sent many productivity missions overseas explicitly to learn why the American and European industries were so much more efficient (Rowthorn, 1975a). However, it is by no means clear that the lower level of productivity in Europe compared with the United States was necessarily due to any lack of knowledge of best-practice techniques. Salter (1966 p. 72) notes that Working Party and Productivity Mission Reports found that the productivity of the best plants in the UK was comparable with that of the best plants in the US. The lower average productivity in the UK was due to a much greater 'tail' of low-productivity plants, resulting from a lower level of real wages. It was not due to ignorance in the UK of the best-practice techniques. As Van der Wee points out, in many cases it was not that Europe and Japan were unaware of such techniques, but that they were not so good at innovating.

The basic techniques for the production of titanium were discovered in Luxemburg. Much of the fundamental work that led to the development of the modern computer technology was undertaken in Europe. The invention of the tunnel diode was based on Japanese research. But in these cases and many others American companies were able to convert invention into innovation. Europe and Japan were better at inventing than innovating, whereas the United States proved very creative in both fields. Over the years there was little change to this pattern . . . . The concepts 'technological gap' and 'catching up movement' as used by some economists such as Cornwall and Maddison, must therefore be somewhat refined. (Van der Wee, 1987, pp. 208, 210)

The regression results cited above in support of the catch-up hypothesis must, moreover, be viewed with a certain amount of caution. The first point to note is that such cross-country regressions can be highly dependent on the presence of outliers, namely Japan (with a high growth rate and initially a low level of productivity) and the United States and Canada (with the converse). The gap variable is often statistically insignificant if the sample is confined to just the European countries and the US (see, for example, the section entitled 'Empirical estimation of the *New View* model' in the Appendix to this chapter). Furthermore, as Feinstein (1982) pointed out, in commenting on Marris (1982), even if the diffusion hypothesis is correct, we should expect the growth rates to have fallen over the postwar period. 'Average growth rates should have been higher in the early postwar period, say in 1951–60, than they were from 1960–73. This is not true for the sample as a whole, and the individual countries for which growth rates were markedly lower in the earlier period include Italy, Japan and Finland, which were among the least advanced at the beginning of the 1950s' (Feinstein, 1982, p. 147).

Perhaps even more important is the fact that the production function studies given by equations (1.26a and b) do not make any allowances for those factors that the growth accounting approach finds to be important. For example, no adjustment is made for changes in the quality of the labour force, which is likely to be important when such relatively backward countries as Greece, Turkey and Portugal are included in the sample. Again, no allowance is made for the temporary increase in growth of total factor productivity due to the reallocation of labour from the low to high productivity sectors. This was an important source of disparities in growth in the advanced countries, especially in the earlier postwar period (see Chapter 2) and is likely to remain so for the less advanced countries still with a substantial low productivity agricultural sector. These factors, together with the effect of increasing returns, should be taken into account when constructing the proxy for the gap variable. In other words, ideally the gap variable should be constructed using what Denison (1967, p. 289) terms 'differences in residual productivity', rather than differences in actual productivity. Kaldor, for example, placed great emphasis on the importance of increasing returns to scale and this alone could account for a substantial part of the international differences in both productivity levels and productivity growth rates. The United States has the largest domestic market of all the advanced countries and is therefore able to benefit most from economies of scale. Michl (1985) estimated a regression model for the manufacturing sector that allows for increasing returns to scale (the Verdoorn law – see Chapter 2) and finds that his proxy for the technological gap, based on per capita income, is statistically insignificant. Productivity levels are also affected by such factors as the degree of managerial efficiency and the level of X-inefficiency, factors which are ignored by the growth accounting approach and the above studies. It should be noted, however, that Dowrick and Nguyen do not interpret their results as necessarily supporting the diffusion of innovations argument and point out that further research is needed to discriminate between the possible underlying causes of the TFP catch up.

Finally, it is unlikely that the introduction of new superior techniques of production will be costless and hence would be reflected in an increase in total factor productivity. The diffusion hypothesis assumes that US capital goods are more efficient than European and Japanese machines. If this were the case, it is likely that this greater efficiency (or at least a greater part of it) would be capitalised into the price of the US machines. The contribution to growth of the more efficient technology would therefore largely be already captured in the estimates of the growth of the capital stock (which, of course, includes both imported and domestic capital equipment). To the extent that this occurs, the introduction of more advanced technology would not appear as a further independent explanation of the residual.

It may be that the diffusion of technology has been a factor in causing differences in the postwar growth rates, but its importance has not yet been conclusively demonstrated. Rather, the Scottish verdict of 'not proven' would seem most appropriate at the present. We are therefore sceptical of the merit of attributing the final residual to this factor, *pace* Kendrick.

THE POST-1973 SLOWDOWN IN TOTAL FACTOR PRODUCTIVITY GROWTH

We saw earlier that 1973 marks something of a watershed, with the advanced countries' (unweighted) average growth per annum of both GDP and manufacturing falling to about one-half of the 1950–73 value. This has been the most serious macroeconomic disturbance since the Second World War. As Fischer (1988) points out, a 4 per cent growth rate per annum of per capita income means that it doubles every 18 years, but if the rate falls to 2 per cent per annum, it takes 35 years to double. He graphically illustrates the implications: 'Taking a generation as 33 years, children in Italy who might have expected to start out with a standard of living nearly five times the level at which their parents began, would on the basis of the lower output growth from 1973 to 1986 expect to start out at less than double the material standard at which their parents began' (Fischer, 1988, p. 3). It is not surprising, therefore, that much time and effort has been devoted to trying to understand the causes of the slowdown, with mixed results, as we shall see.

The slower growth in output cannot be explained in terms of a fall in the growth of the labour input because there was a commensurate fall in the growth of labour productivity. Moreover, as may be seen from Table 1.11, total factor productivity growth also fell *pari passu*, suggesting that the cause could not be attributed to a slowdown of the growth of the combined factor inputs. (The data in the table are for only the business sector because of the difficulties inherent in measuring the growth of total factor productivity in the rest of the economy.) The growth of total factor productivity in Table 1.11 is defined as the growth of output minus the weighted growth of the factor inputs. In other words, there has been no adjustment for changes in the quality of the factor inputs, improvements in the sectoral allocation of resources, increasing returns, etc. Nevertheless, even when these have been made there is still a marked decline in the residual for some countries, as may be seen from Table 1.12.

If we divide the post-1973 period into two subperiods, 1973–9 and 1979–86 (1979 being the year of the second large increase in oil prices and a peak year in terms of economic activity), 1973–9 showed a widespread decline in total factor productivity growth. In the period 1979–86, the picture is rather more complex with manufacturing industries showing a slight recovery in some countries, but not in others, and service industries experiencing a further fall in growth

Table 1.11   The growth of output and total factor productivity (per cent per annum)[a]: business sector

	1960s to 1973[b]		1973–79[c]		1979–86	
	Output	*TFP*	*Output*	*TFP*	*Output*	*TFP*
OECD Average[d]	5.2	2.8	2.9	0.7	2.3	0.6
United States	3.8	1.5	2.8	–0.1	2.2	0.0
Japan	9.7	6.1	3.8	1.8	3.8	1.7
Germany	4.6	2.8	2.4	1.8	1.6	0.8
France	6.4	4.3	3.5	2.1	1.5	1.3
United Kingdom	3.2	2.0	1.1	0.2	1.4	1.1
Italy	5.6	4.7	2.9	1.6	1.9	0.7
Canada	5.7	2.2	4.9	1.1	2.5	–0.3
Austria	4.5	2.8	3.5	1.8	1.7	0.7
Belgium	5.4	3.7	2.0	1.4	1.6	1.3
Denmark	3.4	1.7	0.9	0.1	1.9	0.8
Finland	4.7	3.4	2.2	1.5	3.0	1.6
Greece	8.4	6.6	3.5	1.7	1.2	–0.5
Ireland	4.6	4.0	6.1	4.2	–1.2	–0.9
Netherlands	5.6	3.1	2.7	1.1	1.0	0.4
Norway	3.7	2.0	5.4	2.9	3.1	1.5
Spain	6.4	3.4	2.7	1.5	0.5	0.7
Sweden	2.4	1.4	1.8	0.8	0.8	0.1
Switzerland	4.0	1.7	–0.6	–0.8	2.0	0.7
Turkey	5.2	0.7	4.8	0.3	3.5	1.9
Australia	5.6	2.1	2.2	0.6	2.9	0.5
New Zealand	3.9	0.6	0.1	–2.5	2.6	0.6

Notes:

[a]Output is value added in the business sector (GDP at factor cost excluding value added in general government) at constant prices. TFP growth is equal to to either (i) output growth minus factor input growth (a weighted index of capital and labour inputs), or (ii) a weighted average of the growth of labour and capital productivity. In both cases, 1985 capital and labour shares are used as weights. Differences are due to rounding.

[b]The starting years are as follows: United States, 1960; Japan, 1967; Germany, 1961; France, 1965; United Kingdom, 1960; Italy, 1961; Canada, 1962; Austria, 1961; Belgium, 1961; Denmark, 1960; Finland, 1962; Greece, 1962; Ireland, 1961; Netherlands, 1962; Norway, 1964; Spain, 1966; Sweden, 1966; Switzerland, 1963; Turkey, 1972; Australia, 1961; New Zealand, 1963.

[c]1979–85 for Turkey.

[d]weighted average of the above countries based on 1985 business sector output at 1985 prices and exchange rates.

Source: Englander and Mittelstädt (1988, table 1, pp. 18–19).

Table 1.12 The slowdown in the growth of total factor productivity (percentage points per annum), business sector[a]

	1973/79 on 1960s/73[b]	1979/86[c] on 1960s/73	1979/86 on 1973/79
OECD Average[d]	−2.1	−2.2	−0.1
United States	−1.6	−1.5	+0.1
Japan	−4.3	−4.4	−0.1
Germany	−1.0	−2.0	−1.0
France	−2.2	−3.0	−0.8
United Kingdom	−1.8	−0.9	+0.9
Italy	−3.1	−4.0	−0.9
Canada	−1.1	−2.5	−1.4
Austria	−1.0	−2.1	−1.1
Belgium	−2.3	−2.4	−0.1
Denmark	−1.6	−0.9	+0.7
Finland	−1.9	−1.8	+0.1
Greece	−4.9	−7.1	−2.2
Ireland	+0.2	−4.9	−5.1
Netherlands	−2.0	−2.7	−0.7
Norway	+0.9	−0.5	−1.4
Spain	−1.9	−2.7	−0.8
Sweden	−0.6	−1.3	−0.7
Switzerland	−2.5	−1.0	+1.5
Turkey	−0.4	+1.2	+1.6
Australia	−1.5	−1.6	−0.1
New Zealand	−3.1	0.0	+3.1

For *Notes* and *Sources* see Table 1.11.

rates in most economies. It is perhaps surprising that there was no tendency for the information-intensive industries (wholesale and retail trade, transportation, storage and communications, and finance, insurance, real estate and business services) to recover. These are the industries that should have benefitted most from the information technology revolution. Suggestions as to why this may have been the case include the well-known measurement problems inherent with these industries; over-investment in hardware and under-investment in training necessary to use the rapidly changing equipment; and the long training period normally required to learn to use the software most effectively (Englander and Mittelstädt, 1988). But in spite of all this diversity in economic performance, overall the slowdown persisted through the period 1979–86, and to date there are still no signs of a general recovery to the rates of growth experienced in the 1950–73 period.

Table 1.12 reports the magnitude of the slowdown in total factor productivity between the various sub-periods. The largest decrease in total factor productivity growth was in Japan which experienced a decline of over 4 percentage points per annum in both sub-periods compared with its pre-1973 growth rate. Overall, the (weighted) average slowdown in total factor productivity growth was 2.1 percentage points in 1973–9 compared with the period from the 1960s to 1973 and slightly larger in 1979–86 (2.2 percentage points per annum) compared with the same period. In 1973–9, only Norway and Ireland of the 21 countries escaped a fall in their growth rates, while in the later sub-period this was true of only Turkey and New Zealand. The third column in the table reports the change in the growth rates between 1979–86 and 1973–9. It may be seen that 7 countries experienced some improvement in their growth rates while 14 saw a worsening in their situation. This confirms our earlier conclusion that on the whole there was a slight further deterioration in the position in the period 1979–86.

It is somewhat ironical that the original impetus for the growth accounting approach in the 1960s was the attempt to explain why the residual was so large, but since then the focus has shifted to trying to account for why it has been so relatively small since 1973.

Two points are worth emphasising from the start. The first is that, as we have mentioned earlier, the slowdown affected all the advanced countries, to a greater or lesser extent, simultaneously, from the years 1973/4 onwards (although there is some evidence that the United States experienced the slowdown somewhat earlier in the mid-1960s).[12] The rather obvious implication is that there is likely to be some common factor at work. Nevertheless, much of the detailed and painstaking work in trying to account for the slowdown has been by American economists concerned with the United States economy and, while the international aspect may not have been completely overlooked, it has not always been given the prominence it deserves. For example, Denison (1979), after examining a large number of hypotheses, came to the conclusion that there may have been no one single cause; everything just happened to go wrong at once. 'Several developments may have combined to slow the advance in knowledge itself, and others to retard the incorporation of new knowledge into production. Similarly inflation, regulation, soaring energy prices, high taxes and changing attitudes may have conspired to exert a large adverse impact on the miscellaneous determinants of output that forced the residual series into an actual decline' (Denison, 1979, p. 145). While inflation and soaring energy prices were common to most of the advanced countries in the early 1970s, it is by no means clear that the other factors were equally important in Japan and Europe. And if they were, why did their adverse effect on productivity growth occur at precisely the same time?

Secondly, the slowdown hit all the industries of the various economies to some degree, regardless of whether they were manufacturing or services. This again poses the same question as to why this was the case. One could perhaps make a case that the potential for technical change had become exhausted in, for example, one industry, as the number of inventions dried up. Maddison (1984) terms this argument 'Wolf's Law' after Wolf (1912), and it is the thesis that 'technical progress will ultimately be retarded because we will have exploited the easier innovations, there will be less left to discover, and the unknown will be harder to penetrate' (Maddison, 1984, p. 70). A moment's reflection, though, suggests that this is not as plausible as it may at first seem as an explanation of the slowdown as a whole. The ease of scientific discovery and its commercial application, at any one time, depends very much on the prevailing state of technology. What, a few years ago, may have seemed almost impossible to solve, now, with the advance of knowledge, may become almost child's play. Maddison notes that it is Jorgenson (1981) who perhaps comes nearest to accepting the position of Wolf's Law. Jorgenson notes the productivity slowdown is pervasive throughout the US economy, ascribes it to a fall in the rate of technical progress and is pessimistic about the future prospects for productivity growth. However, it seems to be stretching coincidence rather far to assert that the pace of technical progress just happened to decelerate in all US industries at the same time, let alone concomitantly in all the industries of the other advanced countries.

From Table 1.11 it can be seen that in the case of New Zealand there was actually technical regress at the substantial rate of 2.5 per cent per annum over the period 1973–9: on the above argument this must be interpreted as a severe case of 'forgetting by doing'! There is, however, no conclusive evidence that the pace of scientific advance or the rate of inventive activity has slowed down since the early 1970s. If anything, the annual number of significant inventions has been progressively accelerating since the turn of the century. Predictions of when major breakthroughs will occur generally turn out to be very much on the conservative side (e.g. in the 1950s the date of the first lunar landing was often predicted to occur after the turn of the century). The information technology revolution also postdates the 1973 watershed.

The fact that some industries have experienced negative rates of growth of total factor productivity over long periods has also been observed, *inter alios*, by Griliches (1988a). Commenting on estimates for the growth of total factor productivity for the US over 1949–85, Griliches (1988a, p. 11) asks rhetorically 'is it reasonable to conclude that total factor productivity in mining and construction is significantly lower today than had been its level in the early 1950s and even earlier, and that there has been no growth in productivity during the whole post-World War II period and in the financial and other service sectors?' Could it be that the slowdown is simply due to measurement errors in the growth of output? There are certainly many problems with the measurement of productivity growth in the service industries. Output growth in this sector is often measured simply as the growth of inputs with, or without, an arbitrary imputation for productivity growth. It is for this reason that some studies exclude the service industries. But this cannot be the whole answer, because the slowdown, as we have noted, is pervasive. To account for it in those industries where we should have greater confidence in the data, such as manufacturing, it is necessary to postulate that output growth has been progressively under-recorded. It could be that the change in the quality of goods and services has become of greater importance more recently and there has been less allowance for this in the official statistics. However, the consensus is that, if anything, the adjustment for quality changes and the construction of output indices has improved over the years. It is possible, of course, that the greater measurement problems in the early postwar period led to an overestimate of the growth of output during the Golden Age, but this is unlikely. Denison (1984, p. 33) cites Rees (1980, p. 342), the chairman of a National Academy of Sciences Task Force on Productivity Measurement as follows: 'In short, the lag in measured productivity growth seems to me to be entirely a real phenomenon and in no part attributable to measurement error. Indeed, if anything the deceleration has been understated.'

A related argument by Bruno (1984) is that the rapid rise in the price of raw materials could have caused a measurement bias in the double deflated value added, but Grubb (1986) has shown convincingly that this was insignificant. Moreover, if it were important, the effect should have been reversed by the rapid fall in raw material prices in the mid-1980s, but there is no evidence that this occurred. The slowdown must, therefore, be seen as a real, rather than a statistical, phenomenon.

There has been no dearth of other explanations as to why it occurred, and this has led Matthews (1982a, p. 14) to comment: 'If we add together everyone's econometric estimate of the consequences of his favourite cause, the slow-down would be many times over-explained, rather than unexplained as it seemed to Denison.' However, to be fair, Denison describes the decline in the residual as a 'mystery', not because there have been no explanations, but because none of the myriad hypotheses are, in his opinion, totally convincing. Denison (1979 and 1984) examined 17 such explanations and concluded that: 'None, in my opinion, were *demonstrably* able to explain more than a small part – if any – of the slowdown' (Denison, 1984, p. 23, emphasis in the original). According to Denison, the problem is that many popular explanations are simply based on asserting that because a particular cause is now present, it has been responsible for the slowdown. A good example is the 'people don't want to work anymore' hypothesis and the putative effect of the growth of the 'black economy'. What such arguments need to show and what they fail to do, according to Denison, is that the impact of these factors suddenly changed for the worse around 1973, with a deleterious effect on productivity growth.[13] A problem with more sophisticated explanations based on econometric evidence is that 'one could explain the productivity slowdown fifteen times over by correlating productivity with each of twenty other economic time series chosen almost at random'. This is because most time-series show a structural break at around 1973 and there will be high correlation coefficients if any one such time-series is regressed on another. But determining the direction of causation (if any) between the variables is quite another matter. A further difficulty is that those elements which we can quantify and whose effect can be measured both pre- and post-1973 are, by definition, not those factors that affect the residual since their effects have already been accounted for. Or to put this another way, those factors that led to a worsening in the residual are by their very nature going to be difficult to quantify.

Matthews (1982a) has pointed out that the answer to the question why the slowdown occurred depends very much upon the answers given to two other great conundrums: why was growth so much faster in the 1950s and 1960s than earlier and why did stagflation arise in the

1970s? Since there is no consensus on these issues, there is unlikely to be any general agreement on the causes of the slowdown.

It is beyond the scope of this chapter to provide a comprehensive review of all the theories that have been advanced. Nevertheless, in the next section we shall briefly consider the insights of the growth accounting approach, concentrating on Kendrick's study, and then briefly discuss the major theories that have been put forward to explain the slowdown.

THE GROWTH ACCOUNTING APPROACH AND THE SLOWDOWN

Table 1.13 provides a summary of the results of Kendrick's (1981) study for the period 1973–9 and Table 1.14 provides an estimate of the size of the slowdown using Kendrick's data. R_0 is the growth of total factor productivity calculated as output growth minus the *unadjusted* weighted growth of the factor inputs. Hence, it is identical to the definition of total factor productivity growth in Tables 1.11 and 1.12, but differs from R_1 reported in Tables 1.7 and 1.13 where the growth of the labour input is adjusted for changes in quality, sex and age composition, and output growth is corrected for variations in capacity utilisation.

We have used Kendrick's study merely to illustrate the orders of magnitude involved. It should be emphasised that although Kendrick closely follows Denison's procedure there are small differences in their methods and assumptions that cumulatively can lead to not insignificant differences in their estimates. Kendrick (1981) finds that the slowdown is completely explained in the case of the US. Denison, by contrast, finds that the contribution of the residual for non-residential business national income fell from 1.4 percentage points per annum over the period 1948–73 to −0.3 percentage points per annum in 1973–81: a fall of 1.7 percentage points. (It will be recalled that Denison interprets the residual as the contribution of knowledge and miscellaneous determinants.) Part of this discrepancy may be attributable to differences in the exact periods chosen; part is due to differences in opinion of the importance of certain factors. For example, Denison (1985, p. 42, footnote 14) considers Kendrick over-emphasises the fall in the contribution of R&D to economic growth. Creamer (1972) and Norsworthy (1984) have undertaken a detailed

Table 1.13 Sources of growth of gross business product; selected advanced countries, 1973–9 – Kendrick's estimates

Sources of growth	Belgium	Canada	France	W. Germany	Italy	Japan	Sweden	United Kingdom	United States
Gross Business Product (GBP)	2.1	3.2	3.2	2.2	2.6	4.2	0.1	0.5	2.9
Total Factor Input	-0.1	3.8	1.4	0.2	2.4	3.0	0.0	1.0	2.8
(i) Labour input[a]	-1.1	1.5	-0.2	-1.2	1.3	0.9	-1.3	-0.1	1.6
(ii) Capital input	1.0	2.3	1.6	1.4	1.1	2.1	1.3	1.1	1.2
Capacity utilisation	-1.0	-0.5	-0.5	-0.1	-0.2	-0.3	0.0	-0.8	-0.2
Total Factor Productivity or residual R_1 (% of GBP)	**3.2** (152)	**-0.1** (n.m.)[b]	**2.3** (72)	**2.1** (95)	**0.4** (15)	**1.5** (36)	**0.1** (100)	**0.3** (60)	**0.3** (10)
Economies of scale	0.2	0.3	0.3	0.2	0.3	0.4	0.0	0.1	0.3
Improved allocation of resources	0.1	-0.1	0.1	0.1	0.2	0.0	-0.2	-0.1	-0.1
Residual R_2 (% of GBP)	**2.9** (138)	**-0.3** (n.m.)[b]	**1.9** (59)	**1.8** (82)	**-0.1** (n.m.)[b]	**1.1** (26)	**0.3** (300)	**0.3** (60)	**0.1** (3)

61

Advances in technology	0.7	0.6	0.6	0.7	0.5	0.6	0.5	0.5
(i) Exogenous technical progress[c]	0.4	0.4	0.4	0.4	0.4	0.4	0.4	0.4
(ii) Direct effects of R&D	0.2	0.2	0.2	0.4	0.1	0.3	0.2	0.1
(iii) Domestic technical diffusion	0.1	0.0	0.0	-0.1	0.0	-0.1	-0.1	0.0
Residual R_3 (% of GBP)	2.2 (104)	-0.9 (n.m.)[b]	1.3 (41)	1.1 (50)	-0.6 (n.m.)[b]	0.5 (12)	-0.2 (n.m.)[b]	-0.2 (n.m.)[b]
Effect of government regulation	-0.3	-0.3	-0.3	-0.4	-0.2	-1.0	-0.3	-0.2
Residual R_4 (% of GBP)	2.5 (119)	-0.6 (n.m.)[b]	1.6 (50)	1.5 (68)	-0.4 (n.m.)[b]	1.5 (36)	0.1 (100)	0.0 (n.m.)[b]

Notes:
[a] Adjusted for changes in hours of work, age–sex composition, and education.
[b] Denotes not meaningful.
[c] Taken as the final residual of the US, the most advanced country.

Source: Calculated from Kendrick (1981, tables 1 and 7, pp. 128 and 141 respectively).

Table 1.14   The slowdown in the growth of total factor productivity; 1973–9 compared with 1960–73. Kendrick's data for gross business product

	Change in the residual	
	R_0	R_4
Belgium	−1.8	+1.0
Canada	−3.4	−2.0
France	−1.9	+0.3
Germany	−1.3	+0.2
Italy	−4.6	−2.3
Japan	−4.7	−0.1
Sweden	−3.5	−2.1
United Kingdom	−2.2	−0.6
United States	−1.7	0.0

Notes: R_0: Residual calculated as output growth minus the weighted growth of the factor inputs, unadjusted for changes in capacity utilisation.
R_4: Fully adjusted residual (see Table 1.13).

Source: Kendrick (1981).

comparison of the assumptions made by the three leading researchers into the growth accounting approach; namely, Denison, Jorgenson and Kendrick. Given the relatively low growth of total factor productivity in the US – however precisely measured – compared with the other advanced countries, these differences can make quite a difference to how much of the US residual is considered to have been explained. However, it is beyond the scope of this chapter to go into this any further.

R_0 in Table 1.14 confirms the picture found in Table 1.12 of a substantial slowdown in total factor productivity growth in the 1973–9 cycle compared with 1960–73. It should be noted, however, that there are significant differences in the growth of total factor productivity of, especially, Sweden and Italy compared with the figures reported in Tables 1.12 and 1.13. This may be due either to the fact that the exact pre-1973 periods are not strictly comparable or to statistical revisions. Nevertheless, these discrepancies are not severe enough to alter the general impression of a substantial fall in the growth of total factor productivity. R_4 is the residual that remains after Kendrick's adjustments for changes in the quality, age and sex composition of the labour force; for changes in capacity utilisation; for the impact of economies of scale and improvements in the efficiency of the allocation of resources; and for advances in technology and the effect of changes in government regulation. (It should be remembered that unlike Kendrick we do not attribute the residual to the catch-up, but follow Denison's procedure.) Once all these factors have been taken into account, a substantial fall in the residual remains in only three of the nine countries, namely, Canada, Italy and Sweden. The dramatic fall in Japan's total factor productivity growth of 4.3 per cent per annum is nearly completely explained.

Kendrick found that, except for Japan and Germany, education is estimated to have made a bigger contribution to output growth in 1973–9 than in the earlier period. Taking this into account accentuates the slowdown, though quantitatively the effect is small. Adjusting the growth of the labour input for changes in sex and age composition also has only a small impact. The fall in the growth of output automatically reduces the contribution of increasing returns to scale to economic growth. The extent of the fall depends, of course, on the degree of returns to scale to which the economy is assumed to be subject. Kendrick, as we have noted, assumes that, on the whole, the influence of returns to scale is much less than that postulated by Denison. The contribution of the improved allocation of resources also declines in the second period. This is partly due to the fact that the size of the agricultural sector (and hence the potential for the inter-sectoral transfer of labour) was much smaller. Furthermore, the main determinant of the rate of transfer was the growth of demand for labour in the manufacturing sector. With the rapid fall in the growth rate of the latter associated with the widespread phenomenon of de-industrialisation in the advanced countries, the gains from the reallocation of labour were further curtailed. Kendrick also considers that the exhaustion of the technological catch-up possibilities played a significant role in the deceleration of growth rates, accounting for about half the slowdown. However, we are not convinced by this conclusion, for reasons outlined earlier.

One possible explanation of the slowdown which has attracted a good deal of attention within the growth accounting framework is the proposition that the estimates of the growth of the capital stock may have been overstated since 1973, thereby leading to an under-estimate of the residual. This is because the rapid rise in energy prices may have made capital equipment obsolete more rapidly than the allowance made for the rate of obsolescence in the conventional estimates of the capital stock (calculated via the perpetual inventory method). The most widely cited study is Bailey (1981) who concluded that the increase in energy prices caused a 20 per cent loss of effective capital in the US over the period 1968 to 1978. This figure was more an illustration of the order of magnitude involved than a precise estimate. Bailey estimated the loss by introducing Tobin's q as a component in the calculation of the capital stock. Tobin's q is the ratio of the market value of corporate securities to the replacement value of corporate assets. The marked decline in q that occurred in the 1970s was due partly to the overestimate of the replacement value of corporate assets due to the increase in obsolescence. Maddison (1984), however, is not convinced of the importance of the 'Bailey effect', as he terms it, because the fall in Tobin's q is also caused 'by other factors that influence demand, as Bailey himself was aware, *viz* capacity use, profit expectations, interest policies, and so forth'. Maddison assumes that premature obsolescence only reduced the 1980 capital stock by 5 per cent compared with its 1973 level. (Bailey's figures suggested a fall of 14 per cent in the 1978 figures compared with 1973. This would be sufficient to account for most of the fall between 1948–73 and 1973–8 in the growth of US total factor productivity in non-financial corporations and manufacturing.) Denison is, if anything, even more sceptical. He cites the fact that automobiles, the one asset for which real service lives can be obtained, actually remained in service for *longer* after the oil price rises. 'In any case, after reviewing the composition of the stock, by type of structure and equipment, I find it hard to believe that regulation, oil prices and foreign competition changed service lives enough in either direction to have a major effect on the calculation of output per unit of input in nonresidential business as a whole' (Denison, 1984, p. 14).

It has been suggested that the rapid increase in oil prices could account for the slowdown. A direct effect of the oil price rise could lead to a substitution effect of capital and labour for energy and/or raw materials in general. The effects have generally been found to be low. Lindbeck (1983, p. 24), for example, concludes that 'the main effects on productivity growth of the relative price increases for oil and raw materials must be by way of . . . "indirect effects", via the various macroeconomic variables, i.e. via capacity slack, slower growth of output, capital accumulation, etc., rather than by way of the "direct effects" on production via substitutions away from energy and raw materials.' This view is shared by Feinstein and Matthews (1990, p. 89): 'This view [of the importance of substitution effects caused by the oil price rises] has never enjoyed much favour as applied to the UK. It has fallen further in esteem in the 1980s, when the fall in the oil price should have put things into reverse in the world as a whole but appeared not to.'

PROXIMATE VERSUS FUNDAMENTAL CAUSES

One of the limitations of the growth accounting approach (though by no means the major one, as we shall shortly see) is that it attempts to quantify only the proximate causes of the slowdown. Nevertheless, there is no shortage of proffered explanations of possible fundamental causes (see, for example, the symposia published in the March volume of the 1988 *Economic Journal* and the Fall issue of the 1988 *Journal of Economic Perspectives*). Lindbeck (1983, p. 13) covered most of the broad categories when he saw the slowdown as being the result of three closely related effects, namely '(I) a long-term deterioration in the efficiency and flexibility of some basic mechanisms of the economic and political systems of these countries; (II) the fading away of a number of uniquely favourable circumstances for productivity growth during the 'fifties and 'sixties; and (III) the exposure of these economies to unusually severe macroeconomic disturbances in the 'seventies'. The problem is not one of finding plausible explanations, but how to weight their importance.

Lindbeck's first suggestion is partly based on the assumption that by the end of the 1960s the rise of government expenditure and high marginal rates of taxation had stultified incentives. The long period of full employment and the belief of workers that unemployment was a thing of the past led to greater trade union militancy with the consequence of high inflation and distortions in the price signals. There was an increase in bargaining with governments for subsidies and protection ('rent seeking') at the expense of normal production and marketing activities. In other words, the cause is seen to be mainly on the supply side (Olson, 1982).[14] 'When all these various system changes, in the form of market distortions, disincentives, inflexibilities and uncertainties, are considered, it is tempting to speak of an emerging "arteriosclerosis" of the Western economic systems accentuated by a resistence to change and the fights about income shares, by organised interest groups' (Lindbeck, 1983, p. 17). The attempts to reduce government expenditure and to lower income tax rates, and the extensive privatisation of public enterprises together with the reduction of legal immunities that the Trade Union movement previously enjoyed, can all be seen as supply-side policy responses to the slowdown.

If the slowdown was primarily due to exhaustion of the favourable conditions that existed for the first quarter of a century after the Second World War (Lindbeck's category II), then the slowdown was to a large extent inevitable and the 'severe macroeconomic disturbances in the 'seventies' probably did no more than influence the timing of the slowdown and ensured that it was widespread. This is the view of Giersch and Wolter (1983 p. 46) who argue that 'in a more historical perspective, the advanced countries are now repaying in terms of slower growth what they borrowed from land and nature in a period of accelerated growth'. The Golden Age should therefore be seen as the abnormal period and the Climacteric merely represents a return to more normal growth rates.

There may be a certain amount of truth in this thesis, in so far as the potential gains from the improved allocation of resources diminished over the postwar period. But this does not explain the occurrence of the slowdown in those countries where the intersectoral reallocation of labour was never an important source of growth (e.g. the United States, the United Kingdom and Australia). It also does not explain the slowdown in industry, since the inter-industry transfer of labour has never been an important source of productivity growth.

If either of the explanations (I) and (II) were largely correct, then we should expect the slowdown to have commenced at different times in different countries, given the international differences in the degree of economic maturity and economic structure that existed, and still do exist. This, of course, did not happen, and to argue that the macroeconomic disturbances acted as a trigger gives rise to the suspicion of *post hoc ergo propter hoc* reasoning. It really does not explain why the slowdown was so widespread, simultaneously hitting not only most countries but also most industries, whether they were high-technology capital-intensive or low-technology labour-intensive. Neither manufacturing nor the services industries escaped. It is difficult to believe that the above two explanations can satisfactorily explain either the suddenness of the slowdown, or its all-pervasiveness.

The final explanation suggests that the slowdown was to a large extent policy-induced, at least in the initial stages. This hypothesis is dealt with at much greater length in Chapter 2; but, briefly, it argues that much of productivity growth is *endogenous*, determined by the growth of output. The rate of capital accumulation is not exogenous but is largely a function of the (expected) growth of sales. Lamfalussy (1963) has made an important distinction between what he terms 'defensive investment' and 'enterprise investment'. The former occurs mainly in stagnating industries (or economies) and is investment that is undertaken on a piecemeal or *ad hoc* basis when particular capital machines require replacing. Enterprise investment, on the other hand, takes the form of large co-ordinated investment; for example, the building of a fully integrated plant on a new site. This is more characteristic of a rapidly growing industry. A given pound's worth of enterprise investment is more productive (has a lower capital–output ratio) than a pound of defensive investment. A large part of the rate of technical progress is induced by the growth of output through learning by doing, dynamic economies of scale and embodied technical change.

Consequently, this explanation sees the fall in productivity growth as primarily the result of policy responses to the various balance of payments crises and inflationary pressures that arose because of OPEC I and II. The deflationary policies that were introduced putatively to curtail inflation in a number of the larger OECD countries, and the abandonment of the commitment to full employment, severely reduced the growth of output. This had a damaging effect on entrepreneurial expectations and led to a severe cut back in investment, together with expenditure on 'on the job' training, etc. Moreover, the balance-of-payments constraint, which was not removed through the floating of exchange rates, effectively limited the freedom of other countries to increase their rate of growth through expansionary domestic demand management policies (see Chapter 7). Indeed, the importance of the balance-of-payments constraint, which forms the central tenet of this book, is totally neglected in these theories and explanations of the slowdown. An implication is that in the early 1970s there was nothing immutable about the slowdown (McCracken *et al.*, 1977). But as the slowdown persisted, hysteresis set in. High unemployment led to de-skilling, and reduced expenditure on training also reduced the proportion of skilled workers. The rate of investment adjusted to the lower expected growth rates; expansionary phases were seen as merely temporary and not a return to higher trend rates of growth and so any resurgence in growth rates quickly met capital shortages. Skill shortages also appeared and both these factors set up inflationary forces that, together with the deterioration in the balance of payments, led to the reintroduction of deflationary policies.

CRITICISMS OF THE NEOCLASSICAL GROWTH ACCOUNTING AND PRODUCTION FUNCTION APPROACHES

It is convenient to separate criticisms of the neoclassical approach (both the growth accounting and the econometric approaches) into three distinct, though related, categories.

The first criticism, although perhaps shortcoming is a better word, concerns the taxonomic nature of the growth accounting approach. While the approach attempts to quantify the proximate contributions the various factors make to economic growth, it sheds no light on why these factors differ between countries. However, it can be legitimately argued that an assessment of the proximate causes is a *sine qua non* for the understanding of the more fundamental or determining causes of why growth rates differ. We have examined this distinction between proximate and fundamental causes in the previous section and so will not pursue this further here.

We may group in the second category those views which consider that, while the neoclassical methodology provides an appropriate starting point for organising our thoughts about the growth process, diminishing returns have long since set in. Typical of this view is Griliches (1988b, p. 363) who, in reflecting on research into productivity growth over the last three decades (to which he has made a notable contribution), concluded: 'Despite all of this work there is still no general agreement on what the computed productivity measures actually measure, how they are to be interpreted and what are the major sources of their fluctuations and growth.' Undoubtedly, part of the problem is that many of the important influences of productivity growth, such as the impact of institutional factors, are too nebulous to have any chance of being accurately quantified and are hence omitted by default from the growth accounting framework. Further progress is therefore only likely to come from studies, for example, at the level of the firm, looking at the effects of the organisational structure of firms on the speed of the adoption of new techniques, etc. (Nelson, 1981).

The third set of criticisms, while accepting that a macroeconomic approach can provide useful insights into 'why growth rates differ', argues that the assumptions underlying the neoclassical approach are incompatible with the complex structural change that characterises the growth of the advanced countries. This critique considers that the neoclassical approach not only cannot be regarded as a useful first approximation, but also denies, on theoretical grounds, the whole rationale of trying to separate the contributions of the various factors of production to output growth and the validity of the aggregate production function.

Obviously, the demarcation between the three groups is far from clear-cut, and at the boundaries the categories tend to merge into each other. Bearing this in mind, we shall look at the last two criticisms in further detail.

LIMITATIONS OF THE EMPIRICAL RELEVANCE OF THE NEOCLASSICAL APPROACH

A good example of this type of criticism is elaborated at some length by Nelson (1981) and it is useful to consider his arguments as representative of this class. Nelson forcefully argues that 'the theoretical model underlying most research by economists on productivity growth over time, and across countries [i.e. that based on the neoclassical aggregate production function] is superficial and to some degree even misleading regarding the following matters: the determinants of productivity at the level of the firm and of inter-firm differences; the processes that generate, screen and spread new technologies; the influence of macroeconomic conditions and economic institutions on productivity growth' (p. 1029). He notes that concern with the long-run growth of nations is as old as economics itself; after all, the first chapter of Adam Smith's *Wealth of Nations* was largely about technical progress and the causes of productivity advance. But what is noticeable is that a central concern of the Classical economists was the effect of a nation's institutions in stimulating or retarding economic growth; an issue almost totally ignored in the later neoclassical approach (with the notable exception of Olson, 1982). Moreover, Adam Smith also placed great stress on increasing returns as a key determinant of the level of productivity (the latter being determined by the division of labour which in turn is a function of the extent of the market). We have already commented on how uneasily this lies with the assumption of competitive markets, and we shall consider this issue in greater detail in the next chapter.

The stimulus to the neoclassical approach was undoubtedly Solow's (1957) celebrated article on technical change and the aggregate production function where he attempted to separate and quantify the contribution to output growth of the growth of the factor inputs and the 'residual' or technical progress. The assumptions underlying this and subsequent approaches are so familiar that they are unfortunately seldom questioned.

The first postulate is that firms are merely abstract entities that represent the efficient transformation of inputs into outputs using technology that is assumed to be freely available to all firms.[15] Markets are generally assumed to be perfectly competitive and prices are treated parametrically by individual agents.

This abstracts from problems of inefficient management; trade union/management conflict; restrictive practices; oligopolistic rivalry and collusion; the manipulation of markets by the multinationals etc. Technological change, while at the heart of economic growth, is treated very cursorily. 'The Schumpeterian proposition that technological advance (via entrepreneurial innovation) and competitive equilibrium cannot co-exist is ignored' (Nelson, 1981 p. 1031). If technical advances become immediately available to all firms (the perfect information assumption of perfect competition) then there would be no incentive for entrepreneurs to make any effort to improve products or processes through, for example, R&D. The institutional framework is conspicuous by its absence; 'there is no particular place in the structure for labour unions, banking systems, schools, or regulatory regimes' (p. 1031).

The neoclassical approach assumes that firms are productively efficient, in other words they are cost minimisers. Indeed, the neoclassical 'theory of the firm' is not a theory about how firms actually operate; rather it is merely an integral part of price theory. The firm in this context is an abstract entity necessary for a theory of resource allocation. To criticise the theory for failing to shed any light on the internal structure and organization of the firm, *per se*, is to commit the error of 'misplaced concreteness' (Machlup, 1967).

Nevertheless, it is now being increasingly appreciated that substantial differences in productivity are due to the efficiency with which the firm carries out the production process. If the neoclassical theory is not designed to analyse this sort of phenomenon, this is another reason for questioning the paradigm.

In a seminal paper, Leibenstein (1966) noted that wide disparities existed between firms producing identical output in the same country and that this could only be attributed to differences in managerial ability. Leibenstein cited as an example two petroleum refineries in Egypt that were less than one mile apart. The labour productivity of one refinery had been double that of the other for many years. But this all changed when the less efficient refinery came under new management and achieved a substantial increase in productivity with the same labour force. If the management change had occurred at an earlier date, Leibenstein speculated that the increase in efficiency would likewise have been achieved earlier. After mentioning a number of other examples, Leibenstein (1966, p. 401) came to the conclusion that 'Clearly, there is more to the determination of output than the obviously observable inputs. The nature of the management, the environment in which it operates, and the incentives employed are all important.' Leibenstein coined the term 'X-efficiency' to denote these various factors. He showed that output losses due to X-inefficiency were several orders of magnitude larger than the traditional welfare losses due to the static misallocation of resources resulting from monopoly power and tariffs.

To understand differences in X-efficiency requires the recognition that the firm is a social organisation comprising many people who need to be co-ordinated and who may well have different objectives. As Nelson (1981) points out, there is now a considerable literature on these issues that has great relevance for the understanding of inter-firm differences in productivity levels, but which has been largely ignored by neoclassical economists.

A further problem with the growth accounting approach is that the variables in the production function are assumed to be *independent* of each other, whereas in practice there is likely to be a close inter-dependence. There exist two major interdependencies in the production process. The first is between capital and labour. The production function treats capital and labour as substitutes, whereas for the most part, capital and labour are complementary. Labour needs capital to work with, and capital needs to be 'manned'. Thus, the growth of capital and labour go hand in hand. This poses the problem of statistical multicollinearity in the estimation of the individual contributions of capital and labour to the growth of output, and can lead to a misleading interpretation and misunderstanding of the contribution that each factor makes to measured growth (Scott, 1989). For example, capital accumulation not only contributes directly to output growth, but also indirectly because it adds to the demand for labour.[16]

Similarly, there is also an interdependence, or complementarity, between capital accumulation and technical progress. Most technical progress is embodied in capital. There would not be very much technical progress without capital accumulation. By the same token, there would be very little capital accumulation if technical progress was static; there would be little or no motive for investment.

Full employment (with no disguised unemployment) is usually assumed, although this is contradicted by the evidence discussed in Chapter 2. Denison's pragmatism allows him to estimate a significant contribution to growth resulting from the improved sectoral reallocation of resources, but this is at variance with the assumption of perfectly competitive markets, as are some of the other influences Denison allows for in his work. (Some neoclassical purists such as Jorgenson and his collaborators maintain the assumption of perfect competition and therefore rule out, *a priori*, the importance of any contributions from the intersectoral reallocation of factors or from increasing returns to scale.) As Nelson (1981, p. 1033) comments: 'It is important to note, however, that where relatively formal theoretical arguments are used in growth accounting studies, these are drawn from the neoclassical model. The non-neoclassical variables are, simply, just added on, in an *ad hoc* way. But variables take on meaning only in the context of a theoretical framework, formal and informal. If these kind of variables, or processes, are important, we need to revise our conceptualization of the growth process.'

Examples of the shortcomings of the neoclassical approach may be best demonstrated by reference to two important examples. The first concerns the role of human capital formation and education in economic growth and the second refers to the impact of the organizational structure of the firm and industrial relations together with trade union restrictive practices. It also discusses the insights of Olson's (1982) influential work. Alternatively, these approaches may be viewed as complementing the growth accounting approach, as they may yield further insights as to why the residual differs between countries. Nevertheless, it is difficult, if not impossible, to quantify their effect on economic growth.

THE CONTRIBUTION OF EDUCATION AND TRAINING TO ECONOMIC GROWTH: A REAPPRAISAL

The deficiency of the British education and training system (both formal and informal) is commonly held to be a major factor in accounting for Britain's poor economic performance. Yet the measured contribution that education makes to productivity growth turns out to be very small in the neoclassical approach and can explain little of the observed international disparities in productivity growth. The problem is that the index that is constructed to allow for changes in the quality of the labour force does so by using as a proxy changes in the number of hours of formal schooling. This procedure does not, however, make any allowance for the fact that an hour's schooling of a particular age group in 1991 may be far more effective in increasing human capital than an hour's schooling in 1951. Similarly, it makes no allowance for the fact that an hour's schooling in Japan may also be more effective than an hour's schooling in Britain. Furthermore, the extent of post-secondary school vocational training in the form of apprenticeships may be equally, if not more, important in raising the level of productivity.

The importance of education and training has been clearly brought out in a number of National Institute of Economic and Social Research (NIESR) studies directed by Prais. Prais and Wagner (1983) compared the amount of vocational training undertaken in both Britain and West Germany in five of the more popular occupations, namely, those of mechanical fitter, electrician, construction worker, office worker and retailing employee. While there is not a great deal of difference between the two countries in the proportion of the labour force with higher degrees (although there is greater emphasis in Germany on applied and vocational degrees), there was a marked disparity in the percentage of the labour force with intermediate vocational qualifications. In Britain, two-thirds of the work force had no form of apprenticeship or other qualifications, while the figure for Germany was only one-third. An obvious question that arises is whether or not the larger numbers of workers in Germany with these qualifications meant that the standard obtained was in any way inferior to that in Britain. To answer this question, Prais and Wagner undertook a detailed study of the various syllabi of the courses that were taught in both countries to the apprentices (who were normally between the ages of 16 and 20 years). They came to the conclusion that more does not mean worse. The greater number of qualifications awarded in Germany is *not* obtained at the expense of lower standards and it may be safely concluded that the German labour force is more highly trained than that of Britain (see Prais and Steedman, 1986, 1987, 1988; and Jarvis and Prais, 1989).

In a subsequent study, Prais and Wagner (1985) found that the greater degree of German craftsmanship was not entirely due to vocational training. A large part could also be attributed to the better schooling of the average and below average ability student in Germany. For example, in Germany these groups were about two years ahead in their mathematical ability compared to British pupils. A similar difference was found in a comparison between British and Japanese students. The better education found in Germany was attributed to the type and excellence of the tuition rather than the amount of resources devoted to education. (Pupil–staff ratios were not significantly different between the two countries and Germany actually devoted a smaller proportion of its GDP to education.)

In terms of the elite students, there was little to choose between the two countries. If anything, British students who went on to university had actually acquired more mathematical skills than their German counterparts. There is also little difference to be found between the advanced countries in terms of the standard of university education. This fact may, indeed, serve to obscure the substantial international differences in the effectiveness of the schooling of the *majority* of the population. Yet, with the introduction of more flexible production systems and greater automation in both manufacturing and the service sector, it is the skill level of the *average* worker that is going to become increasingly more important.

The next question to consider is to what extent disparities in education and training contribute to the level and growth of productivity.

The National Institute's study by Daly, Hitchens and Wagner (1985) provides some interesting answers. Daly *et al.* undertook a 'matched pairs' study of British and German firms. They made a detailed study of 36 British and German plants that were matched in pairs in terms of the products that they manufactured. The study concentrated on plants in the metal trades industry that manufactured very simple products (coil springs rather than, say, washing machines). This was to facilitate the identification of the precise causes of the differences in productivity which might have been obscured in more complex production processes. It might be expected that the simpler the production process, the smaller would be the international differences in productivity. Nevertheless there were still substantial disparities between British and German plants. German productivity turned out to be between 10 per cent and 130 per cent higher than British productivity, with an average value of 63 per cent higher.

Perhaps, rather surprisingly, these differences in productivity were not due to British firms employing older and out-of-date machinery – a common explanation of Britain's comparatively low productivity. In fact, it turned out that there was very little difference between the countries in the age structure of their capital equipment. The main cause of the differences in output per worker turned out to be the many more breakdowns in the British machinery and the larger amount of 'downtime' that resulted. To put this another way, the volume of output per worker of the British firms was roughly comparable to that of the German firms when the equipment was actually fully operational; the only trouble was that British equipment did not run for as long as German machinery. The reason for this Daly *et al.* concluded was primarily due to the differences in the skills of the workforce.

The production foreman plays a key role in both countries in determining the smooth running of production on the factory floor. In Britain, the foreman had often been promoted to this position solely on the basis of the length of time he had spent on the factory floor. In Germany, promotion was on the basis of qualifications as well as experience. The certificate of *Meister* (*mastercraftsman*) was often a necessary prerequisite for promotion. This meant that a German foreman was not only able to supervise production, but could also deal with all but the most serious breakdowns on the spot. His British counterpart was rarely able to do this and any breakdown had to await the appearance of maintenance engineers. These were established as a separate unit which was required to service the whole factory, which was a rational response to the scarcity of skilled workers but led to numerous delays. Consequently, there was considerably more downtime in British factories. Another telling factor is that the machinists in Germany were personally responsible for cleaning their machinery of swarf (metal filings from the machining) once a week – a practice that was rare in Britain. Since excessive swarf is a very common cause of machinery breakdowns, this was an additional reason for the greater time lost in the running of British machinery. A dismal picture is painted of British machinery:

> We were told by a service engineer in Britain that machines here were 'abysmally abused'; maintenance procedures were inadequately followed; machines were not cleaned of swarf; they were used for purposes for which they were not built (for example, cutting hardened steel on a machine intended for soft steel); when they break down there is frequently no in-house ability to carry out a repair or even to diagnose the fault. The ability to use diagnostic tapes on NC [numerically controlled] machinery varied greatly. One NC machine tool manufacturer had analysed their repair problems, and found that 70 per cent should have been dealt with by users themselves if they had employed properly skilled fitters.

In addition, breakdown in the UK took three or four times longer to repair than in Germany, said one German machine supplier, 'because of delays caused by British rules on demarcation, teatime, hometime and dirt on the machines'. (Daly *et al.*, 1985, pp. 56–7)

The lack of skilled workers in the British factories, as the above quotation points out, has also meant that the full benefits could not be obtained from the introduction of NC machinery. The use of NC machinery was relatively new in both countries and the suppliers consequently found it necessary to run courses for the purchasers on the basics of programming, operating and maintaining the machinery. In Germany, the person delegated to attend was normally a craftsman who had little difficulty in following the course of instruction. The same could not be said of the typical British representative who often did not have the necessary mathematical skills to cope with the course. Not surprisingly, if there was a difficulty with the British NC machine, there was not the capability to rectify the problem on the spot. '"The upshot of this," we were told by one British manufacturer of NC machines, "is that almost half of the machines sold in Britain are not used as they might be, because their full capacity is not understood." In Germany, problems of this kind were hardly mentioned; with negligible exceptions participants were capable of following the courses' (Daly *et al.*, 1985, p. 57).

It is not only the level of education of those working on the shopfloor that proved inimical to productivity. Daly *et al.* also found that the *type* of education received by those in especially senior management positions also played an important part. A notable difference was found in the educational backgrounds of German and British managers. German managers were found to be largely graduate engineers while British senior management came predominantly from the sales and financial divisions of the company. It is worth quoting Daly *et al.* on the implications of this.

This difference in technological qualification has become ever more important because, as we were told at several interviews, non-engineers are less receptive to technological innovation; their lack of technical understanding leads to delay in installing complex equipment because they are afraid to 'chance their arm'. For example, a British maintenance foreman told us he could not persuade his management to buy electronic equipment which would reduce their heavy repair costs, because – so he thought – they did not understand the technical potential of the equipment; the management were primarily salesman and were suspicious that the equipment manufacturers were 'trying to pull a fast one'. (p. 56, omitting a footnote)

Thus, it is not only the resistance to the implementation of new technology at the shop-floor level by the trades unions that is important, but also that emanating from senior management.

This shortcoming in British management is not merely confined to the metal manufacturing industry but is pervasive throughout the economy. Swords–Isherwood (1980, p. 88) in reviewing the literature on the background of British managers came to the conclusion that 'the education background of the average British manager is inferior to that of his equivalent in other major industrial countries and that there is ground for believing that British managers may be less likely to be educationally and professionally competent'. This is because not only are most managers promoted on the basis of their social background rather than their innate ability but also because they had a non-technical education. The importance of the 'liberal arts' type of education was also found to be prevalent in the US ('the closest model, but perhaps not the one [the United Kingdom] should choose to follow' (p. 89)) but not, for example, in Germany and France. In the last two countries, engineering was the predominant qualification of the managers. Moreover, in Britain 'management as a career remains unattractive to the most educated group . . . The problem lies mainly in the anachronistic conflict between educational and industrial aims, and a culture that is anti-industrial' (Swords–Isherwood, 1980, p. 97).

It may be seen from this brief discussion that the impact of differences in education and training on the disparities of productivity levels and growth rates is far greater than the rather mechanistic calculations of the growth accounting approach suggest. It also confirms our earlier comment about the interdependency of the factors of production. In the metal trades industry the observed output–capital ratio is much higher in Germany than in the UK, not because the machinery is intrinsically superior, but simply because it does not breakdown so often and when it does it is more quickly repaired. This is, in large part, due to the performance of the other factor of production – labour. It thus proves difficult, if not impossible, to separate their individual contributions to economic growth in any meaningful way. Nelson (1981, pp. 1053–54) has summarised the implications of this rather neatly:

> One can analyze the contribution to output of a worker, or a machine, at the margin. It does not make sense, however, to try to calculate the contribution to output of all labor, or all the machines. Or, to take another example, consider the sources of a well made cake. It is possible to list the number of inputs – flour, sugar, milk, etc. It is even possible to analyze the effects upon the cake of having a little bit more or less of one ingredient, holding the other ingredients constant. But it makes no sense to try dividing up the credit for a good cake to the various inputs.

THE OLSON THESIS AND THE ROLE OF SPECIAL INTEREST GROUPS

In 1982, Mancur Olson published *The Rise and Decline of Nations* which, as its title suggests, is an attempt to provide a broad explanation as to why long-run economic growth may differ substantially between countries. In the book, Olson expressed dissatisfaction with the orthodox growth accounting approach for much the same reason as us; *viz* it does not address the fundamental causes of differences in growth rates. Consequently, he has presented a sweeping theory of why growth rates differ, drawing heavily on public choice theory and the neoclassical theory of politics (and especially his earlier work, the *Logic of Collective Activity* (1965)). The focus of interest is on how and why 'special interest groups' develop, and how they can be inimical to the long-run rate of growth. His book has proved to be an influential contribution to the explanation of disparities in economic growth. For example, Beckerman (1983, p. 919), in his review of *The Rise and Decline of Nations* for the *Economic Journal* described it as 'certainly one of the more interesting contributions to many important questions of the day'.

Olson's argument can be used to explain why the residual found in the growth accounting studies differs between the advanced countries, although he does not put it in these terms. Implicit in his theory is the proposition that it is those countries with the lowest rates of growth of total factor productivity which suffer the most from the pernicious effects of special interest groups. The central tenet of Olson's argument is, thus, that differences between countries in their rate of economic growth can largely be explained by the extent to which 'special' or 'common interest' groups have organised in each country. These special interest groups include trade unions, employers' organisations, cartels, professional organisations and lobby groups. Olson's thesis is that 'on balance, special-interest organizations and collusions reduce efficiency and aggregate income in the societies in which they operate' (p. 47). The rationale is simple and an 'elaboration of a fairly old piece of economic folk-wisdom' as Quiggin (1989, p. 62) puts it. Any political decision that benefits a few individuals or firms while spreading the costs over the whole (or a substantial proportion) of the population is likely to be adopted, even though the net effect may be to actually reduce GDP. Hence, the greater the extent to which these pressure groups, which acquire economic rents through lobbying etc., have developed in a country, the lower will be the overall pace of economic growth.

It is hypothesised that during a long period of political stability a country will progressively acquire more and more of these growth inhibiting coalitions, since once formed they subsequently become entrenched. On the other hand, those nations that have suffered a recent major political disruption, whether it be occupation by a foreign power or a period of totalitarian rule, will find that most of their special interest groups have been disbanded. In Olson's (1982, p. 75) words:

> it follows that countries whose distributional coalitions have been emasculated or abolished by totalitarian governments or foreign occupation should grow relatively quickly after a free and stable legal order has been established. This can explain the postwar 'economic miracles' in the nations that were defeated in World War II, particularly those in Japan and West Germany. The everyday use of the word *miracle* to describe rapid economic growth in these countries testifies that this growth was not only unexpected, but also outside the range of known laws and experience. In Japan and West Germany, totalitarian governments were followed by Allied occupiers determined to promote institutional change and to ensure that institutional life would start almost anew.

To demonstrate Olson's argument, let us assume that there is initially an optimal allocation of resources associated with perfect competition (assuming corrections have been made for all externalities, etc.). This is a situation where no individual agent has any market power. If any group was now to form to achieve some sort of market dominance and thereby increase its distributional share, the group's action must be at the expense of overall economic efficiency. Part of the cost will be the resources devoted to lobbying and the remainder will be the loss resulting from the distortion of market prices and the resulting misallocation of resources. Under these circumstances, the gain by one group will be at the expense of another, usually the general public. But generally the losers, most notably the consumers and taxpayers, do not have the incentives or the small numbers to organise effectively. There will be no 'counter-vailing power' to use Galbraith's term. Thus, there will always be strong incentives for governments to bow to pressure groups by granting, say, subsidies or tariff protection to ailing industries in marginal political constituencies. The political benefits to the government from such an action are obvious, while the economic costs to the nation as a whole are so diffuse as to be largely unnoticeable. Hence, they may be safely ignored by the government. But cumulatively, such costs are likely to have serious implications for economic growth.

In contrast to this scenario, let us now consider the case where there are gains to be had from increasing efficiency, i.e. there is a good deal of X-inefficiency in the economy. A special interest group now has a choice as to how to improve its economic returns. It can try to gain a larger share of the cake, even though by doing this it causes the size of the cake to shrink, or it can increase its efficiency thereby increasing the size of the cake and hence its own reward, even though its own particular share remains fixed. An implication of Olson's analysis is that the larger in size the special interest group is, i.e. the more encompassing it is, the greater will be the incentive for the group to increase the efficiency of the economy. If the returns to a group from improving the efficiency are small, and, *ceteris paribus*, this is more likely to be the case the smaller the size of the group, then it may be more effective for the group to try to obtain redistributional gains by engaging in rent-seeking. This could be true even though its actions reduce total output by what could be a substantial multiple of the extra income the group manages to appropriate for itself.[17]

The result is that symbiotic relationships often develop between a government department responsible for an industry and a pressure group reflecting the interests of that industry. The latter becomes beholden to a particular sector of the government bureaucracy or regulatory body which in turn identifies itself with the interests of that particular special interest group. This phenomenon, known as 'industry capture', is now quite widely documented. It is often reinforced by the widespread interchange of personnel between the two parties.

A consequence of the actions of the special interest groups is that the economy will become increasingly beset by regulations, introduced solely to benefit small sections of society. This will have a subtle but pervasive influence on attitudes throughout the economy. The top talent will be drawn to areas where skills in bargaining, a detailed knowledge of the regulations and ways around them are paramount. What are seen as the more 'mundane' occupations which actually create wealth, such as working in industry, will become relatively unattractive. There will also develop powerful vested interests that actually seek to prevent any simplification of the regulation since this would reduce the need for lobbyist skills, etc.

A characteristic of interest groups is that decision-making takes time because of the need to obtain a consensus of opinion about the most effective group strategy. Price fixing is preferred to quantity restrictions because this makes it easier to detect any cheating on the part of members of the coalition. It also leaves the allocation of costs to the impartial market mechanism. This will, for example, lead to wage rigidity in the labour market to which neoclassical economists attribute, *inter alia*, the rapid rise of unemployment in the advanced countries since 1973. Olson's explanation, consequently, has much in common with the 'insider–outsider' theories of unemployment (Snower and Lindbeck, 1986, 1987). Those in employment, the insiders, have a vested interest in keeping the real wage above the market clearing level, even though this is at the expense of those who are unemployed.

The arguments, so far, do not necessarily imply a slower rate of growth as opposed to a lower level of per capita income (except to the extent that the number of special interest groups are growing over time). But the long time involved before consensus between members of a special interest group is reached, Olson argues, means that the innovation of new techniques or products is likely to be slowed down while the implications for each participant in the coalition is discussed. Moreover, the existence of barriers to entry will prevent resources from moving to the rapidly growing sectors which are also likely to have the fastest growing productivity. The combination of these factors is, according to Olson, likely to ensure that coalitions do, in fact, reduce the growth rate.

Moreover, once an interest group has been established, there are powerful vested interests that will ensure its survival long after its *raison d'être* has disappeared. An example of this is the persistence of many craft unions in the UK even though the specialist skills they once represented have long since vanished. Consequently, with a long period of political stability the number of special interest groups will progressively increase, with an increasingly adverse effect on the growth rate. This will lead to the 'arteriosclerosis' of the economy, to use Lindbeck's evocative term. As we have noted above, Olson considers that it will require nothing short of a massive social up-heaval to eradicate these organisations. But Olson has to qualify this. Stability is necessary for a high level of investment and capital accumulation which will facilitate high growth rates. Consequently, the Olson thesis implies that a long period of stability will bring with it its own internal contradictions.

Olson applies his theory to explain nothing less than the broad sweep of economic development of the now advanced countries. Briefly, the early industrialisation of Britain is seen as the result of its early 'jurisdictional integration', *viz.* the development of a single national or large regional market devoid of internal barriers to trade. This destroyed the monopoly power of the medieval city guilds, which did not have the organisational ability to preserve their privileged position on a regional or national scale. The dissolution of the medieval guilds did not occur until much later on the Continent. It was not until the Zolverein that a national market was developed in Germany, and France had to await the Napoleonic era before the last vestiges of the guilds were swept away. Hence, the industrialisation of these countries was significantly delayed.

As we have already noted, Olson argues that the Second World War and its aftermath destroyed many of the special interest groups in Continental Europe and Japan, and laid the foundation for the subsequent rapid postwar growth. It is seen as significant that those countries with the slowest postwar growth rates, especially during the long boom, were the Anglo-Saxon countries such Australia, Canada, New Zealand, the UK and the US. These were never occupied by a foreign power and, with the exception of the UK, suffered relatively little damage during the war. Thus, the inimical power of the special interest groups was not destroyed, or checked, in these countries. The other contributory factor to the rapid growth rates experienced during the long boom was the rapid freeing of international trade during the 1950s. Not only did this lead to gains from an improve-ment in (static) allocative efficiency, as conventional neoclassical theory predicts would have been obtained, but it also undermined the importance of special interest groups in the various countries through greater international competition. This, so the argument goes, reduced their effect of retarding the pace of technical innovation and the rate of capital accumulation. Barriers to trade such as tariffs are seen as being detrimental to growth and to have resulted primarily from the action of special interest groups.

But as Senghaas (1985) has shown in his careful analysis of the historical evidence, protectionism, far from being harmful to growth, was essential for the successful industrialisation of many of the now advanced countries. It was only through extensive protectionism that, for example, Germany and the US were able to counter the initial British superiority in manufacturing, that arose from its being the first country to industrialise. As Senghaas (1985, p. 42) notes:

> In Britain, from the second half of the 1840s onwards, the free-trade stance thus translated itself into high rates of economic growth which still could be sustained during the general phase of general free trade in Europe between 1860 and the second half of the 1870s. In contrast, it can be shown that the continental European countries enjoyed higher economic growth during the protectionist phases before 1860 and after 1875/80 than during the free-trade period. (Omitting a footnote)

Moreover, the case of Britain shows that free trade, *per se*, is not generally enough to ensure rapid growth. Britain has generally had the most laissez-faire attitude to trade of all the advanced countries, in part because of the influence and dominance of the City of London. Consequently, the fact that Britain has had one of the slowest growth rates for the last hundred years must, according to Olson, be attributed to the action of special interest groups in the non-traded sector. Since no evidence is adduced in support of this contention, however, it is open to the charge of being *ad hoc*; the very criticism that Olson levels at other explanations of disparate growth rates.

Bowles and Eatwell (1983) go further and argue that Olson's interpretation of the British experience is erroneous. The economic development of Britain was based on an era of free trade which, to begin with, was *complementary* to British economic development. The growth of overseas markets with the accompanying growth of demand for Britain's manufactures was a necessary adjunct to Britain's rapid industrialisation. Net export growth was a little under 6

per cent per annum over the period 1836 to 1853. After 1850, industrialisation overseas (often behind tariff walls, as we have noted)
became *competitive* with British industry and net export growth fell to
1.5 per cent over the period 1873–1907. The major cause, according
to Bowles and Eatwell, was the failure of the very same institutional
structure that had originally been the cause of its success, but which
had subsequently failed to adjust to the increasing competition from
overseas.

> For our purpose the significant element in this narrative is the
> manner in which those institutions that were identified with the
> success of British industrialisation – free trade, domestic laissez-
> faire (with the consequent lack of any organisational formation
> comparable to the German banks, the giant Japanese companies,
> or the French Commissariat du Plan), the City of London and its
> financial empire, and outward-looking, internationally mobile
> corporations – have become just those institutions that have con-
> tributed to Britain's industrial decline and that inhibit any fun-
> damental change. (Bowles and Eatwell, 1983, pp. 227–8)

Bowles and Eatwell go on to argue that Britain's revitalisation can
only occur with the abandonment of free trade along with 'a major
reform of industrial and social structures' (p. 228). This certainly is
the antithesis of the implications to be drawn from the Olson argument.

Japan also poses problems for the Olson argument. Special interest
groups are commonly associated with demands for protectionism and
a limitation of market forces, yet Japan's rapid growth in the postwar
period was behind a battery of tariffs, quotas and administrative
protective controls. It is difficult to see Japan as a society with
especially weak pressure groups (Stockwin, 1981; Boltho, 1985).
Indeed, as more than one commentator has pointed out, it would be
difficult to find a country that had had more government intervention
and direction and less reliance on the free market than Japan. In
terms of the Olson thesis, Japan should have been in the throes of
stagnation since 1945! As Abramovitz (1983, p. 89) ruefully pointed
out: 'Evidently, there are subtleties in the operation and effects of
protectionist policy. They take a great deal of study to unravel.'

While Olson's thesis has a certain degree of plausibility, it is
difficult to test statistically the effect that special interest groups have
on economic growth. The problem is twofold: it is difficult, if not

impossible, first, to quantify accurately the influence of the special interest groups and, secondly, to separate the impact of these groups in reducing economic growth from other factors. For example, Olson attempts to test his theory by using data based on the US states. He argues that the influence of the special interest groups increases over time so that, *ceteris paribus*, the longer the time since statehood the lower will be the rate of growth of total and per capita income. (An allowance is made for the disruption to the Southern States caused by the Civil War.) Olson uses growth rates from 1965 to 1973 and finds that the results confirm his theory in that the longer the period since statehood, the slower a state's rate of growth, *ceteris paribus*.

The difficulty is, as Pryor (1983) points out, if an earlier period had been picked (such as 1900–10 or 1920–30), the same result might not have been obtained. Moreover, it is necessary to assume that there had been no other factors in the intervening period since statehood that may have influenced the regional growth rates. Pryor points out that the greater importance of the defence industries in the 'newer states' had a great influence on the states' growth during the Vietnam war. 'Further, given the locational pattern of committee chairmen in Congress and the federal funds flowing to the states for the construction of growth-inducing social-overhead capital, it is not unusual that the southern and western states grew faster' (Pryor, 1983, p. 91). These are just specific examples of the more general point that all the possible factors that could influence a nation's growth rate should be included in the regression analysis not just a proxy for the impact of the special interest groups, however accurately constructed that might be. The difficulty, if not impossibility, of specifying all possible explanations (some of which are very qualitative) of the disparate growth rates of nations in a form amenable to statistical testing is one of the main reasons why the large number of competing theories have persisted for so long. Pryor's own statistical results using cross country data from both the West and the Eastern Bloc gives, he argues, little support for Olson's argument, although Pryor is careful to point out the limitations of his data.

Choi (1983) also attempted to test Olson's argument using cross-country data and differences in the postwar growth rates as the explicandum. Unlike Pryor, he confined his attention to the advanced countries. Rather than merely use the time since the last major disruption as a proxy for the influence of the special interest groups, Choi constructs an index based on the assumption that the effect follows a logistic path. But this rather mechanical approach is still very arbitrary. It is not only assumed that the path is logistic but the exact parameters chosen for the logistic curve are capricious. Although Choi claims that his results support the Olson argument, his estimation procedure is subject to the same objections that have been outlined above, especially that there are numerous other factors that have to be taken into account. Abramovitz (1983), in his critique of Olson, specifies a number of these other important, but omitted, factors, which range from international differences in the elasticity of supply of cheap labour to differences in government support for investment.

Even if it were possible to construct a proxy that accurately captured the power of the special interest groups and it was found that it was significantly inversely related to economic growth, there still remains an insurmountable problem. Is the growth of special interest groups the cause, or consequence, of low growth rates? It is equally plausible that, in those countries with poor economic performances, there will be more of an incentive for trade unions to introduce restrictive practices and resist the introduction of new technology in order to preserve jobs. More generally, it is reasonable to expect that the conflict over the distribution of output will be more intense when the growth rate is lower and this will lead to the formation of more coalitions, each intent on increasing its economic welfare at the expense of the rest of the nation. The problem with regression analysis is that correlation, of course, implies nothing about causality.

There are also other conceptual problems that are equally, if not more, serious. The first is that the above tests are based on the assumption that the deleterious effects of the special interest groups grow over time. This has led to the prediction that the longer the time since the last major disruption, the greater will be the power of the special interest groups and hence the slower the growth rate. But as we have noted, there is what Olson terms an 'internal contradiction' in stable societies. This results from the 'colossal economic and political advantages of peace and stability and the longer-term losses that come from the accumulating networks of distributional coalitions that can survive only in stable environments'. But we have no idea of which will dominate at any point in time and there is the real danger of this argument being an immunising strategem, i.e. one that renders the theory incapable of refutation. If it were found, for example, that a country with a very long period of stability had an above average growth rate it could be argued that the 'colossal economic and political advantages of peace and stability' outweighed the disadvantages of the special interest groups, and *vice versa*. Hence, it would be impossible to refute the theory. A similar problem arises when Olson attempts to explain why Sweden, with its long period of stability, has generally experienced a fast rate of economic growth. The answer, according to Olson, is that Sweden is dominated by large, or encompassing, special interest groups. As we have seen, the larger a special interest group, the more likely it will be in the group's interest to raise the overall level of economic efficiency. Thus, corporarist economies are also likely to have fast rates of growth. But it will always be possible to think up plausible reasons, *ex post*, for why a country does not fit the general rule, thus rendering the theory almost tautological.

Much empirical work which attempts to explain the determinants of the levels of tariff protection for various industries can also be viewed as a test of the importance of special interest groups. This is because these regression analyses nearly always include a measure of industrial concentration as the main variable capturing the strength of special interest groups. Yet Quiggin (1989, p. 64) notes that 'this empirical work is remarkable, both for the regularity with which this central prediction has been invalidated, and for the enthusiasm with which success has been claimed for the neoclassical approach'. He cites studies for Australia (Anderson, 1980), Canada (Caves, 1976) and the US (McPherson, 1972; Finger, Hall and Nelson, 1972; Stigler, 1974) where, paradoxically, the level of industrial concentration has been found to be negatively related to success in attaining assistance. He concludes that 'consistent results of this kind must cast grave doubts on the viability of the "interest group" theory, at least with respect to the explanation of protection. The claim that concentrated industries will be in a good position [to obtain protection] is one of the most distinctive predictions of the neoclassical theory, and one of the few that is common to all presentations of the theory' (Quiggin, 1989, p. 69).

Olson's theory is essentially one about the determinants of disparities in *long-run* economic growth as, in the absence of dramatic shocks, the density of coalitions will increase only slowly over time. Whatever one's views about how successfully it accomplishes this, the theory is much less satisfactory as an explanation of the sudden post-1973 slowdown.

Olson argues that since special interest or distributional groups are generally monopolistic, rather than monopsonistic, prices will be set, on the whole, above their market clearing level. (It should be noted that Olson espouses the traditional neoclassical argument about monopolies leading to distorted prices and a resulting misallocation of resources. There is no room here for the Schumpeterian view of the dynamic benefits of monopoly, which may greatly exceed any short-run losses.) If the coalitions have not experienced persistent high inflation, they will set prices nominally rather than fully indexing them. A surprise price shock, in the form of unanticipated inflation, will temporarily reduce the prices obtained by lobbying or cartelisation. 'Thus the social losses from monopoly and the extent to which prices and wages are above market clearing levels will be temporarily diminished and the productivity of the economy will improve for a time' (Olson, 1988. p. 63).

Real shocks will have similar effects. If there is an unexpected increase in productivity, the price that the coalitions charge will be lower than if they had perfect foresight. It follows that the effect will be to increase '*efficiency* and *reduce unemployment* in a sclerotic economy, and the favorable consequences of the surprise are accordingly *multiplied*' (Olson, 1988, p. 64, emphasis in the original). A boom will also increase the proportion of small businesses, which are generally highly innovative and have the additional benefit of undermining the power of the coalitions. On the other hand, an unexpected fall in productivity will lead to a further fall in efficiency for the converse reasons.

It is, of course, extremely difficult to substantiate these hypotheses directly and Olson does not provide any independent evidence about their plausibility.

Furthermore, when he comes to use these arguments to explain the post-1973 slowdown, the explanation becomes too general to be testable and, in many respects, not very novel. Initially, it is necessary for Olson to explain what would, at first sight in terms of his theory, seem to be the anomalous *increase* in the US's productivity growth in the immediate postwar period. It is anomalous, because as the increase in special interest groups in the US was unhindered by the Second World War, we should expect the growth of productivity to have *fallen* in the immediate postwar period. Olson, however, argues that the memory of the Great Depression prevented the coalitions from setting prices as high as they would otherwise have done. This caused productivity growth to accelerate (although the exact mechanism by which this occurred is not spelt out) and this was reinforced by the exploitation of the backlog of inventions that had not been taken advantage of during the Great Depression or the Second World War. (Why these innovations had not been exploited in the Second World War, when the US experienced a very fast growth rate and high rate of investment, is not made clear by Olson.) Continental Europe not only benefitted from the destruction of its special interest groups but also the gains from the jurisdictional integration of the Common Market. To the extent that the faster growth of productivity was unexpected, it would lead to a further increase in efficiency for the reasons set out above.

The postwar period saw the exhaustion of these putative neglected inventions, the progressive diminution of the gains from the inter-sectoral reallocation of resources and the ending of the technological 'catch-up' process for Japan and Europe. While this did not, *per se*, reduce growth rates to below their historic norms, the decline was unexpected and, hence, this, through the effect of the special interest groups, led to a further decline in productivity. (The problem with this argument is that there is no evidence that there was a general slowdown in growth rates prior to 1973, as would be expected as the 'unexpected' high growth of productivity and income quickly became anticipated.) It might be thought, also, that the rapid inflation in 1973/4 was unexpected and hence this would have actually increased productivity. But Olson argues that, in fact, the high degree of indexation of prices and nominal wages, or the prevalence of real wage bargaining, suggests that its effects were rapidly taken into account. Olson (1988, p. 67) summarises his argument as follows:

Given the coalition density, many prices and wages would have been too high for efficiency and market clearing even with perfect foresight. But decisions based on memorable experience led for a time to coalition prices and wages much higher than they would have been if the natural fall from exceptional levels of productivity growth and the oil shock had been foreseen and the harmful effects of each of them were therefore multiplied. The disinflationary aggregate demand shock came at essentially the same time, and each of the three shocks made the coalitions err in the same direction – the direction that multiplied their adverse effects on economic performance.

To account for the fact that there has been no subsequent recovery in productivity growth, Olson relies on the hysteresis argument.

To conclude: our discussion of the Olson thesis, and the evidence supposedly in support of it, have been somewhat critical. This should not obscure the insights that Olson has shed. In particular he has shown why it is possible for small groups, in rationally pursuing their own self interests, actually to reduce the overall growth of the economy. Whether international differences in the power of these groups is sufficient to account for a significant proportion of the observed differences in long-term growth rates is another matter.

Nevertheless, the role of trade unions in the UK would appear to lend some support to Olson's argument and we next briefly consider this as another possible explanation for the UK's slow rate of economic growth.

TRADE UNIONISM IN THE UNITED KINGDOM

In the United Kingdom, bargaining occurs both nationally and at the plant level with the latter assuming far greater importance than in nearly all other advanced countries. Kilpatrick and Lawson (1980), who have provided a useful survey of the issues, argue that plant level bargaining 'is essentially a defensive strength: workers attempt to maintain working conditions and living standards' (p. 88). (Our discussion draws heavily on their article.) Workers are able to delay the introduction of new techniques or modes of new organisation which they feel threaten their customary working practices. The UK, compared with the other advanced countries, has a large number of small craft unions organised within any one industry. The Olson hypothesis suggests that this would generate a great deal of solidarity amongst the workers and hence increase their bargaining power. It also encourages a more parochial view than would exist in an industry-wide union.

The large number of unions is primarily a result of the early legal recognition that the trade unions received in the United Kingdom. This occurred in the late nineteenth century when production was based mainly along craft lines and when mass production based on the assembly line had not been developed. The legalisation of unions and the right to peaceful picketing became enshrined in law in 1871. The first unions were thus comprised of skilled workers organised along craft lines. Unskilled workers were increasingly unionised during the 1880s and while they were initially critical of the high degree to which the craft unions looked inward, by the turn of the century the unskilled workers were themselves emulating these very same practices. The decentralised union structure seems to have resulted also from the early dominance of the subcontracting system. The subcontractor, through his power to hire and fire, was able to exert great influence on the workers. This structure of control persisted long after formal subcontracting had ended since the demise of the subcontractor was brought about by the workers who themselves retained much of the existing practices. Customs and agreements conceded by management were jealously guarded and preserved long after they had become obsolete.

Consequently, the structure of unionism developed along decentralised lines and in a form that was unsuitable for the later modes of mass production. Even the Second World War which brought about a social revolution in Britain served only to strengthen the power of the shop stewards. The spirit of co-operation during the war and the setting up of the Joint Production Committees led to the spread of shop stewards into industries where they were previously absent. Thus, the war accelerated the growth of the shopfloor influence at the expense of the national union movement.

The end result is that a typical industry can now contain upwards of twenty individual unions with associated rigid demarcation lines. In 1975 there were 488 unions which, although fewer than the 1269 that existed in 1913, testifies to the decentralised nature of the British trade union movement. This not only presents great problems for management in terms of the complexity of consultation and negotiation, but also means that the introduction of new technology, which blurs traditional job descriptions, takes a long time.

Britain's experience stands in marked contrast to that of other countries which industrialised in the nineteenth century. These nations not only had a more rapid industrialisation, but also experienced major upheavals of a political nature that profoundly affected the structure of their unions. In Germany, for example, unions were abolished in 1933 and were only allowed to reform in 1945 after Germany's defeat in the Second World War. The new structure was highly centralised with unions based on industries rather than occupations within a particular industry. Thus, the 16 industry-based unions avoided the highly fragmented union structure with its large number of craft unions that existed during the Weimar Republic. In France the suppression of the 1871 Paris commune broke up the French unions and although legal recognition was granted seven years later it was not until 1971 that penalties were introduced against any party refusing to enter into collective bargaining. In Italy, Mussolini replaced the independent unions with government controlled syndicates. These were never completely dismantled after the war and so a strong centralised bias remained. 'Indeed, for most of the postwar period there has been no direct union presence in factories in Italy or in France. Only since 1970 in Italy and since 1968 in France has this begun to change' (Kilpatrick and Lawson, 1980, p. 88).

Trade Unions were slow to develop in the United States and it was only with the passing of the Wagner Act in the 1930s that there was a major expansion of trade union activity. But federal government employees have no legal right to strike and there are limitations on the rights of collective bargaining. 'A limited number of union practices have been banned since 1947, when employers successfully challenged the Wagner Act on the basis that it conceded too much to unions (Labor/Management Relations Act). The legal framework of collective bargaining has remained essentially unchanged since 1947' (Kilpatrick and Lawson, 1980, p. 88).

BRITISH UNIONS AND THE DELAY IN THE INTRODUCTION OF NEW TECHNOLOGY

There is now a plethora of case studies that support the widespread view that unions have been a major factor in Britain's slow rate of innovation over the last century.

For example, although the 'ring frame' in textile production was primarily manufactured in the United Kingdom, British textile manufacturers were very slow to adopt it. In 1907, ring spindles only accounted for 15 per cent of total spindles in the UK; in Germany the comparable figure was 40 per cent; France, 38 per cent; Austria, 36 per cent; Italy, 65 per cent; Russia, 56 per cent, and 80 per cent in the United States. Lazonick (1978) attributes this to the power of the mule spinners (the ring was designed as a more efficient replacement for the mule) through their union to protect their jobs right up until the 1960s. Any attempt to replace the mule would have led to industrial confrontation that the employers could not be sure of winning. By way of contrast, in the United States the employers had complete control over the way the labour force was organised and thus had little hesitation in adopting the new technology.

There are numerous contemporary examples that could be cited ranging from the restrictive practices of the dock workers to the successful (until very recently) resistance of the newspaper print workers to the introduction of new technology. Of course, such practices require the acquiesence of management. It is ironical that for many years there were numerous newspaper editorials scathing of British management for allowing itself to be dictated to by the unions. But the major British national papers themselves provided, *par excellence*, examples of such 'weak' management. On the other hand, the industrial unrest that resulted when management belatedly did challenge the unions to some extent explains their reluctance to do so. There was undoubtedly a marked change in the industrial climate brought in by the Thatcher government after 1979 (the removal of many legal immunities of the trades unions including the outlawing of secondary picketing; the defeat of the miners' strike of 1984; and the high unemployment levels).

The extent to which trade unions may be held accountable for the United Kingdom's slow rate of growth is still controversial. But such issues are totally ignored in the growth accounting approach.

THEORETICAL CRITICISM OF THE NEOCLASSICAL APPROACH: THE SIMON/SHAIKH CRITIQUE[18,19]

Another set of criticisms is concerned more with the theoretical basis of the growth accounting approach than with its empirical relevance, and we next turn to a consideration of these. In particular, it is argued that the marginal productivity theory of distribution *when used in combination with the aggregate production function* is highly questionable. At the one extreme, there are the well-known highly trenchant criticisms of the Cambridge (UK) School, most notably by Eatwell, Pasinetti, Kaldor, Robinson and Sraffa. These criticisms were mainly articulated as part of the well-known capital controversy that arose in the mid-1960s and inconclusively petered out in the mid-1970s. (See Harcourt (1972) for a blow-by-blow account of the debate, and Kaldor (1966a) for a pithy comment of the inadequacies of the marginal productivity theory.)

We deliberately added the rider 'when used in combination with the aggregate production function' because many economists in the neoclassical tradition (or, at least, not as hostile to it as the Cambridge School) are also sceptical of the aggregate marginal product theory while accepting its validity at the microeconomic level (see, for example, Blaug, 1974.) Thus, the use of factor shares as weights may not even provide a close approximation to the contribution various factors make to economic growth and the whole approach is subject to spurious accuracy. For example, what are the confidence limits of Denison's estimates that environmental and health/safety regulations reduced productivity growth in the United States by 0.1 percentage points before 1973 and by 0.3 after this date? We just do not know. Indeed, does it make sense even to try to aim at this degree of disaggregation and precision?

The capital controversy poses a severe challenge to the very notion of the aggregate production function. But it should not be forgotten that severe reservations had arisen about the concept even earlier as a result of the inherent aggregation problems that are involved (Walters, 1963). For example, if the firms' production functions are of the Cobb–Douglas form, they cannot be aggregated into an aggregate production functions that is itself a Cobb–Douglas. Nevertheless, there is little doubt that the use of aggregate production functions of ever increasing sophistication (from the original Cobb–Douglas specification, to the CES and finally to the most general translog production function) has been encouraged by the fact that they 'work'. That is to say, statistical estimations normally provide high correlation coefficients and low standard errors for the estimated coefficients. Furthermore, the estimated output elasticities are very close to the value of the relevant factor shares, which is in accord with the aggregate neoclassical theory of distribution. For neoclassical economists imbued with Friedman's (1953) methodological stance of instrumentalism, this is in itself sufficient justification for using aggregate production functions. At the inevitable risk of oversimplification, Friedman's argument is that the usefulness of a theory should not be judged by the realism or otherwise of its assumptions; what is crucial is its predictive ability. This view rests on the symmetry thesis; explanation and prediction are seen as merely different sides of the same coin. The high goodness-of-fit and the low standard errors of the estimated coefficients is often cited as sufficient justification of the continued use of the aggregate production function, notwithstanding the theoretical criticisms that have been levelled at its use. (See Caldwell, 1982, chapter 8, for a discussion and critique of this methodology.)

The work, however, by Phelps Brown (1957), Simon and Levy (1963), Simon (1979) and Shaikh (1974, 1980, 1987) *inter alios* would lead us to be sceptical of such assertions (McCombie, 1987). They have separately shown that the observed good fits of the Cobb–Douglas and the CES relationships 'are very likely all statistical artifacts. The data say no more than that the value of product is approximately equal to the wage bill plus the cost of capital services' (Simon, 1979, p. 469). This critique by Simon and Shaikh is not only applicable to the aggregate production function but also to any micro-production function that is estimated using constant price value data. It is not applicable, however, to engineering production functions where the output and inputs are measured in physical units.

In spite of the fact that Simon's and Shaikh's critique would seem to be a most damning indictment of the very notion of the production function, and that one of the critics is a Nobel laureate in Economics, it appears to have been largely ignored in the literature.[20]

THE AGGREGATE PRODUCTION FUNCTION AND THE ACCOUNTING IDENTITY

The heart of the Simon/Shaikh criticism is that the estimates of so-called aggregate production functions are merely reflecting an underlying accounting identity. This will produce good statistical fits whether or not there is a well-defined aggregate production function. It will also ensure that the estimated output elasticities closely approximate the relevant factor shares, whether or not the aggregate marginal productivity theory of distribution holds.

Shaikh's (1974, 1980, 1987) critique was couched in terms of the Cobb–Douglas function. After first discussing and amplifying this, we shall show that it is but a special case of an argument applicable to more general production functions. We shall explicitly demonstrate this with respect to the translog production function.

The value of total output (value added) at time t is *defined* as:

$$TC_t \equiv Q_t \equiv w_t L_t + r_t K_t \tag{1.28}$$

where TC, Q, w and r are the values of total costs, output, the wage rate and the rental price of capital, all expressed in real terms. K is the capital stock and L is the level of employment or the total hours worked.[21]

Equation (1.28) may be expressed in terms of instantaneous growth rates as:

$$q_t \equiv \varphi_t + a_t \ell_t + (1 - a_t)k_t \tag{1.29}$$

where $\varphi_t = a_t \varphi_{wt} + (1 - a_t)\varphi_{rt}$.

The variables q, ℓ and k denote the proportionate growth rates of output, labour and capital. φ_w and φ_r are the growth rates of wages and of the rental price of capital. a_t is labour's share in total output (i.e. $a_t = (w_t L_t)/Q_t)$) and $(1 - a_t)$ is capital's share.

The factor shares may, of course, change over time (except in the special case of the Cobb–Douglas) which is why they have a time subscript. To begin with, though, let us assume that the shares are constant (i.e. $a_t = a$). Furthermore, initially and for expositional convenience, we postulate that w and r each grow at a constant rate. It must be emphasised that the argument in its general form does not depend upon either of these assumptions, as will be seen below. Nevertheless, it is shown in McCombie and Dixon (1991, appendix A) that $a \ln w_t + (1 - a) \ln r_t$ generally has a strong linear trend with only a small irregular component. In other words, φ_t may be taken to approximate to a constant growth rate, so that $\varphi_t = \varphi$.

Integrating equation (1.29) with respect to time we obtain:

$$Q_t \equiv A_0 e^{\varphi t} L_t^a K_t^{(1-a)} \tag{1.30}$$

or:

$$Q_t \equiv B_0 w_t^a \, r_t^{(1-a)} L_t^a K_t^{(1-a)} \tag{1.31}$$

where A_0 and B_0 are constants.

Compare equation (1.31) with the specification of the Cobb–Douglas production function with constant returns to scale, *viz*:

$$Q_t = A_0 e^{\lambda t} L_t^\alpha K_t^{(1-\alpha)} \tag{1.32}$$

where λ is the constant growth of total factor productivity and α and $(1 - \alpha)$ are the output elasticities of labour and capital. Under the assumption of perfect competition and the marginal productivity theory of distribution, the output elasticities should equal the relevant factor shares. (This is considered in greater detail below when a more general case of the production function is discussed.) Empirically, it is often confirmed that the output elasticities are equal to the relevant factor shares (Douglas, 1976).

If, however, the equation:

$$\ln Q_t = b_0 + b_1 t + b_2 \ln L_t + b_3 \ln K_t + v_t \tag{1.33}$$

(where v_t is the error term) were to be estimated, we should expect a perfect fit with the estimates of the coefficients b_2 and b_3 always equalling the values of the shares of labour and of capital respectively. This is because of the underlying identity which is given by equations (1.28) and (1.30). b_1 will equal the weighted average of the growth of wages and of the rental price of capital, namely φ.[22]

Since equation (1.28), $Q_t \equiv w_t L_t + r_t K_t$, is compatible with *any* underlying production technology (e.g. a fixed coefficients production function), or indeed with the complete absence of any well-defined production function, no inference can be drawn from the statistical results about, for example, the aggregate elasticity of substitution between the factors of production. Moreover, the close approximation of the output elasticities to the appropriate factor shares cannot be taken as providing any confirmation of the neoclassical theory of distribution.

It does not seriously affect the argument if the growth of wages and the growth of the rental price of capital show some variation over time. If, however, a linear time trend does not give a very good approximation to $a\ln w_t + (1 - a)\ln r_t$, then the estimate of technical progress, if proxied by a linear time trend in the production function (when specified in terms of the logarithms of the levels of the various variables), will *pari passu* have a large standard error. This may also lead to a bias in the estimates of the output elasticities so that they may diverge from the values of the corresponding factor shares. It will, however, always be possible to improve the goodness of fit of the estimation of the production function by finding a non-linear time trend that closely approximates to the fluctuations over time of $a\ln w_t + (1 - a)\ln r_t$. The goodness of fit will increase the closer the specification of the production function approximates to the underlying identity. Usually, the sole criterion of choice of which is the most preferable specification of a production function is in terms of the best statistical fit. The search for the latter is merely the search for the best approximation to the accounting identity!

Shaikh (1980) has also shown that the accounting identity explains why the computer simulations of Fisher (1971) demonstrated that even though the underlying technological relationships of the individual firms were not consistent with any aggregate production function, the data still gave a good fit to the aggregate Cobb–Douglas function so long as factor shares were constant. According to Fisher (1971, p. 325):

> The suggestion [of the simulation experiments] is clear, however, that labor's share is not roughly constant because the diverse technical relationships of modern economies are truly

representable by an aggregate Cobb–Douglas but rather that such relationships appear to be representable by an aggregate Cobb–Douglas *because* labor's share happens to be roughly constant. (emphasis in the original)

We should perhaps amplify our argument somewhat. It is theoretically possible that the underlying technology is, by a remarkable coincidence, an aggregate Cobb–Douglas production function. The above argument concerning the accounting identity thus cannot be taken to imply that the Cobb–Douglas production function does not exist. But nor can the plethora of studies which find remarkably good fits for the Cobb–Douglas relationship be taken as providing any independent evidence about the nature of the underlying technology. A further example is to be found in Shaikh (1987, p. 691) where he shows that 'when the wage share is constant, *even a fixed proportion technology undergoing Harrod-neutral technical change is perfectly consistent with an aggregate pseudo-production function*' which is a Cobb–Douglas in form (emphasis in the original).

This argument also helps to explain the almost embarrassingly good closeness of fit that the Cobb–Douglas relationship actually produces. Given the numerous other factors that would be thought also to influence the level of output, such as variations in X-efficiency, etc., it is remarkable that, if the estimation is interpreted as being that of a production function, often over 90 per cent of the variation in the logarithm of output can be explained simply by variations in the logarithms of labour and of capital together with a time trend.[23] Once it is realised, though, that all that is being estimated is an identity then this problem disappears, since now a very good fit is only to be expected.

The relative constancy of factor shares does not rely solely upon the existence of a Cobb–Douglas production function. For example, if firms pursue a mark-up pricing policy and the average mark-up on unit labour costs is stable over time then factor shares will be constant. If the mark-up is $(1 + \pi)$ then labour's and capital's shares are $1/(1 + \pi)$ and $\pi/(1 + \pi)$. Alternatively, there is the Kaldorian macroeconomic theory of distribution which will also produce the same result of constancy of factor shares if the investment ratio and savings propensities are constant without any recourse to the neoclassical theory of distribution or an aggregate production function.

A GENERALISATION OF THE SIMON/SHAIKH CRITIQUE

What about the case where factor shares are changing over time? As has been noted above, this does not affect the argument as we shall now show.

The production function may be expressed in a more general form as:

$$Q_t = F(L_t; K_t; t) \tag{1.34}$$

where the time variable, t, is included to allow for technical change.

Differentiating equation (1.34) with respect to time (and omitting the time subscripts) we obtain:

$$\frac{dQ}{dt} = \frac{\partial F}{\partial L} \cdot \frac{dL}{dt} + \frac{\partial F}{\partial K} \cdot \frac{dK}{dt} + \frac{\partial F}{\partial t} \tag{1.35}$$

Invoking the usual neoclassical assumptions, the following side relations may be derived from the marginal productivity conditions:

$$\frac{\partial Q_t}{\partial K_t} = r_t \tag{1.36a}$$

and:

$$\frac{\partial Q_t}{\partial L_t} = w_t \tag{1.36b}$$

Substituting equations (1.36a) and (1.36b) into equation (1.35), the latter may be expressed, with some additional manipulation, as:

$$\frac{(dQ_t/dt)}{Q_t} = \frac{w_t L_t}{Q_t} \cdot \frac{(dL_t/dt)}{L_t} + \frac{r_t K_t}{Q_t} \cdot \frac{(dK_t/dt)}{K_t} + \lambda_t \tag{1.37}$$

or:

$$q_t = \lambda_t + a_t l_t + (1 - a_t) k_t \tag{1.38}$$

where $\lambda_t = \dfrac{\partial F_t}{\partial t} \cdot \dfrac{1}{F_t}$

Thus, at any point of time, the production function in terms of growth rates is given by equation (1.38) and, by virtue of the marginal productivity conditions, the coefficients on ℓ_t and k_t are the relevant factor shares. Recall, however, equation (1.29):

$$q_t \equiv \varphi_t + a_t\ell_t + (1 - a_t)k_t \tag{1.29}$$

It may be seen that a_t and $(1 - a_t)$ must always be equal to the relevant factor shares because of the underlying identity. Equation (1.29) (or, identically, equation (1.38)) will always hold exactly. This is true even if the neoclassical assumptions are either invalid or there is no well-defined production function or both.

We may demonstrate this proposition by considering a particular specification of a production function, namely the translog production function. This is a very flexible production function because it provides a local approximation to any production frontier. One version, where A_t is an index of technology, is:

$$\ln Q_t = c + \ln A_t + \alpha\ln L_t + \beta\ln K_t + \gamma\ln L_t \ln K_t + \delta(\ln L_t)^2$$
$$+ \epsilon(\ln K_t)^2 \tag{1.39}$$

Differentiating equation (1.39) with respect to L gives:

$$\left(\frac{1}{Q}\frac{\partial Q}{\partial L}\right)_t = \frac{\alpha}{L_t} + \frac{\gamma\ln K_t}{L_t} + \frac{2\delta\ln L_t}{L_t} \tag{1.40}$$

Multiplying equation (1.40) by L_t and given that, from the marginal productivity condition, $\partial Q/\partial L = w_t$, we obtain an expression for labour's share:

$$\left(\frac{wL}{Q}\right)_t = a_t = \alpha + \gamma\ln K_t + 2\delta\ln L_t \tag{1.41}$$

Similarly, an expression for capital's share may be derived, *viz*:

$$\left(\frac{rK}{Q}\right)_t = (1 - a_t) = \beta + \gamma\ln L_t + 2\epsilon\ln K_t \tag{1.42}$$

It will be noticed that the factor shares are a function of the logarithms of labour and capital and will vary as these change, so long as γ and ϵ do not equal zero.

The growth of output may be obtained by differentiating equation (1.39) with respect to time (where $d\ln A_t/dt = \lambda_t$) as:

$$q_t = \lambda_t + \alpha\,\ell_t + \beta k_t + \gamma\ln K_t\,\ell_t + \gamma\ln L_t k_t + 2\delta\ln L_t\ell_t + 2\epsilon\ln K_t\,k_t \qquad (1.43)$$

Substituting equations (1.41) and (1.42) into (1.43) we obtain:

$$q_t = \lambda_t + a_t\ell_t + (1 - a_t)k_t \qquad (1.44)$$

which is formally equivalent to equation (1.29)

Most production function studies are, however, concerned with finding a specific functional form that will give the best fit when estimated using time series data (i.e. finding a function that will be best capable of tracking the time path of the factor shares). In terms of the translog production function this would involve determining the values of α, β, γ, ϵ, and δ by estimating equation (1.39). It is also generally assumed that $\lambda_t = \lambda$, i.e. λ, the rate of technical change, is constant. If this is approximately true and factor shares are also roughly constant then the Cobb–Douglas will give a very good fit, but, as we have argued, this provides no independent evidence for the existence of a production function. Likewise, if shares are changing then a more flexible functional form is needed such as the CES or translog function, but the same interpretation problem remains by virtue of equations (1.29), (1.38) and (1.44).

The implications of this argument may be seen more clearly with the aid of a simple example. Let us assume that, notwithstanding the necessary heroic assumptions, there is a 'true' aggregate production function that accurately represents the technology of the economy. Furthermore, let us say that it is a CES production function with an elasticity of substitution of 0.4. But, in our hypothetical economy, the labour market is not competitive and the result of trade union power is that the share of labour in total output remains constant over time. The best statistical fit would therefore be given by the Cobb–Douglas function. The estimated output elasticities would equal the relevant factor shares, which is just what the assumptions of a Cobb–Douglas and a perfectively competitive market would predict. Alternatively, if we start out by making these assumptions, the data will not refute the model *even though the latter is erroneous*. Because of the underlying identity, the data cannot provide an independent test of the hypothesis which consequently can be neither falsified nor confirmed.

THE GROWTH ACCOUNTING METHODOLOGY REVISITED

Solow (1988, p. 313), in reviewing the development of modern growth theory, in which he has played a major role, still took the view that 'the main result of that 1957 experiment was startling. Gross output per hour of work in the US economy doubled between 1909 and 1949; and some seven-eighths of that increase could be attributed to "technical change in the broadest sense" and only the remaining eighth could be attributed to conventional increases in capital intensity.' As we have mentioned earlier, this result was very important in providing a major impetus for the growth accounting approach.

But, given the Kaldorian 'stylised facts' of economic growth, what is surprising is that anyone should have found this result surprising. A simple calculation shows that it is logically impossible for 'technical change', as conventionally defined, to have played a minor role. The stylised facts of growth may be summarised as:

  (i)   real output per worker grows at more or less a constant rate,
 (ii)   factor shares are constant, and
(iii)   the rental price of capital is constant.

These are by no means controversial propositions and, in fact, were put forward by Solow (1970) himself as facts that growth theory needs to explain.

We have shown that technical progress is formally equivalent to:

$$\lambda \equiv a\varphi_w + (1 - a)\varphi_r \qquad (1.45)$$

or, given the stylised fact that the rental price of capital is roughly constant:

$$\lambda \simeq a\varphi_w \qquad (1.46)$$

Since factor shares also do not greatly vary, it follows that:

$$\varphi_w \simeq q - \ell \qquad (1.47)$$

Consequently, it follows from equations (1.46) and (1.47) that the rate of technical progress is given by the expression:

$$\lambda \simeq a(q - \ell) \qquad (1.48)$$

Since *a* takes a value of about 0.75 for the whole economy, technical progress must 'explain' about 75 per cent of the growth of output per worker, but this is a far from surprising result! The rate of growth of the labour input also tends to be small relative to q, so λ will also account for a substantial proportion of the growth of output. (It may be recalled in our earlier example using the growth of the UK manufacturing sector, q equalled 3.18 per cent per annum while ℓ took a value of only 0.13 per cent per annum.)

THE BACON AND ELTIS THESIS OF THE CAUSES OF THE UK's SLOW RATE OF ECONOMIC GROWTH

In their original work, Bacon and Eltis (1976) focused primarily on Britain's poor economic performance. The essence of their argument was that most of the conventional scapegoats for Britain's inferior economic record (e.g. labour shortages, balance-of-payments constraints etc.) were all symptoms of a fundamental change in the structure of the economy since the Second World War, namely the growth of what they called 'non-marketable' output, largely produced by government, which the public had not been willing to pay for by reduced consumption of marketable output. Attempts to tax directly or 'forcibly' by monetary expansion (the inflation tax) simply led to wage inflation through workers attempting to maintain their real post-tax incomes. The result of the growth of non-marketable output 'unfinanced' by reduced consumption of marketable output was that industry and the foreign sector were starved of resources. Inflation, low investment (leading to low productivity growth) and a poor balance of payments all resulted from this change in the structure of the economy. The Bacon and Eltis argument originally focused on the decade up to 1973. The argument has provided, however, a justification for more recent attempts in the UK to curb radically government spending, especially during the Thatcher years of the 1980s. Not only politicians of Conservative persuasion found the argument appealing. Denis Healey, the Labour Chancellor of the Exchequer in 1975 when the argument first appeared, expressed the view that Bacon and Eltis's articles in the *Sunday Times* on 'Declining Britain' provided 'the most stimulating and comprehensive analysis of our predicament which I have yet seen in a newspaper'.[24] As Hadjimatheou and Skouras (1979) remarked in an evaluation of the Bacon and Eltis (BE) thesis: 'so ready and unequivocal praise is indicative of the BE thesis's significance'. Yet they conclude their own evaluation by saying 'neither theoretical considerations nor empirical evidence seem to support their [Bacon and Eltis's] thesis which, therefore, can by no means be adopted as a serious basis for the formulation of economic policy'.

Here we outline in some detail the Bacon and Eltis hypothesis concerning slow growth (with particular reference to Britain) and make our own assessment. We find that although Bacon and Eltis emphasise the lack of investment, their argument and evidence comes close to our own that Britain suffers a chronic (structural) balance-of-payments problem, which may be considered as both cause and a consequence of a poor investment record.

Eltis (1979) starts off from the neo-physiocratic view that:

> All economies have a sector which produces a surplus off which the rest of the economy lives. This is one of the oldest propositions in economics. It has always been understood that if the surplus is large, the country will be able to support strong but unproductive armed forces and an extensive state establishment which meet their material needs from the extra output of agriculture, industry and commerce. If the surplus is small, the country cannot afford to employ many non-producers and if it attempts to finance them, it will push taxation to the point where agriculture, industry and commerce fail to function as they should. (p. 118)

After initially considering the industrial sector and the tradeable sector, Bacon and Eltis finally settle on the market sector as the 'surplus creating sector of economies'. The market sector is a wider category than the other two, and consists of all goods and services that are sold in the market, including not only manufactured goods but also construction, transportation, retail and wholesale services and financial services. It also encompasses the output of the nationalised industries to the extent that their costs are covered by sales (in other words, excluding any subsidies). The non-market sector by definition does not produce any marketed output but has to be financed by taxation e.g. the health service, defence, the civil service, the police and state education.

This is not to imply that non-market production is necessarily less valuable than marketed output. Indeed, the demand for many components such as health, education and subsidies to the arts has an income elasticity of demand greater than unity. The reason why the market sector is regarded as more fundamental is that a major determinant of the rate of economic growth is the proportion of output that is invested, and investment has to be supplied by the market sector. Furthermore, the market sector must also provide the economy's exports to pay for imports and hence a satisfactory performance is vital if a country is to pay its way in the world.

The market sector must also supply from its surplus the consumption goods of those employed in providing non-marketed output, as well as the investment requirements of the non-market sector. The larger the non-market sector, the greater will be its claims on the market sector's surplus and the less there will be available for other uses.

The proportion of market output that goes to those employed in the non-market sector is not determined directly as a result of consumers' preferences for market and non-marketed output. Rather, it is determined by the government through its taxation and expenditure policies. The problem Bacon and Eltis point to is that the proportion of marketed output appropriated by the government rose dramatically after 1965, and was far greater than if the allocation could somehow have been left to the market mechanism (which, of course, for the most part it cannot). There was also a ratchet effect at work; public expenditure increased during the downturn of the economic cycle but did not fall at the peak. Workers were thus faced with an inextricable rise in the claims on the marketed output which potentially meant a corresponding fall in the rate of growth of their consumption of market goods. Rather than acquiescing and allowing this increase in non-marketed output to be substituted for consumption, the workers attempted to maintain their share of marketed output (and to some extent succeeded). Greater trade union militancy led to claims for higher money wages. Firms were not able to pass on fully these extra costs, partly because of the incomes policies that were periodically introduced to try to curtail the rapidly escalating rate of inflation, and partly because of the competition from overseas firms and a fixed exchange rate. Consequently, net-of-tax profits were squeezed and this led to a fall in the proportion of marketed output invested. Thus, that part of the market surplus that went to finance the increase in non-market output mainly came at the expense of investment. The economy was, in effect, eating its seed-corn. Strictly speaking, the growth of the non-market sector could also be financed by a deterioration in the balance of payments, but Bacon and Eltis place much greater emphasis on the reduction in investment.

> Hence, Britain's non-market sector grew, not at the expense of the economy's consumable surplus which any society can afford, but instead at the expense of investment in job creation, the economy's seed-corn. The effect of what happened was that employment in British industry fell at a rate of 155,000 a year from 1966 until 1973, the final year before the world recession. (Eltis, 1979, p. 129)

The Bacon and Eltis argument can be illustrated using the National Income Accounts. From the expenditure side, national income (Y) is equal to the sum of consumption, investment and the balance of payments surplus (or deficit). The balance of payments, by definition, is made up of marketable output, $(X - M)_m$, but consumption (C) and investment (I) may be in either the marketable output (m), or non-marketable output (nm), sectors, i.e.

$$Y = C_m + C_{nm} + I_m + I_{nm} + (X - M)_m \qquad (1.49)$$

It follows that if there is an increase in the amount of expenditure devoted to non-marketable output, and the consumption of marketable output does not fall, then investment in the marketable output sector, and/or the balance of payments, must suffer. Or, in terms of shares of national income, if the share of expenditure in the non-marketable sector increases, and the consumption of marketable output does not decline as a proportion of income, then the share of investment plus the trade balance must deteriorate.

The argument can also be illustrated from the output and income sides of the national income accounts. From the output side:

$$Y = C_m + I_m + O_{nm} + (X - M)_m \qquad (1.50)$$

where C_m is the value-added of marketable consumption goods; I_m is the value-added of marketable investment goods; O_{nm} is the value-added of non-marketable output; and $(X - M)_m$ is the balance of payments. If O_{nm} rises and C_m does not fall, then either I_m or $(X - M)_m$ is squeezed.

From the income side of the national accounts:

$$Y = (W_m + P_m) + (W_{nm} + P_{nm}) + (X - M)_m \qquad (1.51)$$

where $(W_m + P_m)$ is wages and profits in the non-traded goods marketable output sector; $(W_{nm} + P_{nm})$ is wages and profits in the non-traded goods non-marketable output sector; and $(X - M)_m$ is the balance of payments. If the wage bill in the non-marketable output sector rises (through the growth of employment or wage rate increases in the non-marketable output sector) then profits in industry or the balance of payments will suffer unless the wages bill in the marketable output sector falls. If profits fall, investment in industry will fall. In fact, Bacon and Eltis claim that employment outside the marketable output sector rose by roughly one-third relative to employment in the marketable output sector from 1961 to 1974, apparently far in excess of other countries. The biggest increase in employment was in education (76.4 per cent). By category, local government employment (producing largely non-marketable output) increased by 54 per cent; central government employment by 9.4 per cent; and other employment by 13.2 per cent. Local and central government employees also received wage increases in excess of the average for all workers. Bacon and Eltis claim that what bore the brunt of the massive increase in the wage bill in the non-marketable output sector was net of tax profits, to the detriment of investment in the marketable output sector. Thus, the UK's macroeconomic performance would not have deteriorated so markedly had the industrial base been strengthened by more investment in the marketable output sector, which alone can feed the balance of payments and meet the consumption demands in both the marketable and non-marketable output sectors.

The argument, while ostensibly convincing, is open to criticism, on at least three counts. First, it deduces causation from a set of (national income) identities. This is always dangerous. Secondly, it is very difficult to derive their prediction of a fall in the profits' share from any plausible *a priori* model.[25] Thirdly, the story is not consistent with the empirical evidence. We will concentrate here on the first and third points.

CAUSE AND EFFECT

According to Bacon and Eltis, deterioration in the British economy began in 1965. It is admitted, however, that industrial productivity actually grew faster on average between 1965 and 1973 than between 1959 and 1965. The problem was that output growth did not match productivity growth, causing a fall in industrial employment and increased unemployment. But why? According to Bacon and Eltis, what should have happened is that employment released by productivity growth in industry should have been reabsorbed into industry. Instead, it went into the non-marketable output sector. Why it did so is not made clear. Was it an 'autonomous' expansion of the non-marketable output sector that was the cause of the industrial malaise (and a weakening of the balance of payments), or was the expansion of the non-marketable output sector itself a symptom of a much more basic malaise and structural phenomenon associated with the inability of the marketable output (and industrial) sector to grow as fast as productivity growth without the economy coming up against a balance-of-payments constraint owing to the UK's high income elasticity of demand for imports and the low income elasticity of demand for its exports? Over the period 1965 to 1974 industrial productivity grew at roughly 4 per cent per annum, while output increased by only 1.7 per cent per annum. The question arises, could the industrial sector have grown at 4 per cent in line with productivity and thereby retain its resources? If not, should not the growth of the non-marketable output sector be seen as a consequence of this failure rather than as a cause, and, instead, as a blessing in disguise, maintaining the level of resource use above what it would otherwise have been? If industry had grown at 4 per cent, the consequences for the UK balance of payments would have been very severe. The income elasticity of demand for imports is close to 2, while the income elasticity of demand for UK exports is no greater than unity (see Chapter 3). Assuming an equiproportional relation between industrial growth and GDP growth, this would have generated a growth of imports close to 8 per cent while exports grew at no more than 4 per cent (assuming 4 per cent GDP growth in the rest of the world). This would have had to be curtailed, and was indeed curtailed after the Maudling boom of 1963/4. Any fall in investment during this period, or fall of employment in the marketable output sector and rise in employment in the non-marketable output sector, is more likely to have been the *consequence* of slow growth caused by a balance of payments constraint than the cause of slow growth and immediate balance of payments difficulties.

Mr Maudling, the Chancellor of the Exchequer, made a dash for industrial growth in 1963 with disastrous consequences. Public investment and consumption were expanded far too rapidly and the current account of the balance of payments deteriorated from a surplus of £114 million in 1963 to a deficit of £381 million in 1964. In those halcyon days, a deficit of a few hundred million was regarded as a 'problem' and sufficient to cause a run on sterling. Bacon and Eltis castigate Mr Maudling for missing the golden opportunity to increase industrial investment in 1962 when there was slack in the economy. But who would have wanted to invest with spare capacity already existing?

The abrupt worsening of the 'full' employment balance of payments in 1964 and the ultimate necessity to devalue in 1967 were decisive turning points in the UK's postwar economic history. It is no accident that from 1967 inflation accelerated, and that the traditional inverse relationship between unemployment and inflation broke down. Rising import prices sparked off wage rate increases, and unemployment rose as a result of expenditure-reducing policies to improve the balance of payments. The balance of payments did improve but the price in terms of wasted resources, low investment and slow growth was heavy. There was certainly no scope at all for the industrial sector to grow at the underlying trend rate of growth of productivity of 4 per cent. If it had not been for the growth of the non-marketable output sector, unemployment would undoubtedly have been higher.

Almost exactly the same experiment was tried by the Chancellor, Mr Barber, in 1971, with equally disastrous results. Having inherited a healthy balance-of-payments surplus on the Conservative return to office in 1970, this was frittered away on a consumption-led boom *par excellence*. As Bacon and Eltis frankly admit, Mr Barber's period of office as Chancellor was ultimately a failure. Investment in industry, and exports as a proportion of industrial output, both fell at the expense of consumption and investment outside industry, and employment increased rapidly in the non-market sector. By 1972 the turn-around in the balance of payments had become so huge – over £1 billion – that foreign holders of sterling panicked, and the decision was taken in June, 1972 to float the pound. The pound immediately depreciated and fell almost continuously to 1976 against a weighted average of other currencies without noticeably – if at all – improving the underlying balance of payments. Indeed the balance of payments worsened by a further £1 billion between June 1972 and the rise in oil prices in the fourth quarter of 1973. The rate of inflation nearly doubled as a direct result of the depreciation of sterling and then more than doubled again under the impact of a four-fold increase in the price of oil.

None of these features of the steadily deteriorating macroeconomic position of the UK economy were the direct result of the growth of the non-marketable output sector. It may have been so in the trivial accounting sense that if the claims of the non-marketable output sector on the marketable output sector increase, then something within the marketable output sector must by definition decrease (for example investment in industry or the balance of payments). But it does not follow that the former is the cause of the latter. The United Kingdom's poor record since 1964, and the growth of the non-marketable output sector, must be regarded as the joint products of the UK's inability to grow as fast as the industrial sector would allow without running into a balance-of-payments constraint. The only outlet for surplus labour that could not be used in industry because of this fundamental constraint was the non-marketable output sector.

Had the Maudling experiment worked because there was no balance-of-payments constraint there is no reason why industry should not have retained its resources, with investment and the balance of payments both flourishing. Likewise there would have been no particular reason for floating the pound in 1972, or at least for the pound to depreciate, if it was possible to grow at 4 per cent without running into balance-of-payments trouble. But the simple fact is that a country cannot grow as fast as productivity growth in industry, or as fast as the outside world, if the income elasticity characteristics of its imports and exports lead to a faster rate of growth of imports than exports. Had successive Conservative Chancellors heeded this fact, the UK's macroeconomic record since 1964 would not look nearly so bad. There would still have been some growth of the non-marketable output sector relative to the marketable output sector but aggregate demand would not have had to be depressed so much and for so long. Likewise, inflation would not have been so rampant since excessive currency depreciation would have been avoided; growth would have been faster, investment higher, inflation lower and the underlying balance of payments stronger.

EMPIRICAL EVIDENCE

The above is argument. Far more damaging to the Bacon and Eltis thesis is that the empirical evidence does not support the interpreta-

Table 1.15   Non-market sector growth: market sector consumption and fixed investment (excluding dwellings) plus net exports (all as percentages of net marketed output)

	1961	1965	1969	1973	1974
Non-market purchases	33.7	34.5	36.8	39.8	43.8
Market-financed consumption	56.1	54.1	51.5	51.8	51.9
Fixed market sector investment plus exports less imports	6.3	6.1	6.8	2.7	–1.0
Other categories	3.9	5.3	4.9	5.6	5.3

Source: Bacon and Eltis, 1979, p. 407, table 4.

tion they impose on it. There are a number of statistical problems involved in measuring precisely the value of the market sector and Bacon and Eltis (1979) provide a revised set of estimates to which we shall refer.

The main empirical evidence they cite in support of their argument is contained in Table 1.15.

From the table it may be seen that up until 1969 the increasing claims of the non-market sector on marketed output were met by a squeeze on personal consumption and *not* investment plus net exports. Bacon and Eltis (1979) admit in reply to Hadjimatheou and Skouras that the authors 'are right to point out that workers financed some of the growth of the non-market sector and they more than financed it all up to 1969' (p. 408). This represents a considerable weakening of their original argument which variously placed the date that investment and net exports began to be crowded out as 1961 or 1965. Since 1973 was the final boom year before the severe recession that was ushered in by the oil crisis, 1974 should be excluded from the analysis. Thus, the theory is only relevant for the five-year period, 1969–73. But its applicability is even narrower than this. 'It is central to our argument as presented in Bacon and Eltis that it is in the boom when the economy is working most nearly to full capacity that full effects of the non-market sector are felt' (Bacon and Eltis, 1979, p. 405). The theory is thus reduced to explaining the 'failure' of the boom of 1972–3 – a period when GDP in purchasers' values grew by

Table 1.16 Percentage shares of net industrial investment, other market sector net investment, non-market sector net investment and the balance of payments in net total final sales of the market sector

Year	Industrial share (1)	Other market share (2)	Total market share (1 + 2)	Non-market share (3)	Total share (1 + 2 + 3)	B of P share
1975	3.3	3.5	6.5	2.9	9.4	−4.1
1974	3.0	4.8	7.8	3.2	11.0	−8.8
1973	2.0	5.2	7.2	3.7	10.9	−4.5
1972	1.7	4.3	6.0	3.5	9.5	−1.4
1971	2.7	4.0	6.7	3.3	10.0	0.8
1970	3.7	3.6	7.3	3.3	10.6	−0.1
1969	3.7	3.6	7.3	3.0	10.3	−0.5
1968	3.9	3.7	7.6	3.1	10.7	−1.9
1967	4.7	3.0	7.7	2.8	10.5	−2.0
1966	5.0	2.7	7.7	2.4	10.1	−0.8
1965	4.7	3.1	7.8	2.3	10.1	−1.7
1964	4.4	3.3	7.7	2.5	10.2	−3.3
1963	3.7	2.7	6.4	2.1	8.5	−1.3
1962	4.1	2.7	6.8	2.1	8.9	−1.2
1961	4.6	3.1	7.7	1.8	9.5	−1.4
1960	4.0	3.4	7.4	1.5	8.9	−2.8
1959	na	na	6.9	1.4	8.3	−0.9
1958	na	na	6.7	1.3	8.0	0.1
1957	na	na	6.8	1.3	8.1	−0.3
1956	na	na	6.1	1.2	7.3	−0.4
1955	na	na	5.6	1.1	6.7	−2.9

Source: Bacon and Eltis (1979, appendix A, pp. 412–14).

over 7 per cent, so it is hardly surprising that a capacity constraint was encountered!

As we have noted, the impression given by the Bacon and Eltis thesis is that the increase in the non-market sector has been directly responsible for reducing the market sector's investment ratio. But this is simply not borne out by the evidence, even over the period 1969–73, as may be seen from Table 1.16.

The first two columns, (1) and (2), report the industrial and other trading companies' share of investment. The sum of these is the share of the market sector's investment and corresponds to the 'fixed market sector investment' component in the category 'fixed market sector investment plus exports less imports' in Table 1.15. It is this investment on which Bacon and Eltis place so much emphasis. But there is no discernible secular decline in this share as may be readily seen from Table 1.16. The share in 1973 of 7.2 per cent is not far short of the average for the whole of the period 1955–73 which is 7.4 per cent. The dramatic fall in 1973 in 'fixed market sector investment plus exports less imports' which is reported in Table 1.15 is entirely due to the rapid deterioration in the balance of payments. While this balance-of-payments deficit may well have posed problems for the future even in the absence of the world recession, the simple fact is that the growth of the non-market sector was *not* associated with any decline in the investment share of the market sector. Bacon and Eltis (1979) are careful in their paper to couch their argument in terms of investment *plus* net exports, but nevertheless they give the impression that it was investment that bore the brunt of the squeeze (and this is certainly true of their 1978 book). Certainly, investment plus net exports did fall substantially over the cycle 1965–73 by 3.4 per cent of marketed output. But, as we have noted, this decline is more than explained by a deterioration in the balance of payments to − 4.5 per cent of marketed output. Yet Bacon and Eltis (1979, p. 407) argue that 'Hadjimatheou and Skouras are inclined to consider shifts of the order of magnitude of 3 per cent of marketed output as unimportant . . . Small swings in consumption therefore become very large swings if they are taken from investment.' This is very true, but unfortunately for their thesis such swings as occurred were *not* taken from investment.

We have already commented on the neglect by Bacon and Eltis of the share of investment by the non-trading, or non-market sector, which is merely included in total non-market purchases. The non-market sector investment share is reported in Table 1.16 as column (3), and when we consider the total share of investment (columns 1 + 2 + 3) there is, in fact, a pronounced steady increase from 6.7 per cent in 1955 to 10.9 per cent in 1973. There is little evidence here of increased 'crowding out'.

The fact that there has been no marked deceleration in the rate of capital accumulation is also confirmed by Table 1.17 which reports the growth of the United Kingdom's net capital stock over three of the postwar growth cycles.

As may be seen, the growth of the net capital stock, excluding

Table 1.17   Growth of the UK's net capital stock, per cent per annum, 1955–73

Sector	% Share 1955	% Growth rates per annum		
		1955–65	1965–69	1969–73
Agriculture	3.0	4.05	3.58	3.61
Industry	48.1	4.56	4.36	2.33
(Manufacturing)	(32.9)	(4.11)	(3.70)	(2.87)
Services excluding dwellings	31.5	4.40	4.63	5.21
Government	17.5	4.58	7.21	6.86
Total excluding dwellings	100.0	4.81	4.97	4.19

Source: *Flows and Stocks of Fixed Capital, 1955–1980*, OECD, Paris, 1983.

dwellings, is slightly lower in 1969–73 than in the other two periods but the decline is hardly enough to warrant the emphasis Bacon and Eltis place on it.

One possible explanation for Bacon and Eltis's mistaken belief in the collapse of the share of the market sector's investment is that they formulated their thesis initially with regard to industry. For example, Chapter 1 of their book *Britain's Economic Problem* (1976) begins by outlining the problems posed by the declining industrial base, and the discussion and charts are all of 'where *industrial* production went' (our emphasis). Certainly, if we confine our attention to industry there is no doubt that both the growth of the net capital stock and the investment ratio did indeed fall dramatically. As may be seen from Table 1.18 the growth of manufacturing also declined *pari passu* by about a third during 1969–73 compared with the earlier periods. There was no noticeable change in the growth of total output.

Moreover, Bacon and Eltis's discussion of the fall in post-tax profits also stresses the manufacturing sector. 'The mechanism that the workers used to more than pass on the extra taxes that fell on them after 1969 was to squeeze the share of profits successfully. In Bacon and Eltis we documented a fall in the share of profits of manufacturing companies, in value-added (net of capital consumption, stock appreciation and taxation) from 12.5 per cent in 1969 to

Table 1.18   Growth of the UK's GDP and manufacturing output, per cent, per annum, 1955–65, 1965–9 and 1969–73

Period	Growth of GDP	Growth of manufacturing
1969–73	2.82	2.09
1965–69	2.52	3.23
1955–65	2.83	3.10

Source: *OECD National Accounts*, various years.

7.2 per cent in 1973' (Bacon and Eltis, 1979, p. 408). The rider is added that 'We . . . found virtually no fall in this period outside industry' but the implications of this are not pursued for Britain's overall growth rate. If we consider the category 'all companies' the figures, using Bacon and Eltis's own data, are 13.2 per cent in 1969 and 12.0 per cent in 1973 – again hardly a significant fall.

A possible alternative version of the thesis is that while there has been no noticeable decline in the British investment ratio up until 1974, the lower investment ratio compared with the faster growing advanced countries could explain the UK's poorer performance over the whole of the sustained boom. Bacon and Eltis (1978, p. 106) quote with approval the findings of Smith (1975) that:

> Until further, and better, estimates can be provided by others the authors would like to suggest that, as a simple rule of thumb to concentrate the mind, it be assumed that each 5 per cent increase in the share of national disposable income absorbed by direct state consumption (on the narrow definition excluding transfer payments) implies a 1.0 per cent drop in the growth rate.

Smith's conclusion is based on the results of a number of cross-country regressions where the growth rate was regressed, *inter alia*, on the investment ratio or the share of public expenditure.

There are a number of conceptual problems in such an approach. We have already mentioned the difficulty of inferring the direction of causality from an identity and this applies equally to a regression analysis. Furthermore, ideally, all the other factors that could cause disparities in the growth rates should also be included in the regression. There are, though, difficulties in satisfactorily quantifying many of the other possible causes. Thus the regressions are likely to suffer from serious mis-specification errors. Furthermore, Smith's results are not confirmed by other studies.

A more recent study is that of Saunders (1985) for the period of 1960 to 1981. Saunders divided the period into the two sub-periods 1960–73 and 1975–81. (The period 1973–5 was excluded on the grounds that it was an abnormal period with the deep world recession.) For the two periods the rate of economic growth of 20 OECD countries was regressed on the share of investment, and on the share of government expenditure, in GDP.

The results for the period 1960–73 would seem to provide some, albeit weak, support for the Bacon and Eltis thesis. The growth of output was positively related to the investment share and negatively related to the government expenditure share. The reliability, however, of these results must be seriously questioned. An examination of the scattergram of the relationship between economic growth and government expenditure (Saunders, 1985, figure 1, p. 12) suggests that the inverse relationship is due entirely to the inclusion in the sample of the relatively underdeveloped countries of Portugal, Turkey and Spain, together with Japan. If these countries were excluded, limiting the sample to the advanced countries, it is highly probable that the already weak relationship would become statistically insignificant.

Saunders finds no evidence of a statistically significant relationship for the post-1975 period. On the basis of these and other results, he concludes: 'Overall, the results provide little evidence that government size and growth have been detrimental to economic growth particularly during the period since 1975, although an inverse relation existed in the sixties between government size and economic growth' (1985, p. 1).

Further evidence is provided by Ram (1986). Adapting a model of Feder (1983), Ram divides the economy into two sectors. The output of the government sector is specified as a function of the inputs of capital and labour, through the production function. This output is also specified as an argument in the production function of the rest of the economy, to capture a possible externality effect. The other arguments are the traditional factor inputs. It is also postulated that the marginal products of capital and labour may differ (by the same amount) between the sectors. A reduced form equation for the production function of the whole economy is derived and is expressed in growth rate form. The growth of the government sector, weighted by its size in total output, appears as a regressor and enables the effect of the government sector to be directly estimated. The equation is estimated using a cross-country sample of 115 advanced and less developed countries and the analysis is also supplemented by time-series estimations for a number of individual countries. Ram (1986, p. 202) concludes that 'the main result is that it is difficult not to conclude that government size has a *positive* effect on economic performance, and the conclusion appears to apply in a vast majority of the settings considered. Even more interesting seems to be the nearly equally pervasive indication of a positive externality effect of government size on the rest of the economy' (our emphasis). The results were challenged, *inter alios*, by Rao (1989) who found that there were significant differences between the less developed countries and the advanced countries. For the latter, the government sector exerted no statistically significant effect on the growth rate; but this still provides scant comfort for the Bacon and Eltis thesis.

A CONCLUDING ASSESSMENT OF THE BACON AND ELTIS THESIS

It must be concluded that there is no empirical support for what may be termed the 'strong' Bacon and Eltis thesis, i.e. that the growth of the non-market sector led to a squeeze on post-tax corporate profits which in turn led to a collapse in the total investment ratio. Not only was the fall in post-tax profits small but there was no secular decline in the investment ratio.

Bacon and Eltis do (belatedly) admit to the possibility that the major constraint on Britain's economic growth was provided by the balance of payments. They argue that:

> Even if planned investment had been just as high as at equivalent points of previous cycles, and these plans had successfully been pushed through, the necessity for the share of investment and the balance of payments in the marketed sector to be lower would have meant that the current account of the balance of payments would then have to take the *full* strain of the higher share of consumption and investment in the non-market sector. As the country could not possibly have run a long-term current account deficit of that magnitude, the authorities would have had to react to a large negative balance of payments at high capacity working by deflating the economy. This would in turn have forced investment in the mar-

keted sector down to a level insufficient to maintain the country's long-term growth potential. (Bacon and Eltis, 1979, p. 411).

One possible elaboration of this argument along the supply-side lines of Bacon and Eltis is that the profits squeeze occurred in the tradeable sector (and we have already seen that there was a significant fall in post-tax profits of the manufacturing sector). This resulted, as in the strong thesis, in a collapse in the investment ratio but this time confined to the tradeable sector. Hence, as demand expanded full capacity was quickly reached and firms were not able to export sufficient goods and services to pay for the rapid induced growth of imports. This led to successive governments having to deflate the economy as a boom developed in order to prevent the balance-of-payments deficit becoming out of manageable proportions. This engendered the 'stop' phase of the familiar 'stop-go' cycle that has been the characteristic of Britain's post-war growth. One effect was a lower rate of investment in the remainder of the economy. The central tenet of this argument is that companies that produced for the overseas markets or competed with imports at home faced a capital constraint and that if they had been able to invest more, Britain's overall rate of growth could have been higher.

If this were the case, there should be a mass of evidence that firms in the tradeable sector were constrained from exporting by insufficient capacity – the orders were there, but British companies could not fulfil them even by increasing capacity utilisation.

The problem for this version of the authors' argument is that the evidence suggests the opposite. It was lack of demand that determined the low investment ratio (especially when compared with Continental Europe and Japan) and not that a low investment ratio limited the supply of exportables. The econometric evidence suggests overwhelmingly that it is the expected demand for output through the flexible accelerator principle that is the main determinant of investment. As Stout (1979, p. 115) states: 'Very few of the variables that we should expect to influence non-accelerator investment – such as relative wage changes, labour constraint, or changes in tax rates – play a significant role in any gross investment functions.' At best these factors can explain fluctuations around the average investment ratio but shed no light on why there are such large international differences in the average proportion of output invested.

Stout (1979, p. 101) likens the British economy to an 'aspiring but seriously out-of-condition fell runner'. He may never rise to the first rank but only after he gets fit is there any point in urging him to eat more. 'He sets out, after all, with little appetite and even less capacity to burn energy. Under-utilization is already a problem for him. He will not so much run faster as to run to fat.'

Commenting on British industry's decline, Stout (1979, p. 105), drawing on the extensive work undertaken by NEDO, comments:

> In some cases British producers have fallen irretrievably behind; in some, they have deliberately continued to produce too many elderly products; in some, they have been discouraged by institutional pressures or by lack of size, from introducing new techniques; in others, out of lack of confidence or lack of access to risk capital for long-term intangible investment, they have refrained from determined and persistent advance marketing in major customer countries. One thing that does *not* emerge from all this is a clear cut proposition about the role of capital adjustment. What the aspiring fell-runner needs to begin with is appropriate training, not more food. (Emphasis in the original)

British industry has not been limited in its rate of capital accumulation below that which entrepreneurs' expectations of future sales would have warranted. The problem is that British industry has progressively found that it cannot compete with foreigners in terms of quality, reliability, after-sales service and marketing efficiency. There is indeed a relationship between productivity, price and non-price competitiveness and investment. But, as Stout argues, investment is not necessarily the main place to break into the vicious circle, which may be difficult even with the most generous of investment grants. Britain did, indeed, already have investment incentives for most of the postwar period. What is needed is to increase productivity growth in the form of an increase in the quality of the inputs, rather than merely relying on an attempt to increase the volume of investment.

As we shall set out in much greater detail in later chapters, the balance of payments has been the major factor limiting the growth of the United Kingdom but not because British exporters have not had the capacity to meet overseas demand. It has been the inability of British producers to match overseas competitors primarily in terms of non-price competition that is the root of Britain's economic problem. To conclude this chapter, we take a brief look at the balance-of-payments positions of the advanced countries since the Second World War.

INTER-COUNTRY GROWTH AND BALANCE-OF-PAYMENTS EXPERIENCE

The average growth and balance-of-payments performance of a selection of 21 countries for the 1970s and 1980s are outlined in Table 1.19. Four categories of countries are distinguished: (a) countries that grew fast with a balance-of-payments surplus; (b) countries that grew fast with a balance-of-payments deficit; (c) countries that grew slowly with a balance-of-payments surplus; and (d) countries that grew slowly with a balance-of-payments deficit. The (arbitrary) dividing line between fast and slow growth is put at 3 per cent per annum.

Taking first the period of the 1970s, the countries in category (a) were growing fast, but not the fastest. The average growth of the six countries in the group was 3.9 per cent. Since they had a balance of payments surplus, they could have grown faster without running into foreign exchange difficulties. Germany ran an average annual surplus on current account of over $3 billion. France and Italy also accumulated substantial surpluses over the period.

The average growth of the ten countries in category (b) was 4.9 per cent per annum. All these countries, however, ran balance-of-payments deficits, some very substantial, so that a proportion of this rapid growth was financed by capital inflows. These countries were up against the constraint of the balance of payments.

Greece, Turkey, Spain and Yugoslavia all ran annual deficits of close to $1 billion, while Canada's annual deficit was over $2 billion.

In category (c) only one country grew relatively slowly with a balance-of-payments surplus and that was Switzerland, which was the only country with a lower recorded growth rate during the 1970s than the UK.

Category (d) contains the 'problem' countries with slow growth and balance-of-payments deficits. Along with the UK there was the US, Denmark and Sweden with an average growth of 2.5 per cent per annum. These countries were balance-of-payments constrained at a low level.

Taking the period of the 1980s, the first significant point to note is that only Japan managed to grow at 3 per cent or more and maintain a balance-of-payments surplus. All the other fast growing countries ran deficits. Only four countries apart from Japan, however, managed to grow in excess of 3 per cent per annum, and those four also grew fast in the 1970s – Turkey, Finland, Canada, Norway. All other fast growers slipped, and most ran into deficit at the same time.

Table 1.19   Balance-of-payments surpluses and deficits and the annual growth of GDP of OECD countries in the 1970s and 1980s

Country groups	Growth rates of GDP (% p.a.): 1970s		Growth rates of GDP (% p.a.): 1980s	
(a) Fast growth with balance-of-payments surplus	Japan	5.9	Japan	4.0
	France	4.1		
	Belgium	3.6		
	Netherlands	3.4		
	Italy	3.3		
	Germany	3.1		
(b) Fast growth with balance-of-payments deficit	Turkey	6.3	Turkey	5.2
	Yugoslavia	6.1	Finland	3.5
	Greece	5.4	Canada	3.1
	Portugal	5.4	Norway	3.1
	Canada	4.7		
	Ireland	4.6		
	Norway	4.5		
	Austria	4.1		
	Spain	4.0		
	Finland	3.8		
(c) Slow growth with balance-of-payments surplus	Switzerland	1.5	Switzerland	2.2
			United Kingdom	2.2
			Germany	1.7
			Netherlands	1.4
			Yugoslavia	0.7
(d) Slow growth with balance-of-payments deficits	United States	2.8	United States	2.7
	Denmark	2.5	Portugal	2.6
	Sweden	2.5	Italy	2.5
	United Kingdom	2.4	Spain	2.4
			Ireland	2.1
			France	1.9
			Sweden	1.9
			Austria	1.9
			Belgium	1.7
			Denmark	1.7
			Greece	1.4

Source: *OECD Economic Review* (various years).

Switzerland continued to grow slowly and accumulate surpluses and so did Germany, the Netherlands and the UK. All these countries, particularly Germany, could have grown faster while maintaining on average balance-of-payments equilibrium. The UK's average surplus in the 1980s, however, was the product of large surpluses in the early

1980s when the economy was in deep recession and when North Sea Oil revenue was at its maximum. In 1986 the surplus turned to deficit and in 1989 the deficit was £19 billion, with growth slowing. In the fourth category of countries, the US, Denmark and Sweden continued to grow relatively slowly and run deficits. A number of other countries were also forced into this position as a result of the slow-down of the world economy in the 1980s and the continual expansion of the Japanese surplus.

What is apparent from the analysis is that the factor that distinguishes the slow growing countries from the fast growing countries is the performance of exports. In the 1970s for the fast growing countries, the unweighted average growth per annum of exports is 7.4 per cent compared with 5.3 per cent for the slow growing countries. In the 1980s, the comparison is 8.4 per cent and 4.2 per cent. Indeed, in Chapter 3, it will be formally shown that for most countries, the growth rate of output can be approximated by the rate of growth of exports relative to the income elasticity of demand for imports, which is the dynamic Harrod trade multiplier result.

NEOCLASSICAL BALANCE-OF-PAYMENTS ADJUSTMENT THEORY

As we mentioned above, before the Keynesian revolution, the assumption of the full employment of resources was basically taken for granted. It was price adjustment not quantity adjustment that restored equilibrium following any disturbance in the economy. The assumption of full employment output (or a tendency towards long-run full-employment equilibrium) is central to many of the tenets of classical and neoclassical economics. It underlies the concept of general equilibrium; it is crucial to the predictions of the quantity theory of money, and the Ricardian proof of the mutual profitability of trade is based on it. When it comes to the balance of payments, whether under the gold standard with fixed exchange rates, or under freely flexible exchange rates, it is prices that are assumed to adjust to rectify balance-of-payments disequilibrium, not output. The balance of payments does not affect the level of resource utilisation because it is never a 'problem'; full employment is assumed.

Under the old pre-First World War gold standard there are many variations on the theme about how balance-of-payments equilibrium was achieved (if, indeed, it was). The classical theory, and the standard textbook story, derives from the price–specie flow mechanism outlined by David Hume (1752). In this account, gold movements themselves were the instrument by which payments-balance was effected. Countries with a payments deficit would lose gold causing an internal price deflation which would induce a rise in exports and a fall in imports, and vice versa for surplus countries. This is also sometimes referred to as the Ricardo–Mill adjustment mechanism, retaining the classical presumption of continuous full-employment.

More refined versions of this story were developed in the late nineteenth century, when the operation of the gold standard was at its height, in recognition of the fact that no gold standard country operated a rigid 100 per cent reserve monetary system backed by gold. Fiduciary issues of currency were permitted. In other words, most monetary systems were mixed, with a narrow gold base and a large superstructure of credit money. Changes in the base, however, were assumed to cause changes in the amount of credit money, assuming no sterilisation. On this assumption, the story of how the gold standard was supposed to achieve payments-equilibrium is essentially the same as the classical theory, namely that countries in payments deficit would experience monetary contraction driving down the price level (in accordance with the quantity theory of money) making a country's goods more competitive, and vice versa for countries in payments surplus. The model was then extended to capital flows, where gold moves in the same direction as the capital transfer, and the trade surplus generated in the country 'exporting' capital is the real counterpart of the capital transfer. Again, there is no adjustment of output.

It has been noted, however, by many economists and monetary historians (e.g. Triffin, 1964; Cooper, 1982; McClosky and Zecher, 1976) that instead of the price levels of countries moving in opposite directions, as assumed by the classical adjustment mechanism, there was a tendency in the nineteenth century for countries' price levels to move together, as did the prices of individual traded commodities. International commodity arbitrage seems to have exerted a powerful force. In practice, it appears that it was not relative price changes that operated to achieve payments-balance, but expenditure (and, therefore, output) changes associated with interest rate differentials. Capital importing countries with higher interest rates would have expenditure damped relative to capital exporting countries with lower interest rates. Income adjustment is therefore implied. Few people were teaching this story, however, even as late as the 1930s. One exception was P. Barrett Whale at the London School of Economics (see Barrett Whale, 1937).

The story of how flexible exchange rates is supposed to rectify payments-imbalances without income adjustment is equally suspect and implausible as the old gold standard mechanism. A country in deficit on the current account of the balance of payments is supposed to experience a depreciation of its currency in real terms, through a fall in the nominal exchange rate, while a country in surplus is supposed to experience appreciation. The depreciation is supposed to reduce the price of tradeable goods in foreign currency and raise the relative price of tradeable *vis-à-vis* non-tradeables in domestic currency – and currency appreciation is supposed to do the opposite. This adjustment of relative prices, in turn, is supposed to so change the relative demand for exports and imports that the balance of payments improves in the depreciating countries and worsens in the appreciating countries. There are, however, many problems with such a story. First, the currency of the country in payments-deficit may not depreciate because high expected real interest rates attract enough foreign capital to finance the deficit. Domestic production many contract, while consumption is allowed to exceed production by buying from abroad. This is one explanation of why in the 1980s, the US dollar frequently continued to rise despite a huge payments deficit, and why in the UK in 1988–9, the pound sterling remained high despite a colossal current account deficit of over £19 billion. Secondly, even if the exchange rate does fall in the deficit country, the price elasticities of demand for exports and imports may not be right for the total change in foreign currency receipts to be positive. Taken together, the demand for exports may not rise and/or the demand for imports may not fall in sufficient proportion to offset the fall in the price of exports in foreign currency and the rise in the price of imports in domestic currency. This may be particularly true in the short-run leading to the so-called J-curve effect whereby net foreign currency earnings fall with depreciation before they start to rise (if ever). Thirdly, even if the elasticities are 'right' (i.e. sum to greater than unity), the effect of depreciation on the domestic price level may be such as to leave relative prices measured in a common currency unchanged. There are a number of mechanisms through which this might happen. If import demand is price inelastic, import price increases will raise the import bill in domestic currency. This will cause producers to seek more credit which will allow other prices to rise. Rising import prices may also lead to higher wages which will also tend to increase the demand for credit. Greater export demand will also require financing. If real exchange rates do not change in the face of balance-of-payments disequilibrium, the burden of adjustment must fall on output and incomes.

RECENT EXCHANGE RATE AND
BALANCE-OF-PAYMENTS EXPERIENCE

Since the onset of floating exchange rates in 1972, it is clear from the historical evidence that the massive nominal exchange rate realignments that have taken place have not rectified payments-disequilibrium. Indeed, in some cases the balance-of-payments response has been perverse; and in the case of the American dollar in recent years, the movement in the exchange rate itself has also been perverse. For the early years from 1972 to 1977, both Triffin (1978) and Kaldor (1978c) have shown how the surpluses and deficits remained largely impervious to both nominal and real exchange rate movements. According to Triffin: 'the most striking feature of the last six to eight years of floating rates is that they scarcely changed the broad pattern of previous disequilibrium among the major trading countries. The countries that experienced the largest surpluses before the increase of oil prices have about doubled them, in spite of the strong appreciation of their currencies, and the countries then in deficit saw their deficits more than triple in the following years, in spite of the sharp depreciation of their currencies.' The evidence is outlined in Table 1.20.

The five surplus countries of Japan, Switzerland, Germany, the Netherlands and Belgium-Luxembourg increased their joint surplus by $8 billion from 1972 to 1977 while their exchange rates appreciated on average against the dollar and other currencies by approximately 50 per cent. In the five deficit countries of the United States, Canada, United Kingdom, Italy and France, their joint deficits increased by $16.7 billion, while their exchange rates depreciated on average by approximately 25 per cent. Kaldor makes the same point in his work: 'The general picture that emerges from a study of the trade record of the last five or six years is that the main industrialised countries remained remarkably impervious to very large changes in effective exchange rates. The surplus countries tended to remain in surplus and the deficit countries to remain in deficit in much the same way as in the 1960s . . . The important thing is that Britain and America, who seemed to be losing out to new industrial giants, Germany and Japan, continued to do so after the real exchange rates between them underwent drastic alterations.' From Triffin's table it can be seen that

Table 1.20   The unchanging pattern of major OECD countries' surpluses and deficits on current account, 1972–8 (in billions of US dollars)

| | Exchange rate changes[a] | | Surpluses and deficits | | | |
	Vis-à-vis the $	Effective rates	1972	1973	1974–6 (average)	1977
Surplus countries			10.2	8.0	9.8	18.2
Japan	+35	+28	6.6	−0.1	−0.6	11.0
Switzerland	+83	+62	0.2	0.3	2.1	3.7
Germany	+58	+43	0.8	4.3	5.8	3.8
Netherlands	+48	+22	1.3	2.4	2.2	0.2
Belgium-Luxembourg	+40	+12	1.4	1.2	0.3	−0.5
Deficit countries			−8.0	−5.9	−12.7	−24.7
United States	. . .	−13	−9.9	−0.4	2.6	−20.2
Canada	+1	−2	−0.7	0.0	−3.3	−3.9
United Kingdom	−27	−37	0.3	−2.2	−4.4	0.3
Italy	−29	−41	2.0	−2.7	−3.5	2.3
France	+13	−1	0.3	−0.7	−4.1	−3.2

Note: [a]Percentage appreciation (+) or depreciation (−) of dollar rates and of multilateral exchange rates from May 1970 to 1977.

Sources: Exchange rates: *International Financial Statistics*, lines *ah*, *x* and *am* of country tables. Surpluses or deficits on current account: OECD, *Economic Prospects*, July 1978 (Triffin, 1978).

the Japanese surplus nearly doubled from $6.6 billion to $11.0 billion with an effective appreciation of 28 per cent and the German surplus rose sevenfold with an effective appreciation of 43 per cent. The American deficit doubled with an effective depreciation of 13 per cent.

The experience since 1977 has been little different except for the 'perverse' appreciation of the dollar by 34 per cent from 1977 to 1985 despite a growing US current account deficit from $20 billion to over $100 billion. Both the Japanese yen and the German mark continued to appreciate, and their surpluses have grown. The 1986 Japanese surplus was over $80 billion while the German surplus stood at over $40 billion. The dollar fell by more than 30 per cent after the Plaza agreement of September 1985, but the US deficit continued to grow, reaching $130 billion in 1986. The experience between 1977 and 1989 is shown in Table 1.21

127

Table 1.21   The current balance of payments and changes in exchange rates in major industrial countries

(Current balance (US$ billion) and current balance as a percentage of GDP in parentheses)
Triffin's surplus countries

Year	Japan		Switzerland		Germany		Netherlands		Belgium-Lux.	
1977	10.9	(1.6)	1.9	(3.2)	4.0	(0.8)	1.2	(1.1)	-0.5	(-0.7)
1978	16.5	(1.7)	2.0	(2.4)	9.2	(1.4)	-1.2	(-0.9)	-0.8	(-0.8)
1979	-8.7	(-0.9)	1.3	(1.3)	-5.7	(-0.7)	0.2	(0.1)	-3.1	(-2.8)
1980	-10.8	(-1.0)	-1.6	(-1.5)	-13.9	(-1.7)	-1.0	(-0.6)	-4.9	(-4.1)
1981	4.8	(0.4)	1.5	(1.5)	-3.3	(-0.5)	3.7	(2.6)	-4.2	(-4.2)
1982	6.9	(0.6)	3.9	(4.1)	5.0	(0.8)	4.5	(3.2)	-2.6	(-3.0)
1983	20.8	(1.8)	1.2	(1.2)	5.4	(0.8)	5.0	(3.7)	-0.5	(-0.6)
1984	35.0	(2.8)	6.2	(6.8)	9.8	(1.6)	6.6	(5.3)	-0.1	(-0.1)
1985	49.2	(3.7)	6.0	(6.5)	17.0	(2.7)	4.0	(3.2)	0.7	(0.8)
1986	85.8	(4.4)	4.7	(3.4)	40.1	(4.5)	3.6	(2.1)	3.0	(2.7)
1987	87.0	(3.6)	6.3	(3.7)	46.1	(4.1)	3.7	(1.7)	2.8	(2.0)
1988	79.6	(2.8)	8.3	(4.5)	50.5	(4.2)	5.5	(2.4)	3.4	(2.2)
1989	56.8	(2.0)	na	(na)	55.5	(4.7)	7.0	(3.1)	na	(na)

Exchange rate changes, 1977–89

	Japan	Switzerland	Germany	Netherlands	Belgium-Lux.
Against US$	+96% (+85%)[a]	+47%	+24%	+16%	-9%
Effective exchange rate	+103% (+52%)[a]	+47%	+27%	+21%	-9%

(continued on page 128)

Table 1.21   cont.

Triffin's deficit countries

Year	United States	Canada	Italy	France	United Kingdom
1977	-14.5 (-0.7)	-4.1 (-2.0)	2.5 (1.0)	-0.4 (-0.1)	-0.2 (-1.0)
1978	-15.4 (-0.7)	-4.3 (-2.0)	6.3 (2.1)	7.0 (1.5)	1.9 (0.6)
1979	-1.0 (-)	-4.1 (-1.8)	5.5 (1.5)	5.1 (0.9)	-0.9 (-0.2)
1980	1.8 (0.1)	-1.0 (-0.4)	-10.0 (-2.2)	-4.2 (-0.6)	7.5 (1.4)
1981	6.2 (0.2)	-5.1 (-1.7)	-9.7 (-2.4)	-4.8 (-0.8)	14.5 (2.8)
1982	-7.0 (-0.2)	2.2 (0.7)	-6.4 (-1.6)	-12.1 (-2.2)	8.0 (1.7)
1983	-44.3 (-1.3)	2.5 (0.8)	1.4 (0.3)	-5.2 (-1.0)	5.8 (1.3)
1984	-104.2 (-2.8)	2.0 (0.6)	-2.5 (-0.6)	-0.9 (-0.2)	2.6 (0.6)
1985	-112.8 (-2.8)	-1.5 (-0.4)	-3.5 (-0.8)	-0.4 (-)	4.8 (1.0)
1986	-133.2 (-3.2)	-7.6 (-2.1)	2.9 (0.5)	2.4 (0.3)	0.2 (-)
1987	-143.7 (-3.2)	-7.1 (-1.7)	-1.7 (-0.2)	-4.4 (-0.5)	-7.4 (-1.1)
1988	-126.6 (-2.6)	-8.3 (-1.7)	-5.4 (-0.7)	-3.5 (-0.4)	-26.7 (-3.2)
1989	-105.9 (-2.0)	-16.6 (-3.0)	na (na)	-4.2 (-0.4)	-34.1 (-4.1)

Exchange rate changes, 1977–89

	United States	Canada	Italy	France	United Kingdom
Against US$	–	-10%	-36%	-23%	-6%
Effective exchange rate	-5% (+34%)[b] (-29%)[c]	-11%	-39%	-24%	-9%

Notes:
[a] 1984–1988 (4-year period)
[b] 1977–1985 (8-year period)
[c] 1985–1989 (4-year period)

Sources: *International Financial Statistics, Yearbook, 1989* (IMF), lines *ah x* and *am* of country tables, current account balance (pp. 142 and 154).

APPENDIX: MAURICE SCOTT'S
'NEW VIEW OF ECONOMIC GROWTH'[26]

A second fundamental criticism of orthodox growth theory, in addition to the Simon/Shaikh critique, may be found in the writings of Maurice Scott (1976, 1981, 1986, 1989, 1990, 1991a, 1991b, 1991c, 1992a and b). For some time now, Scott has argued that the orthodox approach to explaining the sources of economic growth is fundamentally flawed. The exogenous growth of technology is not the 'dominant engine of growth', as Solow (1988), for example, claims. The definitive statement of Scott's views is to be found in his book *A New View of Economic Growth*, published in 1989, where he does not pull his punches. On the first page of chapter 1, Scott argues that his thesis 'demolishes the foundation of orthodox growth theory'. Six hundred pages long, and a decade in the writing, Scott's book is truly a *tour de force* which seriously questions the conventional theory of economic growth. Scott contends that the treatment of technical progress in growth theory as an exogenous factor distinct from the rate of investment is meaningless. He argues that the residual found in the growth accounting approach must be attributable to measurement error, and, in particular, is the result of the way that the capital stock is conventionally measured. Once this error is corrected, Scott finds that the residual completely disappears. He also asserts, equally controversially, that capital cannot be used, as it traditionally has been in orthodox growth theory (including the 'new' growth theory). (Scott's critique, though, has nothing to do with the 'Cambridge controversies' which are dismissed in a couple of sentences.)

Scott's central thesis is that, as a matter of definition, all technical change should be attributed to investment, if the latter is broadly defined to include all expenditures incurred to increase future consumption at the cost of forgoing some present consumption. 'If output is to grow, the static economy must be changed. It seems to me inevitable that this will involve incurring expenditures which need not be incurred in a static economy, for the building of new buildings, roads, vehicles, machines etc., and the improvement of existing ones, for moving labour from places where its marginal product is low to where it is high, for improving labour quality through better health, education and skills, for developing new products, processes, markets and sources of supply, and so on' (Scott, 1981, pp. 212–13). All these costs, Scott asserts, are necessary for technical progress to occur. He argues that it is a self-evident proposition that if there were no investment, there would be little or no technical change. The vintage approach to economic growth provides no help either, since, while it is undoubtedly true that technical change is embodied to some degree in new capital goods, this approach still assumes that more recent vintages of capital goods are more efficient than earlier ones because of costless technical progress. The absurdity of the conventional approach, Scott (1989, pp. 95–6) maintains, may be easily seen by considering a hypothetical closed economy which has remained static over the last hundred years, and in which maintenance expenditures have kept assets intact but have not improved them. After a century capital accumulation restarts and what do we find? 'According to standard vintage theory, the machines available will be capable of producing jet aeroplanes, lasers, microcomputers, the whole array of modern drugs, and all the rest. Silently, without the need for any intervening investment, technical progress will have gone on, and the modern vintages actually available will miraculously be available in the hypothetical present too. This is all wildly implausible' (Scott, 1989, p. 86, omitting a footnote). Consequently, Scott, like Kaldor (1957), argues that it is pointless to try to distinguish either between investment and technical change or between shifts of the production function and shifts along the production function; such a distinction is meaningless.

Such sentiments would probably command a fair degree of agreement. (An exception would be Usher (1980a) who suggests that without technical progress there would be no growth, rather than Scott's converse contention.) After all, the whole purpose of the growth accounting approach is to try to explain the residual which, by default, is classified as technical change. (The residual is interpreted by some commentators as being ultimately due to measurement and specification errors, although this is not the view of Denison, who believes that conceptually there will be a part of growth that must be assigned to 'advances in knowledge, not elsewhere classified'.)

What is controversial, however, is Scott's contention that the fault lies in the failure to measure the capital stock correctly and 'if one corrects the error, one thereby destroys the empirical evidence for the belief that technical progress is a very important factor in economic growth independent of investment.' Denison (1991, p. 224), for example, in a review article about the *New View* argues that Scott's analysis 'does little to advance the understanding of *growth*' (emphasis in the original). This reaction is not perhaps surprising as Scott challenges the fundamentals of Denison's growth accounting methodology and, hence, the whole rationale of Denison's approach.

Orthodox Measures of Gross and Net Capital Stocks

To understand better the full implications of Scott's critique, it is useful first to consider how the real capital stock is conventionally measured in practice. The most widespread approach is what is termed the 'perpetual inventory model'. Under this procedure, the value of the real *gross capital stock* at time *t* is simply measured by summing the value of gross investment, expressed in constant prices, undertaken in each year prior to *t* and subtracting the value of scrapped capital goods. The cost of maintenance and depreciation is not deducted from gross investment, but each capital machine is assumed to have a fixed life of *n* years. The value of gross investment added into the capital stock estimate at time *t* is net of the value of gross investment undertaken *n* years ago, as the latter is assumed to have been retired or scrapped. (In practice, more complex assumptions are made about the length of the service lives of various machines and structures.) It is assumed that the efficiency of a particular machine remains constant over its life. If depreciation is deducted from gross investment and this is summed, we obtain a value for the *net capital stock*. (See Ward, 1976, for a detailed exposition of the perpetual inventory model.)

The great advantage of the perpetual inventory model is that given a long enough period of investment data it is possible to construct reasonably easily a measure of the capital stock. So long as the period extends further back than n years, the necessity is avoided of having to obtain a base year valuation of all the capital stock in existence at that time – always a difficult task. This is because all capital equipment and structures older than n years will have been scrapped or demolished. Hence, data on investment, *per se*, over the last n years will be sufficient to construct an index of the capital stock presently existing. As Usher (1980b, p.7) puts it: 'At no point in the perpetual inventory method is it necessary to compare quantities of capital goods directly – to make inventories of the capital goods available in the year 0 and capital goods in the year t, and to decide which inventory constitutes the larger capital stock.' This stands in marked contrast to constructing capital stock estimates by, for example, direct surveys of the capital goods in existence at any one time. Such surveys have been carried out in the Soviet Union but are very expensive and encounter the almost insurmountable problems of classifying the heterogenous machines and structures into standard categories that can then be used to construct an aggregate index.[27]

Whatever the pros and cons of the perpetual inventory method, it has become the standard procedure adopted by the various national statistical bodies including the CSO, the OECD and the US Bureau of Economic Analysis. Thus, if for no other reason than *faute de mieux*, the growth rates of the capital stock (either gross or net or a weighted average of the two, depending upon the preferences of the individual investigator) calculated this way are often used in the growth accounting approach.

Of importance is the question of how and to what extent quality changes should be incorporated in the constant price estimates of the capital stock. It is almost impossible to find any capital equipment being built today that is exactly the same in all respects as that existing in, say, the 1950s and producing comparable output. How are we to equate these vastly different capital goods, an undertaking which is necessary for the construction of an aggregate index of the capital stock? One approach which is approved by Denison is described by him as follows:

> The value, in base period prices, of the stock of durable capital goods (before allowance for capital consumption) measures the amount it would have cost in the base period to produce the actual stock of capital goods existing in a given year (*not* its equivalent in ability to contribute to production). Similarly, gross additions to the capital stock and capital consumption are valued in terms of base year costs for the *particular* types of capital goods added or consumed. This must be modified immediately, in the case of durable goods not actually produced in the base year, to substitute the amount it would have cost to produce them if they had been known and actually produced. But a similar modification is required in all deflation or index number problems. (Denison, 1957, cited by Denison, 1967, p. 134, emphasis in the original)

Thus, no account is deliberately taken of quality change since, according to Denison, one of the aims of the growth accounting approach is to obtain a separate measure of the contribution of quality changes to economic growth.

Investment measured by the above procedure is summed in the perpetual inventory model with a deduction for scrapping to give an estimate of the gross capital stock.

Very few capital goods, however, are retired or scrapped because they literally fall to bits. Normally before this happens, the capital goods have become economically unviable or obsolescent owing to competition from newer and technically better machines and the increased cost of the complementary factor, *viz.*, a higher real wage. In other words, there is a progressive loss in the value of existing machines because of this economic depreciation. According to Miller (1983), this forms the rationale for an alternative method of valuing the capital stock which attempts to take account of the improved quality of newer capital goods. The procedure is to adjust for the increase in quality of the more recent capital goods so that the improved quality is represented as an increase in the quantity of capital. To achieve this, obsolescence is deducted, since the net improvement to the capital stock obtained by replacing an older by a newer machine is the difference in the contribution of the new capital good to production and the contribution of the displaced capital good. As Miller (1983, p. 291) puts it: 'One must revalue old capital for obsolescence. The intuitively attractive idea of thinking of a particular piece of equipment as always representing the same quantity of capital must be abandoned.' In practice, the measurement of obsolescence is often very difficult and, to a certain extent, arbitrary (Usher, 1980b).

Denison (1969, p.14), not surprisingly, strongly disagrees with this procedure: the 'use of a net stock series is always inappropriate on theoretical grounds: net value drops as the length of the remaining service life declines, and this has no relevance to the ability to contribute to production *currently*' (emphasis added). 'The appearance of better goods does not reduce the ability of existing goods to produce and therefore should not be allowed to affect capital input' (Denison, 1972). In *Why Growth Rates Differ*, Denison (1967) assumed that there was a decline over time in the volume of output that a machine could produce, because of physical wear and tear. He therefore suggested that the growth of an appropriate measure of the capital stock should be a weighted average of the growth of the gross and net stocks, with the weights being 0.75 and 0.25 respectively. It should be emphasised that the inclusion of the net capital stock is merely to capture physical depreciation, *not* obsolescence.

Another method of incorporating quality changes into the capital stock estimates is to adjust the current investment for embodied technical change. This means that rather than the value of old capital goods being reduced, the value of the newer investment is increased. A new machine that provides twice the services of an older machine would be treated as representing twice as much capital, even though it cost the same to produce when measured in base year prices. One way of doing this is to incorporate the quality effect into the price index. An example given by Miller (1983) is that the introduction of the jet plane might have been treated as a reduction in the price index of aircraft. Instead the index was constructed by chaining on the basis of cost and showed a rise of 2.6 per cent per annum from 1957 to 1971. On the other hand, Gordon (1983, p. 209) has shown that if quality adjustments had been incorporated into the price index, there would have been a 7.5 per cent annual decline. This would have greatly increased the capital value of the more modern aircraft. It would, of course, be double counting to adjust both the price index and to deduct obsolescence. A good deal of ingenuity and effort has gone into improving the estimates of economic depreciation in order to improve the estimates of the net capital stock (see, for example, the various papers in Usher, 1980b).

In practice, the growth rates of both the gross and net measures are remarkably similar. The reason is that the net capital stock has had obsolescence (capital consumption) deducted from both investment and the existing capital stock to which investment is being added. In other words, it is deducted from both the numerator and denominator of $\Delta K/K$, and this leaves the growth rate relatively unaffected by the definition of capital stock chosen. This is shown in Table A1.1 where, with the possible exception of Japan, the disparities are very small. The difference made to capital's contribution to output growth, which is obtained by weighting the growth rates by capital's share (approximately one-quarter), is negligible. (Denison uses the net factor share as the appropriate weight whereas Norsworthy (1984) argues that, since capital consumption is a cost of production, the appropriate measure is the gross factor share. But again, this does not make much difference to the results.)

However, Scott argues that both the gross and net measures will provide a misleading estimate of the contribution of capital to economic growth, and we turn next to a consideration of his argument.

Table A1.1   Growth rates of the gross and net capital stocks, selected advanced countries, 1963–87

Country	Period	Gross capital stock (% p.a.)	Net capital stock (% p.a.)	Difference (% p.a.)
Japan	1965–73	12.21	14.32	−2.11
	1973–87	7.04	4.21	2.83
France	1963–73	n.a.	n.a.	n.a.
	1973–87	3.36	3.78	−0.42
Germany	1963–73	5.07	5.18	−0.11
	1973–87	3.02	2.57	0.45
UK	1963–73	3.89	4.41	−0.52
	1973–87	2.45	2.16	0.29
US	1963–73	3.55	3.92	−0.37
	1973–87	3.02	2.72	0.30

Source: *Flows and Stocks of Fixed Capital, 1962–87* (OECD, Paris).

Depreciation and Maintenance and the Measurement of the Growth of the Capital Stock

Scott argues that theoretically an asset should be valued by its marginal product and not by its replacement cost in some base year. But even so, for reasons outlined below, he does not believe that obsolescence should be deducted from gross investment. This, of course, is in marked contrast to those who, unlike Denison, believe that the effects of quality change should be incorporated in the capital stock estimates, but do this by making an allowance for obsolescence. Neither, Scott argues, is the gross capital stock the most appropriate measure because the value of scrapped capital equipment should also not be deducted from gross investment. The increase in the capital stock is equal to gross investment (measured as consumption forgone in base year prices) 'minus nothing'. According to Scott, this implies that little meaning can be given to the growth of the conventionally measured capital stock, per se, as a factor of production contributing to the growth of output. (This is not to say that conventional measures of the capital stock have no meaning. For example, the net capital stock can be taken as a measure of the capitalists' wealth.)

As we have noted, because of economic obsolescence the value of the marginal product (which is generally equal to the asset's quasi-rent) declines over the length of the asset's life until, under the assumptions of perfect competition, it is scrapped when the marginal product is zero. The reason for the decline in the quasi-rent is primarily due to the rise in the real wage; the cost of the co-operating factor. A crucial tenet of Scott's argument is that *if the marginal product of the asset is zero, then, by definition, its scrapping will cause no loss in output*. 'The other factors of production associated with the asset must then be able to go elsewhere and produce as much as they were earning when they worked with the asset, and this must equal the whole of the output they then together produced. The economic contribution of the asset is then zero, and scrapping it does not reduce total output' (Scott, 1986, p. 279). If scrapping an asset does not reduce total output then its value should not be deducted in measuring the increase in the capital stock as a contribution to the change in output.

At first sight, this line of reasoning may seem counter-intuitive. But we can illustrate the point by using an example of a simple vintage model, following Scott (1991c). It is assumed that the output of a machine of vintage v at time t (denoted by Y_v) is produced with one worker. The machine does not suffer any wear and tear but, as we shall see, is eventually scrapped because of the rising real wage rate. A total of I machines is installed each year and each machine produces σ more output than a machine of the immediately preceeding vintage. In other words, machines brought into production at time t, and hence are of vintage t, benefit from an increase in output per machine of $dY_t/dt = \sigma$. However, this increase is not shared by machines already installed. For the moment, we shall not discuss exactly why output per machine increases, but the orthodox approach would attribute it to exogenous technical progress. (The vintage approach is seen by some commentators to be more realistic than the malleable capital model because improvements in efficiency are embodied in the new investment and, as already noted, do not benefit previously installed machines. Nevertheless, the causes of the improvement in efficiency are still left unexplained.)

The vintage of the oldest machine still currently in production at time t is m, with machines of vintage $m-1$ having just been scrapped as a result of the new investment. The real wage is equivalent to the output on the machine of vintage m and is equal to $Y_t - \sigma(T-1)$, where $T = t - (m-1)$. The quasi-rents on machines of vintage t are $r_t = \sigma(T-1)$, and on the marginal machines of vintage m are zero. The total increase in production caused by the introduction of machines of vintage t is equal to the quasi-rent r_t plus the resulting increase in the real wage rate σ, which equals σT. (However, if we consider a marginal increase in the machinery of vintage t which, because of its incremental magnitude, did not increase the real wage, the increase in output would simply be the quasi-rent of the new machine. But, the former approach has certain expositional advantages.) We may interpret the increase in production as the marginal product of capital, even though each machine is subject to a fixed coefficients technology. This is because the increase in production necessitated the release of workers from marginal machines of vintage $m-1$ (which, consequently, went out of production) and their employment on machines of vintage t. Similarly, the marginal product of vintage v, r_v, equals $\sigma(v-m)$ and it declines over time solely as the result of a relative price change (the rise in the real wage) caused by the introduction of new more efficient machines.

Each machine is assumed to cost £1 and so I may represent either the number of machines or the value of investment. We further assume that there is a fixed labour force L which equals IT.

The situation is shown in Figure A1.1. The vertical axis represents output per machine (or output per worker) and the horizontal axis shows the number of machines (or the past rate of investment) for each vintage. The marginal vintage after the investment at time t is m and so there are machines of $t-m+1$ ($= T$) vintages still in production. The distance fg is the quasi-rent and fh the marginal product on a machine of vintage t. The area $fgkj$ is the total profits earned by the machines of vintage t and $gink$ is the wage bill for those machines. The value of total output Q is equal to the average of the output of the latest and oldest machine multiplied by the total number of machines in operation. This equals $IT[Y_t - (\sigma T/2)]$ or $L[Y_t - (\sigma T/2)]$.

Let us consider the effect of bringing I new machines into production at time t. The output per machine is σ higher than that of vintage $t-1$ and competition increases the real wage by $dw/dt = \sigma$ as I machines of vintage $m-1$ are scrapped. (This is because I workers have to be released to work on the new machines.) The increase in total output dQ/dt is $I\sigma T$, which comprises the total of quasi-rents on the new machines $r_t I$ and the increase in the wage bill, σI, for the most recent vintage. These are represented by the areas $fgkj$ and $ghlk$ in Figure A1.1. The value of output depicted by the rectangle $hinl$ does not represent a net gain, since it is exactly offset by the loss of output, $abed$, on the machines of vintage $m-1$.

The growth of total factor productivity is defined as:

$$\lambda = q - a\ell - (1-a)k \tag{A1.1}$$

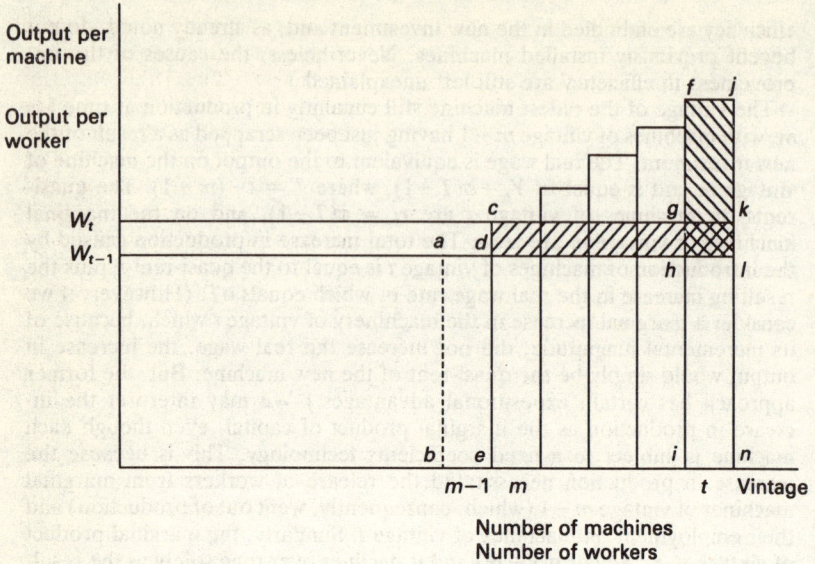

Figure A 1.1

where it will be recalled that q, ℓ and k denote the growth rates of output, quality-adjusted labour and capital. a and $(1-a)$ are the shares of labour and capital in income.

Since there is no growth in the labour force in the model under consideration, equation (A1.1) becomes:

$$\lambda = q - (1-a)k \qquad (A1.2)$$

The rate of growth of output equals $\sigma/[Y_t - (\sigma T/2)]$ and in order to determine λ we need to calculate the growth of the capital stock. Scott considers that the best procedure is to weight the change in capital inputs by their relative marginal products, measuring the latter either from the base or terminal year (or perhaps some average of both). (See Oulton, 1992, for an example of the orthodox approach where this procedure is also adopted.)

As Scott (1991b) points out, there is an obvious analogy with the measurement of real consumption, where changes in the quantities are weighted by the base year (Laspeyres index) or terminal year (Paasche index). Relative prices can be regarded as the best practical proxy for relative marginal utilities – the relative 'marginal products' in the 'production' of utility. However, when we estimate the change in consumption we do not include the relative price changes, i.e. the quantities consumed multiplied by the *changes* in their prices. Likewise, obsolescence, which is the result of a price change (and represents a transfer of income from capitalists to workers) should not be deducted from the growth of the net capital stock because there is no loss to society involved. It is here that Scott and the orthodox approach part company, because the latter does deduct obsolescence in calculating the net stock. Moreover, scrapping should not be deducted (as in the conventional estimates of the gross capital stock) because, while it does represent a quantity change, it is one that receives a zero weight as the rentals of the scrapped machines are zero. If these assumptions are accepted an increase in the capital stock is equal to gross investment, as we shall see, and logically there can be no resulting increase in output unaccounted for. It is only by (erroneously) deducting obsolescence from the capital stock that a residual appears.

This argument may be demonstrated as follows. A measure of the capital stock is defined as (in continuous time):

$$K_t = \int_m^t \frac{r_v}{r_t} I_v \, dv = \frac{1}{r_t} \int_m^t (Y_v - w_t) \, I_v \, dv \qquad (A1.3)$$

Each machine is weighted by its relative marginal product (r_v/r_t), which we now take to be equal to the quasi-rents, (i.e. $\partial r_v/\partial t = 0$, but this is not true of $\partial r_v/\partial t$). The values are summed to give an estimate of the capital stock at time t. Consequently, according to the orthodox approach, the increase in the capital stock is given by:

$$\frac{dK}{dt} = \frac{1}{r_t} \left[(Y_t - w_t)I - (Y_m - w_t)I \right] + \frac{1}{r_t} \int_m^t \frac{\partial(Y_v - w_t)}{\partial t} I_v \, dv \quad (A1.4)$$

Since $(Y_m - w_t) = 0$ and $\partial(Y_v - w_t)/\partial t = -\partial w_t/\partial t = -\sigma$ (so the last term equals $-I$, remembering that $r_t = \sigma(t-m)$), equation (A1.4) may be written as:

$$dK/dt = I - 0 - I = 0 \qquad (A1.5)$$

The logic behind equation (A1.5) is as follows. It can be seen that gross profits are constant, despite the investment of I. Consequently, there must be depreciation equal to I and net investment is zero. The term $\partial(Y_v - w_t)/\partial t$ is the fall in the quasi-rent on a machine of vintage v and this occurs because of the increase in the wage rate equal to gh which is caused by the gross investment at time t. Thus, the last term in equation (A1.4) represents the effect of obsolescence.

Under this orthodox approach, the growth of output must all be attributed to the growth of total factor productivity since there is no increase in the conventionally defined capital stock. Output growth therefore equals:

$$\frac{dQ/dt}{Q} = \frac{I\sigma T}{Q} = \frac{(\partial w/\partial t)L}{Q} = a\varphi_w = \lambda \qquad (A1.6)$$

where, it will be recalled, φ_w denotes the growth of the real wage.

Thus, what the conventional approach sees as technical progress is equal to the growth of the real wage rate (weighted by the share of labour in income). This, in turn, is a function of the rate of decline of the quasi-rents.

Oulton (1992) has shown in a similar vintage growth model that this result generalises to the case where the capital stock and the labour force are both growing. (Oulton's model differs slightly in that he postulates that each successive machine requires less labour to produce the same level of output.) Total factor productivity growth still equals the growth of the real wage rate multiplied by its share in total income. As a consequence of his analysis, Oulton maintains that 'Scott's claim of a flaw in the conventional analysis is incorrect'. It is difficult to agree with this statement since both Oulton's and the above analyses show that the conventional result is only obtained by deducting obsolescence. But should obsolescence be deducted? As we have seen, Scott makes a plausible case that it should not and Oulton does not address this point. From Figure A1.1, it can be seen that the value of obsolescence is equal to the rectangle *cdlk* and this is equal to the gain in total wages that labour experiences from the increased investment. It is definitionally equal to the loss in total gross profits of *cdlk* (and the corresponding increase in gross profits fhl_j). It thus reflects the transfer of income from gross profits to wages and as such is a *price effect* and not a *quantity effect*. It should not therefore be deducted from the growth of the capital input. Or to put it another way, if we include the effect of changes in the relative prices on gross profits, we should also include, for consistency, the effect on total wages. The two effects will cancel each other out. Scott (1990, p. 1178) is aware that 'because of its unfamiliarity [his argument] may leave some readers puzzled or incredulous. I can only plead that they should ask themselves whether a rise in the real price of labor, such as normally occurs every year in a progressive economy, does not in itself (and abstracting from consequential quantity changes) transfer income from capitalists to workers, does not increase workers' wealth, defined as the present value of their future expected consumption, and hence amounts to appreciation of their human capital.'

If we do not deduct obsolescence, the increase in the measured capital input is given by:

$$dK^*/dt = I \text{ and } dQ/dt = r_t I = r_t dK^*/dt \tag{A1.7}$$

where K^* is, according to Scott, the correctly measured capital stock from a growth accounting point of view.

The whole of the increase in output is explained by the increase in capital. There is no residual.

An implication of this argument is that there is no uniquely correct measure of the capital stock. On the one hand, suppose, for example, we wished to estimate a conventional production function using time-series data, where the time trend would capture the putative effect of technical progress (i.e. using the logarithmic values of the *levels* of the variables). The use of a measure of the capital stock defined by equation (A1.3) is inappropriate since this would give an unexplained growth rate of output equal to λ. As we have noted above, the theoretically correct measure is the sum of *all* past gross investments. The reason for this may be seen by considering Figure A1.2. Just as the increase in the total wage bill from investment at time *t* is *cdlk*, so the component of the total wage bill *aoqp* is due to the investment at

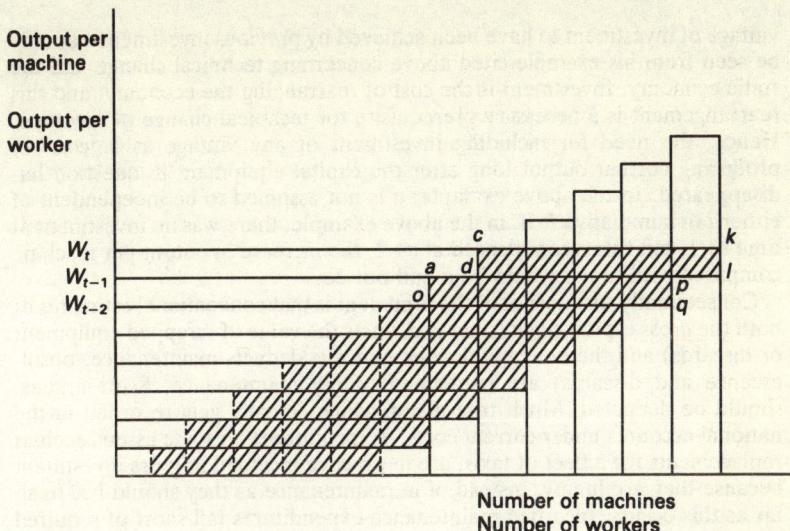

Figure A1.2

time $t-1$, and so on. In this case, where there is no growth in the labour force, the total wage bill is equal to the sum of obsolescence of all past investment. Thus cumulative past investment accounts for all of current output. One might almost call this a 'capital theory of value'! (Of course, this is no longer true if there is growth in the labour force, but this does not alter the conclusion that the capital input should be measured by cumulative investment, even though many of the machines will no longer be in production.)

On the other hand, it is correct to use the measure of the capital stock given by equation (A1.3) to explain the level of output in terms of factor incomes, i.e. $Q_t \equiv w_t L_t + r_t K_t$, but it is *not* correct to use it in any growth accounting exercise.

But what of λ as measured by the orthodox growth accounting approach? Scott (1992b) argues that:

> one is not . . . explaining some unexplained part of growth by postulating labour-augmenting technical progress. There is no residual to explain. Essentially, one is measuring the rate of transfer of income from capital to labour. That is certainly an interesting magnitude, and it is the result of the growth process. What is interesting is an understanding of what it is that enables investment to persist year after year without, it seems, there being any long-run tendency for real rates of return to fall despite rising real wage rates. Let us put the question that way, and not in terms of explaining a residual which disappears if measurements are correctly made.

This really brings us to the crucial difference between Scott and the orthodox approach. Scott regards the increase in efficiency of the latest vintage of investment to have been achieved by previous investments, as may be seen from his example cited above concerning technical change and the static economy. Investment is the cost of rearranging the economy, and this rearrangement is a necessary prerequisite for technical change of any type. Hence, the need for including investment of any vintage as a 'cost' of producing current output long after the capital equipment in question has disappeared. In the above example, σ is not assumed to be independent of either I or cumulative I. If, in the above example, there was no investment at time $t+1$, but this recommenced at $t+2$, the increase in output per machine compared with time t would be σ and not 2σ.

Consequently, the upshot of the argument is that conventional estimates of both the gross capital stock (since it deducts the value of scrapped equipment or discards) and the net capital stock (since it deducts maintenance, obsolescence and discards) are inadequate. Only maintenance, Scott argues, should be deducted. Much true maintenance actually gets recorded in the national accounts under current costs. 'Expenditures on some assets, such as replacements for a fleet of taxis, are in practice included in gross investment because they are lumpy, instead of in maintenance as they should be. In so far as this occurs, recorded maintenance expenditures fall short of required maintenance. However, this shortfall is made good, or more than good, by the inclusion of maintenance (or other current costs) of a great many expenditures that should be classified as gross investment: research and development expenditures, some managerial costs, some advertising expenditures, some costs of financial intermediaries, and so on' (Scott, 1989, p. 32). On balance, he concludes that those expenditures treated as current costs, but which should really be included in gross investment, probably exceed the maintenance costs that ought to be deducted from gross investment. It follows that conventionally estimated maintenance costs should not in practice be deducted from gross investment. The latter, because of these classification errors, actually provides a good estimate of investment net of maintenance costs. Consequently, the best readily available estimate of the growth of the capital stock is simply the total gross investment over the period under consideration without any deduction for retirements.

McCombie (1990) and Denison (1991) both take the view, outlined above, that Scott's approach implies that the correct measure of the capital stock is cumulative gross investment from time immemorial. Denison (1991, p. 225), for example, notes that 'it follows from Scott's views that the correct series would be gross investment . . . cumulated from the beginning of time until each year to be estimated'. But Scott himself, notwithstanding the above arguments, paradoxically would seem to disagree. After outlining the implications of his approach along the lines noted above, Scott (1989, p. 38) notes, almost as an aside, that supporters of the use of the conventional production function would argue that 'a capital stock which includes capital goods that have been scrapped long ago cannot be used for this purpose'. He goes on to say that he agrees with this sentence, although, in his view, this does not rescue the conventional production function. In Scott (1991a, p. 7) this view is given much greater emphasis. 'The cumulative gross stock will include machines and buildings bought, not just 20 years ago, but 200 years ago, or even, in principle, 2,000 years ago, few of which will still exist.

Cumulative gross investment cannot, therefore, be used as an argument in a production function explaining both the level and change in the level of output. Such a function seeks to relate current output to current input, *but there is no sense in which a machine or building scrapped years ago is still a current input* (emphasis added).

These two quotations, initially, would seem to be difficult to reconcile with our interpretation of Scott's view. For example, consider the level of output given by the orthodox Cobb–Douglas production function, $Q_t = A_o e^{\lambda t} L_t^\alpha K_t^{(1-\alpha)}$, with the usual notation, but where K is the net capital stock adjusted for capacity utilisation. When the logarithmic transformation of this production function is estimated using time-series data, the value of λ, which, it will be recalled, is the rate of growth of total factor productivity, is usually found to be substantial. This is for precisely the same reason, which Scott has shown to be erroneous, that the growth accounting approach finds such a large residual. Consequently, for the reasons set out above, the appropriate measure of the capital stock is cumulative gross investment.[28]

However, the paradox is more apparent than real.[29] Scott, in the quotations cited above, implies that current output can be 'explained' by the net capital stock in the sense that if we were either to remove or add a marginal unit of a particular asset (or a worker), it would be possible to predict the effect on output. This hypothetical experiment may be described as a *static* analysis, since the change in the factor of production occurs at one particular instance in time. We are not concerned with explaining how output changes *over time*. (This is, of course, the purpose of the estimation of the Cobb–Douglas production function, notwithstanding that the data are the logarithmic transformations of the *levels* of output and the inputs.) Let us assume that marginal products are directly proportional to factor rewards and also that the net capital stock is valued by using relative marginal products. This means that the ratio of gross profit to the net value of the capital stock is the same for each unit of the stock. To put the matter another way, it implies that increasing any item of the capital stock by, say, one pound's worth increases output by the same amount as increasing any other asset by a pound. In these circumstances, it is correct to use the net capital stock as the capital measure. The same principle holds for workers, although the analysis would be simply in terms of wages rather than capitalised values. But what we are not attempting to explain is the causes of changes in output over time and it is here that Scott considers that a confusion has arisen that has misled many growth theorists. In the static case, the net additions (or subtractions) of capital are, by assumption, identical to existing items of the capital stock. But once we introduce time into the analysis, we find that additions to the capital stock are not 'just more of the same'. As we have noted earlier, the very act of investment opens up new and superior investment opportunities which prevent diminishing returns setting in. The effect of this is a relative price change, which leads to the decline in the value of existing assets (and a rise in the human capital of workers). This is simply depreciation and in trying to account for growth should *not* be deducted from the growth of the capital stock. This is where, according to Scott, the orthodox growth accounting approach errs. Depreciation is deducted in constructing the net capital stock and hence the use of this to measure the growth of the capital input understates the latter's contribution to output growth (by an amount equal to the residual). In the case of explaining current output described above, adding an additional incremental unit of capital will also depress the price of the asset and raise the wage rate, but the effect is ignored this time by the conventional approach. As Scott points out there is an inconsistency here; if it is correct not to deduct depreciation in the static case (as it is), then it follows that this must be equally true in the dynamic case.

The other case where the net stock of capital is the appropriate measure is when we wish to 'explain' current output in terms of the current costs of production (which also involves the use of only current inputs) i.e. $Q_t \equiv w_t L_t + r_t K_t$.

The Growth Accounting Approach in the Light of Scott's Critique

The importance of Scott's approach may be further demonstrated by comparing his method directly with the traditional growth accounting approach. It is useful to begin by considering an approach that Scott discusses and which is similar in many ways to the growth model he develops in chapter 6 of the *New View*, although it is not identical. (It does, however, provide the justification for Scott's (1981) earlier criticism of Denison and the traditional growth accounting approach.)

The increase in output, gross of capital consumption, resulting from an increase in the labour force with a given rate of gross investment is given by:

$$\Delta Q = rI + w\Delta L \qquad (A1.8)$$

where r is the rate of profit on gross investment, I, and w is the real wage rate. L is employment. (Scott takes L to be the quality adjusted labour force and w the price of quality adjusted labour. This does not materially affect the argument.) It is assumed that r is constant (see Scott, 1989, p. 97).[30] It might be thought that the increase in investment would lead to an increase in the real wage, so that there ought to be a term $(\Delta w)L$ added to the right hand side of equation (A1.8). However, it should be remembered that this increase in the wage rate is implicitly included in I, since economic depreciation should not be deducted. The latter is caused by the increase in the price of labour and so by not deducting it, we are attributing its contribution to growth to investment, for Scott's reasons outlined above.

Equation (A1.8) can be expressed as:

$$\frac{\Delta Q}{Q} = \frac{rI}{Q} + \left[\frac{wL}{Q}\right]\frac{\Delta L}{L} \qquad (A1.9)$$

or identically as:

$$q = rs + a\ell \qquad (A1.10)$$

where $s = I/Q$.

Equation (A1.10) may also be expressed as:

$$q - a\ell = rs \qquad\qquad (A1.11)$$

As we have noted above, value added is defined as $Q \equiv wL + rK$. Expressing this in terms of proportionate growth rates, assuming factor shares are constant, and rearranging, we obtain:

$$q - a\ell = rs = a\varphi_w + (1 - a)\varphi_r + (1 - a)k \qquad\qquad (A1.12)$$

where φ_r and φ_w are the growth rates of the real rental price of capital and the real wage, and $a\varphi_w + (1 - a)\varphi_r$ is, by definition, equal to the growth of total factor productivity. As we have assumed that φ_r is zero, total factor productivity growth is equal to the growth of the real wage rate weighted by labour's factor share. The variable k is the growth of the conventionally measured net capital stock. (It should be noted that if the growth of the labour force is adjusted for changes in quality, the growth of real wages will have to be reduced (increased) by the same percentage point by which the growth of the labour input is increased (reduced). This does not, however, significantly affect our argument.)

Hence, the contribution that investment makes to growth is:

$$rs = a\varphi_w + (1 - a)k \qquad\qquad (A1.13)$$

Consequently, it can be seen from equations (A1.11) and (A1.13) that rs, which is the contribution of the growth of the capital stock (now correctly measured, according to Scott's approach) to the growth of output, captures the contribution of both the residual (the growth of total factor productivity) and the growth of the capital input (as conventionally measured). Hence, using the accounting identity, we have provided an alternative demonstration that if Scott's measurement of capital is correct, it follows that its growth will be equal to the sum of the growth of the conventionally measured capital stock and the orthodox rate of technical progress. The latter is equal to the growth of the real wage weighted by labour's factor share. Consequently, by definition, there can be no residual in this approach.

As we have noted above, equations (A1.11) and (A1.13) provide the rationale that Scott (1981) uses to recalculate Denison's estimates of the sources of growth to remove the residual (attributing the gains due to the improved allocation of resources to the growth of the labour input, treating the gains analogously to improvements in the quality of labour). He finds that the contribution of the growth of capital increases from the one-quarter Denison found to just under three-quarters. (This is after economies of scale have been allocated *pro rata* to labour, capital and the residual.) (See Scott, 1981, table 1, p. 223.)

However, this approach differs somewhat from the model presented in chapter 6 of the *New View*. There is not the space to discuss the model, but the 'growth equation' Scott derives as a linear approximation of the model takes the form:

$$q = As + \mu\ell \tag{A1.14}$$

where A and μ are constants and $\mu = a/(1 - s)$.

Scott (1989, p. 183) also derives the result, obtained above, that:

$$q = rs + a\ell \tag{A1.15}$$

It may be seen, from equations (A1.14) and (A1.15), that $A = r - \mu\ell$. Consequently, equation (A1.14) may be written as:

$$q = [r - \mu\ell]s + \mu\ell \tag{A1.16}$$

or, equivalently, as:

$$q = \left[r - \frac{a}{(1 - s)}\ell \right] s + \frac{a}{(1 - s)}\ell \tag{A1.17}$$

This compares with the earlier growth accounting equation, viz:

$$q = rs + a\ell \tag{A1.18}$$

Equations (A1.16) and (A1.17) are mathematically the same as equation (A1.18). But there are important differences between the assumptions underlying the two 'growth accounting' equations. In equations (A1.16) and (A1.17), it is assumed that $\partial[r - \mu\ell]/\partial\ell = \partial A/\partial\ell = 0$ and $\partial\mu/\partial s = 0$. Moreover, $\partial q/\partial s = A$ (and does not equal r, as implied by equation (A1.18)) and $\partial q/\partial\ell = \mu$ ($\neq a$). The marginal product of labour implicit in equations (A1.16) and (A1.17) is $w/(1 - s)$ instead of w, as is implicit in equation (A1.18). These results are derived from the present value maximisation of the representative firm (see Scott, 1989, pp. 154–5).

Consequently, so long as $s > 0$ and $\ell > 0$, the contribution of the growth of labour to the growth of output is higher, and the contribution of investment lower, in the *New View* approach compared with the earlier version. 'For example, for the USA for 1948–73, Denison has estimated that, including an allowance for economies of scale, investment accounted for less than a fifth of the growth of non-residential business output, whereas my estimates put its share at over half' (Scott, 1989, p. xl).

In terms of the accounting identity, the contribution of investment to the growth of output may be obtained from equations (A1.13) and (A1.14) and is given by:

$$As = a\varphi_w + (1 - a)k - \mu s\ell \tag{A1.19}$$

instead of $rs = a\varphi_w + (1 - a)k$, as before.

It can be seen that the contribution of investment to the growth of output includes the growth of the real wage weighted by labour's share in total income and the growth of the conventionally measured net capital stock weighted by capital's share. But it differs from that given by equation (A1.11) in that investment has an effect that enhances the contribution of the growth of labour and this effect is ascribed to the growth of labour rather than to investment, *per se*. This accounts for the term $-\mu s\ell$ included in the right hand side of equation (A1.19).

Scott (1989, p. 173), himself, contrasts his model with the orthodox approach in a slightly different way. An expression for the growth of output derived from his model is:

$$q = (1 - \mu)(I/K) + \mu\ell \qquad\qquad (A1.20)$$

where μ, it will be recalled, equals $a/(1 - s)$ and K is the value of net capital stock as conventionally measured.

$(1 - \mu)$ is less than $(1 - a)$, taking an average value of 0.20 as opposed to 0.33, but I can be some three times larger than ΔK; the precise relationship depends on the country and period. Consequently, it can be seen that the contribution of the growth of capital will considerably exceed that of the conventionally measured growth of the capital stock, *viz* $(1 - a)k$.[31]

Denison on Scott

Although Scott generously acknowledges his debt to Denison's work, the *New View* poses a fundamental challenge to the orthodox growth approach. Denison's work, which, of course, has been very influential in analysing economic growth, is seen as being profoundly flawed. It is, therefore, perhaps not surprising that Denison's (1991) review article of the *New View* is somewhat hostile.

Denison disputes that most capital goods and structures are scrapped because of obsolescence or depreciation before they physically wear out. This is, of course, an empirical issue. Nevertheless, obsolescence is just the mirror image of the increase in real wages earned by quality-adjusted labour. Scott's estimates, for example, suggest that, for the UK and the US, during the postwar years to 1973, the total gains accruing to labour from an increase in the real wage rate (adjusted for changes in the quality of labour) were, in fact, greater than the conventional estimates of capital consumption. The inference is that capital consumption must be either wholly, or largely, due to obsolescence resulting from relative price changes, *pace* Denison.

As we noted earlier, Denison considers that there is a conceptually meaningful residual; this is the growth in output resulting from advances in knowledge, including changes in business organisation and management techniques. We have seen that he argues that, in order to estimate the contribution of these factors to economic growth, capital goods should be valued at their cost of production in some base year. In other words, no allowance should be made for the fact that later machines, costing the same as those built in the base year, are likely to be more efficient. It is the contribution of this rate of change of efficiency to output growth that Denison wishes to calculate. To attribute this contribution to the growth of capital, he argues, is to assume that people, 'and especially the rare and priceless Edisons of this world' do not matter. But to Scott, this is simply a misunderstanding on Denison's part. The proximate causes of growth involve changes in the 'economic arrangements', to use Scott's term. 'In general, these will consist of changes in the numbers and quality of the workforce, and changes in the physical environment in which they work, including changes in buildings, machines, vehicles, stocks of goods etc.' (Scott, 1991b, p. 239). This implies nothing about the *causes* of the changes in these economic arrangements. The efficiency of investment will depend very much on the efforts of management and of the much rarer Edisons, but the quantitative effect of these efforts will be captured by the value of investment. Scott also suggests, on the basis of Schmookler's (1966) work, that much inventive activity is induced by investment. The effects will not, and should not, appear as a residual which would have to be attributed to some classification as 'advances in knowledge'.

Denison's approach is essentially one of attempting to estimate what the growth of output would be if the growth of the gross capital stock was simply the replication of every item of machinery, structures etc. in existence in the base year. In other words, the growth of the capital stock by x per cent is taken to be the growth of each and every piece of capital by the same amount and, if the share of capital in total income is, say, 0.20, the contribution of the growth of this capital stock to the growth of output is 0.20 multiplied by x per cent per annum. Such replication, Denison argues, will exclude, by definition, any quality change and hence the use of such a measure will enable an estimate of the contribution of 'advances in knowledge' to be arrived at. But it is difficult to know precisely what is meant by an increase in inputs independent of any advances in knowledge. Equally, can there be any significant advances in technical knowledge independent of investment? It is difficult not to agree with Scott, for the reasons set out above, that there cannot be. If so, the rationale for the orthodox growth accounting approach becomes problematic.

Empirical Estimation of the *New View* Model

Unlike the growth accounting approach, Scott (1989) uses regression analysis to estimate his model. Although various time and country dummies, together with a proxy for technological catch-up, are also sometimes included, the basic specification is given by:

$$q = b_0 + b_1 \ell^* + b_2 s + \varepsilon \tag{A1.21}$$

where ℓ^* is the quality adjusted growth of the labour force and s is the gross investment–output ratio. ε is the error term.

The data used were for the non-residential sector of ten now advanced countries over a number of sub-periods from the mid-nineteenth century to 1973. A weighted regression analysis was used, with a specially constructed index of the reliability of data used for the weighting.

Scott's preferred regression specification gives the following result:

$$q = \underset{(8.05)}{0.9119\ell^*} + \underset{(2.93)}{0.06879s} + \underset{(3.35)}{0.06756d_p s} - \underset{(-3.16)}{0.05401d_p s \ln cu}$$

$$\bar{R}^2 \text{ (weighted residuals)} = 0.954$$
$$SER \text{ (weighted residuals)} = 0.491$$

(The figures in parentheses are *t*-values. In this, and the subsequent regression results, Scott's data for growth rates and the investment-output ratio have been multiplied by a factor of 100 to express the data in a per cent per annum, and a percentage form, respectively.)

d_p is a dummy variable that takes the value one for the postwar years, and zero otherwise. ln*cu* is the logarithm of an index for the degree of catch-up, measured as the ratio of output per quality adjusted worker in the country concerned to that in the US. Scott postulates that the degree of efficiency of investment is a linear function of ln*cu*. Including the variable *s*ln*cu* in the regression equation provides a test of this hypothesis.

As may be seen, the preferred specification of the regression gives a very good fit. The coefficient of the investment–output ratio is found to take values of 0.07 and 0.14 for the interwar and postwar periods respectively. Most importantly, the intercept which would capture exogenous technical progress does not significantly differ from zero and hence is dropped from the regression equation. This is what Scott's theory predicts. (With no constant in the regression, the R^2 and $\bar{R}^2$ are not well defined. The raw moment R^2 of the regression is 0.990. The intercept, if it is included in the regression, takes a *t*-value of -0.13. Nevertheless, the estimate of s becomes statistically insignificant at the 95 per cent confidence level, although its value does not greatly alter. There is no change in the significance of the other variables and their values remain approximately the same.)

In the above regression, each of the contributions of the investment–output ratio and the growth of the quality-adjusted employment explains nearly half of the growth of output, with the catch-up variable explaining a small but significant portion in the period since the Second World War. Consequently, the increase in capital explains considerably more than in the conventional growth accounting approach, because, according to Scott, it is now correctly measured and is capturing the effect of what the orthodoxy sees as technical change.

The estimated coefficient of ℓ^* at 0.9119 is somewhat high since the unweighted average value of $\mu = (1 - a)/(1 - s)$ is 0.78. (The average value of $(1 - a)$ is 0.65.) Nevertheless, Scott does not find the estimated value implausible, since the existence of imperfect markets, the taxation of investment and savings, and the effect of borrowing should raise the value of the estimate above 0.78.

As Denison (1991) points out, the model does not explain why the coefficient of *s* increased dramatically in the postwar period (doubling, according to the above regression result). Moreover, a further result requiring explanation is why the catch-up variable is significant only in the postwar period. 'The contribution of investment, including catch-up, is merely a residual, and a much more inclusive residual than that which appears in the more refined growth accounting studies' (Denison, 1991, p. 232). It is difficult to understand this criticism. The contribution of investment is not 'merely a residual' since it is the estimated contribution from a regression analysis; it is no more a residual than is labour's contribution. Moreover, Scott's regression results should be seen as merely a preliminary, although encouraging, investigation. It focusses attention on certain anomalies that have to be explained within this framework and Scott does, indeed, put forward some reasons to account for these two phenomena. It is true that the acceleration of growth after the Second World War needs to be explained as does the post-1973 slowdown, but this is equally true of Denison's results. Moreover, Denison never subjects his approach to regression analysis. We have no way of assessing the degree of confidence to be had in his quantification of the individual sources of growth.

The inclusion of Japan in the sample of advanced countries is perhaps debatable, since, until recently, it lagged far behind the other countries in terms of its technology and has such a different socio-economic milieu. Moreover, in other cross-country regressions that have been used to explain disparities in economic growth, Japan has turned out to be an outlier (Rowthorn, 1975a). We therefore repeated the regression, but with Japan omitted. The result is:

$$q = 0.022 + 0.670\ell^* + 0.109s + 0.055d_p s - 0.013d_p s \ln cu$$
$$\quad (0.04) \quad (3.80) \quad (2.06) \quad (2.44) \quad (-0.39)$$

$$\bar{R}^2 \text{ (weighted residuals)} = 0.781$$
$$SER \text{ (weighted residuals)} = 0.461$$

It can be seen that the coefficient of ℓ^* has declined from 0.9119 (or 0.9120 if an intercept is included) to 0.670 which is now below the unweighted average value of μ, which is 0.799 (excluding Japan). The intercept is still statistically insignificant at the 95 per cent confidence level, but this is now true of the estimate of the catch-up variable. There is no evidence that catch-up (as measured by the proxy $s \ln cu$) was a significant factor explaining disparities in growth rates for the remaining nine countries (the US, the UK, Belgium, Denmark, France, Germany, Netherlands, Norway, and Italy). Thus, the emphasis that Scott places on this factor would seem to be unwarranted (except for Japan), at least as far as the regression results are concerned.

There is a further problem as to just how satisfactory the variable $s \ln cu$ is in capturing changes in technology. Variations in output per quality-adjusted worker could vary for reasons other than differences in technology, e.g. economies of scale, the amount of capital (however measured) per worker, and the efficiency and skills of the labour force. (Inter-country differences in the effectiveness of schooling and training are not captured in the quality-adjusted employment index.)

Dropping the catch-up variable slightly improves the goodness of fit and gives the following result:

$$q = -0.044 + 0.634\ell^* + 0.121s + 0.055d_p s$$
$$\quad (-0.10) \quad (4.30) \quad (2.86) \quad (2.48)$$

$$\bar{R}^2 \text{ (weighted residuals)} = 0.793$$
$$SER \text{ (weighted residuals)} = 0.449$$

The *New View* and the 'Old' and 'New' Growth Theory

In the 1980s, a series of growth models was devised that also sought to dispense with exogenous technical progress. This approach was initially developed by Romer (1986, 1987a) and Lucas (1988), although there have now been numerous other contributions. (See Romer, 1987b, Stern, 1991, and Shaw, 1992, for surveys.) The rationale of these 'new' growth models is to explain steady state growth endogenously, i.e. within the model, rather than relying on exogenous technical progress, as does the traditional neo-classical 'old' growth theory, pioneered by Solow (1956). Thus, like Scott's *New View*, there is no residual in the new growth theory and, hence, it is interesting to compare these three approaches.

A standard result of the old growth theory is that, in the steady state, the growth of output equals the growth of capital and these are both determined by, and equal to the sum of, the rate of Harrod neutral (labour-augmenting) technical progress and the growth of labour. Since both these last two growth rates are assumed to be unaffected by policy measures, the growth of output and per capita income are exogenously determined. An implication of this is that an increase in the savings ratio (which causes an equal increase in the investment ratio) has no effect on the steady state growth rate. There is, however, a temporary acceleration in the growth of output as the economy moves to a higher level of output per capita, compared with the position that would have occurred if there had been no increase in the investment ratio. (In practice, the transitory period could be quite long (Sato, 1963).) A reduction in current consumption will lead to an increase in consumption some time in the future; but the steady state growth rate is unaltered. Thus, increasing the proportion of income invested raises the level of output but not the rate of growth. For the latter to occur, it would be necessary for the rate of technical progress to be increased. This could occur through increased expenditures on R&D or, temporarily, through the diffusion of innovations from the technologically advanced to technologically backward countries, but generally the old growth theory has relatively little to say on the matter.

The key assumption that generates the result that the investment ratio has no effect on steady state growth is that there are diminishing returns to capital which raises the capital–output ratio. What is new about both the *New View* and the new growth theory is that, in one way or another, they abandon this assumption. This has the effect of permitting an increase in the invest-ment ratio to increase the trend growth rate, because the productivity of investment is not reduced. Each act of investment opens up new oppor-tunities for profitable investment. It was noted in footnote 30 that Scott argues that the law of diminishing returns does not apply to capital, even in the long run. If investment and technical change are inextricably interwoven, then capital accumulation will result in a qualitative change in the economic environment. Investment does not mean 'more of the same' but 'more that is different'; more that is an improvement. The assumption that an increase in capital accumulation will lead to a fall in the rate of profit, *ceteris paribus*, rests on the belief that investment merely duplicates existing capital and that, given a fixed co-operating factor, this will lead through the law of diminishing returns to a fall in the rate of return. But once it is accepted that the economic milieu is itself altered by the act of investing, then 'investors can see further opportunities of which they were unaware before, and which yield as much as their previous investments did' (Scott, 1989, p. 85). Thus, as Scott

(1991a, p. 28) puts it: 'Because investment creates and reveals further invest-ment opportunities, this conclusion [that the steady state rate of growth is independent of the investment ratio] no longer holds. A bigger share of investment will increase the steady state rate of growth.'

The big difference between the *New View* and the new growth theory is that the latter does not abandon the conventional production function. In one version of the new growth theory, output is determined through the production function by the inputs of capital and labour and the stock of human knowledge, $Y = F(K,L,E)G(E')$ (Romer, 1987b). E is knowledge available only to a firm whereas E' represents the amount of generally available knowledge. If it is assumed that E' increases at the same rate as E which in turn increases at the same rate as K; and that F is a Cobb–Douglas production function; then total output can be expressed as:

$$Q = F(L,K)G(K) = (L^{\alpha}K^{(1-\alpha)})K^{\psi} \tag{A1.22}$$

The fact that the increasing returns are external to the firm ensures that a competitive equilibrium is preserved. If $(1 - \alpha + \psi) < 1$, there are dim-inishing returns to capital and an increase in the investment ratio will not permanently increase the growth of output. A growing labour force will, nevertheless, lead to an increase in per capita output as the benefits from economies of scale are obtained. If, however, $(1 - \alpha + \psi) \geq 1$, so that there are either constant or increasing returns to capital alone, an increase in the investment ratio will increase the long-run growth rate of output. Growth will occur even in the absence of exogenous technical change and population growth, which is not possible with either constant returns to scale with respect to K and L jointly or with $(1 - \alpha + \psi) < 1$ (i.e. diminishing returns to capital). Steady growth will occur if $(1 - \alpha + \psi) = 1$ but it will be (implaus-ibly) explosive if $(1 - \alpha + \psi) > 1$.

The growth accounting equation given by equation (A1.22) is:

$$q = \alpha \ell + (1 - \alpha + \psi)k \tag{A1.23}$$

and there is no residual.

An alternative variation due to Romer (1987a) is to assume, following Adam Smith and Allyn Young, that the greater the degree of specialisation, or division of labour, the greater, *ceteris paribus*, the level of output. To capture the degree of specialisation, output is specified as a function of the number of specialised capital inputs (rather than just the aggregate volume of the capital stock) as well as of labour. It is assumed that there is a fixed cost in producing the specialised capital goods, otherwise there would simply be an infinite number of them. Under certain simplifying assumptions, Romer (1987b) shows that the production function can be expressed as:

$$Q = AL^{\alpha}K \tag{A1.24}$$

and, in growth rate form, as:

$$q = \alpha\ell + k \tag{A1.25}$$

Once again, there is no residual.

On the basis of the empirical analysis, Romer concludes that the appropriate growth accounting equation is $q = \alpha\ell + \beta k$ with the value of α in the range of 0.1 to 0.3 and β between 0.7 and 1.0. For the developed countries, he suggests that the value of α may be somewhat lower and the value of β may be higher.[32] Since α is lower than labour's observed share in national income, there must be a significant negative externality associated with labour. Romer accounts for this by suggesting that the rate of labour-saving innovations could be a function of the growth of real wages, and that a faster growth of labour, by depressing the growth of real wages, could lead to a slower rate of innovations. Thus, the effect of an increase in the labour supply has a positive effect in allowing more output to be produced but a negative effect in slowing the rate of innovation. Romer suggests how a model may be constructed along these lines.

Lucas (1988) adopts a similar approach to the first new growth model discussed above. Each worker is assumed to be endowed with a certain amount of human capital (H) that not only raises the individual's productivity (the *internal effect*) but also has an *external effect* from which all workers benefit (denoted by H', which for simplicity is assumed to equal H). Each worker spends a fraction u of his or her working time engaged in active production and $(1 - u)$ acquiring human capital.

Output is given by:

$$Q = (uHL)^{\alpha}K^{(1 - \alpha)} H'^{\gamma} \tag{A1.26}$$

or:

$$Q = (uH^{\theta}L)^{\alpha}K^{(1 - \alpha)} \tag{A1.27}$$

where $\theta = (\alpha + \gamma)/\alpha$. We may further define the labour input in efficiency units as $L^* = H^{\theta}L$.

To make growth endogenous, we need to specify the rate at which H is acquired. Following Lucas, one possibility is:

$$dH/dt = H^{\zeta}\delta(1 - u) \tag{A1.28}$$

where δ is a constant.

However, there is a problem if $\zeta < 1$. This is because with diminishing returns to the accumulation of human capital it can be seen that eventually the growth rate of human capital (h) will decline to zero. The growth of human capital is given by:

$$h = \delta(1 - u)/H^{(1 - \zeta)} \tag{A1.29}$$

As H steadily increases, h will decline towards zero. In these circumstances, the accumulation of capital cannot take the place of exogenous technical progress in the growth process. However, all that is necessary to obviate the problem is to postulate that ζ is equal to (or greater than) unity. In other words, to assume that there are no diminishing returns to the production of human capital. If ζ equals unity, h will vary depending upon $(1 - u)$, taking a maximum value of δ, when $u = 0$, and a minimum value of 0, when $u = 1$.

It should be noted that it is also necessary to assume that the initial human capital stock with which an individual starts is proportional to the existing human capital stock. In other words, it is not necessary to keep re-inventing the wheel. Knowledge does not totally disappear with the death of a worker. (It should be noted that this is different from the way labour is adjusted for changes in quality in the traditional growth accounting approach. Here, an allowance is made for the increased quality of the labour force resulting from an increase in the average number of hours spent in education. It does not make any adjustment for the fact that an hour's schooling in 1992 increases the efficiency of labour considerably more than an hour's schooling did in 1892. As we shall see, it is for this reason that Lucas's approach explains the residual in terms of the growth of the quality of labour while traditional growth accounting does not.)

If u is constant, so that H grows at a constant rate, equation, (A1.27) can be written as:

$$Q = (uLe^{\lambda t})^{\alpha} K^{(1 - \alpha)} \tag{A1.30}$$

We may simply show why this model also must logically explain the whole of the residual. The wage is given by $\partial Q / \partial L = \alpha Q / L$ and its growth by $\varphi_w = q - \ell$. But the steady state solution is that $q = \lambda + \ell = \ell^*$, where ℓ^* is the growth of the labour input in terms of efficiency units. Hence, it follows that $\varphi_w = \lambda$. Substituting this expression for the growth of wages into the accounting identity we obtain:

$$q = \alpha(\lambda + \ell) + (1 - \alpha)k = \alpha\ell^* + (1 - \alpha)k \tag{A1.31}$$

It will be readily seen that the Romer and the Lucas models differ in their explanation of why there is no residual, but because of the observational equivalence problem, there is no easy way of discriminating between the two theories.

There is a certain similarity between the new growth theory and Scott's approach. However, Lucas attributes the residual entirely to labour (through cumulative knowledge) while Scott attributes it to capital (through cumulative investment). A further implication of the Lucas model is that if K and L are held constant, output would grow over time solely as a result of the increase in human capital. Scott disputes the validity of this conclusion. He does 'not believe that knowledge which was useful for economic output could accumulate independently of changes in K and L' (Scott, 1991a).

Neither of these points are true of the first new growth model we discussed, but this model merely *assumed* that the growth of knowledge increased one-for-one with the capital stock. The second new growth model discussed also attributed the residual to the growth of the capital stock, although this time because of increasing returns. However, Scott argues that the use of K

in the traditional production function in the new growth theory is inappropriate for the reasons we have discussed at length above.

Scott's Critique: A Concluding Comment

We have argued above that the difference between Scott and the orthodox
approach in measuring the sources of economic growth involves the question
as to what is the most appropriate definition of the capital stock. Denison, for
example, considers that the growth accounting approach ought to provide
separate estimates of the contribution to output growth of the growth of
capital and that of the rate of increase in its quality. Hence, he advocates the
use of the gross capital stock measured by the perpetual inventory model,
with investment measured at some base year prices. The value of wear and
tear and scrapping, but not obsolescence, should be deducted from gross
investment. The commonly used alternative that does deduct obsolescence is
the net capital stock, but we have seen that not a great deal depends upon the
choice; both leave a substantial residual when used in the growth accounting
approach.

Scott has shown that the residual is entirely due to a relative price effect. In
other words, it is a measure of the rate of transfer of income from capital to
labour. But the purpose of any growth accounting approach is to explain the
growth of the *volume* of output in terms of the growth of the *quantities* of
inputs. It is entirely inappropriate to deduct from the growth of capital the
effect on profits of a relative price change. Certainly, no one has ever
suggested that, for example, in the measurement of the growth of real
consumption, we should include the rate of change of the various relative
prices. (It is disappointing that Denison (1991), in his review of *The New
View*, never really addresses this central tenet of Scott's critique.) Scott has
shown that the correct measure of the growth of capital may be proxied by
simply gross investment, with no deduction for scrapping or obsolescence. If
this approach is adopted there is (can be) no residual. Scott confirmed this by
estimating his model by regression analysis.

Of course, explanations of why there are international differences in the
growth of the real wage of quality-adjusted labour are still of importance.
These differences are largely explicable by disparities in the gross-investment
ratios without any need to posit international differences in the rates of technical progress. (It is necessary, however, to account for why the efficiency
of investment seems to differ between time periods.) The policy implications are radically different from the 'old growth theory', stemming from the
work of Solow (1956) in that an increase in the rate of investment can
permanently raise the trend rate of growth.

But even in Scott's approach the amount of output each machine and
structure produces is seen to increase over time. Is this not due to exogenous
technical progress? It could be assumed that this is the case and this is the
implicit rationale of the orthodox growth accounting approach. However,
Scott has convincingly shown that this increase in efficiency is part and parcel
of the whole process of investment. There would be little or no improvement
in the efficiency of the capital goods without investment. Thus, it makes no

sense to try to distinguish between technical progress and the rate of investment in the growth process.

The traditional growth accounting approach, with its emphasis on the residual, implicitly took its justification from the fact that, from the early work of Abramovitz and Solow, a large proportion of output growth could not be accounted for by the growth of the traditional inputs. The obvious interpretation was to attribute a large proportion of the residual to advances in knowledge. But if Scott's measure of the growth of the capital stock had been adopted from the outset, would any prominence have ever been given to 'exogenous technical progress', whether embodied or disembodied? We suspect not.

2 Alternative Theories of Growth Performance: II The Demand Orientated Approach

INTRODUCTION

By way of introduction to the demand orientated theories, it is useful to briefly recapitulate the conclusions of the 'old' neoclassical growth theory, pioneered by Solow. The 1970s saw a proliferation of theoretical neoclassical one sector growth models based on the aggregate production function, although a few models were constructed with separate consumption and capital goods sectors. Under the usual neoclassical assumptions there is always the full and efficient utilisation of all resources. That is to say, countries are assumed to exhibit both allocative and producer efficiency. Resources are optimally distributed between firms so that no redistribution could lead to a net increase in output. Firms are also technically efficient and costs are always minimised; there is no X-inefficiency in Leibenstein's (1966) sense of the term. In the steady state, the growth of the capital stock is equal to the growth of output. The Cobb–Douglas production function, expressed in terms of growth rates, takes the form:

$$q = \lambda + \alpha\ell + (1 - \alpha)k \tag{2.1}$$

where q, ℓ and k denote the growth rates of output, labour and capital. The parameters α and $(1 - \alpha)$ are the output elasticities of labour and capital, and under the assumptions of the marginal productivity theory of distribution, are also equal to the relevant factor shares. λ is exogenous technical progress, or the growth of total factor productivity.

Given that, in the steady state, the growth of the capital stock equals the growth of output, the growth of output is given by:

$$q = (\lambda/\alpha) + \ell \tag{2.2}$$

155

and the growth of productivity by λ/α. Thus, the growth of output is ultimately determined by the growth of the labour force and the rate of technical progress. The analysis has nothing to say about what determines either of these; the growth of the labour force is presumably a function of the growth of the indigenous population, and technical progress is merely treated as exogenous. This approach is, as we have stressed earlier, pre-Keynesian, in that whatever is produced is automatically sold and the growth of supply creates its own growth of demand.

However, the empirical evidence with regard to the advanced economies in the postwar period provides scant support for the assumption that the growth of the labour input can be treated as autonomous, independent of demand. This is true even of the conditions experienced during the 'long boom' of 1950–73 when, with recorded unemployment normally at less than 2 per cent of the labour force in many of the countries, it might be thought conditions were most propitious for the applicability of the neoclassical model. Two detailed studies by Kindleberger (1967) and Cornwall (1977), however, came to the conclusion that it is much more useful to analyse the advanced countries as exhibiting the characteristics of 'dual economies', in much the same way as Arthur Lewis (1954) sought to explain the growth of the less developed countries. It was found that the growth of the labour input in the advanced countries, far from exogenously determining the growth of output, largely responded passively to the growth of demand for labour, especially demand emanating from the industrial sector.

THE DUAL NATURE OF THE ADVANCED COUNTRIES

The Lewis model divides the economy of a typical less developed country into two sectors; a high productivity, relatively capital-intensive industrial sector with rapid technical change and an agricultural sector with low productivity and 'surplus labour'. Surplus labour is generally defined as a situation where the marginal product of labour is at or below the subsistence wage. Consequently, the loss of a worker from agriculture in these circumstances would hardly reduce output, and simply induce an increase in average productivity. The wage in agriculture is also very low, fluctuating around the subsistence level. A further characteristic of the dual economy is that the wage in the industrial sector is higher than that prevailing in the agricultural sector, for a comparable worker. The proviso 'for a comparable worker' means that this wage differential cannot be explained by differences in the human capital of the workers employed in the two sectors. It thus means that the labour markets are in disequilibrium.

The agricultural sector acts as a reservoir of surplus labour for industry. It absorbs workers when the increase in the labour force exceeds the increase in the demand for labour by industry, and, conversely, it releases labour when industry's requirements cannot be met by the increase in the working population. An implication of this is that industry is faced with a perfectly elastic labour supply schedule at the prevailing industrial wage rate. Jobs in the industrial sector are scarce and there is an excess demand for them. There are always agricultural workers willing to take jobs in industry when these are available, but such jobs are rationed. Wages do not act in an equilibrating manner to clear the labour market, as postulated in the hypothetical neoclassical price auction model. Consequently, the rate of transfer of labour from agriculture to the industrial sector is solely a function of the growth of industry's derived demand for labour. Industry is seen as the 'engine of growth'. Industrial profits rise with the growth of sales of this sector, because of the stable industrial wage. Lewis assumes that all of these profits are reinvested in industry, thereby generating further growth and stimulating a further transfer of labour from agriculture to industry. This process proceeds until the surplus labour is exhausted in the agricultural sector. Once this has occurred, the marginal product of agricultural labour rises, and with it, the agricultural wage, as labour moves off the land. The wage differential progressively narrows until it is eliminated entirely and the dual sector model ceases to be applicable.

Both Kindleberger and Cornwall argue that, with certain modifications, the Lewis model is necessary for understanding the growth process of the advanced countries. They both argue that in the 1950s and 1960s much of Continental Europe and Japan were characterised by large and inefficiently organised agricultural sectors. Clearly, there was unlikely to be surplus labour in the sense that the marginal product in agriculture was zero. But all that is needed for the model to have a great deal of relevance for the developed countries is for there to be a perfectly elastic supply of labour to industry at the going industrial wage. Thus Cornwall (1977, p. 46), following Kaldor, defines surplus labour in agriculture as occurring 'if a more rapid increase in the demand for labour in the high-productivity, high-wage sector will give rise to a more rapid increase in supply without a change in wage differentials'.

He identifies four conditions for this definition of surplus labour to be satisfied.

(1) There must be a labour force willing to undertake substantial complex inter- and intra-sectoral mobility patterns.
(2) Even if the above condition is met, the inter-industry wage differential must remain stable.
(3) Labour markets must not act according to the price auction model. If this condition is inappropriate, then any wage differential would represent, for example, differences in human capital and so would not act as a market signal for the inter-sectoral transfer of labour.
(4) The demand for output and the derived demand for labour is sufficiently strong that the rates of growth of output and of employment in industry exceed that of the whole economy.

Cornwall carefully considers the diverse evidence concerning each of these conditions and finds that they are generally satisfied for most of the advanced countries. Many of the Continental European countries and Japan had large agricultural sectors and there was a substantial net transfer of labour from this sector to industry. Over the period 1950–73, agricultural employment declined in every country by amounts ranging from 10 per cent in Denmark to 38 per cent in Italy. In many of the advanced countries, especially in the early postwar period, agriculture was based on small family-owned spatially fragmented farms. The process of consolidation of these farms that occurred in many countries after the war (e.g. the French process of *remembrement*) allowed substantial economies of scale to be achieved, together with a widespread increase in the degree of mechanisation. This resulted in a rapid growth of agricultural productivity as may be seen from Table 2.1. The considerable numbers of agricultural workers who were released from working on the land rapidly moved into industry. This was accomplished in the advanced countries, with the exception of Belgium and Canada, without any appreciable narrowing of the income differential between agriculture and industry (see Table 2.2).

There were, nevertheless, a number of the advanced countries that even immediately after the Second World War had a small and efficient agricultural sector with little potential for supplying labour to

Table 2.1   The growth of agricultural output, employment and productivity (per cent per annum) in the early postwar years; selected advanced countries

Period	Country	Output growth	Employment growth	Productivity growth
1951–65	Japan	4.45	–2.68	7.13
	West Germany	1.20	–3.52	4.72
	Italy	2.36	–2.66	5.02
	France	1.92	–3.57	5.49
	Netherlands	2.20	–2.73	4.93
	Denmark	0.92	–3.01	3.93
	Austria	0.86	–3.31	4.17
	Canada	1.84	–3.45	5.29
	Norway	–0.12	–3.14	3.02
	Belgium	2.79	–2.77	5.56
	US	1.28	–3.61	4.89
	UK	2.55	–2.47	5.02
1965–73	Japan	3.57	–3.89	7.46
	West Germany	3.04	–4.83	7.87
	Italy	1.80	–5.05	6.85
	France	2.26	–3.97	6.23
	Netherlands	4.20	–2.84	7.04
	Denmark	0.51	–4.38	4.89
	Austria	2.05	–4.51	6.56
	Canada	0.18	–1.73	1.91
	Norway	–0.76	–3.84	3.08
	Belgium	0.52	–5.65	6.17
	US	7.20	–2.03	9.23
	UK	2.48	–3.48	5.96

Notes:

	1951–65	1965–73
Japan	1953–64	1964–73
West Germany	1951–65	1965–73
Italy	1951–65	1963–73
France	1957–64	1964–73
Netherlands	1951–65	1965–73
Denmark	1957–65	1965–69
Austria	1957–66	1966–73
Canada	1951–66	1966–73
Norway	1951–65	1965–70
Belgium	1951–64	1964–73
US	1951–66	1966–73
UK	1951–65	1965–73

Sources: Cripps and Tarling (1973) updated and revised using *National Accounts*, OECD (various years), *Labour Force Statistics*, OECD (various years).

Table 2.2   Per capita income in agriculture as a percentage of that in the rest of the economy (agricultural productivity as a percentage of that in manufacturing in 1963, in parentheses)

Country	1953–55 %	1959–61 %	1961–67 %	(1963) (%)
Austria	41	42	39	(41)
Belgium	86	100	110	(120)
Canada	49	47	69	(59)
Denmark	70	62	57	(n.a.)
France	n.a.	39	47	(48)
Germany	40	47	45	(50)
Italy	50	46	49	(57)
Netherlands	86	90	91	(90)
Norway	45	43	40	(39)
Sweden	52	49	54	(49)
UK	104	95	106	(102)
US	54	53	60	(50)
Japan	n.a.	n.a.	n.a.	(36)

Source: Cornwall (1977, table 4.1, p. 51, and table 4.2, p. 61).

the industrial sector. Most notably, these were Belgium, the Netherlands, the UK and the US. It may be seen from Table 2.2 that in the case of the first three, there was little difference in per capita income between agriculture and the rest of the economy, and, by implication, industry.

Nevertheless, agriculture was not the only source of labour for industry. For certain countries, a rapid growth of the population may be sufficient to supply all the necessary labour requirements so that no labour supply constraint is encountered. This, as Kindleberger (1967) argued, was true of the Netherlands. As Van der Wee (1987, p. 180) commented in the case of this country: 'the post-war labour surplus was primarily based on the powerful growth of the working population. This was countered by the government's policy on emigration, which was designed to get rid of surplus labour.' But by the 1960s 'the labour reserve was totally exhausted' and 'the replacement of labour by capital was encouraged and the recruitment of foreign workers supported.'

Belgium had a comparatively low growth rate in the 1950s and early 1960s but this was not primarily due to labour shortages. 'Although a sizeable labour reserve was available in Belgium, growth remained strikingly low' (Van der Wee, 1987, p. 181). The main reason was structural factors, especially weak export demand in Belgium's traditional heavy industries. It was with the creation of the EEC and the greater export opportunities this presented to Belgium that its growth rate increased. 'Belgium was able to respond speedily to this [the creation of the EEC] by absorbing open and concealed unemployment and bringing in a large number of guest workers from Italy, Turkey, and the Iberian Peninsula' (Van der Wee, 1986, pp. 181–2). Consequently, the Lewis model fits Belgium well, notwithstanding the country's highly efficient agricultural sector and negligible intersectoral wage differential.

The case of the UK in the 1960s is also interesting. Kaldor (1966b) in his inaugural lecture on the *Causes of the Slow Rate of Economic Growth of the United Kingdom* argued that the UK displayed a case of 'premature maturity'. Even though the UK had a standard of living considerably below the most advanced country, namely the US, it had a structure of demand more akin to the US, with a much greater emphasis on the demand for services than that found in other advanced countries. This was reflected in the service sector in the UK having the largest share of employment compared with the other advanced countries, with the exception of the US and Canada. Kaldor argued that this, combined with a small efficient agricultural sector, meant that the growth of industry was restricted by the availability of labour. It was for this reason that Kaldor recommended the introduction of the Selective Employment Tax (SET), which was a payroll tax on service industries, but not on firms in the manufacturing sector. The aim was to encourage the more efficient use of labour in the service sector, which would thereby release workers for industry. Later work by Sleeper (1970), however, suggested that the distribution and miscellaneous service sectors acted as a conduit for workers on their way to other industries. Sleeper's results showed that, even before the introduction of the SET, the net outflows of labour from these service industries into manufacturing was greater than the net flows from all industries into manufacturing. This evidence, *inter alia*, was sufficient to persuade Kaldor (1975b) that the UK did not face a serious labour constraint in the late 1960s. It suggested that the service sector also contained disguised unemployment and may also be a significant source of labour for industry.

Immigration is another major source of labour supply that is clearly the direct result, rather than the exogenous cause, of the growth of the demand for output. Many countries, in addition to Belgium, adopted a policy of deliberately encouraging immigration as their

Table 2.3   (a) net immigration as percentage of population increase and (b) the percentage share of immigrants in the total labour force

	(a) As a percentage of population increase 1950–72	(b) Percentage share in total labour force 1973
Belgium	25	7
France	33	11
Germany	47	11
Luxembourg	66	35
Netherlands	3	3
Sweden	30	n.a.
Switzerland	39	n.a.
United Kingdom	n.a.	7

Sources: Cornwall (1977, table 5.5, p. 86) and Van der Wee (1987, table 16, p. 162).

labour markets tightened and of subsequently restricting immigration as the developed economies moved into recession after the oil crisis of 1973/4. Van der Wee (1987, p. 160) has succinctly summarised the position as follows: 'The 1950s and 1960s witnessed an astonishing surge in the number of foreign workers in EEC countries. In France, Germany, Italy and the Benelux countries (Europe of the Six) there were 1.5 million foreign workers in 1960 and more than 4.5 million in 1973. When Great Britain, Ireland and Denmark (Europe of the Nine) are included the total number of foreign workers in 1973 were 6.4 million, of which nearly 2.5 million were in West Germany.' It may be seen from Table 2.3 that immigration formed both a significant share of the increase in the total population and a significant proportion of the labour force. This also helps explain the high elasticity of labour supply that the advanced countries experienced during the 'Golden Age'.

Cornwall concluded that his first two conditions, the high flexibility of the labour force and the stability of the inter-wage differential, were amply met in the postwar period. After surveying the evidence concerning the allocative mechanism in the various labour markets, he argues that this corresponds more to the 'job competition' or 'job vacancy' theories than to the neoclassical model. Empirical work suggests that workers are indeed rationed in the type of occupation they can undertake by the number of vacancies. Changes in relative wages do not act to clear the labour market. (See the evidence cited by Cornwall, 1977, pp. 52–9, and his evaluation of it.) This meets the requirement of his third condition. Finally, turning to his fourth condition, *viz*, that the growth of both industrial output and employment should exceed that of the whole economy, Cornwall finds that this is satisfied for all twelve of the advanced countries in the case of output growth and all but Canada, the Netherlands, the UK and the US in the case of employment growth.

We have only been able to sketch the main evidence concerning the dual structure of the advanced countries and, for this reason, we shall leave the summing up to Cornwall (1977, p. 95):

> For all practical purposes employment patterns were demand-determined in the various market economies in the postwar period. It is undoubtedly true that the supply of labour available for manufacturing was more elastic in some countries than in others. But the evidence, however limited, consistently suggested that, when entrepreneurs in the manufacturing sectors of the different economies wanted labour, they found it one way or another. . . . What took place in the postwar period up to the early 1970s was a situation in which the developed capitalist economies were uninhibited in their growth and transformation process by any serious or prolonged supply of labour constraint.

A corollary of this is that in no sense can the growth of the labour force be seen as a major exogenous driving force behind the growth of the advanced countries during the long boom of 1950–73, as is maintained in the neoclassical approach. The rise of recorded unemployment since 1973 means that it would be most implausible to argue that the growth of the labour force has become the autonomous determinant of the growth of output. Given that the rate of capital accumulation is itself largely determined by the rate of growth of output and, likewise, the rate of technical progress (as we shall see), we have to look elsewhere for an explanation of the disparate growth rates of the advanced countries.

THE KALDORIAN VIEW OF THE ECONOMIC GROWTH PROCESS

The production function approach to the measurement of the sources of growth is not only very supply orientated (treating factor supplies as exogenously given), but is also very aggregative. It treats all sectors of the economy – agriculture, industry, services – as if they have the same production, or growth, characteristics. In practice, however, aggregate growth is likely to be related to the rate of expansion of the sector with the most favourable growth characteristics. Nicholas Kaldor has argued in many of his writings that it is impossible to understand the growth and development process (and divisions between rich and poor countries within the world economy) without taking a sectoral approach, distinguishing between increasing returns activities on the one hand and diminishing returns activities on the other. Increasing returns is largely a characteristic of manufacturing industry, while diminishing returns characterises primary product activities which are land-based. There is, indeed, a lot of historical, empirical evidence to suggest that there is something special about manufacturing industry. There is a close association across countries in the world between the level of per capita income and the share of resources devoted to manufacturing industry, and there also appears to be a close association between the growth of manufacturing and the overall growth of GDP. Is this merely coincidence? Kaldor believes not.

Kaldor first articulated his own theory about why growth rates differ in two lectures: one in Cambridge in 1966 entitled *The Causes of the Slow Rate of Economic Growth of the U.K.* which we have already noted; the other at Cornell University in the same year published as *Strategic Factors in Economic Development* (1967). In these lectures he presented a series of 'laws' or 'empirical generalisations' which attempt to account for growth rate differences between advanced capitalist countries. The basic thrust of the model consists of the following propositions:

(i) The faster the rate of growth of the manufacturing sector, the faster will be the rate of growth of GDP, not simply in a definitional sense in that manufacturing output is a large component of total output, but for fundamental economic reasons connected with induced productivity growth inside and outside the manufacturing sector. This is a consequence of the large transfer of labour from the low productivity agricultural sector to the high productivity industrial sector that was experienced in many of the advanced countries especially prior to the mid-1970s.

(ii) The faster the rate of growth of manufacturing output, the faster will be the rate of growth of labour productivity in manufacturing owing to static and dynamic economies of scale, or increasing returns in the widest sense. Kaldor, in the spirit of Allyn Young (1928), conceives of returns to scale as a macroeconomic phenomenon related to the interaction between the elasticity of demand for and the supply of manufactured goods. It is this strong and powerful interaction which accounts for the positive relationship between manufacturing output and productivity growth, otherwise known as Verdoorn's Law (see later in this chapter and Chapter 8).

(iii) The faster the rate of growth of manufacturing output, the faster the rate of transference of labour from other sectors of the economy where there are either diminishing returns, or where no relationship exists between employment growth and output growth. A reduction in the amount of labour in these sectors will raise productivity growth outside manufacturing. As a result of increasing returns in manufacturing on the one hand and induced productivity growth in non-manufacturing on the other, we expect that the faster the rate of growth of manufacturing output, the faster the rate of growth of productivity in the economy *as a whole*.

(iv) As the scope for transferring labour from diminishing returns activities dries up, or as output comes to depend on employment in all sectors of the economy, the degree of overall productivity growth induced by manufacturing growth is likely to diminish, with the overall growth rate correspondingly reduced.

(v) It is in this latter sense that Kaldor believed that countries at a high level of development, with little or no surplus labour in agriculture or non-manufacturing activities, suffer from a 'labour shortage' and will experience a deceleration of growth; not in the sense that manufacturing output is constrained by a shortage of labour, which he originally suggested was the UK's problem but then retracted (1968).

(vi) The growth of manufacturing output is *not* constrained by labour supply (as we have seen above), but is fundamentally determined by demand from agriculture in the early stages of development and exports in the later stages. Export demand is the major component of autonomous demand in an open economy which must match the leakage of income into imports. The level of industrial output will adjust to the level of export demand in relation to the propensity to import, through the working of the Harrod trade multiplier (see Chapter 3).

(vii) A fast rate of growth of exports and output will tend to set up a cumulative process, or virtuous circle of growth, through the link between output growth and productivity growth. The lower costs of production in fast growing countries make it difficult for other (newly industrialising) countries to establish export activities with favourable growth characteristics, except through exceptional industrial enterprise (see Chapter 8).

Kaldor substantiates the role of manufacturing as the 'engine of growth' by showing a strong positive correlation between GDP growth and manufacturing growth across 12 developed countries over the period 1952/4 to 1963/4. This is not simply a spurious correlation resulting from the fact that manufacturing output is a large fraction of total output, since Kaldor also shows a strong correlation between GDP growth and the *excess* of manufacturing growth over non-manufacturing growth and between non-manufacturing output growth and manufacturing growth. These results have been confirmed by other investigators (e.g. Cripps and Tarling, 1973; Thirlwall, 1982a).[1] Moreover, there is no correlation between GDP growth and the growth of either agricultural output or mining. There is a correlation between GDP growth and the growth of services, and the relation is virtually one to one, but Kaldor believes that the direction of causation is almost certainly from the growth of GDP to service activity rather than the other way round, since the demand for most services is derived from the demand for manufacturing output itself. This is an interesting question in the debate on deindustrialisation: to what extent service activities have an autonomous existence and to what extent they are vertically integrated with the process of manufacturing.

What accounts for the fact that the faster manufacturing output grows relatively to GDP, the faster GDP seems to grow? Since differences in output growth rates are largely accounted for by differences in productivity growth, there must be some relationship between the growth of the manufacturing sector and productivity growth in the economy as a whole. There are two main reasons for expecting this. The first is that wherever industrial production and employment expand, labour resources are drawn from other sectors which have open or disguised unemployment, so that the labour transference to manufacturing does not cause a diminution in the output of these sectors and therefore productivity growth increases outside manufacturing. Kaldor's sample of developed countries showed overall productivity growth to be positively associated with employment growth in manufacturing and negatively associated with employment growth outside manufacturing. The second reason for expecting overall productivity growth to be linked with manufacturing growth is the existence of increasing returns in industry, both static and dynamic.

THE VERDOORN LAW AND INCREASING RETURNS TO SCALE

Kaldor (1966b), in his discussion of increasing returns in manufacturing industry, makes reference to what he terms Verdoorn's Law. This law is the close statistical relationship that is often found to occur between the growth of labour productivity and output in both manufacturing and industry (defining the latter as comprising manufacturing, plus construction and public utilities). A very weak, or no relationship at all, is generally found between these two variables for the other sectors of the economy.

Ever since Kaldor's Inaugural Lecture, the Verdoorn Law has been surrounded by considerable controversy. The importance of the law is that it forms the basis of the cumulative causation model of economic growth. This, with the introduction of a balance-of-payments constraint, has been advanced to explain the persistent disparities in the growth rates of the advanced countries and their regions. The law is also an important, though not indispensable, component of the demand orientated approach to economic growth (see Chapter 8 and Kaldor, 1978b, especially the Introduction).

The criticisms have been largely directed at the plausibility or otherwise of the assumptions implicit in Kaldor's interpretation of the law. At one time or another, it has been suggested that the law suffers from: specifying an endogenous variable as a regressor; simultaneous equation bias; the undue influence of an outlying observation; omitted variable bias; an 'errors in variables' problem; and finally, but not least, being spurious. In fact, the debate over the Verdoorn Law would make a good textbook example of the problems that can beset statistical inference! In spite of a number of attempts either to test these assumptions or to specify alternative models, there has not yet been any general agreement as to the seriousness of the various critiques. The purpose of the remainder of this chapter is briefly to outline the debate over the Verdoorn Law and to show that a good deal does, in fact, still remain of Kaldor's second law (as the Verdoorn Law is also sometimes known).

As the title of his inaugural address suggests, Kaldor (1966b) was concerned with explaining why the UK was, at that time, experiencing one of the slowest growth rates of all the advanced countries. In the course of his analysis, he was struck by the close relationship that existed between productivity growth and output growth and which is apparent from a consideration of Table 2.4 (taken from the Inaugural Lecture). It may be seen that a faster growth of output is associated with a faster growth of productivity. In fact, Kaldor went further than this and argued that a faster growth of output *causes* a faster growth of productivity. He called this relationship the Verdoorn Law after the Dutch economist P.J. Verdoorn who had identified this association in a paper published in an obscure Italian journal, *L'Industria*, in 1949. In fact, because of this obscurity, and also because the paper was written in Italian, Verdoorn's work generally went unnoticed until Kaldor first drew attention to it in print. Kaldor, however, did hear Arrow in conversation use earlier the term Verdoorn's Law in connection with models of 'learning by doing' (Thirlwall, 1987, p. 189). But priority perhaps really ought to go to Colin Clark since the relationship seems to have been first discussed in his book *The Conditions of Economic Progress* (1940). Notwithstanding this, it was Kaldor (1966b) who first stressed the importance of the law for the understanding of the determinants of economic growth, and it is from the mid-1970s in response to his lecture (and a critique by Rowthorn, 1975a, discussed below) that much of the work on the law stemmed. (It is true that in the 1950s and 1960s there had been a number of studies confirming the relationship using 'cross-industry' data but the implications for economic growth were never fully realised at the time. See Kennedy, 1971, for a discussion of much of this literature.)

The Verdoorn Law was specified by Kaldor as

$$p = a + bq \tag{2.3}$$

where p and q are the exponential growth rates of productivity and output. The slope coefficient, b, is the 'Verdoorn coefficient'.

Using the data in Table 2.4, we obtained the following regression result:[2]

$$p = \underset{(2.27)}{1.048} + \underset{(6.82)}{0.480q} \qquad \begin{array}{l} \bar{r}^2 = 0.805 \\ SER = 0.681 \end{array}$$

The figures in parentheses are the t statistics and *SER* is the standard error of the regression.

There is a minor problem with the specification of equation (2.3) stemming from the fact that p is definitionally equal to q minus e, where e is the growth of employment. (We use the notation e, rather than ℓ, in keeping with the tradition of the Verdoorn Law literature.) Hence, q appears on both sides of the equation and this will impart a degree of spurious correlation between p and q. Moreover, as Kaldor

Table 2.4   Kaldor's original data: rates of growth of production, employment and productivity in manufacturing, per cent per annum, average 1953–4 to average 1963–4

Country	Production[a]	Employment[b]	Productivity[c]
Japan	13.6	5.8	7.8
Italy[d]	8.1	3.9[e]	4.2
West Germany	7.4	2.8	4.5
Austria[f]	6.4	2.2	4.2
France[g]	5.7	1.8	3.8
Denmark[g]	5.7	2.5[e]	3.2
Netherlands[h]	5.5	1.4	4.1
Belgium	5.1	1.2[e]	3.9
Norway	4.6	0.2	4.4
Canada	3.4	2.1	1.3
UK	3.2	0.4	2.8
US[f]	2.6	0.0	2.6

Notes: [a]GDP in manufacturing, at constant prices.
[b]Wage and salary earners adjusted for changes in weekly manhours.
[c]Output per manhour, derived from the first two columns.
[d]1954/5 to 1963/4.
[e]Incorporates estimated change in weekly manhours.
[f]1955/6 to 1963/4.
[g]1953/4 to 1962/3.
[h]Industrial production including mining.

Source: Kaldor (1966b, table 2).

(1975b, p. 892) pointed out, because of this definitional relationship 'in any situation in which *e* is either zero or a constant there *must* be a perfect correlation between *p* and *q* but one which does not assert anything, since it is the automatic consequence of measuring the same thing twice over' (emphasis in the original). This problem may be easily obviated by re-specifying the Verdoorn Law as:

$$e = a^* + b^*q \tag{2.4}$$

This is the mirror image of equation (2.3) and $b = 1 - b^*$ and $a = -a^*$. The standard errors of b and b^* are identical. We are primarily concerned with testing whether or not b^* is statistically significantly different from unity or, equivalently, whether b significantly differs from zero; both specifications will lead to the same conclusion.

Table 2.5   Verdoorn's original data: rates of growth of output and productivity in manufacturing, per cent per annum, and the Verdoorn Elasticity

Period	Country	Output growth (per cent	Productivity growth per annum)	Verdoorn Elasticity[a] (V)
1913–1930	Switzerland	2.40	1.03	0.43
1841–1907	UK	2.40	0.98	0.41
1907–1930	UK	1.28	0.61[b]	0.47
1869–1899	US	5.61	2.31	0.42
1899–1939	US	3.35	1.91	0.57
1882–1907	Germany	4.38	2.14	0.49
Inter-war period				
1924–1938	Switzerland	5.0	5.3	1.06
1926–1938	Japan	6.7	3.4	0.51
1924–1938	Finland	5.1	3.2	0.63
1927–1938	Hungary	3.4	2.8	0.82
1924–1938	Holland	2.3	2.6	1.13
1924–1938	Norway	2.6	2.5	0.96
1924–1938	Denmark	3.5	1.9	0.54
1927–1938	Poland	1.6	1.9	1.18
1924–1938	UK	1.4	1.5	1.07
1924–1939	US	0.6	1.0	1.67
1924–1938	Canada	1.6	1.0	0.63
1924–1938	Czechoslovakia	0.4	0.7	1.75[c]
1927–1938	Estonia	0.8	0.4	0.50
1924–1938	Italy	0.8	0.2	0.25

Notes: [a]Defined as the ratio of productivity to output growth (i.e. $V \equiv p/q$).
   [b]Rounding up Verdoorn's original value.
   [c]Verdoorn did not report any figure here, presumably because he did not consider the value of 1.75 to be plausible.

Source: Verdoorn (1949, table 1).

Regressing e on q using Kaldor's data provides confirmation of these arguments:

$$e = \begin{array}{cc} -1.048 & + \ 0.520q \\ (-2.27) & (7.39) \end{array} \qquad \begin{array}{l} \bar{r}^2 = 0.830 \\ SER = 0.681 \end{array}$$

The t statistic based on the null hypothesis that b^* does not differ from unity is 6.82 and this is the same value as the t statistic of the Verdoorn coefficient, b, based on the null hypothesis that it does not differ from zero. The value of the t statistic is significant at the 95 per cent confidence level and so b^* is significantly less than unity, and b significantly greater than zero. While Kaldor preferred equation (2.4) to equation (2.3), our main interest is on the determinants of productivity growth and we generally use the original Verdoorn specification. However, when this is the case we also report $\bar{r}^2_{adj}$ which is the $\bar{r}^2$ adjusted, or corrected, for the element of spurious correlation, i.e. it is the correlation coefficient obtained when e is regressed on q.

The data used by Kaldor contain only 12 observations which does not provide many degrees of freedom. However, Cripps and Tarling (1973) have provided data for the same 12 advanced countries for the various growth cycles of the postwar period up until 1970 which has enabled the Verdoorn Law to be estimated with a greater number of observations. Cripps and Tarling chose as initial and terminal years of the growth cycles years when output was at a peak and where there was full capacity utilisation to minimise the influence of short-run cyclical factors.

The period 1951–65 contains approximately three such subperiods and Kaldor's result is confirmed using these data (see Table 2.6). (These results were computed by us since Cripps and Tarling specified and estimated the Verdoorn Law in a different form, regressing productivity growth on *employment* growth – this is discussed below.) It can be seen that the Verdoorn Law broke down in the period 1965–70. The 'adjusted' $\bar{r}^2$ falls to 0.092 and the estimate of the slope coefficient obtained in regressing e on q is statistically insignificant. This, of course, does not imply constant returns to scale, but rather that there is no statistical relationship between the two variables e and q. It follows that no inferences can be drawn about the degree of returns to scale. McCombie (1982c) found that the law also broke down in the subsequent periods, 1970–3 and 1973–9. Michl (1985) also estimated the Verdoorn Law for the advanced countries for a number of sub-periods from 1950 to 1980 using a similar, although not identical, sample of advanced countries to Cripps and Tarling. In constructing the growth of productivity, Michl used the growth of output per hour rather than the growth of output per wage and salary earners, which was used by Cripps and Tarling. This may explain the fact that while the goodness-of-fit of the Verdoorn Law deteriorated in the growth cycles after 1960 (e.g. the SER increased) the estimate of the Verdoorn coefficient still remained between 0.680 and 0.579 and was statistically significantly greater than zero. This implies that the slope coefficient of e on q is significantly less than unity. Never-

Table 2.6   The Verdoorn law ($p = a + bq$): regression results

Source and period	$\hat{a}$	$\hat{b}$	SER	$\bar{r}^2$	$\bar{r}^2_{adj}$
Cripps and Tarling (1973)					
(i) 1950–65[a]	1.313	0.475	0.787	0.762	0.797
n = 32	(4.00)	(10.02)			
(ii) 1965–70	0.163	0.841[b]	0.997	0.841	0.092
n = 12	(0.24)	(7.71)			
Michl (1985)					
(iii) 1950–80[a]	2.568	0.479	1.448	0.528[c]	n.a.
n = 71	(8.01)	(8.80)			
Verdoorn (1949)					
(iv) 1924–38	0.480	0.606	0.779	0.688	0.470
n = 14	(1.36)	(5.44)			

Notes: [a]Pooled sub-periods.
   [b]The Verdoorn coefficient from regressing e on q is not significantly different from zero at the 95% confidence level.
   [c]r^2.

   Countries in sample:
   Cripps and Tarling – Japan, West Germany, Italy, France, Netherlands, Denmark, Austria, Canada, Norway, Belgium, UK, US.
   Michl – Same as Cripps and Tarling except Austria is replaced by Sweden.
   Verdoorn – See Table 2.5.

   For exact periods see Cripps and Tarling (1973, appendix 3), Michl (1985, table 1), and Table 2.5 above.

Sources: Cripps and Tarling (1973), Michl (1985), Verdoorn (1949).

theless, the slope coefficient of e on q is *not* significantly different from *zero* at the 95 per cent confidence level for three of the four post-1960 subperiods; namely 1960–5; 1970–4; and 1974–80. These results are not reported by Michl who therefore gives the impression that the Verdoorn Law is more robust than it actually is. Pooling all the periods, however, does give confirmation of the Law; the Verdoorn coefficient is 0.479 and is significantly greater than zero at the 95 per cent confidence level.

   Table 2.5 reports Verdoorn's original data, and the estimation of the Verdoorn equation using these statistics is included in Table 2.6. They are mentioned more for historical interest than anything else because the reliability of the data cannot be guaranteed and much of the data are for the years which include the Great Depression.[3]

KALDOR'S INTERPRETATION OF THE VERDOORN LAW

The Verdoorn Law shows that an increase in the growth of output by one percentage point increases the growth of productivity by roughly one-half of a percentage point and the growth of employment by a similar amount. Kaldor interprets this as evidence of substantial economies of scale. His implicit argument is that if there were constant returns to scale we should expect an increase in output to be accompanied by a proportionate increase in the growth of labour. In this case, there would not be any association between p and q and the Verdoorn coefficient would not be statistically significantly different from zero. A corollary of this is that the alternative specification of the Verdoorn Law (regressing e on q) should have a slope coefficient that does not differ significantly from unity. For there to be increasing returns to scale we should expect the slope coefficient of e on q to be significantly less than unity. As Kaldor (1975b, p. 693) stated:

> I conclude . . . that a *sufficient* condition for the presence of static or dynamic economies of scale is the existence of a statistically significant relationship between e and q, with a regression coefficient which is significantly less than 1.
>
> If this condition is not satisfied, there are several possibilities. First, that there *is* a significant relationship, but the coefficient of e on q is either not significantly different from unity or is significantly greater than unity. This latter case is sufficient to reject the increasing-returns-to-scale hypothesis.
>
> Second, that there is *no* significant relationship between e and q at all – and this is consistent with all kinds of interpretations. It is in this second case that the Verdoorn Law can be said to have 'broken down' in the period 1965–70.

Kaldor did not discuss in any great depth the rationale for the Verdoorn Law, presumably because in presenting his arguments in a lecture he was constrained by time. But it is clear that he regarded the law as a form of the technical progress function (McCombie, 1982a). Kaldor had long argued that it was fallacious to make a distinction between movements along the production function due to capital deepening and shifts of the function due to technical progress. As an alternative he proposed the technical progress function which originally was specified as a non-linear relationship between the *growth* of labour productivity and that of the capital–labour ratio. In steady state growth, this may be approximated by a linear function. Kaldor (1966b) wrote with respect to the Verdoorn Law: 'It is a dynamic rather than a static relationship – between the rates of change of productivity and output, rather than between the *level* of productivity and the *scale* of output – primarily because technical progress enters into it, and is not just a reflection of the economies of large-scale production.'[4]

Static increasing returns relate to the size and scale of production units and are a characteristic largely of manufacturing where in the process of doubling the linear dimensions of equipment, the surface increases by the square and the volume by the cube (e.g. to make a box to hold twice as much does not require twice as much material). Dynamic increasing returns refer to economies brought about by 'induced' technical progress; learning by doing; external economies in production, and so on. Kaldor draws inspiration from Allyn Young's pioneering paper on 'Increasing Returns and Economic Progress' (1928), with its emphasis on increasing returns as a macro-economic phenomenon. It was Young's contention that, because economies of scale result from increased product differentiation, new processes, new subsidiary industries and so on, they cannot be discerned adequately by observing the effects of variations in the size of an *individual* firm or of a *particular* industry. Economies of scale and increasing returns derive from general industrial expansion which should be seen as an interrelated whole, or as an interaction *between* activities. For example, an increase in the demand for product X may make it profitable to use more machinery in its production which reduces both the cost of X *and* the cost of machinery, which then makes the use of machinery profitable in other industries and so on. The precise conditions in Young's model for a cumulative expansion to take place are that there are increasing returns and that the demand for each commodity is price elastic, so that proportionately more is bought as its exchange value falls, and hence proportionately more is offered in exchange (in a model of reciprocal demand). Take the example of two industries – steel and textile production. Steel is subject to increasing returns, its supply increases and its exchange value falls. If the demand for steel is price elastic, textile producers demand proportionately more steel (and offer proportionately more textiles in exchange). Textile production is subject to increasing returns; the exchange value of textiles then falls, and if demand is elastic steel producers demand proportionately more textiles (and offer proportionately more steel in exchange). Under these circumstances, there are no limits to the process of expansion except the limits beyond which demand is not elastic and returns do not increase.

It was Adam Smith (1776) who first introduced into economics the notion of increasing returns, based upon the concept of the division of labour. He saw the division of labour, or specialisation, as the very basis of a social economy. If there are no advantages from specialisation, everyone might as well be their own Robinson Crusoe. The principle of the division of labour also lay at the heart of Smith's vision of economic progress as a self-generating process (far removed from the later pessimism of the nineteenth-century classical economists and from the later statics of the neoclassical school). Productivity depends on the division of labour, which in turn depends on the size of the market. As the market expands, productivity increases, but the increase in productivity resulting from a larger market in turn enlarges the market for other things, and this causes productivity in other industries to rise. As Young (1928) observed, 'Adam Smith's famous theorem amounts to saying that the division of labour depends in large part on the division of labour. [But] this is more than mere tautology. It means that the counter forces, which are continually defeating the forces which make for equilibrium, are more pervasive and deep rooted than we commonly realise . . . change becomes progressive and propagates itself in a cumulative way.'

INTRODUCING THE CONTRIBUTION OF CAPITAL

As noted in McCombie (1983) and McCombie and de Ridder (1984) there is a problem with the law because the initial specification excludes the contribution of the growth of the capital stock. Clearly, the growth of the capital stock (proxying for the growth of capital services) will be an important factor in determining the growth of productivity and we should expect that a faster growth of capital would, *ceteris paribus*, lead to a faster growth of productivity. We may demonstrate the implications by first considering a Cobb–Douglas production function, expressed in dynamic form:

$$q = \lambda + \alpha e + \beta k \tag{2.5}$$

where λ is exogenous technical progress, k is the growth of capital services and α and β are the elasticities of output with respect to labour and capital.

It is straightforward to manipulate equation (2.5) to give:

$$p = \frac{\lambda}{\alpha} + \frac{(\alpha - 1)}{\alpha} q + \frac{\beta}{\alpha} k \tag{2.6}$$

and a more correctly specified Verdoorn Law is given by:

$$p = a_1 + b_1 q + b_2 k \tag{2.7}$$

denoting now the Verdoorn coefficient by b_1.

It can be seen that unless q and k are orthogonal the original Verdoorn coefficient (b) from equation (2.3) will be biased by the omission of k. However, this may not be a serious problem as it is one of Kaldor's 'stylised facts' that the capital–output ratio of the advanced countries has remained roughly constant over time.[5] If this is the case, $q = k$ and the estimate of b from the original specification of the law is:

$$\hat{b} = (\alpha + \beta - 1)/\alpha \simeq \tfrac{1}{2} \tag{2.8}$$

Let us assume that the output elasticities for manufacturing, α and β, are equal. In these circumstances the degree of returns to scale, v, is equal to 1.33. Alternatively, if we assume that the elasticity of labour is greater than that of capital, say $\alpha = 3\beta$, it transpires that v equals 1.60. Both these estimates indicate very substantial static and dynamic economies of scale (including induced technical progress), but, as we shall see, is in accord with other estimates of the Verdoorn Law where the growth of the capital stock is explicitly included. However, if the growth of the capital stock were one-and-a-half times that of output and $\alpha = \beta$, a Verdoorn coefficient of one-half would imply *constant returns to scale*. This demonstrates that it is important to include, either explicitly or implicitly, the contribution of the growth of the capital stock in the analysis.

Kaldor (1966b) was aware of this problem, but it was not until the mid-1980s that estimates of the capital stock for a number of advanced countries became readily available. He therefore used the incremental capital–output ratio (ICOR) to explain the residuals obtained from the regression of the Verdoorn Law. The ICOR is defined as the ratio of gross investment to output, divided by the growth of output. He found that, with the exception of Canada, investment behaviour as evidenced by the ICOR could explain the deviations of the individual countries' actual productivity growth from their predicted values. In his extended lectures at Cornell University in the following year, Kaldor (1967) included the gross investment–output ratio (I/Q) explicitly in the Verdoorn equation as a proxy for k. Since net investment (i.e. gross investment less scrappings) is definitionally equal to the increase in the capital stock, ΔK, the relationship between the k and I/Q is given by:

$$k = \frac{\Delta K}{K} \simeq \frac{I}{Q}\frac{Q}{K} \qquad (2.9)$$

A possible shortcoming of this proxy is that the *gross* investment–output ratio makes no allowance for either scrapping (and so is a poor proxy for the growth of the gross capital stock) or depreciation (and is therefore an even worse proxy for the growth of the net capital stock). (However, it will be recalled from Chapter 1 that Maurice Scott actually sees this as a reason for preferring the gross investment–output ratio to estimates of k based on the perpetual inventory method.) It also has to be assumed that the capital–output ratio does not differ greatly between countries.

Kaldor (1967) found that the I/Q ratio (expressed as a percentage) is insignificant when included in the Verdoorn equation, but this changes once Canada is excluded. The result for the *industrial* sector for the remaining eleven countries over the period 1953/4 to 1963/4 is:

$$p_{IND} = 0.709 + 0.268q_{IND} + 0.073(I/Q)_{IND} \quad R^2 = 0.960$$
$$\text{(n.a.)} \quad (5.70) \quad\quad (4.29)$$

(The R^2_{adj} and SER are not available.)

If we follow Kaldor (1978a, p. 129) and assume the capital–output ratio is 3, the estimated regression coefficients imply a scale elasticity of output with respect to both capital and labour of 1.53. A similar result is obtained using Cripps and Tarling's (1973) data for *manufacturing* for the period 1950–65:

$$p = 0.816 + 0.403q + 0.050\ I/Q \quad \bar{R}^2 = 0.843\ \bar{R}^2_{adj} = 0.863$$
$$(2.71) \quad (9.02) \quad (3.68) \quad\quad SER = 0.659$$

However, the inclusion of I/Q in the Verdoorn equation for the period 1960–65 does not improve the goodness-of-fit and the coefficient of I/Q is statistically insignificant at the 95 per cent confidence level.

The publication of data on capital stocks for several advanced countries by the OECD (*Flows and Stocks of Fixed Capital*, Paris, 1983, 1985, and 1987) makes it possible to estimate the Verdoorn Law explicitly including the the growth of capital. This was undertaken by Michl (1985) and we extend his work. The Verdoorn Law was estimated for seven countries, namely, Australia, Canada, Norway, Sweden, West Germany, the US and the UK, for sub-periods over the period 1955–87. The sub-periods were approximately 1955–60; 1960–5; 1965–70; 1970–3; 1973–9; and 1979–87. It was found that it was not possible to refute the hypothesis that all sub-periods are drawn from the same population and, consequently, the estimates of the various specifications of the Verdoorn Law are presented for all the sub-periods pooled. The results are reported in Table 2.7.

Not surprisingly in view of the results reported earlier, it is found that the simple Verdoorn Law gives a Verdoorn coefficient of 0.587, which is statistically significantly greater than zero at the 99 per cent confidence level.

However, when the contribution of the growth of capital is included directly into the Verdoorn equation there is severe multicollinearity between q and k. (The r^2 obtained by regressing k on q exceeds that of the multiple regression.) This means that it is not possible to obtain directly an estimate of the degree of returns to scale because the coefficients of q and k are not well-determined. Nevertheless, this is not true of the sum of their coefficients and this makes it possible to gain some idea of the magnitude of the returns to scale.

Defining the coefficient of q as b_1 and of k as b_2 it follows from equation (2.6) that:

$$(\alpha + \beta - 1)/\beta = \hat{b}_1 + \hat{b}_2 \tag{2.10}$$

The estimate of $\hat{b}_1 + \hat{b}_2$ is 0.594. It can be seen from equation (2.10) that a sufficient condition for increasing returns is for $\hat{b}_1 + \hat{b}_2$ to be significantly greater than zero. This is the case, since the t statistic associated with the sum of the coefficients is 9.05. To determine the degree of returns to scale (v), we need to make some assumption about the relative sizes of α and β. If we assume, as before, that $\alpha = 3\beta$, v equals 1.80. This may seem implausibly large but it should be remembered it also captures the effect of induced technical progress.

Table 2.7   The Verdoorn law: 7 advanced countries 1955–87

Regressand	Intercept	q	k	k-e	SER	$\bar{r}$ $(\bar{R}^2)$	$\bar{r}^2_{adj}$ $(\bar{R}^2_{adj})$	v
p	1.928 (7.16)	0.587 (10.13)	–	–	1.036	0.708	0.543	–
p	1.878 (5.57)	0.562 (8.58)	0.032 (0.25)	–	1.048	0.701	0.532	1.80*
p	0.536 (1.62)	0.445 (8.58)	–	0.400 (5.38)	0.799	0.826	n.m.	1.80*
tfp	1.168 (5.06)	0.329 (6.62)	–	–	0.888	0.505	0.812	1.49*

Notes: For definition of variables, see text.
Number of observations is 43.
$\bar{r}^2_{adj}$ ($\bar{R}^2_{adj}$) is the $\bar{r}^2$ ($\bar{R}^2$) adjusted to remove the spurious correlation, i.e. it is the $\bar{r}^2$ ($\bar{R}^2$) when e, rather than p, is the regressand.
n.m. denotes not meaningful. It is not possible to adjust the $\bar{R}^2$.
* denotes significantly greater than unity at the 99% confidence level.
k is calculated over the period that q and e are calculated, lagged one year (see footnote 3).
e is the growth of total hours worked or the growth of employment adjusted for changes in average hours worked.

Sources: Michl (1985); *National Accounts*, OECD (various years); *Main Economic Indicators, Historical Series*, OECD, Paris; *Flows and Stocks of Fixed Capital, 1955–80* and *1960–1985* and *1962–1987*, OECD, Paris.

Michl (1985) chose a different specification and preferred to regress the growth of productivity on output growth and the growth of the capital–labour ratio $(k - e)$. From the estimates in Table 2.7, it can be seen that this overcomes the problem of multicollinearity.[6] The degree of returns to scale is given by $v = 1/(1 - \hat{b}_3)$ where $\hat{b}_3$ is the coefficient of q. This gives a value of 1.80 which is identical to the value obtained above. Notwithstanding this, Michl's equation is poorly specified. This may be seen more easily by considering the Verdoorn Law with e as the regressand. This specification may be written in a general form as $e = f(\lambda, q, k - e)$. The regressors include both output growth and the growth of *both* inputs. The fact that the coefficients of k and minus e are constrained to be equal does not remove the problem. Suppose that, for example, k does not vary, then Michl's specification will, in effect, consist of regressing e on itself (which, by definition, will explain all the variation in the regressand!) and on q. This problem is obviated by the previous specification e (or p) $= f(\lambda, q, k)$. But even this is not wholly satisfactory, because it assumes that the growth of the capital stock is an exogenous factor in economic growth, whereas it can be argued, as Kaldor (1968) does, that it is largely endogenous, determined by the growth of output itself.

> Because savings and capital accumulation in a capitalist economy do not represent an independent variable – a faster rate of growth induces a higher rate of investment; it also brings about a higher share of savings to finance investment, through its effect on the share of profits. It is, therefore, more correct to say that a fast rate of growth of capital accumulation is a *symptom* of the fast rate of growth than a cause of it. (emphasis in the original)

This suggests that it makes more sense to consider the growth of both inputs as endogenous. One possibility is to specify the Verdoorn law as the relationship between the growth of total factor productivity and output growth (McCombie and de Ridder, 1984). The Cobb–Douglas production function may be written in terms of growth rates as:

$$q = \lambda + v[ae + (1 - a)k] \qquad (2.11)$$

where a and $(1 - a)$ are the shares of labour and capital in output. Under these circumstances, the Verdoorn Law becomes:

$$tfp = q - [ae + (1 - a)k] = \lambda/v + [(v - 1)/v]q \qquad (2.12)$$

where *tfp* is the growth of total factor productivity.

We are, of course, aware that the neoclassical assumptions normally associated with the concept of total factor productivity are somewhat at variance with Kaldor's whole methodology, but the results may be of some interest – if only to those of the neoclassical persuasion. (As we shall see, Verdoorn himself took a very neoclassical view of the Law.) It may be seen from Table 2.7 that the results suggest a somewhat lower value of returns to scale of 1.49.

'WHAT REMAINS OF KALDOR'S LAW?' – ROWTHORN'S CRITIQUE

Nearly a decade after Kaldor (1966b) had presented his inaugural lecture, Rowthorn (1975a) rekindled interest in the law by suggesting that it was incorrectly specified. When this was corrected, he argued, Kaldor's data provided no support for the hypothesis of increasing returns to scale. Consequently, the question Rowthorn posed in the title of his paper, 'What Remains of Kaldor's Law?', was obviously intended to be rhetorical! Rowthorn's critique was straightforward. In his inaugural lecture, Kaldor had argued, as we have seen, that manufacturing productivity growth was, apart from a small exogenous component, largely a function of the growth of manufacturing output. The problem with the UK economy, he contended, was that it suffers from 'premature maturity'. By virtue of the UK's early industrialisation, it had a small highly efficient agricultural sector and there was no scope for any significant intersectoral transfer of labour from agriculture to manufacturing. The result, as Kaldor (1966b) noted, was that: 'In postwar Britain periods of faster growth in manufacturing invariably led to severe labour shortages and which continued for some time after production reached its cyclical peak – in fact, on almost every occasion, employment continued to rise after output had begun to fall. All this suggests that a higher rate of growth could not have been maintained unless more manpower had been made available to the manufacturing industry.'

Rowthorn argued, however, that if output growth is constrained by labour growth, it follows that the Verdoorn Law should be specified as:

$$p = c + de \qquad (2.13)$$

The traditional Verdoorn Law is mis-specified because the *endogenous* variable, q, is used as a regressor which violates the assumptions underlying ordinary least squares. This will produce a biased estimate of the Verdoorn coefficient. Indeed, the subsequent study by the Cambridge economists, Cripps and Tarling (1973), actually used the specification of equation (2.13) regressing p on e rather than on q, as Kaldor had done.[7]

To avoid confusion, Rowthorn termed equation (2.13) 'Kaldor's Law', but for reasons that will become apparent below, we prefer the term 'Rowthorn's Specification'.

Cripps and Tarling's results also provided support, so it seemed, for the hypothesis of increasing returns over the period 1950–65, since the estimate of d was statistically significantly different from unity. The coefficient took a value of 0.559 with a t statistic of 4.10. (This implies a Verdoorn coefficient of 0.345. Note that the latter is *not* identical to the value obtained by directly estimating the Verdoorn Law, which as we have seen from Table 2.5, is 0.475 with a t statistic of 10.02. This is for the reason, noted above, that the estimation of the Verdoorn Law will lead to a biased estimate if e is the correct regressor.) Kaldor's data give a value of d, obtained by regressing p on e, of 0.626 with a t statistic of 2.85.

The difficulty for Kaldor's thesis was that, as Rowthorn (1975a) demonstrated, the significance of the regression coefficient depended crucially on the inclusion of one country in the sample, namely Japan. If Japan is omitted the coefficient d becomes statistically insignificant, using either Cripps and Tarling's or Kaldor's data. Rowthorn further argued that at the beginning of the 1950s Japan was very much a 'backward' country and a great part of its productivity growth was due to a 'catching-up' process as it imported both new technology and superior organisational techniques from the more advanced countries. Thus a large part of Japan's above average productivity growth was due to this factor and not simply to increasing returns to scale accruing from a fast growth of employment. Consequently there are strong *a priori* grounds for not including Japan in the sample. (Alternatively, the sample could be widened to include other less developed countries – but again there is no significant relationship between p and e even with Japan in the sample (see Rowthorn, 1975a, especially figure 1).)

Kaldor's (1975b) reply to Rowthorn was telling. First, he never implied that the manufacturing growth of *all* the advanced countries was constrained by the growth of employment, but only in the case of the UK. As he explicitly stated in his 1967 lectures at Cornell University: 'Inelasticity in the supply of labour seems to me the main constraint limiting the growth potential of the United Kingdom in a way which is not true of any other advanced country, with the possible exception of Germany in the last few years' (Kaldor, 1967, p. 42). Moreover, Kaldor argued that he had since changed his mind about the growth of the UK's manufacturing sector being constrained by the growth of its labour supply. Although he did not explicitly say so in the inaugural lecture, he considered that in the other advanced countries much of the service sector exhibited surplus labour and he now believed this to be true of the UK. 'Statistical studies that have come to light [Kaldor here footnotes Sleeper (1970)] make it doubtful whether I was correct in thinking that . . . the growth of manufacturing industry in the United Kingdom was constrained by labour shortages other than in a purely short-term sense – e.g. of not having sufficient skilled labour in engineering to sustain a rapid expansion of engineering production (which from a long-run point of view is itself a consequence of a low trend rate of growth of demand).' In fact, he became convinced that ultimately the growth of the United Kingdom was constrained by its repeated balance of payments crises and the poor performance of its exports, and he had considerable sympathy with the central tenet of this book. The upshot of all this was that Kaldor (1975b) maintained that the *original* specification of the Verdoorn Law was correct and this still implied substantial economies of scale *even when Japan is omitted*. Using Kaldor's (1966b) data, the estimation of the Verdoorn Law without Japan gives:

$$p = \begin{matrix} 1.359 \\ (1.91) \end{matrix} + \begin{matrix} 0.417q \\ (3.22) \end{matrix} \qquad \begin{matrix} \bar{r}^2 = 0.484 \\ SER = 0.704 \end{matrix}$$

or, equivalently,

$$e = \begin{matrix} -1.359 \\ (-1.91) \end{matrix} + \begin{matrix} 0.583q \\ (4.51) \end{matrix} \qquad \begin{matrix} \bar{r}^2 = 0.659 \\ SER = 0.704 \end{matrix}$$

The goodness of fit is somewhat reduced by the exclusion of Japan but the results still suggest increasing returns to scale, at least by Kaldor's criterion.

We are thus left with a paradox; if it is assumed that output growth is exogenous, the results imply substantial economies of scale in manufacturing, but if employment growth is assumed to be the predetermined variable there is no such finding. The statistical reason for this is quite straightforward and may be seen most easily by considering the two specifications expressed as:

$$e = -a + b^*q, \quad \text{where } b^* = (1 - b)$$
$$\text{(the Verdoorn Law)} \qquad (2.14)$$

and

$$q = c + d^*e, \quad \text{where } d^* = (1 + d)$$
$$\text{(Rowthorn's Specification)} \qquad (2.15)$$

The relationship between the ordinary least squares estimates of b^* and d^* are given by:

$$\hat{b}^* . \hat{d}^* = r^2 \qquad (2.16)$$

If the r^2 is one-half, it can be seen that a value of b^* of one-half will be associated with a value of d^* of unity (rather than two, which is the reciprocal of b^*). If we were to plot e against q, the ordinary least squares procedure is to minimise the sum of the squared residuals measured *vertically*. The regression of q on e minimises the sum of the squared residuals measured *horizontally* on the same diagram. It is only when there is a perfect fit (the correlation coefficient equals unity) that it will be immaterial which of the two specifications is used. Given that the fit is never perfect, it can be seen that Rowthorn's Specification will always provide a lower estimate of the degree of increasing returns to scale, and often it will refute the hypothesis of increasing returns to scale. (Rowthorn found that when he reworked the *cross-industry* studies undertaken in the 1950s and 1960s to determine the slope coefficient of the regression of p (or q) on e, it did indeed prove to be the case that nearly always no support for increasing returns to scale could be found.)[8]

THE DIFFUSION OF INNOVATIONS AND THE SPURIOUS VERDOORN LAW

Even though the exclusion of Japan from the sample of countries does not seriously affect the Verdoorn Law using the original specification, it is possible that the 'catch-up' phenomenon could be responsible for producing the law. This possibility is demonstrated in Figure 2.1 which shows how a spurious Verdoorn Law may be engendered even if constant returns to scale prevail, but there are significant differences in 'exogenous' productivity growth (McCombie, 1983). These differences may be due to, for example, the diffusion of innovations (Gomulka, 1971) from the more, to less, advanced countries, or differences in trade union restrictive practices which affect the adoption of new techniques of production (Kilpatrick and Lawson, 1980). With no economies of scale, there exists no relationship between p and q for an individual country, and the true Verdoorn Law is given by the horizontal lines. However, 'exogenous' productivity growth (λ) varies between each country for the reasons

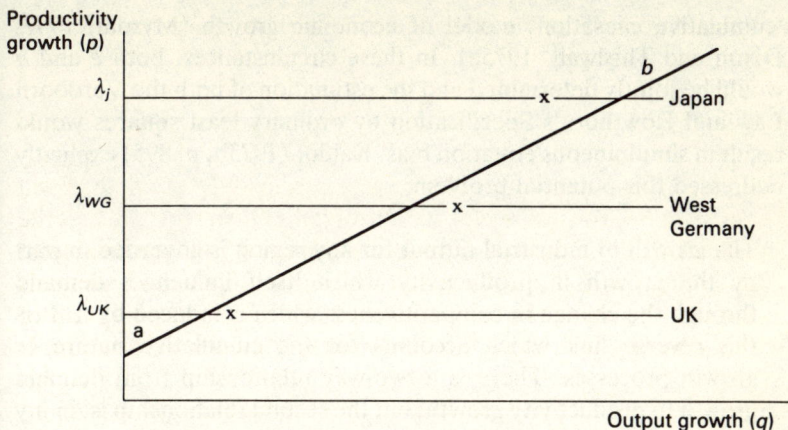

Figure 2.1   The 'Spurious Verdoorn Law'

noted above. The spurious Verdoorn Law is obtained when p is regressed on q using cross-country data (the line ab in Figure 2.1). It occurs because those countries with the fastest growth of productivity also have the fastest growth of output. This may be either coincidental or because a faster growth of productivity has a causal effect on the growth of output (see the next section). The argument is also applicable if, alternatively, we consider the relationship between productivity and employment growth. While it is likely that much of Japan's rapid early postwar productivity growth was due to this catching-up process, it is by no means clear that it was an important feature in the growth of the remaining advanced countries, as we argued in Chapter 1.

THE VERDOORN COEFFICIENT AND SOURCES OF BIAS

The absence of a supply constraint is a necessary but not a sufficient condition for output growth to be treated as exogenous. Even if there were surplus labour, it is also necessary that there should be no feedback from the growth of productivity to that of output. Such a reverse causation could happen if a faster growth of productivity led to an improvement in the rate of change of relative export prices. This, in turn, could stimulate the growth of demand for the country's exports which would lead to an increase in the growth of output through the super-multiplier. Such a mechanism is at the heart of the 'cumulative causation' model of economic growth (Myrdal, 1957; Dixon and Thirlwall, 1975a). In these circumstances, both e and q would be jointly determined and the estimation of both the Verdoorn Law and Rowthorn's Specification by ordinary least squares would result in simultaneous equation bias. Kaldor (1975b, p. 895) explicitly addressed this potential problem:

> The growth of industrial output for any region is governed in part by the growth in productivity which itself influences demand through the change in competitiveness which is induced by it. It is this reverse link which accounts for the cumulative nature of growth processes. There is a two-way relationship from demand growth to productivity growth; but the second relationship is, in my view, far less regular and systematic than the first.

But as Rowthorn (1975b, p. 898) was quick to point out this 'hardly squares with his [Kaldor's] own apparent vision of capitalist development as a continuous interaction between supply and demand'. While Kaldor (1975b) pointed out that the correlation between prices and output growth 'is not perfect' (to use Rowthorn's words), Rowthorn countered by noting that 'the correlation between productivity and output is not very high and does not require a very strong correlation between prices and output to explain it'.

It is one of the central tenets of this book that changes in international relative prices do not explain very much of the international differences in the growth of exports, and so we have rather more sympathy with Kaldor's position than Rowthorn's. Nevertheless, a faster growth of productivity could have a feedback effect in improving a country's non-price competitiveness, which we argue is crucial in explaining differences in countries' performance in overseas markets. This is, nevertheless, likely to be a very long-term effect, but it still admits the possibility of simultaneous equation bias in the estimation of the Verdoorn Law.

Furthermore, Rowthorn pointed out that once the labour supply to manufacturing ceases to be perfectly elastic, so that the manufacturing sector has to attract additional labour by offering higher wages, output growth cannot be deemed to be exogenous, independent of the conditions of the labour supply. The position could only be resolved by estimating the Verdoorn Law in a simultaneous equation model which also explicitly modelled the supply side.

Finally, as the Verdoorn Law is a production relation we should expect a causation from the growth of inputs to that of output for purely technological reasons.

The question is not whether or not simultaneous equation bias exists but how serious a problem it is. We have seen that if the r^2 is unity then we have no problem; both the Verdoorn Law and Rowthorn's Specification will produce identical results, i.e $b^* = 1/d^*$. This is an example of Wold's 'proximity theorem', which states that if the ratio of the standard error of the error term to that of the regressor is small, the asymptotic bias will be negligible, even if there is a high correlation between the error term and the regressor. This result was generalised by Wold and Faxer (1957) to the case of multiple regression.

Rowthorn's critique, therefore, results, to a large extent, from the poor statistical fit of the Verdoorn Law, after Japan has been excluded from the sample. If regression produced a very close fit, then it would make little difference to the estimate of the degree of returns to scale whether q or e is assumed to be the regressor. (Rowthorn, though, did not express it precisely this way.) To put this another way, if the Verdoorn Law gave a perfect fit, it would be immaterial which variable, q or e, was used as a regressor. But since the fit is not perfect, the way the equation is normalised does matter. Regressing p on q suggests substantial increasing returns to scale while regressing p on e does not. But we have seen that the poor statistical fit results largely from the omission of the growth of the capital stock. It is therefore instructive to see whether the discrepancy between the two specifications arises when the growth of the capital stock is included in the regression. We therefore estimated Rowthorn's Specification using Cripps and Tarling's data and included the I/Q ratio as a proxy for the growth of the capital stock. The results were as follows:

Period 1950–65

Including Japan (n = 30)

$$p = \ \ 1.688 \ + \ 0.455e \ + \ 0.091 \ I/Q \qquad \bar{R}^2 = 0.617 \ \bar{R}^2_{adj} = 0.888$$
$$\ \ \ \ \ \ (4.02) \ \ \ \ (4.17) \ \ \ \ \ (4.73) \qquad\qquad SER = 1.028$$

Excluding Japan (n = 28)

$$p = \ \ 1.915 \ + \ 0.313e \ + \ 0.096 \ I/Q \qquad \bar{R}^2 = 0.319 \ \bar{R}^2_{adj} = 0.683$$
$$\ \ \ \ \ \ (3.04) \ \ \ \ (1.67) \ \ \ \ \ (3.48) \qquad\qquad SER = 1.375$$

Excluding Japan reduces the goodness of fit as may be seen from the increase in the *SER* and the fall in the $\bar{R}^2_{adj}$. The coefficient of *e* falls from 0.455 to 0.313 and the latter value is not significantly different from zero at the 95 per cent confidence level. However, our main concern is with the size of returns to scale.

Rowthorn's Specification with the growth of capital included in the equation is:

$$p = \lambda + (\alpha - 1)e + \beta k \tag{2.17}$$

It should be noted that unless there are increasing returns to scale to employment alone, the coefficient of *e* will be negative.

If we follow Kaldor again and assume a capital–output ratio of 3, with Japan in the sample $v = 1.73$. The *t* statistic based on the null hypothesis that *v* is unity is 6.42, which refutes the hypothesis. Excluding Japan causes *v* to fall to 1.60 and the associated *t* statistic is 2.90 which again confirms that *v* is significantly greater than unity. Both these values are close to those obtained from the Verdoorn Law and hence considerably reduces the force of Rowthorn's strictures. (Including the *I/Q* ratio did not improve the fit for 1960–5 when the Verdoorn Law and Rowthorn's Specification both broke down.)

Table 2.8 reports the results using sub-periods over the period 1955–87 *with Japan included in the sample*, since excluding Japan does not, in this case, statistically significantly affect the results. Unlike the case of the Verdoorn Law, it was found that a dummy variable to capture the post-1973 slowdown was statistically significant and so with this specification at least part of the slowdown still remains to be explained. The specification of regressing *p* on *e* gives a coefficient that is not significantly different from zero which, by Kaldor's criterion, implies constant returns to scale. Introducing *k* into the equation increases the goodness-of-fit and *v* takes a value of 1.17. However, not only is this considerably less than the comparable Verdoorn estimate of 1.80 (see Table 2.7), but it does not differ significantly from unity. (The value of the *t* statistic based on the null hypothesis that *v* is significantly different from unity is 1.09, which refutes the hypothesis at the 95 per cent confidence level.) The last regression reported in Table 2.8 is that of output growth on the growth of total factor inputs (*tfi*) where the latter is defined as ($ae + (1 - a)k$) and *a* is the share of labour in total output, i.e. $tfi \equiv q - tfp$. The degree of returns to scale is 1.08, but again this is considerably less than the comparable estimate from the Verdoorn specification

Table 2.8   Rowthorn's specification: 7 advanced countries, 1955–87
(pooled sub-periods)

Regressand	Intercept	Dummy	e	k	tfi	SER	$\bar{r}^2$ $(\bar{R}^2)$	$\bar{r}^2_{adj}$ $(\bar{R}^2_{adj})$	v
p	4.817 (13.15)	−1.605 (−2.32)	0.021 (0.09)	–	–	1.773	0.143	0.589	–
p	1.264 (2.20)	−0.845 (−1.74)	−0.516 (−2.30)	0.683 (6.87)	–	1.208	0.602	0.808	1.17¶
q	2.694 (7.99)	−0.955 (−2.21)	–	–	1.083 (10.27)	1.144	0.828	n.a	1.08¶

Notes: The number of observations equals 43.
The sample includes Japan.
¶ denotes that the value of v does not differ from unity at the 95% confidence levels.
Dummy takes a value of 0 for 1955–73 and 1 for 1973–87.
n.a denotes not applicable.
See also notes to Table 2.7.

Sources: As for Table 2.7.

($v = 1.49$) and is not significantly greater than unity (the relevant t statistic is 0.79). Excluding Japan, as we have noted, does not alter these conclusions.

Contrary to the results reported when I/Q is included in Rowthorn's Specification, these results show that the estimates of the degree of returns to scale, unfortunately, remain extremely sensitive to the specification chosen. This is further confirmed by using data from Englander and Mittelstäd (1988). We excluded the observations on the less developed European countries and the essentially rural economy of New Zealand although doing this does not substantially alter the results. The Verdoorn Law for the business sector gives a good fit and shows substantial dynamic and static increasing returns to scale. An intercept dummy proved to be insignificant suggesting that the slowdown in total factor productivity growth is explained by the fall in the growth in output. But once again we find contradictory results when output growth is regressed on that of the factor inputs. The estimated degree of returns is 1.14 but this does not differ significantly from unity at the 95 per cent confidence level. Excluding Japan makes little difference to the results. The intercept dummy is now significant and a slowdown of 1.781 percentage points per annum remains unexplained.

Table 2.9   The Verdoorn Law and Rowthorn's Specification using the growth rates of total factor productivity, output, and total factor input, for the business sector, advanced countries, 1960s–86 (three pooled sub-periods)

tfp =	-0.456	+	$0.633q$		$\bar{r}^2 = 0.772$	$\bar{r}^2_{adj} = 0.530$
	(-2.40)		(12.25)		$SER = 0.643$	
q =	2.508	+	$-1.781dum$	+ $1.142tfi$	$\bar{R}^2 = 0.705$	
	(5.52)		(-5.14)	(6.49)	$SER = 1.021$	

Notes: Sub-periods are 1960s–1973, 1973–1979, and 1979–1986 (n = 45).

Countries in sample and starting years are: US 1960, Japan 1967, Germany 1961, France 1965, UK 1960, Italy 1961, Canada 1962, Austria 1961, Belgium 1961, Denmark 1960, Netherlands 1962, Norway 1964, Sweden 1966, Switzerland 1963, Australia 1961.

dum is a dummy variable taking 0 for 1960s–1973 and 1 for 1973–1979 and 1979–1986.

Source: Englander and Mittelstädt (1988).

MEASUREMENT ERRORS AND THE VERDOORN LAW

Another possible contributory factor to the divergence in Kaldor's and Rowthorn's estimates may be due to the presence of measurement errors (McCombie, 1981a). In particular, the volume indices of output (and hence their growth rates) may be subject to serious measurement errors. These arise from the method of deflation employed (whether single or double deflation), the treatment of quality change and the usual sampling errors (Hill, 1971). There is little doubt that this is true of the service sector. The methodology involved in the construction of the OECD National Accounts statistics has been examined in detail by Hill and McGibbon (1966). They came to the conclusion that the slow rate of growth of the service sector output compared with that of industry cannot be attributed entirely to either variations in income elasticities of demand or differential rates of technical progress. 'In practice, the main reason for the comparatively slow rate of growth of services in all countries seems to be that a substantial proportion of the real output indicators used in this sector consists simply of employment changes. Whereas substantial increases in labour productivity may be recorded in other sectors, including agriculture, the output indicators in use over a wide range of general services permit little or no increase in output per person' (p. 38). The method of deriving the statistics for service output growth also varies considerably between countries and this, together with the practice of often *assuming* that service productivity growth is either negligible, or of making an arbitrary allowance for it, renders the estimates largely, if not totally, devoid of economic or any other significance. It is thus dangerous to draw any conclusions from the failure of the Verdoorn Law in the tertiary sector. It would be surprising if there were not some economies of scale in, for example, wholesaling and retailing, as evidenced by the recent growth of hypermarkets and the demise of the corner grocery shop, etc.

In the case of industry, the measurement errors are likely to be less serious but may still pose an 'errors in variables' problem for the Verdoorn Law. If the growth of output is measured with error, then it may easily be shown that in the probability limit the relationship between the 'true' Verdoorn coefficient $(\tilde{b})$ and the ordinary least squares estimator (b) is given by:

$$b = \tilde{b} + \frac{(1 - \tilde{b})k}{(1 + k)} \tag{2.18}$$

where k is the ratio of the variance of the measurement error to the variance of the true rate of growth of output. It can be seen from equation (2.18) that if $\tilde{b}$ is less than unity (and it would be most implausible if this were not the case) the Verdoorn coefficient will be biased upwards and in favour of accepting the hypothesis of the existence of increasing returns to scale. However, for measurement errors to be solely responsible for generating a Verdoorn coefficient of one-half, when the true value $(\tilde{b})$ equals zero, requires the variance of the measurement errors to equal that of the true output growth rates, which is most implausible. On the other hand, if we are prepared to treat the Verdoorn Law as an equation with the only error being the measurement of output, then since e is error free, Rowthorn's Specification may be interpreted as being, in effect, an inverse regression and the coefficient on the employment term will be unbiased.

McCombie (1981a) used various instrumental procedures (Wald's two group method, Bartlett's three group method and Durbin's ranking method) but this did not resolve the controversy. The way the equations were normalised still proved important (since the instruments take different values depending upon whether q or e is the regressor). Excluding Japan from the sample, the Verdoorn Law still provided evidence of substantial returns to scale while Rowthorn's Specification did not.

The position is more complicated when the growth of capital is included in the equations as there is a distinct probability that this is also measured with error. We therefore recomputed the regressions in Tables 2.7, 2.8 and 2.9 using Durbin's method and also, where possible, the regressors lagged one growth cycle as instruments. Unfortunately, whether the hypothesis of returns to scale was accepted or rejected still depended upon the way the normalisation was carried out.

PARIKH'S SIMULTANEOUS EQUATION MODEL

It was argued earlier that one of the problems with the estimation of the Verdoorn Law relationship is that the coefficient may be subject to simultaneous equation bias because output growth may depend upon productivity growth, working through relative price changes and demand.

Parikh (1978) has attempted to resolve the controversy of whether growth was supply or demand constrained during the postwar period by explicitly estimating a simultaneous equation model. Superficially, the study would appear to be of great importance for the debate concerning the Verdoorn Law. The results of the estimations of a number of slightly different versions of a simultaneous equation model led Parikh to conclude that growth was ultimately demand constrained as Kaldor had maintained. These results have been accepted by, *inter alios*, Chatterji and Wickens (1982), Michl (1985) and Stafford (1989) but not by Bairam (1987). While Parikh's results would seem to support the position taken by us, the models suffer from specification problems that preclude them from shedding any light on the various issues. Parikh (1978) specifies two basic models.

Model 1 is estimated as a two-equation model (which is the reduced forms of the structural equations), namely:

$$e = c_1 + b_1 q + b_2 nme + \mu_1 \tag{2.19}$$

$$q = c_2 + b_3 e + b_4 x + b_5 (I/Q) + \mu_2 \tag{2.20}$$

where e is the growth of manufacturing employment, q is the growth of manufacturing output, *nme* is the growth of non-manufacturing workforce (which includes the unemployed), x is the growth of exports and I/Q is the gross investment–output ratio. μ_1 and μ_2 are the error terms.

His second model (Model 2) is identical to Model 1 above except that he includes I/Q in equation (2.19) and excludes it from equation (2.20). (It is surprising that I/Q was not included simultaneously in both the equations.)

Parikh seems to regard equation (2.19) as a Verdoorn relationship and equation (2.20) as a relationship determining the growth of manufacturing output. The models are interpreted as a test of the labour surplus hypothesis as follows: Parikh argues with respect to the models that if the coefficient of q in the putative Verdoorn equation (equation (2.19)) is significant while that of e in equation (2.20) is not, this would confirm the contention that output growth was not labour constrained. A corollary is that it is to be expected that the 'demand' factors x and I/Q will also be significant. On the other hand, if Rowthorn were correct, we should presumably expect the converse results, although we would have problems with the identification of equation (2.19), and its counterpart in the second model (Model 2), if x and I/Q had no explanatory power. The fact that the coefficient of q turns out to be significantly different from zero means that 'the growth of employment is constrained by the manufacturing sector's output growth' (Parikh, 1978, p. 87). However, there are certain problems with this inference, as we shall now show.

We have seen that the Verdoorn Law is essentially a dynamic production relation or a form of the technical progress function. The Verdoorn coefficient is a technological parameter which may be interpreted as a measure of the degree of returns to scale if either the investment–output ratio is included as a proxy for the growth of the capital stock (in the absence of data directly on the latter) or an assumption is made about the growth of the capital–output ratio. This, of course, suggests that I/Q should, indeed, be included in equation (2.19). However, as we discussed above, there are strong grounds for considering I/Q to be endogenous, determined by the growth of output. We should also expect there to be a significant relationship between the growth of output and the growth of the inputs in the Verdoorn equation, which may be interpreted as a technical progress function, regardless of whether output growth was labour or demand constrained. The crucial question is not whether or not the Verdoorn coefficient (b_1) is statistically significant, since, if it is reflecting a production relationship, *a priori* it always should be, but whether or not it is biased. If a simultaneous equation model could be correctly specified which included the influence of the elasticity of the labour supply and demand factors, we should still expect the coefficient of q to be a measure of returns to scale, although now hopefully free of simultaneous equation bias. Parikh does not explicitly consider the interpretation or implications of the size of the estimated coefficient beyond concluding that Kaldor's result is confirmed as 'every 1 per cent growth in output leads to about 1/2 per cent growth in employment'.

But it is difficult to understand why Parikh considers that the fact that the Verdoorn coefficient is significant *per se* shows that output was demand constrained, and hence, how the model can be regarded as a test of the significance of demand and supply factors in determining the growth of output.

There are further problems with the specification. Since the Verdoorn equation is a production relation, it is also difficult to comprehend why Parikh includes the growth of the non-manufacturing workforce in this equation. (The growth of the total workforce is included in the structural equation, but using the identity that the growth of the workforce is equal to the weighted growth rate of manufacturing and the growth rate of the non-manufacturing workforce, the growth of the latter is substituted for the growth of the workforce in deriving the reduced form equation (2.19).) Neither the growth of the total nor non-manufacturing workforce makes any contribution as an input to the growth of manufacturing output. If the supply of labour to the manufacturing sector were not perfectly elastic, then it is true that, *ceteris paribus*, a faster growth of the labour force would allow a faster growth of the labour supply available for manufacturing. But such a relationship should be modelled explicitly as a labour supply function and provides no justification for its *ad hoc* inclusion in the Verdoorn equation. Parikh himself comments at the end of the paper that 'the model uses the rate of growth in the non-manufacturing workforce as an exogenous variable, and what is required is an endogenous workforce variable'. Since equation (2.19) is identified solely by the growth of the non-manufacturing workforce, to conclude by arguing that it should not be regarded as an exogenous variable, by itself, raises problems concerning the whole rationale of the model.

Let us turn next to equation (2.20) where q is specified as a function of x, I/Q and e. There are a number of difficulties of interpreting the significance or otherwise of these variables as demonstrating the importance of either demand or supply factors. This equation, as Parikh notes, is similar to a model used by Cornwall (1976) except Cornwall did not include e in his equation. Cornwall assumed that the growth of output was not supply constrained and hence was determined by the growth of exogenous demand factors. The rate of growth of exports affects the growth of output through the dynamic foreign trade multiplier (see Chapter 3). Investment influences the growth of demand, according to Cornwall (1976, p. 311), since 'the higher is $[I/Q]$, the greater should be the demand pressures and the lower will be the "macro risks" of investment'. (We have already commented on the fact that I/Q, to the extent that it is a proxy for the growth of capital, is likely to be as much a function of q as its cause.) Parikh, thus, includes, in a rather *ad hoc* way, the growth of manufacturing employment into Cornwall's equation as a supply side variable.

It is strange, however, that Parikh who is attempting to test for the possibility that the growth of manufacturing output may be labour constrained, makes the assumption that x and I/Q are predetermined variables. Thus the implausible assumption is implicitly made, for example, that the export sector is faced with a perfectly elastic supply of labour schedule irrespective of the state of the labour market in the manufacturing sector. (The vast majority of exports are manufactured products.) Indeed, when Balassa (1963) criticised Beckerman's demand orientated export-led growth model for its neglect of supply factors, he argued that the slow growth of labour would constrain the growth of output through its effect on the growth of exports. As labour became progressively scarcer, manufacturing real wages would be bid up. The international competitive position of the country would decline together with its export growth. This is also likely to weaken the rate of capital accumulation thereby causing I/Q to fall also. If the purpose is to allow for the possibility of supply constraints, then it seems strange to specify x and I/Q as exogenous variables.

Related to this is the oft-quoted criticism of the export-led growth theories that there is no statistical criterion by which to judge whether or not the existence of the close correlation that is found between q and x is due primarily to an expanding home market being the cause or effect of a buoyant export sector. If the former is correct, then a significant coefficient of x is perfectly compatible with the fact that the growth of manufacturing is labour constrained. Parikh briefly acknowledges, again at the end of the article, problems of the direction of causality between q, x and I/Q and this raises 'the issues on the observed association between variables versus ultimate causes of differences in growth'. But once again this is tantamount to conceding that the models cannot resolve the issue of whether growth is essentially supply or demand constrained.

We are also faced with the problem of the rationale for the inclusion of e in equation (2.20) (i.e. $q = f(x, I/Q, e)$) which is not discussed by Parikh. One possible interpretation is that e is regarded as a proxy for the influence of the elasticity of the labour supply on the growth of demand, through, for example, its effect on the growth of real wages and hence the rate of change in relative prices of exports compared with both competitor countries' exports and with imports. However, e is the *ex post* outcome of the interaction of the supply and demand schedules for labour in each country and hence an identification problem arises. There is no way of discriminating between whether a given growth of the labour force is due to demand increasing along a perfectly elastic labour supply curve or to a larger increase in demand shifting along a more inelastic labour supply curve. It follows that it is illegitimate to infer that if the coefficient of e is insignificant the rate of growth of output was not labour constrained.

It may be that Parikh does not envisage such an explanation but merely expects that if the supply of labour is inelastic, then the growth of output will be simply a function of the growth of the labour supply and, hence, expects this to be demonstrated by a significant coefficient of e. Of course, if the supply of labour is 'strictly limited', the growth of q will be determined by e. However, this will occur through the production function (i.e. the Verdoorn equation) since, in this case, the given growth of employment would limit the growth of output through the technological conditions of production. (This demonstrates once again the problem of expecting the significance or otherwise of the Verdoorn coefficient – the coefficient of q in equation (2.19) – to be a test of the importance of demand and supply factors.) What Parikh seems to have done is essentially to have taken the Verdoorn equation and Cornwall's demand equation and included e in the latter to engender the simultaneity of the equations, but there seems no theoretical rationale for this last procedure.

Parikh proceeds to modify Models 1 and 2 by including the reciprocal of per capita income as a proxy for the international diffusion of innovations, but in view of the fundamental problems associated with the first two models we shall not deal with the extensions here.

TIME-SERIES ESTIMATION OF THE VERDOORN LAW

Since the Verdoorn Law is a *long-run* relationship between the growth of productivity and output it has usually been estimated using cross-country or cross-industry data and exponential growth rates calculated over a period of several years (normally from peak to peak of the growth cycle). However, there have also been a number of time-series estimations of the law using either quarterly or annual data for manufacturing or separate industries for a particular country (Katz, 1969; Chatterji and Wickens, 1981, 1982,[9] 1983; and McCombie and de Ridder, 1983). In this section we shall briefly consider the work of Chatterji and Wickens as representative of this approach.

Chatterji and Wickens are concerned with explicitly testing Kaldor's views with time-series data, yet unfortunately they misrepresent his position. (See especially Kaldor's (1981) comment on their first paper.) For example, in Chatterji and Wickens (1982, p. 22) they simply state that 'Kaldor's view of Verdoorn's Law as it applies to manufacturing can be interpreted as yielding the productivity function . . . $p_m = \beta e_m$' (where the subscript m denotes manufacturing). In Chatterji and Wickens (1981) they again state that Verdoorn's Law is defined as $p_m = \alpha + \beta e_m$, $\beta > 1$ (their notation). In this earlier paper, they provide an (unsatisfactory) rationale for their choice of Rowthorn's Specification which is as follows. (In Chatterji and Wickens (1982) no justification is given.) They estimated both the simple Verdoorn equation and Rowthorn's Specification with quarterly data (unadjusted for cyclical changes in the pressure of demand) and used the first four lags of e_m as instruments. Rowthorn's Specification does not give a statistically significant fit. The Verdoorn Law, on the other hand, gives a Verdoorn coefficient of 0.673 with a t-value of 6.63. However, a diagnostic statistic suggests that the instrument for the Verdoorn equation is unacceptable. As Chatterji and Wickens (1981) admit, the unacceptability of the instrument could be due to mis-specification of the model. Clearly, both Rowthorn's Specification and Verdoorn's Law are indeed mis-specified – there is no correction for variations in capacity utilisation nor is there any inclusion of the growth of capital services in the model. In spite of this, they surprisingly argue that 'these results suggest that Rowthorn's version of Verdoorn's law is to be preferred to Kaldor's [which they now correctly but confusingly take to be $p_m = f(q_m)$] which (i) produced implausibly large estimates of β, and (ii) given the massive residual serial correlation in [the Verdoorn equation] seems to indicate some misspecification.' Leaving aside the question of the size of β which begs the question of what is implausible, Chatterji and Wickens thus prefer to use Rowthorn's Specification on the basis of diagnostic tests on the regression of the Verdoorn equation which they concede is likely to be mis-specified.

The issue is essentially which way the specification of the productivity relationship should be normalised. This may be seen more clearly if we write the two specifications as $q_m = f(e_m)$ and $e_m = f(q_m)$.[10] Normally, economic theory is used to decide the normalisation (Maddala, 1977, p. 236). By choosing e_m as the regressor, Chatterji and Wickens are implicitly assuming that, over the growth cycle, variations in output growth are determined by input shocks. A case for this could be made out along New Classical lines in terms of the theory of the real business cycle. But Kaldor unequivocally takes a Keynesian perspective and assumes that such fluctuations are demand determined; as is long-term growth. And, after all, one of Chatterji and Wickens's stated aims is to test the Kaldorian hypothesis. Notwithstanding this, they specify the 'Verdoorn Law' as the regression of manufacturing productivity growth on employment growth and the growth of the capital stock.

One of the problems of using time-series data is that 'Okun's Law' becomes intermingled with the Verdoorn Law, as Chatterji and Wickens recognise. Over the growth cycle, employment growth does not fluctuate as much as changes in demand conditions would warrant. Labour is a 'quasi-fixed factor of production' (Oi, 1962). Because of rehiring costs and the damage to labour relations, labour is, to a large extent, hoarded over the cycle. This means that as output growth falls in the downswing of the cycle so, *pari passu*, will productivity growth and vice versa. This short-run effect will, when productivity growth is regressed on output growth, produce a slope coefficient similar to the Verdoorn coefficient, although this has nothing to do with the presence or otherwise of economies of scale. It is this which undoubtedly accounts for the 'implausibly large' coefficient of the Verdoorn Law noted above. Kaldor, in his regression analysis, used the growth of total hours worked as a measure of the growth of the labour input and this is undoubtedly a better measure than employment growth, especially for time-series estimation. It will capture the effect of changes in, for example, overtime working but not variations in the intensity of use of the labour input. Similarly, the growth of capital has to be adjusted for changes in capacity utilisation.

Chatterji and Wickens attempt to correct partially for these cyclical

influences by including the growth of average hours worked to capture the effects of changes in capacity utilisation.[11] Thus their specification of the function determining long-run productivity growth is:

$$p_m = a + \beta e_m + \gamma h_m + \delta k_m \qquad (2.21)$$

with the usual notation, and where h equals the growth of average
hours worked.

The model is estimated by ordinary least squares in a dynamic
framework with a lagged structure of the regressors and with lagged
values of p_m also included as explanatory variables. The results of the
steady-state solution is given by:

$$p_m = -0.011 + 0.742h_m - 0.96e_m + 1.00k_m$$

Chatterji and Wickens also found some short-run Verdoorn
effects, but from the above equation they infer that there is 'no
Verdoorn's Law effect in the long run'. But it is not clear that the
above long-term relationship necessarily unequivocally refutes the
hypothesis of increasing returns to scale. The equation may be
equivalently written as:

$$q_m = -0.011 + 0.742h_m + 0.04e_m + 1.00k_m$$

These results suggest that there are small increasing returns to the
growth of employment and capital with the sum of their coefficients
equalling 1.04, although the coefficient of e_m is implausibly low. The
small value of the coefficient of e_m could be due simply to the fact
that, for the reasons outlined earlier, there is little fluctuation in this
variable and the changes in the growth of the labour input are being
picked up by the growth in average hours worked. To the extent this
is true and h_m is not merely capturing the effect of changes in capacity
utilisation, the degree of increasing returns will be understated.
(Chatterji and Wickens (1982) suggest that the small coefficient of e_m
could be due to a fixed coefficient technology with employment
growth only affecting output growth in the long run so long as it is
accompanied by the growth of capital.)

However, it is very doubtful whether very much reliance can be
placed on these and other time-series results. The estimated coefficients are likely to be very sensitive to the exact method used to
calculate changes in both capacity utilisation and the intensity of use

of the labour input. The Verdoorn Law is a long-term relationship between the *trend* growth rates of productivity, output and the capital stock which for an individual country show very little variation over time (except for the decline after 1973). The actual quarterly growth rates are thus a combination of cyclical variations and the trend growth rate. Any estimate of the long-run relationship is thus likely to have coefficients that are not well-defined, even if accurate corrections could be made for the cyclical variations. McCombie and de Ridder (1983, p. 387) using US time-series annual data and adjusting the capital stock using the Federal Reserve Board's index of capacity utilisation came to the somewhat nihilistic conclusion that they were 'not sanguine about the possibility of disentangling the short-run cyclical (Okun) and the long-run (Verdoorn) relationship between the growth of employment, output and capital, even though the data have been adjusted for variations in excess capacity.'[12]

Stoneman (1979) estimated the Verdoorn Law for the United Kingdom using time-series data over the period 1880 to 1969. The growth rates were calculated over subperiods ranging from four to ten years, which should reduce the distortion due to variations in capacity utilisation. Unfortunately, no proxy is included for the growth of the capital stock. This may be a potentially serious mis-specification since it is by no means clear what was happening to the capital–output ratio over such a long time-span; it certainly cannot be assumed that it was constant. A further and equally serious problem lies in the implausibility of the assumption that the growth of exogenous productivity is the same for all periods. Given that the time period from which the data are drawn includes the fossil fuel, the hydrocarbon and electronic revolutions, it would be most surprising if the rate of technical progress did not show considerable variation over time. If this is the case, the Verdoorn Law may be mis-specified in a manner analogous to Figure 2.1.

SCOTT'S *NEW VIEW* AND THE VERDOORN LAW

In Chapter 1, we examined the contention of Scott (1989) that the correct way to measure the increase in the capital stock was by gross investment. While Scott does not consider that economies of scale, *per se*, are of overwhelming importance in explaining growth, his argument that each act of investment increases the scope for further equally profitable projects is similar to Kaldor's (1972) argument which he advanced in his *Economic Journal* article 'The Irrelevance of Equilibrium Economics'. (Scott, however, does not dismiss increasing returns to scale entirely: see Scott, 1989, pp. 376, 387 and 389.) The only difference is that Kaldor attributes to increasing returns to scale the fact that each act of investment opens up further avenues of opportunity that were initially unknown to entrepreneurs. By definition, increasing returns to scale means that there must be some qualitative change involved as output increases. (Even increasing returns due to an increase in volume – a favourite example of Kaldor's – will generally need some qualitative change. New construction techniques and advances in engineering were needed before the building of supertankers became feasible.) If a doubling of inputs increases output by, say, 120 per cent there must be some qualitative change; the extra 20 per cent increase in output could not have been accomplished by mere reduplication. Kaldor (1972, p. 1245) considers that 'every change in the use of resources – every reorganisation of productive activities – creates the opportunity for a further change *which would not have existed otherwise*' (emphasis in the original). (The Kaldorian emphasis on increasing returns is, of course, very similar to, and anticipates, the new growth theory.)

Using Scott's data for 10 now advanced countries for the pre-1973 postwar period, the following results are obtained from the estimation of the Verdoorn Law by ordinary least squares:

$$e^* = 0.055 + 0.770q - 0.091s + 0.015s\mathrm{lncu} \qquad \bar{R}^2 = 0.786$$
$$(0.05) \quad (5.16) \quad (-1.37) \quad (0.26) \qquad SER = 0.783$$

where e^* is the growth of quality-adjusted employment (expressed as a per cent per annum), q is the growth of output, $s = I/Q$ (expressed as a percentage) and $s\mathrm{lncu}$ is Scott's proxy for the degree of technological catch-up. We used ordinary least squares in the regression analysis, instead of Scott's procedure of a weighted regression, to maintain comparability with the estimation procedure of Kaldor *et alios*.

The data used differ from those of Kaldor (1966b) in that they refer to the non-residential business sector, instead of industry or manufacturing. The growth of the labour input has also been adjusted for the change in quality, a procedure not adopted by Kaldor. It should be noted that there are only 12 observations and so the results should be regarded as indicative, rather than conclusive.

The coefficient of q is significantly less than unity at the 90 per cent confidence level (one-tailed test), but not at the 95 per cent confidence level. A value of less than unity suggests increasing returns to scale to labour alone. It will be noticed that, as in Scott's results, the intercept is statistically insignificant suggesting that there is no exogenous technical progress. Although the sample includes Japan, the catch-up variable is also insignificant. Dropping this last variable gives the following result:

$$e^* = \underset{(0.18)}{0.160} + \underset{(6.47)}{0.748q} - \underset{(-1.95)}{0.101s} \qquad \begin{aligned} \bar{R}^2 &= 0.808 \\ SER &= 0.699 \end{aligned}$$

If we follow Scott and also omit the intercept, the following result is obtained:

$$e^* = \underset{(6.83)}{0.745q} - \underset{(-3.44)}{0.093s} \qquad \begin{aligned} RMR^2 &= 0.930 \\ SER &= 0.664 \end{aligned}$$

The conventional R^2 and $\bar{R}^2$ are not well defined when there is no intercept. We have reported the raw moment R^2 (RMR^2) instead.

The coefficient of q is statistically significantly less than unity at the 95 per cent confidence level. The regression result supports Kaldor's contention that there are substantial returns to scale in the non-residential business sector, *pace* Scott (1989, chapter 12). Omitting Japan from the sample does not affect the conclusions drawn.

For completeness, Scott's (and Rowthorn's) specification was re-estimated by ordinary least squares using the same data. The result is as follows:

$$q = \underset{(0.15)}{0.170} + \underset{(5.16)}{0.998e^*} + \underset{(1.30)}{0.099s} - \underset{(-1.08)}{0.066slncu} \qquad \begin{aligned} \bar{R}^2 &= 0.867 \\ SER &= 0.840 \end{aligned}$$

Omitting first the catch-up variable, and next the catch-up variable together with the intercept, we obtain:

$$q = \underset{(-0.31)}{-0.331} + \underset{(6.47)}{1.101e^*} + \underset{(3.02)}{0.159s} \qquad \begin{aligned} \bar{R}^2 &= 0.865 \\ SER &= 0.848 \end{aligned}$$

and:

$$q = \underset{(6.83)}{1.105e^*} + \underset{(8.46)}{0.145s} \qquad \begin{aligned} RMR^2 &= 0.981 \\ SER &= 0.699 \end{aligned}$$

In the last two regressions, the coefficient of the quality-adjusted labour force is greater than unity suggesting increasing returns to labour alone. It should, however, be noted that the coefficient of e^* does not differ significantly from unity at the 95 per cent confidence level. If we adopt the same procedure as previously and assume a capital-output ratio of 3, the implied degree of returns to scale is 1.54, which is statistically significantly greater than unity. There is, however, a problem of multicollinearity between s and $slncu$ making it difficult to precisely separate the contributions of these two variables. (This is not such a problem with the Verdoorn Law.) Dropping Japan does not materially affect the results, although the coefficient on e^* falls somewhat.

THE REGIONAL VERDOORN LAW

McCombie and de Ridder (1984) estimated the Verdoorn Law using US state data for the last decade of the Long Boom, 1963–73. This data set avoids a large number of objections that can be levelled at the use of international data and this procedure was largely anticipated by Kaldor (1970) himself:

> The primary question that needs to be considered is what *causes* these differences in 'regional' growth rates – whether the term "regional" is applied to different countries (or even groups of countries) or different areas within the same country. The two questions are not, of course, identical; but up to a point it is illuminating to consider them as if they were and to apply the same analytical technique to both.

The first advantage is that there are few, if any, economic barriers to the interregional mobility of capital and to interstate migration. Indeed, the US is a highly mobile society. This makes it plausible to assume that the growth of a state's output is essentially demand rather than supply constrained. As one of us remarked some time ago:

> Regional growth is demand determined for the obvious reason that no region's growth rate can be constrained by supply when factors of production are freely mobile. For a region in which capital and labour are highly mobile in and out, growth must be demand

determined. If the demand for a region's output is strong, labour and capital will migrate to the region to the benefit of that region and to the detriment of others. We cannot return to the pre-Keynesian view that demand adjusts to supply. (Thirlwall, 1980b)

Nevertheless, we wish to qualify this position somewhat with respect to the short-run. It could be that the existence of spatial and other frictions prevent the growth of factor inputs being fast enough to sustain the anticipated growth of output. If this is the case, then labour should be treated as the independent variable, notwithstanding the importance of demand factors. Even so, given that the time period over which the Verdoorn Law is estimated is a decade, it is unlikely that these frictions will be of any great importance in the context of long-term growth. For completeness, though, we also estimate Rowthorn's Specification which treats employment growth as a regressor.

Secondly, it seems reasonable to assume that there is little reciprocal effect from productivity growth to output growth through the price mechanism. Given the oligopolistic nature of manufacturing industry in the US where a large percentage of manufactured goods is sold on the national market, there is likely to be little variation in the growth of state producer prices. (Unfortunately, it is not possible to test this directly because of the absence of state price deflators.) However, it is possible that simultaneity could occur through those states with a faster growth of productivity achieving a larger growth of retained profits and hence a higher rate of investment and output growth. Consequently, in view of the potential problem of simultaneous equation bias, both the Verdoorn Law and Rowthorn's Specification were estimated using a number of instrumental variable techniques.

Another advantage of state data is that differences in socio-economic factors are likely to be much smaller between states than between countries. For example, the degree of trade union resistance to the introduction of new technology is likely to be much smaller between states than between, for example, the UK and Germany. It is also likely, given the highly oligopolistic nature of manufacturing, that all US firms have access to the same blue-print of technology and that there should be little spatial variation in productivity growth due to the diffusion of innovations from the more to less technologically advanced states. McCombie (1982b) tested this hypothesis by including the relative state level of total factor productivity (after making due allowance for increasing returns to scale) in the Verdoorn Law as a proxy for the level of technology. This variable was found to be statistically insignificant.

It is likely that the estimate of the Verdoorn coefficient in the case of regional statistics will represent a lower bound of the 'true' magnitude obtained using international data in a correctly specified model. This arises because economies of scale at the national level are likely to be captured in the intercept term rather than the slope coefficient of the regional Verdoorn Law because such increasing returns are, by definition, a function of national output growth rather than state variations in growth. It follows that this will impart a bias in favour of accepting the hypothesis of constant returns to scale, and so the regional Verdoorn Law provides a stringent and conservative test of the Kaldorian thesis.

The Verdoorn Law was first estimated by ordinary least squares regression analysis and was specified in the traditional form as:

$$e = a_1 + b_1 q + b_2 k \qquad (2.22)$$

with the usual notation. The degree of returns to scale (v) is given by $(1 - \hat{b}_2)/\hat{b}_1$ and its standard error is calculated by the use of a Taylor series expansion.[13]

Rowthorn's Specification is given by:

$$q = a_1' + b_1' e + b_2' k \qquad (2.23)$$

and the degree of returns to scale is given by $\hat{b}_1' + \hat{b}_2'$.

Three separate proxies were constructed for the growth of the state capital stock as there are no readily available constant price estimates. The first is the traditional gross investment–output ratio, but a necessary condition for this to be a reasonable proxy is that the state capital–output ratios are the same, a condition which our other proxies suggested was not found in practice. (The use of the investment–output ratio also gave implausible results which are not reported here.) The second estimate for the growth of capital (k_1) was calculated by us and is based on a form of the perpetual inventory model and the use of cumulative gross investment at constant prices. Statistics are also available for the gross book value of depreciable assets which is the historic cost of capital equipment. The third proxy (k_2) was the growth of this historic cost valuation which we adjusted to constant prices using national weights and price deflators. Although there must be reservations about this proxy, it is reassuring to note that there is a close association between k_1 and k_2 with a coefficient of determination of over 0.8. As the choice of these two capital proxies does not make a significant difference to the results, those obtained using only k_1 will be reported here.

The results of the estimation of the Verdoorn Law, together with Rowthorn's Specification, are reported in Table 2.10. Dummy variables were introduced to allow for differences in the estimated coefficients resulting from the influence of regional specific factors. The four regional groupings are those delineated by the US Bureau of Economic Affairs and are the North East, the North Central, the South and the Far West. The dummies proved to be significant in the case of the intercept (i.e. exogenous technical progress) and hence are included in the various regression equations. Dummies allowing for shifts in the regression slope coefficients proved to be insignificant.

As may be seen from Table 2.10, the estimate of the size of returns to scale given by the Verdoorn Law is 1.45 while Rowthorn's Specification gives a value of 1.33. Both estimates are significantly greater than unity at the 99 per cent confidence level. These results would seem to provide strong confirmation of the hypothesis that manufacturing industry is subject to substantial economies of scale.

We have already mentioned the argument that under the assumptions of the Verdoorn Law, the growth of capital should be an endogenous variable, determined by the expected growth of output. (This may explain the relatively large standard error of the coefficient of capital growth in the Verdoorn Law, since the latter will be mis-specified.)

The Verdoorn Law, consequently, was also specified as:

$$tfp = a_2 + b_3q \tag{2.24}$$

or, in order to remove the spurious correlation engendered by q being on both sides of the equation, it may expressed equivalently as:

$$tfi = a_3 + b_4q \tag{2.25}$$

where tfi is the weighted growth of the total factor inputs, $tfi = (ae + (1-a)k)$. The weights a and $(1-a)$ are the shares of labour and capital in total output. The degree of returns to scale, v, is equal to the estimate of $1/b_4$. The results together with Rowthorn's Specification are also reported in Table 2.10. The estimates of the returns to scale are slightly larger than those of the more traditional specifications and are also significantly greater than unity at the 99 per cent confidence level.

It may well be, however, that the assumptions of ordinary least squares are still not fulfilled because of the reciprocal effect that an above-average rate of productivity growth has in leading, through a greater rate of investment, to an above-average rate of growth of output. Another issue is that there may be measurement errors in the construction of the estimates of the growth of output and of the capital stock. These errors may arise because of the necessity of using national rather than regional price deflators for converting current price series for output and investment to a constant price series. Given the potential importance of the simultaneity and measurement error problems, the total factor input specifications of the Verdoorn Law and Rowthorn's Specification were estimated using instrumental variable methods. Three procedures were used, namely, Bartlett's grouping method, Durbin's ranking method and the use of lagged variables as instruments. In the last approach, the instruments used for the Verdoorn Law were output growth over the periods 1947–58 and 1958–63. (In the case of Rowthorn's Specification, employment growth is used as the instrument.) These results are reported in Table 2.11 and it is reassuring to note that they confirm the results of the ordinary least squares estimation. McCombie and de Ridder (1984, p. 276) concluded that 'we may, therefore, have a high degree of confidence in accepting that there are substantial economies of scale in manufacturing as Kaldor originally argued in his inaugural lecture'.

A subsequent study by McCombie (1985b), however, suggests that this conclusion must be somewhat qualified. The Verdoorn Law and Rowthorn's Specification were estimated for 17 2-digit SIC industries using US state data over the period 1963–72 (or 1963–9 for some industries). Both the usual specifications and those using the growth of total factor inputs were used. The estimating procedure was again both ordinary least squares and instrumental variable methods. In practice, the results were insensitive to the choice of the method of estimation, but not whether the Verdoorn Law or Rowthorn's Specification was used. The Verdoorn Law using *tfi* as the regressand produced estimates of large increasing returns in all but one industry (Leather and Leather Products). Conversely, Rowthorn's Specification, with either *tfi* or *e* and *k* as the regressors, gave estimates that were not significantly different from unity at the 95 per cent confidence level for all but two industries (Textile Mill Products and Furniture and Fixtures). Thus, at this more disaggregated level, the

Table 2.10 The Verdoorn Law and Rowthorn's Specification: US state data – total manufacturing; 1963–73

(a) e =	-2.813 (-9.07)	$+$ $1.536d_1$ (5.32)	$+$ $0.915d_2$ (2.89)	$+$ $1.874d_3$ (6.21)	$+$ $0.770q$ (12.56)	$-$ $0.117k$ (-1.38)	$\bar{R}^2 = 0.887$ $SER = 0.649$
(b) q =	3.179 (8.63)	$-$ $1.212d_1$ (-3.14)	$-$ $0.466d_2$ (-1.19)	$-$ $1.653d_3$ (-4.07)	$+$ $1.020e$ (12.56)	$+$ $0.305k$ (3.45)	$\bar{R}^2 = 0.876$ $SER = 0.746$
(c) tfi =	-1.412 (-5.52)	$+$ $0.972d_1$ (3.86)	$+$ $0.321d_2$ (1.21)	$+$ $1.161d_3$ (4.41)	$+$ $0.606q$ (14.44)		$\bar{R}^2 = 0.866$ $SER = 0.568$
(d) q =	2.640 (8.75)	$-$ $0.945d_1$ (-2.29)	$-$ $0.082d_2$ (-0.20)	$-$ $1.319d_3$ (-3.07)	$+$ $1.363tfi$ (14.44)		$\bar{R}^2 = 0.838$ $SER = 0.853$

Estimates of Returns to Scale (v)

Equation	(a)	(b)	(c)	(d)
v	1.45^*	1.33^*	1.65^*	1.36^*

Notes: * denotes the estimate is greater than unity at the 99 per cent confidence level.
d_i denotes a regional dummy, where i = 1, 2, and 3.

Sources: Census of Manufactures and Annual Survey of Manufactures, US Bureau of the Census (various years).

Table 2.11 Instrumental estimates of increasing returns: US state manufacturing data, 1963–73

Verdoorn Law[a]:	$tfi = a_3 + b_4 q$
Rowthorn's Specification[a]:	$q = a_3' + b_4' q$

Estimating procedure	Verdoorn Law $\hat{b}_4$	(t-ratio)	v	Rowthorn's Specification $\hat{b}_4'$	(t-ratio)	v
Barlett's grouping method	0.644	(13.09)	1.55*	1.489	(13.46)	1.49*
Durbin's ranking method	0.635	(14.61)	1.57*	1.357	(14.21)	1.36*
Lagged variables as instruments	0.695	(6.32)	1.44*	1.406	(9.32)	1.41*

Note: [a]Includes regional intercept dummies.
　　　　*Denotes v is significantly greater than unity at 99 per cent confidence level.

Sources: See Table 2.10.

way the equations are normalised becomes of crucial importance for the acceptance or rejection of the hypothesis of increasing returns to scale. This is, of course, the same problem found using international data.

We find the assumption that output growth is fundamentally demand, rather than supply, determined more plausible at both the international and the regional level. Hence, we place greater reliance on the estimates of the Verdoorn Law rather than Rowthorn's Specification. But the fact that the acceptance or rejection of Kaldor's thesis of the importance of increasing returns depends on the normalisation of the estimating equation is disconcerting.

THE STATIC-DYNAMIC VERDOORN LAW PARADOX

The most plausible interpretation of the Verdoorn Law is that it is a specification of Kaldor's linear technical progress function. However, just as Black (1962) has shown that the latter may be derived from a conventional production function, so one possible underlying structure of the Verdoorn Law for cross-country or regional data in any *one* year, in log-linear form, is:

$$\ln P = (1/\alpha)\ln A + [(\alpha - 1)/\alpha]\ln Q + (\beta/\alpha)\ln K \qquad (2.26)$$

or:

$$\ln TFP = (1/v)\ln A + [(v-1)/v]\ln Q \qquad (2.27)$$

with the usual notation and where the upper-case letters denote the *levels* of the appropriate variable.

If these are the correct underlying specifications, it is to be expected, *a priori*, that both the 'dynamic' Verdoorn Law (estimated using exponential growth rates) and the 'static' Verdoorn Law (estimated using logarithmic values of the levels) should demonstrate the same degree of returns to scale. (The static Verdoorn Law could also be estimated using cross-country data but pooling a number of years – preferably the initial and terminal years of the growth cycles. In this case, time, or intercept, dummies would have to be introduced to capture the shift of the production function between the years.)

When the simple static Verdoorn Law (i.e. without the contribution of the capital stock being included) is estimated using international data drawn from the postwar period, a paradox is found (McCombie, 1982a). The static Verdoorn Law was estimated by regressing $\ln E$ (or $\ln P$) on $\ln Q$ for a number of years separately and also for all the observations pooled. The estimates of the Verdoorn coefficient obtained by regressing $\ln E$ on $\ln Q$ either do not differ significantly from unity or, where they do, the estimate is small being around 0.90. This compares with the value of 0.5 typically found when the dynamic Verdoorn Law is estimated. Rowthorn's Specification regressing $\ln Q$ on $\ln E$ also produces slope coefficients that are not significantly different from unity. If we assume that the capital–output ratio is constant, these results imply either that constant returns to scale exist, or that there are increasing returns to scale – but very small. It becomes of crucial importance to determine why this paradox occurs and which of the two specifications – the static or dynamic – is to be preferred.[14]

McCombie and de Ridder (1984) estimated the static Verdoorn Law and Rowthorn's Specification (both explicitly including the capital stock) using pooled US state data for manufacturing for 1963 and 1973. The regressions gave a very close fit with the $\bar{R}^2$ in both cases exceeding 0.99. Moreover, both estimates suggested that the estimate of the degree of returns to scale was not significantly different from unity at the 95 per cent confidence level. The Verdoorn and Rowthorn specifications using total factor productivity or total factor inputs each gave estimates of returns to scale of 1.02 which proved to be significantly greater than unity at the 95 per cent confidence level. But these returns to scale are small compared to those obtained from the dynamic specifications.

The explanation of this divergence of the static and dynamic estimates may be purely statistical, being the result of differing bias due, for example, to measurement errors. A more plausible reason is theoretical and involves the contention that, in fact, the technical progress function is not derived from the static Cobb–Douglas production function. This argument has been dealt with at length in McCombie (1982a) and so we shall only briefly recapitulate the argument here. The discrepancy may arise because there are numerous underlying structures of the 'dynamic' Verdoorn Law, depending upon the constant of integration. It may well be that the orthodox Cobb–Douglas is not the correct structure underlying the Verdoorn Law and so the static law will be mis-specified and will yield biased estimates of the returns to scale. Kaldor himself long ago pointed out there was a difference between the linear technical progress function and the Cobb–Douglas production function. Nevertheless, this argument seems to have been largely ignored in the literature. For example, Jones (1975, p. 197) notes that 'Black has shown that if the technical progress function is *linear* then the underlying technology *must* [our emphasis] be representable by a Cobb–Douglas production function.' There is no *must* about it.

VERDOORN'S ORIGINAL MODEL

Verdoorn (1949), in his seminal paper, derived the relationship between productivity and output growth from a simultaneous equation model which contained a *static* Cobb–Douglas production function (with no exogenous technical change) and a labour supply function. Verdoorn was impressed by the stability of what may be termed the Verdoorn Elasticity, *viz* the ratio between the growth of productivity and output (see Table 2.5). Verdoorn was presumably impressed by the stability of the Elasticity for the first six observations. The Elasticity appears most unstable for the inter-war period.

However, if we assume the underlying structure of the Verdoorn Law is simply the production function then once an allowance is made for exogenous technical progress it would be most surprising if the Elasticity were, in fact, stable. To see this, consider the simple Verdoorn Law:

$$p = a_1 + b_1 q \tag{2.28}$$

The Elasticity (V) is defined as:

$$V \equiv p/q \equiv a_1/q + b_1 \tag{2.29}$$

and this will alter with differences in q.

The problem with Verdoorn's argument, is, in fact, rather more complex than this. As Rowthorn (1979) has pointed out, Verdoorn's simultaneous equation model also contains a labour supply function, which specifies the growth of employment as a function of the growth of wages. Since the growth of wages is equal to the growth of productivity (through the marginal productivity conditions), there is a labour supply relationship between e and p (and, hence, q). The Elasticity derived by Verdoorn includes parameters of both the production function and the labour supply relationship. (It also includes two variables, namely, the growth of capital and labour (Thirlwall, 1980a).) Therefore, it is not possible to interpret the Elasticity as a measure of returns to scale. Verdoorn's full simultaneous equation model is, in fact, identified and estimating it by two-stage least squares tends to confirm Kaldor's hypothesis about the existence of surplus labour. Kaldor argues that there is no systematic relationship between the growth of manufacturing wages and the supply of labour to that sector, which is confirmed by regression analysis (McCombie, 1986). (See also Verdoorn, 1980.)

THE VERDOORN LAW AND THE ACCOUNTING IDENTITY

In Chapter 1, it was pointed out that the good fits obtained in the estimation of aggregate production functions merely reflect the fact that they are tracking an underlying accounting identity. This raises the question as to what are the implications for the Verdoorn Law. The analysis in Chapter 1 suggests that the accounting identity would ensure that estimates of the elasticities of production functions would, definitionally, sum to unity and would equal the relevant factor shares. Since the accounting identity must also underlie the Verdoorn Law, then how is it that the estimates suggest substantial increasing returns to scale?

To briefly recapitulate the argument, output (value added) for any one country is defined as:

$$Q_t \equiv w_t E_t + r_t K_t \tag{2.30}$$

In terms of exponential growth rates, this may be expressed as:

$$q_t \equiv a\varphi_{wt} + (1-a)\varphi_{rt} + ae_t + (1-a)k_t \tag{2.31}$$

or:

$$q_t \equiv \varphi_t + ae_t + (1-a)k_t \tag{2.32}$$

where φ_w and φ_r are the growth rates of real wages and of the real rental price of capital and $\varphi_t \equiv a\varphi_{wt} + (1-a)\varphi_{rt}$. For convenience, we have assumed that the factor shares do not change over time, although this is not essential for the argument.

The Cobb–Douglas production function, expressed in growth rates, is given by:

$$q_t = \lambda + \alpha e_t + \beta k_t \tag{2.33}$$

If φ_t reflects a well-defined time trend and so may be approximated by a constant, φ (as empirically it can be – see McCombie and Dixon, 1991), then the estimation of equation (2.33), using time-series data (or its counterpart expressed in the logarithmic values of the levels of the variables), will be merely capturing the underlying identity.

The case of the Verdoorn Law differs somewhat. It will be recalled that the law is usually estimated using cross-country (or cross-regional) data with the growth rates calculated over a period of a number of years. The weighted growth of wages and the rental price of capital differ considerably between countries. In other words, it is not plausible to assume that φ_i or λ_i (where i denotes a particular country or region) is a constant and identical for each country. To see the implications of this, let us express equation (2.32) as:

$$ae_i + (1-a)k_i \equiv -\varphi_i + q_i \tag{2.34}$$

or, equivalently:

$$tfi_i \equiv -\varphi_i + q_i \tag{2.35}$$

where, it will be recalled, tfi denotes the weighted growth of the factor inputs. The time subscript has been dropped for notational convenience.

From the estimation of the Verdoorn Law obtained by regressing the growth of total factor productivity, tfp_i ($\equiv \lambda_i \equiv \varphi_i$), on q_i, we know that there is an empirical relationship of the form:

$$\lambda_i = \lambda_o + \rho q_i \tag{2.36}$$

where λ_o is a constant and ρ takes a value that is approximately equal to one-third (see Table 2.7).

Given that $\varphi_i \equiv \lambda_i$, and substituting equation (2.36) into equation (2.35), we obtain:

$$tfi_i = -\lambda_o + (1-\rho)q_i \tag{2.37}$$

or, equivalently:

$$tfp_i = \varphi_i = \lambda_o + \rho q_i \tag{2.38}$$

In other words, notwithstanding the underlying identity, the Verdoorn Law does have a behavioural component. This is an 'auxiliary' relationship between two components of the identity which shows that a faster growth of output results in, or is associated with, a faster weighted growth of wages and the rental price of capital. This is not without interest since the latter represents the growth of an index of the material standard of living of a country. What the statistical analysis cannot tell us is the individual contributions made by exogenous technical progress, increasing returns to scale and the rate of the capital accumulation. This is by virtue of the underlying identity, and indeed it is not possible to unambiguously interpret equation (2.38) as a specification of an aggregate production function in dynamic form; it is probably best regarded as another of Kaldor's 'stylised facts', or rather a 'stylised relationship'.

The argument can be expressed in similar fashion for the simple Verdoorn Law. Empirically, the growth of the weighted real rental price of capital, $(1-a)\varphi_{ri}$, is small or zero. If factor shares are constant, this implies that $k_i \simeq q_i$. Constant shares also mean that $\varphi_{wi} = p_i$. Consequently, $\varphi_i = \lambda_i \simeq a\varphi_w \simeq ap_i$. Under these assumptions, equation (2.38) may be written as:

$$p_i = p_o + (\rho/a)q_i \qquad (2.39)$$

where p_o is a constant and is equal to λ_o/a.

Given that a, labour's share in income, for manufacturing generally lies between 0.5 and 0.6 for the advanced countries, we should expect the simple Verdoorn coefficient to be between 2 and 1.67 times the size of the Verdoorn coefficient (ρ) obtained using total factor productivity growth as the regressand. This is confirmed by Table 2.7 where it may be seen that the simple Verdoorn coefficient takes a value of 0.587 which is 1.78 times the estimate of ρ, which is 0.329.

Not surprisingly, Rowthorn's Specification raises a similar issue. It will be recalled that the accounting identity is given by (assuming that factor shares are again constant):

$$\begin{aligned} q_i &\equiv a\varphi_{wi} + (1-a)\varphi_{ri} + ae_i + (1-a)k_i \\ &\equiv \varphi_i + ae_i + (1-a)k_i \end{aligned} \qquad (2.40)$$

Rowthorn's Specification is given by:

$$q_i = \lambda_o + v[ae_i + (1-a)k_i] \qquad (2.41)$$

or, alternatively, by:

$$tfp_i = \lambda_i = \lambda_o + (v-1)[ae_i + (1-a)k_i] \qquad (2.42)$$

Comparing equations (2.41) and (2.42) with (2.40), it may be seen that if $v-1$ is found to be statistically significantly greater than zero, and hence v greater than unity (as it is for manufacturing in the US regions), variations in the weighted growth of wages and the rental price of capital can be explained, to a certain extent, by the weighted growth rates of labour and capital. This, again, is of interest.

On the other hand, where v is not statistically greater than unity (as in the case of the cross-country data for the advanced countries) all that, for example, equation (2.41) is capturing is the identity, although mis-specified to the extent that a constant λ_o (or φ_o) has been imposed in the equation, instead of λ_i (or φ_i) which varies between countries or regions.

To summarise, notwithstanding the existence of an underlying identity, the Verdoorn Law and Rowthorn's Specification can reflect behavioural relationships. But the close statistical fit and the low standard errors found in the regressions will, to a certain extent, reflect the identity and the precise interpretation of these relationships is problematical.

THE QUANTITATIVE IMPORTANCE OF INCREASING RETURNS AND THE INTERSECTORAL TRANSFER OF LABOUR IN EXPLAINING PRODUCTIVITY GROWTH[15]

We saw earlier in the chapter that it has been argued that disparities in growth rates of the advanced countries depend, to a large extent, on the effect of increasing returns to scale in industry, together with a fast growth of this sector, and on the presence of surplus labour in agriculture and, possibly, the service sector. The importance of these effects has been succinctly summarised by Kaldor (1968):

> [T]he rate of growth of industrialisation fundamentally depends on the exogenous component of demand (a set of forces extending far beyond the income elasticities of demand for manufactured goods). The higher the rate of growth of industrial output which these demand conditions permit, the faster will be the rate at which labour is transferred from the surplus-sectors to the high-productivity sectors. It is my contention that it is the rate at which this transfer takes place which determines the growth rate of productivity of the economy as a whole. The mechanism by which this happens is only to a minor extent dependent on the *absolute* differences in the levels of output per head between the labour-absorbing sectors and the surplus-labour sectors. The major part of the mechanism consists of the fact that the *growth* of productivity is accelerated as a result of the transfer at both ends – both at the gaining end and at the losing end; in the first, because, as a result of increasing returns, productivity in industry will increase faster, the faster output expands; in the second because when the surplus-

sectors lose labour, the productivity of the remainder of the working population is bound to rise. (Emphasis in the original)

As we have seen, a common feature of those countries that experienced exceptionally fast growth rates of productivity prior to 1973
(most notably Japan, West Germany, France and Italy) was that
initially they had a large and highly inefficient agricultural sector.
There was little mechanisation and the production unit was often the
small spatially fragmented farm, with the result that agricultural
productivity was low compared with the other sectors. These countries also experienced a rapid growth in industrial production and the
resulting growth of the derived demand for labour in industry was
met largely by drawing labour from agriculture and, to a lesser
extent, from the service sector. Some countries also benefitted from a
high rate of immigration. The reallocation of labour from low to high
productivity sectors led to an increase in the rate of growth of
aggregate productivity for purely arithmetical reasons, quite apart
from the mechanism described by Kaldor. On the other hand, those
countries, such as the United Kingdom and the United States, with a
relatively small and efficient agricultural sector were not able to reap
such gains from the improved reallocation of resources. A corollary is
that any large gains in productivity growth from this transfer of
labour, especially in Japan and some of the Continental European
countries, could only be of a temporary nature since these benefits
would inevitably diminish over time as the agricultural sector became
smaller and more efficient.

Two interesting questions arise; to what extent can this phenomenon explain the disparate growth rates of the advanced countries
and to what extent can it account for the productivity slowdown after
1973? The purpose of the last part of this chapter is to attempt to
provide a quantitative answer to these questions.

The approach we adopt is the same as in McCombie (1980) and is
as follows.

The level of productivity for the whole economy at time t may be
expressed in terms of its sectoral components as:

$$P_{wE}(t) \equiv \sum_i Q_i(t)/E_{wE}(t) \tag{2.43}$$

$$\equiv \sum_i P_i(t)a_i(t) \tag{2.44}$$

where P, Q and E are the levels of productivity, output and employment, *WE* denotes the whole economy and *i* denotes the various sectors, namely, agriculture, industry (consisting of manufacturing, construction and public utilities) and the rest of the economy. a_i is the share of sector *i*'s employment in total employment.

Consequently, the annual growth of aggregate productivity is defined as:

$$p_{WE} \equiv (1/T)[ln(\sum_i P_i(T)a_i(T)) - ln(\sum_i P_i(0)a_i(0))] \qquad (2.45)$$

where p_{WE} denotes the annual exponential growth of the productivity of the whole economy.[16] The base and terminal years are denoted by 0 and *T*. Multiplying equation (2.45) by one hundred gives the per annum growth rate in percentage terms.

The growth of aggregate productivity may be dichotomised into two components which we shall term the *standardised* and *structural* productivity growth rates.

The standardised growth is the growth rate of aggregate productivity that would have occurred if all three sectors had experienced the same growth rate of employment, i.e. if their employment had grown at the same rate as that of total employment. The structural productivity growth rate is that due to the differential growth of employment in the various sectors. It therefore captures the effect on productivity growth of the net transfer of labour between the sectors. The structural growth rate is simply the difference between the observed and standardised productivity growth rates.

Formally:

$$p_{WE} \equiv (1/T)\{[ln(\sum_i P_i(T)a_i(0)) - ln(\sum_i P_i(0)a_i(0))]$$
$$+ [ln(\sum_i P_i(T)a_i(T)) - ln(\sum_i P_i(T)a_i(0))]\} \qquad (2.46)$$

where the expression in the first square brackets is the annual growth of standardised productivity and the expression in the second square brackets is the growth of the structural component (when the expressions are divided by *T*).

Equation (2.46) may be interpreted as implying constant returns to scale in all three sectors. The gain (or loss) in transferring a worker between two sectors is simply the difference in the sectoral levels of productivity. In other words, a gain in aggregate productivity growth will arise because, if a net transfer is occurring from a low to a high productivity sector, the loss in output growth in the sector losing labour is less than the gain achieved by employing that labour in the other sector. Under these circumstances, which we shall call *Assumption 1*, the standardised productivity growth will be less than the actual productivity growth and the structural productivity growth will be positive. Differences in sectoral employment growth will have no effect on aggregate productivity growth when all sectors have the same level of productivity. In this case the structural productivity growth will be zero and the gains from the inter-sectoral transfer of labour will have been exhausted. It should be noted that it is possible for the structural component to be negative. Consider, for example, the case where the demand for services is growing sufficiently fast compared with the other sectors to have induced a net transfer of labour into this sector. Negative structural productivity growth would occur if the level of productivity in the service sector was below average. (This is discussed in greater detail below.)

The assumption of constant returns to scale in all sectors, however, may not be appropriate for the advanced countries during the post-war years. A number of the advanced countries should be viewed as 'dual economies', especially during the early postwar period. As we have mentioned, there was a great deal of disguised unemployment in agriculture in many of the countries during this time.

In the limiting case, with surplus labour in agriculture, the growth of agricultural output is unrelated to the growth of the labour input. Empirical confirmation of this hypothesis can be found in Cripps and Tarling (1973). On the basis of a cross-country regression analysis using data drawn from the advanced countries over the period 1950–70, they came to the conclusion that the 'Growth rates of [agricultural] output and employment are almost exactly independent' (Cripps and Tarling, 1973, p. 26). Cornwall (1977) provides a useful survey of other evidence in support of the surplus labour hypothesis.

Consequently, in this case, the standardised level of agricultural output at time T is equal to that which was actually produced, *viz*:

$$Q^*_{AG}(T) = Q_{AG}(T) \qquad (2.47)$$

where the superscript * denotes a standardised value.

In calculating the standardised level of productivity, it is assumed that agricultural employment grows at the same rate as the whole economy, *viz* e_{WE}. Therefore, the standardised level of employment in agriculture at time T is given by

$$E_{AG}^*(T) = E_{AG}(0) \exp(e_{WE}T) \tag{2.48}$$

where exp denotes the natural exponential function.

The standardised level of productivity at time T is defined as:

$$P_{AG}^*(T) = \frac{Q_{AG}^*(T)}{E_{AG}^*(T)} \tag{2.49}$$

Agriculture's contribution to the level of standardised aggregate productivity at time T is therefore $P_{AG}^*(T)a_{AG}(0)$. Alternatively, this may be expressed as:

$$P_{AG}^*(T)a_{AG}(0) = \left[\frac{Q_{AG}^*(T)}{E_{AG}(0) \exp(e_{WE}T)} \right] \left[\frac{E_{AG}(0) \exp(e_{WE}T)}{E_{WE}(0) \exp(e_{WE}T)} \right] \tag{2.50}$$

If we simplify equation (2.50) and multiply both the denominator and numerator by $E_{AG}(0) \exp(e_{AG}T)$ (i.e. by $E_{AG}(T)$) we obtain:

$$P_{AG}^*(T) \, a_{AG}(0) = P_{AG}(T) \, a_{AG}(T) \tag{2.51}$$

At first sight, it may seem strange that the contribution of agriculture to the level of aggregate standardised productivity at time T is the same as it makes to the actual level of productivity, namely $P_{AG}(T)a_{AG}(T)$. This becomes intuitively more obvious once it is remembered that if, for example, all the sectors had surplus labour then the intersectoral transfer of labour would have no effect on the observed growth of aggregate productivity. In other words, under these circumstances, the growth of aggregate standardised productivity would be identical to the actual growth of aggregate productivity which is given by equation (2.45). The growth of the structural component would be zero.

A further complication arises from the fact that the industrial sector exhibits substantial economies of scale of both the 'dynamic' and 'static' variety, captured by Verdoorn's Law, discussed above. Estimates of the Verdoorn coefficient find that it typically takes a value of one-half. The Verdoorn Law thus implies that an increase in the growth of output by one percentage point will result in the growth of employment of half a percentage point and an increase in productivity growth of an equal magnitude. The Law also implies that the gain in output obtained by employing an additional worker is about twice the average productivity.

The Verdoorn Law, specified as $p = a + bq$, may be expressed in terms of productivity growth and employment growth as:

$$p_{IND} = a/(1 - b) + (b/(1 - b))e_{IND} \qquad (2.52)$$

(where b is the Verdoorn coefficient). Since b equals one-half, equation (2.52) may be expressed as:

$$p_{IND} = 2a + e_{IND} \qquad (2.53)$$

Under the assumptions used in calculating the standardised rate of productivity growth, employment in industry is deemed to grow at the same rate as the whole economy.

Consequently, the standardised rate of industrial productivity growth is obtained by substituting e_{WE} for e_{IND} in equation (2.53) and is:

$$p_{IND}^* = 2a + e_{WE} \qquad (2.54)$$

From equation (2.53), it may also be seen that $2a = p_{IND} - e_{IND}$. Substituting this expression into equation (2.54), we obtain:

$$p_{IND}^* = \rho = p_{IND} - e_{IND} + e_{WE} \qquad (2.55)$$

The level of standardised productivity in industry at time T is given by:

$$P_{IND}^*(T) = P_{IND}(0) \exp(\rho T) \qquad (2.56)$$

Finally, it seems plausible to maintain the assumption of constant returns to scale for the 'rest of the economy' (which, it will be recalled, does not include agriculture).

The growth of standardised aggregate productivity (p_{WE}^*) under the assumptions of surplus labour in agriculture, increasing returns to scale in industry and constant returns in the rest of the economy is given by:

$$p_{WE}^* \equiv (1/T)\{\ln[(P_{AG}(T)a_{AG}(T) + P_{IND}^*(T)a_{IND}(0)$$
$$+ P_{ROE}(T)a_{ROE}(0)] - \ln[\sum_i P_i(0)a_i(0)]\} \qquad (2.57)$$

The notation is the same as before and the subscript *ROE* denotes the rest of the economy. As was noted earlier, industry consists of manufacturing, construction and public utilities. For convenience, we shall term collectively the assumptions underlying equation (2.57) as *Assumption 2*.

THE RESULTS: THE LONG BOOM

The long boom was divided into two sub-periods, 1951–65 and 1965–73. The last period was when the simple Verdoorn Law broke down in a statistical sense, although not when the contribution of the growth of capital is included. However, because of the latter and other evidence that suggests the Verdoorn coefficient takes a value of one–half, as we noted above, this estimate was imposed in both periods (i.e. $b/(1 - b) = 1$ in equation (2.52)), allowing exogenous productivity growth to differ between countries. The results for 1951–65 are reported in Table 2.12. Where we assume that constant returns to scale prevail in all the three sectors, namely *Assumption 1*, it can be seen that the inter-sectoral transfer of labour accounts for relatively little of the growth of productivity. The (unweighted) average growth of productivity of the 12 advanced countries was just under 4 per cent per annum and the intersectoral transfer of labour accounted for about one-tenth of this. Not surprisingly, it made the greatest contribution in the case of Japan where the structural component accounts for 15.7 per cent of Japan's observed productivity growth. At the other extreme, the transfer of labour actually retarded growth for the Netherlands.

However, once we allow for increasing returns in industry and surplus labour in agriculture (*Assumption 2*), the contribution of the transfer of labour increases dramatically. For the advanced countries as a whole, it explains 30 per cent of productivity growth. The greatest absolute increase in productivity is again to be found for Japan where the structural productivity growth explains 2.81 percentage points of Japan's productivity growth rate of 7.64 per cent per annum. The greatest percentage contribution to productivity growth accounted for is Denmark. The smallest contribution, both absolutely and relatively, is to be found for the US and the UK. It may be objected that the assumption of surplus labour is unrealistic in these two countries with their heavily commercialised and efficient agricultural sectors. However, the numbers transferred in these countries are sufficiently small that, even under the labour surplus assumption, the intersectoral transfer of labour makes little contribution to overall productivity growth. The degree of disparity in the standardised productivity growth rates under *Assumption 2* is less than that exhibited by the observed productivity growth rates, but significant differences still remain. This is not surprising given the multitude of other factors that determine economic growth. The intersectoral transfer of labour and increasing returns to scale can explain a lot, but not all, of the story.[17]

The period 1965–73 actually saw a slight increase in the average productivity growth rates of the 12 countries from 3.96 per cent per annum (1951–65) to 4.27 (1965–73). (See Table 2.13.) However, under both assumptions, the contribution of the transfer of labour declines. Under *Assumption 1* it explains only 6.3 per cent of the average productivity growth of the twelve countries. Under *Assumption 2* the percentage of total productivity growth explained by the structural component declines from 30 per cent to 13 per cent. Nevertheless, it is still important in the cases of Italy, Japan and Norway where it explains over one-quarter of productivity growth. In both periods, there is a tendency for the growth of the structural component to be greatest for those countries which had the greatest growth rates of productivity; the Spearman rank correlation coefficients of 0.804 (1951–65) and 0.664 (1965–73) are significant at the 95 per cent confidence level.

An interesting finding is that in spite of the decline in the contribution of the structural component, overall productivity growth did not fall commensurately, but, as we have noted, actually increased slightly. A counterpart to this is that in the period 1965–73, the variation in the growth of employment in the manufacturing sectors converged, but there was no such diminution of disparities in manufacturing productivity growth. It may well be that as surplus labour became exhausted, X-inefficiency in industry was progressively reduced leading to an increase in 'exogenous' productivity growth. Cripps and Tarling (1973, p. 32) suggest that 'where the manufacturing sector still managed to achieve a rapid growth of sales, the more successful producers may have been increasingly forced to find labour from within the manufacturing sector itself, either by direct competition in the labour market or by direct acquisition and reorganisation of low productivity plants'.

To conclude; these results suggest that Kaldor is correct, at least for the period 1951–65, in his emphasis on the importance of the transfer of labour if surplus labour in agriculture exists and there are large economies of scale in manufacturing.

Table 2.12   Aggregate productivity growth and its standardised and structural components (% per annum); 1951–65

Country	Productivity growth	Standardised productivity growth	Structural productivity growth	Structural as a % of actual productivity growth
Assumption 1 (Constant returns in all sectors).				
Austria	4.79	4.16	0.63	13.2
Belgium	3.06	3.06	0.00	0.0
Canada	2.41	2.21	0.20	8.3
Denmark	3.65	3.39	0.26	7.1
France	4.91	4.35	0.56	11.4
Germany	4.95	4.32	0.63	12.7
Italy	4.20	3.64	0.56	13.3
Japan	7.64	6.44	1.20	15.7
Netherlands	3.71	3.73	−0.02	n.m.
Norway	3.83	3.36	0.47	12.3
United Kingdom	2.05	2.03	0.02	1.0
United States	2.34	2.20	0.14	6.0
Unweighted mean	3.96	3.57	0.39	9.8
Assumption 2 (Surplus labour in agriculture, increasing returns in industry and constant returns in the rest of the economy).				
Austria	4.79	3.63	1.16	24.2
Belgium	3.06	2.65	0.41	13.4
Canada	2.41	1.58	0.83	34.4
Denmark	3.65	1.91	1.74	47.7
France	4.91	3.44	1.47	29.9
Germany	4.95	3.26	1.69	34.1
Italy	4.20	2.31	1.89	45.0
Japan	7.64	4.83	2.81	36.8
Netherlands	3.71	3.11	0.60	16.2
Norway	3.83	2.81	1.02	26.6
United Kingdom	2.04	1.79	0.25	12.2
United States	2.34	2.03	0.31	13.2
Unweighted mean	3.96	2.78	1.18	30.0

Notes: Periods covered – Japan   1953–64   West Germany 1951–65
                              France   1957–64   Netherlands   1951–65
                              Denmark   1957–65   Austria   1957–66
                              Canada   1951–66   Norway   1951–65
                              Belgium   1951–64   Italy   1951–63
                              UK   1951–65   US   1951–66

n.m. denotes not meaningful.

Sources: OECD *National Accounts* (various years); OECD *Labour Force Statistics* (various years).

Table 2.13   Aggregate productivity growth and its standardised and structural components (% per annum); 1965–73

Country	Productivity growth	Standardised productivity growth	Structural productivity growth	Structural as a % of actual productivity growth
Assumption 1 (Constant returns in all sectors).				
Austria	6.04	5.53	0.51	8.4
Belgium	4.15	4.17	−0.02	n.m.
Canada	2.14	2.14	0.00	0.0
Denmark	3.42	3.18	0.24	7.0
France	4.51	4.21	0.30	6.7
Germany	4.59	4.36	0.23	5.0
Italy	5.21	4.61	0.60	11.5
Japan	8.64	7.64	1.00	11.6
Netherlands	4.55	4.68	−0.13	n.m.
Norway	3.54	3.10	0.44	12.4
United Kingdom	2.75	2.68	0.07	2.5
United States	1.78	1.80	−0.02	−1.1
Unweighted mean	4.27	4.00	0.27	6.3
Assumption 2 (Surplus labour in agriculture, increasing returns in industry and constant returns in the rest of the economy).				
Austria	6.04	5.06	0.98	16.2
Belgium	4.15	4.17	−0.02	n.m.
Canada	2.14	2.34	−0.20	n.m.
Denmark	3.42	2.64	0.78	22.8
France	4.51	3.84	0.67	14.9
Germany	4.59	4.13	0.46	10.0
Italy	5.21	3.77	1.44	27.6
Japan	8.64	6.31	2.33	27.0
Netherlands	4.55	4.89	−0.34	n.m.
Norway	3.54	2.57	0.97	27.4
United Kingdom	2.75	2.93	−0.18	n.m.
United States	1.78	2.02	−0.24	n.m.
Unweighted mean	4.27	3.72	0.55	12.9

Notes: Periods covered – Japan   1964–69   West Germany 1965–73
France   1964–73   Netherlands 1965–73
Denmark   1965–69   Austria   1966–73
Canada   1966–73   Norway   1965–70
Belgium   1964–73   Italy   1963–73
UK   1965–73   US   1966–76

n.m. denotes not meaningful.

Sources: See Table 2.12.

EXPLAINING THE SLOWDOWN: THE RESULTS FOR 1973–85

The year 1973 marks something of a watershed since it was from this date that the (unweighted) average productivity growth rate of the advanced countries fell by over one-half. A similar pattern is found for GDP growth (see Chapter 1).

The process of de-industrialisation accelerated after 1973 and the decline in the growth of demand for labour emanating from the industrial sector provides another reason why the rate of transfer of labour from the agricultural to the industrial sector declined. There were also less gains in productivity growth to be had from the Verdoorn effect from this date. As may be seen from Table 2.14, under *Assumption 1* the structural component on average explained a negligible proportion of the observed productivity growth of the 13 advanced countries (the sample has been extended to include Australia). Under *Assumption 2* the contribution of the structural component overall is actually negative. This is largely because the growth of industrial employment over the period 1973–85 was slower in all the advanced countries than the growth of total employment and in many countries it was actually negative. Thus the net transfer of labour was out of industry rather than the converse as was the case in the Long Boom.

The main question we wish to examine in this section is whether or not these factors can largely explain the productivity growth slowdown. If this were the case, the structural component of productivity growth should be sufficiently small compared with that of the pre-1973 period to make the standardised growth rates in the period 1973–85 comparable with those calculated for 1951–73.

The results of the calculations of the standardised and structural components of aggregate productivity growth under *Assumptions 1* and *2* for 1973–85 are, as we have already noted, reported in Table 2.14 The slowdown in the actual and the standardised productivity growth rates are reported in Table 2.15.

Turning first to the results under *Assumption 1*, where it will be recalled it is postulated that there are constant returns to scale in all sectors, it may be seen from Table 2.14 that the structural component is relatively insignificant for all the advanced countries. As we have noted, if the structural component could explain all of the slowdown then there should be no difference between the standardised growth rates in the two periods. In the vast majority of cases, however, the standardised growth is less than that in 1951–73 and the difference may be interpreted as the 'unexplained' productivity growth slowdown. Thus, as may be seen from Table 2.15, under *Assumption 1* there was an (unweighted) average slowdown of 1.91 percentage points in the standardised growth rate of the advanced countries which means that 86 per cent of the actual slowdown still remains to be explained.

Under *Assumption 2* which assumes that there is surplus labour in agriculture, increasing returns to scale in industry and constant returns to scale in the rest of the economy, the effect of the transfer of labour explains considerably more of the slowdown. On average there was only a slowdown of 0.84 percentage points in the standardised growth rate leaving a little over a third of the actual productivity slowdown to be explained.

The reason for this difference between the two sets of assumptions is as follows. There is generally no great difference between the relative levels of productivity between industry and the rest of the economy at least when compared with the difference between these two sectors and agriculture. (Australia proves to be the major exception.) The sector the 'rest of the economy' has an employment growth rate which is significantly faster than that of industry for all the countries. But under *Assumption 1* this does not greatly influence the size of growth of the structural component compared with that which would be obtained if industry was still the most rapidly growing sector. This is because the relatively small difference in the productivity levels of industry and the rest of the economy means that the growth of the structural component is going to be small regardless of which of the two sectors is the faster growing. When increasing returns to scale are assumed in industry, the Verdoorn Law, as we have noted, implies that the productivity of the marginal worker is twice the average product in industry, and is also considerably larger than that of the marginal worker in the rest of the economy. Hence, the fall in industrial growth has a commensurately larger effect in explaining the productivity slowdown than under *Assumption 1*.

It may be legitimately argued, as we noted above, that the assumption of surplus labour in *Assumption 2* is not appropriate for those countries with a highly productive agricultural sector such as Australia, Belgium, the United Kingdom and the United States. We therefore recomputed the estimates of the two components on the assumption of constant returns in agriculture and the rest of the economy and increasing returns in industry. This did not make very

Table 2.14   Aggregate productivity growth and its standardised and structural components (% per annum); 1973–85 (1951–73 in parentheses)[a]

Country	Productivity growth		Standardised productivity growth		Structural productivity growth	
Assumption 1 (Constant returns in all sectors).						
Australia[b]	1.51	(2.46)	1.47	(2.53)	0.04	(−0.07)
Austria	1.56	(5.34)	1.40	(4.76)	0.16	(0.58)
Belgium	1.96	(3.50)	2.16	(3.51)	−0.20	(−0.01)
Canada	0.52	(2.32)	0.61	(2.19)	−0.09	(0.13)
Denmark	1.36	(3.57)	1.28	(3.32)	0.08	(0.25)
France	2.11	(4.68)	2.19	(4.27)	−0.08	(0.41)
Germany	2.25	(4.82)	2.14	(4.33)	0.11	(0.49)
Italy[c]	1.40	(4.66)	1.38	(4.08)	0.02	(0.58)
Japan	3.01	(7.95)	2.76	(6.81)	0.25	(1.14)
Netherlands[d]	1.91	(4.02)	2.06	(4.04)	−0.15	(−0.02)
Norway	3.00	(3.75)	2.76	(3.29)	0.24	(0.46)
Norway[e]	1.41	(3.75)	1.37	(3.29)	0.04	(0.46)
United Kingdom	1.54	(2.31)	1.63	(2.27)	−0.09	(0.04)
United Kingdom[e]	1.06	(2.31)	1.22	(2.27)	−0.16	(0.04)
United States	0.62	(2.16)	0.75	(2.07)	−0.13	(0.09)
Unweighted mean[f]	1.75	(3.96)	1.74	(3.65)	0.01	(0.31)
Assumption 2 (Surplus labour in agriculture, increasing returns in industry and constant returns in the rest of the economy).						
Australia[b]	1.51	(2.46)	2.19	(2.83)	−0.68	(−0.37)
Austria	1.56	(5.34)	1.44	(4.25)	0.12	(1.09)
Belgium	1.96	(3.50)	3.37	(3.27)	−1.41	(0.23)
Canada	0.52	(2.32)	1.20	(1.82)	−0.68	(0.50)
Denmark	1.36	(3.57)	1.58	(2.15)	−0.22	(1.42)
France	2.11	(4.68)	2.73	(3.66)	−0.62	(1.02)
Germany	2.25	(4.82)	2.70	(3.58)	−0.45	(1.24)
Italy[c]	1.40	(4.66)	1.79	(2.97)	−0.39	(1.69)
Japan	3.00	(7.95)	2.94	(5.32)	0.06	(2.63)
Netherlands[d]	1.91	(4.02)	2.97	(3.76)	−1.06	(0.26)
Norway	3.00	(3.75)	3.07	(2.75)	−0.07	(1.00)
Norway[e]	1.41	(3.75)	1.71	(2.75)	−0.30	(1.00)
United Kingdom	1.54	(2.30)	2.67	(2.20)	−1.13	(0.10)
United Kingdom[e]	1.06	(2.30)	2.31	(2.20)	−1.25	(0.10)
United States	0.62	(2.16)	1.25	(2.03)	−0.63	(0.13)
Unweighted mean[f]	1.75	(3.96)	2.30	(3.12)	−0.55	(0.84)

Notes: ᵃThe productivity growth rates for 1951–73 differ marginally from those reported in Table 1.2 (see p. 7) because the latter incorporate subsequent statistical revisions.
ᵇElectricity, gas and water are included in the rest of the economy.
ᶜMining and quarrying is included in industry.
ᵈCoal mining is included in industry.
ᵉExcludes crude petroleum and natural gas production.
ᶠNorway and UK with crude petroleum and natural gas production included.

Sources: *National Accounts*, OECD, Paris (various years); *Labour Force Statistics*, OECD, Paris (various years); McCombie (1980 and 1991).

---

much difference to the results. The standardised annual growth rate of Australia was 2.30 per cent (compared with 2.19 per cent under *Assumption 2*); Belgium was 3.43 per cent (3.37 per cent); the United Kingdom was 2.69 per cent (2.67 per cent) and the United States was 1.34 per cent (1.25 per cent). The small sizes of these differences are mainly due to the relatively small number of workers leaving the agricultural sector over the period 1973–85.

In the case of Norway and the United Kingdom, the occurrence of a positive value in Table 2.15 for the standardised productivity growth slowdown under *Assumption 2* indicates that the structural component actually over-explains the slowdown. The rate of Norway's productivity growth was about the average of the advanced nations during the pre-1973 period, but from 1973 to 1985 it was virtually identical to the growth of Japan which, in turn, had the fastest productivity growth of all the countries. A large proportion of both Norway's and the United Kingdom's post-1973 productivity growth was due to the windfall gain of North Sea oil and gas production. The rapid growth of oil and gas production since the mid-1970s was accomplished with only a relatively small growth of employment in this industry. This had a significant effect of increasing the growth of aggregate productivity of both the countries.

As may be seen from Table 2.14, if crude petroleum and natural gas production and employment are excluded from the data, Norway's productivity growth during the post-1973 period falls by over half, from 3.00 per cent to 1.41 per cent per annum. The standardised productivity growth rate falls concomitantly. A similar picture is found for the United Kingdom where oil and natural gas production accounts for nearly a third of the United Kingdom's productivity growth of 1.54 per cent per annum.

Table 2.15   The slowdown in actual and standardised productivity growth
rates between 1973–85 and 1951–73[a] (% per annum)

Country	Actual productivity growth slowdown	Standardised productivity growth slowdown	
		Assumption 1	Assumption 2
Australia	−0.95	−1.06	−0.64
Austria	−3.78	−3.36	−2.81
Belgium	−1.54	−1.35	−0.10
Canada	−1.81	−1.58	−0.62
Denmark	−2.21	−2.04	−0.57
France	−2.57	−2.08	−0.93
Germany	−2.57	−2.19	−0.88
Italy	−3.26	−2.70	−1.18
Japan	−4.94	−4.05	−2.38
Netherlands	−2.11	−1.98	−0.79
Norway	−0.75	−0.53	+0.32
United Kingdom	−0.77	−0.64	+0.47
United States	−1.54	−1.32	−0.78
Unweighted mean	−2.22	−1.91	−0.84
Norway[b]	−2.34	−1.92	−1.04
United Kingdom[b]	−1.25	−1.05	+0.11
Unweighted mean[c]	−2.37	−2.05	−0.97

Notes: [a]The initial years are the same as those in Table 2.12 and the terminal
years as those in Table 2.13.
[b]Excludes crude petroleum and natural gas production.
[c]Average of the 13 countries, but the figures for Norway and the
United Kingdom exclude crude petroleum and natural gas
production.

Sources: The same as for Table 2.14.

The results of *Assumption 2* thus suggest that a substantial part of
the very rapid productivity growth experienced during the sustained
boom of the earlier postwar years was of a transitory nature.
Obviously, the gains in productivity induced by the transfer of labour
would diminish over time with the contraction of the size of the
agricultural sector.

Another important explanation lies in the decline in the growth of
the industrial sector and a consequent net transfer of labour to the
rest of the economy, the majority of which comprises the service

sector. Industry, under the assumption of increasing returns to scale, has a marginal product of labour that is considerably higher than that in the rest of the economy. The result is that the inter-sectoral transfer of labour in the post-1973 period away from industry generates a large negative structural growth rate for a number of countries.

The question arises as to what caused the process of 'de-industrialisation'. One explanation is that, with increasing per capita income, demand has shifted away from manufactured goods towards services. There are also a number of other reasons why the growth of the rest of the economy should be less sensitive than industry to the output growth slowdown. The rest of the economy includes such large non-market services as health and education which tend to grow under their own momentum. Moreover, the government sector as a whole may have expanded relatively faster in an attempt to reduce the increasing level of unemployment that emerged after 1973.

Finally, mention must be made of the well-known measurement errors that are inherent in the estimates of output for the tertiary sector. Such errors may well lead to an underestimate of the true rate of productivity growth in this sector.

3 The Balance-of-Payments Constraint as an Explanation of International Growth Rate Differences

We outline in this chapter the concept of the balance-of-payments equilibrium growth rate, as originally developed by Thirlwall (1979, 1982a), and then show its empirical application to a wide range of developed and less developed countries, drawing also on the recent work of Bairam (1988, 1990). The two original papers by Thirlwall are presented here basically in their original form, but with some modifications.

THE THEORY

As we saw in Chapter 1, the neoclassical approach to the question of why growth rates differ between countries, typified by the meticulous studies of, *inter alios*, Denison (1967, 1985), Kendrick (1981) and Maddison (1970, 1972) concentrates on the supply side of the economy using the concept of the production function. Having specified the functional form, the growth of output is apportioned between the growth of capital, the growth of labour, and the growth of total factor productivity obtained as a residual. By this approach, growth rate differences are 'explained' in terms of differences in the growth of factor supplies and productivity. While the approach is considered by some to be fruitful, interesting and mathematically precise, it does not tell us *why* the growth of factor supplies and productivity differs between countries. To answer this question a more Keynesian approach is required which stresses demand. In Keynesian theory it is demand that 'drives' the economic system to which supply, within limits, adapts. Taking this approach, growth rates differ because the growth of demand differs between countries. The question then

232

becomes why does demand grow at different rates between countries? One explanation may be the inability of economic agents, particularly governments, to expand demand. This explanation by itself, however, is not very satisfactory. The more probable explanation lies in constraints on demand. In an open economy, the dominant constraint is the balance of payments. In this chapter, it is shown how closely the growth experience of several developed countries approximates to the rate of growth of exports divided by the income elasticity of demand for imports, which, on certain assumptions, can be regarded as a measure of what may be called the balance-of-payments equilibrium growth rate. In fact, the rate of growth of exports divided by the income elasticity of demand for imports gives such a good approximation to the actual growth experience of major developed countries since 1950 that a new economic rule, or 'stylised fact' to use Kaldor's term, might almost be formulated.

The importance of a healthy balance of payments for growth can be stated quite succinctly. If a country gets into balance-of-payments difficulties as it expands demand before the short-term capacity growth rate is reached, then demand must be curtailed; supply is never fully utilised; investment is discouraged; technological progress is slowed down, and a country's goods compared with foreign goods become less desirable so worsening the balance of payments still further, and so on. A vicious circle is started. By contrast, if a country is able to expand demand up to the level of existing productive capacity, without balance-of-payments difficulties arising, the pressure of demand upon capacity may well raise the capacity growth rate. There are a number of possible mechanisms through which this may happen: the encouragement to investment which would augment the capital stock and bring with it technological progress; the supply of labour may increase by the entry into the workforce of people previously outside or from abroad; the movement of factors of production from low productivity to high productivity sectors, and the ability to import more may increase capacity by making domestic resources more productive. It is this argument that lies behind the advocacy of export-led growth, because it is only through the expansion of exports that the growth rate can be raised without the balance of payments deteriorating at the same time. Believers in export-led growth are really postulating a balance-of-payments constraint theory of why growth rates differ. It should be stressed, however, that the same rate of export growth in different countries will not necessarily permit the same rate of growth of output because the import requirements associated with growth will differ between countries, and thus some countries will have to constrain demand sooner than others for balance-of-payments equilibrium. The relation between a country's growth rate and its rate of growth of imports is the income of elasticity of demand for imports. The hypothesis we shall be testing, from the model to be outlined below, is that, if balance-of-payments equilibrium must be maintained, a country's long-run growth rate will be determined by the ratio of its rate of growth of exports to its income elasticity of demand for imports.

THE DETERMINATION OF THE BALANCE-OF-PAYMENTS EQUILIBRIUM GROWTH RATE

Balance-of-payments equilibrium on current account measured in units of the home currency may be expressed as:

$$P_d X = P_f ME \tag{3.1}$$

where X is the quantity of exports; P_d is the price of exports in home currency; M is the quantity of imports; P_f is the price of imports in foreign currency; and E is the exchange rate (i.e. the home price of foreign currency).

In a growing economy, the condition for balance-of-payments equilibrium through time is that the rate of growth of the value of exports equals the rate of growth of the value of imports, i.e.:

$$p_d + x = p_f + m + e \tag{3.2}$$

where lower-case letters represent (continuous) rates of change of the variables.

Using standard demand theory, the quantity of imports demanded may be specified as a multiplicative function of the price of imports (measured in units of the home currency), the price of import substitutes, and domestic income. Thus:

$$M = a \left(\frac{P_f E}{P_d} \right)^{\psi} Y^{\pi} \tag{3.3}$$

where a is a constant, ψ is the price elasticity of demand for imports

($\psi < 0$). Y is domestic income, and π is the income elasticity of demand for imports ($\pi > 0$).

The rate of growth of imports may be written:

$$m = \psi(p_f + e - p_d) + \pi y \tag{3.4}$$

where lower-case letters again represent continuous rates of change of the variables.

The quantity of exports demanded may also be expressed as a multiplicative function in which the arguments in the demand function are: the price of exports; the price of goods competitive with exports (measured in units of domestic currency), and the level of world income. Thus:

$$X = b\left(\frac{P_d}{P_f E}\right)^\eta Z^\varepsilon \tag{3.5}$$

where b is a constant, η is the price elasticity of demand for exports ($\eta < 0$); Z is world income and ε is the income elasticity of demand for exports ($\varepsilon > 0$).

The rate of growth of exports may be written:

$$x = \eta(p_d - p_f - e) + \varepsilon z \tag{3.6}$$

Substituting equations (3.4) and (3.6) into (3.2), we can solve for the rate of growth of domestic income consistent with balance-of-payments equilibrium which we shall call the balance-of-payments equilibrium growth rate, y_B:

$$y_B = \frac{(1 + \eta + \psi)(p_d - p_f - e) + \varepsilon z}{\pi} \tag{3.7}$$

Remembering the signs of the parameters ($\eta < 0$; $\psi < 0$; $\varepsilon > 0$; and $\pi > 0$), equation (3.7) expresses several familiar economic propositions:

(i) Inflation in the home country relative to abroad will lower the balance-of-payments equilibrium growth rate if the sum of the price elasticities of demand for exports and imports is greater than unity in absolute value (i.e. if $|\eta + \psi| > 1$).

(ii) A continuous devaluation or currency depreciation, i.e. a sustained rise in the home price of foreign currency ($e > 0$), will improve the balance-of-payments equilibrium growth rate provided the sum of the price elasticities of demand for imports and exports exceeds unity in absolute value, which is the Marshall–Lerner condition (i.e. if $|\eta + \psi| > 1$). Notice, however, the important point that a once-for-all depreciation of the currency will not raise the balance-of-payments equilibrium growth rate permanently. After the initial depreciation, e will equal zero and the growth rate would revert to its former level. To raise the balance-of-payments equilibrium growth rate permanently would require continuous depreciation i.e. $e > 0$ in successive periods.

(iii) A faster growth of world income will raise the balance-of-payments equilibrium growth rate, but by how much depends crucially on the size of ε, the income elasticity of demand for exports.

(iv) The higher the income elasticity of demand for imports (π), the lower the balance-of-payments equilibrium growth rate.

To calculate the balance-of-payments equilibrium growth rate from equation (3.7) for a number of countries requires a substantial amount of data and estimates of parameters which are not readily available. If the assumption is made, however, that relative prices measured in a common currency do not change over the long run, equation (3.7) reduces to:

$$y_B = \frac{\varepsilon z}{\pi} = \frac{x}{\pi} \tag{3.8}$$

i.e. a country's balance-of-payments equilibrium growth rate equals the rate of growth of export volume divided by the income elasticity of demand for imports.

Many models (see Ball *et al.*, 1977; and Wilson, 1976), and the empirical evidence, suggest that over the long period movements in relative prices measured in a common currency are comparatively small. Models of both perfect competition (the neoclassical interpretation of the 'law of one price') and oligopoly predict this, although we shall show that international trade is, in fact, characterised by highly differentiated products produced under conditions of oligopoly (see Chapter 4). Also when exchange rate changes take place, domestic price movements tend to mirror those changes to keep real exchange rates relatively stable.

The result in equation (3.8) has been recently called by Krugman (1989) the 45-degree rule since the growth of one country (y_B) relative to all the others (z) will be equiproportional to the ratio of the income elasticities of demand for exports and imports (ε/π). That is to say, $y_B/z = \varepsilon/\pi$. Unlike us, however, he wishes to reverse the direction of causation: instead of the ratio of income elasticities determining relative growth rates, he argues that relative growth rates determine relative income elasticities. In Chapter 5, we shall criticise this (neoclassical) view.

THE HARROD FOREIGN TRADE MULTIPLIER

The simple growth rule, specified in equation (3.8), that growth will approximate to $y = x/\pi$ in the long run, can be shown to be the dynamic analogue of the static foreign trade multiplier, first put forward by Sir Roy Harrod (1933). In his book, *International Economics*, Harrod put forward the idea that the pace and rhythm of industrial growth in open economies was to be explained by the principle of the foreign trade multiplier which at the same time provided a mechanism for keeping the balance-of-payments in equilibrium.

The original Harrod foreign trade multiplier assumes that the real terms of trade are constant; that there is no saving and investment, and no government activity. Output or income is generated by the production of consumption goods (C) and exports (X), and all income is spent either on home consumption goods (C) or imports (M). On these assumptions trade is always balanced, and income adjusts to preserve equilibrium. We have:

$$Y = C + X \tag{3.9}$$

and:

$$Y = C + M \tag{3.10}$$

$$\therefore \quad X = M \tag{3.11}$$

Now let the import function be:

$$M = M_0 + \mu Y \tag{3.12}$$

where M_0 is the level of autonomous imports and μ is the marginal propensity to import. (We use μ rather than the conventional notation, m, since the latter is used by us to denote the rate of growth of imports.) We then have:

$$X = M_0 + \mu Y \tag{3.13a}$$

or:

$$Y = \frac{X - M_0}{\mu} \tag{3.13b}$$

It follows that:

$$\frac{\Delta Y}{\Delta X} = \frac{\Delta Y}{\Delta M_0} = \frac{1}{\mu} \tag{3.14}$$

This is the static Harrod foreign trade multiplier. The multiplier, $1/\mu$, will always bring the balance of payments back into equilibrium through changes in income following a change in exports or autonomous imports.

The assumptions used by Harrod to derive his original result are clearly unrealistic, but the Harrod result will still hold if (i) other induced expenditures and withdrawals from the circular flow of income balance each other in the aggregate or (ii) balance-of-payments equilibrium is, for one reason or another, a policy objective or requirement so that the level and growth of income must of necessity be constrained in the long run to preserve a balance between exports and imports.

Equation (3.l4) when it is made 'dynamic', becomes the simple growth rule $y = x/\pi$. We have:

$$\frac{\Delta Y}{Y} = \frac{\Delta X}{X} \frac{1}{\pi} \tag{3.15}$$

where $\Delta Y/Y$ is the rate of growth of income, and $\Delta X/X$ is the rate of growth of export volume. If the real terms of trade remain unchanged, we can use the equilibrium condition under which the Harrod foreign trade multiplier works and multiply the left hand side of equation (3.14) by X/Y and the right hand side by M/Y (since $X = M$) to give:

$$\frac{\Delta Y}{\Delta X} \frac{X}{Y} = \frac{\Delta Y}{\Delta M} \frac{M}{Y} \qquad (3.16)$$

or:

$$\frac{\Delta Y}{Y} = \frac{\Delta X}{X} \left(\frac{\Delta Y}{\Delta M} \frac{M}{Y} \right) = \frac{\Delta X}{X} \frac{1}{\pi} \qquad (3.17)$$

There are only two factors which may cause a country's growth rate to deviate from this rate: first, changes in the real terms of trade, and secondly capital flows allowing there to be a difference between domestic expenditure and income and a current account disequilibrium.[1] If equation (3.17) predicts well, the presumption must be either that these two factors are relatively unimportant, or that they are working in opposite directions, and by exactly the same amount to offset each other (which would seem to be highly coincidental).

EMPIRICAL EVIDENCE FOR THE DEVELOPED COUNTRIES

The interesting question is how well does the actual growth experience of countries approximate to the balance-of-payments equilibrium growth rate? There may, of course, be an asymmetry in the system. While a country cannot grow faster than its balance-of-payments equilibrium growth rate for very long, unless it can finance an ever-growing deficit, there is little to stop a country growing slower and accumulating large surpluses. This may particularly occur where the balance-of-payments equilibrium growth rate is so high that a country simply does not have the physical capacity to grow at that rate. This typifies many oil producing countries and would also seem to typify the experience of Japan, especially in the postwar period prior to 1973, as we shall see below.

Applying equation (3.8) to international data gives a remarkable approximation to the growth experience of many countries over the last thirty years, and *ipso facto* provides an explanation of why growth rates differ. It might almost be stated as a fundamental rule that, except where the balance-of-payments equilibrium growth rate exceeds the maximum feasible capacity growth rate, the rate of growth of a country will approximate to the ratio of its rate of growth of exports and its income elasticity of demand for imports. The approximation itself vindicates the assumptions used to arrive at the simple rule in equation (3.8). The hypothesis is tested here on two sets of data on the growth of output and exports: one for the period 1953 to 1976 (Kern, 1978), and the other from a different source (Cornwall, 1977) for the period 1951 to 1973.[2] On the income elasticity of demand for imports, Houthakker and Magee's estimates (1969) have been taken as applying to the whole of these periods even though they were only estimated over the period 1951 to 1966. They are one of the best consistently estimated international estimates available, but are probably now on the low side. The data and the results of applying equation (3.8) are presented in Tables 3.1 and 3.2.

In both tables there is a general tendency for the estimates of the balance-of-payments equilibrium growth rate to be higher than the actual growth rate, which, if true, would produce a balance-of-

Table 3.1   Calculations of the growth rate consistent with balance-of-payments equilibrium 1953–76

Country	% Change of real GNP (y)	% Change in export volume (x)	Income elasticity of demand for imports (π)	Balance-of-payments equilibrium growth rate from applying equation (3.8)
USA	3.23	5.88	1.51	3.89
Canada	4.81	6.02	1.20	5.02
West Germany	4.96	9.99	1.89	5.29
Netherlands	4.99	9.38	1.82	5.15
Sweden	3.67	7.16	1.76	4.07
France	4.95	8.78	1.62	5.42
Denmark	3.58	6.77	1.31	5.17
Australia	4.95	6.98	0.90	7.76
Italy	4.96	12.09	2.25	5.37
Switzerland	3.56	7.20	1.90	3.79
Norway	4.18	7.70	1.40	5.50
Belgium	4.07	9.24	1.94	4.76
Japan	8.55	16.18	1.23	13.15
Austria	5.17	11.12	n.a.	–
United Kingdom	2.71	4.46	1.51	2.95
South Africa	4.97	6.57	0.85	7.73
Spain	5.94	11.10	n.a.	–
Finland	4.55	6.63	n.a.	–

Table 3.2   Calculations of the growth rate consistent with balance-of-payments equilibrium 1951–73 using data given by Cornwall (1977)

Country	% Change of real GNP (y)	% Change in export volume (x)	Income elasticity of demand for imports (π)	Balance-of-payments equilibrium growth rate from applying equation (3.8)
Austria	5.1[a]	10.7	n.a.	–
Belgium	4.4[a]	9.4	1.94	4.84
Canada	4.6	6.9	1.20	5.75
Denmark	4.2[b]	6.1	1.31	4.65
France	5.0	8.1	1.62	5.00
Germany	5.7	10.8	1.89	5.71
Italy	5.1	11.7	2.25	5.20
Japan	9.5	15.4	1.23	12.52
Netherlands	5.0	10.1	1.82	5.55
Norway	4.2	7.2	1.40	5.14
United Kingdom	2.7	4.1	1.51	2.71
USA	3.7	5.1	1.51	3.38

Notes: [a]1955–73; [b]1954–73.

payments surplus. For countries which have built up surpluses, the estimates are consistent with the empirical evidence. Japan is a striking example of a country where the gap between its actual growth rate and its balance-of-payments equilibrium growth rate has resulted in the build up of a huge payments surplus. Presumably Japan could not grow faster than it did because of an ultimate capacity ceiling. But Japan still grew considerably faster than other countries because demand was unconstrained and induced its own supply of factors of production. For countries which have moved into deficit over the period, the estimate of their balance-of-payments equilibrium growth rate must be too high. As suggested above, this may be because the assumed income elasticity of demand for imports is an underestimate for the period stretching into the late 1960s and 1970s. Also, adverse relative price movements combined with various price elasticity conditions cannot be entirely ruled out as determinants of the balance of payments even though they may be of minor significance compared with income movements and income elasticities of demand for imports and exports.

Despite the overestimation of the balance-of-payments equilibrium growth rate in some cases, and the fact that some countries may grow slower and build up payments surpluses, nonetheless, the rank correlations between the predicted growth rates from applying our simple rule and the actual growth rates are very high for both sets of data. For the sample of countries in Table 3.1 the Spearman rank correlation is 0.764 and in Table 3.2 the Spearman rank correlation is 0.891.

More recent work by Bairam (1988) has applied the above model to a wider range of developed countries over the more recent time period 1970–85. The results are shown in Table 3.3.

Bairam concludes: 'The results obtained . . . consistently suggest that the overall economic growth is determined by the Harrod foreign trade multiplier. This means that overall economic performance of a country depends upon the values of its income elasticities of exports and imports.'

There are two formal tests of whether or not the actual growth experience of countries can be predicted from its balance-of-payments equilibrium growth rate. One is to regress y on y_B and test whether the regression coefficient is equal to unity. If it is, y_B will be a good predictor of y. The test, however, suffers three drawbacks.

First, there may be bias (i.e. systematic overprediction or underprediction) if only an incomplete sample of countries is taken in which balance-of-payments surpluses and deficits do not cancel out (i.e. if there is a systematic tendency for $y_B > y$ or $y_B < y$).

Secondly, there may well be outliers where y does not equal y_B (such as Japan). The inclusion of such countries in the sample may well give rise to a regression coefficient that is significantly different from unity, thereby erroneously leading us to reject the rule for *all* countries. Moreover, all countries cannot logically be balance-of-payments-constrained at the same time. Any test that tries to test the hypothesis that they can be, as in the case of regression analysis, is mis-specified.

Thirdly, the estimate of π used to calculate y_B has an associated standard error because π itself is estimated from a regression analysis. A better procedure is to regress y_B on y but this does not obviate the first two criticisms. Consequently, the use by McGregor and Swales (1985, 1991) of ordinary least squares in regressing y on y_B is inappropriate (see Chapter 5).

An alternative test which avoids these problems is to take each country separately and to estimate π (i.e. π') that would make $y = y_B$, and to compare that estimate with the estimated π from time-series

Table 3.3 Calculations of the growth rate consistent with balance-of-payments equilibrium 1970–85 using data given by Bairam (1988)

Country	% Change of real GNP (y)	% Change in export volume (x)	Income elasticity of demand for imports (π)	Balance-of-payments equilibrium growth rate from applying equation (3.8)
France	3.5	6.3	2.42	2.6
W. Germany	2.4	5.0	1.92	2.6
Italy	2.6	5.2	2.83	1.8
UK	1.9	4.7	2.14	2.2
Austria	3.3	6.8	2.24	3.0
Belgium	2.7	5.0	2.64	1.9
Denmark	2.2	4.6	4.12*	1.1
Finland	3.4	5.9	1.94	3.0
Ireland	3.7	13.8	2.63	5.2
Netherlands	2.4	4.3	2.00	2.2
Norway	3.9	4.4	1.43	3.1
Sweden	2.2	3.8	2.53	1.5
Greece	3.8	8.7	2.13	4.1
Portugal	4.1	6.1	1.69	3.6
Spain	3.1	4.8	2.67	1.8
Turkey	5.0	18.5	2.68	6.9
Yugoslavia	4.3	5.8	1.83	3.1
Canada	3.4	5.0	1.77	2.8
USA	2.5	5.7	2.32	2.5

Note: * Estimate not significantly different from zero at the 95% confidence level.

Source: Bairam (1988).

regression analysis ($\hat{\pi}$) for the country under consideration. If π' does not differ significantly from $\hat{\pi}$, nor will y and y_B differ significantly. When these tests are performed on our samples of countries, the model is supported in the vast majority of cases, as will be shown in Chapter 5.

IMPLICATIONS OF THE MODEL

The simple policy conclusion for most countries is that if they wish to grow faster they must first raise the balance-of-payments constraint on demand. In other words, in an open economy, relevant economic management is the one that manipulates the Harrod foreign trade multiplier. To raise the rate of growth of productive capacity (by improving productivity, for example) without being able to raise the rate of growth of demand because of the balance of payments will merely lead to unemployment. If the balance-of-payments equilibrium growth rate can be raised, however, by making exports more attractive and by reducing the income elasticity of demand for imports, demand can be expanded without producing balance-of-payments difficulties; and, within limits, demand can generate its own supply by encouraging investment, absorbing underemployment, raising productivity growth and so on. Thus, the explanation of growth rate differences must lie primarily in differences in the rate of growth of demand, and the major constraint on the rate of growth of demand in most countries is the balance of payments. The model and the empirical evidence lends strong support to the advocates of export-led growth.

The deeper question lies in why the balance-of-payments equilibrium growth rate differs between countries. This must be primarily associated with the characteristics of goods produced which determine the income elasticity of demand for the country's exports and the country's propensity to import. For countries with a slow rate of growth of exports, combined with a relatively high income elasticity of demand for imports, the message is plain: the goods produced by the country are relatively unattractive at both home and abroad. We have concentrated so far on growth rate differences between developed countries. The argument probably has even greater relevance for developing countries.

APPLICATION TO DEVELOPING COUNTRIES[3]

It has been argued above that for most countries the major constraint on the rate of growth of output is likely to be the balance-of-payments position because this sets the limit to the growth of demand to which supply can adapt. Most developing countries, apart from the oil producing countries of the Middle East, can absorb foreign exchange without difficulty; and most cannot earn enough. It is true, of course, that the world as a whole cannot be balance-of-payments-constrained, but it only requires one country or block of countries not to be constrained, for all the rest to be so. There cannot be many developing countries that could not utilise resources more fully given the greater availability of foreign exchange.

It was shown above how closely the actual growth experience of several developed countries over the post-war period has approximated to the rate of growth of export volume (x) divided by the income elasticity of demand for imports (π). This ratio defines the balance-of-payments constrained growth rate on the assumptions that balance-of-payments equilibrium on current account is preserved and that the real terms of trade remain unchanged. The fact that the growth rate of so many advanced countries seems to approximate to this simple rule suggests that for most countries capital flows are relatively unimportant in contributing to deviations of a country's growth rate from that consistent with current account equilibrium, and that relative price changes between countries measured in a common currency play only a minor role in balance-of-payments adjustment and in relaxing the balance-of-payments constraint on growth. It is largely real income (and employment) that adjusts to bring the value of imports and exports into line with one another to preserve balance of payments equilibrium.

The growth experience of the developing countries over the last thirty years has been even more diverse than that of the developed countries, and can hardly be explained by reference to differences in the autonomous rate of growth of factor supplies. Capital accumulation, labour supply and technical progress are partly, if not mainly, endogenous to an economic system and respond to variations in the pressure of demand. In this section we attempt to see how well the Harrod foreign trade multiplier model fits the growth experience of a sample of developing countries, where in general foreign exchange is a more acute bottleneck than in the developed countries. It must be recognised, though, that developing countries are often able to build up ever-growing current account deficits financed by capital inflows (which are then written off!) which allow these countries to grow permanently faster than otherwise would be the case. If this is so, growth becomes constrained ultimately by the rate of growth of capital inflows, and, by itself, the simple growth rule enunciated would not be a good predictor of long-run growth performance. The model thus needs some amendment to allow for capital flows. What countries gain from capital inflows, however, they may lose by the adverse effects of relative price movements; indeed, the former may be partly in response to the latter. It is an interesting empirical question what the net effect may be.

In the next section, we shall first model the balance-of-payments constrained growth rate, making allowance for the fact that the economy may both start off in balance-of-payments disequilibrium (with capital flows) and move further into disequilibrium over the time period under consideration. Secondly, both the simple and extended Harrod model will be applied to a range of developing countries where it has been possible to obtain from other studies, or to make ourselves, well-determined estimates of the income elasticity of demand for imports, which is the crucial parameter in the model. Again we shall model under the assumption that relative prices measured in a common currency remain unchanged over the long period, so that any deviation of the actual growth rate from that predicted by the extended model with capital flows would be a measure of the invalidity of that assumption (barring errors in the measurement of variables and parameters).

CAPITAL FLOWS AND THE BALANCE-OF-PAYMENTS CONSTRAINED GROWTH RATE

If the balance of payments is in initial current account disequilibrium, this may be expressed as:

$$P_d X + F = P_f M E \tag{3.18}$$

where again X is the volume of exports; P_d is the domestic price of exports, M is the volume of imports; P_f is the foreign price of imports; E is the exchange rate (measured as the domestic price of foreign currency), and F is the value of nominal capital flows measured in domestic currency. $F > 0$ measures capital inflows and $F < 0$ measures capital outflows. Taking rates of change of the variables in equation (3.18) gives:

$$\theta(p_d + x) + (1 - \theta)f = p_f + m + e \tag{3.19}$$

where the lower-case letters represent rates of growth of the variables, and θ and $(1 - \theta)$ represent the shares of exports and capital flows as a proportion of total receipts (or the proportions of the import bill 'financed' by export earnings and capital flows). $\theta = P_d X/R$ and $(1 - \theta) = F/R$ where R is total overseas receipts and equals $P_d X + F$.

Now let us again assume the normal multiplicative import and export demand functions with constant elasticities:

$$M = a\left(\frac{P_f E}{P_d}\right)^\psi Y^\pi \tag{3.20}$$

and:

$$X = b\left(\frac{P_d}{P_f E}\right)^\eta Z^\varepsilon \tag{3.21}$$

where a and b are constants; ψ is the price elasticity of demand for imports ($\psi < 0$); η is the price elasticity of demand for exports ($\eta < 0$); Y is domestic income; Z is the level of 'world' income; π is the income elasticity of demand for imports, and ε is the income elasticity of demand for exports. From equations (3.20) and (3.21), taking rates of change of the variables, we have:

$$m = \psi(p_f + e - p_d) + \pi y \tag{3.22}$$

and:

$$x = \eta(p_d - e - p_f) + \varepsilon z \tag{3.23}$$

Substituting equations (3.22) and (3.23) into (3.19) gives the balance-of-payments constrained growth rate, starting from initial disequilibrium, of:

$$y_B = \frac{(\theta\eta + \psi)(p_d - e - p_f) + (p_d - e - p_f) + \theta\varepsilon z + (1 - \theta)(f - p_d)}{\pi} \tag{3.24}$$

The first term on the right-hand side of the equation gives the volume effect of relative price changes on balance-of-payments constrained real income growth; the second term gives the terms of trade effect; the third term gives the effect of exogenous changes in income growth abroad; and the last term gives the effect of the rate of growth of capital flows. If $p_d = e + p_f$, i.e. if relative prices measured in a common currency remain unchanged over the long run, equation (3.24) reduces to:

$$y_B^* = \frac{\theta \varepsilon z + (1 - \theta)(f - p_d)}{\pi} \qquad (3.25)$$

In other words, the balance-of-payments constrained growth rate starting from initial current account disequilibrium is the weighted sum of the growth of exports due to exogenous income growth outside the country, and the growth of *real* capital flows, divided by the income elasticity of demand for imports. Given the model, deviations of the actual growth rate from y_B^* will be a reflection of the two relative price terms in equation (3.24). Since we do not have information on εz for all countries we shall assume that $\varepsilon z = x$, thereby incorporating into the analysis from the start any volume changes in exports from relative price movements. The equation we focus on is thus:

$$y_B^* = \frac{\theta x + (1 - \theta)(f - p_d)}{\pi} \qquad (3.26)$$

The difference between the actual growth rate and that predicted by (3.26) will be a measure of the pure terms of trade effect on real income growth and of any import volume response from relative price changes relaxing or tightening the balance-of-payments constraint on growth according to the direction of movement in the terms of trade and whether the import volume response is normal or perverse.

This result may now be compared with the result of the simple model which starts from balance-of-payments equilibrium and assumes no growth of capital inflows. Three observations may be made:

(i) With no initial disequilibrium and no capital flows, i.e. $\theta = 1$ and $(1 - \theta) = 0$, equation (3.26) yields the earlier result:

$$y_B = x/\pi \qquad (3.27)$$

(ii) If there is initial current account disequilibriun but the rate of growth of nominal capital inflows is zero ($f = 0$), the balance-of-payments constrained growth rate will be lowered to:

$$y_B^{**} = \frac{\theta x - (1 - \theta)(p_d)}{\pi} \qquad (3.28)$$

y_B^{**} is obviously less than y_B, assuming that p_d is positive. The explanation of this result is that if export earnings are initially below the value of imports, an equal rate of growth of exports and imports would widen the disequilibrium absolutely, and if the difference is not filled by an increasing level of capital inflows, the growth of income must be lower in order to reduce the growth of imports below that of exports to keep the absolute gap between exports and imports (equal to the initial value of F) unchanged. Subtracting equation (3.28) from (3.27) we see that the absolute reduction in the level of the growth rate is equal to:

$$y_B - y_B^{**} = \frac{(1 - \theta)(p_d + x)}{\pi} \qquad (3.29)$$

(iii) If there is an initial current account deficit financed by capital inflows and the growth rate is not to be lower than without initial disequilibrium, there must be a positive rate of growth of capital inflows to compensate. We can find this rate by setting equation (3.26) equal to (3.29) and solving for f. This yields:

$$f = p_d + x \qquad (3.30)$$

This result should be apparent from equation (3.19). Without initial disequilibrium, the balance-of-payments constrained growth rate is defined where $p_d + x = p_f + m + e$ and for the weighted sum of $(p_d + x)$ and f to equal $(p_d + x)$, f must grow at the same rate as $(p_d + x)$.

We end up therefore with a very simple guideline. If a country starts in balance-of-payments disequilibrium the simple Harrod rule for predicting the growth rate, $y_B = x/\pi$, will underpredict or overpredict according to whether $f \gtrless (p_d + x)$, or, in other words, according to whether the growth of capital inflows is greater or less than the rate of growth of export earnings. The degree of underprediction or overprediction of y_B is given by subtracting equation (3.26) from (3.27) which gives:

$$y_B - y_B^* = \frac{(1 - \theta)\,(p_d + x - f)}{\pi} \qquad (3.31)$$

In real terms: if $f - p_d > x$, the dynamic Harrod foreign trade multiplier result will underpredict; if $f - p_d = x$, the prediction will be unaffected, and if $f - p_d < x$, the Harrod foreign trade multiplier rule will overpredict.

THE EMPIRICAL EVIDENCE FOR THE DEVELOPING COUNTRIES

We are now in a position to fit the basic and extended Harrod foreign trade multiplier models, equations (3.8) and (3.26), to a sample of developing countries. Three samples of countries are taken. First, we use a sample of countries taken by Khan (1974), and his estimates of the income elasticity of demand for imports over the period 1951 to 1969. Out of 15 countries, seven yielded statistically significant elasticity estimates. The countries (excluding Brazil) are listed in the first section of Table 3.4.[4] Secondly, we take the three developing countries for which Houthakker and Magee (1969) made estimates of the income elasticity of demand for imports over the period 1951 to 1966: Mexico, India, and Portugal. These are listed in section II of Table 3.4. Finally, we make estimates ourselves of the income elasticity of demand for imports for a selection of developing countries primarily chosen on the basis of data availability. The countries yielding statistically significant estimates in a traditionally specified import demand function are given in section III of Table 3.4.

For all the countries, Table 3.4 gives data, over the relevant time period, on the actual growth rate (y); the growth of export volume (x); the income elasticity of demand for imports (π); the growth rate predicted by the simple dynamic Harrod foreign trade multiplier ($y_B = x/\pi$); the growth of real capital imports (f_r); and the predicted balance-of-payments constrained growth rate with capital flows (y_B^*). We expect the extended model with capital flows to give a closer prediction of the actual growth rate than the simple Harrod multiplier result except to the extent that adverse or favourable effects of relative price movements may have worked in the opposite direction tending to push the actual growth rate back towards the prediction of the simple rule. The difference between the actual growth rate and that predicted by the extended model is a measure of the extent to which the balance-of-payments constrained growth rate has been affected by relative price movements in international trade. When we look at the prediction of the two models, we find that the mean absolute error of the actual growth rate from that predicted by the extended model is in fact smaller than the error of prediction from the simple rule (1.55 percentage points compared with 2.01), so that complete offsetting movements of capital flows on the one hand and the effects of relative price changes on the other cannot have occurred.

Table 3.4 The annual growth rate of output, exports and real capital flows; and growth rate predictions from the simple and extended Harrod trade multiplier model

Countries	Growth of income (y)	Growth of exports (x)	Income elasticity of demand for imports (π)	Simple Harrod trade multiplier prediction $y_B = x/\pi$	Growth of real capital imports (f_r)	Predicted growth rate from extended model including capital flows y_B^*
I. 1951–1969[1]						
Costa Rica	0.040	0.080	2.046	0.039	0.350	0.053
Ecuador	0.048	0.064	0.555	0.120	−0.231	0.110
Pakistan	0.069	0.062	1.020	0.060	0.199	0.089
Sri Lanka	0.061	0.013	0.218	0.059	0.088	0.067
Philippines	0.053	0.046	0.668	0.068	0.013	0.063
Colombia	0.050	0.025	0.290	0.086	0.138	0.060
II. 1951–1966[2]						
India	0.024	0.040	1.43	0.028	0.134	0.037
Portugal	0.051	0.080	1.39	0.057	0.039	0.050
Mexico	0.060	0.060	0.53	0.110	0.007	0.100
III. Various Dates[3]						
Tunisia	0.064	0.045	0.91	0.050	0.086	0.060
Cyprus	0.034	0.035	1.05	0.035	0.017	0.033
Kenya	0.081	0.085	0.99	0.086	0.017	0.060
Honduras	0.042	0.070	0.89	0.079	0.363	0.082
Jamaica	0.040	0.052	0.70	0.074	−0.022	0.058
Thailand	0.068	0.062	0.93	0.066	0.110	0.073
Sudan	0.054	0.053	0.64	0.083	0.070	0.085
Morocco	0.033	0.030	0.43	0.069	−0.004	0.062
Brazil	0.095	0.083	2.05	0.040	0.350	0.094
Zaire	0.060	0.037	0.53	0.069	−0.180	0.054
Turkey	0.058	0.056	0.92	0.061	0.053	0.059

Sources: [1] from Khan (1974); [2] from Houthakker and Magee (1969); [3] Own estimates.

To throw more light on the question of the relative importance of capital flows and relative price changes in accounting for deviations of growth from the Harrod foreign trade multiplier result, it is interesting to divide the countries in Table 3.4 into two groups: those where growth has exceeded the predicted rate and those where it has fallen below. For those countries with $y > y_B$ we except real capital inflows to have grown faster than the volume of exports, and for this to be the major explanation of the positive difference, unless relative price changes have been favourable to the relaxation of the balance-of-payments constraint on growth. Contrariwise, for those countries with $y < y_B$, we expect real capital inflows to have grown slower than export volume unless the negative difference is wholly accounted for by the (adverse) effect of relative price changes. In Table 3.5 the

Table 3.5   The 'explanation' of divergencies between the actual growth rate and the dynamic Harrod trade multiplier result

A. Countries with Actual Growth Greater than Harrod Trade Multiplier Result (% per annum)

				Contribution to difference of:	
Country	*Actual growth rate (y)*	*Harrod trade multiplier result* $y_B = (x/\pi)$	*Difference*	*Real capital inflows growing faster (+) or slower (−) than exports*	*Effect of relative price movements*
Brazil	9.5	4.0	+ 5.5	+ 5.4	+ 0.1
Tunisia	6.4	5.0	+ 1.4	+ 1.0	+ 0.4
Pakistan	6.9	6.0	+ 0.9	+ 2.9	− 2.0
Thailand	6.8	6.6	+ 0.2	+ 0.7	− 0.5
Sri Lanka	6.1	5.9	+ 0.2	+ 0.8	− 0.6
Costa Rica	4.0	3.9	+ 0.1	+ 1.4	− 1.3
Average deviations			+ 1.38	+ 2.03	− 0.65

B. Countries with Actual Growth Less than Harrod Trade Multiplier Result

Ecuador	4.8	12.0	− 7.2	− 1.0	− 6.2
Mexico	6.0	11.0	− 5.0	− 1.0	− 4.0
Honduras	4.2	7.9	− 3.7	+ 0.3	− 4.0
Colombia	5.0	8.6	− 3.6	− 2.6	− 1.0
Morocco	3.3	6.9	− 3.6	− 0.7	− 2.9
Jamaica	4.0	7.4	− 3.4	− 1.6	− 1.8
Sudan	5.4	8.3	− 2.9	+ 0.2	− 3.1
Philippines	5.3	6.8	− 1.5	− 0.5	− 1.0
Zaire	6.0	6.9	− 0.9	− 1.5	+ 0.6
Portugal	5.1	5.7	− 0.6	− 0.7	+ 0.1
Kenya	8.1	8.6	− 0.5	− 2.6	+ 2.1
India	2.4	2.8	− 0.4	+ 0.9	− 1.3
Turkey	5.8	6.1	− 0.3	− 0.2	− 0.1
Cyprus	3.4	3.5	− 0.1	− 0.2	+ 0.1
Average deviations			− 2.41	− 0.80	− 1.61

countries are so divided. An interesting contrast between the two groups of countries is immediately apparent. In the six countries with $y > y_B$, the mean difference is 1.38. In all countries, the rate of growth of real capital inflows was greater than the growth of exports which, according to the extended model, should have relaxed the balance-of-payments constraint on growth by an average of 2.03 percentage points. Since the average deviation was only 1.38 per cent, however, the conclusion must be that the effect of relative price changes was adverse, tightening the balance-of-payments constraint on growth in these countries by an average of 0.65 percentage points.

In two of the countries out of the six, however, the effect of relative price movements was apparently favourable.

Turning to the countries with $y < y_B$, the explanation of the shortfall of growth appears to lie not so much in a shortfall of capital import growth below export growth but in the adverse effects of relative price movements. The average (negative) deviation of y from y_B is -2.41. In all countries but three, the growth of real capital inflows was lower than the growth of exports, but on average, according to the extended model, this would have contributed to a shortfall of y below y_B of only 0.08 percentage points, leaving a residual of -1.61 which can only be explained by the adverse effects of relative price changes.

The effects of relative price changes on balance-of-payments constrained real income growth comprise two components in our model: one, a pure terms of trade effect, and the second, the effect of relative price changes on the volume of imports (both divided by the income elasticity of demand for imports). Where the effect of relative price changes has been apparently adverse on real income growth, this could be the result of a combination of an adverse terms of trade effect partly offset or reinforced by an import volume effect, depending on whether the price elasticity of demand for imports is 'normal' or perverse. Alternatively, the adverse effect could be the result of a favourable movement in the terms of trade but more than offset by the effect of a high price elasticity of demand for imports.

Where the effect of relative price changes has apparently had a favourable effect on real income growth, the explanation would be the reverse of the above arguments. In Table 3.6, the average annual percentage rate of change of the real terms of trade divided by the income elasticity of demand for imports is given for all the countries in the sample for comparison with the implied effect of relative price movements from the last column of Table 3.5. It can be seen that for most countries where the implied terms of trade effect has been adverse on real growth, the actual real terms of trade has on average deteriorated over time, but in some cases the implied adverse effect is greater than the effect of the actual deterioration suggesting a perverse import volume response to adverse relative price movements. Where the implied terms of trade effect has been positive, however, the effect of the actual terms of trade improvement has generally been greater, which would be consistent with a normal import volume response. In three cases, a favourable pure terms of trade effect on real income growth is associated with an implied adverse

Table 3.6   The actual and implied effect of relative price movements on
real income growth

	Effect of relative price movements (% p.a.)	
Country	Implied effect (from Table 3.5)	Pure terms of trade effect[1]
A. Brazil	+ 0.1	+ 1.1
Tunisia	+ 0.4	+ 4.6
Pakistan	− 2.0	− 4.1
Thailand	− 0.5	+ 1.1
Sri Lanka	− 0.6	− 12.4
Costa Rica	− 1.3	− 0.4
B. Ecuador	− 6.2	− 0.5
Mexico	− 4.2	− 0.4
Honduras	− 4.0	− 1.6
Colombia	− 1.0	+ 1.4
Morocco	− 2.9	− 0.7
Jamaica	− 1.8	+ 0.6
Sudan	− 3.1	− 1.7
Philippines	− 1.0	− 3.1
Zaire	+ 0.6	+ 1.7
Portugal	+ 0.1	+ 0.8
Kenya	+ 2.1	− 0.2
India	− 1.3	− 0.3
Turkey	− 0.1	− 0.9
Cyprus	+ 0.1	+ 2.7

Note: [1]Calculated as the change in the terms of trade divided by π. The terms of trade is calculated as the ratio of the country's export price index to its import price index, where all prices are expressed in US dollars.

Source: International Financial Statistics Yearbooks.

relative price effect suggesting that the unfavourable effect of the import volume response has outweighed the favourable pure terms of trade effect. For the countries as a whole, the annual average deterioration in the real terms of trade has been approximately 0.075 per cent over the years taken for the different countries, which would amount to a deterioration of 1.6 per cent over, say, a twenty-year period. There is some variation in the experience of individual countries, but for most of them the evidence suggests that in the long run relative prices measured in a common currency stay relatively stable.

The conclusion of the analysis must be that the experience of countries is very mixed. On balance, changes in the real terms of trade seem to have constrained countries in their growth by about 0.6 per cent per annum, while capital inflows, on balance, have enabled the countries to grow slightly faster than the Harrod foreign trade multiplier result, by about 0.05 per cent per annum. In some countries, however, the real terms of trade improved, while in many others the rate of growth of real capital imports did not keep pace with the growth of exports, thereby reducing the growth rate below that predicted by the Harrod foreign trade multiplier result starting from initial deficit. Although the mean absolute error of the actual growth rate from the predicted Harrod multiplier result of 2.01 may be regarded as high, it is difficult to believe that the growth process, and constraints on it, can be understood properly in most countries without reference to the balance-of-payments, and the 'dynamic' Harrod foreign trade multiplier provides a simple and useful starting point for analysis.

The model has been applied by others taking different samples of developing countries, with mixed results. Perraton (1990) takes 59 developing countries over the period 1970–84, and calculates a Spearman rank correlation of 0.67 between the actual growth of countries and that predicted by the simple dynamic Harrod foreign trade multiplier result which is significant at the 99 per cent confidence level. Approximately one half of the countries pass the parametric test of the estimated income elasticity for imports not differing significantly (at the 95 per cent confidence level) from the required income elasticity to make the actual growth rate equal to the predicted rate.

Research by Bairam (1990) and Bairam and Dempster (1991) also give qualified support for the model. Their results for a selection of developing countries are given in Table 3.7.

It can be seen that the difference between the actual growth experience (y) and the estimated balance-of-payments equilibrium growth rate (y_B) is generally small, except for India, Japan and Greece. The discrepancy in the case of Japan is consistent with the accumulation of large balance-of-payments surpluses (see also Table 3.1), and the discrepancies in the case of India and Greece are probably accounted for by the poor estimate of the income elasticity of demand for imports. For the rest of the countries y_B is a good predictor of y.[5] See Chapter 5 for a more detailed discussion.

256   *Economic Growth and the Payments Constraint*

Table 3.7   A comparison of actual growth with that predicted
by the dynamic Harrod foreign trade multiplier in a selection of
developing countries

Country/ period	Growth of income % per annum y	Growth of exports % per annum x	Income elasticity of demand for imports π	Simple Harrod trade multiplier prediction $y_B = x/\pi$
India, 1961–83	3.9	9.3	1.0*	9.3
Indonesia, 1966–85	6.5	21.4	2.7	7.9
Israel, 1962–85	5.7	13.8	2.4	5.8
Japan, 1961–85	7.4[a]	16.9	1.5	11.3
Pakistan, 1971–85	5.4	15.4	2.9	5.3
Philippines, 1961–85	4.4	10.0	2.4	4.1
Singapore, 1973–8	8.2	33.2	3.6	9.2
Sri Lanka, 1961–84	5.3	6.4	1.0*	6.4
Syria, 1964–84	6.3	14.3	2.4	6.0
Thailand, 1961–85	6.9	13.3	1.9	7.0
Turkey, 1973–83	4.2	20.7	4.1	5.0

Notes: *Indicates estimate not significantly different from zero at the 95% confidence level.
[a]Bairam and Dempster report a figure of 5.7 in their table 1, but this is clearly too low. The figure 7.4 is the value they use in their calculations reported in their table 2.

Source: Bairam and Dempster (1991).

CENTRE–PERIPHERY MODELS OF GROWTH AND DEVELOPMENT

It is interesting to note that development economists in the past (e.g. Prebisch, 1950, and Seers, 1962) have developed centre–periphery models of growth and development which reduce to the dynamic Harrod foreign trade multiplier result, i.e. the simple rule in equation (3.8).

The Prebisch Model

Raul Prebisch was the first development economist in the post-war era to seriously question the doctrine of the mutual profitability of trade between developed and less-developed countries. The traditional approach to the measurement of the gains from trade is from the classical standpoint of real resource augmentation from special-

isation which trade permits. Prebisch instead concentrated attention on the monetary, or balance of payments, aspects of trade,
arguing, in effect, that the real resource gains from specialisation may
be offset by the under-utilisation of resources if foreign exchange or
the balance of payments is the dominant constraint on output. Classical (Ricardian) trade theory assumes away both unemployment of
resources and monetary balance-of-payments constraints through the
assumptions of constant returns in all activities and relative price
adjustments in trade. But if some activities are subject to diminishing
returns (such as land-based activities) the full employment of resources cannot be guaranteed in these activities; nor can full employment be guaranteed if relative price changes do not work to maintain
balance-of-payments equilibrium on current account. Less developed
countries tend to specialise in diminishing returns activities and also
appear to suffer perpetual balance-of-payments difficulties which
stifle growth and development. Prebisch attributed the latter to the
low income elasticity of demand for primary commodities which
less-developed countries produce and export, compared with the
higher income elasticity of demand for manufactures that developed
countries produce and export. The nature of the problem can be
illustrated with a simple numerical example. Assume two countries: a
less developed country (LDC) exporting solely primary commodities
with an average income elasticity of demand of 0.5 ($\varepsilon_{LDC} = 0.5$), and
a developed country (DC) exporting solely manufactured goods with
an average income elasticity of demand of 2.0 ($\varepsilon_{DC} = 2.0$). The export
elasticity of the LDC is the import elasticity of the DC ($\pi_{DC} = 0.5$),
and the export elasticity of the DC is the import elasticity of the LDC
($\pi_{LDC} = 2.0$). For both countries to grow at the same rate, the
situation is clearly not sustainable. For example, at a growth rate of 5
per cent, the rate of growth of exports (x) and imports (m) in the two
countries would be as shown in Table 3.8.

There would be a perpetual tendency to deficit in the LDC and a
perpetual tendency to surplus in the DC. Balance-of-payments

Table 3.8   Unsustainable import and export growth in a two-country
model: an illustrative example

Less developed country	Developed country
$x = 5 \times \varepsilon_{LDC} = 5 \times 0.5 = 2.5$	$x = 5 \times \varepsilon_{DC} = 5 \times 2.0 = 10.0$
$m = 5 \times \pi_{LDC} = 5 \times 2.0 = 10.0$	$m = 5 \times \pi_{DC} = 5 \times 0.5 = 2.5$

equilibrium in the LDC requires that the growth of output be constrained so that imports grow no faster than exports.

The constrained growth rate is equal to:

$$y_{LDC} = \frac{x_{LDC}}{\pi_{LDC}} = \frac{y_{DC} \times \varepsilon_{LDC}}{\pi_{LDC}} = \frac{5 \times 0.5}{2} = 1.25 \qquad (3.32)$$

Equilibrium balance of payments in both countries implies 1.25 per cent growth in the LDC compared with 5 per cent in the DC. The relative growth of the two countries is given by:

$$\frac{y_{DC}}{y_{LDC}} = \frac{\pi_{LDC}}{\varepsilon_{LDC}} = \frac{2}{0.5} = 4 \qquad (3.33)$$

which is the simple growth rule enunciated in equation (3.8). The centre grows four times faster than the periphery.

Prebisch's other major concern in his path-breaking paper was adverse movements in the barter terms of trade against developing countries which in his model is the means by which the fruits of technical progress are transferred from the 'centre' to the 'periphery'. A deterioration in the net barter terms of trade clearly means a reduction in real income by reducing the purchasing power of exports over imports, unless the balance of payments responds causing exports to rise and the exchange rate to appreciate which improves the real terms of trade (the barter terms of trade adjusted for changes in the exchange rate) and real income. There has been some dispute in the literature whether the net barter terms of trade has moved consistently through history against the primary producing LDCs as Prebisch claimed.[6] We do not want to enter this debate here except to say that the evidence now seems unequivocal that allowing for a structural break during the period of the two world wars, the LDCs and primary commodities have both suffered, on average, a deterioration in purchasing power *vis-à-vis* industrialised countries and manufactured commodities of approximately 0.5 to 1.0 per cent per annum over at least the last hundred years.

If no allowance is made for the war years, however, the terms of trade series look trendless. It appears that long run secular forces working against the purchasing power of primary commodities have been offset by violent short run cyclical improvements. There also appears to be a wide diversity of experience between commodities and primary producing countries; some suffering more than others. The upshot of the controversy is perhaps that the real income loss from terms of trade movements against the 'periphery' should not be exaggerated, particularly as no allowance is made for the possibility that adverse movements *may* have led to an improved balance-of-payments position, and that the major factor to focus on in the Prebisch centre–periphery model is differences in the income elasticities of demand for primary commodities on the one hand and manufactured goods on the other which impose differential balance-of-payments constraints. Prebisch makes no mention of trade multipliers, but as we have seen, his implied result concerning relative growth rate differences between countries is the same as that derived from Harrod's trade multiplier when it is made dynamic.

The Seers Model

In 1962, Seers outlined an elaborate and technically sophisticated centre–periphery model, which was largely ignored by the economics profession and never received the attention it deserved. It was, however, remarkably perceptive, and also had as its basis the disparate income elasticities of demand for goods exported and imported by two sets of countries. Two of the assumptions of the basic model are also the same as those of Prebisch and Harrod: trade is balanced and the terms of trade remain unchanged. The periphery (p) exports only primary commodities, and the centre (c) exports only finished goods. The import functions are expressed in arithmetically linear form:

For the centre: $\qquad\qquad M_c = a_c + b_c Y_c$ $\qquad\qquad\qquad$ (3.34)

For the periphery: $\qquad\quad M_p = a_p + b_p Y_p$ $\qquad\qquad\qquad$ (3.35)

Balanced trade requires: $a_p + b_p Y_p = a_c + b_c Y_c$ $\qquad\qquad$ (3.36)

Therefore,

$$Y_p = \frac{(a_c - a_p) + b_c Y_c}{b_p} \qquad\qquad\qquad (3.37)$$

Consequently,

$$\frac{Y_p}{Y_c} = \frac{a_c - a_p}{b_p Y_c} + \frac{b_c}{b_p} \qquad\qquad\qquad (3.38)$$

Equation (3.38) expresses the relative difference in income levels between the periphery and the centre in terms of the parameters of the import demand functions. What will happen to this relative difference through time? Assume income in the centre grows exponentially at rate r, so that $Y_c = Y_{c0} e^{rt}$.

Equation (3.38) can then be written as:

$$\frac{Y_p}{Y_c} = \frac{a_c - a_p}{b_p Y_{c0} e^{rt}} + \frac{b_c}{b_p} \tag{3.39}$$

Differentiating with respect to time gives:

$$\frac{d(Y_p/Y_c)}{dt} = \frac{-r(a_c - a_p)}{b_p Y_{c0} e^{rt}} \tag{3.40}$$

If $a_c > a_p$ so that $(a_c - a_p) > 0$, the periphery will become relatively poorer through time; in other words, growth must be slower in the periphery than the centre if balance-of-payments equilibrium is to be preserved. If the income elasticity of demand for imports (of manufactures) in the periphery is greater than unity, a_p in the linear import demand function must be negative; and if the income elasticity of demand for imports (of primary commodities) in the centre is less than unity, a_c in the linear import demand function must be positive. Therefore, $(a_c - a_p) > 0$, and relative income levels will diverge. Relative per capita income levels will diverge even more if population growth is faster in the periphery than in the centre. Hypothetically, sufficient capital flows from the surplus centre to the deficit periphery could prevent the relative income gap from widening, but the flow would have to be at a constant proportionate rate through time, implying a higher and higher level of flow and an ever-increasing debt repayment burden. This is feasible in the very short term, but not in the long term. As far as the long-run solution to the problem is concerned, Seers draws the same conclusion as Prebisch, namely that there is no solution without a change in the structure of production to make the import functions of the periphery look more like those of the centre; in other words, to narrow the difference in the income elasticity of demand for exports of the two sets of countries by import substitution in the periphery.

It can be seen in conclusion that the centre–periphery models of Prebisch and Seers both have as their essential feature the lower income elasticity of demand for primary commodities in world trade relative to manufactured goods, and that if long-run balance-of-payments equilibrium on current account is a requirement and the real terms of trade is constant, the relative growth rates of the periphery and centre will approximate to the ratio of the periphery's export elasticity to its import elasticity. It has also been shown that this result is the same as the dynamic Harrod foreign trade multiplier on the same assumptions. The extent to which the terms of trade do remain constant over the long run, and current account balance is maintained, are empirical questions which can only be answered by appeal to the historical facts. The evidence in the post-war period does not suggest that relative price movements in international trade are an efficient mechanism for relieving countries of a balance-of-payments constraint on growth, or that capital inflows can raise the growth rate permanently above the level that otherwise would prevail. To understand relative growth performance in open economies, it is to the income elasticities of demand for exports and imports that we must look.

4 Non-Price Competition, Trade and the Balance of Payments

INTRODUCTION

We showed in the previous chapter that the slow growth of national output (particularly for the UK) has been associated with a very slow rate of export growth relative to other countries. This resulted in a massive decline in the UK's share of world trade in manufactures from just over 20 per cent in 1950 to just under 8 per cent in 1988. It is difficult to argue that this unfavourable trend has been the result of continually declining price and cost competitiveness because, for long periods over the postwar years, measures of price and cost competitiveness moved in Britain's favour. Figure 4.1 shows movements in relative producer prices and unit labour costs from 1963 to 1989.

From 1963 to 1977, there was a trend improvement in competitiveness which continued after 1981 following a serious deterioration between 1977 and 1981. Despite the improvement in the 1960s and 1970s, Britain's share of world trade in manufactures fell from 15 per cent in 1960 to just over 10 per cent in 1977. The major explanation for this declining share must lie in the failure of UK industry adequately to engage in non-price competition; that is, with respect to factors which determine *shifts* in the demand curve for products as opposed to movements *along* the demand curve associated with price.

At the individual industry level, there was a serious imbalance between exports and imports which had been growing steadily, and which led in 1983 to a deficit on trade in manufactured goods for the first time in British economic history. Table 4.1 shows the components of the trade deficit in the major manufacturing sectors in 1990. Several key sectors such as vehicles, electronics, paper and textiles were in substantial deficit. The only major manufacturing sectors then in surplus were chemicals, aerospace and defence equipment.

In this chapter, we consider the role of non-price competitiveness

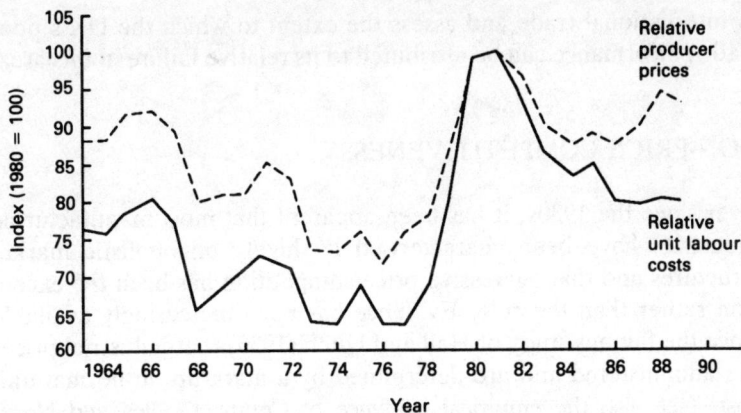

Figure 4.1 Measures of price and cost competitiveness 1963–89

Table 4.1 Components of the trade deficit in manufactured goods 1990 (£million)

Standard industrial trade classification	Exports (FOB)	Imports (CIF)	Balance of trade
5–8: All manufactured goods	84 202	98 149	− 13 947
5: Chemicals & related products	13 181	10 834	+ 2 347
6: Manufactured goods chiefly classified by material, of which:			
64: Paper, paperboard etc.	1 539	4 014	− 2 475
65: Textile yarn, fabrics, etc.	2 446	3 936	− 1 490
7: Machinery and transport equipment of which:			
75: Office machines & automatic data processing equipment	6 341	7 715	− 1 374
77: Electrical machinery, apparatus & appliances	5 648	6 921	− 1 273
78: Road vehicles	7 296	12 594	− 5 298
8: Miscellaneous manufactured goods	13 349	18 252	− 4 903

Source: *Overseas Trade Statistics* 1990.

in international trade and assess the extent to which the UK's poor trade performance can be attributed to its relative failure in this area.

NON-PRICE COMPETITIVENESS

Ever since the 1930s, it has been apparent that most manufacturing industries have been characterised by highly oligopolistic market structures and that aggressive price competition has been the exception rather than the rule. Evidence has been increasingly available since the famous study of Hall and Hitch (1939) that industrial prices are administered and are determined by a mark-up on normal unit costs (see also the empirical evidence of Coutts, Godley and Nordhaus, 1978). Firms have been increasingly engaged in non-price rather than in price competition. Yet, in spite of the evidence, one textbook writer has recently lamented:

> Despite the increasing recognition of the importance of product changes and selling strategy as market weapons, economic theory has remained basically a theory of price, while non-price competition is brushed aside. Various aspects of product diversity and advertising have been discussed in economic literature, but there has been no successful effort to integrate product strategy, price strategy, selling strategy and other major decisions into a general-equilibrium approach of the firm. (Koutsoyiannis, 1982, p. 4)

The same is true of the so-called pure theory of international trade, where the price auction model and the neoclassical tradition still hold sway. Nevertheless, there have been developed the 'new' theories of trade associated with influences on the demand-side which appear to provide a more reasonable explanation of the growth of trade between countries and of the phenomenon of intra-industry trade – at least between industrialised countries. These new trade theories include the technological gap theory (Posner, 1961, Hufbauer, 1970); the idea of the product cycle (Vernon, 1966 and 1970, Wells, 1969 and 1972); and the product differentiation and variety hypotheses (Linder, 1961, Davies, 1976, Barker, 1977). It is true to say, though, that these theories still remain peripheral to the main research programme in international trade theory.[1]

There seem to be two reasons for this neglect of non-price competition.

The first is that it is a very nebulous concept. Non-price competitiveness encompasses, by definition, all those factors other than price that affect consumer choice. These include quality, reliability, speed of delivery, the extent and efficacy of the distribution network and the availability of export credit and guarantees.

There is an obvious problem in quantifying the effects of such non-price factors. Often, in applied work, the impact of non-price factors is taken as the residual growth of exports and imports after due allowance has been made for relative price changes. For example, the time-trend in export and import demand functions is often interpreted as reflecting the effects of non-price competitiveness. Where no time-trend is included in the specification, differences between countries in their income elasticity of demand for exports and imports are commonly seen as reflecting disparities in non-price competitiveness, as we have noted in Chapter 3 and will discuss in greater detail in Chapter 5. (See also, for example, Singh, 1977; Stout, 1977; and Winters, 1985, chapter 18.)

Other studies have included various proxies for non-price competitiveness in regression analyses such as expenditure on R&D as a proportion of GDP and the number of patents. Some of these studies are reviewed later in this chapter. They generally confirm the importance of non-price competitiveness, notwithstanding the almost inevitable reservations that must be borne in mind concerning the adequacy of the proxies.[2]

The imprecision of the concept of non-price competition also poses problems for theoretical modelling. Koutsoyannis's (1982) textbook shows that profit maximising models can be, and have been, easily constructed where the level of quality is the decision variable of the firm while prices remain fixed. In these models, greater quality involves greater cost and, given the demand conditions, there is an optimal level of quality. But this does not get us very far when we compare international differences in non-price factors which do not appear to be the result of a conscious profit maximising process. Rather, differences between countries in non-price competitiveness are analogous to, and indeed reflect, differences in X-efficiency (Leibenstein, 1966). In spite of the empirical importance of X-efficiency, it still remains very much of a 'black box' in economics, as do the causes of the disparities in non-price competitiveness.

The second reason for the neglect of non-price competition is that it is difficult conceptually to draw a hard and fast distinction between poor export performance due to price uncompetitiveness on the one hand and non-price uncompetitiveness, on the other. The decline in the British-owned car industry is often cited as the result of the poor non-price characteristics of British automobiles, especially reliability, handling and styling. But if the price were reduced far enough, it could be argued, then any number of British cars could be sold. Hence, the problem could equally be described as one of lack of price competitiveness. Such an argument, however, serves merely to divert attention from the important deficiencies in British non-price competitiveness. As per capita income grows, so increasingly does the demand for more sophisticated goods. If Britain were to rely purely on price competition, it would find that there would have to be increasingly severe relative price cuts to compensate for lack of non-price competitiveness. These would probably have to be so drastic as to make the British production of cars ultimately untenable. Even if price competition could be pursued indefinitely, it would be unlikely to succeed in maintaining the volume of production as the growth of the demand for low quality cars inevitably diminishes as income increases. (This is considered in greater detail when the Schott model is discussed below.) For example, the low quality cars of the Eastern Bloc such as the Skoda and Lada have made negligible inroads into the markets of the advanced countries in spite of their exceptionally low price.[3] In the long run, in a world of rapid product and process innovation, and where the rapid growth of demand is for increasingly sophisticated products, it would be disastrous to rely to any great extent on price competition to maintain market share. The fact that British manufacturers have been prone to opt out of the production of high-tech products and to 'trade down' reflects the underlying weakness of British manufacturing. British companies have had little choice but to 'trade down' – they just cannot compete in many of the markets for sophisticated high value added goods.

We thus disagree with the arguments of those such as Armington (1977) who, in his review of Stout (1977), dismisses the importance of non-price competition and asserts the primacy of the role of the exchange rate in maintaining equilibrium in the balance-of-payments. *Pace* Armington, it is meaningful to draw a distinction between price and non-price competition however imprecise the demarcation criterion may be. The relative failure of British goods in overseas markets can only be fully explained in terms of the lack of non-price competitiveness. In spite of the relatively little work done on the topic in contrast to the plethora of studies on the effects of exchange rate changes, it is difficult to disagree with Posner and Steer (1979, p. 159) who, after surveying price and non-price competition in international trade, conclude that 'Historically there is no doubt that non-price influences have dominated – the proportion of total change which they "explain" is an order of magnitude greater than the explanatory power of price competitiveness'.

THE NEOCLASSICAL 'LAW OF ONE PRICE' AND NON-PRICE COMPETITION

In Chapter 3, it was mentioned that the observed small movements of relative prices in the long run are compatible with perfect competition as well as oligopolistic market structures. Atomistic competition implies that price elasticities of demand are infinite and that exports are determined by profitability rather than by demand constraints. The concept of the balance-of-payments constraint thus has no meaning as exporters can sell as much abroad as they wish at the going world price, at least on the basis of the small country assumption. Clearly, this interpretation is incompatible with the theoretical model underlying the law of economic growth discussed in the last chapter and also considered in greater detail in Chapter 5. Nevertheless, the pure theory of international trade and the monetarist approach are still largely based on models where exports (and imports) are treated as homogeneous entities.

This assumption is summarised by the so-called neoclassical 'law of one price'. Similar goods are homogeneous regardless of where they are produced and, in the absence of transport costs, arbitrage will ensure that the price (in a common currency) will be equal throughout the world. Strictly, the law of one price states that competition will equate the price of *identical* traded goods. If price differences are observed, it can be argued that as a matter of logic the goods under consideration are by definition not identical, but differ in some non-price characteristics. This, of course, empties the law of any empirical content reducing it to a truism. *Reductio ad absurdum*, there will be as many classifications as there are individual products. As an operational concept, the law must be interpreted as implying that goods at a low level of aggregation are perfect substitutes, whether they be nuts and bolts or 1.3 litre 5-door motor cars.

Tests of the 'law' in this form, however, find that it is empirically refuted and thereby provide indirect evidence of the importance of product differentiation and, hence, of non-price competition. For example, Isard (1977, p. 942) argues that 'in reality the law of one price is flagrantly and systematically violated by empirical data'. Williamson (1983, p. 201) expresses similar sentiments: 'The hypothesis that arbitrage equates goods prices internationally has probably been rejected more decisively by empirical evidence than any other hypothesis in the history of economics.'[4]

Kravis and Lipsey (1971, 1978) have probably undertaken the most detailed study of international price competitiveness. They found some difference in price in all of the six 2-digit SITC categories that were included in their study. In the case of Iron and Steel (SITC 67), 'in 1963, Japanese prices averaged 30% less than those of the US, German prices 24 per cent less and UK prices 22 per cent less' (Kravis and Lipsey, 1978, p. 230). An even greater price difference was found at a more disaggregated level. In the case of iron and steel wire (SITC 677), Japanese prices were some 40 per cent less than those of the US, and German prices also undercut US prices by a similar magnitude in the case of bars and rods (SITC 673.2) and tube and pipe fittings (SITC 678.5). These differences persisted over the whole period studied, namely, 1953–64. Such examples can be multiplied many times. 'German export prices (in dollar terms, i.e. adjusted for exchange rate changes) for "locks, padlocks and keys. . . . of miscellaneous metal" (SITC 698.1) rose by 104.9 per cent between 1970 and 1974 while US export prices rose by 23.3 per cent' (Kravis and Lipsey, 1978, p. 203).

In fact, the extent of the differences in prices for a product produced in two different countries is likely largely to reflect differences in quality.[5] This is especially true of unit values which are simply the value of goods shipped divided by the tonnage. These have been used by some National Economic Development Office (NEDO) studies as a proxy for differences in quality, as we shall see in the next section.

Thus, these studies show that non-price factors differ substantially between similar products and that manufacturers face a downward sloping demand curve. Nevertheless, the evidence suggests that price competition is not of great importance in explaining the differential growth of trade flows.

NON-PRICE FACTORS IN TRADE

The fundamental problem is that there are significant gaps in the UK's product range which have led not only to a trend deterioration in the balance between exports and imports but also to bottlenecks and surges of imports whenever domestic demand has grown rapidly. In this sense, the balance-of-payments is a structural problem. Many British industrialists and public servants share this view. A former Chairman of the Technology Requirements Board wrote: 'Our lack of effectiveness is deepseated. The principal cause is our failure to engineer properly UK products in a way that provides attractive, functionally competent designs associated with manufacturing technology which ensures quality and market satisfaction with profit. Pursuit of this objective requires a big increase in the funds devoted to R&D.'[6] As far as one can tell, the situation is getting worse. The National Economic Development Council (NEDC), which monitored these matters closely, declared in 1988: 'Systematic evidence of supply-side improvements enhancing the UK's non-price competitiveness has not yet emerged.'[7]

The NEDO Report on non-price factors in international trade (Stout, 1977) distinguished two broad aspects of non-price competitiveness: first, the act of selling or marketing, and, secondly, the characteristics of the product including design, ease of maintenance, quality, reliability, delivery time and after-sales service. It appears from both casual empiricism and detailed studies that in most, if not all, major areas of non-price competition, the performance of British industry leaves much to be desired. Mr David Orr, the former Chairman of Unilever, has described marketing as 'the skill of providing the right product for delivery at the right time in the right place at the right price and with the right back-up service for a profit'. He goes on 'the most decisive factors today are concerned with design, styling, packaging, advertising; and for capital goods, particularly credit terms, delivery dates, reliability, technical service and so on'.[8] In a study on the problems of export marketing by *Political and Economic Planning*,[9] it was concluded that the neglect of marketing, especially marketing based on systematic market research overseas, has been one of the main reasons for Britain's poor export performance. A study by the British Export Trade Research Organisation (1975) found that leading British companies had either no, or only a single, permanent export representative in key foreign markets compared with an average of eleven for German and Japanese companies. The NEDC Inquiry on Export Trends (1963) referred to poor marketing: 'the tendency to follow the market rather than lead it – the slowness in initiating or responding to fashion and design changes. . . . inadequate effort by manufacturers to find out about specific requirements or improvements needed by customers and potential customers'.

The Department of Scientific and Industrial Research concluded in its report, *Engineering Design* (1963), that the loss of exports in products where the UK once excelled was 'probably because the design . . . [was] failing to satisfy the customer'. The NEDO study of Imported Manufactures (1965) showed that, on the basis of users' opinions, technical performance was the decisive factor for most imports of mechanical engineering products, electronic capital goods and scientific instruments. It found that 'either a piece of equipment which does a specific job is not available in the UK or there is a difference in its design characteristics which alters the economics or reliability of operating it'. The Design Council of Britain declared in its new three-year Corporate Plan 'uncompetitive product design remains an important element of the national manufacturing deficiencies'.

The responses reported in some of the industry studies by NEDO are revealing. In machine tools, export success was seen to depend primarily on delivery and reliability. In a separate study of the machine tool industry (NEDO, 1965), UK machine tool users were asked why they bought foreign machines: 5 per cent said price was the main factor; 5 per cent, better after-sales service; 8 per cent, willingness of foreign producers to meet special requirements; 20 per cent, quick and reliable delivery; 21 per cent said machine specifications were not available in the UK; and 30 per cent referred to the technical superiority of the foreign product. In the pumps and valves industry, it was felt that the industry lacked the organisational support and resources necessary to match the marketing, delivery and after-sales service of competitors. In the electronics industry, the criticism was made that electronic consumer goods are not designed with the European market in mind and suffered from a reputation for poor quality. In clothing, likewise, it was found that designs and fashions were often out of line with continental preferences. Quality and design were being sacrificed to keep prices down. In the engineering industry, the Sector Working Party mentioned the following non-price factors: the failure to introduce products which are technologically ahead of competitors; concentration on engineering rather than design with insufficient attention to details such as controls, ease of adjustment, etc.; failure to adopt a market-orientated approach; insufficient contact maintained with past customers to ensure that repeat orders are placed; and, lastly, poor delivery.

Poor design, poor quality and poor reliability are reflected in the fact that the UK tends to export relatively low value-added products and to import relatively high value-added products compared with its major industrial competitors. According to research by NEDO on industries covered by 35 Sector Working Parties, the average unit values of German exports were found to be higher than those of British exports in 29 out of 35 industries examined, and in 23 out of 34 in the case of French exports. This suggests that the UK is specialising in 'down-market' or inferior products.

Kravis and Lipsey (1971), in their detailed study of price competition discussed above, also considered the relative importance of non-price factors, although understandably they were not able to obtain quantitative data comparable to those for prices. They relied on the answers to questionnaires which were sent to various firms asking for the factors accounting for the firms' success in exporting in terms of relative percentages. 'Low prices received only 28 per cent of the weight on the average. . . . The greatest importance (57 per cent) was assigned to factors that enabled the US firms to sell abroad even though their products were more expensive than those of foreign competitors; product superiority in one form or another . . . accounted for the largest part (34 per cent out of the 57 per cent), with better after-sales service the leading runner-up (12 per cent). There was, as would be expected, a greater emphasis on relative price in basic products (SITC 2 and 5) than in manufactured goods (SITC 6 and 7). Indeed, over half the firms reporting upon manufactured goods in SITC 6 and 7 did not attribute any of their export success to their ability to match foreign prices' (Kravis and Lipsey, 1971, p. 154).[10] Table 4.2, which is also taken from Kravis and Lipsey, compares the factors that US exporters and German importers of factory equipment (a more limited range of products than described above) considered were important in determining export success and the decision of what imports to buy.

It may be seen that there is a remarkable correspondence between the results of the two countries. In both cases, only 7 per cent of the purchases were for reasons of price, and about three quarters of German imports and US exports were bought for reasons of product differentiation.

This provides further confirmation that as far as the characteristics of goods are concerned, design, performance, reliability and appearance are very important.

The decline in the US's market share of manufactured exports from 25.5 per cent in 1956 to just under 10 per cent in 1990 also seems

Table 4.2   Factors accounting for factory equipment trade (per cent):
German imports versus US exports, 1964

	German imports	US exports
Price	7	7
Product differentiation	77	73
Unique goods	63	22
Superior goods	14	51
(Technical features)	(10)	
(Quality)	(5)	
Service and other factors	16	20
Better service	3	9
Delivery time	9	8
Miscellaneous	4	3
Total	100	100

Source: Kravis and Lipsey (1971, table 7.4, p. 156).

to be due mainly to its deterioration in non-price competitiveness. This may seem surprising since, after all, the US is generally regarded as being at the forefront of the development of new and technologically sophisticated products. A report in *The Economist* (July 1987), suggests, however, that most American firms cater primarily for the domestic market and only attempt to sell overseas when home sales are in relative decline. This means that US firms tend to be seriously handicapped when they attempt to sell overseas. For example:

They mistakenly believe that they can export their products designed for American customers, without any modification to take account of foreign tastes (and without translating their instruction and maintenance manuals into a foreign language). Even such a popular product as American jeans needs changing when sold abroad, because the shapes of the typical American, French and Asian women are different.

Another example: Indonesia has the world's fifth largest population. Although income per person is low, the country has a large rural electricity grid. With its tropical climate, it offers a big market for refrigerators. Why, then, are all refrigerators in Indonesia Japanese and none of them American? Answer: the supply of electricity in Indonesia is subject to large voltage swings, which cause electric motors to burn out. Since Japanese exporters did

their homework, every one of their refrigerators has a small, cheap
voltage regulator, which stops the compressor motor burning out.
(*The Economist*, July 1987, p. 70)

The Economist goes on to detail further shortcomings of the US in
the export field. Typically, US companies do not undertake their own
market research abroad but commission local consultants to undertake feasibility studies that 'are based on misleading and incomplete
market statistics'. Few American banks have set up nationwide facilities to provide international banking facilities for US firms. Consequently, most American companies 'have to rely on their small
hometown bank to provide the necessary international financial services'. The US is the only country that prohibits American businessmen making 'commission' payments (bribes) to government officials
to obtain favourable treatment. Given that corruption is endemic in
many third world countries, this can seriously hinder the sale of US
exports. Exporting requires a long-term commitment yet US managers are paid substantial bonus payments on yearly or quarterly
results. This militates against taking a long-term view which exporting normally requires. Finally, and perhaps surprisingly,

American goods no longer enjoy a reputation for quality. To
compensate for this deficiency at home, a new service industry has
sprung up to maintain defective merchandise. To establish, train
and run such a maintenance and service network abroad is impossible.

This evidence is, of course, somewhat anecdotal and by its nature it
is difficult to quantify its effect; but it does confirm other evidence on
the importance of non-price competitiveness.

Less anecdotal is Connell's (1979) NEDO study of the UK which
provides dramatic confirmation of the importance of non-price competition. Table 4.3 reports the unit values of exports of non-electrical
machinery (SITC 71) for the years 1962 and 1975 for a number of
advanced countries. Non-electrical machinery exports are generally
complex and technically sophisticated products where differences in
non-price competitiveness are likely to be of paramount importance.

These exports account for about one-fifth of the UK's total exports
of goods and broadly correspond to the products of the mechanical
engineering industry. From the table, it can be seen that, over the
period 1962–75, the UK had the second smallest increase in unit

Table 4.3   Average value per tonne of exports of non-electrical machinery
(SITC 71)

| Country | Average value per tonne of exports ($US000 per tonne) | | Change % | Share | Percentage point change in world export share |
	1962	1975	1962–75	1962	1962–75
Japan	1.40	4.11	193	2.7	+5.3
France	2.00	5.11	156	5.9	+2.9
Italy	2.30	4.74	106	5.5	+1.6
Netherlands	2.08	5.77	177	2.2	+0.3
West Germany	1.99	5.94	198	23.8	+0.3
Sweden	2.20	5.99	172	4.0	−0.3
UK	1.75	4.24	142	17.5	−6.3

Source: Connell (1979, table 5, p. 17).

values, after Italy. The slower growth in UK unit values dates from
the latter part of the 1960s. In 1967, if aero engines are excluded, unit
values were equal for France and the UK and 14 per cent higher for
Germany. But by 1976, according to Connell's data, French unit
values were 29 per cent higher and German unit values were 60 per
cent higher than those of the UK.

Connell argues that given international arbitrage there is little
room for price differences between genuinely identical goods and so
the differences in unit values reflect differences in the non-price
elements of the goods involved. Substantial differences between two
countries can reflect either a different mix of products (with the
country with the lower unit value concentrating on technologically
less sophisticated goods) or broad differences in non-price factors
across the whole spectrum of exports, or both. 'In most cases, this
apparent difference is conceptual rather than real as differences in the
current mix of products are usually the result of a series of historical
decisions regarding R&D expenditure and the direction in which
companies have developed their product range' (Connell, 1979,
p. 16).

Under this interpretation, Table 4.3 presents a depressing picture
as far as the UK is concerned; it is one of either the progressive
deterioration in the quality of the UK's exports or the 'trading down
market' into less sophisticated products, or both.

Another explanation is that these differences could be due to the
exchange rate fluctuations that were experienced over the period,

1962–75, which covered both nominal and real sterling devaluations. As Brech and Stout (1981) point out, while much of the increased price competitiveness resulting from the 1967 devaluation of sterling had been lost because of the subsequent inflation, the nominal devaluation of nearly 49 per cent between December 1971 and 1976 had resulted in a 'real' depreciation of about 16 per cent. Connell (1979, p. 17), however, argues that 'It seems unlikely that such large apparent price [unit value] differences could have been sustained for very long if they were not indicative of real underlying variations in product mix, quality or other non-price factors.' The fact that the UK experienced a most dramatic decline in its market share of 6.3 percentage points would seem to refute the explanation that the cause of the relative fall in the UK's unit values was primarily the depreciation of sterling. Sweden, which experienced the second largest fall in market share, only experienced a loss in its share of 0.3 percentage points, in spite of having a higher increase in its unit values than the UK. Germany had the largest increase in unit values over this period, but still actually managed to increase its market share. Clearly, the higher unit values in Germany reflect predominantly their superior quality.[11] Moreover, for the basic product groups where price competition is much more important, there was little difference between the unit values of the UK and Germany.

Brech and Stout (1981 p. 269) report some further NEDO results that provide additional confirmation of this interpretation. In a period of rapid currency depreciation we should expect those products which are relatively homogeneous (i.e. basic products rather than sophisticated manufactured goods) to experience the fastest rates of growth. This is precisely what NEDO found. Over the period 1975 to 1977, a time of rapid devaluation, 'broadly speaking, the most buoyant [exports] were 'commodity' products like chemicals (+75%), plastic materials (+57%), and leather, rubber, wood, paper and non-metallic minerals (+60%). The most stagnant were those at the technology-intensive end of engineering, like professional and scientific instruments (−9%)' (Brech and Stout, 1981, p. 269).

Connell (1979) assumed that short-term fluctuations in unit values reflected changes in prices while changes in the long run were capturing changes in non-price competitiveness. This enabled him to calculate that for the UK to have maintained its market share of mechanical engineering products its prices would have had to have fallen by 4 per cent per annum compared with those of Germany. Compared with France, the figure was 8 per cent per annum. Even if these figures are only of the right order of magnitude, they graphically illustrate the difficulty of relying on improvements in price competition to offset a long-run decline in the non-price elements.

Brech and Stout (1981) also present some interesting evidence that suggests that a depreciation in the UK's exchange rate may actually have worsened the quality of British exports. They constructed an index of 'trading up' or 'trading down' which is based on the changing composition of 40 categories of exports in the machine tool sector as between high and low unit value products. They found that over the period 1970 to 1980, this index was positively correlated with the change in the exchange rate, indicating that a depreciation was associated with trading down or the substitution of low for high unit value goods. (It should be emphasised that this is in addition to the distinct possibility of a general decline in non-price competitiveness of *all* the products which is not captured by the index.)

The hypothesis that Brech and Stout set out to test, and for which they found some empirical support, is consistent with that advanced by us throughout this book and is as follows.

For deep-seated structural and institutional reasons, economic agents in the UK adapt slowly and hesitantly to either market or technology changes. There is, therefore, a trend decline in UK NPC [non-price competitiveness]. This decline is reflected in a relatively low income elasticity of demand for UK manufactures. There are usually strong social and political pressures to try to maintain growth at a rate relative to the rest of the world which is inconsistent with this trend towards product obsolescence. The trend decline is therefore partially compensated for, in its effect on the balance-of-payments, by episodes of nominal and (temporarily *real*) devaluation. However, the remedy is inappropriate, not just because, after a lag of a few quarters, domestic inflation liquidates most of the relative price advantage, but because recourse to devaluation has two effects. The greater ease with which older products, which tend also to be more price elastic, can be sold provides some exporters with a soft short-run option to the painful, expensive and risky process of developing superior products. On top of this, those firms who have launched products early in their life-cycle alongside older products, find, following a devaluation, that the demand for the older products has risen more strongly. Those of them who behave passively, retain labour and expand investment for the production of the older products instead of moving more resources into the new. This type of outcome is consistent with the pricing behaviour to be expected at least in the less concentrated UK industries where some temporary rigidity in sterling prices can be expected following devaluation. On balance, given some short-sightedness among UK entrepreneurs, the devaluation that was a result, in part, of failures of NPC in the past may therefore feed back and further reduce it, leading UK manufacturing even further downmarket. (Brech and Stout, 1981, pp. 271–2, omitting a footnote; emphasis in the original)

Brech and Stout are quick to point out, however, that, even if this hypothesis is correct, it does not imply that the optimal strategy to be pursued is one of artificially keeping the exchange rate up. First, no consideration has been taken of the direct impact of the exchange rate on export earnings. Since conventional estimates of the price elasticities of demand for UK exports and imports suggest that the elasticities sum to greater than one, a devaluation is likely to provide some improvement in the balance-of-payments, albeit only temporarily and at the cost of a deterioration of non-price competitiveness. Secondly, an appreciation of the exchange rate might cut profit margins to such an extent that even manufacturers at the top end of the quality range may not find it worthwhile to export. This possibility was dramatically illustrated by the rapid appreciation of sterling over the period 1979–81 with its deleterious effect on manufacturing output in the UK. It should be pointed out, however, that Landesmann and Snell (1989) found some evidence that the non-price competitiveness of UK exports increased after this recession. An inference that may be drawn is that in the long run the reliance on a continuous real depreciation, even if could be engineered at the necessary substantial rate, to overcome deficiencies in non-price competitiveness is likely to be self-defeating. Not only would this set up a vicious inflation-devaluation circle, but it would also, at the very least, fail to improve non-price competitiveness and possibly worsen it. The solution to the UK's balance-of-payments constraint lies at the microeconomic level and is likely to be impervious to macroeconomic policies such as exchange rate adjustments. There are no quick remedies.

OTHER STUDIES OF NON-PRICE COMPETITION

In practice, it is not easy to measure non-price competition. Proxies have to be taken such as R&D expenditure as a measure of input into the innovative process, the number of patents issued as a measure of the output of innovative activity, or the level of education and skill intensity employed in various industries. All the measures have their weaknesses. Patent statistics may not accurately reflect differences in innovative activity *between* firms, sector or countries, while R&D and education statistics measure inputs not outputs. However, there is evidence that R&D and patent statistics are correlated. As reported by Pavitt and Soete (1980), a comparison among US industrial sectors shows a correlation between a sector's share of total R&D and its share of patents (excluding aerospace and motor vehicles from the sample). This correlation is also evident across OECD countries in 1975, taking patents registered by OECD countries in the US.

In empirically testing the importance of non-price factors in the determination of trade performance, it is also probably wise to make a distinction between capital goods, consumption goods, and the production of basic materials (see Freeman, 1979, in Blackaby, 1979). In capital goods, technical effort is directed mainly towards the design and development of new products which have superior technical characteristics. In this sphere, R&D expenditure will be extremely important. In consumption goods, such as food, textiles, furniture etc., advertising expenditure and design are likely to be more important than R&D. In basic materials, technical effort will be mainly directed towards cost reductions through factor-saving innovation. This being so, price will matter more for consumer goods and basic materials than for capital goods with a high research intensity.

Pavitt (1980) finds no relation between inter-country differences in the rate of growth of manufacturing exports and the rate of change of manufacturing prices. For Britain, Posner and Steer (1979) point out that in the 1960s and 1970s there was a relative decline of UK exports in spite of favourable price competitiveness. Price competitiveness also improved in the latter part of the 1980s, yet export market share was falling and import penetration rising. Hibberd and Wren Lewis (1978) show that the increase in imports of manufactures into the UK cannot be explained by unfavourable relative price movements. All the evidence points to the dominant role of non-price competition.

Many aggregate and industry studies have been undertaken which show a strong link between export performance and various measures of non-price competition, particularly in the capital goods sector. We report here some of the major studies, focusing mainly, although not exclusively, on studies of the UK.

Pavitt and Soete (1980) have examined export performance in forty sectors across twenty-two OECD countries over the period 1963 to 1977. Their measure of non-price competition is the number of patents registered in the US. The hypothesis is that the greater the resources devoted to innovation, and the more patents taken out, the more competitive a country will become in products and processes. Exports in 1977 for each sector (per head of the population) are regressed on the cumulative number of patents per head over the period 1963 to 1976. The correlation coefficient is significant at the 98 per cent confidence level for twenty-three out of the forty industries. The relation is strongest in the capital goods industries and also in chemicals and some transport equipment, and weakest in traditional products and consumption goods.

A study by Mayes, Buxton and Murfin (1988) for NEDO examines UK trade with France, Germany, Japan and the US in fifteen manufacturing industries over the period 1970–83. R&D expenditure is used as the main measure of non-price competition and treated as a stock variable. In every industry, cumulative R&D expenditure is a highly significant determinant of trade performance.

Greenhalgh (1988, 1990) has tried to separate the roles of price and non-price factors in determining UK trade performance in thirty-nine sectors (including twenty-three manufacturing sectors) over the period 1954–81. Three hypotheses are tested: (i) industries with high levels of innovation will be net exporters; (ii) successful innovators will face higher income elasticities of demand for their products and lower price elasticities; and (iii) innovative industries will use more highly qualified manpower and invest more in R&D. Product quality is measured by the number of innovations and patents. The number of innovations appears to be an important explanation of trade performance in about one-half of the sectors covered, although, surprisingly, not in the two sectors of mechanical and electrical engineering where innovation has been most active. In only one-third of the sectors was there a significant price effect. Greenhalgh concludes: 'This lends support to the view that price is not necessarily the most salient characteristic of complex manufactured products, whose typical quality is changing rapidly through time' (Greenhalgh, 1988,

p. 21). Within manufacturing, the relation between *net* exports (exports minus imports) and the income variable is negative in two-thirds of the cases, indicating that the income elasticity of demand for imports is greater than for exports. This in itself is a reflection of the UK's relative inferiority in the production of 'up-market' products.

Schott and Pick (1984) have tested a model in which exports are related to relative prices, the quality of goods (measured by R&D expenditure and the number of employees with higher education) and 'world' income. The model was fitted to UK data for manufacturing industries 3 to 19 of the Standard Industrial Classification for the years 1972, 1975, 1978 and 1981. The analysis therefore used pooled time-series and cross-section data. Both the R&D and education variables turned out to be significant, but so too did the relative price variable. Both price and non-price competition are important.

Goodman and Ceyhun (1976) used principal components analysis to examine the factors determining the performance of US manufactured exports at the two and three-digit SIC level. They explicitly included non-price factors such as proxies for technological innovations, sales promotion etc. as factors affecting export performance. On the basis of their study they concluded that: 'First, it would appear that trade theory to date has been characterized by a fairly general and unwarranted underemphasis of non-price factors. At an earlier point in time, perhaps this could be justified. But with the contemporary revolutions in communications, managerial techniques, marketing institutions, and industry organization, and the rapid transformation of the world economy into a cohesive, tightly interwoven whole, concentration exclusively or even primarily on cost-price factors becomes virtually untenable. Although the results of this study are far from conclusive, they do indicate that there is much to be gained by transferring a large amount of attention to non-price factors' (Goodman and Ceyhun, 1976, p. 551).

RESEARCH AND DEVELOPMENT EFFORT

The UK has been losing market share for some time in almost every sector of the economy. The message of the foregoing analysis is that countries neglect non-price competition and its determinants at their peril. This is also the conclusion to emerge from the extensive research carried out by the Science Policy Research Unit at Sussex University (e.g. Pavitt, 1980): that Britain's performance in technical

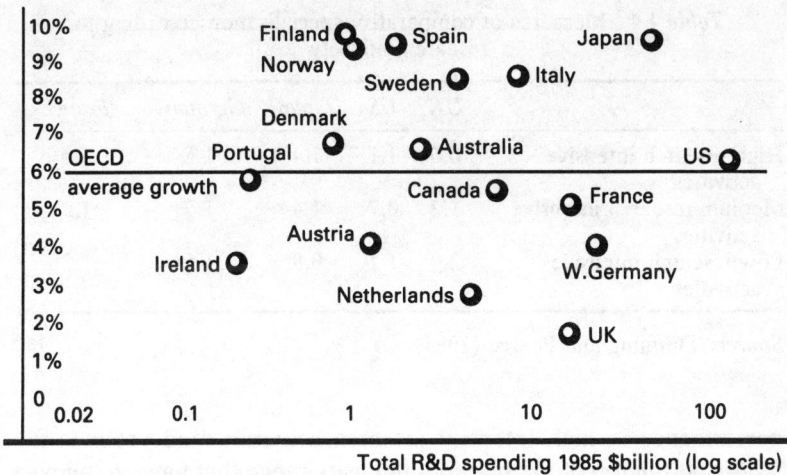

Figure 4.2 R&D growth in OECD countries, 1981–5

Source: OECD.

innovation has been unsatisfactory for a long time relative to competitors, and this is a major explanation of Britain's relative economic decline. R&D effort appears to have been particularly weak. For example, between 1967 and 1975, Britain was the only OECD country where industry-financed R&D declined in absolute terms. The performance continues to be poor absolutely and relative to other countries. From 1969 to 1983, the real growth of total R&D expenditure averaged 1.8 per cent per annum, the lowest rate of all industrialised countries. The experience in the first half of the 1980s is shown in Figure 4.2. The amount of expenditure is large, but the rate of growth of 1.6 per cent has been the lowest of all countries, and slower than the growth of GDP. Much of the expenditure is on defence and aircraft, which does not enhance the competitiveness of British industry directly. Equally worrying is the finding by Dunning and Pearce (1985) that the UK tends to specialise in low research intensity activities.

Research intensity is defined in terms of R&D expenditure relative to sales.[12] Comparative specialisation is measured by a country's share of world export sales in an industry relative to the country's total share of world export sales. The figures are given in Table 4.4. Compared with its major competitors, the UK has a weak sales

Table 4.4   Measures of comparative specialisation according to research intensity

	UK	US	Japan	Germany	France
High research intensive activities	0.6	1.1	1.4	1.5	1.2
Medium research intensive activities	1.2	0.7	1.4	1.5	1.2
Low research intensive activities	2.0	1.1	0.8	1.5	1.2

Source: Dunning and Pearce (1985).

performance in high intensity research activities, and yet it is the sectors at the top of the research intensity range that have in the past recorded the fastest rate of growth (Smith, 1986). Explanations have to be sought for this weakness of British industry. Large firms have a role to play. According to Smith (1986), countries with the largest and fastest growing giant firms have been the most competitive in international markets.

The UK's largest industrial companies are smaller than those in the US, Japan and West Germany. In 1984 the turnover of the UK's twenty largest companies was only 26 per cent that of the twenty largest US companies, 61 per cent of the Japanese level, and 73 per cent of the German. The Sussex Science Policy Research Unit stresses the generally poor academic and professional training of British managers and engineers. Successful technical innovation requires an integration of R&D, marketing and planning and this requires high level personnel.

The UK is particularly weak relative to Germany, which is responsible for a large part of the UK trade deficit. A study by Patel and Pavitt (1989) shows that Germany took out more patents in the US than did the UK in all thirty-three industrial sectors examined. Moreover, there was a much greater concentration of technological activities in twenty-two out of the thirty-three sectors. Freeman (1979) has argued that 'perhaps the biggest single long-term contrast between British and German industry has been in the number and quality of engineers deployed in all managerial functions in manufacturing'.

A much earlier study by Freeman (1965) of the electronic capital goods industry has turned out to be very prescient in its conclusion, and we let Freeman have the final word which lends strong support to the central argument of this book. In discussing the British government's role in R&D, he concluded 'the government should consider the prospective contribution to the balance of payments since an unsatisfactory balance of payments has been – *and is likely to be* – the main obstacle to faster growth in Britain' (emphasis added).

THE 'NEW' TRADE THEORIES

Non-price competition lies at the heart of several new theories of trade that have been developed in recent years to replace the static, price-based theory of comparative cost, and to account for the growing phenomenon of intra-industry trade between countries. As countries get richer through time there tends to be a shift of emphasis within sectors towards product novelty, quality and reliability, and in general towards high value-added products where non-price factors are critically important. These new trade theories are sometimes referred to as neo-technology theories of trade because product quality, reliability, sophistication etc. depend in the main on technical progress and innovation, which in turn depend to a large extent on research and development. The definition of scientific and technological innovation, now used by the OECD,[13] identifies seven stages in the innovation process, *viz*, research and development, new product marketing, patent work, financial, design engineering, tooling-industrial engineering and manufacturing start.

One of the pioneering theories was the technological gap model of Posner (1961) which argued that a country which first introduces a new product may export it, at least until imitators come into the market. Economies of scale enjoyed by the innovators will keep the country ahead as long as the imitation lag is longer than the demand lag. As imitation proceeds and novelty wears off, the theory of comparative costs will reassert itself.

A natural development of this theory of trade was the idea of the product-cycle developed by Vernon (1966) and Hirsch (1967). Trade in products will go through cycles where non-price characteristics are important in the early stages of a product's life; but as production gradually shifts from innovator to imitator, price competition becomes more important.

The growing phenomenon of intra-industry trade, first documented in detail by Grubel and Lloyd (1971), has lent strong support to these theories, and has been a major impetus to their development. Differences in costs and prices cannot explain trade between countries in the 'same' product. The basis of intra-industry trade must lie in non-price competition or product differentiation. Following the characteristics approach to demand theory pioneered by Lancaster (1971), a differentiated product is one that offers a bundle of attributes or characteristics different from its competitors. Countries will export goods intensive in one set of characteristics and import goods intensive in another. Intra-industry trade will be more important the more similar countries are since there will not be specialisation according to cost differences. Davies (1976) has tested this hypothesis for UK trade with the EEC and USA. He looked at trade balances in 945 sectors with France, Germany, Italy, USA and Japan. A broad correspondence was found between the similarity of factor endowments and intra-industry trade.

Barker (1977) has put forward a similar 'variety hypothesis' of trade which argues that 'as real income increases, purchasers tend to buy more varieties of a product, and since a greater number of these varieties is available from abroad rather than from home sources, the share of imports in demand tends to increase. For imports as a whole, the quantity of imports tends to rise more than proportionately with real per capita income.' Both the Davies and Barker models predict that the greater the degree of intra-industry trade, the higher the income elasticity of demand for imports and exports because the greater the product differentiation and variety of products. This prediction has been tested by Barker who finds a high correlation between intra-industry trade and the income elasticities of demand for imports across fifteen countries over the period 1951–66 (using the Houthakker and Magee estimates of income elasticities reported in Chapter 3). Also, the amount of imports supplied by different sources is found to rise as income rises. The enormous trade deficit that the UK has with Germany undoubtedly has something to do with the similarity of industrial structures and the growth of trade based on product differentiation and variety.

A formal model of the relative influence of price and non-price competition has been developed by Schott (1984) and Schott and Pick (1984) which we present here for its simplicity and pedagogic attractiveness.

THE SCHOTT MODEL

Schott, drawing on the work of Gabszewicz and Thisse (1979) and Shaked and Sutton (1982), presents a simple model that has the advantage of emphasising the potential importance of non-price competition, as represented by differences in quality, in consumer choice.[14]

We consider one good which is manufactured by two countries, for example, the UK and Japan. The good, say, a motor car, differs between the two countries in terms of quality. Thus, while both products are five-door 1.3 litre cars, they are not perfect substitutes; the Japanese car is of better quality.

The following plausible assumptions are made. First, if the two goods are of the same quality, then the cheaper will be preferred by the consumer. Secondly, the product with the higher quality will be preferred if both vehicles have identical prices. Thirdly, when consumers face a combination of differing prices and qualities, their choice depends upon their income and tastes. There is a large number of consumers with identical preferences but varying incomes. The consumers have the choice of buying either the Japanese car or the British make or of abstaining from buying either of them. But the representative consumer only buys a maximum of one car.

Let us begin by considering the British domestic market for this type of car. In Figure 4.3(a), all the consumers are ranked by income along the horizontal axis so that consumers to the left of the figure have lower incomes than those to the right and each point on the axis represents one consumer. The prices of the cars are represented on the vertical axis and the price of the UK car is denoted by P_{UK}.

The reservation price is defined as the price at which the consumer is indifferent to buying or not buying the car. In the latter case, more money can be spent on other goods. We further assume that those with a higher income have a higher reservation price. Those on low incomes will view a car as a luxury and will only buy one if the price is comparatively low. Thus, the reservation line denoted by R_{UK} in Figure 4.3(a) has a positive slope. All the consumers to the right of X_0 will buy the car as their reservation price, R_{UK}, exceeds the actual price, P_{UK}, whereas those consumers to the left of X_0 will refrain from making a purchase as their reservation price is below the actual price.

From Figure 4.3(a), it may be readily seen that a reduction in the price to P'_{UK} will increase the number of sales, as all consumers to the right of X_1 will now purchase a vehicle. An improvement in quality

(a)   Price

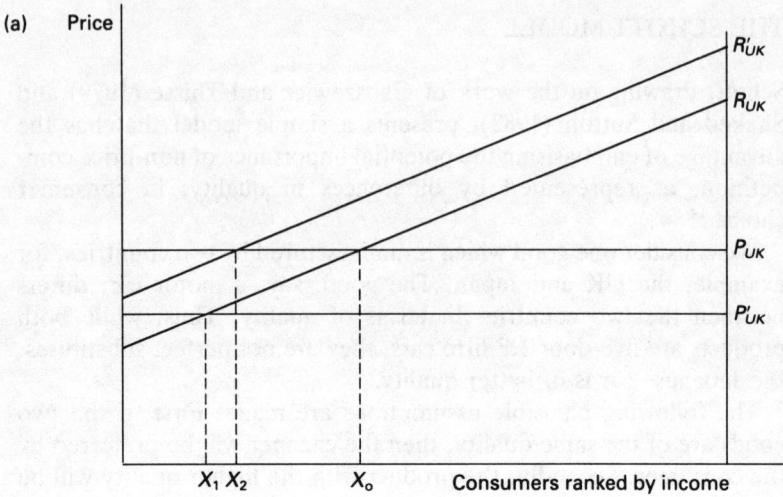

X_1 X_2 X_0 Consumers ranked by income

(b)   Price

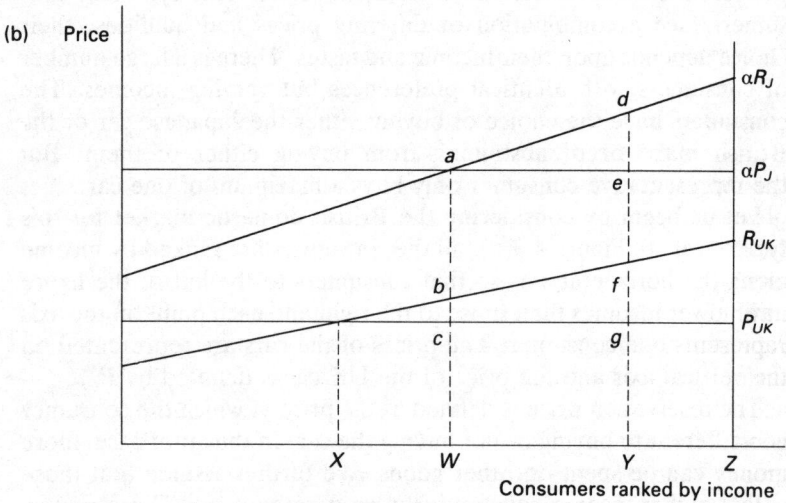

X W Y Z
Consumers ranked by income

with the price remaining constant at P_{UK} will also increase the number of sales. In terms of the diagram, an increase in quality raises the reservation line to R'_{UK} and X_0 shifts leftwards to X_2.

Now let us introduce the better quality Japanese car into the analysis. It is assumed that its price is higher than that of the British car. (If it were not, under the above assumptions, Japanese imports would sweep the market completely wiping out the British domestic motor-car industry.) We are interested in determining initially under what circumstances the higher priced, but higher quality, Japanese

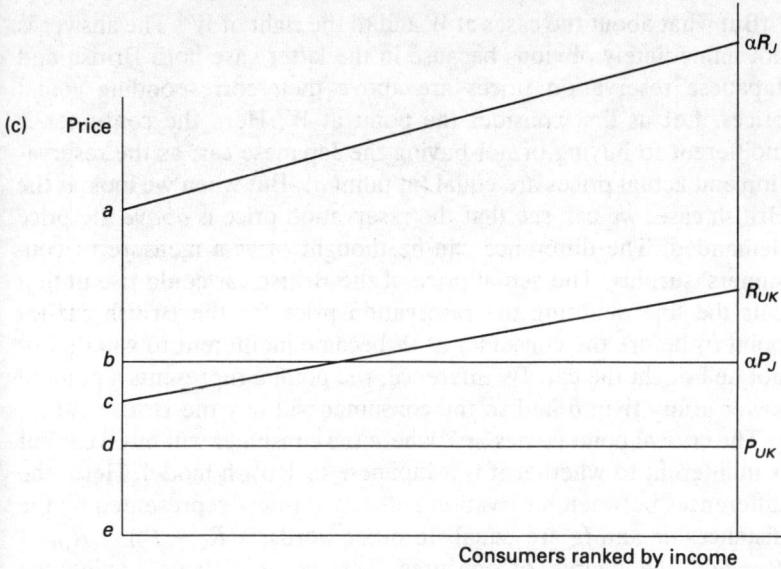

Figure 4.3

car will be purchased in preference to the British make. The most obvious way is to incorporate the actual and reservation prices for Japanese cars in the same diagram. The choice, however, of which product to buy is based on considerations of utility. Using a simple utility function, Schott shows that we may use the same axes if the Japanese asking price and reservation prices are multiplied by a factor α which 'can be thought of as the ratio of the utility of acquiring the foreign good over the utility of acquiring the British good. Because the foreign good is superior in quality, α will be greater than unity' (Schott and Pick, 1984, p. 9).

Figure 4.3(b) considers both the Japanese and British cases. The reservation line for the Japanese car is steeper than that for the British one. This is based on the not unreasonable assumption that as income increases, the better quality product is valued progressively more highly than the poorer quality one. From the figure, it is clear that consumers to the left of X will buy neither good as the reservation prices for both makes of car are below the actual prices. It may also be seen that from X to W consumers will buy the British car, as over this range the consumers' reservation price is above the actual price for the British car only.

But what about the cases at W and to the right of W? The answer is not immediately obvious because in the latter case both British and Japanese reservation prices are above their corresponding actual prices. Let us first consider the point at W. Here the consumer is indifferent to buying or not buying the Japanese car, as the reservation and actual prices are equal (at point a). But when we look at the British case, we can see that the reservation price is *above* the price demanded. The difference can be thought of as a measure of consumers' surplus. The actual price of the British car could rise until it cuts the line denoting the reservation price for the British car (at point b) before the consumer at W became indifferent to whether or not he bought the car. By inference, the point a represents a point of lower utility than b and so the consumer will buy the British car.

The critical point comes at Y where the consumer will buy a car but is indifferent to whether it is a Japanese or British model. Here, the differences between reservation and actual prices represented by the distances *de* and *fg* are equal. In other words, $\alpha(R_J - P_J) = R_{UK} - P_{UK}$ and the degree of consumer surplus at Y from buying the Japanese car is exactly the same as that obtained by purchasing the British car. To the right of Y the consumer will gain more utility by buying Japanese and hence this will be purchased in preference to the British car. Over the range from Y to X the British car will be bought, while to the left of X no car will be purchased.

SOME IMPLICATIONS OF THE MODEL

From Figure 4.3(b), it is clear that if the price of the British car falls, this will increase the value of its sales. X will move to the left and Y to the right. The British car will increase its sales at both ends of the market. If, on the other hand, the price of the Japanese car falls, Y (and W) will move to the left so that the Japanese car will pick up sales at the upper income end of the market.

An improvement in the quality of the British car will shift its reservation line upwards and, *ceteris paribus*, this will increase British sales. X will move to the left and Y to the right. If the Japanese car improves in quality, so its reservation line (αR_J) would shift upwards and both W and Y will move to the left. A quality improvement in the foreign car thus increases its sales in the upper end of the market.

These propositions are self-evident. Both a lower price and an improvement in quality will improve sales. But what is more interesting is the role of consumers' incomes in the analysis. As we have seen, improvements in price and quality affect purchases of those with the higher incomes, since those on the lower incomes will continue to buy the cheaper British car. Equally, as incomes rise over time, the demand for the better quality product will increase proportionately more than that for the inferior quality good. As standards of living rise, there is a commensurate rise in the demand for quality goods and the effect of relative prices becomes less important. It is possible that if a country neglects quality in a product, it may eventually cease to have a viable industry. This is demonstrated in Figure 4.3(c) where the quality of the Japanese good is so much greater relative to its price compared with the British product that even if the latter's price fell to zero it still could not give the product away. This is because the degree of consumers' surplus involved in buying the Japanese vehicle (*ab*) is greater than that obtained from the British good even when the latter is free (*ce*). This is an unrealistic result in that it arises from the assumption that the consumer buys only one car, i.e. that no extra utility is obtained from having a second car even if free. Moreover, the British industry is certain to have gone bankrupt long before its price falls to zero. But it does demonstrate that price competition will eventually prove to be a poor or, indeed, no substitute for lack of non-price competitiveness. Given a British price which, because of the costs of the firm, can be cut no further, it is possible that the better quality Japanese product, even though higher priced, may completely expunge the British industry.

THE 'KALDOR PARADOX'

If the growth of exports and imports were highly responsive to changes in relative prices, then we should expect that those countries which had a noticeable improvement in their relative prices would also experience, *ceteris paribus*, the most rapid increase in their overseas market shares. In practice, and paradoxically, as Kaldor (1978c) first pointed out, the converse holds for much of the postwar period, with those countries which experienced the greatest decline in their price competitiveness also having had the greatest increase in their market share. This may be seen from Table 4.5 which reports the percentage changes in relative unit labour costs (RULCs), relative export prices and export shares for manufacturing for a number of countries.

Table 4.5   Long-run relationship of changes in price competitiveness and changes in trade performance in manufactures 1963–75

	Percentage changes in		
Country	Relative labour costs per unit of output	Relative export prices	Export shares
United Kingdom	−21.4	−12.4	−37.9
United States	−43.7	−14.1	−17.8
France	−8.6	+4.9	+17.8
West Germany	+42.9	+10.1	+3.0
Italy	+24.1	−9.3	+18.3
Netherlands	−10.5	−0.5	+19.0
Belgium-Luxemburg	+7.2	−1.8	+1.7
Sweden	−10.4	+22.0	+8.8
Switzerland	+33.3	+31.7	−11.8
Canada	−22.3	−13.3	+2.3
Japan	+27.1	+4.5	+72.0

Source: Kaldor (1978c, table 2, p. 105) (omitting a footnote).

Theoretically, to the extent that RULCs and relative export prices reflect relative price competitiveness, we should expect the changes in both of these to be inversely related to improvements in export shares. Only in three of the eleven countries (with Belgium and Luxemburg treated as a single entity) is this the case: the Netherlands, Switzerland and Canada (but the last only just). The other countries exhibit perverse behaviour to varying degrees.

The US and the UK both experienced substantial improvement in their RULCs, but this was associated with a rapid decline in their market shares. At the other extreme, both West Germany and Japan experienced a large increase in their RULCs, but nevertheless experienced a substantial increase in their market shares. A similar picture emerges if we take export prices rather than RULCs. But as Kaldor points out, the measure of export prices must be interpreted with a good deal of care. Export prices are 'export unit values' which are simply calculated by dividing the value of exports in a particular category by their weight. As we have seen when discussing the NEDO studies, increases in unit values (especially in the long run) may simply reflect the fact that a country is producing and selling goods of greater sophistication and quality. To the extent that this is true, the positive relationship between increases in unit values and market shares, which has been noted above, is only to be expected.

In order to test more directly the relationship between the rate of change of export shares and the growth of price competitiveness, we regressed the former on the latter using ordinary least-squares. The data consisted of growth rates for 15 countries calculated over the peak-to-peak years of economic activity for four subperiods from 1960 to 1983, namely, 1960–8, 1968–73, 1973–9, and 1979–83.[15] The regression result was as follows:

$$xs = 0.512 - 0.180 \; rulc \quad \bar{r}^2 = 0.019, \; SER = 2.558$$
$$(1.55) \quad (-1.47) \quad n = 60$$

where *xs* and *rulc* are the growth of the countries' shares of the total export market and the growth of relative unit labour costs respectively. The figures in parentheses are t-statistics and *SER* is the standard error of the regression.

As can be seen, there is no statistically significant relationship between the two variables. In other words, the differential growth of RULCs by itself cannot explain differences between the advanced countries in the growth of their export shares. To the extent that the growth of RULCs reflects changes in relative price competitiveness, the latter alone cannot be considered an important factor in explaining the relative performance of countries in the world market. The explanation must lie in disparities in non-price competitiveness.

In many cross-country regressions of, for example, growth performance Japan is found to be an outlier that significantly affects the results (Rowthorn, 1975a). In the case of the 'Kaldor Paradox', however, omitting Japan does not improve the goodness of fit. There is also no significant difference between the various subperiods.

As an alternative proxy for price competition, we also used the growth of relative prices of exports and imports.[16] This gave a slightly more significant relationship than when RULCs were used (excluding Japan, which in this case does prove to be an outlier):

$$xs = 0.014 - 0.336 \; rp \quad \bar{r}^2 = 0.045, \; SER = 2.025$$
$$(0.05) \quad (-1.90) \quad n = 56$$

where *rp* is the growth of relative prices of exports and imports.

The coefficient of *rp* is statistically significant at the 90 per cent confidence level and takes the expected sign, but the differential growth of relative prices still only explains about 5 per cent of the variation in the growth of export shares.[17]

Kaldor (1978c, p. 104) summarised the position with respect to the changes in RULCs and in the export shares reported in Table 4.5 as follows:

> The reason for such a negative correlation [between changes in price competitiveness and in export shares] can only be that the true causal relationship is the other way around: the changes in exchange rates and in 'competitiveness' as conventionally measured were not the cause, but the consequence of differing trends in market shares of different industrial countries, and the 'trends' themselves must then be due to factors not susceptible to measurement.

In other words, these strong trends captured the effects of changes in non-price competition. Those countries such as Germany and Japan which had a rapid improvement in the quality of their exports or an aggressive overseas marketing policy, or both, found that their market shares were rapidly growing, causing their exchange rates to appreciate in spite of the increase in their RULCs. Conversely, the UK and the US found that improvement in their price competitiveness could not compensate for their loss in non-price competitiveness. Kaldor is perhaps rather pessimistic, however, in his contention that the factors behind these trends are not 'susceptible to measurement'. We have seen in the last chapter that the income elasticities of demand for exports and imports are capturing the effects of non-price competition and, as we have noted above, it is likely that so also are changes in unit values.

The same picture emerges when we consider the determinants of the growth of import shares and find that the change in price competitiveness proves to be an insignificant explanatory variable. The result using the growth of RULCs and the full sample of countries is:

$$ms = 2.100 + 0.233 \; rulc \quad \bar{r}^2 = 0.051, \; SER = 2.370$$
$$(6.86) \quad (2.04) \qquad n = 60$$

where *ms* is the growth of the share of imports in a specific country's home market.

But even this weak relationship collapses when Japan is excluded from the sample:

$$ms = 2.171 + 0.154 \; rulc \quad \bar{r}^2 = 0.017, \; SER = 2.226$$
$$(7.30) \quad (1.40) \qquad n = 56$$

Using the growth of relative prices as the proxy for the growth of price competitiveness confirms the above results:

$$ms = 2.231 + 0.337\ rp \quad \bar{r}^2 = 0.042,\ SER = 2.381$$
$$ (7.04) \quad (1.90) \quad\quad n = 60$$

Excluding Japan, the result is:

$$ms = 2.204 + 0.154\ rp \quad \bar{r}^2 = -0.007,\ SER = 2.253$$
$$ (7.19) \quad (0.78) \quad\quad n = 56$$

Fagerberg (1988) has, *inter alia*, attempted explicitly to account for the Kaldor Paradox by estimating a simultaneous equation model where the growth of an index of technology is introduced to try to capture the effects of non-price competition.

Fagerberg's approach is to specify a simultaneous equation model essentially comprising five relationships:

(1) The growth of GDP is expressed as a function of the growth of export shares, the growth of import shares, the growth in the terms of trade (relative prices expressed in a common currency) and the growth of world income. These explanatory variables 'jointly determine the balance-of-trade equilibrium rate, to which the actual growth rate is assumed to adjust'. Fagerberg, consequently, uses the balance-of-payments equilibrium growth rate model derived in Chapter 3, except the model is expressed in terms of the growth of market shares rather than the growth of exports and imports, *per se*. He argues that 'Basically, what is assumed is that countries do not wish, or are not able, continually to increase debts or claims to the rest of the world, so that the balance of payments, with the exception of short-run fluctuations, will have to balance through its current account. This implies that, in the medium and long run, actual growth has to adjust to the balance-of-trade equilibrium growth rate, or the growth rate "warranted" by the current account, to use a Harrodian term' (Fagerberg, 1988, p. 361, omitting a footnote).

(2) The second relationship specifies that the growth of the terms in trade is determined by the growth of RULCs.

(3) The growth of export shares is specified as a function of the level and growth of technology, the growth of world income, the growth of RULCs and the investment–output ratio (the last acting as a proxy for the growth of capital). The major innovation is the new proxy for the level and growth of technology, which acts as a measure

of the degree of non-price competitiveness. Fagerberg constructs an index which is a weighted average of civilian R&D expenditures expressed as a proportion of GDP and external patents applications per capita, adjusted for differences in the openness of the economy as reflected in the ratio of exports to GDP (see Fagerberg, 1988, p. 373).

(4) The growth of import shares is determined by the same variables as the growth of export shares, with the exception that the growth of world income is replaced by the growth of GDP.

(5) The investment–output ratio is a function of the share of government welfare payments in GDP, the share of expenditure on the military, and the growth of GDP. The rationale for this equation is that investment in physical capacity is complementary to growth in 'the number of scientists and engineers, R&D facilities, advanced electronical (*sic*) equipment etc. Some of these are scarce, and to the extent that the government succeeds in attracting these at the expense of the market sectors of the economy, this may hamper investment in physical production capacity too' (Fagerberg, 1988, p. 362).

The model may be summarised as follows (where the functional forms are linear):

$$gdp = f_1 \, (xs, ms, tot, w) \tag{4.1}$$

$$tot = f_2 \, (rulc) \tag{4.2}$$

$$xs = f_3 \, (TG, TL, rulc, I/Q, w) \tag{4.3}$$

$$ms = f_4 \, (TG, TL, rulc, I/Q, gdp) \tag{4.4}$$

$$I/Q = f_5 \, (MIL/Q, WEL/Q, gdp) \tag{4.5}$$

where

gdp is the growth of GDP
xs and *ms* are the growth of export and import market shares
tot is the growth of the terms of trade
rulc is the growth of relative unit labour costs
TG and *TL* are the growth and level of the index of technology
w is the growth of world trade
I/Q, *MIL/Q*, and *WEL/Q* are the shares in GDP of gross investment, military expenditure and non-military government consumption.

Thus, it may be seen that the approach is essentially demand oriented. However, we are rather dubious about the inclusion of the investment–output ratio as a determinant of export and import shares. The rationale is that the growth of capacity is necessary for the production of exports and imports. Hence, the equations for changes in the export and import shares are hybrid supply and demand equations, rather than simply demand equations. While capacity constraints are undoubtedly a factor in short-term growth, in the context of long-term balance-of-payments equilibrium growth we would argue that the growth of capacity is ultimately the result of the growth of exports through the Harrod foreign trade multiplier. If supply factors are thought to be important, it would be better to introduce separate supply functions for exports and imports.

The model was used to explain the growth of the 15 advanced countries mentioned in footnote 15 over the period 1960–83. The growth rates of the appropriate variables were calculated over four subperiods: 1960–8, 1968–73, 1973–9 and 1979–83. The variables expressed as shares were the averages over these periods. The model was estimated using pooled cross-country data for the 15 countries, giving 60 observations in all. Dummies were introduced, where necessary, to allow for the oil-price shocks and country specific influences.

It is found that if dummies are introduced for the US and Norway, there is no statistically significant difference between the balance-of-trade equilibrium growth rate and the actual growth rate. This provides additional support for our finding in Chapter 3 that there was no statistical difference between our definition of the balance-of-payments equilibrium growth rate and the actual growth rates of most of the advanced countries.

The estimates of the various coefficients in the other equations (sections (2) to (5) above) of the model take the expected signs and are statistically significant. It is interesting to note that this is true of the growth of RULCs in the export share and import share equations, although this variable was not quantitatively important in explaining the growth of the export and import shares.

This is demonstrated when Fagerberg uses his model to explain the Kaldor Paradox for three countries, Japan, the UK and the US. He finds that his model actually predicts a strong 'perverse' relationship between the growth of export market shares and the growth of RULCs. In the case of Japan, Fagerberg found that, for the period 1961–73, 85 per cent of the predicted increase of market share (which was 103.3 per cent) could be attributed to the level and growth of the technology variable. He also found that 'the net effect of growth in relative unit labour costs on the growth of market shares for exports measured in value terms turns out to be negligible' (Fagerberg, 1988, p. 376). In the case of the UK and the US, the growth of RULCs also has little explanatory power. Fagerberg (1988, p. 371) argues that 'the main factor behind the losses in market shares seems to have been slow growth in productive capacity caused by the unusually low shares of national resources devoted to investments'.

Although the technological variable is only capturing one aspect of non-price competition, the paper is instructive in demonstrating once again that changes in relative prices are quantitatively unimportant in determining changes in market shares and, by implication, changes in exports and imports. We included the growth and level of Fagerberg's technology variable (TG and TL respectively) in the specification of the export market shares equations estimated by us earlier in this section (pp. 291–3). We are thus testing both the role of technology (as a proxy for non-price competitiveness) and the impact of the growth of RULCs in a purely demand equation.

The result for the pooled subperiods over 1960–83 is as follows:

$$xs = \underset{(2.53)}{1.747} - \underset{(-2.18)}{0.230} \; rulc + \underset{(4.85)}{0.333} \; TG - \underset{(-2.06)}{2.829} \; TL$$

$$\bar{R}^2 = 0.287$$
$$SER = 2.181$$
$$n = 60$$

At first glance, this result would seem to provide striking support for the hypothesis that the level and growth of technology are important factors in determining the growth of export shares. However, the result is very sensitive to the inclusion of Japan in the sample. If Japan is excluded, the relationship collapses:

$$xs = \underset{(1.50)}{1.055} - \underset{(-1.68)}{0.171} \; rulc + \underset{(0.79)}{0.084} \; TG - \underset{(-1.46)}{1.969} \; TL$$

$$\bar{R}^2 = 0.030$$
$$SER = 2.040$$
$$n = 56$$

It makes no difference if we use the growth of relative prices instead of relative unit labour costs. The estimated equation is still not statistically significant. This suggests that *TG* and *TL* are not the good proxies for the multi-faceted aspects of non-price competition that the initial results suggested.[18]

Estimating the equation for the growth of import shares gives the following result:

$$ms = 2.012 + 0.232 \; rulc + 0.005 \; TG + 0.190 \; TL$$
$$(2.68) \quad (1.99) \quad\quad (0.06) \quad\quad (0.13)$$

$$\bar{R}^2 = 0.017$$
$$SER = 2.412$$
$$n = 60$$

where it will be noted that rulc is now significant at the 95 per cent confidence level. But when Japan is excluded none of the explanatory variables is statistically significant.

$$ms = 2.187 + 0.141 \; rulc + 0.144 \; TG + 0.178 \; TL$$
$$(2.93) \quad (1.27) \quad\quad (1.27) \quad\quad (0.12)$$

$$\bar{R}^2 = 0.182$$
$$SER = 2.224$$
$$n = 56$$

A study by Kellman (1983) has provided further evidence of the relative unimportance of relative prices in international trade. He tested not only the relationship between the level of relative prices and the size of the share of exports in various overseas markets, but also the relationship between their respective growth rates. The concern was with the less developed countries (LDCs) and Kellman confined his attention to Japan, Korea and India. His purpose was to test the hypothesis that as the LDCs moved away from a policy of import substitution to one of export promotion and liberalization, there should emerge a negative relationship between the levels of relative prices and relative export market shares. Thus, if we rank the relative prices of n commodities of country A and the world such that

$$P_{1A}/P_{1W} < P_{2A}/P_{2W} < \ldots < P_{nA}/P_{nW}$$

we should expect the market shares to be ranked as follows

$$MS_{1A} > MS_{2A} > \ldots > MS_{nA}$$

where MS_{1A} is the share that country A takes in the world market for commodity 1. (The analysis can be repeated for markets other than the world market, e.g. for the market of less developed countries as a group or for the US.)

Consequently, a negative relationship is to be expected between the relative prices and relative market shares.

We should also expect a similar relationship between the growth rates of the two variables: the greater the growth in relative prices, the lower the growth in the relative market share.

It is hypothesised that the price distortions which accompany the policy of import substitution mean that there is unlikely to be any systematic relationship between these two variables during the early stages of development. Kellman further postulated that there should also be no relationship at the higher stages of development when comparative advantage is determined by R&D and technological advances. We should perhaps add to these last two factors all the other aspects of non-price competition.

To test the hypothesis, Kellman used disaggregated data on relative prices for each of the three countries and reclassified them into 28 three-digit SIC commodities. These ranged from crude oil and coal tar (SITC 521) to sporting goods (SITC 894). These data were used to calculate indicators of international price competitiveness based on purchasing power parities (PPPs) expressed in terms of the ratio of the domestic currency to the US dollar. Thus, if the PPP of a Japanese export was 264 (yen/US$), this means that 264 yen had the same purchasing power in Japan as did one dollar in the US. The relative price of this export would be more competitive than one with a PPP of, say, 326 (yen/US$).

The share was calculated for each of the 28 exports of the three countries in five markets, that is to say, the markets of the world, the advanced countries, the US, the LDCs, and OPEC. For each of these five markets, Kellman estimated separately for Japan, Korea and India the simple correlation coefficient between the levels of price competitiveness (the PPPs) and the market shares of the various 28 commodity exports. The correlations were undertaken for the years 1965, 1970 and 1977 (1978 in the case of Korea). The relationships between the growth rates were estimated over the subperiods 1965–70 and 1970–7 (1970–8 in the case of Korea).

For Japan, Kellman found that for the years 1965 and 1970 there were (the expected) negative correlations between the PPPs and the various market shares, but these had disappeared by 1977. For example, the simple correlations for the shares in the world market were −0.216 in 1965; −0.213 in 1970; and −0.003 in 1977. A similar picture is found for the other markets. The first two years are considered by Kellman (1983, p. 129) to be 'consistent with the operation of classic price competitiveness', but it should be noted that all the above correlation coefficients are *insignificant* at the 90 per cent confidence level. The correlations between the growth of the PPPs and of the market shares are also instructive. For the period 1965–70, there was no significant correlation in the case of the world market ($r = -0.027$) while for the years 1970–7 there was a significant *positive* (perverse) correlation of $r = 0.372$. This picture was repeated for the other markets: the correlations for 1965–70 were all insignificant, while for 1970–7 the correlations were significant but positive for all markets, except for the OPEC market where there was no significant relationship.

The cases of Korea and India are less interesting for our purposes since, unlike Japan, they cannot be regarded as advanced countries, but once again in the vast majority of the correlations there is no significant relationship between the levels of PPPs and market shares. The only significant relationships found were the negative ones between the growth rates of the variables in three cases (out of a possible 20); namely, for India, when considering shares in the world market and in the market of the advanced countries (both for 1970–7), and for Korea in the market of the LDCs for 1970–8. These three results are thus consistent with the neoclassical model of price competition. Notwithstanding this, the overwhelming impression is one of the statistical insignificance of relative prices in determining market shares even in those cases where we would expect it to be relatively important. As Kellman (1983, p.125) summarises: 'Thus the applicability of typical results derivable from standard static trade theories are found to be bound or restricted to special cases defined by stages of economic development, and by policy choices.'

CONCLUSIONS

In spite of the now overwhelming evidence of the importance of non-price competition, it is surprising how many theoretical economic models still persist in making the assumption that the exports from the advanced countries are relatively homogeneous and focus on changes in relative prices to explain changes in export (and import) performance. The extreme assumption of the neoclassical 'law of one price' is often made which implies, in effect, that any country faces a perfectly elastic demand curve for its exports. Clearly, under these circumstances there can be no such thing as a 'balance-of-payments constraint' – a country can sell as much on the world markets as is required to finance its imports.

The evidence, however, suggests that this is an untenable assumption. It is a central tenet of this book that when long-run economic performance is considered, non-price factors are of much greater importance than price competition in determining the success or otherwise of a country in overseas markets. This is not to say that, in the short run, fluctuations of the real exchange rate will have *no* effect on the level of exports and imports. The devaluations of sterling in 1967 and of the franc in 1953 and 1957 did improve the balance of payments, *for a given growth rate of GDP* (Kaldor, 1978c). The rapid appreciation of sterling in the early 1980s also undoubtedly had a deleterious effect on export growth and thereby on the manufacturing sector as a whole. What is far more debatable is the contention that the long-term *growth rate* of exports can be improved by a continuous depreciation of either the nominal or the real exchange rate. The evidence we have cited in this chapter suggests that changes in relative prices have explained very little of the differences between countries in the long-run growth rates of exports and imports.

5 Critiques and Defences of the Balance-of-Payments Constrained Growth Model

The model of balance-of-payments constrained growth put forward in Chapter 3 has generated a lively debate, particularly between Messrs McGregor and Swales and ourselves in the pages of *Applied Economics*. We reproduce here (with minor corrections and changes for consistency of style) the first four papers in full (McGregor and Swales, 1985, 1986; Thirlwall, 1986b; and McCombie, 1989). McGregor and Swales (1991) subsequently presented yet a third version of their critique, largely in response to McCombie (1989). While we do not reproduce their latest paper here, we do briefly address the more important issues that they raise. We also consider the arguments put forward by Crafts (1988, 1990) (following Balassa, 1979) that if the income elasticity of demand for exports is measured 'correctly', the UK's growth rate cannot be considered to be demand constrained by the balance of payments, but supply constrained. Finally, we discuss Krugman's (1989) neoclassical view that it is relative growth rates that determine relative income elasticities rather than the other way around.

THE McGREGOR–SWALES CRITIQUE[1]

I Introduction

In various recent pieces of work, Thirlwall (1979, 1980b, 1980c) and Thirlwall and Dixon (1979) present a theory to explain the differential growth rates of developed nations.[2] They argue that the growth of domestic income (y) is constrained by the requirement that the current account of the balance of payments must, in general, balance in the long run. This is also the view of the Cambridge Economic Policy Group who

> assert that in the medium term the foreign trade performance of the economy is the main determinant of the level of domestic spending, output and income . . . At any given time there is a certain level of domestic spending at which . . . the balance of payments on current account would be in balance. We may call this the level of spending 'warranted' by the country's performance in foreign trade . . . While swings of fiscal and monetary policy . . . have influenced the level of spending from year to year, in the longer run the main determinant was the spending level 'warranted' by the economy's performance in foreign trade. (Cambridge Economic Policy Group, 1981, pp. 10–11)

The theory behind the Cambridge Economic Policy Group's statement is never made explicit. However, it seems unlikely that it can differ significantly from that developed by Thirlwall.

Thirlwall shows that, under certain restrictive assumptions, the growth of domestic income is determined by a simple dynamic Harrod trade multiplier which takes the form:

$$y = \frac{x}{\pi} \tag{5.1}$$

where x represents the rate of growth of export volume, and π represents the domestic income elasticity of demand for imports. He makes strong claims for this theory. He states:

> Applying Equation 1 [i.e. equation (5.1) above] to international data gives a remarkable approximation to the growth experience of many countries over the last twenty years, and *ipso facto* provides an explanation of why growth rates differ. It might also be stated as a fundamental law that, except where the balance-of-payments equilibrium growth rate exceeds the maximum feasible capacity growth rate, the rate of growth of a country will approximate to the ratio of its rate of growth of exports and its income elasticity of demand for imports. The approximation itself vindicates the assumptions used to arrive at the simple rule in Equation 1. (Thirlwall, 1979, p. 50)

In Section II below we outline the theory which Thirlwall uses to derive equation (5.1). In Section III, we argue that crucial elements of this theory appear to be very weak. In Section IV we consider the empirical evidence presented by Thirlwall to support his argument for balance-of-payments constrained growth. The tests that Thirlwall performs are not very strong. When his data are subject to more rigorous testing they do not strictly support his hypothesis, as represented by equation (5.1). However, it is the case that both the rate of growth of exports (x) and the income elasticity of demand for imports (π) are significant variables in explaining cross-sectional variation in the rate of growth of national income (y). In Section V, the causal mechanism operating in equation (5.1) is examined more closely. We question whether empirical support for equation (5.1) can be taken as strong evidence for balance-of-payments constrained growth, as equation (5.1) can be derived from an open economy neoclassical model as well as a Keynesian one. Section VI comprises a short conclusion.

II Theory

The model Thirlwall develops of balance-of-payments constrained growth has the following form. First:

$$p_d + x = p_f + m + e \tag{5.2}$$

where all variables are measured as percentage changes.

p represents prices,
m represents the volume of imports,
e represents the domestic price of foreign currency, and the d and f subscripts refer to the domestic and foreign economies respectively.

Equation (5.2) defines the conditions which must hold for what Thirlwall terms the balance-of-payments equilibrium rate of growth (y_B). That is to say, the rate of growth of the value of exports is equal to the rate of growth of the value of imports. The demand functions for exports and imports are assumed to take a multiplicative form, with relative prices and foreign income (for exports) and national income (for imports) as arguments. Therefore

$$x = \eta(p_d - p_f - e) + \varepsilon z \tag{5.3}$$

$$m = \psi(p_f + e - p_d) + \pi y \tag{5.4}$$

where η and ψ represent the price elasticity of demand for exports and imports (η, $\psi < 0$), ε and π represent the income elasticity of demand for exports and imports and z and y represent the growth in foreign and domestic real income respectively.

If equations (5.3) and (5.4) are substituted into equation (5.2), we find the balanced trade domestic growth rate (y_B) is given by the equation:

$$y_B = \frac{(1 + \eta + \psi)(p_d - p_f - e) + \varepsilon z}{\pi} \tag{5.5}$$

In order to derive equation (5.1) from equations (5.3) and (5.5), it is necessary to argue both that:

$$p_d - p_f - e = 0 \tag{5.6}$$

so that:[3]

$$y_B = \frac{\varepsilon z}{\pi} = \frac{x}{\pi} \tag{5.7}$$

and that:

$$y = y_B \tag{5.8}$$

III   Criticisms of the Theory

Equations (5.3), (5.4), (5.6) and (5.8) are the important behavioural functions for the development of the dynamic Harrod trade multiplier represented by equation (5.1). In this section we shall scrutinise these equations. In particular, we shall consider in detail the arguments that Thirlwall presents for accepting equations (5.6) and (5.8). We shall attempt to show that these arguments are questionable, especially in the context of a demand constrained model.

The Demand for Imports and Exports (Equations (5.3) and (5.4))

The import and export demand functions underpinning equations (5.3) and (5.4) have only relative prices (measured in a common currency) and the relevant incomes as arguments. There are two criticisms of these equations: first, that they are too aggregative and secondly, that they do not incorporate non-price competitive factors.

Equations (5.3) and (5.4) are very aggregative. In these equations no distinction is made between export prices, domestic prices and import competing prices. This implies that in this theory there is no distinction between traded and non-traded goods, or between exported and imported goods. This high level of aggregation is worrying analytically because diversity is generally regarded as the basis for trade, but Thirlwall's model appears to assume away such diversity.

The second criticism is related to the first. There is a growing literature which attempts to explain trade in manufactured goods between developed countries as being driven by economies of scale and consumer demand for variety (Barker, 1977; Lancaster, 1980). Such theories explain the high level of intra-industry trade and the high income elasticity of demand for imports in developed countries. A central notion in these theories is that even in highly competitive industries, rivalry occurs not only in product price but also in other product characteristics. It is therefore a potential weakness of the Thirlwall model that non-price competition does not appear in the demand functions, nor anywhere else in the analysis.

The Law of One Price (Equation (5.6))

Thirlwall and Dixon (1979, p. 184) give two reasons for accepting their view that in the long run the ratio of foreign prices to domestic prices will not vary:

> either the law of one price could be invoked, or in the event of exchange depreciation it could be argued that depreciation will force up domestic prices equiproportionately.

Additionally, Thirlwall has argued, in private correspondence, that relative prices might remain unchanged under other, imperfectly competitive (oligopolistic) market structures. We shall consider the exchange depreciation argument first.

There is a large literature which considers the effect of currency depreciation on domestic prices. This work generally first attempts to model the impact of a devaluation of the domestic currency on domestic costs, then the effect on the domestic price level is determined, usually by the use of a mark-up model. In most simple models a sufficient condition for domestic prices eventually to rise equiproportionally with import prices is for there to be real wage resistance

(Brown *et al.*, 1980) in the sense that labour is presumed to bargain for money wages with a view to achieving an exogenously determined real wage target. However, this condition is not sufficient to guarantee equation (5.6), for these simple models are intrinsically comparatively static in nature, being concerned with the effects of a once over step devaluation. If domestic and foreign prices, measured in a common currency, are to rise at the same rate over time, Ball *et al.* (1977) show that for a simple mark-up model a number of conditions must hold. First, there should be no money illusion in the wage equation. Secondly, if there is a Phillips curve relationship between wage changes and the rate of unemployment, then unemployment must be at the natural rate. Alternatively, if there is no link between unemployment and wage inflation, the exogenous rate of growth of real wages must just equal the rate of growth of labour productivity.

Thirlwall clearly cannot accept the Natural Rate Hypothesis because this would imply that the economy is supply constrained (rather than demand constrained). Consequently, his case is dependent on organised labour bargaining for a real wage target which fortuitously grows at a rate equal to the rate of growth of labour productivity. Thirlwall can claim empirical support from the Cambridge Economic Policy Group on this issue (Coutts *et al.*, 1976), but only because they determine the target real wage growth by fitting a trend through actual real wage growth. Meade (1981) has provided a formal analysis of the Cambridge Economic Policy Group's theoretical model of wage determination which establishes that there is nothing in this model to prevent excessive (relative to productivity) real wage growth and consequential explosive wage-price behaviour. Since neither Thirlwall nor the Cambridge Economic Policy Group suggests any mechanism for ensuring the equality of productivity and target real wage growth, the case for accepting equation (5.6) on present arguments is highly suspect.

Until now we have simply considered the proposition that a process akin to real wage resistance will keep domestic and foreign prices in line: the conditions under which this will be the case seem restrictive. However, Thirlwall has another argument: that the law of one price holds. That is, 'that arbitrage will equalize the price of traded goods in highly competitive markets' (Thirlwall, 1980b, p.432). Now one might worry about the assumption that all trade takes place in perfectly competitive markets, but even if this were the case, export and import prices would not necessarily change at the same rate. That is to say, the acceptance of the law of one price does not imply the acceptance of equation (5.6). For a nation will generally export different commodities from those that it imports and prices for these different sets of commodities might well be varying at different rates.[4] However, as has already been pointed out, the aggregative nature of Thirlwall's model means not only that there is only one price in any one world market, but also that there is only one world market. When the law of one price is imposed, it is as though the whole world is producing the same good: the rationale for trade in these circumstances is unclear.

This having been said, it is the case that the law of one price is often invoked in highly aggregated models of trade determination in a small country. However, the imposition of this law is especially questionable in a model which has no supply side. For a small country, the law of one price means that prices are determined outside the nation in world markets: the price elasticity of demand for both exports and imports (η and ψ) is infinite. In models which assume the law of one price to hold, output is normally determined by equating marginal cost with price. But this is not the case with Thirlwall's model, because costs are not explicitly modelled here at all. In fact the introduction of equation (5.6) amounts to assuming that the nation's exports will maintain a constant share of their world markets and that the nation's imports will similarly maintain their share of relevant national markets despite any changes in the relative costs of production between the nation and the rest of the world.[5]

Since the law of one price implies infinitely elastic demands for UK exports its acceptance would necessitate rejection of the whole notion of export demand constrained growth which is the essence of Thirlwall's theory. Indeed, given the law of one price, output is entirely supply-determined, the very condition to which neoclassical growth theory is intended to apply and in which Keynesian growth theory is inapplicable. Thus the law of one price, whilst (at least in the context of highly aggregative models) validating equation (5.6), is inconsistent with the whole spirit of Thirlwall's model and so can hardly be invoked in support of that model.

The third argument, that in oligopolistic industries price variations between producers might be very limited, has clear support in economic theory. It is often argued that oligopolists fear price competition and various models of price leadership show how a price might be set in an oligopolistic industry which would be accepted by all the firms in that industry. However, there is only a superficial similarity between this case and the perfectly competitive model outlined already. For, under perfect competition, the only characteristic of the product on which firms compete is price. In these circumstances, the intensity of competition means that firms must all charge the same market price. Under oligopoly, we normally assume that firms compete over a number of characteristics of the good. This competition therefore not only includes price but also marketing, advertising, new product innovation, after sales services, speed of delivery, etc. The fact that price competition might be limited does not preclude other, non-price, forms of competition. Therefore, if the argument for equation (5.6) rests on there being explicit or implicit price collusion in oligopolistic markets, the demand equations (5.3) and (5.4) appear to be misspecified: as well as relative price and income terms, they should also include variables to cover various aspects of nonprice competition.

The Balance-of-Payments Constraint (Equation (5.8))

It is clear that the acceptance of equation (5.6) is convenient but problematic. Similarly problems also arise with equation (5.8). Thirlwall (1980b p. 421) merely states:

> The fundamental proposition I wish to make is that no country or region (for very long) can grow faster than its balance-of-payments equilibrium growth rate unless it can continually 'finance' a rate of growth of imports in excess of the rate of growth of exports.

This is a tautology. Presumably Thirlwall must mean that countries in fact cannot continually finance a rate of growth of imports in excess of the rate of growth of exports. Implicit here is a theory of capital flows which is not defended. Clearly equation (5.2) requires only that the ratio of the value of imports to the value of exports be constant (and not necessarily equal to unity). Thus the Thirlwall model is not necessarily inconsistent with persistent capital flows. However, the model does have to be modified significantly to permit autonomous growth in, or income-sensitivity of, capital flows as Swales (1983, section 5) has shown.[6] An additional implicit assumption is that countries do not choose to grow at a rate less than y_B. But if, through choice or necessity, some countries do grow at a rate which is lower than the balance-of-payments constrained growth rate ($y < y_B$), they will run balance-of-payments surpluses. This means that other countries must run balance-of-payments deficits: in these cases $y > y_B$. This might result in economies' actual growth rates diverging systematically from the balance-of-payments constrained growth rate.

In questioning the acceptance of equations (5.6) and (5.8), our arguments have not primarily queried the empirical validity of these two equations. Rather, our arguments have concentrated on whether the use of these equations in this context is analytically sound. In particular, the view that equation (5.6) can be supported by the law of one price appears to render Thirlwall's model incoherent. It becomes a demand constrained model with no demand constraint. Our view is that these analytical problems rob Thirlwall's theory of any real explanatory power (McLachlan and Swales, 1982). However, as we saw earlier, in the introduction, Thirlwall invokes Friedman's methodology in assessing this theory (Friedman, 1953). Thirlwall's position is that the actual growth rates of developed countries in the post-war period are remarkably close to the calculated balanced trade growth rates. These empirical results are thought to vindicate the use of unrealistic assumptions in developing the theory, and to provide strong evidence of the veracity of Thirlwall's theory of balance-of-payment constrained growth. In the next section we look at the empirical results which Thirlwall derives. We argue that they do not constitute strong evidence in favour of his theory.

IV Empirical Testing

Thirlwall tests the balanced trade theory of economic growth in the following way. For two overlapping postwar periods, the balanced trade equilibrium growth rate is calculated using equation (5.1) for a number of developed economies.[7] The Spearman's rank correlation coefficient is then calculated between the estimated balanced trade equilibrium growth rate (y_B) and the actual growth rate (y) for these economies. For both time periods, the size of this coefficient is large, positive and statistically significant. However, the use of a nonparametric test here is very weak: it would seem more reasonable, at least initially, to test equation (5.1) directly using regression analysis.

If equation (5.1) is expressed logarithmically, it can be tested by estimating the following equation:

$$\log y = c_0 + c_1 \log x + c_2 \log \pi \tag{5.9}$$

If the theory holds we expect that $c_0 = 0$, $c_1 = 1$ and $c_2 = -1$.

In Table 5.1 the estimated coefficients are given for the regressions of equation (5.9) using the two data sets given in Thirlwall (1979). These results are interesting. When $\log y$ is regressed against $\log x$

Table 5.1   Results of regressing equation (5.9) using data from various developed economies[a]

Dependent variables	log x	log π	Constant	R^2, F
1953–76				
log y	0.818[b]	−0.499[b]	−0.014	0.907
	(0.648/0.988)	(−0.690/−0.308)	(−0.354/0.326)	58.522[b]
log y	0.685[b]	–	0.064	0.656
	(0.388/0.981)		(−0.556/0.684)	24.826[b]
1951–73				
log y	0.814[b]	−0.581[b]	0.111	0.957
	(0.674/0.955)	(−0.850/−0.313)	(−0.174/0.396)	89.511[b]
log y	0.719[b]	–	0.045	0.824
	(0.468/0.970)		(−0.506/0.597)	42.057[b]

Notes: [a]The data for these regressions are taken from Thirlwall (1979, p. 51), tables 1 and 2. These data are represented in Figures 5.1 and 5.2.
[b]Indicates significant at the 1% confidence level.

The figures in brackets give the 5% confidence interval.

alone, these data suggest that there is a strong positive relationship. When log π is added to these regressions, it enters with the correct (negative) sign, the regressions are generally improved and the coefficient on the log x term is generally increased. The regressions have very high R^2 values and significant coefficients on the explanatory variables. But the crucial test of the balanced trade hypothesis put forward by Thirlwall concerns the size of the coefficients on these variables and the constant term. In particular, for Thirlwall's theory to hold, the constant term should be close to zero, whilst the absolute value of the coefficients on the two explanatory variables should be close to unity. In the results reported in Table 5.1, the constant term is not significantly different from zero at the 5 per cent level. However, the absolute values of the coefficients on log x and log π are significantly less than 1 at the 5 per cent level. In particular, the coefficient on log π never has an absolute value greater than 0.6.[8]

These results do not support Thirlwall's theory as expressed in equation (5.1). However, they do not permit rejection of the hypothesis that the coefficient on log x (c_1) has the same absolute size as the coefficient on log π (c_2). It is therefore interesting to study directly the relationship between y and y_B.

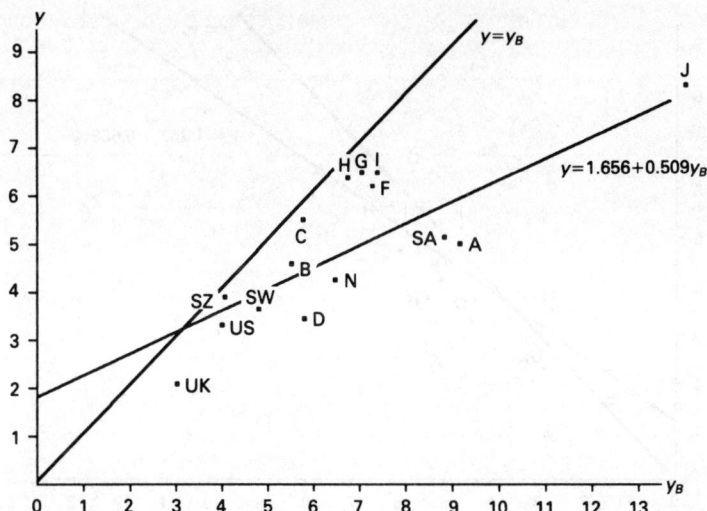

Figure 5.1   The actual growth rate plotted against the estimated balanced trade growth rate for 15 developed economies, 1953–76.

Note: A, Australia; B, Belgium; C, Canada; D, Denmark; F, France; G, Germany; H, Netherlands; I, Italy; J, Japan; N, Norway; SA, South Africa; SW, Sweden; SZ, Switzerland; UK, United Kingdom; US, USA.

Source: These data are taken from Thirlwall (1979 p. 51) table 1.

In Figures 5.1 and 5.2 the actual growth rates are plotted against the estimated balanced trade growth rates for the economies and time periods used in Thirlwall (1979). Thirlwall (1979, p. 50) claims that 'there is a general tendency for the estimates of the balance-of-payments equilibrium growth to be higher than the actual growth rate'. This somewhat understates the case. In the two figures, there is only one observation where the actual growth rate (y) is greater than the estimated balanced trade growth rate (y_B): in 22 out of the 26 cases $y_B > y$. This is particularly noticeable in Figure 5.1 which uses data for the period 1953–76. Here there is no case where $y > y_B$, and many countries appear to be growing at a rate well below that given by the calculated balance-of-payments constraint. In Tables 5.2 and 5.3, the results are given for linear regressions of y against y_B. For Thirlwall's theory to hold the constant term should be zero and the coefficient on y_B should equal one. When all the observations are

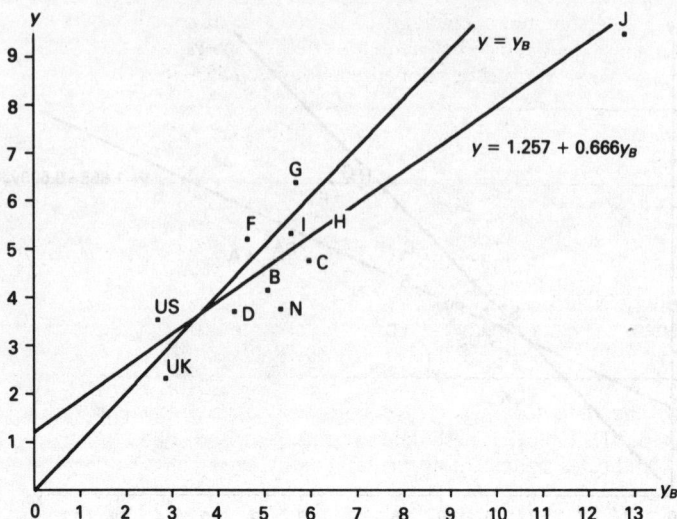

Figure 5.2   The actual growth rate plotted against the estimated balanced trade growth rate for 11 developed economies, 1951–73.

Note: For explanation of abbreviations see Fig. 5.1.

Source: These data are taken from Thirlwall (1979, p. 51) table 2.

included, in both sets of data the constant is significant and positive, and the coefficient on y_B is significantly lower than unity.

Thirlwall (1979) offers three reasons why the economies' actual growth rates in these two time periods are almost all below the estimated balanced trade growth rates. First, Thirlwall (1979) argues that:

> While a country cannot grow faster than its balance-of-payments equilibrium growth rate for very long, unless it can finance an ever-growing deficit, there is little to stop a country growing slower and accumulating large surpluses. This may particularly occur where the balance-of-payments equilibrium growth rate is so high that a country simply does not have the physical capacity to grow at that rate. (p. 49)

The problem with this explanation is that if some countries have balance-of-payments surpluses, others must have deficits. This means

Table 5.2 Estimated coefficients of regressions of actual output growth
(y) against the balance-of-payments equilibrium growth rate (y_B) for
various developed economies, 1953–76[a]

Dependent variables	y_B	*Constant*	R^2, F
Full sample			
y	0.509[b]	1.656[b]	0.855
	(0.384/0.635)	(0.885/2.427)	76.788[b]
Excluding US and Japan			
y	0.414[b]	2.174[b]	0.532
	(0.156/0.671)	(0.787/3.560)	12.509[b]

Notes: [a]The data for these regressions are taken from Thirlwall (1979,
    p. 51), table 1. These data are represented in Figure 5.1.
    [b]Indicates significant at the 1% confidence level.

    The figures in brackets give the 5% confidence interval.

Table 5.3 Estimated coefficients of regressions of actual output growth
(y) against the balance-of-payments equilibrium growth rate (y_B) for
various developed economies, 1951–73[a]

Dependent variables	y_B	*Constant*	R^2, F
Full sample			
y	0.666[b]	1.257[b]	0.952
	(0.554/0.778)	(0.584/1.931)	179.758[b]
Excluding US and Japan			
y	0.817[b]	0.500	0.790
	(0.440/1.193)	(−1.393/2.393)	26.294[b]

Notes: [a]The data for these regressions are taken from Thirlwall (1979,
    p. 51), table 2. These data are represented in Figure 5.2.
    [b]Indicate significant at the 1% confidence level.

    The figures in brackets give the 5% confidence interval.

that if for some countries $y > y_B$, for others $y_B > y$. It might be that
those countries with a high balance-of-payments equilibrium growth
(y_B) will in fact be supply constrained, whilst those with a low value
for y_B run balance-of-payments deficits in an attempt to grow more
rapidly. This would mean that:

$$\frac{y}{y_B} = f(y_B) \quad \text{where } f(0) > 1 \text{ and } f' < 0 \tag{5.10}$$

If this is the case, when y is regressed against y_B one would expect a positive constant term and a coefficient on y_B less than one. Now this seems to be consistent with the data given in Figure 5.2 and Table 5.3. When the figures for the major slow growing deficit country (US) and the most important fast growing surplus country (Japan) are removed, the regression corresponds to equation (5.1).[9] Moreover, for the US, $y > y_B$: for Japan $y_B > y$. However, the data in Figure 5.1 and Table 5.2 do not support these ideas. For these figures there is no country for which $y > y_B$, and when the data for Japan and the US are removed, the regression results do not correspond more closely to equation (5.1).

The second explanation offered by Thirlwall for the relatively low value of y as compared to y_B concerns the data used to estimate y_B. Thirlwall (1979, p. 50) states:

On the income elasticity of demand for imports, Houthakker and Magee estimates have been taken as applying to the whole of these periods even though they were only estimated over the period 1951 to 1966. They are the best consistently estimated international estimates available, but are probably now on the low side.

Implicit here is the idea that the true values of the income elasticity of demand for imports (π_r) are higher than the estimates (π) made by Houthakker and Magee (1969). This would make the actual balanced trade growth rates lower than the balanced trade growth rates estimated by Thirlwall (1979).

Thirlwall is arguing that $\pi_r > \pi$. Let us consider two possible relationships which would satisfy this:

$$\pi_r = g\pi \tag{5.11}$$

where g is a parameter, $g > 1$.

$$\pi_r = \pi^h \tag{5.12}$$

where h is a parameter, $h > 1$.[10]

If equation (5.11) or (5.12) is correct, this should be reflected in the regressions of equation (5.9) reported in Table 5.1. If equation (5.11) holds, the coefficient on log π should be -1, but the constant term should be negative and equal to $-\log g$. If equation (5.12) holds, the constant term should be zero, but the coefficient on log π should have an absolute value greater than 1. From Table 5.1 we know that in fact the constant term is small in these regressions and is never statistically significantly different from zero. The coefficient on log π always has an absolute value significantly less than 1. It is clear that if either equation (5.11) or equation (5.12) represents the specific form of the relationship which Thirlwall believed might exist between π_r and π, the data do not support that belief.

A third explanation offered for the relatively low actual growth rates in these economies is that:

> adverse relative price movements combined with various price elasticity conditions cannot be entirely ruled out as determinants of the balance-of-payments even though they may be of minor significance compared to income movements and income elasticities of demand for imports and exports. (Thirlwall, 1979, p. 52)

It is not clear how relative price movements would systematically generate $y < y_B$. However, a more promising approach, suggested by Kennedy and Thirlwall (1979, 1983), is to consider the effects of trade liberalisation in increasing import penetration. Clearly, if policies such as tariff reductions have increased the competitiveness of imports during the two time periods covered by the data, equation (5.1) will overestimate the balanced trade growth rate.

It is easy to illustrate this point by introducing a proportionate tariff into the simple model developed in Section II. Equation (5.2) still holds, but equations (5.3) and (5.4) have to be augmented to incorporate tariff changes:

$$x = \eta(p_d - p_f - e + t_f) + \varepsilon_z \qquad (5.13)$$

$$m = \psi(p_f + e + t_d - p_d) + \pi y \qquad (5.14)$$

where t_f and t_d represent the proportionate changes in foreign and domestic tariffs respectively. If equations (5.13) and (5.14) are combined with equation (5.2), this gives the balanced trade growth rate as:

$$y_B = \frac{(1 + \eta + \psi)(p_d - p_f - e) + \varepsilon z + t_d\eta - t_d\psi}{\pi} \qquad (5.15)$$

Imposing the law of one price (equation (5.6)) then gives:

$$y_B = \frac{x}{\pi} - t_d\frac{\psi}{\pi} \qquad (5.16)$$

This means that in time periods when domestic tariffs have been falling, equation (5.1) will overestimate the balanced trade growth rate. Note that this is independent of movements in foreign tariffs.[11] In the post-war period tariffs have generally fallen, so that estimates of y_B using equation (5.1) might be expected to be systematically higher than actual growth rates in this period. But this can be invoked to explain Thirlwall's empirical results only at a cost. First, if tariffs are empirically significant, it seems even more difficult to accept the law of one price (equation (5.6)). Secondly, equation (5.1) must be replaced by equation (5.16) as the expression for balanced trade equilibrium growth.

Thirlwall overstates the case when he refers to equation (5.1) as a general law, as a quick glance at Figures 5.1 and 5.2 clearly shows. The actual rates of growth of the countries represented in these diagrams are almost all less than the calculated balance-of-payments growth. Moreover, Thirlwall's attempts to explain the general divergence between y and y_B are really no more than speculation. However, had these empirical results been more impressive, would they have lent 'strong support to the advocates of export led growth' (Thirlwall, 1979, p. 52)? We shall attempt to answer this question in the next section.

V   The Direction of Causation

Equation (5.1) can be derived from the following assumptions:

(i) foreign and domestic prices are the same, measured in a common currency
(ii) demand equations contain as arguments only relative prices and real income
(iii) imports are not supply constrained
(iv) the current account of the balance-of-payments balances.

Given these assumptions, equation (5.1) must hold. The following two points should be noted. First, there is nothing in these assumptions which implies an export led model. Secondly, all these assumptions are generally made in the standard neoclassical theory of trade for a small country. This second point is interesting. It means that equation (5.1) should hold in a standard, supply constrained neoclassical model. How can this be the case?

Thirlwall interprets equation (5.1) in the following way. The rate of growth of exports (x) is exogenous to the domestic economy: it is determined by the rate of growth of real world income and the income elasticity of demand for goods the economy exports. The income elasticity of demand for imports (π) is taken as constant. Therefore the growth of domestic income (y) is demand determined, equal to the growth of exports (x) times the dynamic Harrod foreign trade multiplier ($1/\pi$). However, the direction of causation might be quite different. For instance, we have already argued that it seems illogical to maintain that exports are demand constrained if the law of one price is invoked. The standard neoclassical argument would be that real income growth (y) is determined by supply factors. Again, the income elasticity of demand for imports (π) is a constant. The growth of exports (x) is therefore endogenous and is just enough to maintain the current account of the balance of payments in balance. That is to say, equation (5.1) would be more appropriately written as:[12]

$$x = \pi y \tag{5.17}$$

It is perhaps useful to outline the short-run response of such a neoclassical system to an exogenous shock. The nature of this response will depend, to some extent, on: the exchange rate regime; the degree of (transitory) capital mobility; the extent of feasible short-run deviations from purchasing power parity (PPP); the degree of short-run flexibility in wages and prices; and the expectations formation process. Consider, for example, the impact of an increase in labour productivity in the context of a fixed exchange rate neoclassical model which exhibits zero capital mobility. Imagine that expectations adjustment in the labour market is very rapid, and that commodity prices are flexible, but that trade flows respond very sluggishly to changes in the prices of domestically produced goods. Under these circumstances the excess supply of domestically produced goods (at initial wage and price levels) causes a reduction in the price of domestically produced goods. This stimulates domestic (but not foreign) demand and causes actual output to rise. However, even in the absence of money illusion, the stimulus to actual output will be less than that to natural output given the assumed deviations from PPP.[13] By assumption, the price change has no initial effect on trade flows, but imports are higher due to higher real domestic income. However, imports are considerably below their final equilibrium value at this stage for two reasons: output is below its natural level; real income is even further below its new natural level since the price of domestically produced goods has fallen below the domestic currency prices of the rest of the world's output. The resultant current account deficit is financed by means of foreign exchange reserve reductions.

The crucial equilibrating mechanism is that which underlies the 'law of one price'. In particular, as the overseas sector's demand for domestic exports increases, this demand is willingly met in full by domestic suppliers. The increase in export demand continues until the prices of domestically produced goods are again equal to world price levels. In this model, the money supply adjusts automatically in response to changes in the foreign component of the monetary base, which in turn reflects the overall balance-of-payments position. Once PPP is re-established the new natural level of output must be established. Also, given the law of one price, real income and output are re-equated and imports will have increased by π times the change in the natural level of output. Restoration of relative prices also restores indifference on the part of domestic producers between domestic and overseas sales, so that the level of export sales required to ensure balance-of-payments equilibrium is assured.[14]

Thirlwall (1981) argues:

> The empirical evidence suggests, therefore, that the Harrod trade multiplier works, at least for many advanced countries. In other words, it is income that tends to adjust in the face of imbalance between exports and planned imports, not relative prices.

A neoclassical economist would view the evidence in a different light. In as far as equation (5.1) was found to be true, this would represent exports adjusting to planned imports in an economy with prices determined internationally.

VI Conclusions

We have argued here, first, that equation (5.1) cannot be derived in a manner consistent with the notion of export led growth except under very restrictive assumptions which are unlikely to be met except fortuitously. Secondly, equation (5.1) does not represent a general law, because it is not supported by the evidence which Thirlwall adduces. Thirdly, even if equation (5.1) were a general law, this could not, in itself, be taken as strong evidence for demand constrained growth. This is because equation (5.1) can be derived from a plausible theory of supply constrained growth. However, this is not meant to imply that the reduced form equation on which Thirlwall focuses our attention is not of interest. But if Thirlwall is to properly substantiate the claims he makes for his theory, the evidence must be much stronger and the direction of causation examined more closely in the context of competing structural macroeconometric models of small open economies.

A RESPONSE TO McGREGOR AND SWALES BY THIRLWALL[15]

Introduction

The simple rule, that a country's long-run growth rate will approximate to the ratio of the rate of growth of export volume (x) to the income elasticity of demand for imports (π), seems to have provoked a lot of interest and discussion, not only by McGregor and Swales (1985), but also by Shann (1982), Williamson (1984) and McCombie (1985a), among others. The appraisal of the model by McGregor and Swales, and the policy conclusions drawn, is critical on a number of counts, but can be boiled down to three major concerns. First, to derive the simple rule, relative prices in international trade measured in a common currency must be sticky and they question the mechanisms which were suggested that might produce this stickiness. More important, they argue that if the 'law of one price' is invoked, exports must be supply constrained and the model cannot be interpreted as a demand constrained model of economic growth or used in support of the theory of export-led growth. Secondly, on the basis of various econometric tests, they argue that the evidence presented for the theory gives only weak support. Thirdly, they claim that the assumptions of the model and the end prediction make it indistinguishable from a neoclassical model of growth in which growth is supply determined (independent of demand) with exports endogenous adjusting to the level of planned imports. This is in strong contrast to my own interpretation of the model and the growth process in which income adjusts to equate imports with an exogenously determined level of exports. The formal equivalence of the model with the Harrod trade multiplier has been shown in several places (e.g. Thirlwall 1980b, 1982a; see Chapter 3 of this book).

Relative Prices In International Trade

There are three possible reasons why relative prices measured in a common currency may not change very much over a long period which, if true, and if current account balance-of-payments equilibrium is a requirement, will generate the rule, $y = x/\pi$: (i) domestic price changes mirroring exchange rate changes; (ii) highly competitive markets, and (iii) oligopolistic market structures. Whether exchange rate changes lead to equiproportionate changes in the domestic price of exports in an export demand model (nullifying the effectiveness of devaluation), or in domestic prices in an export supply model of tradeables and nontradeables (also nullifying the effectiveness of devaluation), is an empirical question. Contrary to McGregor and Swales, the assumptions of the London Business School Model (Ball *et al.*, 1977) that might generate this result are not in the least implausible. The same might be said of the Wilson model (Wilson, 1976) which predicts the same result, but this is a relatively minor point.

The 'law of one price' was then invoked. This was, perhaps, using unfortunate terminology that should have been avoided. The term was used loosely to refer to constant relative prices which may be the outcome of highly competitive or imperfectly competitive market structures. The implication was not that all firms (and countries) face infinitely elastic demand curves and the only factor that prevents countries exporting more is supply constraints. That would be absurd. In a closed industrial economy, most firms face downward sloping demand curves, and as long as monopolistic competition prevails, there is no reason to drop this assumption for the open economy. Any form of imperfect competition implies excess capacity, and excess capacity implies that individual producers face a limited demand for their product. But it is not unrealistic to postulate that for many goods, price reductions by some countries will be matched by foreign competitors, while for other goods the structure of production is such that oligopolistic stickiness prevails. Either way, constant relative prices are observed. McGregor and Swales have misconstrued my implied meaning of the 'law of one price' to say that the model is perfectly consistent with a small, open economy, neo-classical model.

Had it been assumed that industrial countries inhabit a perfectly competitive world in which there is a world price of everything, the export function would not have been described as a demand function, nor would income have been one of the independent variables. In all estimated export demand functions for countries, whether they be for aggregate exports, or for sectors, the income variable is always well determined and highly significant. This is not consistent with the small open economy, one world price, assumption. McGregor and Swales are correct when they say (1985, p. 19) that even in highly competitive industries rivalry occurs not only in product price but also in other product characteristics. It is precisely these non-price factors that are captured in the income elasticity of demand for exports.

It is true that in the original model there is no formal model of non-price factors, or inclusion of them as separate arguments in the export demand function, but what are differences in income elas-ticities between countries picking up if not differences in the nature and characteristics of goods produced and exported by different countries? The charge that Friedman's methodological position, that only the predictions of a model matter and not the assumptions, is taken is unjustified. However, there is empirical evidence to support the proposed 'law' which is consistent with the assumption that relative prices are sticky in international trade, and there are good reasons for believing that this assumption is a realistic one. If relative prices were fluctuating wildly over the long run, it would be a chance coincidence indeed to find that the actual growth experience of so many countries corresponded so closely to the balance-of-payments equilibrium growth rate as defined in equation (5.1) above.

Empirical Evidence

McGregor and Swales go on to claim, however, that even if the theory is unambiguous, $y = x/\pi$ does not represent a general 'law' because it is not supported by the evidence which is adduced. To quote directly, they say (1985, p. 18) 'the tests that Thirlwall performs are not very strong. When his data are subject to more rigorous testing they do not strictly support his hypothesis.' Note, however, that they also say 'that both the rate of growth of exports (x) and the income elasticity of demand for imports (π) are significant variables in explaining cross-sectional variation in the rate of growth of national income (y)'. There would seem to be a certain schizophrenia here.

The essence of interesting economics, particularly applied economics, is to get a 'lot from a little'. I thought I had done that by showing how close the actual growth experience of several developed countries over the 1950s and 1960s (and into the early 1970s) had approximated to the balance-of-payments constrained rate, x/π. The perennial question arises, of course, (as with 'stylised facts') of how close is close? Their test of the predictive power of the model is to regress the actual growth rate (y) on the estimate of the balance-of-payments equilibrium growth rate (y_B). They then argue that for these regressions to be consistent with the theory, the constant term should be zero and the regression coefficient unity. This would be a legitimate test taking all countries of the world (where surpluses must equal deficits, or where divergences between y and y_B cancel out), but it is not a legitimate test for a small sample of countries where the combined balances of payments do not balance. For example, a sample of countries may, by chance, have been taken with either a combined surplus or a combined deficit. The simple rule might still be a good predictor of the actual growth of most countries, but because of one or two outlying observations $(y \gtreqless y_B)$ their test would reject the hypothesis that countries' growth rates approximate in the long run to x/π. This is a good example of the inappropriateness of a cross-section test of a model relating to the time-series behaviour of countries in an incomplete sample. It is interesting to note that when Japan, the major deviant observation in the sample, with $y < y_B$, and massive balance-of-payments surpluses over the period, is excluded from the sample (along with the US) for the period 1951–73 (which excludes the turbulent years 1973–6 of the other sample), the hypothesis that the constant term is zero and the regression coefficient is unity cannot be rejected at the 95 per cent confidence level. The position sustained here remains largely unchanged: y is not precisely equal to $y_B \, (= x/\pi)$, but close enough to be interesting and to suggest that there is a common force operating constraining growth.

A number of reasons were given as to why there may be (usually small) divergences between y and y_B, including supply constraints, biased estimates of π, capital flows and terms of trade effects. McGregor and Swales apparently find none of these very convincing. They criticise the model for excluding capital movements, but these are easily incorporated as has been done in Thirlwall and Hussain (1982).[16] They maintain that they do not see how relative price movements (terms of trade effects) would systematically generate $y <$ y_B. Such movements would do so if all the countries experienced terms of trade improvement combined with a price elasticity of demand for imports greater than unity or, alternatively, terms of trade deterioration combined with a price elasticity of less than unity. It is agreed with them that (autonomous) tariff reductions are another likely explanation of $y < y_B$. Their introduction of tariffs is a useful extension to the model. Yannopoulos (1984) has also extended the model in this direction to examine the spatial distribution of the effects of economic integration schemes within a balance-of-payments equilibrium framework. (See Chapter 9.)

What is Cause and What is Effect?

Finally, there is the question of whether empirical support for the 'law' can be taken as evidence of balance-of-payments constrained growth when equation (5.1) ($y = x/\pi$) can be derived (so they claim) from an open economy neoclassical model (as well as a 'Keynesian' one), and is therefore consistent with a plausible theory of supply constrained growth. They would only be right if the 'law of one price' was to be taken literally in the sense of infinitely elastic demand curves for all goods, and income was not an argument in the demand function, but as has been argued above, it is not legitimate to assume this. They say that all the assumptions that are made are generally made in the standard neoclassical theory of trade for a small country. But in these models, relative prices adjust to preserve balance-of-payments equilibrium, leaving income unchanged.

The position here is opposite: that there can be no presumption that relative price changes in international trade work as a perfect adjustment mechanism (and the observation of constant relative prices – perfect arbitrage – is not evidence that they do) with the consequence that the burden of adjustment is thrown on income. In a neoclassical model, export growth would not be the product of the growth of 'world' income and the income elasticity of demand for exports. Exports would be endogenous to supply conditions and relative profitability within the country. McGregor and Swales give an example of a neoclassical productivity shock which leads to higher exports to match planned imports, from which we are led to believe that it is autonomous differences in productivity growth that are the source of growth rate differences with exports responding by exactly an amount equal to the planned level of imports. Why there should be exact matching to preserve balance-of-payments equilibrium is not clear. Nor is it clear how the model works with alternative shocks. Suppose the internal shock is a monetary or fiscal stimulus at less than full employment: output expands, but how then do exports respond endogenously to the new planned level of imports, and if they do what is the mechanism which brings about equilibrium?

To conclude on a conciliatory note, it would be foolish to argue that growth rate differences between countries depend solely on the balance-of-payments, or that supply conditions do not matter with respect to the availability of factor supplies and the characteristics of goods. What is being argued is that if the characteristics of traded goods differ between countries, exports (and to a certain extent imports) must largely be regarded as exogenously determined, and that if relative prices are sticky, or do not work as an efficient adjustment mechanism, then the Harrod trade multiplier will work, i.e. income (and the growth of income) is fundamentally determined by the demand for exports relative to the propensity to import. Economists must decide on the world they think they live in, and what story – the Harrod story or the neoclassical story – is the more plausible.

McGREGOR AND SWALES'S REJOINDER[17]

Earlier, we expressed doubts about the theoretical and empirical basis of what Thirlwall originally referred to as 'a fundamental law of growth'. In his reply, Thirlwall argues that such doubts are unfounded. He clarifies his theory on a number of points. He argues that his theory was subjected to inappropriate empirical tests. And whilst accepting that equation (5.1) or (5.7) can be derived from a strict neoclassical model, he invites the reader to choose between the plausibility of the neoclassical story, as against the Keynesian alternative.

The view taken here is that the points Thirlwall makes in his reply do not meet earlier criticisms. However, his reply does raise issues which should be tackled in more detail.

Theory

Thirlwall reaches his central equation (equation (5.1)) in two steps. First, he argues that the balance-of-payments constrained growth rate (y_B) is determined by the ratio of the growth of exports to the income elasticity of demand for imports:

$$y = x/\pi \tag{5.18}$$

Second, he asserts that the country's actual growth rate (y) normally equals the balance-of-payments constrained growth rate (y_B):

$$y = y_B \tag{5.19}$$

It is difficult to accept either equation (5.18) or equation (5.19). Consider equation (5.18) first.

In order to derive equation (5.18), it is important that foreign and domestic prices do not vary when measured in a common currency. In earlier work Thirlwall suggests three quite different reasons why this might be the case: real wage resistance, the law of one price and price stickiness in oligopolistic markets. In McGregor and Swales (1985), reasons were put forward for rejecting each of these, though the focus was on the law of one price. However, Thirlwall maintains that the interpretation of the law of one price was too strict. In fact, he now says that 'the term was used loosely to refer to constant relative prices which may be the outcome of highly competitive or imperfectly competitive market structures'. If this is Thirlwall's true position, the present authors stand by the conclusion in their earlier paper, that his model is wrongly specified.

In the Thirlwall model, the demand functions for exports (X) and imports (M) are both taken as multiplicative functions of the ratio of domestic to foreign prices, measured in a common currency (P_d/P_f), and the relevant income variable. Therefore:

$$X = (P_d/P_f)^\eta Z^\varepsilon \tag{5.20}$$

and:

$$M = (P_d/P_f)^{-\psi}Y^{\pi} \tag{5.21}$$

where Z is world income, Y is domestic income, ε is the income elasticity of demand for exports, and η and ψ are price elasticities of demand for exports and imports respectively. If, through sticky prices, $P_d = P_f$, equations (5.20) and (5.21) simplify to:

$$X = Z^{\varepsilon} \tag{5.22}$$

$$M = Y^{\pi} \tag{5.23}$$

Using lower-case letters to stand for rates of growth, the dynamic equivalents to equations (5.22) and (5.23) are:

$$x = \varepsilon z \tag{5.24}$$

$$m = \pi y \tag{5.25}$$

If the current account is to balance continuously, the growth of exports must equal the growth of imports. In Thirlwall's model, the growth of world income (z) and the income elasticities of demand for imports and exports (π, ε) are exogenous. Therefore the balance-of-payments constrained growth rate (y_B) is uniquely determined. Imposing the balance-of-payments constraint and using equations (5.24) and (5.25):

$$y_B\pi = \varepsilon z \tag{5.26}$$

Rearranging equation (5.26) and using equation (5.24):

$$y_B = \varepsilon z/\pi = x/\pi \tag{5.27}$$

It is argued that, if firms operating in oligopolistic markets reject price competition in favour of nonprice competition, then the export and import demand functions (equations (5.20) and (5.21)) are badly misspecified. They should be replaced by:

$$X = f(N_d, N_f, Z) \tag{5.28}$$

$$M = g(N_d, N_f, Y) \tag{5.29}$$

where N_d, N_f represent the levels of domestic and foreign nonprice competition.

Put simply, these non-price competitive elements should be included, either directly or indirectly, in the export and import demand functions. In his reply, Thirlwall argues that they are. He maintains that they are captured in the relevant income elasticities of demand. This argument is unacceptable. The income elasticity of demand will determine the growth of the market for a country's exports and imports, but not the changes in the share of that market which the country's exports and imports will take. In this model, changes in market share are determined by nonprice competition; but these changes in market share are not allowed in Thirlwall's formulation.

A country's exports in industry i (X_i) can be tautologically expressed as the product of the world market for that industry (Q_i) and the country's share of that market (S_i):

$$X_i = S_i Q_i \qquad (5.30)$$

Expressed dynamically, again using lower-case letters to denote rates of change,

$$x_i = s_i + q_i \qquad (5.31)$$

The country's export growth rate (x) is the weighted sum of the individual industry export growth rates. So if there are n industries:

$$x = \sum_{i=1}^{n} v_i x_i \qquad (5.32)$$

where v_i is the proportion of the country's total exports which are in industry i $(v_i = X_i/X)$. Substituting equation (5.31) into equation (5.32) gives:

$$x = \sum_{i=1}^{n} v_i s_i + \sum_{i=1}^{n} v_i q_i \qquad (5.33)$$

How can the identity shown in equation (5.33) be made to square with Thirlwall's export demand equation (equation (5.24))? Two assumptions need to be made:

$$Q_i = f(Z) \qquad (5.34)$$

$$\sum_{i=1}^{n} v_i s_i = 0 \qquad (5.35)$$

Equation (5.34) simply states that the size of the world market for good i depends solely on world income. Equation (5.34) can be expressed dynamically as:

$$q_i = \varepsilon_i z \qquad (5.36)$$

where ε_i is the income elasticity of demand for good i.

Equation (5.35) asserts that there has been no change in the share of the country's exports in world markets.

If equations (5.35) and (5.36) are substituted into equation (5.33):

$$x = z \sum_{i=1}^{n} v_i \varepsilon_i \qquad (5.37)$$

so that:

$$x = \varepsilon z$$

where:

$$\varepsilon = \sum_{i=1}^{n} v_i \varepsilon_i \qquad (5.38)$$

The most worrying aspect of this model is the imposition of equation (5.35). In general, non-price competition will produce changes in market share. Let the change in a country's share of export markets ($\sum_{i=1}^{n} v_i s_i$) equal a. This, together with equation (5.38) means that equation (5.33) can be expressed as:

$$x = a + \varepsilon z \qquad (5.39)$$

By exactly the same argument, the demand for imports can be expressed as:

$$m = b + \pi y \qquad (5.40)$$

where π is the weighted sum of the income elasticities of demand for the individual import industries, and b is the weighted sum of the changes in the share of imports in domestic markets. Again, imposing the balance-of-payments constraint, solving for domestic income growth (y_B) and substituting equation (5.39) gives:

$$y_B = \varepsilon z/\pi + (a-b)/\pi = x/\pi - b/\pi \tag{5.41}$$

It is clear that, except for the special case where the shares of exports and imports in their relevant markets do not change ($a, b = 0$), a country's actual growth rate will not be correctly explained by Thirlwall's theory. But Thirlwall claims that non-price competitiveness is captured in the income elasticities of demand. Can this be the case? Consider the demand for exports. Imagine that in industry i the change in the share of the foreign market going to the country's exports is a fixed multiple of the growth of that market. This means that:

$$s_i = c_i q_i \tag{5.42}$$

Equation (5.31) would then be replaced by

$$x_i = (1 + c_i)q_i \tag{5.43}$$

If it is again argued that the rate of growth of the foreign market for each industry depends only on the rate of growth of world income (equation (5.36)), then the rate of growth of exports (x) is given by:

$$x = z \sum_{i=1}^{n} v_i (1 + c_i)\varepsilon_i \tag{5.44}$$

so that $x = \varepsilon z$, where this time:

$$\varepsilon = \sum_{i=1}^{n} v_i (1 + c_i)\varepsilon_i \tag{5.45}$$

Similarly, an argument of the same form could be made for changes in the demand for imports.

The theory now depends crucially on imposing equation (5.42). There appear to be two important problems here. The first relates to the form of equation (5.42). It might appear intuitively plausible that there is a relationship between the change in a country's share of the world market for a particular good (s_i), and the growth of that market (q_i). However, Thirlwall's theory requires more than this. The relationship must take a particular form: it must be linear and homogeneous. This has the implication, for example, that if the world market for a good is static, there is no change in the market share held by individual countries.

The second problem is more fundamental. It is not clear what causal mechanism would underlie equation (5.42). Moreover, with the most plausible candidate, supply side factors are important and the values of the c_i are not choice variables for the national economy. If the general export demand function (equation (5.28)) is expressed in a multiplicative form, similarly to the way in which Thirlwall expresses his demand functions, then the effects of changes in non-price competition are independent of the growth of the industry.[18] The most plausible argument linking changes in the share of the market resulting from changes in nonprice competition to the rate of growth of the market incorporates supply side factors. The argument is that at the level of the industry, the amount of resources devoted to non-price competition is linked to the rate of growth of the world market for that product. Imagine that the c_i values for individual industries are represented as elements of a vector (**c**). If a country has a **c** vector, most of whose elements are positive, it will compete most intensively in those markets which are expanding, whilst withdrawing from those markets which are contracting. The rationale for this might simply be that the most rapidly expanding markets are the most profitable so that they will be the most fiercely contested.

There are two important points about this approach. The first is that the variable which is being identified as the income elasticity of demand (ε) is actually measuring an amalgam of demand and supply side factors. Second, the **c** vector is not a choice variable for the national economy. The situation where most of the elements of the **c** vector are positive has already been discussed. But what if they were negative? This would mean that the economy would increase its share of contracting world markets and reduce its share of expanding ones. It is difficult to think of reasons why individual firms would choose to act in this way. But it must be remembered that changes in the share of the market reflect changes in the relative competitiveness of domestic and foreign goods. It seems reasonable to suggest that a country which has a **c** vector, most of whose elements are negative, does not choose these values, but rather finds it difficult to compete in the most highly contested markets.

These two points have important implications for Thirlwall's theory. Let it be accepted for the moment that Thirlwall's balance-of-payments constrained growth equation (equation (5.18)) holds for the reasons that he puts forward. That is to say, there is no price competition and the effects of non-price competition are incorporated into the measured income elasticity of demand. Can such an equation be given the Keynesian interpretation implied by Thirlwall when he describes this as representing the dynamic Harrod trade multiplier? Clearly not, because embedded in this equation is the **c** vector which is determined by supply side considerations. In fact, in these circumstances, equation (5.18) should be regarded as a side relation of an essentially supply side model of national growth which Thirlwall has failed to specify even in the most general terms.

Up to now the focus has been on the notion that the growth rate which would maintain a current account balance (y_B) can be expressed as the ratio of the rate of growth of exports (x) and the income elasticity of demand for imports (π) (equation (5.18)). The second general theoretical point which was raised in McGregor and Swales (1985) was whether the actual growth rate (y) need equal this balance-of-payments constrained growth rate (equation (5.19)). It was argued that 'Implicit here is a theory of capital flows which is not defended' (McGregor and Swales, 1985, p. 22). By this it was meant that a theory of capital flows is required to ensure that the balance-of-payments constraint is binding. Thirlwall replies by stating that we 'criticize the model for excluding capital movements, but these are easily incorporated as has been done in another paper which McGregor and Swales omit to cite'.

This paper (Thirlwall and Hussain, 1982) does not put forward a theory of capital flows which would ensure that y and y_B are in equality. Rather, it documents in some detail that in conditions where capital flows are important, which they are in many underdeveloped countries, y will not equal y_B. This is a position with which we agree and it will be discussed in more detail in the next section.

Empirical Evidence

Thirlwall prefaces his criticisms of our empirical analysis with the following comments:

> It has always been believed by the present author that the essence of interesting economics, particularly applied economics, is to get a 'lot from a little'. I thought I had done that by showing how close the actual growth experience of several developed countries over the 1950s and 1960s (and into the early 1970s) had approximated to the balance-of-payments constrained rate, x/π. The perennial

question arises, of course, (as with 'stylised facts') of *how close is close?* (Our emphasis)

Thirlwall's answer to the question he poses was (Thirlwall, 1979), and appears to continue to be, that inspection of the data, combined with the calculation of a rank correlation coefficient for y and y_B, suffice to show that the relation is 'close enough' in some sense. There are three main problems with this position. First, the sense in which the relation is 'close enough' is qualitative and impressionistic. Yet there exists a widely accepted method for subjecting hypotheses which can be expressed in simple linear equations to statistical testing. This method, regression analysis, employs rigorous criteria for determining 'how close is close', and this is why it was chosen for use by the present authors. Secondly, the rank correlation between y and y_B gives no indication of the 'predictive ability' of Thirlwall's theory. The rank correlation coefficient could be unity yet there could be a wide disparity (of a systematic nature) between the levels of y and y_B which is clearly inconsistent with the theory which requires that y equals y_B. This relation was tested for directly and it was found that, in general, it is rejected at conventional significance levels. Thirdly, as is clear from the preceding section, $y = y_B$ is only one element of the theory. The other critical relation is that $y_B = x/\pi$. Clearly correlation of the ranks of y and y_B computed by x/π gives no direct test of the appropriateness of assuming $y_B = x/\pi$. Our own tests gave an indication of this by regressing y separately on x and π, and generally resulted in rejection of the hypothesis. In summary, the empirical tests which are adopted in the earlier paper (McGregor and Swales, 1985), in contrast to those used by Thirlwall, employed a widely accepted, rigorous definition of 'how close is close' and led, in general, to the rejection of Thirlwall's theory.

However, Thirlwall raises a number of objections to those tests of his theory, or at least those based on regressions of y and y_B. First, he argues that these regressions (and tests of parameter constraints)

would be a legitimate test taking all countries of the world (where surpluses must equal deficits, or where divergences between y and y_B cancel out), but it is not a legitimate test for a small sample of countries where the combined balances of payments do not balance.

A number of points arise from this. First, the sample used in McGregor and Swales (1985) is identical to the sample on which

Thirlwall conducted his own tests, on the basis of which he proposed the relation that he describes as a 'fundamental law'. Secondly, 'surpluses must equal deficits' only in the limited sense that (in the absence of errors and omissions from accounts) the sum of the surpluses/deficits over all countries must be zero. However, this does not imply that the sum of differences between y and y_B across all countries must similarly cancel out. The impact of a current account deficit or surplus on the rate of growth of any one country will depend on the scale of that country's trade and the elasticity of demand for imports. Only if all countries had the same level of trade in current account equilibrium and the same value of π would the sum of all divergences from the balance-of-payments constrained growth rates necessarily equal zero. Thirdly, even if this were so, it is not necessarily the case that Thirlwall's theory would perform better on a sample which included all trading nations. This is because, as was pointed out in the earlier paper, the divergence of y from y_B might be systematically related to the value of y_B. Fourthly, Thirlwall clearly recognises the existence of divergences between y and y_B, although these are asserted to be 'usually small'. This seems strictly inconsistent with the formal theory. Of course, this begs the question of 'how small is small', but this issue was presumed to have been dealt with in the preceding arguments.

Thirlwall also raised the possibility of the results being biased because of 'one or two outlying observations'. In fact, any 'outliers' would seem to raise problems for Thirlwall's 'law' in that they imply that the balance-of-payments 'constraint' is not a constraint. Furthermore, 'outliers' appear to be the rule rather than the exception. For example, virtually the entire sample of developing countries used by Thirlwall and Hussain (1982) fall into this category, and McGregor and Swales (1985) drew attention to the fact that, in the sample in Thirlwall (1979), $y < y_B$ for almost all countries.

Thirlwall considers our empirical work to be 'a good example of the inappropriateness of a cross-section test of a model relating to the time-series behaviour of countries in an incomplete sample'. This seems to imply an objection in principle to the use of cross-section data in the evaluation of his theory. This point might be legitimate in the sense that any country in any one year might be in a transitory disequilibrium position whereas the theory is intended to apply to long-run equilibria. Perhaps, in principle, matters could be improved by some form of pooling of cross-section and time-series data – even in the form of investigating, say, a cross-section data set based on ten-year averages of the time-series data of each country.

Nevertheless, the only data which Thirlwall has invoked in support of his theory have been of the form of which he now apparently disapproves.

It might be that Thirlwall's main objection is to the 'incompleteness' of the sample, rather than to its cross-sectional nature. This criticism was hopefully dealt with earlier, but it is accepted that *ceteris paribus* the larger the sample size the better. Accordingly, in the Appendix below are reported the results of re-running tests on the data set for developing countries presented in Thirlwall and Hussain (1982) and on original data sets for developed countries from McGregor and Swales (1985) augmented by the data from Thirlwall and Hussain (1982). For developing countries considered as a group, even the hypothesis that y_B exerts an effect on y which is statistically significantly different from zero is rejected. Furthermore, the hypotheses that x and π exert effects on y which are statistically significantly different from zero are also rejected. Perhaps unsurprisingly in the light of these results, augmentation of the initial data sets through inclusion of data from the sample of developing countries results in a marked deterioration, across the board, in the statistical performance of Thirlwall's model. It becomes much more emphatically rejected by the data.

Thirlwall could object to this exercise on two grounds. First, the sample remains 'incomplete'. It is argued above that this is not a telling objection. Secondly, he could legitimately point to the fact that at least an element in the motivation of the Thirlwall and Hussain (1982) paper appears to have been specifically in order to show that developing countries seemed not to conform to Thirlwall's 'law'. To incorporate them in a test of the law might consequently be argued to be illegitimate. Perhaps Thirlwall wishes to confine the theory exclusively to developed countries. However, this too is problematic for his position insofar as this would seem to render selection of an 'incomplete sample' essential to a testing of his theory.

It is clear that the empirical data do not support the notion that $y = x/\pi$, no matter what its causal interpretation, is a fundamental law. It quite simply is not. Whilst it might be aesthetically pleasing to explain a lot by a little, the real world is clearly more complex than Thirlwall's simple model allows, and Thirlwall understands this. His reaction is to assert that the divergence of reality from the simple model can be explained in ways which retain the central Keynesian core of his theory. It is felt such claims, at present, have very weak empirical support. In order to substantiate these views, Thirlwall needs to specify a more general model in some detail and subject this to the standard battery of statistical tests.

Methodology

In our earlier article it was argued that Thirlwall's fundamental equation could be derived from a standard neoclassical model of growth in an open economy. Thirlwall's response is to appeal to the reader's judgement concerning the relative plausibility of the assumptions invoked by the neoclassical and Keynesian models. However, it was not argued that we live in a world where the truth of $y = x/\pi$ is to be explained in a neoclassical way. To begin with, the available evidence is not felt to support the equation $y = x/\pi$. Rather, perhaps too indirectly, a methodological point was being made.

Thirlwall interprets what he takes to be support for his equation as support for a Keynesian approach to the determination of open economy growth. But such a view is misleading because the test fails to distinguish between Keynesian and other major theories of economic growth. A neoclassical model was outlined, but other theories are also compatible with the equation. For example, the very general supply side model developed in the first section of this paper is neither a standard neoclassical nor a simple Keynesian model, yet it is capable of generating the equation as a side relation. Thirlwall might believe that the Keynesian demand-led approach is clearly superior to the supply constrained neoclassical view. However, the empirical work he presents here, even were it more convincing in establishing the veracity of the equation, cannot be used as evidence of this superiority.

Conclusions

In principle, the present authors are sympathetic to the broad approach that Thirlwall is adopting. There remains, however, concern that the conviction with which he expresses his views is not matched by the theoretical and empirical rigour of the work on which these views are apparently based.

Appendix to McGregor and Swales (1986)

Two equations were estimated on each of three data sets. The two equations are:

$$y = \alpha_0 + \alpha_1 y_B \qquad\qquad\qquad (A5.1)$$

and

$$\log y = \beta_0 + \beta_1 \log x + \beta_2 \log \pi \qquad\qquad (A5.2)$$

Thirlwall's theory implies that $\alpha_0 = \beta_0 = 0$; $\alpha_1 = \beta_1 = 1$; $\beta_2 = -1$.
The results of estimating equation (A5.1) on the sample of developing countries presented in Thirlwall and Hussain (1982) are:

$$\hat{\alpha}_0 = 0.048 \qquad \hat{\alpha}_1 = 0.093 \qquad \bar{R}^2 = -0.038$$
$$(4.009) \qquad\qquad (0.551)$$

where figures in parentheses are t-statistics. Estimation of equation (A5.2) on the same data set yields:

$$\hat{\beta}_0 = -1.705 \qquad \hat{\beta}_1 = 0.440 \qquad \hat{\beta}_2 = -0.269 \qquad \bar{R}^2 = 0.067$$
$$(-2.477) \qquad\qquad (1.836) \qquad\qquad (-1.390)$$

Estimation of Equation (A5.1) on the 1953–76 sample of developed countries, augmented to include the sample of developing countries, gives:

$$\hat{\alpha}_0 = 0.031 \qquad \hat{\alpha}_1 = 0.306 \qquad \bar{R}^2 = 0.189$$
$$(4.571) \qquad\qquad (2.990)$$

Estimation of equation (A5.2) on the same sample yields:

$$\hat{\beta}_0 = -1.428 \qquad \hat{\beta}_1 = 0.567 \qquad \hat{\beta}_2 = -0.458 \qquad \bar{R}^2 = 0.305$$
$$(-3.449) \qquad\qquad (3.891) \qquad\qquad (-3.823)$$

Equation (A5.1), estimated on the 1951–73 sample of developed countries, expanded to include the Thirlwall–Hussain sample of developing countries, gives:

$$\hat{\alpha}_0 = 0.033 \qquad \hat{\alpha}_1 = 0.317 \qquad \bar{R}^2 = 0.181$$
$$(4.222) \qquad\qquad (2.764)$$

Finally, estimation of equation (A5.2) on the same sample generates the following results:

$$\hat{\beta}_0 = -1.314 \qquad \hat{\beta}_1 = 0.593 \qquad \hat{\beta}_2 = -0.432 \qquad \bar{R}^2 = 0.323$$
$$(-3.102) \qquad\qquad (3.996) \qquad\qquad (-3.429)$$

A REPLY TO McGREGOR AND SWALES BY McCOMBIE[19]

McGregor and Swales make three major points in their renewed attack on the balance-of-payments constrained growth model.

First, they argue that the model can be interpreted in a neoclassical manner by invoking the neoclassical interpretation of the 'law of one price'. An implication of this is that the causation runs from income growth to export growth and not vice versa.

Secondly, they claim that a supposedly more appropriate test of the goodness of fit between y and y_B provides no empirical support for the model.

Finally, it is argued that even if all the arguments are granted, the model still cannot be regarded as either (a) satisfactorily capturing the effects of non-price competition or (b) reflecting the workings of the dynamic foreign trade multiplier. We will examine each of these objections in turn.

The Direction of Causality and the 'Law of One Price'

The rule that $y = x/\pi$ implies a close correlation between the growth of income and that of exports; but, of course, such correlation implies nothing about causality. It could be that the direction of causality is from the growth of income to that of exports or both could be jointly determined. The direction of causality has to be decided on independently of the regression analysis and depends upon other empirical evidence. Of particular relevance here is the work of Cornwall (1977) who, after surveying the evidence concerning the growth of the advanced countries, came to the conclusion that it was not the exogenous growth of the labour force that determined the growth of output (and exports). '[D]ifferences in growth rates across countries in the postwar period could not be attributed to differences in the degree of flexibility of the labour force because when the demand for additional flexibility arose, the additional (surplus) labour was found' (1977, p. 214). Moreover, the rate of capital accumulation is largely determined by the (expected) growth of output and hence is, to a great extent, endogenous. Given the lack of any factor supply constraint, it is more plausible to assume that causation runs from the growth of exports to that of income via the growth of demand acting through the dynamic analogue of Hicks's super-multiplier (see Chapter 6).

Nevertheless, McGregor and Swales argue that the lack of variation of relative prices reflects the neoclassical interpretation of the 'law of one price' and this implies causation does not run from export to income growth. Relative prices, far from being unimportant, are seen as being the fundamental determinant of the growth of exports. This is because the neoclassical 'law of one price' implies that the price elasticities of demand for exports are infinite. They argue that this appears 'to render the model incoherent. It becomes a demand constrained model with no demand constraint. Our view is that these analytical problems rob the theory of any real explanatory power. . . .'

There are two points to note about this argument. The first is that if the neoclassical interpretation of the 'law of one price' is correct, then there obviously can be no such thing as a balance-of-payments constraint. The concept of export-led growth has no meaning under 'global monetarism'. Under the assumptions of the latter, the price mechanism will always ensure that sufficient exports will be forthcoming to pay for any given growth of imports without there being any need for the growth of income to adjust.

Thus, the question whether the observed small variations in the growth of relative prices are due to the neoclassical 'law of one price' or are the result of oligopolistic pricing (and reflect the importance of non-price competition) is of crucial importance in deciding how the economic system works. Which interpretation of the 'law of one price' is correct is ultimately an empirical question.

We will not discuss here the empirical evidence in detail, but the work of Isard (1977) and of Kravis and Lipsey (1978) suggest that there is significant product differentiation even at very fine levels of product classification and, in the words of Isard, 'In reality, the law of one price is flagrantly and systematically violated by empirical data' (1977, p. 942). (The corollary, the importance of non-price competition, is discussed below.)

Moreover, the 'best' point estimates of the price elasticities of demand from a number of econometric studies for various countries range from -2.00 (UK, manufactures) to -0.93 (Italy, total exports) (Stern, Francis and Schumacher, 1976). These values are somewhat below infinity, to say the least. (See also Cripps (1979) for a simple demonstration of why the 'law of one price' is likely to reflect oligopolistic pricing.)

A second point to note is that even if it is maintained that the neoclassical 'law of one price' is a reasonable assumption, it does not follow that the model would be incoherent or inconsistent – rather, it would be irrelevant. The growth of exports and imports would, under these circumstances, be functions of profitability rather than demand factors. Since the demand for exports is assumed to be perfectly elastic, demand has no independent role to play in this explanation. The specification of the model using, as it does, export and import demand functions, is only compatible with oligopolistic pricing and no supply constraints. In all estimated export demand functions the income variable is always highly significant. This is not consistent with the small open economy, one world price, assumption.

McGregor and Swales are inconsistent in their argument to the extent that they themselves also suggest that non-price competition is important (and erroneously argue that this factor is absent from the model). Either non-price competition is important and the neoclassical 'law of one price' does not hold or the converse is true, but not both. In fact, McGregor and Swales seem to change their tune. They say 'it was not argued that we live in a world where the truth of $[y = x/\pi]$ is to be explained in a neoclassical way'. (From this it must be inferred that they are no longer prepared to defend their lengthy neoclassical analysis as a valid critique of the model.) The main issue is seen as being empirical rather than analytical: 'To begin with, the available evidence is not felt to support equation (5.1), i.e. $y = x/\pi$.' The 'available evidence' they consider is confined to whether or not y and y_B are statistically significantly different. This evidence is considered next.

The Statistical Testing of the Model

McGregor and Swales argue that a rigorous test of the model is to estimate the following equations by ordinary least-squares:

$$\ln y = c_0 + c_1 \ln x + c_2 \ln \pi \tag{5.46}$$

and:

$$y = c_3 + c_4 y_B \tag{5.47}$$

They find for the period 1951–73 and 1953–76 that although the estimated coefficients c_1 and c_2 are statistically significant and the R^2 is over 0.9, the absolute values of the two coefficients are significantly less than unity (at the 95 per cent confidence level). This result, they argue, provides a statistical refutation of the model. Moreover, they also find that whereas the coefficient c_4 in equation (5.47) is also statistically significant, it is likewise significantly less than unity (except when Japan and the United States are excluded from the sample for the period 1951–73).

The first point to notice with this procedure is that the estimation of equations (5.46) and (5.47) by ordinary least-squares is inappropriate and, hence, no conclusions should be drawn from the statistical tests performed on the estimates of the coefficients. This is because the regressor is itself an estimated coefficient from a regression analysis and hence each observation of π in the sample has an associated standard error, i.e. π is a stochastic explanatory variable and the use of ordinary least-squares will lead to bias in the estimates (y_B in equation (5.47) also suffers from this problem since it is calculated using π). The information of the standard error of each observation of π should be explicitly incorporated into the estimation procedure.

However, there is a more fundamental objection to McGregor and Swales's procedure which even correcting for the above would not remove. The problem is that the regression analysis is, as has been pointed out already, a good example of the 'inappropriateness of a cross-section test of a model relating to the time-series behaviour of countries in an incomplete sample.' If a cross-section regression analysis is to be undertaken, it should be undertaken by using the fully specified model, including the growth of capital flows and the rate of change of relative prices. While for the majority of countries the omission of the growth of relative prices and of capital flows is not important, there are a few cases where this is obviously incorrect. Hence, the cross-section test of McGregor and Swales, because of a small number of outliers, misleadingly leads them to reject the relationship for *all* the individual countries.

It is interesting to note, for example, that one of the outliers, namely Japan, was, over the period under consideration, running an increasingly large trade surplus. This suggests that y_B will exceed y and this indeed proves to be the case. Australia also proves to be another extreme observation. This country, 80 per cent of whose exports are primary products, has experienced a steady deterioration in its terms of trade over the post-war period. Each year Australia had to export about 2 per cent more in volume terms just to maintain the same real foreign-exchange earnings. Thus, in this case, the omission of the effect of the rate of decline of the terms of trade from the rule will lead to an over-estimate of y_B which again seems to have occurred.

A more satisfactory test that avoids these objections is to determine whether y and y_B are statistically significantly different for each individual country *separately*.

The test can be undertaken as follows. What may be termed the 'balance-of-payments equilibrium income elasticity of demand for imports' (denoted by π') is first calculated from the expression $\pi' = x/y$. There are hence two expressions for the growth of income, *viz*, $y = x/\pi'$ and $y_B = x/\hat{\pi}$, where $\hat{\pi}$ is the estimate of the income elasticity of demand for imports, and is taken from Houthakker and Magee (1969).

It follows that if π' and $\hat{\pi}$ are not statistically different, this is also true of y_B and y. Thus, the hypothesis to be tested is whether or not $\hat{\pi} = \pi'$. This was undertaken by calculating the t statistic from the standard error of $\hat{\pi}$ for the null hypothesis that $\hat{\pi}$ is equal to π' and ascertaining whether or not the null hypothesis is rejected at the 95 per cent confidence level. (The standard error of $\hat{\pi}$ is also taken from Houthakker and Magee, 1969.) The test was confined to the use of growth rates for the period 1951–73 in order to avoid the effects of the post-1973 shocks to world trade. Moreover, this period more closely accords with that of Houthakker and Magee's original sample. The results are reported in Table 5.4.

It may be seen that for 11 of the sample of 15 advanced countries, the law is not refuted at the 95 per cent confidence level. Moreover, even for the other four countries where there is a statistically significant difference between $\hat{\pi}$ and π', the discrepancy is not large. It must be also remembered that possible errors may be introduced by the estimation procedures of Houthakker and Magee and significant differences between $\hat{\pi}$ and π' may not be due to a failure of the rule to hold. (In particular, Houthakker and Magee's study has been criticised on the grounds that their use of ordinary least-squares may lead to simultaneous equation bias. Furthermore, no allowance is made for the possibility of lags in the various specifications and there may be aggregation errors.)

Taking all these factors into account it seems that these results, *pace* McGregor and Swales, certainly cannot be taken as constituting a rejection of the model.

There is one further difficulty that must be mentioned and which was first pointed out by Williamson (1984). Ideally, y_B should be calculated from $\hat{\epsilon}z/\hat{\pi}$ rather than $x/\hat{\pi}$ since x, being an ex post value, already incorporates the effects (if any) of relative price changes. Unfortunately, it is not possible to undertake a comparable statistical test to that above. Nevertheless, defining y_B as equal to $\hat{\epsilon}z/\hat{\pi}$, it may be seen, from an inspection of Table 5.5 that y_B also, with one or two exceptions, closely approximated to y. (The estimates of the income elasticity of demand for exports, $\hat{\epsilon}$, are also taken from Houthakker and Magee (1969).)

Table 5.4   Testing for whether $\hat{\pi}$ and π' are statistically significantly different; selected advanced countries

Country	Income elasticity of demand for imports[a] $\hat{\pi}$	Balance-of-payments equilibrium income elasticity of demand for imports π'	Absolute value of the t statistic[b, c] $|t|$
Australia	0.90	1.39	2.75*
Belgium[d]	1.94	2.14	1.35
Canada	1.20	1.50	4.08*
Denmark[e]	1.31	1.45	0.49
France	1.66	1.62	0.22
Italy	2.19	2.29	0.30
Japan	1.23	1.62	4.14*
Netherlands	1.89	2.02	0.78
Norway	1.40	1.71	2.38*
South Africa[d]	1.13	1.15	0.10
South Africa[d]	(0.91)	1.15	(0.79)
Sweden[d]	1.42	2.10	1.97
Switzerland[d]	1.81	1.74	0.30
West Germany	1.80	1.89	0.86
United Kingdom	1.66	1.52	0.89
United Kingdom	(1.45)	1.52	(0.44)
United States	1.51	1.38	1.04
United States	(1.68)	1.38	(1.90)

Notes: [a]Figures in parentheses are the values of $\hat{\pi}$ where there have been corrections for autocorrelation in Houthakker and Magee's regression analyses.
[b]The t statistic is based on the null hypothesis that $\hat{\pi} = \pi'$. Figures in parentheses are calculated using the corrected values of $\hat{\pi}$.
[c]*denotes that $\hat{\pi}$ differs significantly from π' at the 95% confidence level.
[d]Period is 1955–73.
[e]Period is 1954–73.

Sources: Cornwall (1977), Houthakker and Magee (1969) and International Monetary Fund (1985).

Non-Price Competition and International Trade

There is a good deal of supporting evidence of both a qualitative and quantitative nature, that non-price competition is of paramount importance in international trade (see Chapter 4). For example, Posner

Table 5.5 A comparison between the actual output growth rates and those predicted by the rule $y_B^* = \hat{e}z/\hat{\pi}$ (% per annum), 1951–73; selected advanced countries

Country	Ratio of the income elasticity of demand for exports to that of imports[a] $\hat{e}/\hat{\pi}$	Balance-of-payments equilibrium growth rate[b, c] y_B^*	Growth of GDP y
Australia	1.31	5.8	4.9
Australia	(1.29)	(5.7)	4.9
Belgium[d]	0.94	4.1	4.4
Canada	1.18	5.2	4.6
Denmark[e]	1.29	5.7	4.2
France	0.92	4.0	5.0
Italy	1.35	5.9	5.1
Italy	(1.22)	(5.4)	5.1
Japan	2.89	12.7	9.5
Netherlands	0.99	4.4	5.0
Norway	1.14	5.0	4.2
South Africa[d]	0.78	3.4	4.8
South Africa[d]	(0.97)	(4.3)	4.8
Sweden[d]	1.24	5.5	3.9
Sweden[d]	(1.23)	(5.4)	3.9
Switzerland[d]	0.81	3.6	4.3
Switzerland[d]	[0.72]	[3.2]	4.3
West Germany	1.16	5.1	5.7
West Germany[f]	(0.51)	(2.2)	5.7
West Germany[g]	[0.49]	[2.2]	5.7
United Kingdom	0.52	2.3	2.7
United Kingdom	(0.69)	(3.0)	2.7
United States	0.66	2.9	3.7
United States	(0.59)	(2.6)	3.7

Notes: [a]Figures in parentheses are the values of $\hat{e}/\hat{\pi}$ where there have been corrections for autocorrelation in Houthakker and Magee's regression analyses of either the import or the export demand functions, or both, and where the price term has not been excluded. Figures in square brackets are where the estimate of π has been corrected for autocorrelation and the price term has been excluded.

[b]$y_B^* = \hat{e}/\hat{\pi}$ where z, defined here as the growth of world income, takes a value of 4.4% per annum.

[c]Figures in parentheses and square brackets are the values of y_B^* obtained using the corrected estimates of $\hat{e}$ or $\hat{\pi}$, or both, and where the price term has been included and excluded respectively.

[d]Period is 1955–73.

[e]Period is 1954–74.

[f]Estimate of only ε has been corrected for autocorrelation and price term has been included

[g]Estimates of both ε and π have been corrected for autocorrelation, but the price term has been dropped from the estimation of π.

⌐r (1979), after surveying the literature on the role of non-
⌐d price competition in determining trade flows, came to the
⌐ng conclusion:

> Our impression of the relationship between price and non-price
> influences may be summarized as follows. Historically, there is no
> doubt that non-price influences have dominated – the proportion of
> the total change which they 'explain' is an order of magnitude
> greater than the explanatory power of price competitiveness. Even
> when price competitiveness works, it may have 'featherbedding'
> effects. (p. 159)

In a similar vein, Stout (1979), drawing on the extensive work that the
National Economic Development Office has undertaken on non-price
competitiveness and the growth of UK exports, argues as follows:

> Given that over a long period and using a variety of indicators of
> price competitiveness, exchange rate changes have broadly com-
> pensated for the relative rise in sterling costs of production and
> given that (as earlier shown) the broad product composition of
> British exports and domestic output of manufactures is very similar
> to that of Germany and not very different from that of France, *the
> difference between the British and the German or French income
> elasticities of demand for manufactured imports, as well as the
> differences in the elasticity of foreign demand for exports support the
> now quite widespread evidence that non-price competitive disadvan-
> tages underlie Britain's industrial decline.* (p. 181, emphasis added)

A lot of other evidence has already been given in Chapter 4.

These arguments are confirmed by the quantitative evidence provided by Fetherston, Moore and Rhodes (1977). They showed that
changes in relative prices could explain very little of the differences in
changes in export shares of six large advanced countries over the
period 1956–76 (although they preferred to use changes in relative
unit costs because of the well-known difficulties associated with the
use of import and export price indices).

As may be seen from Table 5.6, the actual change in manufactured
export shares varied considerably between the countries. At one
extreme, Japan's share increased from 4 per cent of the world market
to 14 per cent while, at the other end of the spectrum, the share of the
US fell from 30 per cent to 17 per cent. Fetherston, Moore and

Table 5.6 Manufactured export shares of six large countries and shares adjusted for cyclical variations and changes in relative costs, 1956–76

		UK	USA	West Germany	France	Italy	Japan
(A) Actual share	1956	17.82	30.02	14.39	6.03	2.58	4.19
	1976	8.27	17.17	17.77	8.42	6.50	14.06
	Change	–9.55	–12.85	+3.38	+2.39	+3.92	+9.87
(B) Adjusted share[a]	1956	16.84	34.69	9.21	8.48	2.43	3.65
	1976	7.80	12.56	19.24	9.10	6.48	16.88
	Change	–9.04	–22.13	+10.03	+0.62	+4.05	+13.23

Note: [a]Assumes a cost elasticity of −1.0.

Source: Fetherston *et al.* (1977).

Rhodes estimated what the share of the various countries would have been after adjusting for changes in relative unit labour costs together with plausible values of the cost elasticity (although the results proved to be relatively insensitive to the exact values of the elasticity used). They also adjusted the shares for cyclical variations in world trade, but the effect of this was negligible. The adjusted shares are also reported in Table 5.6. It can be seen that after allowing for the effects of changes in relative unit costs there still remain considerable changes in the countries' market shares. Indeed, in the case of the US the decline in its market share would have been far worse but for the improvement in its relative costs. On the other hand, the increase in the market shares of West Germany and Japan would have been greater but for the deterioration in their relative costs.[20]

As Fetherston, Moore and Rhodes (1977, p. 66) put it (omitting a footnote):

The general picture to emerge, therefore, is of a trading system dominated by strong long-run trends in export shares whose effects were reduced but not reversed by effective devaluations and re-valuations. This result goes some way to explaining the 'Kaldor Paradox' that ex post the value of net exports appeared to respond perversely to effective devaluations. The reason is that relative cost changes, although moving in the right direction, have not been large or strong enough to reverse the strong underlying trends in export shares.

This is strong additional evidence that corroborates our emphasis on the importance of non-price competition in determining trade flows. It is non-price competition that accounts for the 'strong long-run trends in export shares' mentioned by Fetherston, Moore and Rhodes in the above quotation.

Whereas McGregor and Swales (1986) seem to accept the importance of non-price competition, they nevertheless deny that this is being captured by observed variations in ε and π. 'He [Thirlwall] maintains that they [the non-price competitive elements] are captured in the relevant income elasticities of demand. This argument is unacceptable. The income elasticity of demand will determine the growth of the market for a country's exports and imports, but not the changes in the share of that market which the country's exports and imports will take' (p. 1267).

McGregor and Swales's argument is simply wrong.

McGregor and Swales arrive at the above conclusion by first considering the tautological definition that the level of exports of industry i is given by:

$$X_i = S_i Q_i \tag{5.48}$$

where S_i equals X_i/Q_i, the share that the exports of industry i take in the world market for that product, Q_i.

Consequently, equation (5.48) becomes, in terms of growth rates:

$$x_i = s_i + q_i \tag{5.49}$$

For total exports, equation (5.49) is:

$$x = \sum_i v_i s_i + \sum_i v_i q_i \tag{5.50}$$

where v_i is the share of industry i's exports in total exports of the country (i.e. $v_i = X_i/X$).

McGregor and Swales then assert that there are two necessary assumptions for equation (5.50) to be 'made to square' with the export demand equation used by Thirlwall (*viz*, $x = \varepsilon z$). The first assumption is that:

$$Q_i = f(Z) \tag{5.51a}$$

where Z is the level of world income. More specifically, and in terms of growth rates, equation (5.51a) may be expressed as:[21]

$$q_i = \widetilde{\varepsilon}_i z \tag{5.51b}$$

A tilde has been used over ε_i in equation (5.51b) to distinguish $\widetilde{\varepsilon}_i$, the world income elasticity of demand for the total world market of industry i, from ε_i which is defined as the world income elasticity of demand for a particular country's exports of industry i. To put this another way, $\widetilde{\varepsilon}_i = (dQ_i/dZ)(Z/Q_i)$ and $\varepsilon_i = (dX_i/dZ)(Z/X_i)$.

As will be seen below, it is the failure to make this distinction that is responsible for McGregor and Swales's mistaken criticism of Thirlwall.

Following McGregor and Swales, and substituting equation (5.51b) into equation (5.50), the growth of a country's total exports may be expressed as:

$$x = \sum_i v_i s_i + z \sum_i v_i \widetilde{\varepsilon}_i \tag{5.52a}$$

$$= \sum_i v_i s_i + \widetilde{\varepsilon} z \tag{5.52b}$$

$$= a + \widetilde{\varepsilon} z \tag{5.52c}$$

where $\widetilde{\varepsilon} = \sum_i v_i \widetilde{\varepsilon}_i$ and a is the growth of the country's total export share in world markets (i.e. $a = \sum_i v_i x_i - \sum_i v_i q_i$).

As has been noted, the growth of exports is postulated by Thirlwall to be given by:

$$x = \varepsilon z \tag{5.53}$$

McGregor and Swales assume that ε is always equal to $\widetilde{\varepsilon}$. (The same symbol, ε, is used for both parameters throughout their analysis.) Hence, a comparison of equation (5.53) with equation (5.52c) (and, consequently, equation (5.52a)) suggests that the two approaches are only equivalent if market shares are constant.

Thus, the second necessary assumption, according to McGregor and Swales, is that $\sum_i v_i s_i = a = 0$. If market shares are constant then they are correct and ε and $\widetilde{\varepsilon}$ will indeed be formally equivalent. This may be simply demonstrated. Let:

$$X_i/Q_i = k_i \tag{5.54}$$

where k_i is constant.

The export demand function for industry i is given by $X_i = g_i Z^{\varepsilon_i}$ (where g_i is a constant and the relative price term is omitted). It follows from this and equation (5.54) that:

$$Q_i = (1/k_i)g_i Z^{\varepsilon_i} \tag{5.55a}$$

and:

$$(dQ_i/dZ)(Z/Q_i) = \varepsilon_i \tag{5.55b}$$

But $\tilde{\varepsilon}_i$ is definitionally equal to $(dQ_i/dZ)(Z/Q_i)$. Consequently, when market shares are constant, ε_i equals $\tilde{\varepsilon}_i$ and similarly, at the aggregative level, ε and $\tilde{\varepsilon}$ are also identical.

But this leads McGregor and Swales to infer erroneously that Thirlwall's model will not accurately predict the growth of exports if market shares are changing because there is no corresponding term for a in equation (5.53). They argue that 'In this model, changes in market share are determined by non-price competition; but these changes in market share are not allowed in Thirlwall's formulation.'

The problem with this argument is that when market shares change, ε and $\tilde{\varepsilon}$ are not formally equivalent and the estimate of ε used by Thirlwall does, in fact, capture the effects of changes in market shares.

It is ironical that McGregor and Swales themselves implicitly demonstrate this when they outline one possible way in which the income elasticity of demand in their specification of the export demand function could capture the effects of non-price competition (see equations (5.42) to (5.45)). No explanation, however, is offered as to how this is to be made consistent with their contention that 'This argument is unacceptable' in a quotation cited above. They apparently also fail to appreciate that it vitiates their criticism of Thirlwall's model.

A consideration of McGregor and Swales's argument will make this explicit. Their 'unorthodox' export demand function (expressed in terms of growth rates) for industry i, as has been seen, is given by:

$$x_i = s_i + \tilde{\varepsilon}_i z \tag{5.56}$$

It is now assumed that the rate of change of the market share is a linear function of the growth of the world market, *viz*:

$$s_i = c_i q_i = c_i \tilde{\varepsilon}_i z \tag{5.57}$$

c_i is presumably assumed to vary between countries and its value may be regarded as reflecting the degree of non-price competitiveness.

Substituting equation (5.57) into equation (5.56) and aggregating over industries the following is obtained:

$$\sum_i v_i x_i = \sum_i v_i \tilde{\varepsilon}_i (1 + c_i)z \qquad (5.58)$$

The more conventional specification of an export demand function is given by:

$$\sum_i v_i x_i = \sum_i v_i \varepsilon_i z \qquad (5.59a)$$

or:

$$x = \varepsilon z \qquad (5.59b)$$

It follows that ε equals $\sum_i v_i \tilde{\varepsilon}_i (1 + c_i)$ and not $\sum_i v_i \varepsilon_i (1 + c_i)$.

The implications perhaps may be seen more clearly if we work directly with the aggregate values and postulate that $s = a = cq$. Following the procedure of McGregor and Swales, the counterpart of equation (5.58) is obtained, *viz*:

$$x = (1 + c)\tilde{\varepsilon}z \qquad (5.60)$$

Consequently, it may be seen that when market shares are changing ε and $\tilde{\varepsilon}$ are not equivalent but, from equations (5.59a) and (5.60), $\varepsilon = (1 + c)\tilde{\varepsilon}$. In other words, the relationship between McGregor and Swales's approach (as given by equations (5.52c) and (5.60)) and that of Thirlwall (as given by equation (5.59b)) is:

$$x = a + \tilde{\varepsilon}z = (1 + c)\tilde{\varepsilon}z = \varepsilon z \qquad (5.61)$$

It is clear from equation (5.61) that Thirlwall's model is capturing the change in market share, *pace* McGregor and Swales. The error McGregor and Swales make is to assume that the estimate of ε used by Thirlwall is always formally equivalent to $\tilde{\varepsilon}$.

It may be objected that for ε to capture the change in market shares it is necessary for the condition $s = cq$ (or $s_i = c_i q_i$) to hold. But it is not unusual for conventional export demand functions to be specified so that the coefficient of the world income variable (or the world trade variable, since the two are highly correlated) is assumed to capture the change in market share. For example, Anderson and Dunnett (1987, p. 46) note that 'Some export volumes equations include a time trend to take into account the declining UK share of world trade, but this specification [i.e. the one employed by the National Institute of Economic and Social Research] allows the world trade coefficient (which is less than unity) to capture the effects of this downward trend.'

A further point to note is that McGregor and Swales's confusion between ε and $\tilde{\varepsilon}$ leads them to argue that the observed differences between countries in the estimated values of ε must be determined only by variations in the commodity mix of exports. 'But the value of ε depends *solely* on the product composition of a country's exports. If $\varepsilon > 1$, the country will be maintaining its share of markets which generally have a high income elasticity of demand and are therefore growing rapidly relative to other markets' (McGregor and Swales, 1985, p. 21, footnote 4, emphasis added).

No empirical evidence is cited in support of this assertion which is not surprising as the evidence suggests that precisely the opposite is the case. For example, Cornwall (1977, p. 161) notes: 'Empirical studies of market economies in the postwar period indicate that part of export growth of any country attributable to the changing structure of the area and commodity composition of trade is small.' (See also the references cited by Cornwall.) With respect to the UK, Connell (1979, p. 14) argues with regard to his study that 'Overall the analysis reinforces the view that the deterioration in the UK's export performance is not the result of the broad product structure of its export trade, but is related rather to performance within industries.' (See also Stout, 1979, p. 177, for a similar conclusion.) Differences between countries in the value of ε, as estimated by a conventional export demand function, reflect primarily changes in market shares for the reasons noted above, in spite of McGregor and Swales's assertion to the contrary.[22]

Additional empirical evidence is furnished by Table 5.7 which demonstrates that, for the UK, differences in the income elasticities of demand for imports and exports are important even at very fine levels of disaggregation. For example, it may be seen that the UK's income elasticity of demand for foreign motor vehicles is considerably higher than the world's income elasticity for UK motor vehicles (3.7 as opposed to 0.9). Since it is most implausible that this disparity is due to the UK specialising in a sector of the vehicle market for which world demand is growing relatively slowly, it is difficult to see what else could be responsible other than the impact of non-price competitiveness. Indeed, this argument applies equally to all the industries reported in Table 5.7.

Table 5.7 Industries with a money income elasticity of demand for imports greater than two, and export elasticities of the same commodities, 1963–74

1958 MLH		UK income elasticity of demand for imports	World income elasticity of demand for UK exports
381	Motor vehicles	3.7	0.9
492	Linoleum, leather cloth etc.	3.5	1.2
442	Men's and boys' tailored outerwear	3.2	1.7
364	Radio and other electronic apparatus	2.9	1.8
395	Cans and metal boxes	2.8	0.6
382	Motor cycles	2.7	0.9
496	Plastics moulding and fabricating	2.6	1.7
365	Domestic electric appliances	2.6	1.1
362	Insulated wires and cables	2.6	1.0
313	Iron castings etc.	2.6	1.3
472	Furniture and upholstery	2.5	2.2
240	Tobacco	2.5	1.1
473	Bedding etc.	2.4	0.6
444	Overalls and men's shirts, underwear etc.	2.4	2.0
429	Other textile industries	2.4	1.1
272	Pharmaceutical and toilet preparations	2.3	1.4
443	Women's and girls' tailored outerwear	2.3	1.1
441	Weatherproof outerwear	2.3	0.7
499	Miscellaneous manufacturing industries	2.3	1.8
399	Metal industries not elsewhere specified	2.2	1.2
482	Cardboard boxes etc.	2.2	1.3
445	Dresses, lingerie, infants' wear etc.	2.2	1.3
363	Telegraph and telephone apparatus	2.2	1.0
411	Production of man-made fibres	2.1	1.3
339	Other drink industries	2.1	1.0
463	Glass	2.1	1.2
394	Wire and wire manufactures	2.1	0.9
495	Miscellaneous stationers' goods	2.1	1.1
213	Biscuits	2.1	1.3
369	Other electrical goods	2.1	1.3

Source: Thirlwall (1978, p. 31).

The reason for the error made by McGregor and Swales becomes apparent once it is remembered that $\widetilde{\varepsilon} = \sum_i v_i \widetilde{\varepsilon}_i$. As was noted above, $\widetilde{\varepsilon}_i$ is the world income elasticity of demand for the total world market of industry i (i.e. $\widetilde{\varepsilon}_i = (dQ_i/dZ)(Z/Q_i)$) and its value is the same regardless of which country is being considered. Consequently, $\widetilde{\varepsilon}$ can only differ between countries to the extent that the commodity mix of exports (reflected in the values of the v_is) varies. In the case of the income elasticity of demand for exports, $\varepsilon = \sum_i v_i \varepsilon_i$, both v_i and ε_i are free to vary between countries. But the evidence cited above suggests that international differences in the aggregate income elasticity of demand for exports are nearly entirely due to differences between countries in ε_i while any disparities in the commodity mix have little effect.

The whole issue as to how successfully the estimate of ε captures changes in market shares is essentially an empirical one and it is not a question of 'imposing', *a priori*, a relationship such as $s = cq$ as McGregor and Swales (1986, p. 1269) assert.

If the export demand functions estimated by Houthakker and Magee (1969) were not implicitly capturing those changes in exports due to changes in market shares, then only poor statistical fits and estimated values of ε that were approximately the same for each country would be expected. In fact, the R^2 values are over 0.9 and the estimates of ε are well determined with low standard errors. Indeed, the very fact that Thirlwall's law does explain the observed growth rates of the majority of the countries in his sample provides additional evidence that the model is capturing changes in market shares.

McGregor and Swales are, of course, correct that, if world markets are static, our analysis suggests that there will be no change in market shares held by individual countries. But, as Connell (1979) points out, the loss of the UK's overseas markets is indeed relatively less when the world economy moves into recession.

Of greater importance, though, is the more general point that whereas it is very easy to express an export demand function, as McGregor and Swales do, in the general form $X = f(N_d, N_f, Z)$ (where N_d and N_f represent the levels of domestic and foreign non-price competition), it is far more difficult to specify it in a form suitable for estimation. The interpretation of differences between countries in the values of ε as, for example, estimated by Houthakker and Magee as capturing the effects of N_d and N_f is a useful beginning.

Thirlwall's Law and the Dynamic Harrod Foreign Trade Multiplier

Finally, McGregor and Swales argue that, even if all the arguments are granted and the effects of non-price competition are incorporated into the observed values of the income elasticities, the simple rule $y = x/\pi$ cannot be interpreted as reflecting the foreign trade multiplier because the values of x and π are determined by supply side considerations. The rule 'should be regarded as a side relation of an essentially supply side model of national growth which Thirlwall has failed to specify even in the most general terms' (1986, p. 1270). Here, they simply fail to make the important distinction between, on the one hand, growth being determined by the supply side through the exogenous growth of factor inputs and, on the other, the important role that supply characteristics (reflected in the non-price aspects of competition) play in the growth of income through their effect on the growth of demand for exports and imports. These supply characteristics are determined by, *inter alia*, the innovative ability and adaptive capacity of a country's manufacturers in the field of product development. In our model, it is assumed that there is no long-run supply constraint which is why factor supply functions are not included. Nevertheless, it has always been an important and integral part of this explanation that differences in the non-price characteristics of goods are crucial in determining the growth of exports and imports for any given growth of the income of the rest of the world and of the country under consideration. But while ε and π reflect these supply characteristics, the import and export demand functions are precisely what their name implies – demand functions. This is stated quite explicitly by Houthakker and Magee (1969, p. 111): 'The main purpose of this paper is to estimate *demand* elasticities for both imports and exports with respect to income (or more precisely GNP in constant prices) and price . . . for a number of countries . . .' (emphasis added).

Although the interpretation of the rule $y = x/\pi$ as reflecting the dynamic Harrod foreign trade multiplier is well-known, it is useful to recapitulate briefly the argument.

For expositional ease, it is assumed, following Harrod, that there is no saving, investment or government sector. Trade is initially balanced.

This simple economy may be expressed by the equations:

$$Y = C + X - M \tag{5.62}$$

$$M = \mu Y \tag{5.63}$$

$$X = M \tag{5.64}$$

where Y, C, X and M denote the values of income, consumption, exports and imports, μ is the marginal (and the average) propensity to import. (It will be recalled that we use μ rather than the traditional notation of m because we have reserved the use of the latter for the growth of imports.)

It is assumed that all consumption is induced and so the level of income is determined by the autonomous component of demand, namely, exports. Consequently:

$$Y = (1/\mu)X \qquad (5.65)$$

where $1/\mu$ is the foreign trade multiplier.

From equation (5.65) it follows that an increase in exports will induce an increase in income of:

$$\Delta Y = (1/\mu)\Delta X \qquad (5.66)$$

An increase in income of ΔY, from equation (5.63) induces an increase in imports equal to ΔX, i.e.:

$$\Delta M = \mu\Delta Y = \Delta X \qquad (5.67)$$

Thus, the foreign trade multiplier increases income by an amount sufficient to restore the balance of payments to equilibrium.

The growth of income may be determined from equation (5.66) and is:

$$\Delta Y/Y = (1/\mu)(X/Y)(\Delta X/X) \qquad (5.68)$$

Since $1/\mu = \Delta Y/\Delta X$, $X = M$ and $\Delta X = \Delta M$, it follows that $(1/\mu)(X/Y)$ is equal to $(\Delta Y/\Delta M)(M/Y)$, which is the reciprocal of the income elasticity of demand for imports, $1/\pi$. Hence, equation (5.68) may be expressed equivalently as:

$$y = x/\pi \qquad (5.69)$$

All this is familiar and may be extended to more complicated economies which include savings, taxation, etc. (Thirlwall, 1982a).

It should be noted that the import function given by equation (5.63), *viz*, $M = \mu Y$, is linear. This is best interpreted as a short-run import demand function, and the power import demand function ($M = hY^{\pi}$, where h is a constant) as a long-run relationship. It will be recalled that it is the power function which is used in the determination of the law. The long-run function is thus derived from the

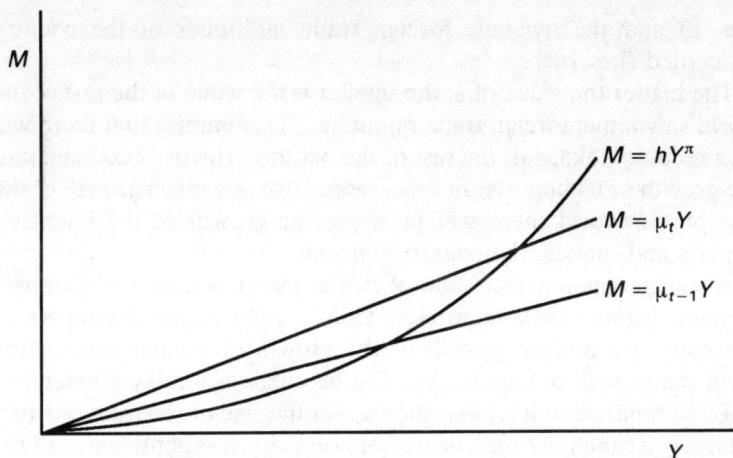

Figure 5.3   The short-run and long-run import demand functions.

short-run linear function, as the slope of the latter changes over time (see Figure 5.3). This change may be regarded as being partly determined by the country's non-price competitiveness. The distinction between the short-run and long-run import demand function reconciles the fact that while the income elasticity of demand for imports derived from $M = \mu Y$ is unity, the value of π derived from the estimation of the power function generally exceeds unity, as may be seen from Table 5.4. The former elasticity may be interpreted as a short-run elasticity and the latter as a long-run elasticity. (In the case where the linear import demand function includes autonomous imports, its shift will be due to changes in either autonomous imports or in the slope, or in both. The short-run income elasticity of demand for imports will be less than or greater than unity depending on whether autonomous imports are positive or negative.)

The export demand function of a particular country is identical to the rest of the world's import demand function. This is because, of course, the country's exports are definitionally equal to the imports of the rest of the world. Thus, the income elasticity of demand for the country's exports will be equal to the rest of the world's dynamic foreign trade multiplier.

Let us consider the law again in the form $y_B = \varepsilon z / \pi$. It may be seen that the equilibrium growth rate is a function of the product of the reciprocal of the rest of the world's dynamic foreign trade multiplier (i.e. ε) and the dynamic foreign trade multiplier of the country concerned (i.e. 1/π).

The higher the value of ε, the smaller is the value of the rest of the world's dynamic foreign trade multiplier. This implies that there will be a greater leakage of the rest of the world's growth of demand into the growth of its imports. In other words, for any given growth of the rest of the world there will be a greater growth of the country's exports and, hence, the country's income.

Also, the smaller the value of π, the larger will be the country's dynamic foreign trade multiplier. Thus, it follows that the impact on the country's income growth of the growth of demand emanating from the growth of exports will also be commensurably greater.

To summarise: it has been shown that the size of the ratio of ε to π is largely a function of the degree of non-price competitiveness of the country *vis-à-vis* the rest of the world. Although the value of this ratio ultimately reflects supply characteristics (and an improvement in, for example, the quality of a country's products will have the effect of increasing this ratio and hence y_B, *ceteris paribus*), ε and π are still demand parameters. Growth is not determined by indigenous factor supplies growing independently of demand and by the autonomous rate of technical progress, as in the neoclassical model.

THE DEBATE CONTINUED: A REJOINDER FROM McCOMBIE[23]

McGregor and Swales (1991) subsequently criticised for a third time the argument that the long-run growth of most of the advanced countries is balance-of-payments constrained. In particular, they address criticisms of their arguments that were made by McCombie (1989) and which were reproduced above. We feel that diminishing returns have set in with respect to the debate and McGregor and Swales's latest critique is not reproduced here. Nevertheless, the new (and some not so new) arguments that McGregor and Swales (1991) advance are briefly discussed below. The discussion is reasonably self-contained, but the interested reader is invited to read McGregor and Swales's (1991) original paper published in *Applied Economics*.

It will be shown that there are no grounds for the 'emphatic' rejection of Thirlwall's Law which they now advocate. It is also demonstrated again that McGregor and Swales are erroneous in their contention which they repeat, notwithstanding the arguments in

McCombie (1989), that the estimated income elasticities of demand for imports and exports cannot logically capture the effects of non-price competition (see the previous section).

McGregor and Swales's (1985, 1986, 1991) critiques of Thirlwall's Law basically rest on three points.

First, if the lack of variation in relative prices reflects the neoclassical 'law of one price' then, as this implies infinite price elasticities, economic growth cannot be balance-of-payments constrained. However, McGregor and Swales (1991) assert that they never subscribed to the law of one price. As neither do the present authors, this criticism of the model is irrelevant.

It is puzzling that McGregor and Swales (1991) should argue that McCombie (1989) simply portrays 'McGregor and Swales (1985) as an attack on this position [that prices are determined oligopolistically] which invokes . . . the neoclassical interpretation of the "law of one price" (McCombie, 1989, p. 612)'.

They further write that:

> McCombie gives quite the wrong impression about the sequence of events and the motives involved in the debate over Thirlwall's Law. His view appears to be that the law is well founded, both empirically and analytically, right from the start. The law was subsequently subject to neoclassical attack from McGregor and Swales which has been successfully fended off. Our interpretation is quite different. (McGregor and Swales, 1991)

With regard to these comments, nowhere in McCombie (1989) is there any speculation on the motives of McGregor and Swales. Motives are irrelevant: what matters is the quality of the arguments. Furthermore, the more I considered the arguments, the more convinced I became of the usefulness of Thirlwall's Law. (It is somewhat strange to be accused of believing in the law 'right from the start' since McCombie (1981b) was the first published criticism of the law! Needless to say, my position has changed since then.) Finally, nowhere in McCombie (1989) is the impression given that McGregor and Swales's criticisms were based *solely* on the law of one price or on the neoclassical model. The neoclassical model and the law of one price were discussed simply because McGregor and Swales (1985) considered them at length in criticising the theoretical rationale of Thirlwall's Law.

Moreover, a few lines below the selective quotation that McGregor and Swales extract from McCombie (1989) is written: 'Finally, it is argued [by McGregor and Swales] that, even if all Thirlwall's arguments are granted, the model still cannot be regarded as either (a) satisfactorily capturing the effects of non-price competition or (b) reflecting the workings of the dynamic foreign trade multiplier.' It is also stated by McCombie (1989, p. 614) that 'by 1986 (p. 1272) the emphasis of McGregor and Swales has altered: "it was not argued that we live in a world where the truth of Equation [5.1, $y = x/\pi$] is to be explained in a neoclassical way."' (From this it must be inferred that they are no longer prepared to defend their lengthy neoclassical analysis of Thirlwall's model.) The main issue is now seen as being empirical rather than analytical.'

As McGregor and Swales had raised the issue of the law of one price (whether they believed in it or not), it still seemed useful to cite evidence which explicitly rebuts this putative 'law'. McGregor and Swales nowhere discuss the empirical evidence on the issue.

McGregor and Swales (1991) argue that they 'were never engaged in attempting to give Thirlwall's law a neoclassical interpretation. We are not predisposed to an extreme neoclassical view of the world, and none of the arguments we invoke here are predicated upon such a vision.' But this contention is very difficult to reconcile with the following:

> The standard neoclassical argument would be that real income growth (y) is determined by supply factors. Again, the income elasticity of demand for imports (π) is constant. The growth of exports (x) is therefore endogenous and is just enough to maintain the current account of the balance-of-payments in balance. That is to say, Equation [5.1] would be more appropriately written as:
>
> $x = \pi y$
>
> It is perhaps useful to outline the short run response of such a neoclassical system to an exogenous shock. (McGregor and Swales, 1985, omitting a footnote and, to avoid confusion, an equation number)

Shortly after this discussion, they argue 'equation [5.1] can be derived from a *plausible* theory of supply constrained growth' (emphasis added). Since the only supply orientated theory McGregor and Swales (1985) discuss was the neoclassical approach, it seemed logical to infer that this was the 'plausible' theory to which they referred.[24] McCombie (1989), as will be apparent from the earlier part of this chapter, critically assessed all of the arguments (both neoclassical and non-neoclassical) of McGregor and Swales and found them wanting.

Secondly, McGregor and Swales (1985) argue that Thirlwall's Law ought to be tested using regression analysis. When this is done, they argue Thirlwall's Law should be rejected. It was demonstrated in McCombie (1989) that this test is mis-specified since, because of one or two outliers, it rejects the hypothesis that economic growth is balance-of-payments constrained for *all* the advanced countries. An alternative test was proposed and, on the basis of this, it was shown that a large majority of advanced countries were, in fact, balance-of-payments constrained. McGregor and Swales (1991) argue that McCombie's test, together with their badly specified regression analysis, leads to an 'emphatic rejection of Thirlwall's Law'. As noted above, we shall examine this conclusion – and show that it is untenable.

Thirdly, throughout McGregor and Swales's (1985, 1986, 1991) various papers, they make what they obviously regard as a telling criticism that even if all Thirlwall's assumptions are granted, the values of the income elasticities of demand for imports and exports cannot *logically* capture changes in market shares. Hence, differences in these elasticities cannot possibly capture the effects of non-price competition. This was mentioned in passing in McGregor and Swales (1985) and was elaborated at greater length in McGregor and Swales (1986) where a mathematical 'proof' was included. In McCombie (1989), it was argued that the question was essentially empirical and evidence was presented to demonstrate that McGregor and Swales were in error on this point. It followed that their proof was also logically flawed and this was demonstrated at some length in McCombie (1989). The empirical evidence is ignored by McGregor and Swales (1991) and the theoretical argument was barely (and misleadingly) examined. It will be shown again that McGregor and Swales are incorrect in what they see as an important criticism of Thirlwall's Law.[25]

To begin with, McGregor and Swales's criticism of the empirical evidence will be considered.

The Evidence

The only empirical evidence McGregor and Swales consider about whether long-term economic growth is balance-of-payments constrained, or determined by the growth of exogenous technical change and the autonomous growth of the labour force in the neo-classical manner, is the statistical tests they impose to determine whether or not there is any difference between y and $y_B = x/\pi$ or $y_B = \varepsilon z/\pi$. Consequently, in this section the examination of their specious arguments will be confined to this point.

As has been noted, McGregor and Swales (1985) argued that a more 'rigorous' test than the use of Spearman's rank correlation coefficient is to regress y on y_B (where $y_B = x/\pi$) using ordinary least squares and to examine whether or not the intercept is significantly different from zero and the regression coefficient significantly different from unity. Since they found that the intercept and the regression coefficient did differ significantly from zero and unity respectively, they argued that this rejected Thirlwall's hypothesis that the countries in the sample could be regarded as balance-of-payments constrained. (They also used x and $\hat{\pi}$ as regressors instead of y_B in a logarithmic specification.)

In McCombie (1989), it was pointed out that there are two problems with this approach.

The first, which McGregor and Swales (1991) accept but do not correct, is that the regression includes an 'extraneous' estimate ($\hat{\pi}$) which has an associated standard error. This information should be included when computing the standard errors of the coefficients in the regression equation; ordinary least squares is not an appropriate or 'rigorous' regression procedure. (The fact that $\hat{\pi}$ is obtained from the two-stage least squares rather than the ordinary least squares procedure does not obviate this criticism as McGregor and Swales (1991) seem to think.)

The second criticism is that it is implicit in McGregor and Swales's approach that either all the sample of the advanced countries are balance-of-payments constrained or none is. They argue that 'even if one accepts that the number of outliers is "small", the existence of *any* outliers is surely problematic for the existence of the law summarized by equation (5.1), since the outliers establish "that the balance-of-payments 'constraint' is not in fact a constraint"' (McGregor and Swales, 1991, p. 11, our emphasis). In other words, they interpret Thirlwall's hypothesis as being that all the advanced countries are simultaneously balance-of-payments constrained. They continue, 'McCombie's view appears to be that since equation [5.1] is so obviously inapplicable to some countries in his chosen data set, it is inappropriate to use observations on these countries to assess the validity of equation [5.1]! The law is clearly not intended to apply universally, but only selectively.' But it is obvious that, for the world as a whole, growth *cannot* be balance-of-payments constrained and, consequently, *all* countries cannot be balance-of-payments constrained at the same time. The law logically cannot apply 'universally'.[26] This point seems to have escaped McGregor and Swales completely, at least on the evidence of the above quotation. Of course, it is theoretically possible that all the advanced countries could be balance-of-payments constrained if some Third World countries were not. However, given that a large majority of world trade is between the advanced countries, it would be most surprising if some of the advanced countries were not, in fact, balance-of-payments constrained. McGregor and Swales do appear to concede this possibility when subsequently they add the qualification that 'the notion that a theory is applicable only to a select group of countries is, of course, defensible provided the conditions under which the theory is intended to apply are clear *ex ante*'. So now they seem to agree that the theory, after all, can apply selectively![27]

Thirlwall (1979) himself was careful to note the possibility that not all countries are balance-of-payments constrained:

> While a country cannot grow faster than its balance-of-payments equilibrium growth rate for very long, unless it can finance an ever-growing deficit, there is little to stop a country growing slower and accumulating large surpluses. This may particularly occur where the balance-of-payments equilibrium growth rate is so high that a country does not have the physical capacity to grow at that rate.

And again:

> Japan is a striking example of a country where the gap between its actual growth rate and its balance-of-payments equilibrium growth rate has resulted in the build up of a huge payments surplus. Presumably Japan could not grew faster than it did because of an ultimate capacity ceiling. (Thirlwall, 1979)

However, this last quotation certainly does not mean that we are back in a neoclassical world. While there was a rapid growth of demand for Japanese goods in world markets, there was a maximum rate at which these goods could be produced. There undoubtedly was a limit to the speed of the intersectoral mobility of labour, especially from agriculture to manufacturing, and to the rate of production of the capital goods industry. It should be remembered that for much of the pre-1973 postwar period Japan's growth of GDP was near 9 per cent per annum and the growth of the manufacturing sector was even faster. This is not, of course, to argue that Japan's growth was determined by the exogenous growth of both the labour force and the rate of technical progress, as in the neoclassical schema.

It is useful to describe such countries in Japan's position as 're-source constrained'. Other countries, however, may be 'policy constrained'; that is to say, for policy reasons such as the putative combating of inflation, the economy may be run at a rate of growth below its balance-of-payments equilibrium growth rate. An important implication of this approach is that the growth of the balance-of-payments constrained countries is thus limited by the growth of the resource or policy constrained countries through trade interlinkages. (See Chapter 7.)

It should be recalled that it is only McGregor and Swales who claim that the law must be specified in the form of a regression equation. In view of McGregor and Swales's (1991) sentiments noted above, it is surprising to find that, in their own regression analyses, 'separate regressions were performed where data from Japan and the US were removed. Data from Japan were excluded on the grounds that Japan's growth is likely to have been supply constrained. Data on the US were excluded as the US had a persistent balance-of-payments deficit on current account in this period' (McGregor and Swales, 1985, p. 23, footnote 7). That is to say, after excluding two countries they suspect may not have been balance-of-payments constrained, McGregor and Swales proceed to test whether or not this is true for the remaining countries in their sample. This procedure is hardly consistent with their position cited above, although perhaps they would argue that these countries were omitted for reasons *ex ante* rather than *ex post*! But in that case, why include Japan and the US in the first place? They found that when this procedure was undertaken for the period 1951–73, the law was not refuted. This result was dismissed in favour of the result using data for 1953–76 where the law was still invalidated. (We shall show below that when a more appropriate regression specification is used the law is not refuted for 1951–73, even though Japan and the US are included in the sample. For 1953–76 data, it was found that, when Japan is excluded, the hypothesis is not refuted.) It seems that McGregor and Swales are ambivalent, to say the least, about whether or not the outliers (or outlier) in the regression analyses are responsible for refuting the law.

It is because certain countries may not be balance-of-payments constrained that an alternative test examined Thirlwall's hypothesis for each country *individually*, rather than by the use of regression analysis. This test was simply that the hypothetical value of π is calculated from the equation $y_B = x/\pi$ that makes $y = y_B$. The hypothesis to be tested is whether or not the actual and the hypothetical values of π are equal. If they are, this would not refute Thirlwall's hypothesis. Over the postwar boom of 1951–73, it was found that there was no significant difference between the two values of π for 11 out of the 15 advanced countries. It was therefore concluded that for the vast majority of the advanced countries the law holds. McGregor and Swales (1991) 'maintain that these results do not support Thirlwall's Law', to which presumably should be added the rider 'except in 75 per cent of the cases'! Furthermore, Bairam's (1988) data show that for the period 1970–85 only two of the 14 advanced countries in his sample fail the test (see McGregor and Swales, 1991).

McGregor and Swales (1991) repeat the exercise for the advanced countries for 1953–76. However, this is a less appropriate test of the law, because the terminal year includes an exceptionally severe recession. Since the law is based on a theory of long-run economic growth, the inclusion of the final years of a period which is a deep recession is highly dubious. The usual procedure is to take years that are peaks in economic activity with roughly the same level of capacity utilisation at the initial and terminal years. (In practice, it does not make very much difference to the results McGregor and Swales obtain.) Related to this is the fact that McGregor and Swales point out that in McCombie (1985a) the hypothesis is refuted in five out of the six large advanced countries[28] over the period 1973–80, but Bairam (1988) and Bairam and Dempster (1991), using longer time periods (1970–85, except for Japan, which is 1961–85) and contemporaneous estimates of the income elasticity of demand for exports, find that the law holds for five of these six countries. (The exception is Italy.)

Since differences in the income elasticities reflect non-price competitiveness, it is to be expected that they would change over time as a country's non-price competitiveness changes, although this is likely to be a slow process. (This is one reason why Landesmann and Snell's (1989) paper, which finds an increase in the income elasticity of demand for UK exports after the early 1980s, is interesting. Landesmann and Snell argue that this reflects an increase in the UK's non-price competitiveness.) Consequently, Houthakker and Magee's (1969) estimates are likely to become less relevant as the more recent sample period progressively departs from their sample period which was 1951–66, *pace* McGregor and Swales.

McGregor and Swales (1991, tables 4 and 5) cite some additional results from Thirlwall and Hussein (1982) and Bairam (1988) which include the less developed countries or different periods, or both. Again, a large majority of the results (28 out of 38) confirm the law. Further evidence is supplied by Bairam and Dempster (1991). They find that Thirlwall's hypothesis is not refuted in *all* the eleven Asian countries considered. Bairam (in Bairam and Dempster, 1991) also now agrees that McCombie's test is more applicable than McGregor and Swales's regression analysis for the reasons advanced by McCombie (1989). Therefore, Bairam would presumably also argue that McGregor and Swales's (1991, equations 5a and 5b) re-working of his regression results to incorporate an intercept is of dubious validity. (These new regression results of McGregor and Swales will be discussed further below.)

McGregor and Swales's Suppression of the Price Term

In McCombie (1989), it was argued that the estimate of π should be taken from the regression where the price term is included, whether or not its coefficient is significant. The reason was that 'to use the estimates of the income elasticities of demand from the specification where the relative price term is omitted is to accept, either *a priori* or *a posteriori*, Thirlwall's contention that relative prices have had no significance on trade flows.' Williamson (1984) remarked that the *ex post* values of x already include the effect of price changes (if any). Hence, a more appropriate test is to use $y_B = \varepsilon z / \pi$. While nothing can be done about x in the expression $y_B = x / \pi$, it is desirable not to exclude the effect of prices from the estimate of π. Unfortunately, it is not possible to calculate the standard error of $\hat{\varepsilon} / \hat{\pi}$ and hence subject the specification $y_B = \varepsilon z / \pi$ to a comparable statistical test.

With regard to the price term, McGregor and Swales (1991) offer the curious argument that 'in so far as relative prices do in fact exert a statistically significant impact on trade flows, this would appear to raise doubts about the validity of Thirlwall's Law'. Related to this, they argue subsequently that 'the problem here is that both Thirlwall and McCombie interpret Thirlwall's Law as implying that prices measured in a common currency do not vary. Therefore, as argued earlier, evidence that trade has been affected by changes in relative prices is evidence against Thirlwall's Law in general, rather than any one theory concerning the causal mechanism underpinning the Law' (McGregor and Swales, 1991). They seem here to propose yet another test of Thirlwall's Law; if either of the price elasticities is significant in the estimated export and import demand equations then Thirlwall's Law is refuted. For example, referring to the sample of the advanced countries, they point out that 'the price variable is significant in the import demand functions for six countries in this sample and in the export demand functions for ten countries. In total, the assumption that relative prices play an insignificant role in trade flows seems, on this evidence, to be inadmissable in 12 out of the 15 cases' (McGregor and Swales, 1991). And again in referring to Bairam's study: 'Relative prices exerted a statistically significant effect in the import functions of 17 of the countries and in the export functions of three of the countries. The sample contained only two countries (Austria and Portugal) for which relative prices exerted no effect on trade flows, so that again there is a strong *prima facie* case against Thirlwall's Law.'

But McGregor and Swales have totally misread Bairam's (1988) results. All, except four, of Bairam's 38 price elasticities are statistically *insignificant*, but even two of the four exceptions take the *wrong sign*! (Bairam, 1988, Appendix A and Appendix B). Moreover, Bairam (1988) explicitly drew attention to this, noting that 'the estimated price elasticities of exports (η), although generally they have the correct sign (negative), they are not large, and what is more, in most equations reported they are not statistically significant'. (In fact, only Austria has a statistically significant coefficient of the price term that takes the right sign. Portugal is the other country with a statistically significant price elasticity but it has the wrong sign.) Bairam further comments on the same page that, with respect to imports, 'the estimated price elasticities (ψ) are insignificant and/or have the wrong sign (negative). Thus, the estimated import equations also imply [in addition to the export equations] that the price elasticity is small relative to income elasticity for the countries under consideration in this study.' (The only country with a statistically significant import price elasticity that takes the right sign is Spain.) These results are contrary to the position as stated by McGregor and Swales. In terms of their own argument, presumably McGregor and Swales would now assert that these results present a strong *prima facie* case *in favour* of Thirlwall's Law.

The crucial point, however, is not whether or not the coefficients of the relative price terms are significant but whether or not the impact of changes in relative prices on trade flows is *quantitatively* important in the long run. McGregor and Swales seem take the curious position that for a variable to be relatively unimportant its coefficient must be statistically insignificant! They have overlooked, for example, the point that the price elasticities may be highly significant but that if they sum to unity, changes in relative prices will have no impact on the balance-of-payments. They also ignore the point that the price elasticities could be both large and statistically significant but that there will be little effect on trade flows if relative prices do not change very much in the medium to long run. The statistical significance or otherwise of the price term is not the crucial issue.

It is thus somewhat strange to be accused by McGregor and Swales of interpreting Thirlwall's Law in general as 'implying that prices in a common currency do not vary'. Nowhere is such an extreme assumption made. In McCombie (1989) it was explicitly stated that 'in the post-war period, changes in relative prices (expressed in a common currency) have played a *quantitatively* small role in determining the growth of a country's trade especially when compared with the impact of the differences in the non-price aspects of competition' (emphasis added).[29] In fact, nowhere is it argued that a depreciation has *no* effect on the balance-of-payments in the short run; what is denied is that in the long run it is feasible for a country to have a continuously depreciating currency that enables it to raise its trend rate of growth. The whole point of the citation in McCombie (1989) of the study of Fetherston, Moore and Rhodes (1977) was to show that, on plausible assumptions about the size of cost elasticities (i.e., values that are comparable to the estimates of price elasticities surveyed in Stern, Francis and Schumacher (1976)) where changes in relative unit costs can, to some extent, explain changes in market shares, they seem do so perversely. This is sometimes known as the 'Kaldor Paradox' after Kaldor (1978c). The paradox is that those countries with the greatest relative improvement in price competitiveness also experienced the greatest losses in their world market shares. Moreover, the converse was also found: *viz* those countries that experienced the greatest deterioration in their price competitiveness nevertheless experienced the largest increase in their world market share. The explanation is that there were consequently strong offsetting trends in the growth of export shares that can only be ascribed to the effect of non-price factors.

As a result of an examination of bilateral trade flows and changes in competitiveness, Kaldor (1978c) argued:

> The general picture which emerges from a study of the trade record of the last five or six years is that the comparative export perform- ance of the main industrialised countries remained remarkably imper- vious to very large changes in effective exchange rates. The surplus countries tended to remain in surplus and the deficit countries to remain in deficit in much the same way as in the 1960s, when the complications caused by the fivefold increase in oil prices and their different impact on different countries are allowed. The important thing is that Britain and America, who seemed to be losing out to the new industrial giants, Germany and Japan, continued to do so after the real exchange rates between them underwent drastic alterations.

McGregor and Swales are nevertheless content to suppress the price term which means that a further four countries in the sample of advanced countries over the period 1951–73 no longer pass the test. McGregor and Swales adopt a curiously inconsistent position. They believe that for these four countries relative prices are 'genuinely irrelevant', yet at the same time contend, somewhat in contradiction, that, when McCombie's test is undertaken with this assumption, Thirlwall's Law is refuted. Since it was never asserted in McCombie (1989) that relative prices are 'genuinely irrelevant', there are no grounds for suppressing the price term. Given though that McGregor and Swales do concede that in these cases relative prices are insig- nificant, the question arises how to account for the discrepancy between y and y_B, as, by definition, this cannot be due to the impact of price competition. One plausible explanation is that the income elasticities are only imperfectly capturing the effects of non-price competition, but this does not refute the argument about growth being balance-of-payments constrained. We shall return to this point below.

It is ironical that a large part of McGregor and Swales 'emphatic' rejection of Thirlwall's Law depends crucially on whether or not a statistically insignificant price term is excluded from the import and export demand functions. The exclusion of this term, by their own implicit admission, is tantamount to assuming Thirlwall's Law in the first place.[30]

McGregor and Swales's Regression Analysis Revisited

It has been argued above that, because of the inclusion of one or two outliers, McGregor and Swales's test is not appropriate. McGregor and Swales (1991), nevertheless, maintain that 'we still believe that the cross-sectional analysis performed after appropriate recognition of stochastic regressors is the optimal approach'. They repeat their regression analysis using Bairam's (1988) data for 17 European countries together with Canada and the United States for the period 1970–85. They further assert that 'Bairam's estimation method should minimize the impact of what we consider to be the only legitimate criticism of our earlier work made in McCombie (1989)' (McGregor and Swales, 1991). Bairam's method of two-stage least squares does not, however, obviate the criticism since the estimated income elasticities still have (sometimes large) associated standard errors and McGregor and Swales's estimating procedure once again ignores this fact. They obtained the following results using ordinary least squares:

$$y = 1.76 + 0.64y_{B1} \qquad\qquad r^2 = 0.58$$
$$\quad\; (5.48) \quad (4.84)$$

$$y = 1.75 + 0.49y_{B2} \qquad\qquad r^2 = 0.64$$
$$\quad\; (6.17) \quad (5.55)$$

where $y_{B1} = \varepsilon z/\pi$ and $y_{B2} = x/\pi$. The figures in parentheses are the t-statistics.

The coefficient of y_{B1} takes a value of 0.73 which is not significantly different from unity at the 95 per cent confidence level. McGregor and Swales, however, discount this result because Bairam (1988) expressed doubts as to the reliability of the estimate of y_{B1} for some of the countries. (They are clearly prepared to reject the implications of a regression result because of outliers when it suits them!) They also claim that y_{B2} is the usual specification of the law. Great importance is attached to the fact that even when the three countries that fail McCombie's alternative test (i.e. those countries which cannot be said to be conclusively balance-of-payments constrained) are omitted, the 'remaining observations reject Thirlwall's Law' (McGregor and Swales, 1991). This may seem somewhat surprising until it is remembered that just because a country fails McCombie's test, this does not necessarily mean that it is an outlier in McGregor and

Swales's regression results and vice versa. For example, the standard error of $\hat{\pi}$ may be so large that the country does not fail McCombie's test in spite of the substantial difference between y and y_{B2}. However, since y_{B2} for this country is included as an observation in McGregor and Swales's regression, it may prove to be an outlier, especially as no information on the size of its associated standard error is included. This demonstrates once again the inappropriateness of McGregor and Swales's procedure.

Since McGregor and Swales seem to attach particular importance to these results, it is useful to consider their approach in further detail, while being sceptical of the whole exercise for the reasons set out above.

Because the regression analysis is used merely as a test of association, rather than with any assumption of causality, it would seem to be purely arbitrary whether y or y_{B1} (y_{B2}) is chosen as the regressor. (McGregor and Swales, as we have seen, choose y_{B1} and y_{B2}.) However, given that y_{B1} is calculated using estimated parameters ($\hat{\varepsilon}$ and $\hat{\pi}$) and hence is subject to errors, and to the extent that this poses an errors in variables problem, McGregor and Swales's estimate of the slope coefficient will be biased. (A further measurement error is introduced into y_{B1} by using the growth of world income for z, instead of the growth of an index of the income of each country's trading partners weighted by the appropriate trade shares.) A better procedure is to regress y_B on y, which, in the usual errors in variables context, is known as 'inverse least squares'. In the case under consideration here, if there were no measurement problems in the construction of y_B there would be no reason for preferring either y_B or y as the regressor.

The results, using Bairam's data, are:

$$y_{B1} = -0.657 + 0.907y \qquad \bar{r}^2 = 0.554$$
$$\phantom{y_{B1} = } (-1.07) \quad (4.84) \qquad |t'| = 0.50*$$

$$y_{B2} = -1.249 + 1.303y \qquad \bar{r}^2 = 0.623$$
$$\phantom{y_{B2} = } (-1.62) \quad (5.55) \qquad |t'| = 1.29*$$

$|t'|$ is the absolute value of the t-statistic based on the null hypothesis that the slope coefficient is unity. The superscript * denotes that this hypothesis cannot be rejected at the 95 per cent confidence level. The figures in parentheses are the usual t-statistics.

It can be seen that in neither case is Thirlwall's Law rejected at the 95 per cent confidence level, *pace* McGregor and Swales. In both equations, it may be seen from the *t*-statistics that, individually, the intercept is not statistically significantly different from zero and the slope coefficient different from unity at this confidence level. Bairam's data do not refute the law, let alone refute it 'categorically'. (Removing the three countries that are not balance-of-payments constrained under McCombie's test does not alter the conclusions. In both regressions, the intercepts and slope coefficients are again individually not significantly different from zero and unity, respectively, at the 95 per cent confidence levels.)[31]

For completeness, we repeated the analysis using the growth rates for the advanced countries over the earlier period from 1951 to 1973. The estimates of the income elasticities of demand for exports and imports are from Houthakker and Magee (1969, tables 1 and 8) and are taken from those regression equations which included the price term and were corrected, where appropriate, for autocorrelation. The following results were obtained for the full sample of advanced countries and for $y_{B1} = \varepsilon z/\pi$:

$$y_{B1} = -1.468 + 1.324y \qquad \bar{r}^2 = 0.624$$
$$\quad (-1.09) \quad (4.92) \qquad |t'| = 1.20^*$$

It can be seen from an inspection of the *t*-statistics that the intercept does not differ from zero and the slope coefficient does not differ from unity at the 95 per cent confidence level. Hence, Thirlwall's Law cannot be said to be refuted by the data.[32]

McGregor and Swales (1985) preferred to use the balance-of-payments equilibrium growth rate defined as $y_{B2} = x/\pi$ in their regression analyses. They regressed y on y_{B2} using data for two periods, namely, 1951–73 and 1953–76. For the first period, they found that Thirlwall's Law was rejected using the full sample of advanced countries, but that this was not the case if Japan and the United States were omitted from the sample. (In fact, when McGregor and Swales's regressions were replicated, it transpired that dropping Japan alone is sufficient to ensure that the law is not refuted at the 95 per cent confidence level. For some reason, McGregor and Swales (1985) omitted to report this.)

The preferable specification gives the following result for 1951–73 using the full sample:

$$y_{B2} = -1.175 + 1.406y \qquad \bar{r}^2 = 0.841$$
$$\quad (-1.44) \quad (8.66) \qquad |t'| = 2.50^{**}$$

where the ** superscript denotes that the hypothesis that the slope coefficient equals unity cannot be rejected at the 99 per cent confidence level.

Once again it can be seen that Thirlwall's Law cannot be categorically rejected. The slope coefficient is significantly different from unity at the 95 per cent, but not at the 99 per cent, confidence level. However, if Japan is omitted, the following result is obtained:

$$y_{B2} = \begin{matrix} -0.173 \\ (-0.11) \end{matrix} + \begin{matrix} 1.176y \\ (3.41) \end{matrix} \qquad \begin{matrix} \bar{r}^2 = 0.449 \\ |t'| = 0.51^* \end{matrix}$$

The slope coefficient is now not significantly greater than unity at the 95 per cent confidence level, although there are problems in precisely interpreting the values of the t-statistics. Hence, Thirlwall's law cannot be said to be refuted. (The data and sample used here differ slightly from those used by McGregor and Swales. The income elasticity of demand for imports for several countries used by McGregor and Swales are from Houthakker and Magee's (1969) regressions where the price term has been omitted. Nevertheless, the use of identical data and the same sample of countries employed by McGregor and Swales does not significantly alter the results.)

McGregor and Swales (1985) also found that Thirlwall's Law was refuted for the period 1953–76 for the full sample and where both Japan and the United States were omitted. Although, as noted above, there are serious reservations about the choice of 1976 as the terminal year, the regression was repeated using the preferable specification. The law is still refuted at the 95 per cent confidence level with the full sample, but when Japan is omitted the following result is obtained:

$$y_{B2} = \begin{matrix} 0.151 \\ (0.12) \end{matrix} + \begin{matrix} 1.179y \\ (3.89) \end{matrix} \qquad \begin{matrix} \bar{r}^2 = 0.521 \\ |t'| = 0.59^* \end{matrix}$$

Hence, unlike in McGregor and Swales's case, Thirlwall's Law is not refuted. This conclusion is not altered if the United States is also omitted from the sample. (Once again, it makes no difference which data set is used.)

To conclude, it is difficult to see how the regression results 'emphatically' reject Thirlwall's Law, at least in the sense that the word is commonly understood.

Income Elasticities of Demand for Imports and Exports and Non-Price Competitiveness

It is strange that McGregor and Swales (1991) should still feel it necessary to ask:

> Does Thirlwall . . . believe that international variations in income elasticities of demand for imports and exports are the result of differences in the composition of exports and imports or non-price competitive elements or some combination of the two?

It is difficult to see how Thirlwall could answer the question more emphatically than by restating his position that is already explicit in his writings on the subject. The response to their question was given unambiguously by Thirlwall (1986b) as 'it is precisely these non-price factors that are captured in the income elasticity of demand for exports'. My own position is summarised in McCombie (1989) as: 'The estimated values of ε and π show considerable variation between countries and this reflects differences in the various aspects of non-price competition.'

McGregor and Swales cite McCombie (1985a) where, in the discussion of income elasticities of demand for *imports*, it was argued that, in particular, Japan's low income elasticity of demand reflected primarily its high import content of primary products. These commodities typically have a relatively low income elasticity of demand.

It should be noted, however, that it is differences in the income elasticities of demand for *exports* that are the more crucial factors explaining differences in y_B. The elasticities of demand for imports show much less variation. Nevertheless, differences in the income elasticity of demand for the import of *manufactured* goods also reflect disparities in non-price competitiveness. Panić (1975), for example, has examined the differences in the income elasticities of demand for imports for the UK, France, and West Germany. His estimates of the income elasticities of total imports were 1.82 (UK), 1.63 (France), and 1.31 (West Germany). Most of these differences, he argues, could be accounted for by differences in the income elasticities of demand for manufactured goods. These differences Panić ascribes to 'structural disequilibrium' factors which mainly reflect disparities in non-price competition.

A theme running throughout McGregor and Swales's (1985, 1986, 1991) three critiques is that, even if all Thirlwall's assumptions are accepted, the values of his income elasticities of demand for imports and exports cannot capture non-price competition. Most recently, McGregor and Swales (1991) contend that 'in McGregor and Swales (1986) some considerable time was spent arguing that international differences in income elasticity of demand for exports and imports *must logically* be the result of differences in the composition of exports and imports for different countries' (emphasis added). If this reference is to the differences in the estimated income elasticities from Houthakker and Magee (1969) used by Thirlwall (as it should be), then this is an empirical question and not a logical issue. In McCombie (1989) empirical evidence was presented that showed this not to be the case. Differences between countries in the estimated income elasticities of demand for exports and imports, as conventionally estimated, do *not* solely reflect international differences in composition of exports and imports, *pace* McGegor and Swales. For example, the UK's low income elasticity of demand for exports was not due to its exports being concentrated in the slower growing export categories (i.e. the ones with relatively low income elasticities of demand). The UK performed badly in all export markets. The empirical evidence presented in McCombie (1989) is totally ignored by McGregor and Swales.[33]

Given the importance of this subject, it is worthwhile making the same point another way. Balassa (1979), like McGregor and Swales, was concerned that no variable that *explicitly* took into account differences in the quality of traded goods appeared in Houthakker and Magee's (1969) export demand functions. (Balassa also considers Goldstein and Khan's (1978) estimated income elasticities of demand for exports for a number of advanced countries estimated over the period 1955–70. Reassuringly, these estimates do not differ greatly from those of Houthakker and Magee.) Because of this concern, Balassa calculated a hypothetical or 'apparent' income elasticity of demand for exports for a number of advanced countries. This 'apparent' income elasticity is based on the assumption that each country maintained its share of exports in world markets for various goods (Balassa used 171 commodity categories).[34] By the Balassa method, inter-country differences in the growth of 'hypothetical' exports, reflecting differences in the 'apparent' elasticities, will be solely due to differences in the commodity composition of exports. His results, however, suggest that this factor is not an important determinant of the disparities in the actual elasticities. There is very little correspondence between the actual elasticities (as estimated by both

Table 5.8 Alternative estimates of the income elasticity of demand for exports

Country	Houthakker–Magee (1969) 1951–66	Goldstein–Khan (1978) 1953–70 (i)	(ii)	Balassa's constant-market-share model 1953–71	Competitive gains and losses from Balassa's constant-market-share model 1953–71
US	0.99	1.01	1.01	2.02	−43.4
Canada	1.41	n.a.	n.a.	1.89	+ 3.8
Belgium	1.83[a](1.87)[b]	1.68	1.90	1.98	+14.6
France	1.53	1.69	1.70	2.04	+11.4
Germany	2.08 (0.91)	1.81	2.09	2.27	+48.9
Italy	2.95 (2.68)	1.96	2.21	2.07	+99.0
Netherlands	1.88	1.91	1.92	1.91	+48.6
Austria	1.59	n.a.	n.a.	2.04	+12.4
Denmark	1.69	n.a.	n.a.	1.82	− 3.8
Norway	1.59	n.a.	n.a.	1.82	+22.9
Sweden	1.76 (1.75)	n.a.	n.a.	1.93	+17.4
UK	0.86 (1.00)	0.92	0.90	2.20	−45.9
Japan	3.55	4.23	3.64	2.00	+375.7
Industrial countries	n.a.	n.a.	n.a.	2.07	

Notes: Figures in parentheses are Houthakker and Magee's elasticities derived from estimates adjusted for autocorrelation.
(i) Estimates from an equilibrium model.
(ii) Estimates from a disequilibrium model.
[a]Houthakker and Magee's figure is 1.83 rather than the 1.87 reported by Balassa.
[b]Price term has been excluded from the regression analysis.

Source: Balassa (1979, table 1).

Houthakker and Magee, 1969, and Goldstein and Khan, 1978) and Balassa's 'apparent' elasticities. (See Table 5.8.) A Spearman rank correlation, in fact, gives a negative correlation between the two measures.

Moreover, there is very little difference between the countries in their 'apparent' elasticities, and what international difference initially existed diminished over the period 1953–71. (Balassa calculated the 'apparent' elasticities separately for the subperiods 1953–62 and 1962–71 as well as for 1953–71 as a whole. The international disparities were less for 1962–71 than for 1953–62. The figures are not reported here.) To take an example: the UK's actual income elasticity of demand for exports is 1.00 using Houthakker and Magee's estimates where there has been a correction for autocorrelation. Goldstein and Khan's figures are 0.92 and 0.90 using an equilibrium and disequilibrium model respectively. All these estimates are the lowest of those for the advanced countries considered.[35] However, the UK had an 'apparent' income elasticity of demand that was actually above the average for the advanced countries. Over the period 1953–62, its 'apparent' elasticity was 1.88 (compared with the advanced countries' average of 1.71). For 1962–71, the UK's 'apparent' elasticity was 2.40 and the average of the advanced countries was 2.32. The UK's poor performance was *not* due to its exports being concentrated in the slower growing markets – in fact, quite the opposite. The UK's exports were concentrated in the faster growing markets.

Balassa also calculates the competitive gains and losses in the exports of the various countries. These are defined as the ratio of the difference between actual and hypothetical exports to hypothetical exports calculated using a Laspeyres formula. As may be seen from Table 5.8, the results show, not unexpectedly, that Japan made the largest gain, while the UK experienced the largest loss. These gains and losses provide a measure of the effect of non-price competition since changes in relative prices are assumed by Balassa to be negligible.

Equivalently, we may use the difference between the actual and 'apparent' elasticities as reflecting the degree of non-price competitiveness of a particular country. As Balassa (1979, p. 607) himself puts it: 'It appears, then, that intercountry differences in export competitiveness, which are shown by competitive gains, are reflected by the Houthakker–Magee and Goldstein–Khan estimates of income elasticities of export demand.' Hence, Balassa himself has to conclude that the estimates of Houthakker and Magee and Goldstein and Khan are capturing the effects of quality (and capacity) variables and that these are measured by the difference between the actual and 'apparent' elasticities or by the degree of bias, as Balassa terms it.

In McCombie (1989), a detailed analysis was given of McGregor and Swales's attempt theoretically to square the empirical circle, i.e. to prove logically that Houthakker and Magee's estimates of the income elasticities of demand do not capture empirically changes in market shares. The problem as McGregor and Swales (1986, p. 1267) saw it was that:

non-price competitive elements should be included, either directly or indirectly, in the export and import demand functions. In his reply, Thirlwall argues that they are. He maintains that they are captured by the relevant [Houthakker and Magee] income elasticities of demand. This argument is unacceptable. The income elasticity of demand will determine the growth of the market for a country's exports and imports, but not changes in the share of that market which the country's exports and imports will take. In this model, changes in market share are determined by non-price competition; but this change in market shares is not allowed in Thirlwall's formulation.

McGregor and Swales refute neither the criticism of their reasoning by McCombie (1989, and equations (5.48) to (5.61) above) nor the conclusion that 'they are simply wrong'. (Moreover, their reasoning was not merely dismissed as flawed on the grounds, as McGregor and Swales (1991) appear to suggest, that the Houthakker and Magee demand equations were empirically well-determined.) Instead of addressing these issues directly, McGregor and Swales (1991) argue that:

The issue appears to be this. Imagine a demand function for the exports of industry i (X_i):

$$X_i = f(Z, NP_i)$$

where Z represents world income and NP_i represents the country's relative non-price competitiveness in industry i.

As we understand it, McCombie's income elasticities (ε_i and $\widetilde{\varepsilon}_i$) are defined as:

$$\widetilde{\varepsilon}_i = (\partial X_i/\partial Z)(Z/X_i)$$

$$\varepsilon_i = [(\partial X_i/\partial Z) + (\partial X_i/\partial NP_i)(\partial NP_i/\partial Z)](Z/X_i)$$

so that:

$$\varepsilon_i = \widetilde{\varepsilon}_i + (\partial X_i/\partial NP_i)(\partial NP_i/\partial Z)(Z/X_i)$$

$\widetilde{\varepsilon}_i$ is the conventionally defined income elasticity of demand whereas ε_i is not.

A number of points follow from this. The first is that in the context of Thirlwall's Law, the term income elasticity of demand (at least as used in recent accounts) does not have the conventional meaning.

Whilst this might appear pedantic, the whole value of technical terms is their lack of ambiguity. [The equation numbers have been omitted to avoid confusion with the numbering in the text.]

It is surprising and regrettable that McGregor and Swales should misrepresent the definitions of $\tilde{\varepsilon}_i$ and ε_i. It was stated quite unambiguously that '$\tilde{\varepsilon}_i = (dQ_i/dZ)(Z/Q_i)$ and $\varepsilon_i = (dX_i/dZ)(Z/X_i)$' (McCombie, 1989). Q_i is the world market of good i or, alternatively, total expenditures in the world market on this good. ε_i is the income elasticity of demand for exports as the term is conventionally understood and as estimated in export demand functions by Houthakker and Magee (1969), Goldstein and Khan (1978), Panić (1975), and other researchers. In other words, it is the value of the coefficient of the logarithmic value of world income in the log-linear specification of the conventional export demand function. It is also the income elasticity used by Thirlwall. $\tilde{\varepsilon}_i$ is the definition used by McGregor and Swales, which they fail to realise is different from the conventional term, ε, except when market shares do not change. McGregor and Swales (1986) do not make any distinction between the two different definitions of income elasticities. This was the reason they seemed unable to comprehend why the Houthakker and Magee estimates empirically capture changing market shares as was formally demonstrated in McCombie (1989). However, it is useful to put this argument about the reason for McGregor and Swales's misunderstanding somewhat differently.

$\tilde{\varepsilon}_i$ is thus the income elasticity of demand for the total world market of good i, say motor vehicles. The aggregate income elasticity $\tilde{\varepsilon}$ for, say, the UK is defined by McGregor and Swales as equal to $\Sigma \, v_i \, \tilde{\varepsilon}_i$, where v_i is the share of the UK's exports of good i in its total exports, *viz*:

$$\tilde{\varepsilon} \equiv \Sigma \, (X_i/X)[(\partial Q_i /\partial Z)(Z/Q_i)] \qquad (5.70)$$

This is analogous to Balassa's 'apparent' or 'constant-market-share' income elasticity of demand for exports discussed above. The 'apparent' income elasticity of demand for the UK's motor vehicles is assumed to be equal to the income elasticity of demand for the world market of motor vehicles and so as world income grows, the UK will, by definition, maintain its share of the world market of motor vehicles. If there is not much difference in the export shares of the internationally traded goods and services (i.e. in (X_i/X)) between the various countries, as is empirically the case, then there will be very little difference between countries in the values of their 'apparent' aggregate income elasticity of demand for exports, $\tilde{\varepsilon}$. On the other hand, if the UK's composition of exports was concentrated in markets with a low income elasticity then the 'apparent' elasticity will be correspondingly lower than average. (In fact, as we have noted above, the UK's 'apparent' income elasticity of demand for exports in the early postwar period was greater than the average.) McGregor and Swales interpret this constant-market-share elasticity as the definition of the conventional income elasticity of demand. But not even Balassa considers this definition to be the conventional one, as may be seen by his terms 'the "apparent" income elasticity of demand for exports' and 'hypothetical' exports. As was pointed out in McCombie (1989), McGregor and Swales's confusion is most apparent in McGregor and Swales (1985) when they argue that 'the value of ε depends solely on the product composition of a country's exports. If $\varepsilon > 1$, the country will be maintaining its share of markets which generally have a high income elasticity of demand and are therefore growing rapidly relatively to other markets.' If the income elasticity of demand is defined in this way (i.e. as a constant-market-share elasticity) then it is no wonder that it cannot explain changes in market shares. But it is not the same income elasticity as that estimated by Houthakker and Magee (1969) and used by Thirlwall. As has been shown, the latter measure is indeed capturing the changes in market shares. It is only when, empirically, a country is performing in overseas markets at the average rate (i.e., maintaining its market shares) that McGregor and Swales's and Houthakker and Magee's measures coincide. Moreover, as we have also seen, the difference between Thirlwall's (Houthakker and Magee's) estimates of the income elasticity of demand and McGregor and Swales's 'apparent' income elasticity provides an estimate of the effect of a country's non-price competitiveness. McGregor and Swales implicitly and erroneously argue, in the quotation cited immediately above, that $\tilde{\varepsilon}$ is the definition of Thirlwall's (Houthakker and Magee's) income elasticity of demand.

We may illustrate the argument with two examples. Balassa's 'apparent' elasticity of, for example, Japan was 2.00 (see Table 5.8). Over the period 1951 to 1973, world income grew at 4.4 per cent per annum. Consequently, the hypothetical growth of exports of Japan that would have occurred if Japan had been merely maintaining its share in world markets would have been 8.8 per cent per annum. In fact, the actual growth of Japanese exports over this period was 15.4 per cent per annum (Thirlwall, 1979, table 2, p. 51). Thus, if the Houthakker and Magee elasticities were not capturing the change in market shares, then the export equation would have had very poor explanatory power. The predicted growth of Japanese exports obtained using the Houthakker and Magee estimate of ε of 3.55 is 15.6 per cent per annum. At the other extreme, if the UK had maintained its share of world markets, its export growth should have exceeded the hypothetical growth of Japanese exports since the UK's 'apparent' income elasticity was 2.20. This implies a growth of its hypothetical exports of 9.7 per cent per annum compared with Japan's 8.8 per cent. Actually, the UK was losing market shares as its actual growth of exports was 4.1 per cent per annum (Thirlwall, 1979, table 2, p. 51). The Houthakker and Magee estimate of ε for the UK was 1.00 which implies an export growth rate of 4.4 per cent. This is again very close to the observed growth rate.

It was for these reasons that McCombie (1989) suggested that, because there was a close statistical fit, the Houthakker and Magee estimates must be capturing the change in market shares. It was also pointed out in McCombie (1989) that if the income elasticities were not capturing the effect of changes in market shares, the estimates should be approximately the same for all countries (i.e. equal to $\tilde{\varepsilon}$), which clearly is not the case. However, McGregor and Swales (1991, p. 17) dismiss this econometric evidence, seemingly because it is based on time-series data. (If they have no confidence in Houthakker and Magee's estimates of ε and π in the first place, it is strange that they should think it worthwhile testing the law at all.)

Of course, the approach using Houthakker and Magee's estimates is by no means definitive. In terms of the aggregate export and import demand functions, a logical extension of the research programme would be to try explicitly to include variables to capture the non-price factors or to use a hedonic goods approach. A more disaggregated approach could lead to further insights into the role of non-price competition. To the extent that the explicit inclusion of a proxy for non-price competitiveness is successful, we should expect the estimate of the income elasticity of demand to converge to its constant-market-share value. See, for example, the studies by Schott and Pick (1984), Fagerberg (1988), and Greenhalgh (1990). (See also Chapter 4.)

McGregor and Swales (1991) seem also to think that because we argue that the income term is capturing the effects of non-price competitiveness, the latter is somehow determined in a *causal* sense by the income term. Hence, they write $NP_i = f(Z)$ where NP represents a country's relative non-price competitiveness and Z is the level of world income. Here they err in assuming that because two variables are collinear one must be determined by the other. Why British goods cannot compete in non-price competition in overseas markets on equal terms with most other countries is a question that is presently giving rise to a good deal of concern. It is related to the whole question why X-inefficiency exists and why it differs between firms. Why do British firms seem to be so bad at commercialising and marketing British inventions? Why is the quality and reliability of British goods so poor? These are complex questions and there is not space to touch on the answers here. But it is not argued and never has been, except by McGregor and Swales, that the degree of non-price competition depends on world income in any causal sense. It is simply that British exports are not so highly in demand as are other countries' exports in third markets. Thus, as world income increases, so British exports grow more slowly than those of most other countries. The determination of the degree of non-price competitiveness is *exogenous* to Thirlwall's model. But because non-price variables are not explicitly included in the import and export demand functions, the estimates of the elasticities of demand are capturing their effect, as Balassa's calculations show.[36] This interpretation has been argued by, *inter alios*, Panić (1975), Stout (1977), Thirlwall (1979), Stout (1979), Brech and Stout (1981), Fagerberg (1988), Landesmann and Snell (1989), and Greenhalgh (1990).

To summarise: the estimates of ε can logically capture the effect of changes in market shares, in spite of McGregor and Swales's argument to the contrary. As was pointed out in McCombie (1989), whether or not they do so is ultimately an empirical question and the evidence shows that Thirlwall is correct in his interpretation. McGregor and Swales are also in error about the relationship between ε and $\widetilde{\varepsilon}$ and in assuming that the degree of non-price competitiveness is in any way causally determined by Z.

Some Methodological Issues

McGregor and Swales (1986, p. 1273) argued that 'perhaps, too, a methodological point was being made'. It is instructive to consider briefly the methodology to which McGregor and Swales appear to be subscribing. Thirlwall's approach is based on a number of underlying assumptions, some of which were sketched in McCombie (1989).

These include the assumptions that the long-run growth of factors of production respond to the growth of demand for them, rather than being autonomously determined, and that the trend growth of exports is relatively insensitive to changes in the exchange rate and in relative prices.

However, throughout their critique of Thirlwall's Law, McGregor and Swales largely ignore all the other evidence relating to whether growth is of a neoclassical or Keynesian nature, etc., some of which is documented in McCombie (1989). They also disregard evidence relating to the plausibility of the underlying assumptions. The only evidence they consider is whether or not there is a statistically significant difference between y and y_B. Because they (erroneously) consider that there is such a significant disparity, they are led to reject the whole post-Keynesian approach. From this point of view, McGregor and Swales would seem to be subscribing to 'naive falsificationism'. This is 'the belief that scientific theories can be faulted by a single decisive test' (Blaug, 1980, p. 122). For example, they consider that because the difference between y and y_B (when y_B is calculated as $\varepsilon z/\pi$) may be as great as 30 per cent for an individual country, this is sufficient to justify the rejection of the whole approach. By this criterion, they would no doubt reject the whole of the 'growth accounting approach' because typically over half the growth of output cannot be accounted for by the growth of factor inputs. Indeed, by this criterion there would be very little left of applied economics! The question that must be addressed is why Thirlwall's model does not completely explain the observed growth of output and whether or not any other theory performs better. Indeed, it is the mark of 'sophisticated falsificationism' that 'there is no falsification before the emergence of a better theory' (Lakatos, 1970, p. 119). The most obvious alternative is neoclassical growth theory, but notwithstanding emphasis placed on this approach in McGregor and Swales (1985), they now argue that they do not subscribe to it.

The explanatory power of Thirlwall's model is good, but not, of course, perfect. Given the simplicity and high level of aggregation of the model, it would be remarkable if it were. One plausible reason why there is not a closer fit between y and y_B is that the estimates of the income elasticities of demand are not completely picking up the effects of non-price competition. What is clear, however, is that export growth is not primarily determined by the rate of change of both the exchange rate and relative prices, as in the neoclassical model. If this were the case (as in the neoclassical law of one price), then export growth would be endogenous and the concept of the balance of payments constraint would be irrelevant. In these circumstances, the theory would indeed be untenable. It was for this reason that other empirical evidence relating to this issue was considered by McCombie (1989). Moreover, a novel prediction of Thirlwall's approach is that even with the introduction of flexible exchange rates in the early 1970s, the balance-of-payments constraint would not be removed. Subsequent evidence from Bairam (1988), *inter alios*, has not refuted this. Moreover, it is now being increasingly realised that exchange rate adjustments have little quantitative impact of trade flows (see, for example, Krugman, 1989). Clearly, an area of further research is to try to specify models that explicitly include the effects of non-price competition on international trade more accurately: this is what the studies referenced at the end of the previous section are attempting to do.

Where McGregor and Swales do consider other evidence, they do so in a most superficial manner. For example, they dismiss as an 'assertion' Cornwall's (1977) finding that the growth in the labour supply of the advanced countries generally responded to the growth of the demand for it. This is in spite of the fact that Cornwall's conclusion was based on a careful assessment of a great deal of empirical evidence. They also seem to think there is a major inconsistency between Thirlwall's (1981) and Cornwall's positions on the nature of the labour supply. Thirlwall's term the 'reserve army of labour' undoubtedly refers to the disguised unemployment in agriculture that many advanced countries experienced in the early postwar period and to the fact that some European countries imported a substantial number of guest workers from abroad as the demand for labour grew. These are two factors that Cornwall (1977) documents in his book as being of major importance in the postwar supply of labour in the advanced countries. Kindleberger (1967) earlier had argued that because of the existence of disguised unemployment, the advanced countries were, in effect, dual economies. This implies that the growth of the labour force was not an exogenous factor in determining the growth of the advanced countries. The argument that disguised unemployment in agriculture (and, to a certain extent, in services) is an important factor in explaining the postwar growth of the advanced countries is also put forward by Denison (1967). It is difficult to disagree with McGregor and Swales when they argue that 'detailed empirical evidence rather than assertion is the appropriate way to deal with this issue [whether or not the UK has been supply constrained] (1991). It is therefore all the more surprising to find them asserting in the preceding sentence, with no empirical evidence, that 'there are strong *prima facie* arguments that, at least over some time periods, UK growth is supply constrained even where national unemployment exists'.

Finally, McGregor and Swales make the rather obvious point that other theories are compatible with a close relationship between export and output growth. As Caldwell (1982, p. 51) notes, 'it is well known that for any set of data, an infinite number of theories can be developed to explain them'. This clearly is not a problem confined to Thirlwall's model. In the alternative neoclassical model, as outlined by McGregor and Swales (1985), the growth of income is determined by the growth of exogenous factor supplies and autonomous technical progress. In this approach, the growth of imports is determined by the growth of income and relative prices expressed in a common currency. Export growth is determined endogenously by the need to pay for the growth of imports. To the extent that there is a close association between import and income growth, there will be a close relationship between export and income growth. (It should be mentioned in passing though that this is incompatible with specifying the growth of exports to be determined by the growth of *world* income.) In fact, Marin (1990) has shown that export growth 'Granger causes' output growth, rather than vice versa, for Japan, West Germany, the UK and the US over the period 1960–87. This provides further evidence in support of Thirlwall's approach. In assessing the competing theories, it is thus necessary to consider all the relevant empirical evidence pertaining to the various approaches. McGregor and Swales (1986, p. 23) assert, for example, that Thirlwall's assumptions are 'unrealistic', but no evidence is adduced in support of this view.

A Concluding Comment on McGregor and Swales's Critiques

McGregor and Swales (1985, 1986, 1991) have now devoted considerable space to a nihilistic critique of Thirlwall's Law; it is nihilistic because nowhere do they contrast the model with what they consider to be a more satisfactory theory of long-run economic growth. Essentially, they make three criticisms.

The first is that the law of one price, in the neoclassical sense of the term, is theoretically incompatible with a post-Keynesian model of economic growth. Even a cursory examination of the structure of Thirlwall's model would confirm that this is correct. There is no disagreement with this rather obvious point of McGregor and Swales. A crucial assumption of the post-Keynesian approach is that prices are determined oligopolistically and that the so-called law of one price is empirically invalid. McGregor and Swales now assert, somewhat surprisingly in view of the arguments advanced in their 1985 paper, they also do not subscribe to the law of one price.

The second is that rather than use Spearman's rank correlation coefficient to determine the degree of association between y and y_B, McGregor and Swales prefer to use the more powerful ordinary least squares regression technique. This is only more 'rigorous' if it is correctly specified. Unfortunately, this is not true of the specification adopted by McGregor and Swales. No allowance is made for the fact that y_B is constructed from either one or two extraneous estimates (i.e. $\hat{\pi}$ and $\hat{\varepsilon}$ in $y_B = x/\hat{\pi}$ or $\hat{\varepsilon}z/\hat{\pi}$ which have associated standard errors). To the extent that this reflects an errors in variables problem, a more preferable procedure is to regress y_B on y, *viz.* the converse of the procedure adopted by McGregor and Swales. When this is done, Thirlwall's Law certainly cannot be said to be 'emphatically' rejected. There is also a further objection that regression analysis may lead to a rejection of the law for *all* the countries because of one or two outliers. In fact, using the preferable specification of the regression equation, it is only in the case of the period 1951–73 with y_{B2} $(= x/\pi)$ as the regressand that Thirlwall's Law is refuted at the 95 per cent (but not the 99 per cent) confidence level. In other words, the slope coefficient is significantly different from unity at the 95 per cent confidence level, but not at the 99 per cent level. Moreover, this refutation depends upon only *one* outlier, Japan. Following Fisher (1966), where this occurs the best procedure is to drop the outlier(s) and re-estimate the regression, although there are now problems in using the normal diagnostic tests. It is for this reason that an alternative test was proposed in McCombie (1989) that considered each country separately. McGregor and Swales find that if the estimates of π are used from the regression analysis where the relative price term has been suppressed in Houthakker and Magee's (1969) original regressions, a few more countries fail the test. It was argued that there are no grounds for suppressing the price term. Moreover, to do so renders the test contradictory, since if it assumed that relative prices play no role at all in determining trade flows, then only income can adjust to bring the balance of payments into equilibrium in the manner outlined in Thirlwall (1979). The failure of the law in these circumstances must be, by definition, that the income elasticity of demand for imports and exports, in the import and export demand functions, are capturing most, but not all, of the effects of non-price competition.

In the third criticism, they repeat their assertion that, even if all Thirlwall's assumptions are granted, the Houthakker and Magee (1969) income elasticities cannot be logically capturing the effects of non-price competition. In McCombie (1989), it was argued that this was erroneous. McGregor and Swales do not satisfactorily address this point. They are confusing 'constant-market-share' income elasticities of demand with the income elasticities of demand as conventionally estimated. Because of this confusion, McGregor and Swales, far from clarifying the role of non-price competition in international trade and its reflection in Thirlwall's Law, have served merely to obfuscate the issue.

Moreover, the methodology of McGregor and Swales underlying these three putative criticisms seems to be one of 'naive falsification'.

The conclusion of McCombie (1989) was that 'Thirlwall has provided a useful, albeit highly aggregated model (but no more than most neoclassical growth models) that provides a fruitful starting point for the analysis of the long-term growth rates of the advanced countries. McGregor and Swales have produced no substantial criticisms that should lead to any qualifications of this conclusion.' There is no reason, as a result of McGregor and Swales (1991), to amend this conclusion in any way. If McGregor and Swales find this approach unconvincing, they would be far better developing an alternative model than making untenable criticisms of the post-Keynesian approach.

CRAFTS' CRITIQUE

In recent work on British growth performance, Crafts (1988, 1990) uses Balassa's (1979) technique for estimating the income elasticity of demand for exports to argue that Britain's growth rate is not constrained by its balance of payments, but by limitations of supply.

Balassa (1979) argued that his results, discussed above, have important implications for the United States, and Crafts quotes Balassa approvingly in reaching his conclusions for the United Kingdom. Balassa remarks: 'While the Houthakker–Magee and Goldstein–Khan estimates lead to the conclusion that, given its unfavourable export structure, the United States would have to accept a lower rate of growth of real incomes through a slowing down of the growth of output or a deterioration of its terms of trade, according to the estimates obtained by the use of the constant-market-share approach, *economic growth in the United States is not constrained by balance-of-payments considerations'* (emphasis added). It can be seen from Table 5.8 that the 'apparent' income elasticity for the US is 2.02 compared with the actual elasticity of roughly unity, and for the UK 2.20 compared with actual estimates of 0.99 and unity respectively.

Crafts argues in exactly the same vein for the United Kingdom that growth is not constrained by balance-of-payments considerations. He accepts the constant-market-share methodology for calculating the income elasticity of demand for exports. He says that 'to calculate an income elasticity of demand for exports for each country based on what would have been the case had they maintained their market shares . . . seems to be a more acceptable methodology. . . . Balassa's estimates suggest that the income elasticities of demand for U.K., Germany and Japan were 2.20, 2.27 and 2.00. Using Balassa's estimates . . . leads to the implication that British growth was less constrained by demand elasticities than French or German growth and only slightly more constrained than Japanese growth' (1988). He arrives at this conclusion by using the Balassa figures to produce a table (reproduced as Table 5.9) to compare the conventionally calculated balance-of-payments equilibrium growth rate (column *a* of Table 5.9) with the estimates of equilibrium growth calculated using the 'apparent' elasticity (column *b*). (It should be noted that the balance-of-payment equilibrium growth rate calculated using the 'apparent' income elasticity of demand for exports should also use

Table 5.9   A comparison of balance-of-payments equilibrium growth rates and actual growth rates, 1951–73

	(a) Equilibrium growth using conventional estimates of export elasticities	(b) Equilibrium growth using 'apparent' estimates of export elasticities	Actual growth of income	Growth of exports
UK	2.8	7.1	2.7	4.1
US	3.2	6.6	3.7	5.1
France	4.6	6.2	5.0	8.1
Germany	5.4	5.9	5.7	10.8
Japan	14.1	8.0	9.5	15.4

the 'apparent' income elasticity of demand for imports. This has important implications for the work done by Crafts, who, in fact, uses the actual income elasticity of demand for imports, rather than the corresponding constant-market-share elasticity.) In the case of the UK, the equilibrium growth rate using the constant-market-share methodology turns out to be 7.1 per cent per annum – nearly three times higher than the actual growth rate! On this basis, Crafts argues that the UK's growth rate has not been constrained by the balance of payments.

It is difficult to see why Balassa, for the US, and Crafts, for the UK, argue this. All that the approach shows is that *if* the US and the UK had been able to match the average of the advanced countries in quality improvements and the efficiency of their overseas distribution networks, then their exports would have grown faster and their output growth, consistent with balance-of-payments equilibrium, would have been higher. But this does not imply that the US and the UK were not, in fact, balance-of-payments constrained. The point is that the US and the UK *cannot* match the other advanced countries in terms of non-price competitiveness. The equilibrium growth rates reported in column *b* of Table 5.9 merely show that the UK and US could have grown as fast as the rest of the advanced countries if their exports had grown at a corresponding rate. But the export growth of both countries has been nowhere near as fast and so the equilibrium growth rates based on the 'apparent' elasticities are of no relevance in determining whether or not growth was demand (or supply) constrained. The technique and argument used is akin to measuring the income elasticity of bread by assuming bread expenditure remains a constant share of total expenditure, and then saying that the output of bread is supply constrained because the share of bread expenditure has actually fallen! Such an assertion would be meaningless and so, likewise, is the interpretation placed on the constant-market-share elasticity of demand for exports.

If all Balassa and Crafts mean is that the growth rate at which the balance-of-payments constraint becomes binding is not immutable and may be raised by supply-side policies designed to improve non-price competition, then this is uncontroversial. But such microeconomic policies are unlikely to have any quick or dramatic impact. Moreover, the cumulative causation model of economic growth indicates just how difficult it is for a slow growing country to break out of the vicious circle of low productivity growth, poor non-price competitiveness and low export and output growth.

KRUGMAN'S 45-DEGREE RULE

Krugman (1989) expresses surprise that despite substantial differences in the growth of output between developed countries in recent decades, real exchange rates have remained relatively unchanged. The two observations, he argues, can only be reconciled if there is a systematic relation between country growth rates and relative income elasticities of demand for exports and imports. He finds such a systematic relation which he calls the 45-degree rule because one country's growth relative to all others will be equiproportional to the ratio of the income elasticity of demand for its exports to its income elasticity of demand for imports. This is none other than the dynamic Harrod trade multiplier result, although Krugman does not recognise it as such.

Krugman recognises that the close association between growth rates and the relative size of income elasticities could have two types of explanation. On the one hand, income elasticities could determine growth by imposing a balance-of-payments constraint on demand. On the other hand, differential growth rates could affect trade flows in such a way as to create apparent differences in income elasticities. Krugman rejects the first explanation that countries with unfavourable income elasticities will have slow growth owing to balance-of-payments problems whenever they attempt to expand. He says: 'I am simply going to dismiss *a priori* the argument that income elasticities determine growth, rather than the other way round. It just seems fundamentally implausible that over stretches of decades balance-of-payments problems could be preventing long term growth, especially for relatively closed economies like the U.S. in the 1950s and 1960s. Furthermore, *we all know* that differences in growth rates among countries are primarily determined in the rate of growth of total factor productivity, not differences in the rate of growth of employment; it is hard to see what channel links balance of payments due to unfavourable income elasticities to total factor productivity growth' (emphasis added).

Krugman essentially reverses the direction of causation arguing that faster growth in one country leads to a greater supply of exports which causes what he calls the 'apparent' income elasticity of demand for exports to be higher and the 'apparent' income elasticity of demand for imports to be lower. As a country's relative growth rate changes, its apparent income elasticities change as well, preserving the 45-degree rule. Krugman presents a model which purports to

describe a mechanism that could account for a causal re
from growth to income elasticities of demand. It is a
based on monopolistic competition and increasing retu
the price of representative goods is equalised between co
the number of product varieties produced in a country is pr
to its effective labour force as a measure of resource availa᠁ty. If
then the labour force grows at different rates between countries, the
faster growing country will be able to increase its share of world
markets by increasing the number of goods faster than other
countries, allowing it to sell more without a reduction in its relative
prices, therefore giving the faster growing country an apparently
higher income elasticity of demand for its exports. In developing the
model, Krugman concedes 'no effort will be made at realism', and
therein lies the problem. It is tautologically true that if faster growing
countries manage to sell more exports, they will be observed to have
a higher income elasticity of demand for exports, but the model does
not explain how faster growth arises in the first place (except by the
assumption of a faster growth of the labour force), or why a faster
growing country will necessarily export more independent of the
characteristics of the goods it produces. Greater supply availability
and/or variety is not sufficient if demand is relatively lacking.

In the final analysis, it is a question of to what extent income
elasticities can be considered as exogenously determined and to what
extent they are endogenously determined by the growth process
itself. In this respect, it should not be forgotten that in many
instances, countries' income elasticities are largely determined by
natural resource endowments and the characteristics of goods produced (e.g. whether they are 'necessities' or 'luxuries') which are the
product of history and independent of the growth of output. An
obvious example is the contrast between primary product production
and industrial production, where primary products tend to have an
income elasticity of demand less than unity (Engels' Law) while most
industrial products have an income elasticity greater than unity. If the
real terms of trade between primary commodities and industrial
goods does not change, the country producing and exporting primary
products will be constrained in its growth by the balance of payments
relative to the industrial country. This is the basic result of centre–
periphery models of growth and development that we consider in
Chapters 3 and 8. Indeed all the famous centre–periphery models of
Prebisch (1950), Myrdal (1957), Seers (1962), Kaldor (1970) reduce
to the 45-degree rule that the periphery's growth rate relative to the

centre will equal the ratio of the income elasticities of demand for exports and imports. Even between industrial countries, with which Krugman is concerned, negative feedback mechanisms of the type already described (associated with Verdoorn's Law) will tend to perpetuate initial differences in income elasticities associated with 'inferior' industrial structures on the one hand and 'superior' industrial structures on the other. To escape this syndrome requires an exogenous shock which Krugman fails to explain.

Krugman dismisses far too readily the idea that growth may be demand constrained by the balance of payments, and that slow growth may itself adversely affect productivity growth. In practice there are many channels linking slow growth imposed by a balance-of-payments constraint to low productivity growth, and the opposite where the possibility of fast output growth unhindered by balance-of-payments problems leads to fast productivity growth. There is a rich literature on export-led growth models (including the Hicks super-multiplier), incorporating the notion of circular and cumulative causation (Myrdal, 1957) working through induced investment, embodied technical progress, learning by doing, scale economies etc., that will produce fast productivity growth in countries where exports and output are growing fast. These ideas we will describe as the book proceeds. The evidence from testing Verdoorn's Law shows a strong feedback from output growth to productivity growth (see Bairam, 1987, and Chapter 2).

In conclusion, Krugman's empirical findings of growth rate differentials between countries are quite consistent with an open economy Keynesian (Harrodian) growth model with a balance-of-payments constraint and sticky relative prices in international trade in which factor supplies are endogenous to demand. Real exchange rate changes are unnecessary if, in the face of different income elasticities (determined by the commodity composition of exports and imports), output can grow at different rates, i.e. no supply constraints. In this case, it is income not prices that adjusts when imbalances occur between exports and imports through the workings of the Harrod trade multiplier. As we have seen in this chapter, for many countries the evidence suggests that growth is demand constrained by the balance of payments before supply constraints bite. Many of the resources for growth can be considered endogenous, including the labour force via migration and the intersectoral transfer of labour, capital accumulation and technical progress embodied in capital. However, this is not to say that supply-side factors do not matter in the growth process. Income elasticities determine the balance-of-payments constrained growth rate, but the supply characteristics of goods (such as their technical sophistication, quality etc.) determine relative income elasticities. In this important respect, there can be a marrying of the demand and supply-side explanations of the comparative growth performance of nations. This seems more plausible than the view that long-run growth rate differences are determined by exogenous differences in the rate of growth of the effective labour supply between countries (in accordance with neoclassical growth theory) and that these growth rate differences lead to a constellation of income elasticities that just keep the balance of payments in equilibrium without any long run shifts in real exchange rates. The model would imply, for example, that if for some reason Japan's growth rate slowed down, this would so change its income elasticities of exports and imports as to leave the trade balance unchanged with no upward pressure on the exchange rate. This seems implausible. Even more implausible is the presumption that faster growth in the United Kingdom would so change the income elasticities of exports and imports as to prevent a deficit developing with no downward pressure on the exchange rate. The historical experience suggests otherwise.

6 Economic Growth, the Harrod Foreign Trade Multiplier and the Hicks Super-Multiplier[1]

INTRODUCTION

As we saw in Chapter 2, the post-Keynesian view of economic growth denies that the postwar economic performance of the majority of the advanced countries has been seriously constrained by the growth of factor supplies. Even during the 'long boom' of 1950–73, when the growth of output of the advanced countries in aggregate was double that of the historic norm, labour shortages were never a limiting factor. There was either sufficient disguised unemployment in the non-manufacturing sectors or enough immigration to satisfy the demand for labour (Kindleberger, 1967). The rate of capital accumulation is never a long-run constraint on economic growth as investment is as much a result of the expansion of output as its cause (Kaldor, 1970). The evidence in support of these conditions has been summarised in Chapter 2.

If growth is indeed demand constrained rather than supply determined, the question naturally arises why some countries have performed so much better than others. Furthermore, why has it not been possible to increase the rate of economic growth simply by the use of traditional expansionary demand-management policies? The answers to these questions have led to a consideration of the importance of the balance-of-payments constraint and a revival of interest in the Harrod foreign trade multiplier.[2]

In an open economy which is not fundamentally resource constrained, the level of income is determined by the volume of exports. Exports represent the autonomous component of demand, analogous to investment in the Keynesian closed economy model. Under fixed exchange rates, or in a situation where the volume of exports and imports are relatively insensitive to relative price changes, it is the level of output that adjusts to ensure equilibrium in the balance of payments. If, as Kaldor (1979b) has noted, the average and marginal propensities to import are constant over time, investment is financed by retained profits, government expenditure is financed by taxation, and the other exogenous components of demand are ignored, then the level of income (GDP) is simply determined by the level of exports (X):[3]

$$\text{GDP} = (1/m)X \tag{6.1}$$

where m is the marginal propensity to import.

A logical corollary is that the growth of output will be determined primarily by the growth in exports through the foreign trade multiplier. Moreover, the latter is often taken to be equivalent to the Hicks 'super-multiplier'.

It is useful to quote Kaldor's (1978a, p. 146) summary of this argument:

> From the point of view of any particular region,[4] the 'autonomous component of demand' is the demand emanating from *outside* the region; and Hicks' notion of the 'super-multiplier' can be applied so as to express the doctrine of the foreign trade multiplier in a dynamic setting. So expressed, the doctrine asserts that the rate of economic development of a region is fundamentally governed by the rate of growth of its exports. For the growth of exports, via the 'accelerator', will govern the rate of growth of industrial capacity, as well as the rate of growth of consumption; it will also serve to adjust (again under rather severe simplifying assumptions) both the level, and the rate of growth, of imports to that of exports.

Dixon and Thirlwall (1975a) have likewise invoked the super-multiplier as an explanation of the relationship between the growth of output and the growth of exports which forms an integral part of their cumulative causation model of economic growth. (See Chapter 8.)

In this chapter, we examine and clarify the relationship between export-led growth, the Harrod foreign trade multiplier and Hicks's super-multiplier in the context of long-run economic growth. It is argued that the Keynesian model which has been traditionally used to examine short-run fluctuations in income and employment also yields insights into the determination of the trend rate of economic growth. Consequently, the argument will be developed later in this chapter in terms of the orthodox Keynesian model and the New Cambridge variant.

It will be shown that, generally, the workings of the Harrod foreign trade multiplier and of the Hicks super-multiplier are not synonymous. In view of this, it is argued that there is no validity in the criticism that the growth of exports cannot be an important determinant of the growth of output for those countries (such as the US) where exports form only a small fraction of GDP.

At the end of the chapter, we discuss the link between the supermultiplier and our rule of economic growth and reconsider the relevance of the law for analysing the postwar growth of the advanced countries.

EXPORT-LED GROWTH AND THE FOREIGN TRADE MULTIPLIER

It is useful to begin the discussion, however, with consideration of the simple empirical relationship between the growth of GDP and the growth of exports that has been often held to confirm the importance of export-led growth. This is given by:

$$y = a_1 + b_1 x \tag{6.2}$$

where y and x are the proportionate, or exponential, growth rates of GDP (or GNP) and exports.

Equation (6.2) is usually estimated by regression analysis using cross-country data and growth rates pertaining to a decade or more. A close fit is commonly found with the regression coefficient b_1 that is statistically significant and which takes a value of about one-half. Since the specification is so parsimonious, Occam's razor suggests it will be a powerful explanation of the disparate growth rates of output, provided it can be shown to have a satisfactory theoretical rationale.

One of the earliest studies along these lines was that of Emery (1967). He estimated the relationship between the growth of GNP per capita and the growth of exports for 50 countries for the period 1953–63. The result obtained was:

$$y_{pc} = 0.663 + 0.333 \, x \qquad \bar{r}^2 = 0.667$$
$$(2.61) \quad (9.94)$$

where y_{pc} is the growth of per capita GNP and the figures in parentheses are t-ratios.

Since the growth of population is small compared with both the growth of GNP and the growth of exports, a similar relationship is likely to be found when the growth of GNP is used as the regressand. To confirm this, we used Emery's data and regressed the growth of GNP on the growth of exports. Following the suggestion of Syron and Walsh (1968), the sample was split into the advanced countries and the less developed countries.[5] The results obtained were:

$$\text{Advanced countries: } y = \underset{(0.57)}{0.418} + \underset{(6.16)}{0.478x} \quad \begin{array}{l} \bar{r}^2 = 0.725 \\ SER = 1.010 \end{array}$$

$$\begin{array}{l} \text{Less developed} \\ \text{countries:} \end{array} \quad y = \underset{(12.12)}{3.426} + \underset{(6.95)}{0.292x} \quad \begin{array}{l} \bar{r}^2 = 0.582 \\ SER = 1.228 \end{array}$$

Some studies include other exogenous variables in the regression equation apart from export growth. These include the ratio of capital flows to GDP and the share of manufactured exports to total expenditure. The theoretical basis of these equations is often not made clear and only Kaldor (1978a) and Thirlwall (1979) have explicitly interpreted the relationship as reflecting the (dynamic) foreign trade multiplier. It will be shown later that the relationship is best regarded as a reduced form equation describing the operation of the super-multiplier. In this case, it is not a mis-specification to exclude the growth of other variables that are often held to be important determinants of growth (such as the rate of capital accumulation). This is because the growth of these variables is, in turn, determined by the balance-of-payments constraint and the rate of growth of exports. Strictly speaking, the rate of growth of capital flows (weighted by the ratio of capital flows to total foreign exchange receipts) should also be included as a regressor in addition to the growth of exports (weighted by the ratio of exports to total receipts). (See Chapter 3.) In practice, for the advanced countries the former is so small compared with the latter that for expositional purposes we can safely ignore it. (This is not the case, however, for the less developed countries. See Thirlwall and Hussain (1982).)

As a further example, we estimated equation (6.2) for the advanced countries for two postwar sub-periods, namely, 1953–73 and 1973–86. The year 1973 represents a turning point after which the advanced countries entered a period of substantially slower growth rates, punctuated by the severe recessions of 1974/5 and 1979/80. The regression results are reported in Table 6.1. It transpires that there is a statistically significant relationship between the growth of GDP and

Table 6.1   The relationship between the growth of output (y) and the
growth of total exports (x)

1953–73:	$y =$	0.788	$+$ $0.518\,x$	$\bar{r}^2$ $= 0.702$
		(1.20)	(6.22)	$SER = 0.730$
1973–86:	$y =$	0.734	$+$ $0.360\,x$	$\bar{r}^2$ $= 0.431$
		(1.57)	(3.62)	$SER = 0.610$

Notes: Figures in parentheses are t-values.
Sample consists of 17 countries, namely, Japan, US, Canada,
Austria, Belgium, Denmark, France, Germany, Italy, Netherlands,
Norway, Sweden, Switzerland, UK, Australia, Finland, and Ireland.

Source: *OECD National Accounts* (various years).

the growth of total exports for both periods, although the fit is better
for 1953–73. The question of how to interpret the results of the
equation arises, because the correlation in the above regressions, of
course, implies nothing about the direction of causality, or indeed
whether there is any causal connection between the variables at all.
For example, it is perfectly possible for those factors (such as entrepreneurial dynamism) that make for a fast rate of growth of GDP to be
likewise responsible for a rapid export growth, so that both variables
are jointly determined. Furthermore, it is possible, as in the neoclassical model, that growth of output may be determined by the exogenous growth of factor inputs. The growth of exports in this case
would be determined by the necessity of paying for the growth of
imports. However, as we noted in Chapter 5, Marin's (1990) study
suggests that export growth 'Granger causes' income growth, rather
than vice versa, for Japan, West Germany, the UK and the US over
the period 1960–87.

As noted above, we assume that there has generally been no
long-run supply constraint on the growth of most of the advanced
countries. (See Chapter 2 for a discussion of these issues.) Under
these circumstances, the interpretation of equation (6.2) is that the
growth of exports predominantly causes the growth of GDP. This is
how Emery interpreted his results. He argued that 'it would appear
from the data that relatively high rates of growth are likely to follow
from relatively high rates of export growth' (Emery, 1967, pp. 483–4).
Certainly, a failure to find any statistically significant relationship
between the growth of GDP and the growth of exports could be taken
as a refutation of the hypothesis that the growth of exports plays a

crucial role in determining the growth of output. Indeed, the weaker correlation that is found for 1973–86 indicates that the balance-of-payments may not have been such a binding constraint as several countries pursued deflationary policies in order to restrict output, with the aim of combating inflation. In other words, since 1973, the growth of GDP for a number of countries was often lower than the maximum made possible by the growth of exports.

If the relationship given by equation (6.2) is supposed to reflect simply the foreign trade multiplier, then one objection, as mentioned in the introduction to this chapter, is that its importance must vary considerably between the advanced countries, depending on the size of the export sector relative to GDP. For example, in 1953 the ratio of the value of exports of goods and services to GDP measured in current prices varied from 5 per cent in the US to 47 per cent in the Netherlands. (By 1986, these ratios had increased to 9 per cent and 54 per cent respectively.) It could be argued that the impact of an increase in the growth of exports of, for example, one percentage point will have considerably less impact in the case of the US than the Netherlands. This suggests that the relationship between the growth of GDP and the growth of exports estimated above is wrongly specified, if its theoretical rationale rests solely on the foreign trade multiplier.[6]

Severn (1968) has pursued this argument by reasoning that an allowance ought to be made in the regression for the degree of openness of the economy. He suggested that the growth of exports should be weighted by an 'openness coefficient', namely the ratio of exports to total output. The regression to be estimated now becomes:

$$y = a_2 + b_2 x^*$$ (6.3)

where $x^* = (X/Y)x$, and X and Y are the levels of total exports and GDP.

We estimated equation (6.3) for the two postwar subperiods 1953–73 and 1973–86. The results are reported in Table 6.2.

It is sufficient to note that there is now no statistically significant relationship between the two variables. It will be shown later, however, that it is a mis-specification to weight export growth by the openness coefficient, if the relationship between the growth of GDP and of exports is interpreted as reflecting the operation of the super-multiplier.

Ideally, in order to discuss the role of the two multipliers (i.e. the

Table 6.2   The relationship between the growth of GDP (y) and the growth of total exports weighted by the 'openness coefficient' (x^*)

1953–73:	$y =$	$4.646 + 0.052x^*$	$\bar{r}^2$	$= -0.066$
		$(5.75)\quad(0.12)$	SER	$= 1.382$
1973–86:	$y =$	$1.923 + 0.303x^*$	$\bar{r}^2$	$= 0.017$
		$(4.54)\quad(1.13)$	SER	$= 0.801$

For notes and sources, see table 6.1.

Harrod trade multiplier and the Hicks super-multiplier) in the context of economic growth, we should use a full-scale econometric model of the economy. Nevertheless, the main arguments can be satisfactorily demonstrated with the use of simple Keynesian models. Clearly, the theoretical rationale must be Keynesian in nature since export-led growth has little or no meaning under neoclassical assumptions, including the neoclassical interpretation of the law of one price. In the latter case, the state of the current account of the balance of payments, *per se*, is a matter of indifference to the extent that it does not affect the long-run rate of economic growth.

We further accept the argument that, in the long run, 'money does not matter' in the sense that the domestic money supply, broadly defined, is endogenous and we abstract from the financial sector. By making this assumption, we are presenting the strong, or, no doubt, some would say, extreme, Keynesian interpretation of export-led growth. The differences in the growth of the advanced countries are seen to reflect ultimately real rather than monetary forces, although it is a monetary phenomenon – the balance-of-payments constraint – that is the proximate cause of why growth rates differ.

The orthodox Keynesian model may be described by the following equations:

$$Y = C + I + G + X - M \tag{6.4}$$

$$C = C_0 + c(Y - T) \tag{6.5}$$

$$I = I_0 \tag{6.6}$$

$$G = G_0 \tag{6.7}$$

$$T = tY \tag{6.8}$$

$$X = X_0 + \gamma P \tag{6.9}$$

$$M = M_0 + mY - \rho P \tag{6.10}$$

Y, C, I, G, X, M, and T denote income, consumption, investment, government expenditure, exports, imports, and tax revenues, all measured in real terms. c, t and m are the marginal propensities to consume, to tax and to import.[7] $P = P_f E/P_d$ where P_f is the foreign price of imports, E is the exchange rate measured as the domestic price of foreign currency and P_d is the domestic price of output which, for convenience we assume to be the same for exports. M is the volume of imports. The subscript o denotes an autonomous component of expenditure. γ and ρ are positive

The relationships of the model are well-known and need not be discussed here.

The level of income is given by:

$$Y = (1/k)(C_0 + I_0 + G_0 + X_0 - M_0 + (\gamma + \rho)P) \tag{6.11}$$

where $k = (1 - c + ct + m)$.

We assume that there is no change in the ratio of foreign to domestic prices measured in a common currency, so the growth of exports can be regarded as exogenous, or, strictly speaking, determined by the autonomously given growth of world income. Thus, the growth of income can be expressed in terms of the growth of the autonomous components of expenditure, *viz*:

$$\overset{\circ}{Y} = (1/k)(\omega_{co}\overset{\circ}{C} + \omega_I\overset{\circ}{I} + \omega_G\overset{\circ}{G} + \omega_x\overset{\circ}{X} - \omega_{MO}\overset{\circ}{M}) \tag{6.12}$$

where ω_x, etc., denote the shares of the relevant variables in total income. (The subscript 0 has been dropped from $\overset{\circ}{X}$, $\overset{\circ}{I}$ and $\overset{\circ}{G}$, and their respective shares, for notational convenience.)

If the only increase in autonomous expenditure comes from exports, the rate of growth of income is given by $\overset{\circ}{Y} = (1/k)\omega_x\overset{\circ}{X}$. This represents the direct impact of export growth on income growth, via the operation of the foreign trade multiplier.

An alternative approach is to use the New Cambridge model of the economy which was developed by the Cambridge Economic Policy Group (CEPG). This model is similar to the orthodox Keynesian approach, but with the important difference that, instead of individual relationships for the determinants of consumption and investment, there is only one for private expenditure. Private expenditure is defined as the sum of consumption and investment expenditure. In other words, investment is now taken to be endogenous. (See Smith, 1976, and Anyadike-Danes, 1982.)

The expression for private expenditure is given by either:

$$PE = (C + I) = (Y - T) - NAFA \qquad (6.13a)$$

$$= c'(Y - T) + H \qquad (6.13b)$$

where *NAFA* denotes the net saving (or the Net Acquisition of Financial Assets) by the private sector and c' is the marginal propensity of the private sector to spend. H is the effect of changes in hire purchase and stock building on private expenditure. Consequently, the equilibrium level of income is now obtained by first substituting equation (6.8) into (6.13b) and then substituting equations (6.7), (6.9), (6.10), and (6.13b) into equation (6.4). We again assume, however, that relative prices do not affect imports and exports and also that there are no autonomous imports. In these circumstances, income is given by:

$$Y = (1/k')(G + X + H) \qquad (6.14)$$

where $k' = (1 - c' + c't + m)$.

In practice, the CEPG assumed that c' is approximately unity and that the NAFA is determined simply by H. The CEPG found that empirically the effect of H (and changes in H) on NAFA was generally small and therefore NAFA (and its changes) were also small (Cuthbertson, 1979, p.64). If we assume that c' takes a value of unity and that NAFA is zero, the determination of the level of income becomes:

$$Y = \frac{1}{(t + m)} (G + X) \qquad (6.15)$$

The multiplier in equation (6.15), $1/(t+m)$, is larger than the conventional Keynesian multiplier. Furthermore, it can be assumed that the Public Sector Borrowing Requirement (PSBR) is an exogenous or a target variable. The PSBR is defined as equal to $(G - T)$.

The level of income is now given by:

$$Y = (1/m)(X + PSBR) \qquad (6.16)$$

The multiplier is now simply the reciprocal of the marginal propensity to import. As Smith (1976, p. 195) points out, though, 'problems may arise in a closed economy when $m = 0$'.

The growth of income may be obtained from equation (6.16) and is given by:

$$\overset{\circ}{Y} = \left(\frac{1}{m}\right)(\omega_x \overset{\circ}{X} + \omega_{PSBR} \overset{\circ}{PSBR}) \qquad (6.17)$$

where ω_{PSBR} is the ratio of the PSBR to income.

If the government's long-run target is to run a balanced budget so the PSBR, and its rate of growth, are zero, then equation (6.17) shows that the growth rate of income will depend entirely upon the growth of exports. The foreign trade multiplier and the super-multiplier are now formally equivalent, as will be shown below. In any event, the quantitative effect of the growth of the PSBR on the growth of income is likely to be small.[8]

THE DIRECT IMPACT OF THE FOREIGN TRADE MULTIPLIER

In this section we report estimates of the percentage point increase in the growth of GDP induced, through the conventional foreign trade multiplier, by an increase in the growth of exports of one percentage point per annum. In order to calculate this it is necessary to know the values of the multiplier for the various advanced countries, but unfortunately these are not always readily available. It is therefore necessary to construct first an estimate of each country's multiplier.

The multiplier used is defined as:

$$1/k = 1/(1 - c + ct_d + t_i + m) \qquad (6.18)$$

where c, t_d, t_i and m are the marginal propensities to consume, to tax directly, to tax indirectly and to import.[9] Direct taxation includes both social security contributions and imputed employee welfare contributions. The marginal propensities were calculated by estimating the increase in the ratios of the relevant variables over the period concerned. For example, the marginal propensity to import was simply taken as $m = \Delta M/\Delta Y$. The data were taken from various issues of the OECD *National Accounts*.

Since the marginal propensity to import is the propensity that varies the most between the countries and, hence, its value is of particular importance, we also constructed an alternative estimate. The marginal propensity to import manufactures was taken to be double the average propensity, while for raw materials and semi-processed goods the marginal and average propensities to import were taken as equal. (It is reassuring to note that, in practice, it makes little difference which procedure is adopted.)

Since this approach was taken as a *pis aller*, the values of the multipliers are best regarded as orders of magnitude rather than precise estimates. Nevertheless, the value obtained for the UK of 1.11 for 1980 seems plausible, especially since Cuthbertson (1979) reports that the NIESR multiplier lies in the range 0.8 to 1.0; the Treasury Model gives a value of 1.1, and the CEPG's value is approximately 1.25.[10] The value for the US of 1.37 also seems reasonable for what is a much more closed economy.

The results of the calculations of the impact on GDP growth of a one percentage point increase in export growth are reported in Table 6.3, column 5a. These were calculated using the expression of the foreign trade multiplier, i.e.

$$\mathring{Y} = \left(\frac{1}{k} \right) \omega_x \mathring{X} \tag{6.19}$$

It follows that an *increase* in the growth rate of income caused by an *increase* in the growth of exports is given by:

$$\Delta \mathring{Y} = \left(\frac{1}{k} \right) \omega_x \Delta \mathring{X} \tag{6.20}$$

It can be seen that there is a wide diversity of results across the countries. The US, although it has the largest multiplier, experiences the smallest increase in output growth through the foreign trade multiplier. Even Japan, often cited as the example *par excellence* of export-led growth, especially since the mid-1960s, experiences only a small impact. In Japan's case, a one percentage point increase in total export growth increases the growth of GDP by only 0.16 percentage points in 1957 and 0.18 in 1980. Alternatively, the very open economies of Denmark, the Netherlands and Norway experienced an increase in their growth rates in the mid-1950s by over a third of a percentage point.

Over time, the impact of the foreign trade multiplier has generally increased slightly as the increase in the relative size of the export sector has more than offset the small decline in the value of the multiplier.

The variation of the importance of the impact of the foreign trade multiplier across the countries would superficially seem to confirm the criticisms noted earlier in this chapter about the importance of the degree of openness of a particular country. Notably, it would tend to substantiate the argument that there will be substantial international variation in the impact that an increase in export growth will have on the growth of GDP, and this variation depends primarily upon the size of the export sector relative to total output. The results also confirm that the contribution of export growth to overall economic growth is low, especially for the more closed economies.

A further objection to the fundamental role of the foreign trade multiplier by itself in determining economic growth may be seen by considering equation (6.12) again. This may be written equivalently as:

$$\overset{\circ}{Y} = \left(\frac{1}{k} \right)(\omega_X \overset{\circ}{X} + \omega_A \overset{\circ}{A}) \qquad (6.21)$$

where $\overset{\circ}{A}$ is the growth of all other autonomous expenditures. It may be questioned why an increase in exports should have any greater impact on the level of economic activity than an equivalent increase in other autonomous expenditures. The answer is, of course, that the growth of exports is the only element that simultaneously relaxes the balance-of-payments constraint while increasing the growth of income. For example, the postwar history of the UK was one of periods of consumption-led expansion which briefly resulted in a growth of output above the trend rate of growth. (The peaks of the growth cycles were in 1954, 1959, 1963, 1967, 1973, 1979 and 1990.) These periods of rapid growth were, especially in 1973 and the earlier peak years, brought to an abrupt end by the rapid increase in induced imports which led to the familiar balance of payments crises. The argument advanced by, for example, Kaldor (1970) is that export-led growth enables the rate of investment to be increased, thereby raising the growth of productive potential. Consumption-led growth, on the other hand, by eventually precipitating a balance of payments crisis which requires correction through deflation, reduces the incentive to invest. This leads to a lower investment–output ratio than would be obtained through export-led growth.[11] It is, therefore, necessary to

Table 6.3 The effect of the growth of total exports on GDP growth through the foreign trade multiplier and the super-multiplier

Country 1	Ratio of total exports to GDP (%) 2	Marginal propensity to import 3	Value of the multiplier 4	Percentage point increase in GDP due to an increase in export growth of one percentage point 5		Ratio of 5a to 5b (%) 6
				Foreign trade multiplier 5a	Super-multiplier 5b	
1980						
Austria	39.0	0.50	0.78	0.30	0.78	38
Belgium	59.7	0.82	0.66	0.39	0.73	54
Canada	29.3	0.31	1.05	0.30	0.94	33
Denmark	33.3	0.36	0.91	0.30	0.92	33
France	22.4	0.29	1.04	0.23	0.77	30
Germany	27.0	0.41	0.88	0.23	0.66	36
Ireland	53.9	0.82	0.73	0.39	0.66	59
Italy	25.2	0.31	1.02	0.25	0.81	32

Japan	14.0	0.19	1.26	0.18	0.74	24
Netherlands	53.0	0.73	0.67	0.36	0.73	49
Norway	47.6	0.38	0.76	0.36	1.25	30
UK	28.4	0.26	1.11	0.32	1.09	29
US	10.0	0.15	1.37	0.14	0.66	21
Mid-1950s						
Austria	25.1	0.38	0.90	0.23	0.66	34
Belgium	33.7	0.52	0.81	0.27	0.65	42
Canada	20.0	0.25	1.07	0.21	0.80	26
Denmark	33.9	0.34	1.12	0.38	0.99	38
France	14.1	0.20	1.18	0.17	0.70	24
Germany	20.1	0.24	1.06	0.21	0.84	25
Ireland	31.0	0.46	0.99	0.31	0.67	46
Italy	10.9	0.21	1.27	0.14	0.52	27
Japan	11.5	0.16	1.43	0.16	0.72	22
Netherlands	43.9	0.60	0.94	0.41	0.73	56
Norway	43.8	0.46	0.76	0.33	0.95	35
UK	21.9	0.31	1.08	0.24	0.71	33
US	5.0	0.08	1.42	0.07	0.62	11

Source: OECD *National Accounts* (various years).

turn to an examination of the role of import growth in constraining growth via the balance of payments, which leads us to a consideration of the super-multiplier.

EXPORT-LED GROWTH AND THE HICKS SUPER-MULTIPLIER

The direct influence of an increase in exports, or an increase in their rate of growth, through the foreign trade multiplier is only one mechanism by which GDP (or its growth rate) will be increased. A secondary route is one through which, by initially relaxing the balance-of-payments constraint, an increase in exports will allow other autonomous expenditures to be increased until income has risen by enough to induce an increase in imports equivalent to the initial increase in exports.

We have seen that, in the short-run, the increase of income through the foreign trade multiplier is given by:

$$\Delta Y = (1/k)\Delta X \qquad (6.22)$$

The increase in imports induced by the expansion of income is given by the marginal propensity to import as:

$$\Delta M = m\Delta Y \qquad (6.23)$$

Substituting equation (6.22) into equation (6.23) and rearranging we obtain:

$$\Delta M = (m/k)\Delta X \qquad (6.24)$$

As $k > m$, the increase in imports will be less than the increase in exports and there will be an improvement in the balance of trade, *viz*:

$$\Delta X - \Delta M = \frac{(k - m)}{m}\Delta X > 0 \qquad (6.25)$$

In the long run, however, the super-multiplier operates and increases the level of economic activity until the induced increase in imports equals the increase in exports. In other words, income will increase until the balance of payments is brought back into equilibrium. This secondary increase in demand may occur, for example, through a faster rate of capital accumulation induced by entrepreneurs' expectations of a sustained faster growth rate or an increased growth of government expenditure, or both. Wealth effects arising from the acquisition of overseas assets as a result of the initial excess of exports over imports may also result in an increase in consumption.

Consequently, starting from balance-of-payments equilibrium, and since $\Delta M = \Delta X$, it follows from equation (6.23) that:

$$\Delta M = m\Delta Y = \Delta X \tag{6.26}$$

and, hence:

$$\Delta Y = (1/m)\Delta X \tag{6.27}$$

This may be expressed equivalently as:

$$\frac{\Delta Y}{Y} = \frac{1}{m} \frac{X}{Y} \frac{\Delta X}{X} \tag{6.28}$$

or

$$\overset{\circ}{Y} = \left(\frac{1}{m}\right)(\omega_x \overset{\circ}{X}) \tag{6.29}$$

Since $m = \Delta M/\Delta Y$ and X/Y equals M/Y, it follows that $(1/m)(\omega_x) = \pi$, the income elasticity of demand for imports. Consequently, equation (6.29) is nothing other than the balance-of-payments equilibrium growth rate:

$$\overset{\circ}{Y}_B = \frac{1}{\pi}\overset{\circ}{X} \tag{6.30}$$

Using equation (6.21), equation (6.30) may be written as:

$$\overset{\circ}{Y}_B = \left(\frac{1}{k}\right)(\omega_x \overset{\circ}{X} + \omega_A \overset{\circ}{A}_B) \tag{6.31}$$

where $\overset{\circ}{A}_B$ is the rate of growth of autonomous expenditures necessary, for a given growth of exports, to maintain the growth of income at the balance-of-payments equilibrium rate. ω_A is the share of A_B in total income.

Equations (6.30) and (6.31) represent the working of the Hicks super-multiplier. From equation (6.31), it may be seen that apart from the direct growth in output through the foreign trade multiplier, viz. $(1/k)\omega_X\overset{\circ}{X}$, the initial relaxation of the balance-of-payments constraint permits (rather than automatically causes) a growth in 'autonomous' expenditure given by subtracting equation (6.31) from (6.29) and rearranging:

$$\overset{\circ}{A}_B = k\left(\frac{1}{m} - \frac{1}{k}\right)\left(\frac{\omega_X}{\omega_A}\right)\overset{\circ}{X} \tag{6.32}$$

If autonomous expenditure does not grow as fast as the rate implied by equation (6.32), then the growth of output will be commensurately less and an increasing balance of payments surplus will occur. (A simple numerical example illustrating this argument is presented in the Appendix.)

Consequently, the balance-of-payments equilibrium growth rate may be expressed as:

$$\overset{\circ}{Y}_B = \left(\frac{1}{k}\right)(\omega_X\overset{\circ}{X} + \omega_A\overset{\circ}{A}_B) = \frac{1}{\pi}\overset{\circ}{X} \tag{6.33}$$

The balance-of-payments equilibrium growth rate of income is thus determined jointly by the growth of exports, via the dynamic foreign trade multiplier (ω_X/k), and the growth of 'induced' autonomous expenditures working through its associated dynamic multiplier (ω_A/k). This is identical to the effect of the growth of exports working through the super-multiplier $(1/\pi)$.

In the case of the New Cambridge model, we have seen that one specification (equation (6.16)) gives the value of the multiplier as $1/m$. In this case it can be seen that an increase in exports will *automatically* induce an increase in imports of the same magnitude. The foreign trade multiplier and the super-multiplier are identical.

An idea of the magnitude of the impact of the super-multiplier may be seen again from Table 6.3 (column 5b) where the percentage point increase in GDP growth resulting from a one percentage point increase in export growth is reported. This is calculated from the expression:

$$\Delta \mathring{Y} = \left(\frac{1}{m}\right)\omega_x \Delta \mathring{X} \tag{6.34}$$

where $\Delta \mathring{X}$ is equal to one percentage point.

It can be seen that the increase in the growth of GDP is greater and shows less inter-country variation than when only the foreign trade multiplier operates. It is noticeable that the US and Japan, especially, now experience a much larger increase in GDP growth resulting from a given increase in exports, compared with the situation when only the foreign trade multiplier is in operation. Table 6.3 also reports the ratio of the growth of output attributable to the Harrod trade multiplier to the effect of the super-multiplier (column 6). In the mid-1950s, the proportion ranged from 11 per cent in the US to 56 per cent in the Netherlands. It may also be seen that the proportion has increased over time.

With these arguments in mind, we are now in a position to reconsider the empirical the relationship between the growth of GDP and exports, namely the regression equation:

$$\mathring{Y} = a_1 + b_1 \mathring{X} \tag{6.35}$$

where the estimate of a_1 does not differ significantly from zero at the 95 per cent confidence level (see Table 6.1).

It is clear that the most plausible rationale for this equation is that it is a reduced form equation reflecting the operation of the super-multiplier, as we suggested earlier, rather than being a mis-specified representation of the workings of the foreign trade multiplier. The slope coefficient b_1 represents an estimate of the average value of $(1/m)\omega_x$, or $(1/\pi)$, for the advanced countries, i.e. the average value of the super-multiplier.

However, it is clear that the use of cross-section data is, to a certain extent, inappropriate as from Table 6.3 it may be seen that the value of the super-multiplier shows some variation between the countries.[12] The assumption underlying equation (6.35) is, of course, that all countries have the same value of b_1 or the same size of the super-multiplier. It may also be seen from Table 6.1 that the estimate of b_1 of 0.5 for 1953–73 obtained by estimating equation (6.35) compares with the average value of column 5b in Table 6.3 of 0.74.

If the growth of exports is weighted by the openness coefficient, as suggested by Severn (1968) and discussed above, the slope coefficient is likely to vary markedly between countries and so it is not surprising equation (6.3) does not give a very good fit. This may be shown as follows.

Since a_1 in equation (6.35) may be taken to be zero, the equation may be written as:

$$\mathring{Y} = b_1\mathring{X} = (1/\pi)\mathring{X} \tag{6.36}$$

This may be written equivalently as:

$$\mathring{Y} = \left(\frac{1}{\pi}\frac{Y}{X}\right)\left(\frac{X}{Y}\right)\mathring{X} = \left(\frac{1}{\pi}\frac{Y}{X}\right)\mathring{X}^* \tag{6.37}$$

where $\mathring{X}^*$ is the growth of exports weighted by the openness coefficient.

Assuming initial balance-of-payments equilibrium and balance-of-payments equilibrium growth, equation (6.37) can be written as:

$$\mathring{Y} = \frac{1}{m}\mathring{X}^* \tag{6.38}$$

which is the same result as equation (6.29).

But m and, hence, $1/m$ are not even approximately constant across countries (see Table 6.3) and this explains why the estimate of equation (6.3) gives such a poor fit. Consequently, it is erroneous to weight the growth of exports by an 'openness coefficient' in the manner suggested by Severn (1968).

THE IMPACT OF AN INCREASE IN AUTONOMOUS IMPORT EXPENDITURE

Hitherto, the analysis has been concerned with the change in output that an increase in exports will induce, both directly through the foreign trade multiplier, and indirectly by allowing other autonomous expenditure to increase through the initial relaxation of the balance-of-payment constraint. There is one important component of autonomous expenditure which it is useful to consider explicitly, namely, autonomous imports. In the above analysis we have implicitly assumed that the growth of all imports is induced by the growth of income. We now relax this assumption.

The import demand function is now given by:

$$M = M_0 + mY \qquad (6.39)$$

where M_0 denotes autonomous imports.

The increase in total imports resulting from an increase in both autonomous imports and income is:

$$\Delta M = \Delta M_0 + m\Delta Y \qquad (6.40)$$

or in terms of proportional growth rates:

$$\overset{\circ}{M} = \left(\frac{M_0}{M}\right)\overset{\circ}{M}_0 + m\left(\frac{Y}{M}\right)\overset{\circ}{Y} \qquad (6.41)$$

For balance-of-payments equilibrium $M = X$ and $\overset{\circ}{M} = \overset{\circ}{X}$. Substituting these expressions into equation (6.39), the following expression is obtained:

$$\overset{\circ}{Y}_B = \left(\frac{1}{m}\right)(\omega_X\overset{\circ}{X} - \omega_{M_0}\overset{\circ}{M}_0) \qquad (6.42)$$

where ω_{M_0} is the ratio of autonomous imports to income.

It can be seen that an increase in the growth of autonomous imports reduces the rate of growth of output analogously to a decline in export growth, acting directly through the foreign trade multiplier and indirectly through the balance-of-payments constraint.[13]

GROWTH IN OPEN ECONOMIES

We have seen from equations (6.30) and (6.33) that the value of the super-multiplier is equal to the reciprocal of the income elasticity of demand for imports if the share of total exports in total income is approximately equal to the share of imports.

If imports are a linear function of income with no autonomous imports, i.e. $M = mY$ as we have assumed earlier in this chapter, then the marginal and average propensity to import should be equal and the value of the income elasticity of demand for imports should be unity. But, as may be seen from Table 6.3, in practice, our estimates of the marginal propensities to import are greater than the shares of exports in GDP, and hence, by inference, the shares of imports in GDP. We calculated the marginal propensity to import as the ratio of the increase of imports divided by the increase in income over the relevant growth cycle $(\Delta M/\Delta Y)$. The ratio of exports to income was calculated for the base year. The super-multiplier was estimated as $(\Delta Y/\Delta M)(X/Y)$ which, for most countries, was less than unity. Consequently, the implied value of the income elasticity of demand given by the reciprocal of the super-multiplier is greater than unity. We did, in fact, confirm this directly by calculating $(\Delta M/\Delta Y)(Y/M)$ which also generally proved to exceed one, although the estimates are not reported here. In Chapter 5, it will be recalled that we postulated that the linear import function is a short-run relationship while the power specification was interpreted as a long-run relationship. This distinction does not, of course, affect the theoretical interpretation of equation (6.30) as representing the super-multiplier.

Differences will occur between the super-multiplier and the inverse of the income elasticity of demand to the extent that the shares of exports and imports in GDP are not the same. Also, in calculating the marginal propensity to import, we have assumed that changes in relative prices are quantitatively insignificant in affecting the demand for imports.[14] To summarise: it may be seen that the rule given by equation (6.30) represents, in general, the workings of the Hicks super-multiplier, of which Harrod's foreign trade multiplier is a component. It is only under a strong set of assumptions associated with the New Cambridge model that the super-multiplier and the foreign trade multiplier are formally equivalent.

If the growth of exports is determined by the growth of world income, $(\overset{\circ}{X} = \varepsilon \overset{\circ}{Z})$, we may derive the alternative specification, namely:

$$\overset{\circ}{Y}_B = \frac{\varepsilon \overset{\circ}{Z}}{\pi} \tag{6.43}$$

Table 6.4 reports the values of the world income elasticities of demand for the exports of the six largest countries, together with their income elasticities of demand for imports. Before considering the implications of equations (6.33) and (6.43) it is useful to digress briefly and discuss the differences between the countries in their income elasticities of demand for imports.

In the case of the UK, the value of the super-multiplier for 1980 is 1.09. This is somewhat higher than the estimates of the reciprocal of

Table 6.4   Export and import income elasticities of the six largest
advanced countries

Country	World income elasticity of the demand for exports	Domestic income elasticity of demand for imports	
		(a)	(b)
Japan	3.55	1.23	n.a.
Italy	2.95	2.19	n.a.
West Germany	2.08[a]	1.80[b]	1.31
France	1.53	1.66	1.63
United States	0.99	1.68[c]	n.a.
United Kingdom	0.86	1.45[c]	1.82

Notes: [a] See Chapter 5 note 32.
  [b] The estimate from the regression where there has been a correction for serial correlation is 1.85, but the price term was excluded.
  [c] Estimate from regression where there has been a correction for serial correlation.

Sources: Houthakker and Magee (1969), except for the income elasticities in column (b) which are from Panić (1975).

the income elasticities of demand for imports for the UK reported in Table 6.4 which are 0.69 and 0.55. Part of the reason is that we calculated the various marginal propensities to import in terms of ratios measured in nominal terms, i.e. implicitly deflating both the numerator and denominator by the GDP deflator. If we use, however, separate import and GDP price deflators to calculate the marginal propensity to import at 1975 prices, the value of the super-multiplier falls to 0.71 and the value of the income elasticity of demand for imports rises from 0.92 to 1.41.

Panić (1975) has examined the differences in the income elasticity to import between the UK, West Germany and France. As may be seen from Table 6.4, according to Panic's estimates, the UK has the largest import elasticity of 1.82 while France and West Germany have values of 1.63 and 1.31 respectively. These estimates are taken from regression analyses where the effects of changes both in the pressure of demand and relative prices are included. Panić argues that generally these two additional variables have little to contribute in explaining the growth of imports, especially when compared with the influence of the growth of domestic income. This provides additional confirmation of our contention that it is the income elasticity of demand that is the important determinant of the growth of imports.

Table 6.5   Income elasticities of demand for imports: UK, West Germany
and France

	UK	W. Germany	France
Food, beverages and tobacco	0.35	0.86	0.84
Basic materials	0.66	1.22	0.70
Fuels	2.47	2.66	1.26
Manufactured goods	3.09	2.14	2.19
(Semi-manufactures)	(2.37)	(2.06)	(n.a.)
(Finished products)	(4.30)	(3.52)	(n.a.)
Total Imports	1.82	1.31	1.63

Note: n.a. denotes not available.

Source: Panić (1975, table 2, p. 4).

It is instructive to disaggregate the income elasticity of demand for imports into the major commodity groups. These elasticities are reported in Table 6.5.

As Panić points out, the most significant differences in the elasticities occur in manufactured goods, which account for between 57 per cent (UK) and 66 per cent (France) of total imports. Panić attributes these differences to 'structural disequilibrium' factors which reflect the disparities in non-price competitiveness. Thus, those factors which we have seen cause substantial differences between countries in their growth of exports are, not surprisingly, also reflected in the growth of imports.

In the case of Japan, a part of the reason for its low income elasticity of demand for imports is due to the composition of its imports. As we have seen, the highest income elasticities of demand are to be found for manufactured goods. In 1973, the share of manufactures in Japan's total imports was only 33 per cent, whereas for the remaining five advanced countries reported in Table 6.4 the next lowest was the UK with 57 per cent. This disparity is due to the greater reliance Japan has on international trade for its raw materials, the greater preponderance of both formal and informal ('administrative') import controls and the high degree of non-price competitiveness of its manufactured goods, especially since the mid-1960s.

Returning to a consideration of the rule $\overset{\circ}{Y} = \overset{\circ}{X}/\pi$, Table 6.6 reports the balance-of-payments equilibrium rates of growth of GDP, together with the growth of exports and of GDP for the six largest advanced countries. The growth rates were calculated for two

Table 6.6 Observed and balance-of-payments equilibrium growth rates of GDP and growth of exports for the six largest advanced countries

| Country | 1951–73 | | | 1973–86 | | |
| | *Growth of* | | *B. of P. equilibrium growth of* | *Growth of* | | *B. of P. equilibrium growth of* |
	(i) GDP	(ii) Exports	GDP	(i) GDP	(ii) Exports	GDP
Japan	9.79	12.67	10.30	3.63	8.00	6.50
Italy	5.22	11.13	5.08	2.80	4.43	2.02
West Germany	5.64	9.88	5.49(7.54)	1.78	4.14	2.30(3.16)
France	5.11	7.59	4.57(4.66)	2.16	3.88	2.34(2.38)
United States	3.58	5.04	3.00	2.39	3.73	2.22
United Kingdom	2.91	4.27	2.94(2.35)	1.52	3.19	2.20(1.75)

Note: The balance-of-payments equilibrium growth of GDP is derived using import elasticities from Houthakker and Magee (1969) except for those in parentheses which use Panić's estimates.

The figures for 1951–73 differ slightly from those used in Chapter 3 and 5 because of different sources and statistical revisions.

Sources: OECD *National Accounts* (various years).

periods, namely, the 'long boom' of 1951–73 and the 'slowdown' of 1973–86. The equilibrium growth rates of GDP in the first period are found to approximate closely the observed growth rates, confirming the results of earlier chapters. The test described in Chapter 5 using π and π' (the hypothetical income elasticity of demand for imports that equates y and y_B) shows that the differences between the equilibrium and the actual growth rates are not statistically significant. (Houthakker and Magee's (1969) estimates of π and their standard errors were used.) In the period 1973–86, three countries (Japan, Germany and the UK) have equilibrium growth rates that were statistically significantly above their actual growth rates. This was undoubtedly because growth was restricted for fear of inducing inflationary pressures; the result was that all three countries improved their balance-of-payments position. In 1973, Japan's current account was in balance, but by 1986 it had a current account surplus that was 4.3 per cent of GDP (measured in current prices). Germany had a surplus of 1.3 per cent in 1973 and this increased to a surplus of 4.4 per cent in 1986. The UK reduced its deficit from 2.0 per cent in 1973 to a deficit of 0.9 per cent in 1986.

In the context of long-term growth, it is readily apparent that the differing export elasticities are more important in explaining the different GDP growth rates than disparities in the import elasticities. For example, the countries with the fastest and the second fastest growth of GDP from 1951 to 1973, namely, Japan and Italy, had the lowest and highest income elasticities of demand for imports respectively (using the estimates of Houthakker and Magee, 1969). It was the high world income elasticities of the demand for their exports that was responsible for their high balance-of-payments equilibrium growth rates. To put the matter another way: if the UK had Japan's income elasticity of demand for imports then the equilibrium growth rate would only increase by a little over 0.5 percentage points per annum, *ceteris paribus*. If, however, the UK's exports were in sufficient demand that the world income elasticity of demand for its export matched, say, that of West Germany, this would have had the effect of doubling the UK's balance of payments equilibrium growth rate.

Our approach to economic growth described here is, as we have seen in Chapter 2, sometimes termed 'demand orientated' because of its stress on the role of the multiplier. Nevertheless, it is worth reiterating that the approach places great emphasis on the importance of supply characteristics which determine the disparities in the world income elasticity of demand for the various countries' exports. It provides no justification for the conventional Keynesian demand-management policies that were applied particularly to the postwar UK economy prior to 1979 which merely resulted in the 'stop–go' pattern of economic growth.

The key to the long-run growth of the economy is the rate of growth of exports. This has more to do with such factors as quality, design and delivery dates than with pure price competitiveness (Chapter 4). Thus, attempts to increase the trend rate of growth of exports through macroeconomic policies, such as exchange rate adjustments, are unlikely to be very successful. The problem of the poor performance of UK exports is a structural one requiring an industrial strategy at the microeconomic level. The fallacy underlying past UK policy has rested in the belief that if only growth generated by fiscal policies could be maintained for long enough (albeit at the expense of a 'temporary' balance of payments deficit) there should be no reason why the growth of the UK could not match that of the other European countries. This myth should have been finally laid to rest with the Barber boom of 1971–3, but the folly was repeated with the UK's rapid consumer-led boom from 1986 to 1989 which plunged the UK into an even larger balance-of-payments deficit and precipitated the severe recession from 1990 to the time of writing (1992). Even an 18 per cent devaluation during the Barber boom did not prevent the occurrence of an untenable balance-of-payments deficit. An attempt to increase the underlying rate of growth of output by a consumption-led boom leads to an immediate increase in imports and a rapid deterioration in the balance of payments. It may be that increasing the trend rate of growth of output would eventually increase the growth of exports (through, for example, the Verdoorn effect), but such results are achievable only in the long term and would not have very much influence over a period of two or three years. It was hardly surprising that such attempts at demand-management, based as they were on a theory essentially concerned with a closed economy, were bound to end in failure. But this does not imply the irrelevance of Keynesian economic theory as some, such as Eltis (1976), have argued. In fact, it implies quite the opposite.

CONCLUSION

The most satisfactory basis of the export-led growth theory is that it represents the operation of the Hicks super-multiplier. A corollary to this is that while some of the faster growing countries (most notably Japan and West Germany) may have experienced a labour supply constraint, the growth of factor inputs has never been the exogenous determinant of growth. This role belongs to the growth of exports which, by relaxing the balance-of-payments constraint, determines the maximum growth of GDP even though this may not be sufficient to ensure the full utilisation of the factors of production. The reason why the slower growing countries did not experience a marked acceleration in the rate of unemployment until the early 1970s was that the primary and tertiary sectors acted as a resevoir of labour even though it resulted in disguised unemployment.

Although the theory outlined in this chapter is Keynesian in the sense that it is demand-orientated, nevertheless, it emphasises the importance of the supply side of the economy. The efficiency with which goods destined for the foreign market are produced ultimately determines the performance of the economy as a whole. Of course, it is unlikely that the UK could ever have matched the economic performance of Japan especially during the 'long boom', but if exports had grown consistently at about 7 per cent p.a. over the postwar period the UK must surely have been capable of a growth of GDP of between 4 and 4.5 per cent p.a. instead of the 2.8 per cent actually experienced.

APPENDIX: THE LEVEL OF INCOME, THE FOREIGN TRADE MULTIPLIER AND THE SUPER-MULTIPLIER: A NUMERICAL EXAMPLE

The purpose of this appendix is to present a simple numerical example to demonstrate the arguments that were made in the main body of the chapter. For expositional ease, however, we shall deal in terms of levels of and discrete changes in expenditure, rather than exponential growth rates. The example is based on a simple Keynesian model described by the following equations:

$$Y = C + I + G + X - M \tag{A6.1}$$
$$C = c(Y - T) \tag{A6.2}$$
$$I = I_0 \tag{A6.3}$$
$$G = G_0 \tag{A6.4}$$
$$T = tY \tag{A6.5}$$
$$X = X_0 \tag{A6.6}$$
$$M = mY \tag{A6.7}$$

(with the usual notation).

Let the values for c, t, and m be 0.8, 0.25 and 0.2. To begin with, we assume that the balance of payments is in equilibrium and $Y = 100$ units. Potential or full employment output, Y_p, is taken to be 120. The equilibrium values of the variables are:

$$Y = 100$$
$$C = 60$$
$$I = 15$$
$$G = 25$$
$$T = 25$$
$$X = 20$$
$$M = 20$$

The balance of payments $= X - M = 0$; the budget deficit $= (G - T) = 0$; and $Y_p - Y = 20$.

The foreign trade multiplier $(1/k) = 1/(1 - c + m + ct) = 1.667$

It may be easily confirmed that the level of income is determined by the exogenous components of demand, namely, exports, government expenditure and investment.

$$Y = (1/k)(X + I + G) = 1.667 (20 + 15 + 25) = 100$$

(1) The Effect of an Increase in Investment

Suppose that for some reason business expectations improve, leading to an increase in investment of 12 units. Total investment becomes 27. The equilibrium values are now:

$$Y = 120$$
$$C = 72$$
$$I = 27$$
$$G = 25$$
$$T = 30$$
$$X = 20$$
$$M = 24$$

The government is now running a budget surplus of 10 and the economy is at full employment. The balance of payments, however, has moved into deficit by 4 units which we assume is not sustainable indefinitely. Under the assumptions of the model, the only way to correct this deficit is to deflate the economy. To bring the balance of payments back into equilibrium requires a cut in government expenditure of 12 units. The equilibrium values after this has occurred are:

$$Y = 100$$
$$C = 60$$
$$I = 27$$
$$G = 13$$
$$T = 25$$
$$X = 20$$
$$M = 20$$

The balance of payments is now back in equilibrium and there is a budget surplus of 12 units. It is likely that investment will eventually fall to its initial level of 15 units and government expenditure will have to increase to 25 units to maintain the economy at its balance-of-payments equilibrium output. This restores the economy to its original position.

(2) The Direct Effect of an Increase in Exports

Let us now suppose that exports increase by 4 units when the economy is in its initial equilibrium position. The increase in income is 6.67 units and the values of the various variables are:

$$Y = 106.67$$
$$C = 64$$
$$I = 15$$
$$G = 25$$
$$T = 26.67$$
$$X = 24$$
$$M = 21.2$$

It can be seen that there is now a balance-of-payments surplus of 3.8 units and a small budget surplus. Income is still 13.33 units below its maximum potential.

(3) The Effect of the Super-Multiplier

Since the economy has a balance of trade surplus, the government can reflate the economy by increasing its expenditure without precipitating a balance of payments crisis. In fact, demand can be increased until the maximum level of income is reached, as this is the level of income that brings the balance of payments back into equilibrium. It is also likely that the rate of investment will increase with the increase in output. Let us assume that the investment–output ratio is constant at 15 per cent. The equilibrium values will now be:

$$
\begin{aligned}
Y &= 120 \\
C &= 72 \\
I &= 18 \\
G &= 30 \\
T &= 30 \\
X &= 24 \\
M &= 24
\end{aligned}
$$

Government expenditure exactly equals the tax revenue. The economy is now resource constrained, in that any further increase in demand will not increase Y, but will merely result in both inflation and a change in the distribution of the expenditures.

This simple example shows that the direct result of the increase in exports through the foreign trade multiplier, which takes a value of 1.667, is to increase income by a third of the eventual outcome. Nevertheless, by relaxing the balance-of-payments constraint, exports have been both directly and indirectly responsible for all of the increase in income. This is the working of the super-multiplier which, in our example, takes a value of 5.

7 Export-Led Growth and the Balance-of-Payments Constraint

INTRODUCTION[1]

There are two main reasons for believing in the importance of export-led growth; one uncontroversial, the other more contentious. The first is that export growth can lift a balance-of-payments constraint on demand and therefore permit faster growth if factor supplies are available to be utilised. The second is that export growth may create a virtuous circle of growth by virtue of the link between output growth and productivity growth. A number of models of this genre have appeared in the literature in recent years (e.g. Lamfalussy, 1963; Beckerman, 1962; Kaldor, 1970; Dixon and Thirlwall, 1975a) and they are surveyed later. There is a problem with these models, however, and that is they do not incorporate an explicit balance-of-payments equilibrium condition or constraint, which means that the equilibrium growth rate specified may be inconsistent with the long-run requirement of payments balance.[2] The implicit assumption seems to be that provided it is exports that are the engine of growth, as distinct from domestic demand, the balance of payments will look after itself. Indeed, it is assumed in some models that the initial export growth and trade surplus generates such favourable responses in the economy that the balance-of-payments surplus actually grows. No consideration is given to the possibility that the rate of growth of income determined by the model may generate a rate of growth of imports in excess of the rate of growth of exports, thereby imposing a constraint on the export-led growth rate if balance-of-payments equilibrium must be preserved. Import behaviour in export-led growth models seems to have been neglected. This is not to pour cold water on export-led growth models. If the balance of payments is constraining the actual growth rate before the capacity rate is reached, then growth led by export demand, as opposed to other elements of demand, will raise the constraint; and if the actual growth rate can reach the capacity rate, the capacity rate itself may be raised. But it cannot be taken for granted in export-led models that there is no constraint on growth at all. If balance-of-payments equilibrium is a requirement, the equilibrium growth rate in an export-led growth model must reflect this requirement, otherwise the model may be useless for predictive purposes.

Models of export-led growth are typically very unspecific about the precise relationship between the rate of growth of exports and income, and how much income growth might be associated with a given growth of exports. It is clear from the historical and contemporary evidence, however, that exports tend to grow faster than income, which must make one immediately suspicious of models, for predictive purposes at least, which set the rate of growth of income equal to the rate of growth of exports. There is no doubt a variety of explanations as to why the rate of growth of exports typically exceeds the rate of growth of income through time, but a balance-of-payments constraint, related to the characteristics of goods traded, is one powerful explanation. It is intuitively obvious, and has be shown formally earlier (Chapter 5), that if the income elasticity of demand for imports is greater than unity, and there is no continual compensating improvement in price competitiveness, an equality between the rate of growth of exports and income would generate a higher rate of growth of imports than exports, and income growth would sooner or later have to be curtailed. Thus, as long as the income elasticity of demand for imports is greater than unity, which it appears to be for most countries, the ratio of export growth to income growth will almost certainly show an historical tendency to exceed unity. Indeed, one could go further and say that if the income elasticity of demand for imports exceeds unity the export sector *must* expand relative to the total economy if growth is to be sustained. This simple truth has important policy implications for all countries that wish to raise their growth rate but which at the same time are confronted with a high income elasticity of demand for imports. If the growth rate is specified as $y = \gamma x$, where x is the growth of exports, and $0 < \gamma < 1$, it was shown in Chapter 3 that γ does indeed approximate to the reciprocal of the income elasticity of demand for imports for a number of countries.

In this chapter we first briefly consider the importance of export-led growth and survey the main models. The balance-of-payments equilibrium condition is then specified and incorporated into a model of export-led growth. We then consider the importance of export-led growth in a situation where the growth of one group of countries directly limits the growth of another group through the impact of trade flows together with the balance of payments constraint.

THE IMPORTANCE OF EXPORT-LED GROWTH

The importance of export-led growth is best discussed and understood within the framework of the relationship between the balance-of-payments equilibrium (constrained) growth rate (y_B) on the one hand and the actual and capacity rates of growth $(y_A$ and $y_C)$ on the other. The possible sets of relationships between y_B, y_A and y_C are outlined below:

(i) $y_B = y_A = y_C$: balance-of-payments equilibrium and full employment
(ii) $y_B = y_A < y_C$: balance-of-payments equilibrium and growing unemployment
(iii) $y_B < y_A = y_C$: increasing balance-of-payments deficit and full employment
(iv) $y_B < y_A < y_C$: increasing balance-of-payments deficit and growing unemployment
(v) $y_B > y_A = y_C$: increasing balance-of-payments surplus and full employment
(vi) $y_B > y_A < y_C$: increasing balance-of-payments surplus and growing unemployment.

It is a fundamental proposition in economics that in the long run when all resources are fully utilised, a country's actual growth rate cannot exceed its capacity rate as determined by the rate of growth of the labour force and the productivity of labour: the Harrodian natural rate of growth. For countries with perpetual balance of payments and unemployment difficulties, the lure of export-led growth lies in the possibility of moving from situation (iv) to at least (i) if not (v), where the balance of payments equilibrium growth rate lies above the capacity growth rate, thus allowing the actual growth rate to equal the capacity growth rate without balance of payments difficulties arising. In this situation, the buoyancy of demand at full employment will then raise the capacity growth rate. There are a number of possible mechanisms through which this may happen: the encouragement to investment which would augment the capital stock, and bring with it technical progress; the supply of labour may increase by the entry into the workforce of people previously outside or from abroad; the movement of factors of production from low productivity to high productivity sectors; and the ability to import more may increase capacity by making domestic resources more productive. In this spirit, Cornwall (1977) argues persuasively that the major explanation of growth rate differences between countries is differences in the pressure of demand to which supply adjusts, although for reasons we shall consider later (and question) he does not believe that the balance of payments is a constraint on demand.

As far as the British economy is concerned, it is difficult to know what a faster rate of growth of exports might do for the capacity growth rate because export performance in the past has never been good enough to escape a balance-of-payments constraint before the capacity growth rate has been reached. Britain has approximated to situation (iv) above. It is frequently argued, however, that if only Britain did not run into balance-of-payments difficulties before full employment is reached, demand would not have to be contracted, investment would remain high, and that these conditions in the long run would raise the capacity growth rate closer to that of other countries. While the argument is speculative, it would be surprising if Britain's growth record relative to other countries since the Second World War did not have something to do with the characteristics of its trading position compared to other countries, particularly its low rate of growth of exports combined with a relatively high income elasticity of demand for imports. Certainly part of Japan's phenomenal success must be related to the fact that, as the figures in Tables 3.1 and 3.2 in Chapter 3 show, its growth rate consistent with balance-of-payments equilibrium has exceeded by a considerable margin its actual growth rate which has continually pressed on its capacity rate. Kaldor (1974) has argued that the main cause of unemployment in the UK throughout the last century, barring periods of acute depression, has not been over-saving but insufficient exports relative to the level of imports which would be required at full employment: 'despite commitment to full employment from 1944 it took a very long time – in fact until 1963[3] – before it was realised that the true effect of the new system (i.e. commitment to full employment) was simply to transmute the chronic pre-war unemployment problem into the chronic post-war balance-of-payments problem'. Kaldor goes on to say that what the UK has really suffered from has been the slow growth of exports, an historical fact which can be explained by the industrialisation of other regions of the world which have constantly narrowed the markets for British goods. Kaldor was a strong believer in the importance of export-led growth, maintaining that the common feature of all industrial economies is that their economic growth has been invariably led by a faster growth of exports which has given a higher rate of growth of industrial productivity. He claims that the UK could have grown at 5 per cent per annum had it achieved export growth of 10–15 per cent per annum.

To sum up, we can make two propositions about the importance of export growth. First, that up to the capacity growth rate, a country's actual growth rate is fundamentally determined by its rate of growth of exports (in relation to the rate of growth of imports) if it is to maintain balance of payments equilibrium. Secondly, it is probable that a country's capacity rate is also partly determined by its export performance because of the link between high demand and the response of factor supplies, and because faster growth itself generates faster productivity growth. This is the idea of a virtuous circle of growth led by exports, which we now develop.

MODELS OF EXPORT-LED GROWTH

In the European context, Lamfalussy (1963) was one of the first economists to propound an export-led growth theory to account for differences in the growth performance of Western European countries. In Lamfalussy's model, export-led growth is important for three main reasons: (i) the rate of growth of exports, as a determinant of demand, is assumed to be an important determinant of investment; (ii) growth requires imports, and if exports do not rise as fast as import requirements, growth will be constrained by the balance of payments; and (iii) the smaller the domestic market, the greater the importance of external demand in enabling economies to reap economies of scale in production to make enterprises viable that would otherwise not be so. Lamfalussy envisaged a virtuous circle commencing with higher exports leading to more investment, which in turn leads to a higher rate of growth of productivity, lower export prices and thus higher exports. There is, however, no explicit treatment of the balance of payments in the model.

Beckerman (1962) develops a similar virtuous circle of export-led growth, but his model also lacks a balance-of-payments constraint. Demand determines investment and growth; an important component of demand is exports (and it is only this component of demand that can help to balance the import requirements at a higher level of demand); a high level of demand and investment is favourable to growth which contributes to greater competitiveness and further export demand. Beckerman claims that the growth of exports is closely related across countries to the growth of competitiveness, and that differences in competitiveness are mainly a function of differences in productivity growth. While not wanting to prejudge the cause of the relationship, there is certainly a close relationship across countries between the rate of growth of output and the rate of growth of exports. The rank correlation between the two variables for the selection of countries in Table 3.1 is 0.84.

As Caves (1970) rightly noted, Beckerman's model in its original form lacks an equilibrium condition. Also the export demand function is very *ad hoc*, making the rate of growth of exports a function of the absolute difference between domestic and foreign prices. We will make use of the more conventional multiplicative export demand function, which makes the rate of growth of exports depend on the difference between the rate of growth of domestic and foreign prices (see equation (3.5) in Chapter 3). This also gives the model an equilibrium condition. The (modified) Beckerman model runs as follows: export growth is a function of the difference in the rate of growth of domestic and foreign prices; faster export growth leads to faster productivity growth; faster productivity growth contributes to a lower rate of growth of wage costs per unit of output if wages do not rise in line with productivity; a lower rate of increase in wage costs per unit of output leads to a lower rate of domestic price increase; and a lower rate of domestic price increase leads to a faster rate of growth of exports. The virtuous circle is complete. If the model is formulated algebraically, using linear relations, with signs correctly specified in the model, we have:

$$x = a_0 - b_0(p_d - p_f - e); \quad a_0 > 0, b_0 > 0 \tag{7.1}$$

where x is the rate of growth of exports; p_d is the rate of growth of domestic prices; p_f is the rate of growth of foreign prices; e is the rate of growth of the exchange rate (the domestic price of foreign currency); b_0 is the price elasticity of demand for exports, and a_0 represents the rate of growth of exports determined by other factors (e.g. the growth of world income):

$$r = a_1 + b_1 x; \quad b_1 > 0 \tag{7.2}$$

where r is the rate of growth of labour productivity;

$$w = a_2 + b_2 r; \quad 0 < b_2 < 1 \tag{7.3}$$

where w is the rate of growth of wages, and:

$$p_d = w - r \tag{7.4}$$

Substituting (7.2) and (7.3) into (7.4) and the result into (7.1) gives an expression for the equilibrium rate of growth of exports of:

$$x = \frac{a_0 - b_0(a_2 - a_1 + b_2 a_1) + b_0(p_f + e)}{1 + b_0 b_1(b_2 - 1)} \tag{7.5}$$

Notice that the virtuous circle of export-led growth depends crucially on the rate of increase in wages being less than the rate of increase in productivity (i.e. $b_2 < 1$). If $b_2 = 1$ there would be no 'circular' process; that is, no induced rate of growth of exports from the initial expansion of exports itself. Balassa (1963) has also argued that if wages respond to the level of employment, the virtuous circle may be choked. He is concerned that if $b_2 < 1$, Beckerman's model may lead to diverging country growth rates which are not observable in practice. The model is easily modified by relating changes in wages to the level of unemployment, using a Phillips curve relation. This makes for stability by causing wages and prices to rise faster in regions where export growth is high than in regions where export growth is sluggish and unemployment high. Divergence of growth rates may take place until full employment is reached but then the virtuous circle would break down. Beckerman (1963) replies that wage rate increases between countries bear little relation to unemployment rate differences. This is clearly an empirical matter. A lot would seem to depend on the extent to which labour supply can adjust to demand across countries. The work of Cornwall (1977) suggests that labour is very flexible and that demand and growth have not been constrained in Europe in the postwar period by a lack of factor supplies. Beckerman stresses an economy obtaining its initial advantage in trade through a favourable movement in relative prices; that is, through some competitive shock such as devaluation.[4] By contrast, we stress the importance of countries obtaining their initial trading advantage in goods with a high income elasticity of demand in world markets, which affects the term a_0 in equation (7.1).

Before proceeding to develop our own model, incorporating a balance of payments equilibrium condition, a brief examination of Caves's (1970) comments on the empirical content of the individual functions making up the export-led growth models of Lamfalussy and Beckerman will be useful to clarify the argument. He makes two major points but neither, in our view, is substantial enough to undermine the importance of export growth for simultaneous balance of payments equilibrium and a high rate of growth of income. First Caves asks 'what is special about the growth of exports compared to the growth of any other component of aggregate demand of equal size?' Beckerman himself gives the answer when he argues that if other items of demand are expanded businessmen may fear that demand growth will not continue smoothly because of the balance of payments implications of the expansion of other types of demand. Caves seems to recognise this as the crucial point, but then says 'but it does attribute to business enterprises an aversion to demand fluctuations induced by public authorities that defies easy credibility'. Caves appears to be questioning the influence of the level of demand on investment. But if investment is sensitive to the pressure of demand in relation to capacity output, the point made by the export-led growth school remains valid if export-led growth raises the rate of growth at which a balance-of-payments constraint becomes operative. Caves's second point concerns the relationship between higher export growth and a higher rate of productivity growth. He contends that there may be a link between export and output growth on the one hand and productivity growth on the other, but the direction of causation is anything but clear. This question relates to the controversy over the Verdoorn relationship.[5] Suffice it to say that while productivity growth is obviously a source of output growth, there are also good economic reasons why higher output growth should be a stimulus to productivity growth. The question is not whether there is a relationship but whether the estimate of the relationship is biased because of its two-way nature.

Another critic of the idea that growth is constrained by the balance of payments is Cornwall (1977) who argues that the forces that lead to the rapid growth of output, e.g. technological change and entrepreneurial dynamism, also work to relieve a country of a balance-of-payments constraint. He rightly observes that the developed countries with recurring balance of payments difficulties have also been the slow growers, but wants to argue from this that it is the slow growth that has caused the balance of payments difficulties – rather than the other way round. It is hard to accept this view. It is not the case that all of the forces that lead to rapid output growth in a country necessarily improve the balance of payments. Technological change may be expected to improve productivity at home and also increase the desirability of a country's goods abroad, but this is only one of many factors behind the growth of output. Cornwall's argument does not fit the British experience where, if anything, productivity growth and the capacity growth rate have risen, and yet the balance-of-payments constraint has not improved because the forces making for the rise in productivity have not improved the demand characteristics of the goods exported.

THE KALDOR MODEL OF EXPORT-LED GROWTH

As we indicated earlier, Kaldor was a strong advocate of export-led growth, and we shall use his model here for the incorporation of a balance-of-payments constraint (or equilibrium condition). Kaldor's argument is essentially the Hicksian view (1950) that it is the growth of autonomous demand which governs the long-run rate of growth of output. In open economies, export demand is the main component of autonomous demand, so that the rate of growth of exports governs the long-run rate of growth of output to which investment and consumption adjust. We can therefore write $y = \gamma x$.[6] Kaldor is not explicit on the form of the export demand function, but seems to be suggesting the conventional multiplicative function. We adopt this, and relate the quantity of exports to relative prices measured in domestic currency and world income:

$$X = k_1 \left[\frac{P_d}{EP_f} \right]^\eta Z^\varepsilon \tag{7.6}$$

where the notation is as before: X is the quantity of exports; k_1 is a constant; P_d is the domestic price of exports; P_f is foreign prices; Z is the level of world income; E is the domestic price of foreign currency; η is the price elasticity of demand for exports ($\eta < 0$); ε is the income elasticity of demand for exports ($\varepsilon > 0$). The rate of growth of exports may be written:

$$x = \eta(p_d - p_f - e) + \varepsilon z \tag{7.7}$$

where lower-case letters represent proportional rates of change of the variables. The rate of growth of income outside the economy (z), the rate of change of foreign prices (p_f), and changes in the exchange rate are taken as exogenous. The rate of growth of domestic (export) prices (p_d) is assumed to be endogenous, however, and is derived from a pricing equation of the form:

$$P_d = (W/R)(T) \tag{7.8}$$

where W is the level of money wages; R is the average product of labour, and T is $1 + \%$ mark-up on unit labour costs. From equation (7.8) we can write the approximation:

$$p_d = w - r + \tau \tag{7.9}$$

The third relation in Kaldor's model, which gives a virtuous circle of export-led growth, is the dependence of the growth of labour productivity on the growth of output, which is Verdoorn's Law discussed in Chapter 2:

$$r = r_a + \lambda y \tag{7.10}$$

where r_a is the rate of autonomous productivity growth and λ is the Verdoorn coefficient. Equation (7.10) makes the model 'circular' since the higher the rate of growth of output, the faster the rate of growth of productivity, and the faster the rate of growth of productivity, the lower the rate of increase in unit costs and hence the faster the rate of growth of exports and output. It is also the Verdoorn relation which gives rise to the possibility that once an economy obtains a growth advantage it will tend to keep it. Suppose, for example, that an economy obtains an advantage in the production of goods with a high income elasticity of demand in world markets which raises its growth rate above that of other economies. Through the Verdoorn effect, productivity growth will then be higher and the economy will retain its competitive advantage in these goods, making it difficult for other countries to establish the same commodities. The income elasticity of demand for exports is, in our view, probably the most important determinant of comparative export performance. Likewise, the income elasticity of demand for imports must assume key importance in an export-led growth model with a balance-of-payments equilibrium condition. The lower the income elasticity of demand for imports, the higher the growth rate consistent with balance-of-payments equilibrium, other things remaining the same. In models of cumulative causation (Myrdal, 1957, and Hirschman, 1958),[7] in which some economies produce goods which are expanding fast in demand while other economies produce goods which are sluggish in demand, it is the difference between the income elasticity characteristics of exports and imports which is the essence of the theory of divergence between 'centre' and 'periphery' and between industrial and agricultural economies. This is also the essence of Kaldor's view that the opening up of trade between economies may create growth rate differences which are sustained or even widened by the process of trade, viz. the United Kingdom in the European Economic Community.

THE BALANCE-OF-PAYMENTS EQUILIBRIUM CONDITION

Starting from initial balance-of-payments equilibrium, the condition for a moving equilibrium through time is that the rate of growth of exports equals the rate of growth of imports. Let the initial equilibrium be defined as:

$$P_d X = P_f M E \qquad (7.12)$$

where M is the quantity of imports, E is the domestic price of foreign currency, and P_d, X, and P_f are defined as before. Taking rates of change of the variables, gives the condition for a moving equilibrium through time of:

$$p_d + x = p_f + m + e \qquad (7.13)$$

The quantity of imports demanded may be specified as a multiplicative function of the price of imports, measured in units of domestic currency; the price of import substitutes (which we assume to be approximated by the domestic price level), and domestic income. Thus:

$$M = k_2 \left[\frac{P_f E}{P_d} \right]^{\psi} Y^{\pi} \qquad (7.14)$$

where Y is domestic income, k_2 is a constant, ψ is the price elasticity of demand for imports ($\psi < 0$), and π is the income elasticity of demand for imports ($\pi > 0$). The rate of growth of imports may be written as:

$$m = \psi(p_f + e - p_d) + \pi y \tag{7.15}$$

Substituting equation (7.15) into (7.13), the condition for balance-of-payments equilibrium through time is:

$$p_d + x = p_f + \psi (p_f + e - p_d) + \pi y + e \tag{7.16}$$

and thus the rate of growth of income consistent with balance-of-payments equilibrium is:

$$y_B = \frac{x + (1 + \psi)(p_d - p_f - e)}{\pi} \tag{7.17}$$

An increase in x will raise the balance-of-payments constraint on growth. Within this framework, we are free to specify any export demand function we choose. In the simplest case, without going on to develop a virtuous circle model of export-led growth, equation (7.7) could be used. Substituting (7.7) for x in equation (7.17) gives:

$$y_B = \frac{(1 + \eta + \psi)(p_d - p_f - e) + \varepsilon z}{\pi} \tag{7.18}$$

Alternatively, if we use the specification of the rate of growth of exports in equation (7.11), which contains the idea of a virtuous circle of growth led by exports, and substitute in equation (7.17) we obtain:

$$y_B = \frac{(1 + \eta + \psi)[w - r_a + \tau - p_f - e] + \varepsilon z}{\pi + \lambda(1 + \eta + \psi)} \tag{7.19}[8]$$

Both models, showing the importance of exports and incorporating the balance-of-payments equilibrium condition, have interesting properties, some of which are very familiar. First, in both equations (7.18) and (7.19), domestic prices rising faster than foreign prices will lower the equilibrium growth if the sum of the (negative) export and import price elasticities exceeds unity. Secondly a depreciation of the currency, i.e. a rise in the home price of foreign currency ($e > 0$), will improve the equilibrium growth rate if the sum of the two elasticities exceeds unity in absolute value. This is the Marshall–Lerner condition for a successful devaluation ($|\eta + \psi| > 1$). Notice, however, that the improvement in the growth rate can only be once-for-all unless depreciation is continuous. In subsequent periods when the exchange rate settles at its new level, the growth rate would revert to its former level (since $e = 0$). Thirdly, the equilibrium growth rate varies positively with the growth of world income, and inversely with the income elasticity of demand for imports. The difference between the two export growth models is that the virtuous circle version of the model (equation (7.19)) will give a higher equilibrium growth than otherwise would be the case if the bracketed term in the denominator of the equation is negative; in other words, if the Marshall–Lerner condition is satisfied. If it is not fulfilled, the growth rate consistent with balance-of-payments equilibrium will be lower than it otherwise would have been. If, of course, there is no virtuous circle through the Verdoorn effect, so that $\lambda = 0$, the two models are the same: that is, equations (7.18) and (7.19) are identical.

The balance-of-payments constrained export-led growth model used here is certainly a far better predictor of the actual British growth experience than the unconstrained export-led model of equation (7.19a) (see footnote 8). When the unconstrained model was applied to the data for the period 1951–66 (Dixon and Thirlwall, 1975a) it predicted a growth rate of 4 per cent on the basis of the following values for the variables and parameters: $\eta + \psi = -1.5$; $w + \tau = 0.06$; $r_a = 0.02$; $p_f = 0.02$; $\varepsilon = 1.0$; $z = 0.04$; $\lambda = 0.5$ and $\gamma = 1.0$. Since the actual growth rate over the period was 2.8 per cent, it was concluded that the model may be overpredicting because of a balance-of-payments constraint – apart from any constraint on capacity. If 4 per cent was a permissible rate consistent with balance-of-payments equilibrium, the country should have enjoyed a growing surplus, which it did not. Application of the same model, but with a balance-of-payments constraint (equation 7.19), assuming $\pi = 1.51$ and that imports are insensitive to price, gives a growth rate consistent with balance-of-payments equilibrium of 2.4 per cent. This is closer to the actual growth rate of 2.8 per cent, and the discrepancy between the two rates is consistent with the balance-of-payments moving into deficit over the period. Making imports sensitive to price would raise the rate slightly.

Applying the equations to the post-1966 period gives rather less satisfactory results probably because the period has been one of general economic upheaval, and the model is very sensitive to small variations (errors) in the variables and in the assumed parameter values. When the constrained virtuous circle model (equation (7.19)) is applied to the data over the period 1967–76, the estimated growth rate is 5.5 per cent compared with the actual growth rate of 1.8 per cent per annum.[9]

Since the country moved into substantial deficit over the period, the model is clearly overpredicting. It could be that the income elasticity of demand for imports is much higher than the assumed value of 1.51 or that the sum of the price elasticities of demand for UK exports and imports is less than the assumed −1.5.

The application of our simple growth rule in Chapter 3 gives a balance-of-payments equilibrium growth rate of 2 per cent. This looks much more consistent with the facts, particularly if the income elasticity of demand for imports has risen. A value of approximately 2 would give a balance-of-payments equilibrium growth rate of 1.5 per cent per annum over the period, which would be consistent with the actual growth experience and the balance of payments on current account moving into deficit. Despite the effort of formulating a fairly sophisticated export-led growth model, incorporating the idea of a virtuous circle led by exports but constrained by the balance of payments, it seems from the empirical evidence that a simpler model will suffice. Specifically, that growth performance, and growth rate differences between countries, can be approximated by the rate of growth of a country's exports divided by the income elasticity of demand for imports. This is not to disparage the idea of the possibility of a virtuous circle. It is to suggest that the link between exports and growth via the Verdoorn effect may not be very important either because relative prices change very little or because the price elasticities of demand for exports and imports are not sufficiently high. The main importance of export growth lies in raising the balance-of-payments constraint on growth, simply allowing countries to reach their capacity rate.

EXPORT-LED GROWTH IN A TWO-COUNTRY MODEL[10]

Up to now, our modelling of the relationship between the balance of payments and economic growth has been essentially a partial equilibrium approach, with the growth of GDP specified as a function of export growth which, in turn, is determined primarily by the exogenously given rate of growth of 'world' income. In this section, explicit allowance is made for trade interlinkages and it is shown how the economic performance of one group of countries may deleteriously affect that of another group, working through the balance-of-payments constraint.

When a country expands its domestic demand, it simultaneously increases the demand for its imports. This induces an increase in demand in the countries supplying those imports which, in turn, increases the import supplying countries' demand for the initiating country's exports. This sets up a secondary multiplier effect and so on. The 'linked' multiplier explicitly allows for these feedback effects from the rest of the world. However, the values are not radically different from the conventional multiplier estimates. The value of the linked multiplier for the United Kingdom, for example, is only about 1.16, which compares with the unlinked multiplier of 1.10 (authors' estimates).

The total effect, however, of a number of countries simultaneously expanding or contracting demand can be much larger than these linked multiplier figures suggest. The multiplier for the OECD countries as a whole is of the order of 3, more than double the average value for the individual countries. Thus, the expansionary (deflationary) impact acting through the foreign trade multiplier on a particular country which results from a number of the larger OECD countries simultaneously increasing (reducing) their growth rates can be substantial. This is even before we consider the ramifications of the 'super-multiplier'.

While numerous countries correctly consider many of their growth difficulties as originating overseas, for the OECD countries as a whole such problems are largely internally generated. This is because the OECD in aggregate only trades about 7 per cent of its GDP with the rest of the world – a figure which is exceeded by all the individual advanced countries, with the exception of the United States. (The United States has the smallest share of exports in output of the advanced countries, with a figure of 7 per cent, while at the other extreme Belgium exports about 65 per cent of its output.)[11] Consequently, to understand the causes of, for example, the post-1973 slowdown in output growth, it is necessary to consider the interlinkages between, in particular, the individual advanced countries.

Of particular importance, especially since 1973, is the 'deflationary bias' that the asymmetry in balance-of-payments adjustment has imparted into the international economy. This asymmetry results from the fact that a country is able to run a balance-of-payments surplus almost indefinitely, while there are strong pressures on countries to correct a deficit, normally through deflationary measures to reduce the growth of output and, hence, the growth of imports. The severe deflationary pressures that were introduced in the 1970s, supposedly to reduce the inflation generated by the commodity boom and oil price rises of 1973/4 and 1979, led to a global recession from which it became difficult for any one country to escape through the use of domestic demand management policies. It will be shown that, when we consider the interlinkages between the advanced countries, the export-led growth theory has to be extended. Attempts by any one country to relax its balance-of-payments constraint by expenditure switching policies (if, indeed, this is possible) may well lead to *competitive growth*, i.e. to an increase in output which is at the expense of another country's production. This is a situation which may eventually lead to reciprocal devaluation and other protectionist measures to control trade that may ultimately render such expenditure switching policies self-defeating. An implication is that the most effective way of increasing growth and reducing unemployment is the generation of *complementary growth*: this involves the politically more difficult problem of co-ordinated reflation. Only by nations acting in concert in a manner analogous to a closed economy (which obviates the balance-of-payments constraint) can a faster rate of growth be generated.

In the next section, we extend the Harrod dynamic multiplier model to a two-sector case. We consider two groups of countries. The growth of one group is either at its maximum potential ('resource constrained' growth) or at a rate which the relevant governments do not wish to increase for policy reasons such as, for example, combating inflation ('policy constrained' growth). The model shows how the growth of this group limits the growth of the other group through the balance-of-payments constraint, and the latter group may therefore be described as being 'balance-of-payments constrained'. We next introduce capital flows and relative prices into the model. If the change in relative prices is sufficiently important in determining the growth of exports and imports, the balance of payments ceases to act as a constraint. Likewise, a sufficiently fast growth of long-term capital flows may achieve the same result. Nevertheless, we have argued earlier that both these conditions are very unlikely to be met in practice. But this extension of the analysis does demonstrate how the change in both relative prices and capital flows may be incorporated into the model and how these factors may partially relax the balance-of-payments constraint. We next show how import controls may enable a country to circumvent the balance-of-payments constraint. In the long run, however, the imposition of such controls may reduce a country's competitiveness through encouraging 'feather-bedding' and X-inefficiency in the domestic economy. Following this discussion, we briefly review the problems of the international co-ordination of demand management. We conclude by discussing some illustrative examples of countries that have been balance-of-payments constrained and discuss the postwar growth record in the light of our model.

RESOURCE CONSTRAINED, POLICY CONSTRAINED AND BALANCE-OF-PAYMENTS CONSTRAINED GROWTH

In this section, we discuss how the existence of international trade flows is an important factor in determining the maximum growth rate that a number of advanced countries are able to achieve. Notwithstanding the fact that the industrialised countries, in aggregate, are almost a closed economy, all that is necessary for the balance of payments to act as a factor constraining growth is for one country (or group of countries) to have an exogenously determined growth of output.

Prior to 1973, this condition was fulfilled by such countries as Japan and possibly West Germany, both of which achieved growth rates that were sufficiently fast to induce domestic factor supply shortages.[12,13] These countries may be termed 'resource constrained'. It is difficult to argue convincingly that any country has been resource constrained since the mid-1970s in the sense that the factor supplies have, in the long run, limited the growth of GDP. (There have been times, of course, when short-term capacity shortages may have restricted a country's rate of expansion.) Nevertheless, various countries have, at different times and to differing degrees, resorted to deflationary policies in the belief that therein lay the solution to the problem of inflation. From the point of view of the remainder of the advanced countries, the result is similar to the effect of resource constrained economies – it restricts the degree of freedom possessed by these countries to pursue policies to raise their individual rates of growth.

For expositional purposes, it is convenient to divide the countries into two categories. 'Group One' consists of those countries which are growing below their maximum potential and are constrained from growing faster by their balance-of-payments problems. 'Group Two' are those countries which are either resource or policy constrained and, hence, are either unable or unwilling to increase their growth rate. Clearly, the composition of the two groups will vary from time to time. For example, the United Kingdom from 1945 to 1979 should be classified as being balance-of-payments constrained (Group One), whereas for the period 1979–86 it was policy constrained (Group Two). Since 1986, the United Kingdom is again encountering severe balance-of-payments problems, putting the country once more into Group One.

The level of real income of the two groups (measured in Group One's currency) may be expressed in terms of the familiar Keynesian identity as:

$$Y_1 = C_1 + I_1 + G_1 + X_1 - M_1(EP_2/P_1) \tag{7.20}$$

and

$$Y_2 = C_2 + I_2 + G_2 + X_2 - M_2(P_1/EP_2) \tag{7.21}$$

with the same notation as before and where C, I and G denote consumption, investment and government expenditure.

The following relationships are assumed to hold for each group:

$$C_i = \bar{C}_i + \delta(Y_i - T_i) \qquad i = 1, 2; \quad i \neq j \tag{7.22}$$

$$T_i = \tau Y_i \tag{7.23}$$

$$I_i = \bar{I}_i + \theta Y_i \tag{7.24}$$

$$G_i = \bar{G}_i + \zeta Y_i \tag{7.25}$$

where T is the amount of taxation. A bar over a variable denotes autonomous expenditure. Equations (7.22), (7.23), (7.24) and (7.25) are the consumption, taxation, investment and government spending functions.

The level of aggregate autonomous expenditure, from equations (7.22), (7.24), and (7.25), is defined as:

$$A_i = \bar{C}_i + \bar{I}_i + \bar{G}_i \tag{7.26}$$

The sum of induced consumption, induced investment and induced government spending may be determined from equations (7.22), (7.24) and (7.25) as:

$$B_i = (\delta(1-\tau) + \theta + \zeta) Y_i \tag{7.27}$$

Substituting equations (7.26) and (7.27) into equation (7.20) and expressing the results in terms of exponential growth rates, we obtain:

$$y_i = \omega_{Ai} a_i + \omega_{Bi} b_i + \omega_{Xi} x - \omega_{Mi} m_i \tag{7.28}$$

where ω_{Ai} is the share of autonomous expenditure in the total income of group, or country, i, etc. The lower-case letters denote the exponential growth rates of the variables with the usual notation. In deriving equation (7.28), we assume that the terms of trade do not alter in the long run, i.e., $(e + p_2 - p_1) = 0$.

The growth of relative prices, therefore, is also absent from the (dynamic) import and export demand functions. The growth of imports is given by the import demand function, $m_i = \pi_i y_i$. Expressing equation (7.27) in growth rates gives $b_i = y_i$. Using these two results and the definition that the growth of the exports of one group equals the growth of imports of the other, the growth of income of the first group may be expressed in terms of the growth of its autonomous expenditure and the growth of income of the other group as:

$$y_i = \alpha_i a_i + \beta_i \pi_j y_j \qquad i, j = 1, 2; \quad i \neq j \tag{7.29}$$

where $\alpha_i = \dfrac{\omega_{Ai}}{(1 - \omega_{Bi} + \omega_{Mi}\pi_i)}$

and $\beta_i = \dfrac{\omega_{Xi}}{(1 - \omega_{Bi} + \omega_{Mi}\pi_i)}$

α and β are the (dynamic) domestic expenditure and foreign trade multipliers, respectively.

The relationships for Groups One and Two are given by equation (7.29). These, for convenience, may be termed the 'growth equations' and are shown diagrammatically in Figure 7.1(a) as the lines A and B respectively. The actual growth rates of the two groups are determined by the intersection of the two lines. (This is assumed to occur initially at point a in Figure 7.1(a) where the lines A_0 and B_0 intersect.)

It may be seen that the growth of Group One is positively related to that of Group Two. This is because, as the growth of the latter increases, so does its growth of demand for Group One's exports and this will raise Group One's growth of output through the foreign trade multiplier.

The growth of Group One is thus a function not only of the growth of its own autonomous domestic expenditure (as in a closed economy), but also of the growth of comparable expenditure undertaken by Group Two. The growth of Group One is given by:

$$y_1 = \rho(\alpha_1 a_1 + \beta_1 \pi_2 \alpha_2 a_2) \tag{7.30}$$

where $\rho = 1/(1 - \beta_1 \beta_2 \pi_1 \pi_2) > 0$[14]

Given any value of a_2, the growth of Group Two's autonomous expenditure, equation (7.30) suggests that Group One could achieve any desired rate of growth by simply determining the appropriate rate of growth of its own autonomous expenditure and achieving this through domestic demand management policies. This may not be possible, however, because of the existence of a balance-of-payments constraint which it is now necessary to incorporate into the model.

The line BP in Figure 7.1(a) is the locus of points where the growth of the two groups is such that there is no change in the balance of payments. The equation of the BP line is derived from the import and export demand functions together with the balance-of-payments identity (see Chapter 3, p. 248). Assuming, for the moment, that there is no change in relative prices or in the exchange rate, and that Group One has an initial trade deficit, the equation of the BP locus is given by:

$$y_1 = \frac{\varphi \pi_2}{\pi_1} y_2 + \frac{(1 - \varphi)}{\pi_1} (f - p_1) \tag{7.31}$$

where φ is Group One's share of exports in its total foreign exchange receipts. f is the growth of long-term or autonomous net nominal capital flows from Group Two to Group One. The growth of these capital flows is assumed to be independent of the growth of Group One.[15]

For expositional ease, it is convenient to assume $\varphi = 1$, which means that there are no autonomous capital flows and that trade

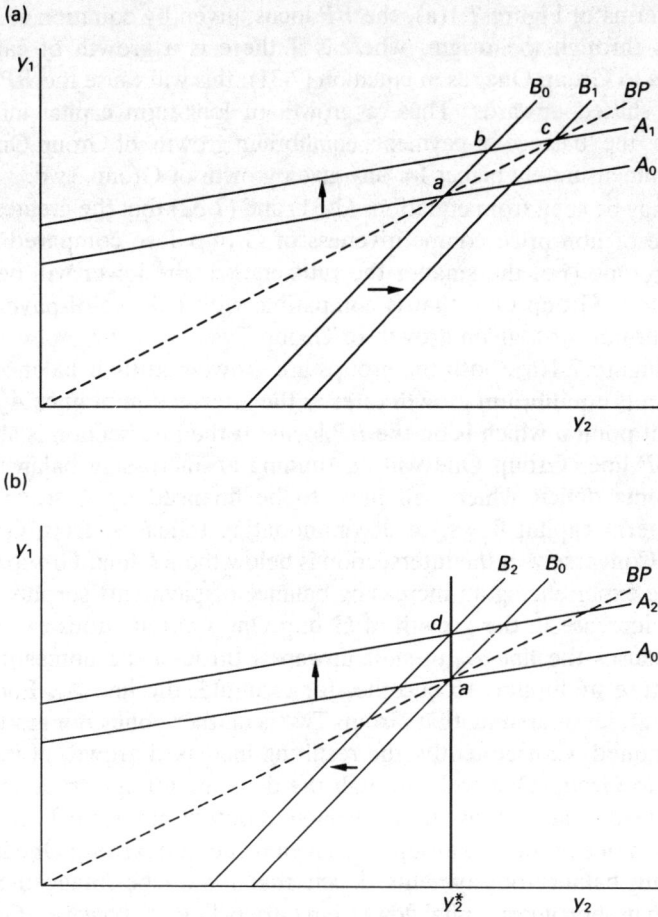

Figure 7.1 Economic growth and the balance-of-payments constraint

between the two groups is initially balanced. The equation of the *BP* locus is now given by:

$$y_1 = \frac{\pi_2}{\pi_1} y_2 \tag{7.32}$$

which is formally equivalent to the dynamic Harrod trade multiplier (or the Hicks super-multiplier) result.

In terms of Figure 7.1(a), the *BP* locus, given by equation (7.32), passes through the origin, whereas if there is a growth of capital inflows to Group One, as in equation (7.31), this will cause the *BP* line to be shifted upwards. Thus, a growth of long-term capital inflows enables the 'balance-of-payments equilibrium growth' of Group One to be commensurately higher for any given growth of Group Two.

It may be seen from equations (7.31) and (7.32) that the greater the degree of non-price competitiveness of Group Two compared with Group One (i.e. the smaller the ratio π_2/π_1), the lower will be the growth of Group One that is compatible with balance-of-payments equilibrium for a given growth of Group Two.

In Figure 7.1(a), both the groups are growing at their balance-of-payments equilibrium growth rates as the intersection of lines A_0 and B_0 is at point *a* which is on the *BP* locus. If the intersection is above the *BP* line, Group One will be running an increasing balance-of-payments deficit which will have to be financed by a growth of short-term capital flows, or accommodating transfers, from Group Two. Conversely, if the intersection is below the *BP* line, Group One will be experiencing an increasing balance-of-payments surplus.

An increase in the growth of Group One's autonomous expenditure causes the line A_0 to shift upwards, through the domestic expenditure multiplier, to become, for example, the line A_1. For the moment, let us assume that Group Two is neither policy nor resource constrained. Consequently, the resulting increased growth of its exports to Group One will, through the dynamic foreign trade multiplier, lead to an increase in the growth of output of Group Two. The growth rates of the two groups are given by point *b*. Group One has a growing balance-of-payments deficit that has to be financed by a growth in short-term capital flows from Group Two. If, however, Group Two takes the opportunity of increasing its growth of domestic autonomous expenditure so that the output growth rates are given by point *c*, the balance of payments will be brought back into equilibrium. The overall movement from *a* to *c* represents the working of the Hicks super-multiplier. We have previously termed this type of economic growth as complementary and we shall return to its importance.

Figure 7.1(b) depicts the situation where Group Two is resource or policy constrained and has a constant growth rate of y_2^*. An expansion in the growth of Group One's autonomous expenditure now results in a movement from *a* to *d*. Once again, the growth of short-term capital flows from Group Two has to finance Group One's growing trade imbalance. In the short run, the growth of Group

Two's autonomous domestic expenditure has to decrease to release resources for the increased growth of exports sold to Group One (i.e. the line B_0 shifts to B_2).

In the long run, however, the increasing balance-of-payments deficit becomes unsustainable as the ratio of international debt to GDP increases. In the absence of effective expenditure switching policies to increase the growth of Group One's exports and reduce its import growth, the only remedy is to reduce its growth of output. Thus, in Figure 7.1(b), Group One's balance-of-payments constrained growth is that given by the point a. It would be purely fortuitous and highly unlikely if this rate of growth were such as to be associated with a full utilisation (or a desired level of utilisation) of Group One's factors of production. More likely, Group One's rate of growth would be below its full employment rate of growth, leading to rising unemployment (either overt or disguised) over time.

Since Group One is constrained by the balance of payments to grow below its maximum potential, if Group Two is policy constrained but decides to raise its rate of growth, it is assumed that Group One will simultaneously increase its own rate of growth to the greatest extent compatible with balance-of-payments equilibrium. Hence, the growth of Group One is fundamentally determined by the growth of Group Two's autonomous expenditure (a_2^*):

$$y_1 = \frac{\pi_2 \alpha_2}{\pi_1 (1 - \beta_2 \pi_2)} a_2^* \quad ; \quad (1 - \beta_2 \pi_2) > 0 \qquad (7.33)$$

If, on the other hand, Group Two is resource constrained, then:

$$y_1 = \frac{\pi_2}{\pi_1} y_2^* \qquad (7.34)$$

where y_2^* is the growth of Group Two which is limited by its growth of factor inputs. (Equation (7.34) can also describe Group One's balance-of-payments equilibrium growth rate when Group Two is policy constrained, except that y_2^* is now determined by a_2^*, rather than by the growth of factor inputs.)

While it has been argued that in the long run a depreciation of the exchange rate is unlikely to be effective in overcoming the balance-of-payments constraint, nevertheless, it may provide some amelioration in the short run. In the next section, the effect of a devaluation on the growth rates of the two groups is considered.

THE IMPACT OF A DEVALUATION

In order to analyse the effect of a devaluation or depreciation of Group One's currency, it is convenient to assume that trade is initially balanced and to commence again with the national income identities of the two groups expressed in real terms:

$$Y_1 = A_1 + B_1 + X_1 - (EP_2/P_1)M_1 \qquad (7.35)$$

and

$$Y_2 = A_2 + B_2 + X_2 - (P_1/EP_2)M_2 \qquad (7.36)$$

where again E is the exchange rate and P_1 and P_2 are the price levels of Groups One and Two. A and B, it will be recalled, are autonomous and induced expenditures.

The export and import demand functions (expressed in growth rate form) are given by:

$$x_1 = m_2 = \pi_2 y_2 - \eta_1(e + p_2 - p_1) \qquad (7.37)$$

and:

$$m_1 = x_2 = \pi_1 y_1 + \psi_1(e + p_2 - p_1) \qquad (7.38)$$

where, as has been noted, the price elasticities of demand, η_1 and ψ_1, are negative. (In the two-region model under consideration here, $\eta_1 = \psi_2$; $\eta_2 = \psi_1$; $\varepsilon_1 = \pi_2$; and $\varepsilon_2 = \pi_1$, where η_2, ψ_2, ε_1, and ε_2 are the relevant elasticities of the other (redundant) export and import demand equations.)

The growth of the two groups may be determined by expressing equations (7.35) and (7.36) in growth rate form and substituting equations (7.37) and (7.38) into them. The resulting equations are given by (dropping, for notational convenience, the subscripts of η_1 and ψ_1):

$$y_1 = \alpha_1 a_1 + \beta_1 \pi_2 y_2 - \beta_1(1 + \eta + \psi)(e + p_2 - p_1) \qquad (7.39)$$

and:

$$y_2 = \alpha_2 a_2 + \beta_2 \pi_1 y_1 + \beta_2(1 + \eta + \psi)(e + p_2 - p_1) \qquad (7.40)$$

The balance-of-payments equilibrium growth rate becomes:

$$y_1 = \frac{\pi_2}{\pi_1} y_2 - \frac{(1 + \eta + \psi)(e + p_2 - p_1)}{\pi_1} \qquad (7.41)$$

It is important to note that in order to alter the growth rate of Group One, given the growth of Group Two, a *continuous* real depreciation is required rather than a once-and-for-all devaluation, because of the multiplicative nature of the demand functions. (For convenience, we shall henceforth take the term 'devaluation' as referring to a continuous depreciation of the currency.)

If the Marshall–Lerner condition just fails to be satisfied in the sense that the price elasticities sum to minus unity, it follows from equations (7.39), (7.40) and (7.41) that a devaluation will have no effect upon the equilibrium growth rate of either group of countries. The growth equations and the balance-of-payments equilibrium locus are in this case given by equations (7.29) and (7.32). Empirical studies, however, suggest that the sum of the price elasticities for aggregate exports and imports falls within the range of -1.0 to -2.5, although the estimates are sometimes found to be statistically insignificant. (See, for example, Houthakker and Magee, 1969; and Stern, Francis and Schumacher, 1976.)

In the circumstances where the Marshall–Lerner condition is satisfied, equation (7.41) demonstrates that, in terms of Figure 7.2, a devaluation will have the effect of shifting the BP locus upwards from

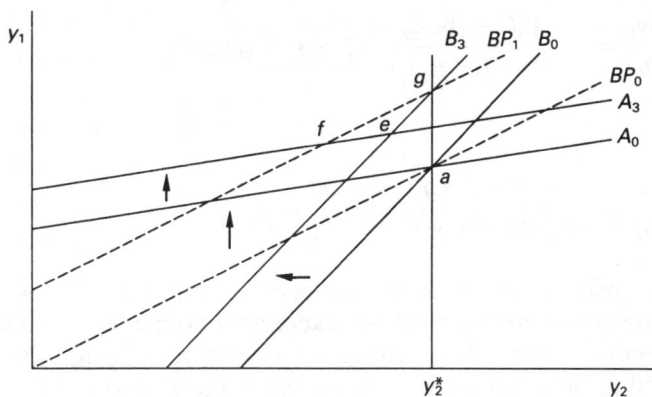

Figure 7.2   The effect of a devaluation

BP_0 to BP_1. The devaluation also results in the line A_0 moving upwards to A_3. The shifts of the BP_0 locus and of the line A_0 are given by $-(1 + \eta + \psi)(e + p_2 - p_1)/\pi_1$, and $-\beta_1(1 + \eta + \psi)(e + p_2 - p_1)$, respectively.

Since β_1 is equal to $\omega_{x1}/(1 - \omega_{B1} + \omega_{M1}\pi_1)$, which is less than $1/\pi_1$, the shift of the BP line exceeds that of the line A_0. A corollary is that, from equation (7.40), the devaluation, *ceteris paribus*, shifts the line B_0 to the left to become line B_3.

The direct impact of the devaluation (i.e. the effect on the growth rates assuming no change in the growth of autonomous expenditure in either group) may be seen by considering the growth equations expressed in terms of a_1 and a_2 and the rates of change of the terms of trade. These are given by:

$$y_1 = \frac{(\alpha_1 a_1 + \beta_1 \pi_2 \alpha_2 a_2) - \beta_1(1 - \beta_2 \pi_2)(1 + \eta + \psi)(e + p_2 - p_1)}{(1 - \beta_1 \beta_2 \pi_1 \pi_2)} \tag{7.42}$$

and:

$$y_2 = \frac{(\alpha_2 a_2 + \beta_2 \pi_1 \alpha_1 a_1) + \beta_2(1 - \beta_1 \pi_1)(1 + \eta + \psi)(e + p_2 - p_1)}{(1 - \beta_1 \beta_2 \pi_1 \pi_2)} \tag{7.43}$$

The effect of a devaluation on the growth rates of the two groups may be determined by partially differentiating equations (7.42) and (7.43) with respect to e. Thus,

$$\frac{\partial y_1}{\partial e} = -\frac{\beta_1(1 - \beta_2 \pi_2)}{(1 - \beta_1 \beta_2 \pi_1 \pi_2)}(1 + \eta + \psi) > 0 \tag{7.44}$$

and:

$$\frac{\partial y_2}{\partial e} = \frac{\beta_2(1 - \beta_1 \pi_1)}{(1 - \beta_1 \beta_2 \pi_1 \pi_2)}(1 + \eta + \psi) < 0 \tag{7.45}$$

It is apparent that the direct impact of a devaluation is to increase the growth of Group One at the expense of Group Two: growth is *competitive*. Group Two, seeing its growth rate being adversely affected by the devaluation, may engage in a retaliatory devaluation, thus rendering Group One's initial attempt to raise its rate of growth self-defeating. Moreover, Group One experiences an increasing surplus on the balance of payments whereas the other group suffers from a worsening deficit. With reference to Figure 7.2 again, the effect is that the growth rates move from the values given by point *a* to those designated by point *e*.

The eventual equilibrium position depends upon the reaction of both groups to the devaluation. To take one example: Group Two, in the face of an increasing balance-of-payments deficit, may consider that the most effective remedy is to engage in a competitive devaluation. If this were successful, it would return the economies to point *a*. Alternatively, Group Two might seek to improve its balance-of-payments by reducing its growth rate even further than that induced by the initial devaluation. In this case, the line B_3 would shift to the left (not shown in Figure 7.2 for clarity) and the equilibrium solution would be given by point *f*.

If, on the other hand, the desired rate of growth of Group Two is its original rate, y_2^*, and Group One simultaneously increases its rate of growth of autonomous expenditure thereby shifting the line A_3 upwards (not shown), the eventual equilibrium will be at point *g*. Thus, with a sufficiently fast rate of currency depreciation, Group One may be able to achieve its own resource or policy constrained rate of growth. Given this, the question arises why flexible exchange rates do not seem to have de-linked the national economies and removed the balance-of-payments constraint.

In fact, the introduction of flexible exchange rates with the breakdown of Bretton Woods has not proved to be the panacea originally envisaged. As we have noted above, the existence of real wage resistance makes it difficult, if not impossible, to translate variations in the nominal exchange rate into long-run changes of the real exchange rate. Associated with this is the possibility of a vicious circle developing which comprises rising inflation, initially generated by the devaluation, and a depreciating exchange rate. Oligopolistic pricing and the effect of uncertainty induced by exchange rate changes also make trade flows unresponsive to changes in relative prices. The experience since the 1970s has shown that all these factors have effectively prevented flexible exchange rates from de-linking the national economies. The failure of flexible exchange rates is perhaps best seen by the emergence of the Exchange Rate Mechanism of the European Community, which represents a substantial but fragile move back to the type of regime experienced under the Bretton

Woods arrangement. There is, however, still exchange rate flexibility between countries in the Exchange Rate Mechanism and the US and Japan. Moreover, the evidence cited earlier in this paper suggests that the magnitude of real exchange rate adjustments would have to be substantial to compensate for the differences in non-price competitiveness between countries.

THE IMPOSITION OF IMPORT CONTROLS

The second method by which a country may attempt to relax the balance-of-payments constraint is through the imposition of import controls. These may take the form of tariffs or quotas.

The imposition of tariffs by, for example, Group One, would raise the price of imports in terms of domestic currency. (It should be noted that in order to reduce the rate of growth of imports the tariff must be increasing over time: once again the term 'tariff' will be taken to refer to a continuously increasing tariff. A continuously increasing tariff, however, does seem implausible.) The effect of a tariff is thus analogous to that of a devaluation, with the exception, of course, that there is not the direct stimulus to export growth that a devaluation provides. As the case of a devaluation has been discussed in the last section, the impact of a tariff will not be dealt with separately here. (It is perhaps worth pointing out, though, that the effect of a retaliatory tariff imposed by Group Two may well vitiate any advantage provided to Group One by the original tariff.)

We assume that quotas are introduced to reduce the growth of imports. This may be viewed as a fall in the income elasticity of demand for imports. It is normally postulated that the licences to import would be auctioned off, thus providing a source of revenue.

If Group One introduces a quota, its income elasticity of demand for imports will fall from π_1 to π_1' and hence the slope of the BP locus will increase from π_2/π_1 to π_2/π_1'. This is shown in Figure 7.3 where the BP locus will rotate from BP_0 to BP_2. The slope of the line A_0 will also increase from $\beta_1\pi_2$ to $\beta_1'\pi_2$ (where $\beta_1' = \omega_{X1}/(1 - \omega_{B1} + \omega_{M1}\pi_1')$), but the increase is not so great as that of the BP locus. The size of the dynamic foreign trade multiplier increases as there is less leakage of the growth of expenditure into imports. There is also an increase in the contribution that autonomous expenditure growth makes to that of output, since $\partial\alpha_1/\partial\pi_1 < 0$ and, consequently, a fall in π_1 has the effect of increasing α_1, the dynamic domestic autonomous expendi-

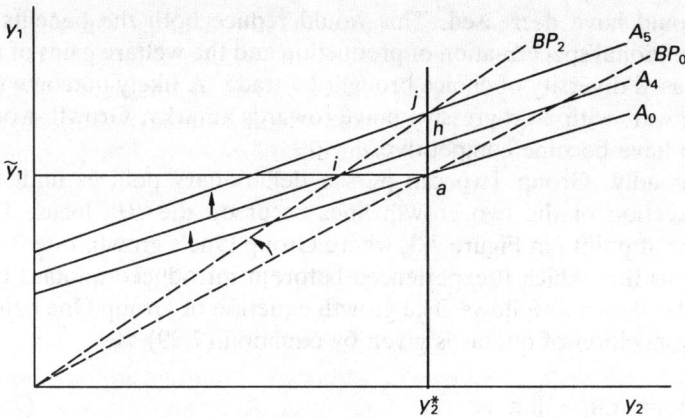

Figure 7.3   The effect of import quotas

ture multiplier. (See equation (7.29).) The post-import quota situation from Group One is given by the line A_4, where we assume that the growth of Group One's autonomous expenditure growth is the same as in the pre-quota case. (Note that the corresponding line B for Group Two is not shown in Figure 7.3 for clarity.)

Group Two now faces a decline in the rate of growth of demand due to a fall in the growth of its exports. Let us suppose it attempts to maintain its rate of growth at y_2^* by increasing its autonomous expenditure to compensate (Figure 7.3). In this case, the intersection of the line A_4 and the corresponding line for Group Two will occur at point h. In the long run, this is not sustainable, since Group Two is now running a growing balance-of-trade deficit. The reason for this is simple. The imposition of quotas by Group One has reduced the growth of its imports, which are, of course, the exports of Group Two, while the imports of Group Two remain at their pre-quota rate of growth. Unless Group Two is willing to finance an increasing inflow of capital, it will have to take measures to correct this disequilibrium.

There are fundamentally two choices open to Group Two.

First (and more likely, as the experience of the 1930s suggests), Group Two can retaliate by imposing its own import quotas in an attempt to return the ratio of the import elasticities to its original value. Even if this were successful, it should be noted that the growth of world trade would have fallen, since the absolute values of π_1 and

π_2 would have decreased. This would reduce both the benefits of international specialisation of production and the welfare gains of the increased diversity of choice brought by trade. A likely outcome is a trade war, with a progressive move towards autarky. Growth would again have become competitive.

Secondly, Group Two can pursue deflationary policies until the intersection of the two growth lines occur on the BP_2 locus. This occurs at point i in Figure 7.3, where Group One's growth rate is the same as that which it experienced before it introduced quotas. This may be shown as follows. The growth equation of Group One before the imposition of quotas is given by equation (7.29) as:

$$y_1 = \alpha_1 a_1 + \beta_1 \pi_2 y_2 \tag{7.46}$$

Group Two is assumed to be initially either resource or policy constrained, and we assume that Group One is growing at its balance-of-payment equilibrium growth rate:

$$\tilde{y}_1 = \frac{\pi_2}{\pi_1} y_2^* \tag{7.47}$$

where $\tilde{y}_1$ is Group One's balance-of-payment constrained growth, given that Group Two is growing at y_2^*.

Substituting equation (7.47) into equation (7.46), we obtain the growth of Group One's autonomous expenditure, given the balance-of-payments constraint:

$$\tilde{a}_1 = \frac{(1 - \beta_1 \pi_1)}{\alpha_1} \tilde{y}_1 \tag{7.48}$$

After the imposition of import quotas, and assuming that the growth of autonomous expenditure remains the same, the growth equation of Group One is:

$$y_1 = \frac{\alpha_1' (1 - \beta_1 \pi_1)}{\alpha_1} \tilde{y}_1 + \beta_1' \pi_2 y_2 \tag{7.49}$$

where α_1' and β_1' are the multipliers after the imposition of import quotas.

To preserve its balance-of-payments equilibrium, Group Two must reduce its growth to:

$$y_2 = \frac{\pi_1'}{\pi_2} y_1 \tag{7.50}$$

Substituting equation (7.50) into equation (7.49), we obtain Group One's new balance-of-payments equilibrium growth rate:

$$y_1 = \frac{\alpha_1' (1 - \beta_1 \pi_1)}{\alpha_1 (1 - \beta_1' \pi_1')} \tilde{y}_1 \tag{7.51}$$

From the definitions of α_1 and β_1 (and, hence, α_1' and β_1') from equation (7.29), it can be simply shown that:

$$\frac{\alpha_1' (1 - \beta_1 \pi_1)}{\alpha_1 (1 - \beta_1' \pi_1')} = 1 \tag{7.52}$$

The outcome is thus that Group One obtains no benefit from the imposition of quotas, while Group Two finds that its growth rate is reduced. The question then arises why Group One should ever introduce quotas. The answer is that, if at the same time as introducing quotas, Group One increases its growth of autonomous expenditure then its balance-of-payments equilibrium growth rate will be higher than in the pre-quota situation, even though this is not true for Group Two.

Moreover, the growth rate of Group Two need not fall if Group One, at the same time as imposing quotas, takes other measures to increase its growth of autonomous demand *and thereby ensures that its growth of imports remains at the previous rate*. (This was the policy prescription argued by the Cambridge Economic Policy Group. See, for example, Cripps and Godley, 1978.) This action will ensure that Group Two will no longer be faced with a trade deficit. In terms of Figure 7.3, Group One's growth line shifts up to A_5 and the post-import control growth rates are given by the point j. The outcome is that both countries are growing at their maximum or desired growth rates. The gains for Group One include a greater utilisation of labour, a faster rate of capital accumulation and an increase in the growth of income.

The Cambridge Economic Policy Group argued that the major advantage of import controls, compared with a devaluation, is that they are likely to be less inflationary. If Group One were to introduce reflationary measures to accompany a devaluation so that, assuming no retaliation, the end result would be a growth rate equivalent to that obtained with import controls, the former would be likely to set up larger inflationary pressures. The depreciation would, as we have mentioned above, lead to an increase in the growth of the prices of imported goods (in terms of the domestic currency) leading to an inflationary wage–price spiral. On the other hand, under import controls, all the tariff and quota revenues could be returned to the economy through tax reductions and so the effect would be likely to be less inflationary than with a devaluation.

The effectiveness, however, of import controls is controversial, not least because of the problem of retaliation. Even the advocates of import controls regard them as necessary only because of the lack of a better alternative. A devaluation would be preferable if it had a sufficiently large quantitative impact on trade flows, but, for the reasons already discussed, this is not seen as a feasible remedy. Import controls are, though, superior to the only other policy which consists of restricting the growth of Group One to the rate determined by the value of its income elasticities of demand for imports and exports, together with the growth of Group Two. In the long term, it is possible that increased inefficiency induced by protectionism may eventually cause π_2 to fall and π_1 to rise, thus offsetting any short-run gains in the growth rate due to the imposition of the quotas.

THE POST-1973 SLOWDOWN IN ECONOMIC GROWTH

The model outlined above may be used to illustrate the post-1973 recession and the slowdown from that date in the economic growth of the advanced countries. The oil crisis of 1973/4 exacerbated the 'deflationary bias' inherent in the asymmetry of the adjustment pressures on deficit and surplus countries. Given the high savings propensities of the OPEC countries, the initial quadrupling of oil prices meant that to sustain growth, the OECD countries, collectively, would have to maintain a substantial current account deficit; indeed, this was appreciated by the policy makers at the time. Nevertheless, countries such as Japan and West Germany, accustomed to low inflation rates and annual surpluses on the balance of payments,

introduced restrictive monetary and fiscal policies in order to curtail
the rate of price increases (through a belief in some sort of short-run
Phillips curve trade-off). The US initially pursued expansionary policies, but this led to a marked deterioration of its current account
between 1975 and 1978. The counter-inflationary policies that were
introduced in October 1978 were not sufficient to prevent a speculative run on the dollar, which necessitated the corrective action of a
marked tightening of monetary policy. As Larsen *et al.* (1983, p. 56)
commented: 'This episode suggests that even the largest OECD
country, with a relatively small share of trade in GNP, is not immune
from the pressures of international linkages.' The inevitable result of
the Japanese, West German, and, later, United States policies was
that deflationary pressures were transmitted to the advanced countries as a whole.

This is shown in Figure 7.4, where the policy constrained rate of
growth of Group Two falls from y_2^* to y_2^{**} in an attempt, for example, to restrain inflation. Given the ineffectiveness of expenditure
switching policies for the reasons outlined earlier, the growth of
Group One has also to fall (regardless of whether or not this is a
desired objective) to bring the balance of payments back into equilibrium. Thus, for the advanced countries as a whole, the balance-of-
payments deficit fell as the growth of output declined.

This may have given the misleading impression that there was no
longer a 'balance-of-payments problem'. Although, *ex post*, the
balance-of-payments deficits were extinguished, this occurred at the

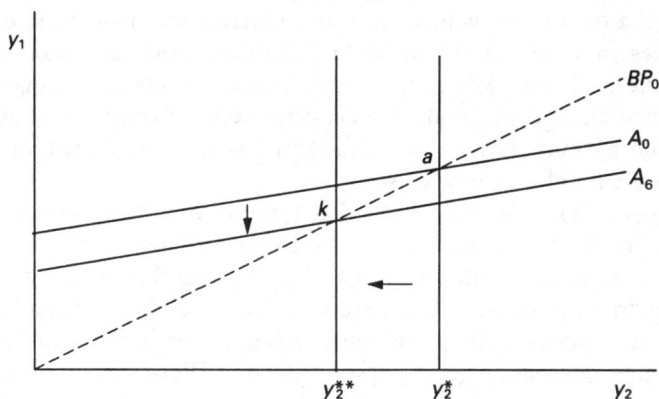

Figure 7.4   The international transmission of deflationary forces

cost of increasing under-utilisation of resources and the social cost of rising and prolonged unemployment. Nevertheless, there were some explicit balance-of-payments crises in countries that tried to expand faster than their balance-of-payments equilibrium growth rate permitted. These included the UK's sterling crisis of 1976 which led to IMF intervention and consequent deflationary policies; Italy in 1980–1 and France in 1982. During the 1980s, there were still the large structural imbalances of the US deficit and the Japanese and West German surpluses. In the 1980s, the US went from being the world's largest net creditor to the largest net debtor as a result of a growth rate that was faster relative to Japan and Europe than it had been in the past. However, there was increasing pressure from the world financial markets for the US to undertake restrictive measures to reduce the external deficit. Once again, even the US was not immune from the balance-of-payments constraint. (See Stewart, 1983, for a discussion of the problems facing the international management of demand subsequent to 1973.)

FINANCIAL INTERLINKAGES

The analysis so far has abstracted from considerations of the financial sector. A higher growth of output is assumed to be a function of a faster growth of autonomous expenditure, and this gives rise to a deterioration in the balance of payments. The exact method of the financing of this expansion (whether it is, for example, by bond issue or by an increase in the money supply) and whether exchange rates are fixed or floating will, of course, influence the magnitude of the changes in many of the variables. Perhaps most importantly, no account has been taken of the interrelationship between changes (or expected changes) in both interest rates and exchange rates, and in the international flows of the substantial volume of short-term speculative capital that now exist.

Nevertheless, the fundamental determinant of the external constraint is the 'basic' account of the balance of payments (i.e., the current account together with long-term capital flows); the working of the financial markets has merely served to reinforce this mechanism. Larsen *et al.* (1983) have summarised the experience of flexible exchange rates since the collapse of Bretton Woods as follows:

Following the breakdown of the fixed rate system in 1973, it was hoped that floating would permit countries to pursue more independent domestic objectives than had hitherto been the case, insulating them from monetary policies of dominant partners. In part, this view rested on the assumption that capital movements would tend to offset temporary current account disequilibria and play a stabilising role. These hopes proved too optimistic, however: *the exchange rate has remained a constraint and financial linkages have often compounded real linkages*. Moreover, exchange rates are, at times, affected by incipient capital movements induced by foreign financial disturbances or international political considerations. (Our emphasis)

Since the financial sector generally reinforces the effect of the balance-of-payments constraint, it would be desirable to include this formally in any subsequent development of the approach outlined in this chapter.

CONCLUSION

The close interlinkages that have developed between the advanced countries through the medium of trade have progressively circumscribed the latitude that individual countries have in implementing domestic policies. In particular, there is not much scope for a country to increase its rate of growth relative to that of its trading partners faster than in the past. This comparative economic performance is largely dependent upon the values of its export and import income elasticities of demand compared with those of its competitors. These primarily reflect differences in non-price competitiveness which result from supply characteristics, not very amenable to change by macro-economic policies. Attempts to raise the growth rate ignoring this balance-of-payments constraint have invariably resulted in large trade deficits (of over 2 per cent of GDP) which could not be sustained for long in most countries. In this sense, Eltis (1976) is correct when he points out that British policy makers, brought up on the closed economy model of the *General Theory*, simply generated the familiar 'stop–go' cycle by the use of Keynesian demand management policies. But it should be noted that the 'failure of the Keynesian conventional wisdom', as Eltis entitled his critique, is not a failure of the theory, but one of drawing the appropriate policy prescriptions from that theory, *pace* Eltis. The approach we have adopted here is, of course, avowedly Keynesian in nature.

It has been shown that attempts by individual countries to overcome the balance-of-payments constraint through exchange rate adjustments and by the use of tariffs and quotas will be self-defeating if they generate a depreciation–inflation circle or competitive growth which involves retaliation. We have also argued that there are strong reasons for doubting the efficacy of these instruments in permanently raising a country's growth rate. From an individual country's point of view, the most effective solution is to improve the non-price competitiveness of its exports through industrial policies which focus on research and development and training; but these are unlikely to achieve spectacular results in the short run.

This leaves the possibility of raising the growth rate of all the advanced countries through some form of co-ordinated reflation, thereby generating complementary growth. However, not only are there political problems in this approach, but the fact that countries are initially at differing levels of the pressure of demand also poses complications for the so-called 'locomotive theory of expansion'. If demand is simultaneously expanded, certain countries will become resource constrained before others have reached their full employment growth rates. The balance-of-payments constraint will again operate in a manner similar to that appertaining to the pre-1973 period. Nevertheless, a return to the growth rates experienced during those years would be regarded as something of an achievement in itself.

8 Export-Led Growth, Regional Problems and Cumulative Causation[1]

INTRODUCTION

In this chapter we use the ideas of Kaldor, already introduced in Chapter 7, to consider the role of the Verdoorn relationship in a model of 'circular and cumulative causation'. Kaldor was a long-standing critic of the application of neoclassical modes of thought to the analysis of economic growth and development. He supported Myrdal's (1957) notion of vicious circles of success and failure (the principle of 'cumulative causation'), and attacked the predictions of neoclassical theory that regional (national) growth rate differences would tend to narrow with trade and the free mobility of the factors of production. The essence of the argument is that once a region gains a growth advantage it will tend to sustain that advantage through the process of increasing returns that growth itself induces – the Verdoorn effect. Kaldor first articulated his theory in a purely verbal way in a lecture given to the Scottish Economic Society in 1970 (Ka'dor, 1970). We discussed the structure of the model in the previous chapter. Here we shall use the model to consider such questions as: the role of the Verdoorn effect in contributing to regional growth rate differences; whether regional growth rate differences will tend to narrow or diverge through time; and how policies of regional 'devaluation' can raise a region's growth rate (if at all). Kaldor sets up the problem by assuming two regions, initially isolated from one another, each with an agricultural area and an industrial and market centre. Trade is then opened up between the two regions with the effect that the region with the more developed industry will be able to supply the needs of the agricultural area of the other region on more favourable terms so that the industrial centre of the second region will lose its market and will tend to be run down without any compensating advantage in the form of increased agricultural output. The way that we can capture the spirit of this idea is to model an individual region's growth rate and then to consider the sources of interregional differences – stable or divergent – in terms of the parameters of the model. For example, in the two-region case a necessary condition for the persistence of stable regional growth rate differences is that the steady-state equilibrium growth rates of the two regions differ. For the growth rates of two regions to diverge, a necessary condition is that the growth rate of one of the regions diverges from its own equilibrium rate. It is also a sufficient condition if the growth rate of the other region is stable or diverges from equilibrium in the opposite direction. If Kaldor's arguments are first used to examine equilibrium growth in one region, therefore, the assumptions implicit in the hypothesis that regional per capita incomes and/or growth rates may diverge can then be readily seen. This is the approach adopted here in an attempt to formalise the model without violating its spirit. His more complex verbal argument is easily accommodated within the framework outlined. The approach is essentially partial equilibrium in the sense that each region is considered in isolation from all others, and interregional relationships are not considered explicitly. Interregional relationships are considered implicitly, however, since we argue that it is the Verdoorn effect which can sustain high growth in one region once it obtains an initial growth advantage, which then makes it difficult for other regions to compete on equal terms.

In discussing the model, we have four specific purposes in mind: first, to make clear the role of the Verdoorn relationship as it affects regional growth rate differences; secondly, to suggest that while the model in theory can generate divergent or convergent regional growth paths, in practice, given reasonable parameter values for the model, regional *growth* divergence is not likely, and that the model is best interpreted as predicting constant persistent regional growth rate differences sustained by the Verdoorn effect;[2] thirdly, to bring out the importance of regional structure in determining the equilibrium growth rate, a feature of regional growth which Kaldor does not stress, and fourthly, to evaluate wage subsidies as a policy device for reducing persistent regional growth rate differences.

THE KALDOR MODEL

As we saw in the previous chapter, the structure of the model can be reduced to four equations, *viz*, equations (8.1) to (8.4):

$$y_t = \gamma x_t \tag{8.1}$$

where y_t is the rate of growth of output and x_t is the rate of growth of exports at time t.[3] γ is the (constant) elasticity of output growth with respect to export growth ($\gamma = 1$ if exports are a constant proportion of output).[4]

$$x_t = \eta p_{dt} + \delta p_{ft} + \varepsilon z_t \tag{8.2}$$

where p_{dt}, p_{ft} and z_t are the rates of growth of the region's prices, prices outside the region and the growth of income outside the region. η and δ are the own and cross-price elasticities of demand for exports and henceforth we shall make the usual assumption that $\eta = -\delta$. ε is the income elasticity of the demand for the region's exports.

This export demand function given by equation (8.2) is easy to handle, but it leads to some difficulty if one wishes to interpret Kaldor's model as predicting that wage subsidies can raise permanently a lagging region's growth rate. On the other hand, there is no reason why Kaldor should be interpreted in this way; he is (perhaps deliberately) vague on this point.[5] Presumably few people would want to argue that a once-for-all currency devaluation, which is analogous to a continual wage subsidy at the regional level, could raise a nation's growth rate permanently. We return to this point later.

Regional (export) prices are derived from a mark-up on unit labour costs, and the growth of regional prices is given by:

$$p_{dt} = w_t - r_t + \tau_t \tag{8.3}[6]$$

where w_t, r_t and τ_t are the growth rates of nominal wages, labour productivity and one plus the percentage mark-up (henceforth referred to simply as the mark-up).

Finally:

$$r_t = r_a + \lambda y_t \tag{8.4}[7]$$

where r_a is the rate of autonomous productivity growth and λ is the Verdoorn coefficient.

Combining equations (8.1) to (8.4) to obtain an expression for the equilibrium growth rates gives:

$$y_t = \frac{\gamma[\eta(w_t - r_a + \tau_t - p_{ft}) + \varepsilon z_t]}{1 + \gamma\eta\lambda} \tag{8.5}$$

Remembering that $\eta < 0$, the growth rate is shown to vary positively with r_a, z, ε, p_{ft} and λ, and negatively with w and τ.[8]

Note that the Verdoorn effect is a source of regional growth rate differences only to the extent that the Verdoorn coefficient (λ) varies between regions, or initial differences exist with respect to other parameters and variables in the model such that $0 < \lambda < 1$ serves to exaggerate the effect of the differences. In other words, the dependence of productivity growth on the growth rate *per se* is not sufficient to cause differences in regional growth rates unless the Verdoorn coefficient varies between regions or growth rates would diverge for other reasons anyway.

It is equally clear, however, that it is the Verdoorn relation which makes the model circular and cumulative, and which gives rise to the possibility that once a region obtains a growth advantage, it will keep it. What this means is that the Verdoorn relationship plays a sustaining role in the regional growth process, and a sustaining role in the persistence of regional growth differences once they have arisen due to initial differences in the other parameters of the model.

Suppose, for example, that a region obtains an advantage in the production of goods with a high income elasticity of demand (ε) which causes its growth rate to rise above that of another region. Through the Verdoorn effect, productivity growth will be higher; the rate of change of prices lower (assuming w and r are the same in both regions), and the rate of growth of exports (and hence the rate of growth of output) higher and so on. Moreover, the fact that the region with the initial advantage will obtain a competitive advantage in the production of goods with a high income elasticity of demand will mean that it will be difficult for other regions to establish the same activities. In models of cumulative causation, this is the essence of the theory of divergence between 'centre' and 'periphery' and between industrial and agricultural regions. This is also the essence of Kaldor's view that the opening up of trade between regions may create growth differences which are sustained or even widened by the process of trade.

Notice that an autonomous shock which raises a region's growth rate is not sufficient for its growth advantage to be maintained through the Verdoorn effect unless the autonomous shock affects favourably the parameters and variables of the model (or is a sustained shock). This consideration is important when we come to consider the role of wage subsidies as a device for improving the growth performance of a region.

The dependence of the equilibrium growth rate on the parameters of the model, and the sustaining role of the Verdoorn effect, is illustrated in Figure 8.1. For illustration, but without discussion for the moment, the growth rate is shown converging to its equilibrium rate. The disequilibrium behaviour of the model is considered explicitly in the next section.

The distance of the curves from the origin reflects factors affecting each variable other than the variable specified in the functional relation. Figure 8.1 shows clearly the link that the Verdoorn relation provides between exports and growth via productivity and prices, and its sustaining influence. The steeper the slope of the Verdoorn relation (i.e. the larger λ), the higher the equilibrium growth rate will be and the greater the divergence between regional growth rates for given differences between regions in other variables and parameters.

DIVERGENT OR CONVERGENT GROWTH?

We come now to the second purpose of formalising Kaldor's model which is to consider under what circumstances there will be a tendency for regional growth rates to diverge. In a two-region model, a necessary condition for divergence is that the growth rate of one of the regions diverges from its equilibrium rate. Whether divergence will take place is essentially an empirical issue depending on the stability conditions of the model in disequilibrium. It is an unfortunate feature of cumulative causation models in general that none seem to be specific as to what the stability conditions are in their various models. In order to consider the growth rate in disequilibrium, a variety of lag structures could be introduced into the equations which constitute the model.

If, for simplicity, we confine ourselves to a first-order system, inspection of the model shows that, since the model is 'circular', a one-period lag in any of the equations gives the same stability conditions, namely that convergence to or divergence from the equilibrium growth rate depends on whether $\gamma \eta \lambda \gtrless 1$, as illustrated in Figure 8.1.[9] To consider the growth rate in disequilibrium it would not be unreasonable on economic grounds to specify exports in time t as a lagged function of its determinants. It can take time for exporters

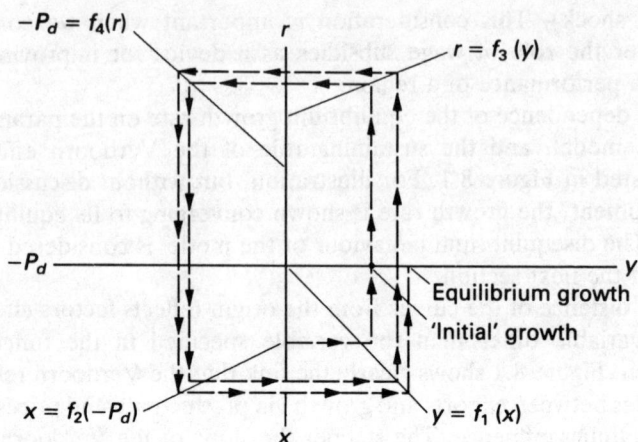

Figure 8.1

and/or foreign buyers to adjust to changes in prices and income. Thus we could write $X_t = (P_{dt-1}/P_{ft-1})^\eta Z_{t-1}^\varepsilon$ giving the approximation:

$$x_t = \eta(p_{dt-1} - p_{ft-1}) + \varepsilon z_{t-1} \qquad (8.6)$$

where the lower-case letters are discrete rates of growth as before. Using equation (8.6) instead of (8.2), and combining with (8.1), (8.3) and (8.4), and assuming the rate of growth of the exogenous variables to be constant, gives the first order difference equation:

$$y_t = \gamma[\eta(w_{t-1} - r_a + \tau_{t-1} - p_{ft-1}) + \varepsilon z_{t-1}] - \gamma\eta\lambda y_{t-1} \qquad (8.7)$$

the general solution to which is:

$$y_t = A(-\gamma\eta\lambda)^t + \frac{\gamma[\eta(w_{t-1} - r_a + \tau_{t-1} - p_{ft-1}) + \varepsilon z_{t-1}]}{1 + \gamma\eta\lambda} \qquad (8.8)$$

where A is the initial condition.

The behaviour of y depends on the value of $\gamma\eta\lambda$. Since $\eta < 0$, $(-\gamma\eta\lambda)$ will be > 0. The condition for cumulative divergence from equilibrium is that $(-\gamma\eta\lambda) > 1$.[10] In our view, this is unlikely because: $\gamma = 1$ if exports are a constant proportion of output; the price elasticity of demand for exports (η) rarely exceeds 2; and the Verdoorn coefficient (λ) rarely exceeds 0.5.[11] Taking realistic values for the parameters of the model, therefore, the most likely prediction must be one of constant differences in regional growth rates determined by differences in the equilibrium rates; not divergence. Admittedly, our disequilibrium specification is arbitrary, but the fact that a one-period lag in any one of the equations gives the same stability conditions, and likewise when more than one equation is lagged, considerably enhances the generality of the result. It also serves some purpose to give a (not unrealistic) specification which suggests on empirical grounds that divergence is not very likely, if only to induce those who adhere to the cumulative causation school to specify more precisely the model they have in mind and to show the conditions under which regional growth rates would diverge through time. In our specification we suggest that diverging regional growth rates would seem to be possible only if the equilibrium rates themselves diverged through time because the determinants of the equilibrium rates were themselves time dependent. For example, the price and income elasticities of demand could change in the course of time as the structure of production changed. This possibility is not pursued further because of the obvious difficulties it would present for the solution to equation (8.7).

REGIONAL STRUCTURE AS A DETERMINANT OF GROWTH

The second term on the right-hand side of equation (8.8) (i.e. the particular solution to the first-order difference equation) shows that the equilibrium growth rate depends on six main economic parameters and variables that may vary from region to region: η, w, r_a, τ, ε, and λ.[12] If it is assumed that the percentage mark-up on unit labour costs is constant in each region, and that for institutional reasons w is fairly uniform from region to region,[13] we are left with differences in η, r_a, ε and λ as explanations of differences in regional growth rates. The price and income elasticities of demand for regional exports will depend on the nature of the products produced. The rate of autonomous productivity growth, r_a, and the Verdoorn coefficient, λ, will depend on the technical dynamism of productive agents in the region and the extent to which capital accumulation is induced by growth and embodies technical progress. The determinants of r_a and λ are closely related to the determinants of the position and shape of

Kaldor's technical progress function (Kaldor, 1957). The technical progress function in linear form may be specified as:

$$r = d + \alpha(\kappa) \qquad (8.9)$$

where r is the rate of growth of output per worker
    κ is the rate of growth of capital per worker
and d is the rate of disembodied technical progress.

Now let d and κ be functions of the rate of growth of output so that:

$$d = a_1 + \beta_1 y \qquad (8.10)$$

and:

$$\kappa = a_2 + \beta_2 y \qquad (8.11)$$

where β_1 is a measure of 'learning by doing' and β_2 is an 'accelerator' coefficient.

Substituting (8.10) and (8.11) into (8.9) gives:

$$r = (a_1 + \alpha a_2) + (\beta_1 + \alpha \beta_2)y \qquad (8.12)$$

Hence:

$$r = r_a + \lambda y$$

where $r_a = (a_1 + \alpha a_2)$ and $\lambda = (\beta_1 + \alpha \beta_2)$.

The autonomous rate of growth of productivity, r_a, is determined by the autonomous rate of disembodied progress, the autonomous rate of capital accumulation per worker, and the extent to which technical progress is embodied in capital accumulation. The Verdoorn coefficient, λ, is determined by the rate of induced disembodied technical progress (learning by doing), the degree to which capital accumulation is induced by growth and the extent to which technical progress is embodied in capital accumulation. To the extent that the determinants of r_a and λ vary between industries, r_a and λ may also vary between regions depending on the industrial composition of the regions.

From this analysis, it would appear that the message of Kaldor's model is that raising a region's growth rate is fundamentally a question of making regions more 'competitive' and/or altering the industrial structure so that goods are produced with higher income elasticities of demand and higher Verdoorn coefficients attached to them.[14,15]

REGIONAL COMPETITIVENESS

To make regions more competitive, a policy of wage subsidies to manufacturers in lagging growth regions is sometimes advocated, to achieve the same effect regionally as a policy of currency devaluation nationally. The argument needs to be treated with some caution, however. It is easy to show that a wage subsidy in a regional context is equivalent to a devaluation of the currency in a national context, but the argument that wage subsidies can raise a region's growth rate permanently is no more convincing. To show the equivalence of wage subsidies and currency devaluation, let the price of domestic exports in terms of the overseas currency equal P_o. Then P_{ot} equals P_{dt} divided by the exchange rate (E, which is the domestic price of foreign currency), or in terms of growth rates:

$$p_{ot} = p_{dt} - e_t \qquad (8.13)$$

where p_{ot} is the rate of change of home prices expressed in overseas currency in time t, e_t is the rate of change in the exchange rate in time t and p_{dt} is the rate of growth of prices in domestic currency in time t.

Expressing the domestic price in the same units as the overseas currency, equation (8.2) becomes:

$$x_t = \eta(p_{dt} - p_{ft} - e_t) + \varepsilon z_t \qquad (8.14)$$

and the equilibrium growth rate is:

$$y_t = \frac{\gamma[\eta(w_t - r_a + \tau_t - p_{ft} - e_t) + \varepsilon z_t]}{1 + \gamma\eta\lambda} \qquad (8.15)$$

Partially differentiating (8.15) with respect to e or w gives the same result:

$$\frac{\partial y_t}{\partial e_t} = \frac{\partial y_t}{\partial w_t} = \frac{\gamma\eta}{1 + \gamma\eta\lambda} \qquad (8.16)$$

Hence, wage reductions and currency devaluation are formally equivalent.

But neither devaluation, nor wage subsidies, can have a permanent effect on the rate of change of the exchange rate or money wages, only on the level of the exchange rate or money wages. The effect of devaluation and wage subsidies on the rate of change of the exchange rate and the rate of change of money wages is once-for-all. Unless the export pricing function, or the export demand function, is additive (as opposed to multiplicative), the effect of devaluation, or the introduction of flat-rate wage subsidies, on the growth rate cannot therefore be permanent.[16] e and w become zero in the periods after wage subsidies have been introduced or devaluation has taken place.[17] As far as an additive export demand function is concerned, it is not at all clear what demand function would generate the argument that the rate of growth of exports is related to the absolute difference between domestic and foreign prices.[18] It seems unfortunate that the success or otherwise of government policies with respect to regional wage subsidies will depend on the (unknown) form of the pricing and export demand functions. The relation between export prices and the growth of output is a subject which seems to be treated far too casually in the theory of trade and growth. We believe that it is much more satisfactory to regard the level of exports as determined by relative prices in a multiplicative demand function than by the absolute difference between domestic and foreign prices in an additive demand function. If this argument is accepted, wage subsidies at the regional level are equivalent at the most to an autonomous shock which, as we argued earlier, could only affect the growth rate permanently if the structural parameters of the growth model were thereby affected favourably. If anything, however, policies of 'devaluation' tend to ossify a region's or country's industrial structure, impeding structural change. Export promotion and import substitution properly directed offer a much more hopeful solution to lagging growth caused by unfavourable price and income elasticities of demand for exports and slow autonomous productivity growth. At the regional level, this policy conclusion points to the need to relate regional taxes and subsidies to activities with particular structural characteristics rather than to particular factors of production, either capital or labour. We believe the income elasticity of demand for exports to be a particularly important parameter at both the national and regional level. Regional policy for stimulating regional growth could usefully direct its attention to identifying activities with a high income elasticity of demand and encouraging these to locate in depressed regions by policies of capital incentives and labour subsidies.

In conclusion, the formalisation of Kaldor's model has the pedagogic virtue of bringing into the open the structure of the model and the main determinants of regional growth rate differences. The model presented captures the main elements of an open economy growth model which has relevance to regions within countries and to open developed and developing countries alike. At the national level, a built-in balance-of-payments constraint would make the model more realistic.[19] At the regional level there is no requirement that exports and imports must balance to preserve the value of a currency in the foreign exchange market, which may be required at the national level. This is not to say, however, that regional problems are not balance-of-payments problems; they simply show up in other ways, e.g. high unemployment (see later in the chapter).

KALDOR'S MODEL AND THE DYNAMIC FOREIGN TRADE MULTIPLIER[20]

The link between Kaldor's regional growth model and the dynamic foreign trade multiplier can be seen if we make two further plausible assumptions. The first is that prices are determined in the national market and so grow at the same rate in all regions. The second is that the increase in money wages is determined through national bargaining and, consequently, the growth of money wages is spatially invariant. There may, of course, be an element of regional wage drift with money wages in the prosperous areas growing slightly faster than in the peripheral regions, but we shall ignore this complication because it does not significantly affect our argument.

Let us consider two regions, the periphery and the centre. Denoting these two regions by the subscripts p and c respectively, the Kaldorian model becomes:

$$y_c = \gamma \, x_c \tag{8.17}$$

$$x_c = \eta p_c - \eta p_p + \varepsilon y_p \tag{8.18}$$

(making the conventional assumption again that $\delta = -\eta$).

$$p_c = w_c - r_c + \tau_c \tag{8.19}$$

$$p_p = w_p - r_p + \tau_p \tag{8.20}$$

$$p_c = p_p \tag{8.21}$$

$$w_c = w_p \tag{8.22}$$

$$r_c = r_{ac} + \lambda y_c \tag{8.23}$$

$$r_p = r_{ap} + \lambda y_p \tag{8.24}$$

The notation is as before, except that the growth of the centre and periphery are now denoted by y_c and y_p.

From equations (8.17), (8.18) and (8.21), the equilibrium growth rate of the centre is given by:

$$y_c = \gamma \varepsilon y_p \tag{8.25}$$

Comparing this with equation (8.5), it can be seen that the Verdoorn coefficient, λ, no longer has a direct influence on the equilibrium growth rate. The reason for this is straightforward. In the earlier model, the positive feedback from a faster growth of productivity to a faster growth of output occurs through an improvement in the region's growth of relative prices. As prices, by assumption, are now growing at the same rate in both regions, this mechanism is no longer in operation. This, however, does not mean that there is no longer a cumulative causation mechanism at work; it is simply that it works through the induced disparities in the regional rates of capital accumulation in the following way.

From equations (8.19) to (8.24), and assuming the exogenous growth of productivity is the same in both regions, the following relationship may be derived:

$$\tau_c - \tau_p = \lambda(y_c - y_p) \tag{8.26}$$

This demonstrates that if the centre is growing faster than the periphery, its mark-up will likewise be growing faster.

The rate of growth of the mark-up is equal to:

$$\tau_i = -\overset{0}{a_i} = \frac{(1 - a_i)}{a_i}(1 - \overset{0}{a_i}) \qquad i = c, p \tag{8.27}$$

where a and $(1 - a)$ are labour's and capital's shares in regional output, respectively. The superscript ^{0} denotes an exponential growth rate. If we further assume that nationally there is a constant mark-up, it follows that the faster growing centre will have $\tau > 0$ and, conversely, the periphery will have $\tau < 0$. Thus, capital's share in output will be increasing in the centre and decreasing in the periphery. If we assume that investment is substantially internally generated, then the rate of capital accumulation is likely to be proportionately higher in the faster growing centre. This is likely to lead to an improvement in non-price competitiveness and a superior industrial structure through diversification into the rapidly growing industries. The result will be a steady increase in the value of ε. If the growth of the capital–output ratio is constant in both regions, then the rate of return will be increasing in the faster growing region and decreasing in the slower growing region. This may well lead to a flow of net investment (and labour) from the periphery to the centre, further exacerbating the situation. Alternatively, if there is only limited labour mobility there is likely to be increasing unemployment, whether disguised or overt, in the periphery.

So far, no consideration has been given to the role of the balance-of-payments constraint in the regional context. This requires the condition that $\gamma = 1/\pi$ in equation (8.25), where π is the centre's income elasticity of demand for imports. Therefore, $y_c = x_c/\pi = \varepsilon y_p/\pi$. This is the dynamic Harrod trade multiplier result.

BALANCE-OF-PAYMENTS CONSTRAINED GROWTH IN A TWO-REGION MODEL

In Chapter 7, we outlined a model which analysed the impact of trade flows in constraining growth rates within the context of two groups of countries, one of which was resource or policy constrained and the other balance-of-payments constrained. It was shown how the growth of the former determined the maximum growth of the latter through the balance-of-payments constraint. This analysis may also be applied to the regional context. For expositional ease, we again assume that the national economy is closed (although this does not seriously affect the argument).

From equation (7.29) in Chapter 7, the growth of the periphery may be expressed as a function of the centre's growth:

$$y_i = \alpha_i a_i + \beta_i \pi_j y_j, \qquad i, j = p, c; \quad i \neq j \tag{8.28}$$

where $\alpha_i = \dfrac{\omega_{Ai}}{(1 - \omega_{Ci} + \omega_{Mi} \pi_i)}$, and $\beta_i = \dfrac{\omega_{Xi}}{(1 - \omega_{Ci} + \omega_{Mi} \pi_i)}$.

The variable denoted by a is the growth of domestic or regional autonomous expenditure. ω is the share of a particular category of expenditure in the total. A, C, X, and M denote autonomous expenditure, consumption, exports and imports. The 'growth function' for the periphery is given by the line p in Figure 8.2, and for the centre by the line c. The balance-of-payments equilibrium growth rate of the periphery is given by:

$$y_p = (\pi_c/\pi_p) y_c \tag{8.29}$$

and this is represented by the line BP. ($\varepsilon_p \equiv \pi_c$ for a closed two-region economy.) It is assumed, to begin with, that there are no capital transfers between the regions.

It is further assumed that the government has a target rate of growth for the economy as a whole, dictated by considerations of inflation, or, in the case of an open economy, by the national balance-of-payments constraint. Consequently, the growth of the periphery can be expressed in terms of the growth of total income and the growth of the centre as:

$$y_p \equiv \frac{1}{\theta} y_n + \frac{(1 - \theta)}{\theta} y_c \tag{8.30}$$

where y_n is the growth of national income and θ is the share of the periphery's income in the national total. Equation (8.30) is represented by the line n in Figure 8.2. The growth functions of the periphery and centre intersect with the balance-of-payments equilibrium growth locus at point A, which is on the national growth constraint. Thus, the two regions are initially experiencing equilibrium growth at the rates y_p' and y_c', and the aggregate growth of the two regions is at the government's desired rate. Let us suppose that the centre is growing at a rate consistent with the full utilisation of its resources, while the periphery experiences a growing underutilisation of its factors of production, especially labour. (It is assumed that there is only limited mobility of labour between the two regions.) If

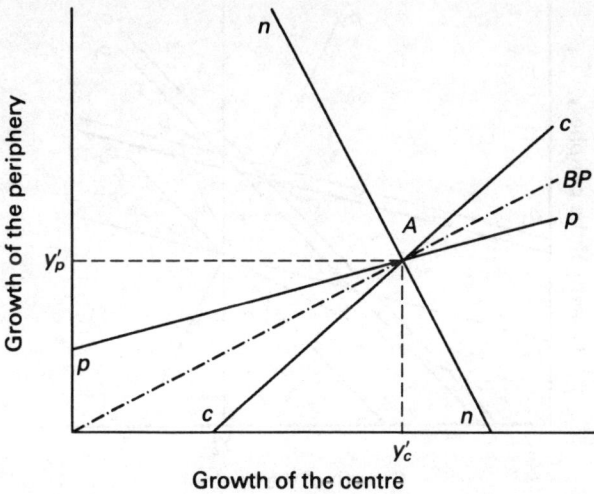

Figure 8.2 Regional growth and the regional balance-of-payments constraint

the intersection of the lines *p* and *c* were above the *BP* line so that the periphery was growing faster than y'_p, the growth of imports to the periphery would exceed its growth of exports. The periphery would thus be running an increasing deficit in its trade with the centre and there must be a compensating growth of *short-term* capital inflows, or accommodating transfers.

The question that arises is whether or not the periphery could achieve the required rate of growth of output necessary to bring about the full-utilization of its resources merely by increasing its borrowing from the centre, and hence its growth of consumption. There is, of course, no regional counterpart to a national balance-of-payments crisis. With a common currency, there is no rapidly de-preciating exchange rate to cause concern and, furthermore, inter-regional trade flows are unrecorded so any current account deficits are concealed. It could therefore be argued that there can be no such thing as a regional balance-of-payments problem. However, we shall show that this view is mistaken.

In order to answer the question as to whether or not the periphery could raise its growth rate merely by borrowing, let us assume that there is an autonomous increase in the periphery's growth of con-sumption expenditure. The resulting increase in the growth of imports

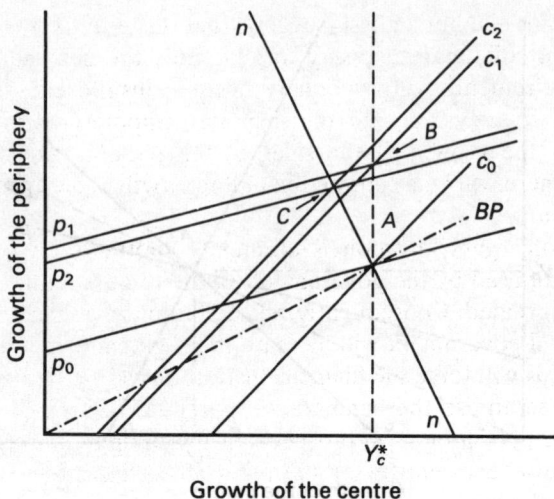

Figure 8.3 The effect of an increase in the growth of the periphery's autonomous expenditure

is financed by short-term capital inflows from the centre. In terms of Figure 8.3, this increased growth of the periphery's exogenous expenditure has the immediate effect of causing the line p_0 to shift up to the line p_1. The growth rates of the two regions move from point A to point B, with the growth of the periphery increasing, while that of the centre remains constant at its full employment rate y_c^*. There is a decline in the growth of the centre's autonomous expenditure to allow resources to be released for the increased growth of exports to the periphery. Hence, the line c_0 shifts to c_1.

The overall result is a growth rate of the national economy that is faster than the central government's target and, consequently, deflationary national macroeconomic policies will be implemented. This has the result of shifting the lines p_1 and c_1 to p_2 and c_2 respectively. The growth rates of both the periphery and centre are now given by point C. It may be seen that the growth of the periphery has increased at the expense of the centre (i.e. growth is competitive).

Are these growth rates sustainable in the long run? For this to be possible, there would have to be an increasing rate of capital inflows into the periphery so that the BP line shifts permanently upwards and to a position that passes through point C. The mechanism and the impact of the transfer of capital has been usefully discussed in detail by Dow (1986) and her analysis suggests that this is unlikely to occur. The regional collateral necessary to guarantee the periphery's borrowing requirements will eventually become insufficient. There is also a limit to how much of the increased import growth can be financed by the growth of the sales of the region's assets. Thus, eventually there will be a contraction in the growth of credit available to the region.

One region's gain in credit is ultimately another's loss, given a constraint imposed by the government on the total amount of credit that may be created. Consequently, the deflationary policies imposed by the central government will increase the regional competition for credit and this will force the financial institutions and potential investors *etc.* to scrutinise the comparative potential returns of the two regions. The poor long-term prospects of the periphery are likely to act as a major disincentive for the financial institutions to provide indefinitely the necessary growth of capital which is required to finance the difference between the growth of the periphery's exports and its imports.

At point C, the growing balance of trade deficit has to be financed either by a growing sale of assets by the periphery or by increasing claims on the region's assets by the centre. (It is assumed that the government is not prepared to finance the deficit indefinitely by the redistribution of income from the centre to the periphery through the tax mechanism or through regional grants or both.) The increasing decline of the region's assets will have a depressing effect on the periphery's growth of spending.

This will result in the periphery's growth function (denoted by the line p_2) shifting downwards. Concomitantly, the accumulation of assets by the centre and the resulting increase in the centre's autonomous expenditure will shift its growth function (the line c_2) to the right.

It should be noted, however, that a reduction in the growth of the income of the periphery to the rate where the growth of imports and exports are once again equal will not, of itself, be sufficient to re-establish the balance-of-payments equilibrium growth rate. This is because the *level* of imports will now exceed that of exports as a result of the temporary faster growth of imports. There will have to be a further downward adjustment of income and output to bring the level of imports and exports back into equality. Once this has occurred, the balance-of-payments equilibrium growth rate will again be given by point A.[21]

The effect of the temporary divergence of the periphery's growth rate from its balance-of-payments equilibrium growth rate is to increase the cumulative output produced by the region over the period of the disturbance.

The only way for the periphery to generate a sustained increase in its rate of growth is for it to increase its growth of exports. This could be achieved both by diversifying into those industries for which there is a high income elasticity of demand by the centre and by increasing the non-price competitiveness of the periphery's products. Success in accomplishing these objectives is also likely to lead to an increased substitution of imports by goods produced in the periphery.

This case is shown in Figure 8.4 where the BP locus rotates upwards from BP_0 to BP_1. This is a result of an increase in π_c and a decrease in π_p, as may be seen from equation (8.29). The effect is to allow the growth of regional autonomous expenditure to increase in the periphery, causing the line p_0 to shift upwards to the line p_3. The equilibrium position moves from point A to point D and the increase in the growth of the periphery leads to a decline of that of the centre, resulting in competitive growth. (In an open economy, part of the increase in the periphery's export sales is likely to be sold overseas which would have the effect of shifting the national growth constraint – the line n – outwards if the latter is the result of a national balance-of-payments constraint.) The important point to note is that the higher growth of the periphery which is generated by a faster growth of exports is sustainable indefinitely, unlike the case where a faster output growth requires financing by growing capital flows from the centre.

There are likely to be substantial obstacles, however, in the path of the periphery autonomously increasing its growth of exports. As we saw above, the Verdoorn effect will give the initially faster growing region, the centre, a competitive advantage over the periphery which the latter may find difficult to overcome. The process of cumulative causation will result in a secular decrease in the ratio of π_c/π_p thereby causing an increase in the growth of the the centre at the expense of the periphery, given the national growth constraint. In terms of Figure 8.4, the slope of the BP locus will decline from, say, an initial position given by BP_1 to BP_0, which is the converse of the case just discussed. A temporary acceleration of the growth of the periphery is, for a time, likely to stop or even reverse this decline in π_c/π_p, but the effect is unlikely to be permanent. As we have noted above, if there is not sufficient interregional labour mobility, there will be

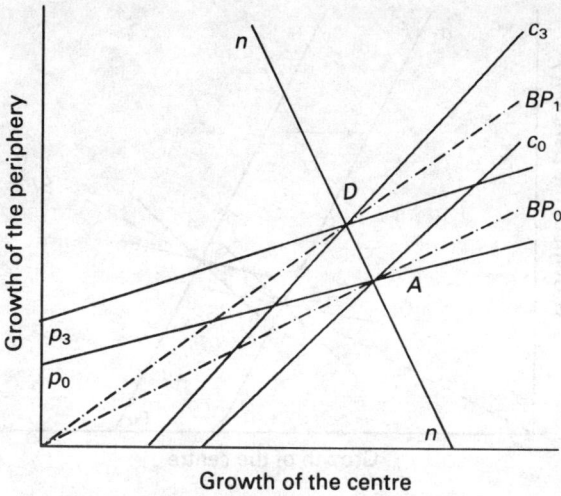

Figure 8.4   The effect of an increase in the growth of the periphery's exports

rising long-term unemployment in the periphery due to an inadequate growth of effective demand.

A region's relative income elasticity of demand for imports is likely to change only slowly in response to differences in its productivity growth, when compared with other regions. Consequently, it is useful to distinguish between two mechanisms. First, there is the almost instantaneous impact that a change in output growth of one region has on another through interregional trade flows and the operation of the dynamic foreign trade multiplier. Secondly, there is the effect on a region's output growth of a change in its relative income elasticity of demand for imports, caused by a change in both non-price competitiveness and the structure of its economy, together with the composition of its exports. In practice, the structural factor is likely to be the more important, since there are not very great differences in non-price competitiveness between regions. (On the other hand, we have seen that differences in the composition of exports can explain very little of the relative export performance at the international level. The primary cause of disparities in nations' export performance is difference in non-price competitiveness.) For the purposes of short-run analysis, the slope of the *BP* locus may be taken as constant; but in the long run, changes in the slope become crucial in determining changes in the relative economic performance of a region.

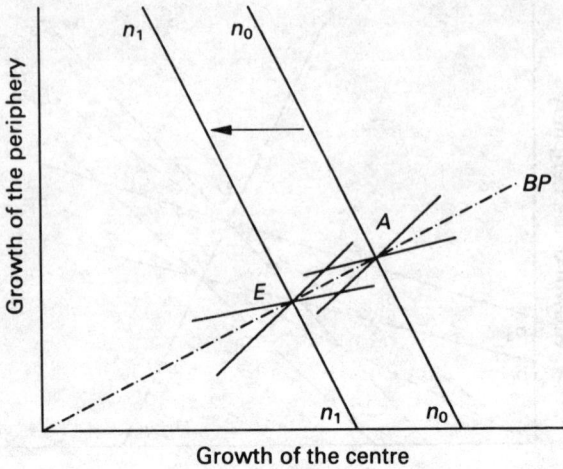

Figure 8.5 The effect of a national recession on regional growth rates

Eventually, increased congestion, shortage of land and the appearance of other external diseconomies of scale may begin to reduce the attractiveness of the centre for entrepreneurs compared with the periphery. This may be reinforced by government expenditure, either deliberately through regional policies or indirectly through interregional income transfers both of which benefit the periphery. The effect of these may be to improve the growth of the periphery at the expense of the centre and may result in a convergence in both the levels of productivity and unemployment rates. But all the time there are powerful underlying forces working in the opposite direction.

Finally, Figure 8.5 depicts the impact of a recession on the growth rates of both regions. A decline in the rate of growth of the national economy results in a leftward shift of the national growth constraint from the line n_0 to the line n_1. The decline in the growth of both regions is given by a movement from point A to point E. Clearly, if the decline in the national growth rate is substantial, the resulting regional and national unemployment problems become, to a large extent, synonymous.

The remedy is to increase the growth of the whole economy and thereby shift the line n outwards again. This means that it is necessary to adopt effective national macroeconomic policies, rather than regional policies, *per se*, in order to increase the growth of both regions simultaneously. This would generate complementary, as opposed to competitive, growth and is the regional equivalent to expansion of the world economy through co-ordinated international policies (as discussed in Chapter 7).

REGIONAL PROBLEMS ARE BALANCE-OF-PAYMENTS PROBLEMS[22]

The view that regional growth is demand constrained and that regional problems are balance-of-payments problems is in contrast to the models of regional growth and unemployment of the so-called neoclassical variety. First, in neoclassical theory, growth is resource-based. Regional growth performance is determined by, or constrained by, the rate of growth of indigenous factor supplies and productivity, exogenously given independent of demand. In our model, by contrast, regional growth is demand determined for the obvious reason that no region's growth rate can be constrained by supply when factors of production are freely mobile. For a region in which capital and labour are highly mobile in and out, growth must be demand-determined. If the demand for a region's output is strong, labour and capital will migrate to the region to the benefit of that region and to the detriment of others. Supply adjusts to demand. We cannot return to the pre-Keynesian view that demand adjusts to supply. If we could, the solution to any region's lagging growth rate would be for it to save more and breed more! Production function studies of interregional growth performance, which approach growth from the supply side, have their uses, but the question still has to be answered: why does the rate of growth of labour, capital and total factor productivity differ between regions? The major explanation must lie in differences in the strength of demand for regions' products. The only true supply constraint on growth is land-based resources, but economic activity in most regions in mature economies is not land-based.

Secondly, in neoclassical theory, regional balance-of-payments difficulties, while disguised by the fact of a common currency, make no difference to the long-run performance of regions because relative prices in regional trade adjust to preserve long-run balance-of-payments equilibrium. By contrast, in our model it is income that adjusts to bring exports and imports into balance through the workings of the Harrod trade multiplier.

Thirdly, in neoclassical theory, high unemployment is voluntary because the real wage is too high. In our model, unemployment is of the Keynesian involuntary variety.

A fourth feature of neoclassical theory in a regional context is that migration, and the free flow of factors of production between regions, are assumed to act as an equilibrating mechanism to equalise growth, income and unemployment rate differences between regions. In practice, it seems that once an initial disequilibrium develops between regions, most social and economic processes in the dynamic context of development work on balance to perpetuate or to worsen the disequilibrium rather than to narrow it. Supply and demand curves for factors of production are not independent but interdependent. Thus factor prices do not necessarily equilibrate between regions, nor do unemployment rates necessarily equilibrate as the unemployed migrate from depressed to prosperous regions. Vanderkamp (1970) found in Canada that for every five unemployed persons leaving the Atlantic region, two more persons became unemployed. This is the notion of circular and cumulative causation that we expounded earlier in the chapter. This principle is based on the existence of increasing returns in the widest sense; a phenomenon which the neat theorems of neoclassical economics do not admit. The Verdoorn relationship between the rate of growth of output and the rate of growth of labour productivity plays a key role.

The neoclassical approach to an understanding of regional growth performance needs to be replaced by a model in the Keynesian spirit appropriate to an open economy, where exports are treated as the major component of autonomous demand which must pay for imports if output and employment are not to contract in the absence of capital transfers. In the model, supply must be endogenous (through migration) and adjust to demand (not the other way round), and regional income not relative prices, which in practice are very inflexible, must be the main adjustment mechanism balancing imports and exports in the absence of monetary transfers.

GROWTH AND UNEMPLOYMENT IN THE REGIONAL ECONOMY

Once the growth of output is determined, the growth of employment and the behaviour of unemployment is also determined, given the rate of productivity growth, the natural rate of increase in the workforce and the propensity to migrate. This can be shown in a simple Harrodian growth framework.

Let:

$$y_t = \ell_t + r_t \tag{8.31}$$

where y, ℓ, and r are the growth rates of income, employment, and labour productivity.

Thus:

$$\ell_t = y_t - r_t \tag{8.32}$$

Now if the actual growth rate (y_t) approximates to the balance-of-payments equilibrium growth rate $(y_B = x/\pi)$ in the long run, we have:

$$\ell_t = \frac{x_t}{\pi} - r_t \tag{8.33}$$

By the Verdoorn relationship:

$$r_t = r_{at} + \lambda \frac{x_t}{\pi} \tag{8.34}$$

where r_{at} is the autonomous rate of growth of labour productivity and λ is the Verdoorn coefficient $(0 < \lambda < 1)$. Substituting equation (8.34) into equation (8.33) gives:

$$\ell_t = \frac{x_t}{\pi}(1 - \lambda) - r_{at} \tag{8.35}$$

The behaviour of unemployment depends on the difference between the rate of growth of labour supply (n) and the rate of growth of employment (ℓ). If $n > \ell$, there will be a growing rate of unemployment, and vice versa. The rate of growth of labour supply will consist of two components: an indigenous component plus migration, which can be expressed as a positive function of the rate of growth of labour demand or employment, and as a negative function of the difference between the percentage level of unemployment inside the region and outside.[23]

Thus:

$$n_t = n_{at} + \rho\ell_t - \mu(\%U_{rt} - \%U_t) \tag{8.36}$$

where n_{at} is the indigenous rate of growth of labour supply, ρ is the elasticity of labour supply from outside the region with respect to demand, $(\%U_{rt} - \%U_t)$ is the difference between the regional rate of unemployment and the rate outside the region and μ is the sensitivity of migration to unemployment rate differences.

Taking equation (8.35) from equation (8.36) and substituting for ℓ_t, gives an expression for the change in the unemployment rate of (approximately):[24]

$$\Delta(\%U_{rt}) \simeq n_{at} - [\frac{x_t}{\pi}(1-\lambda) - r_{at}](1-\rho) - \mu(\%U_{rt} - \%U_t) \tag{8.37}$$

from which the level of the unemployment rate in time t is:

$$\%U_{rt} \simeq \{n_{at} - [\frac{x_t}{\pi}(1-\lambda) - r_{at}](1-\rho)$$

$$+ \mu\%U_t + \%U_{rt-1}\} \left(\frac{1}{1+\mu}\right) \tag{8.38}$$

The unemployment rate in time t depends on its level in the previous period and the current balance between the rate of growth of the supply and demand for labour.

Given the balance-of-payments equilibrium growth rate, what happens to unemployment depends on the values of the variables n_{at} and r_{at}, and on the parameters λ, ρ and μ.[25,26] The higher the values of n_{at}, r_{at} and λ, and the lower μ, the more unemployment will rise or the less it will fall, for any given value of x_t/π. From a policy point of view, if there is growing unemployment in a region, there is not much that can be done to affect n_{at}, r_{at}, λ, ρ or μ, although no doubt some of these variables and parameters will adjust with growing unemployment in such a way as to act as a 'safety valve'. Policy must be directed at raising the rate of growth of exports and reducing the income elasticity of demand for imports. How? As we have argued earlier in the chapter, the export growth rate cannot be raised by currency depreciation or by flat-rate subsidies to make a region's exports cheaper. The only way the rate of growth of exports can be raised is by operating on the income elasticity of demand for exports. That is, policy must encourage activities in the region which produce goods which are as income elastic as possible in markets outside the region.[27] It is of little use encouraging activities producing goods with low income elasticities of demand because this will simply perpetuate the region's dynamic problem. Activities with high income elasticities of demand must be identified, and then financial incentives must be selective – geared to activities within regions rather than to regions as such. The generosity of subsidies could vary according to some index of growth potential. It matters little whether the subsidies are to capital or to labour. Both have an 'income' effect, and the labour intensity of the new industries attracted will depend not on the nature of the subsidy but on the nature of the activities brought within the margin of profitability.

From the simple model outlined above, one could go on to develop a model of cumulative causation, as we have seen earlier in the chapter, showing that once a region obtains a growth advantage it will tend to sustain it through the Verdoorn effect, making it difficult for other regions to establish those activities which give the favoured region its growth advantage. This is the essence of the regional problem in most countries and the essence of the development gap in the world economy. The favoured regions are producing goods with a high income elasticity of demand in export markets, and since the more rapid the growth, the faster the rate of growth of productivity, other regions find it difficult to secure a competitive foothold in the production of these commodities.[28]

9 Applications of the Balance-of-Payments Constrained Growth Model

INTRODUCTION

In this chapter we consider some of the applications to which our balance-of-payments constrained growth model can be put – other than the analysis of growth within or between countries and regions. First, we use the model to consider the effects on growth of the removal of tariff barriers within Customs Unions. Secondly, we show that in a closed economy model of industry and agriculture, the equilibrium level of industrial output is determined by the Harrod trade multiplier result. Thirdly, we see how the model can be used for forecasting the rate of growth of output consistent with balance-of-payments equilibrium given assumptions about the growth of world income and changes in the nominal and/or real exchange rate.

THE EFFECTS ON GROWTH OF THE REMOVAL OF TARIFF BARRIERS IN CUSTOMS UNIONS[1]

A customs union has several effects on both the integration bloc and the rest of the world. These can be separated into static allocative effects (namely, trade creation, trade diversion and, in the presence of economies of scale, trade suppression, with each one of these encompassing both production and consumption effects), static technical efficiency effects (X-efficiency), and dynamic allocative and technical efficiency effects (including investment creation and diversion). Some of these effects are amenable to economic analysis; others are difficult to subject to more than qualitative analysis. The distribution of these effects among the partners of an integration bloc is a matter that requires more systematic treatment in economic analysis. We start this inquiry by taking the case of an integration scheme involving two partners forming a customs union. The questions to be raised refer to the factors that determine the distribution of costs and benefits from the formation of the customs union. We start first with the trade creation effects of customs unions (Lipsey, 1970; Robson, 1980).

The question of the interregional distribution of the gains from trade creation does not arise in the orthodox theory. Where (intra-union) imports are substituted for domestic production, each partner benefits by the resulting savings in the real costs of previously produced domestic goods, and from the substitution of lower cost for higher cost means of satisfying local demand. Both partners benefit from the expansion of their own domestic production and the opportunities for specialisation according to comparative advantage. If this view is taken of the nature of the trade creation effects, it is apparent that the issue of their interregional distribution becomes irrelevant. But this view can be challenged for a number of reasons.

Implicit in the analysis of the trade creation effects of the orthodox theory of customs unions is the assumption that the factors of production released from the inefficient production are put to other uses, particularly to the production of exports. Once the importance of this assumption is recognised then it is easy to see that the process of trade creation may generate certain short-term and, in a few instances, long-term costs which are likely to affect differently the countries and regions participating in a customs union. Let us see what these costs are and what factors determine their spatial distribution within the customs union.

The first source of costs is the short-run adjustment cost of channelling the productive factors from inefficient production to other, relatively more efficient, uses. The inter-regional distribution of this burden of adjustment depends first on the differences in the pre-union level of tariffs that each partner imposed on the other's trade (in other words, on the size of tariffs to be eliminated on intra-union trade), secondly on the size of the new external tariff of the union in relation to each partner's pre-union tariff rates *vis-à-vis* the rest of the world, and thirdly on the partner's 'reallocative ability in the form of response to profit opportunities' (Linder, 1961). Regions with an ability to reallocate factors of production will tend to maximise the gains from trade creation and to accumulate them faster over time. The less developed partner of a customs union is likely to have a higher tariff regime. Furthermore, if its bargaining in setting the common external tariff is weak then the new tariff level *vis-à-vis* third countries will be closer to the rates and structure of the tariff of the stronger partner. The latter happens especially in cases of customs union extensions. It follows, therefore, that the size of adjustment will be larger for the more protected and the smaller of the partners. There will thus be a certain asymmetry in the extent of tariff dismantling. This asymmetry is all the more important, first, because the capacity for industrial restructuring is often lacking in the less developed economies where the quality of entrepreneurship and labour imposes considerable inflexibilities, and secondly, because lack of speedy adjustment will aggravate the balance-of-payments constraint under which the development process often operates. In this case inability to reap the static allocative benefits from trade creation may well lead to an adverse effect on economic growth.

GROWTH EFFECTS

Now let us consider how the formation of a customs union may be expected to affect the growth rate of an individual country or region. The dynamic effects are measured through the impact of the discriminatory dismantling of tariffs between participating countries on the equilibrium growth rate of national income, where the equilibrium growth rate is defined as the maximum attainable rate of growth of national income consistent with balance-of-payments equilibrium on current account.[2] In the traditional, non-dynamic, models of customs unions it has long been recognised that the whole set of the static allocative effects of trade creation, trade diversion, external trade creation and supply-side diversion will exert an impact (positive or negative) on the balance of trade of the participating nations. In the traditional approach, however, these trade imbalances are assumed to be corrected automatically, without output having to adjust, either through exchange rate movements or via counterbalancing capital flows. One of the standard assumptions of the theory of customs unions (besides full employment, pure competition in commodity and factor markets etc.) is that trade is always balanced (Robson, 1980). The dynamic effects of customs unions can therefore be conveniently modelled within a (dynamic) Harrod trade multiplier framework, assuming also that the real terms of trade remain unchanged.[3]

Take the case of two countries, A and B, contemplating the formation of a customs union. The two countries trade with each other and with the rest of the world, W. We examine how the rate of growth of country A is likely to be affected by the tariff realignment expected to take place upon the formation of the customs union, i.e. from the abolition of tariffs on mutual trade with B, and the establishment of an agreed common external tariff that may be different from the level of tariffs currently imposed by A on exports originating from W. Before the formation of the customs union, country A exports to both B and W, and also imports from both these areas. When exporting to B and to W, A's exports are faced with tariff (ad valorem) levels T_b and T_w, respectively. Importers into A pay a non-discriminatory tariff T_a when trading with A. The exports and imports of country A are described by the following multiplicative export and import demand functions (equations (9.1) to (9.4) below):

$$X_{ab} = \left[\frac{P_a (1 + T_b)}{P_b} \right]^{\eta} Z_b^{\varepsilon} \tag{9.1}$$

$$X_{aw} = \left[\frac{P_a (1 + T_w)}{P_w} \right]^{\theta} Z_w^{\zeta} \tag{9.2}$$

$$M_{ab} = \left[\frac{P_b (1 + T_a)}{P_a} \right]^{\psi} Y^{\pi} \tag{9.3}$$

$$M_{aw} = \left[\frac{P_w (1 + T_a)}{P_a} \right]^{\omega} Y^{\rho} \tag{9.4}$$

where:

X	is the export volume of goods and services
M	is the import volume of goods and services
P_a	is the price of A's exportables
P_b	is the price of imports from B
P_w	is the price of imports from the rest of the world (W)
T_a	is the ad valorem tariff imposed by A on products originating from either B or W (before the formation of the customs union)
T_b	is the ad valorem tariff imposed by B on all outside imports
T_w	is the ad valorem tariff imposed by W on imports from either A or B

Z_b is the income of country B

Z_w is the income of the rest of the world (W)

Y is the income of country A

η is the price elasticity of the demand for the exports of A in the market of B

θ is the price elasticity of the demand for the exports of A in the markets of the rest of the world (W)

ψ is the price elasticity of A's demand for imports from country B

ω is the price elasticity of A's demand for imports from W

ε is the income elasticity of country B's demand for exports of country A

ζ is the income elasticity of the demand for exports of country A in the rest of the world

π is the income elasticity of A's demand for imports from B

ρ is the income elasticity of A's demand for imports from W

The subscripts a, b and w refer to countries A and B and the world, respectively.

It is assumed that $T_a \neq T_b$ and that $\eta < 0$, $\theta < 0$, $\psi < 0$, and $\omega > 0$. It is also assumed that before the formation of the customs union, country A's balance of payments is in equilibrium. This equilibrium is defined as:

$$P_a (X_{ab} + X_{aw}) = P_b M_{ab} + P_w M_{aw} \tag{9.5}$$

or

$$P_a (X_{ab} + X_{aw}) = P_b(M_{ab} + M'_{aw}) \tag{9.6}$$

where

$$M'_{aw} = M_{aw} \frac{P_w}{P_b} \tag{9.7}$$

Substituting equations (9.1), (9.2), (9.3) and (9.7)[4] into (9.6), we can solve for the level of income in country A consistent with its balance-of-payments equilibrium (Y_a^*).

The condition for a moving equilibrium through time is that the growth of exports should equal the growth of imports. Taking rates of change of the variables in equation (9.6) (denoted by lower case letters) gives:

$$p_a + x_{ab} \, S^x_{ab} + x_{aw} \, S^x_{aw} = p_b + m_{ab} \, S^m_{ab} + m'_{aw} \, S^m_{aw} \qquad (9.8)$$

where S^x and S^m represent shares of exports and imports in total exports and imports, respectively.

Expressions for x_{ab}, x_{aw}, m_{ab} and m'_{aw} can be derived by taking rates of change of equations (9.1), (9.2), (9.3) and (9.7) (after substitution of equation (9.4)). This gives:

$$x_{ab} = \eta(p_a + t_b - p_b) + \varepsilon z_b \qquad (9.9)$$

$$x_{aw} = \theta(p_a + t_w - p_w) + \zeta z_w \qquad (9.10)$$

$$m_{ab} = \psi(p_b + t_a - p_a) + \pi y \qquad (9.11)$$

$$m'_{aw} = \omega(p_w + t_a - p_a) + \rho y + p_w - p_b, \qquad (9.12)$$

where y, z_b and z_w are the rates of change of income in countries A, B and W (rest of the world), respectively, and t_a, t_b and t_w are the rates of change of the tariff markup expressions $(1 + T_a)$, $(1 + T_b)$ and $(1 + T_w)$, respectively.

Substituting equations (9.9) to (9.12) into (9.8) we can solve for y to obtain country A's growth rate consistent with balance-of-payments equilibrium, namely:

$$
\begin{aligned}
y^*_a = \Big[& \eta \, t_b \, S^x_{ab} - \psi \, t_a \, S^m_{ab} + \theta \, t_w \, S^x_{aw} - \omega \, t_a \, S^m_{aw} \\
& + (p_a - p_b)[1 + \eta \, S^x_{ab} + \psi \, S^m_{ab}] + (p_a - p_w)[\theta \, S^x_{aw} + \omega \, S^m_{aw}] \\
& + (p_b - p_w)S^m_{aw} + \varepsilon \, z_b \, S^x_{ab} + \zeta \, z_w \, S^x_{aw} \Big] \Big(\frac{1}{\pi \, S^m_{ab} + \rho \, S^m_{aw}} \Big)
\end{aligned}
$$

$$\qquad (9.13)$$

Equation (9.13) gives the maximum attainable growth rate consistent with balance-of-payments equilibrium in terms of a set of predetermined or policy variables, *viz.* price and income elasticities, income growth rates in the countries trading with A, export and import shares, price changes and tariff movements. To isolate the effects of tariff changes following the formation of a customs union between A and B, we assume initially that prices and incomes outside A remain unchanged.

Focusing simply on the realignment of tariffs, it is clear from equation (9.13) that y_a^* is inversely related to the rate of decline of B's tariff on A's exports (since $\eta < 0$). However, the magnitude of the effect on A's growth rate depends on the size of the price elasticity of A's exports in country B and on the share of A's total exports that go to B. On the other hand, y_a^* is positively related to the rate of decline of A's tariff against B's goods, so that the greater the reduction in A's tariffs, the lower its balance of payments equilibrium growth rate. Again, however, the magnitude of the effect will depend on the price elasticity of demand for goods from B, and on B's share of total imports into A. The replacement of A's tariff *vis-à-vis* the rest of the world by a common external tariff (CET) will affect y_a^* upwards or downwards depending on the relationship between T_A and CET. The relative importance of this effect on y_a^* will depend on the price elasticity of A's demand for imports from the rest of the world and on the share of the rest of the world in A's imports. Here, t_w is assumed to be zero unless the rest of the world retaliates in response to the discretionary treatment of its exports in the markets of the customs union. Equation (9.13) also shows that the higher the (weighted) sum of the income elasticities of demand for imports (π and ρ) from B and W, the smaller will be the incidence of any changes (positive or negative) from tariff realignment on the maximum sustainable growth rate. High income elasticities of demand for imports in A will tend to attract high levels of imports as national income rises, thus dampening any effects on y_a^* from tariff realignment.

It is fairly clear from what has been said so far that no safe generalisations can be made about the impact of economic integration on the growth rate of the economy. In this respect, the dynamic analysis of custom unions effects is not substantially different from the static analysis. To give the analysis more precision, however, it is useful to take three benchmark cases:

(i) where $T_a = T_b$ = Common External Tariff (CET)
(ii) the case of a tariff averaging customs union where $T_a > T_b$ and therefore CET $< T_a$.
(iii) the same as above, but where $T_a < T_b$ so that CET $> T_a$.

Case (i). Before the formation of the customs union, we assume $T_a = T_b$. This tariff is then adopted as the Common External Tariff. In this case, the size of t_a and t_b (for trade with the partner country) will be the same. This does not imply no change in the value of y_a^*.

The effect of the equiproportionate change in the tariff barriers on intra-area trade will depend on the relative size of the price elasticities (of A's exports to B and of A's imports from B) and the relative importance of partner country B in the structure of A's exports and imports. Assuming $\eta = \psi$, then $y_a^* > 0$ if B dominates A's exports more than it does A's imports. Thus, the extent to which trade links are symmetrical or not (symmetrical in the sense that a given country has the same share in another country's exports as it has in that country's imports) appears to be of some importance in influencing the final outcome of a customs union on the growth rate of the participating countries. If a country buys relatively more from its customs union partners than it sells to them, tariff realignment in the case under consideration, and assuming $\eta = \psi$, tends to reduce the growth rate consistent with the maintenance of balance-of-payments equilibrium. Thus, the gross trade creating effects of the customs union do not produce unambiguous effects on the growth rate, whilst any trade diversion effects that the relative discrimination against exporters from third world countries may produce will have a neutral impact on the growth rate. Adverse static allocative effects do not necessarily imply income growth reduction.

Case (ii) is the case where $T_a > T_b$ and the customs union is tariff-averaging implying $CET < T_a$. The elimination of tariffs in intra-union trade will produce a negative impact on the growth rate if $\eta = \psi$ and $S_{ab}^x = S_{ab}^m$ (i.e. under conditions of symmetric trade links). If country A has weak trade links with its partner B (low share of B in the total imports of A) and if A's price elasticity of demand for imports from B is less than the price elasticity of A's exports in B's markets, then the positive effect from the elimination of T_b may in the end outweigh the negative effect from the removal of tariffs on B's imports, thus exerting a favourable impact on the growth rate. Again the result of the gross trade creating effect of the customs union on the growth rate is not unambiguous. The adoption of a lower tariff on imports from the rest of the world ($CET < T_a$) will have a negative impact on the growth rate. The final result of these changes on the participating country's growth rate will depend on the change in the level of the CET, the values of ψ and ω in relation to η and the pre-union geographic distribution of A's imports between the two sources of supply, B and W.

Case (iii) is where $T_a < T_b$ but $CET > T_a$. The abolition of trade barriers in intra-area trade will raise the sustainable equilibrium growth rate if $\eta = \psi$ and $S_{ab}^x = S_{ab}^m$. In the event that $\eta = \psi$ but $S_{ab}^x \neq$

S_{ab}^m, then the positive impact of intra-union trade liberalisation on the growth rate will be higher the larger is the share of A's exports directed to B and the smaller the contribution of B's products in the structure of A's imports. If the shares are more or less symmetrical, but η is substantially lower than ψ, then the effect becomes indeterminate. Notice, however, that the impact from the adoption of the CET is always positive irrespective of the share of the rest of the world in A's total imports.

It is clear that without a knowledge of the values of the relevant price elasticities (the price elasticity of demand for A's exports in B's markets; the price elasticity of A's demand for imports from B; and the price elasticity of A's demand for imports from the rest of the world), and of the nature of trade links between the participating countries, it is not easy to predict the impact of tariff changes on the maximum sustainable growth rate compatible with balance-of-payments equilibrium. Despite this limitation the above analysis can be used to explain why policy makers have not been guided by the prescriptions provided by the orthodox theory of customs unions. According to the analysis of the static allocative effects of customs unions, a country is likely to gain from its membership of a customs union the higher the initial level of its tariffs, the more elastic is the domestic demand for the goods produced by the partner and the lower the level of the CET after the establishment of the customs union compared to the level of its tariff before the formation of the customs union (Lipsey, 1970). Yet, in practice, despite the policy prescriptions stemming from this analysis, successful and durable customs unions have been established among countries with relatively low initial levels of tariffs. Furthermore, policy makers have appeared to be more concerned with the price elasticity of the demand for their exports in their partners' markets, whilst they have not particularly welcomed relatively lower CETs. The nature of the trade links among the participating countries, and particularly the extent to which they tend to be symmetric or not, has also featured prominently in policy discussions in countries negotiating membership of a customs union. The reasons why policy makers have been concerned with these issues instead of following the prescriptions of the orthodox customs union theory can be readily understood from the above analysis of the impact of tariff realignment on the growth rate of national income compatible with balance-of-payments equilibrium.

In the analysis so far, it has been explicitly assumed that there is no change in income in the partner country. This is clearly unrealistic, but can easily be remedied. The analysis carried out for the impact of tariff realignment on *A*'s maximum sustainable equilibrium growth rate can also be repeated for country *B* and for the rest of the world (*W*) simultaneously. The macro-approach developed by El-Agraa and Jones (1981) can be incorporated into the model.

The model can also be extended to cover cases where there exists balance-of-payments disequilibrium, and the imbalance is met by capital inflows. Indeed, an interesting feature of this dynamic analysis is that the link between the maximum sustainable growth rate and tariff changes established in equation (9.13) can be used to calculate the capital (or other financial) transfers required among partner countries (i.e. through a common budget) to enable them to reap the static allocative effects of customs unions without a downwards adjustment in their maximum sustainable equilibrium growth rate.[5] For example, suppose that, after the tariff changes brought about through the establishment of the customs union, the expression $\eta\, t_b\, S_{ab}^x - \psi\, t_a\, S_{ab}^m - \omega\, t_a\, S_{aw}^m$ in equation (9.13) is negative. This means that the maximum sustainable equilibrium growth rate of country *A* will decrease by:

$$\Delta y_a^* = \frac{\eta\, t_b\, S_{ab}^x - \psi\, t_a\, S_{ab}^m - \omega t_a\, S_{aw}^m}{\pi\, S_{ab}^m + \rho\, S_{aw}^m} \qquad (9.14)$$

unless counterbalancing financial transfers from the partner countries rise by an appropriate amount.

CAPITAL AND FINANCIAL TRANSFERS

As indicated above, the constraints imposed by the balance of payments can to some extent by smoothed out, at least in the short run, by compensatory financial flows that may become more accessible as a result of economic integration. If the formation of a customs union is accompanied by the formation of a monetary union as well, then the short-run balance-of-payments adjustment mechanism is likely to be more efficient because of the higher degree of integration of the banking system and the relative ease with which debt can be raised in highly integrated securities and capital markets in such a union. However, the relatively easier access that a region of an integrated market has to compensatory financial flows is not sufficient to eradicate the structural causes of the disequilibrium generated from differential tariff dismantling effects. The smoothness of the short-run adjustment mechanism of the regional balance of payments does not guarantee that the long-run adjustment mechanism is necessarily less painful or protracted. The long-run adjustment mechanism of the regional balance of payments may in fact be slower because, for one thing, the effects from the reduction in the stock of money in the region as a result of its deficit position will not cut very deep owing to the existence of a highly integrated banking system and to the limited variation in the prices of the financial assets resulting from the high degree of integration of the financial markets over the domain of the whole union (Ingram, 1959; Allen, 1976). The adjustment process may be further slowed down because in a unified state, or a federation, the cost of supporting unemployed labour shifts to taxpayers located in other jurisdictions.

As already mentioned, an implicit assumption of the orthodox customs union theory is the local existence of alternative uses to which factors can be employed from activities that have ceased operation or declined as a result of trade creation. A further implication of this assumption is that interregional patterns of production specialisation are determined by comparative advantage. The fact that regional depopulation and decline have continued in many cases for a long time indicates that regional patterns of specialisation may be determined by absolute rather than relative costs (Nevin, 1972). If absolute and not relative advantage determines trade between regions then a region forming part of an integrated market may find it difficult to establish prices at which it can sell its products to the other regions if its resources are inferior or is unable to gain economies of scale (McCrone, 1969b). Thus, dislocation of production from trade creation effects may entail in the long run a relocation outside the region of the labour and other (mobile) resources released from the cessation or decline of production. The dependence of regional specialisation on absolute advantages is not a direct consequence of the customs union. Rather, it is the result of factor market integration that leads to inter-regional equality in factor earnings. Both the freer inter-regional movement of labour and the development of union-wide collective bargaining practices are conducive to this development. How strong is the evidence that comparative advantage is not relevant in determining inter-regional patterns of specialisation? Most of the empirical analysis in this field is handicapped by the lack of appropriate data. The resort to various proxies and surrogates to measure the relative factor intensity of industry and the relative factor abundance of a region often yields contradictory results (Moroney and Walker, 1966; Moroney, 1975; Dixon and Thirlwall, 1975b; Smith, 1975; Swales, 1979; Norcliffe and Stevens, 1979). The possibility of factor intensity reversal, the problem of excluded variables (notably natural resources), and differences in the quality of essentially heterogeneous factors further complicate the issue and render the results of such investigations inconclusive. Dixon and Thirlwall (1975b) suggest that absolute advantage determines regional specialisation in those activities where resources are industry specific. If resources are regional specific then regions will continue to specialise according to their comparative advantage. Resources are industry specific if they are highly mobile across regions. The distinction made by Dixon and Thirlwall suggests that insofar as integration encourages resource mobility (either actual or potential), it will tend to increase the number of resources which will become industry specific and in this respect make regional specialisation dependent upon absolute cost differences. In such cases, the more industry specific a region's resources become, the lower will be its ability to adjust if its other (natural) resources are of inferior quality.

It is possible that a region may be characterised by adequate reallocative ability and regional specific resources and yet incur costs from trade creation. This may occur if the (positive) externalities of the activities that ceased operations were higher than the corresponding externalities of the new activities that replaced them. The integration induced resource reallocation is brought about through changes in market price signals. There is no reason to expect that social costs and benefits will be properly reflected in market prices. It is thus possible that the potential for generating agglomeration economies may be smaller from the new activities that the economy is directed to specialise in. This development is of course related to the type of specialisation encouraged by the process of integration.

In summary, trade creation undoubtedly brings the benefits assigned to it by the orthodox theory of customs unions but it also entails costs of industrial adjustment. These costs of industrial adjustment will be borne differently by the various areas taking part in the integration scheme. Slow progress towards adjustment affects adversely the regional balance of trade. In the absence of an exchange rate policy and in the absence of accommodating financial flows, this will tend to reduce the growth rate of income consistent with balance-of-payments equilibrium. The regions that bear the largest share of the cost of industrial adjustment are those with a higher pre-integration tariff on intra-union trade, those with high pre-integration tariffs towards third countries in relation to the post-integration common external tariff and those with a price elasticity of demand for their exports substantially higher than the corresponding elasticity of the demand for their imports. Furthermore, the benefits from trade creation will be captured more by regions with: (a) a high 'reallocative ability', and in particular more flexible factor markets and better entrepreneurial quality; (b) a high proportion of resources that are regional specific; and (c) low absolute costs in activities utilising industry specific resources. What is clear is that the inter-regional distribution of benefits from trade creation is not automatic. A lot depends on the strategic response of firms to changes in the new cost conditions they are faced with.

So far, the discussion has focused on the distribution of costs and benefits from trade creation. A few words must be added on the distribution of costs and benefits from trade diversion. The costs of trade diversion are the higher prices at which the product is sold. The benefits are production gains and increased employment. The effects of a customs union in diverting imports to higher cost sources within the union are larger the higher the proportion of a member's pre-integration external trade with non-union, third, countries. The crucial question in this case is whether one region reaps all the benefits whilst another shares only in the costs. If the switch from external sources of supply is to the domestic producers of region *A*, then that region, whilst it shares in the losses, enjoys all the gains of increased production and employment. If the switch is to region *B*, then *A* shares in the losses but reaps no benefits. A switch to the domestic producers of region *A* is likely to occur if the new common external tariff on third countries is higher than the pre-union national tariff. Much depends, therefore, on the relative bargaining position of each partner in fixing the common tariff towards non-union countries. The region with the weakest bargaining power in this respect will probably end up with no benefits while sharing in all the losses from the diversion of trade (Hazlewood, 1975).

Finally, a brief comment on trade suppression. In this case there is the possibility of perverse specialisation. The region with the smallest internal market is likely to suffer most from this effect. The corresponding industry in the region with the largest domestic market would have already reached (before integration) more competitive costs per unit of output, not necessarily because of more favourable long-run cost conditions but because it would have operated on a larger scale. It is then possible that the region with the less favourable long-term cost conditions, but the largest pre-union domestic market, could suppress the most efficient producers in the long run in the smaller partner-region and thus dominate the whole market in the integrated area (Robson, 1980).

THE REGIONAL EFFECTS OF FACTOR MARKET INTEGRATION

In discussing the regional impact of factor market integration, it is useful to distinguish between labour markets and markets for financial assets and capital. Removal of the various administrative and legal impediments to labour mobility, and improvement in the dissemination of information about the state of demand and supply in spatially separated labour markets, will increase potential labour mobility. This enhanced labour mobility is expected to lead to convergence – rather than equalisation – in labour rewards, and also in regional unemployment rates. There are two main channels through which convergence in labour rewards might be brought about. Integration (even in its simplest form of a customs union) increases the intensity of trade between the partners in an integration scheme. As Ohlin, Samuelson and Lerner have shown, freer trade in commodities acts as a partial substitute for the free movements of factors thus reducing intra-union inequalities in factor rewards (Tovias, 1982). A second channel leading to convergence in labour rewards is added when factor markets are integrated. This channel acts through the removal of impediments to labour mobility thereby facilitating such movements across regional frontiers. It is argued that it is not actual mobility that matters but also potential mobility. High potential mobility makes entrepreneurs susceptible to the threat of quits or migration in wage negotiations. The real effectiveness of this type of quit threat may not be so important if regions are in a state of chronic excess supply in their labour markets. That is, the threat of quits or migration on wage settlements may be scale dependent in the sense that it becomes ineffective at the inter-regional level.

Far more important are the changes in the frame of reference in pay comparisons that labour market integration brings about. 'Reference' group comparisons form an integral part of modern money wage setting processes. Industrial relations studies often point to the importance of external groups in earnings comparisons (Weddeburn and Crompton, 1972) and tend to emphasise that the frame of reference for judging the work–wage bargain is provided by those labour groups (occupational or regional) with whom the closest and most frequent contacts are maintained. Proximity is regarded as an important factor that encourages consciousness of earnings differences between workers in similar jobs (Hyman and Brough, 1975). Integration increases the sense of belonging to the same broader group, removes communications barriers and improves contacts between groups located at different parts of the integrated area not merely through trade union integration but also through the operations of multiplant, multi-regional enterprises. If, in addition to the integration of the labour markets, monetary integration also takes place, then the 'proximity' factor is further strengthened through the removal of money illusion that the use of different currencies encourages (Pearce, 1973). Perceptions of wage movements are more accurate when a common currency is in use. But even in the absence of monetary integration, factor market integration will enlarge the domain of the reference groups in pay comparisons. One factor that contributes to this is the changes in the structure of collective bargaining institutions and procedures.

The geographical extension of the domain of the reference groups in pay comparisons will turn certain labour markets into leading markets and others into markets experiencing wage leadership from other regions. Integration of labour markets changes the process of money wage transmission between different regional markets. Regions which have the more serious structural problems are likely to experience wage leadership from outside their markets in most of their occupations. When earnings increases are transmitted through wage leading markets then money wages will not respond to differences in local labour market conditions thus generating persistent differences across regions in efficiency wages. This will have further consequences on the pattern of regional specialisation and on the emergence of persistent differences in unemployment rates. Social pressures to negotiate for comparability and to introduce uniform social security contributions and taxation payments will lead towards equalisation of factor earnings. They will also make regional production and trade dependent upon absolute advantages (McCrone, 1969b). Inter-regional differences in efficiency wages and unemployment will be mitigated if money wage levels are inversely and systematically related to distances from leading markets (Anderson, 1976) or if recruitment for at least unskilled jobs can be done without difficulties. In this last case, the earnings structure for unskilled jobs will behave differently from the corresponding regional earnings structure of skilled jobs (Hart and Mackay, 1977). However, the ability of firms to cope with and absorb wage increases transmitted via institutional bargaining mechanisms may vary from one regional market to another. Clark (1981), for example, found in Canada that labour markets in the western part of the country display a greater ability to absorb wage-rate increases from leading markets whereas in the eastern provinces of the country wage inflation generates increases in regional unemployment. The difference must be attributed to a capacity to speed up productivity rises – a factor essentially related to differences in the strategic response of firms to differential increases in factor costs. Leaving aside for the moment the question of alternative strategic responses firms make in situations of differential changes in factor costs, let us see how the process of labour rewards convergence will affect the process of income growth in the region experiencing the impact of wage leadership from other markets.

The model developed in the previous section can be adapted to deal with the present problem. The adapted model is essentially a Kaldor-type export-led regional growth model similar to the one presented in Dixon and Thirlwall (1975a) and subsequently developed by Swales (1983) (see Chapter 8). The novel feature is the application of the model to elucidate the problems arising from the process of labour market integration and money wage convergence. The model starts with the identity of balanced trade equilibrium, taking just two regions, A and B. All rates of change are given a time subscript. B represents the leading labour market, high wage region; A represents the market experiencing convergence in money wages towards the levels of the leading market region. Thus, we start with:

$$p_{at} + x_{at} = p_{bt} + m_{bt} \tag{9.15}$$

The rates of change of exports and imports are related to the differences in the rates of change of the prices of the two competing regions, the rate of change of the income of the importing region (z for region B, y for region A) and the relevant price elasticities (η for region A, ψ for region B) and income elasticities (ε for region B and π for region A) of export and import demand, i.e.:

$$x_{at} = \eta(p_{at} - p_{bt}) + \varepsilon z_{t-1} \tag{9.16}$$

$$m_{at} = \psi(p_{bt} - p_{at}) + \pi y_{t-1} \tag{9.17}$$

Notice that exports and imports respond to changes in incomes one period earlier. The rates of changes of prices are defined as the difference between the sum of the changes in money wages (w) and profit mark-ups (τ) and the rate of change of productivity (r):

$$p_{at} = w_{at} + \tau_{at} - r_{at} \tag{9.18}$$

$$p_{bt} = w_{bt} + \tau_{bt} - r_{bt} \tag{9.19}$$

Productivity changes depend on the rate of change of output and an autonomous element (r_a). This relationship is described by means of the Verdoorn coefficient (λ) and is explained by the idea of embodied technological progress and the economies of learning by doing. So:

$$r_{at} = r_{aat} + \lambda_a y_t \tag{9.20}$$

$$r_{bt} = r_{abt} + \lambda_b z_t \tag{9.21}$$

Substituting and solving for the equilibrium income growth rate in region a consistent with balance-of-payments equilibrium (y_a), we get:

$$y_a^* = \frac{(1+\eta+\psi)(w_{at} - w_{bt} + r_{abt} - r_{aat} + \tau_{at} - \tau_{bt} + \lambda_b z_t) + \varepsilon z_{t-1}}{(1+\eta+\psi)\lambda_a + \pi} \tag{9.22}$$

The question that now arises is how this equilibrium growth rate is affected when money income convergence, stimulated from factor market integration via union-wide collective bargaining, is taking place. In this case $w_{at} > w_{bt}$. Under the assumption that as a result of factor market integration only the rates of money wage change, with the rate of change in the low wage region rising faster than the corresponding rate of change in the leading region, we have:

$$\Delta y_a^* = \frac{\Delta(w_a - w_b)(1 + \eta + \psi)}{\pi + (1 + \eta + \psi)\lambda_a} \tag{9.23}$$

where Δ stands for increment in the value of the relevant variable. If $(1 + \eta + \psi) < 0$, it follows that y_a will fall if:

$$\left| \frac{\pi}{(1 + \eta + \psi)} \right| > \lambda_a, \text{ and will rise if } \left| \frac{\pi}{(1 + \eta + \psi)} \right| < \lambda_a$$

The price elasticities of the demand for exports and imports, the income elasticity of the demand for imports and the size of the Verdoorn coefficient (a measure of the response of productivity growth to changes in the rate of change of output) will determine how a region can cope with the convergence in money wages brought about through institutional and social pressures.

There are a number of options that firms can follow in order to overcome rising wage costs (Cable, 1983). One route the firm can follow is that of horizontal specialisation. The firm can shift its resources within the enterprise to commodities manufactured with the use of more capital-intensive methods. In this case, the capital intensity of production will be raised without the undertaking of new investment. Larger firms may follow the route of inter-industry switch whilst others – not necessarily the big ones – could follow upmarket quality strategies channelling their efforts to exports.

Defensive adjustment is the second major option a firm can follow in response to differential factor cost changes. Rationalisation to cut fixed and overhead costs, or investment in capital deepening, can be tried. The question may be raised here as to why firms will invest in the face of falling profit rates. Demand expectations are of course crucial here as is the relationship between the scrap value of assets and their profit value (Lamfalussy, 1961). Furthermore, small-scale entrepreneurs are likely to judge what is the proper size of normal profits by reference to the relatively small geographical domain over which they can afford to scan for alternative business ventures. Still a third option is location specialisation. It could involve transfer of plant location to areas with relatively lower wage costs within the economic union, restricting activities to finishing touch assembly operations or reducing into manufacturer importing. Locational specialisation within the economic union implies that labour cost differentials continue to exist. These differentials may not be necessarily in favour of regions with relatively lower money wages. Regions where money wage increases outpace labour productivity rises will suffer from locational specialisation, i.e. it will be the firms operating in these regions that will seek new locations elsewhere in the union.

Regions that experience a deterioration in their efficiency wages may still, in one sense at least, remain 'cheap labour' regions. Labour is a quasi-fixed factor of production, not a purely variable one (Oi, 1962). Because of this characteristic of labour inputs, firms operating in traditionally tight labour markets prefer to use more extensively the internal labour market rather than the external one. On the contrary, firms operating in labour markets chronically in surplus will use more often the external labour market. Using more intensively the internal market over the course of the trade cycle entails higher costs to the firms. This cost of operating internal labour markets is smaller in regions experiencing traditionally high levels of unemployment. If these are the regions that during the integration process increase their money wages at rates faster than changes in labour productivity, then their higher labour costs per unit of output may be mitigated over the period of the business cycle if firms are not forced by circumstances to rely heavily on internal labour markets. Ability to rely on external labour markets may prove an incentive to firms operating in tight labour markets to establish plants in labour markets with chronic excess supply.

The integration process may enhance the location specific advantages that multiplant, multi-regional, enterprises can exploit on the basis of the ownership specific advantages they possess and the internalisation incentives they have. This trend will not be general. Indeed, opposite cases can be stated. In Table 9.1, we use Dunning's (1981) taxonomy of location specific advantages and indicate (in the right-hand side of the table) how the integration process is likely to affect them, i.e. whether it enhances or suppresses them. If it enhances them, then investment creation effects will work in favour of the region; if it suppresses them, then investment creation effects will work against the region. The table gives on the left-hand side the sources of locational specific advantages, and on the right-hand side the impact of the integration process on them.

The operations of multiplant, multi-regional enterprises will exert a further impact on the region's economy through the opportunity they offer to 'transplant' into the less developed region part of the agglomeration economies of the more developed ones. Agglomeration economies are often thought of as a kind of immobile 'resource'. Some of them may not actually be so. For example, economies of joint supply (in production, input procurement, marketing, finance etc.) can reasonably be regarded as a component of agglomeration economies. These economies could still be enjoyed by branch plants

Table 9.1   Taxonomy of location specific advantages

1. Input prices, quality and productivity	Convergence in labour rewards reduces the attractiveness of this location specific advantage; however, attraction for operations that can rely on the use of external labour markets will increase.
2. Spatial distribution of inputs and markets	Affected by the direction of factor movements, but also the trend for balanced income growth; result uncertain but most likely will work against less developed regions.
3. Control on imports including tariff and non-tariff barriers	Liberalisation of intra-union trade makes sites in less developed regions more attractive for export oriented production towards union markets but not for import substituting (domestic market oriented) activities.
4. Climate for investment, political stability	Enhanced; increases attractiveness of sites in the developing regions.
5. Government intervention	Unified government policies lead to reductions in costs of dealing with government departments and thus increase locational advantages.
6. Infrastructure	Fiscal union may help towards improving infrastructure through the unification of the standards of public services and fiscal transfers.
7. Psychic distance	As consumer goods markets become more unified, special problems of dealing with markets with different consumer habits and tastes are reduced. Increased attractiveness of location.
8. Economies of research and development, production and marketing	No impact.

of multi-regional enterprises located outside their 'home' regions. Furthermore, a branch plant of a multi-regional enterprise has access to inputs such as skilled labour, finance or information even if it is located in a peripheral region. The process of integration can thus be seen as a mechanism for redistributing agglomeration economies. The emergence of the branch plant economies raises, however, the question of the external control of a region's industry (Firn, 1975).

We have examined so far how labour market integration affects differently the regions participating in an integration bloc. The integration of securities and capital markets will tend to distribute fairly evenly changes in monetary policy rather than limiting them to the initial target region. Interest rate pressures will be distributed in a balanced way across the integration bloc and so will be the pressures on the goods and services markets (Allen, 1976). Well-integrated capital markets also enable the easy financing of the regional short-run current account deficits through the capital account thereby reducing the need for adjustment in relative product prices. All this presupposes that the domestic capital markets were not initially compartmentalised (Woolley, 1974).

Morgan (1973) has argued that the securities and capital market integration implies centralisation of capital markets – given the externalities from the concentration in space of the institutions supplying financial services. Centralisation of capital markets may make certain regions enforced exporters of capital. Whilst capital markets become more centralised, information about the geographical distribution of investment opportunities remains essentially imperfect. Ignorance or prejudice in informationally imperfect markets can lead to a systematic overestimation of the risks in peripheral, less developed, regions and to a systematic underestimation of the risks in central more developed regions. A region which is characterised by a weak demand for its exports and strong domestic demand for imports must experience a depression of its aggregate demand if it is to become a forced lender. This is more so if the region participates in a currency union that rules out exchange rate devaluation.

Monetary integration within a common market will not automatically ensure an equal distribution of the resulting gains and costs. This distribution is crucially influenced by the extent to which a region satisfies the criteria for belonging to the domain of a given currency area (Ishiyama, 1975). On the gains side, small and open regions with a narrow export base and considerably fluctuating export earnings will gain most in terms of economies in the use of foreign exchange reserves and in terms of reducing the misallocation of resources arising from the distortions in the price of raising capital caused by speculative exchange rate movements. Furthermore, by increasing the smoothness of the regional balance-of-payments adjustment mechanism, monetary integration will enhance the positive aspects of trade creation (Robson, 1980). An additional benefit for low wage regions will be the promotion of convergent income growth because monetary integration strengthens the wage emulation phenomenon of the factor market integration process as a result of the removal of money illusion from collective bargaining pay negotiations (Pearce, 1973).

However, monetary integration will force inflation rate convergence. Inflation rate convergence may lead to an increasing overall unemployment rate because the deflating region will experience a higher rate of increase in its unemployment rate than the inflating region. Thus balanced income growth could be accompanied by an unequal distribution of the costs of unemployment. The size of the unemployment effects of inflation rate convergence depends on the extent to which regions possess different types of inflation–unemployment trade-offs, and how far these trade-off relationships are stable and different from the long-run natural rate of unemployment. Depending on the situation, inflation rate convergence may lead not only to temporary but also to lasting unemployment effects. Wage emulation encouraged by monetary integration increases labour market rigidities in the regions experiencing these 'demonstration' effects in pay comparability norms. This process will shift the region's natural rate of unemployment to a higher level since it can be argued that the long-run aggregate supply schedule has its position determined – among other factors – by the level of real wages. The regions to suffer more from these unemployment effects of monetary integration are those with the stronger wage emulation phenomenon (mainly the low wage regions) and with the relatively lower opportunity cost of leisure (Williamson, 1976). Monetary union will lead to a reduction in the inter-regional disparities in wage earnings but at the same time it will fail to equalise unemployment differentials and may indeed raise in some instances the overall unemployment rate of the union. Labour mobility across regional boundaries becomes the main channel to reduce unemployment differentials. In view, however, of the consequences of migration on regional expenditure (since the expenditure financed through the transfers received by migration unemployed individuals is 'taken out' of the region), the efficacy of this adjustment mechanism is seriously doubted (Vanderkamp, 1970). Here, it should also be added that Canadian evidence (Wrage, 1981) further suggests that there is a strong positive relationship between the rate of immigration into a region and the rate of growth of regional productivity.

The regional aggregate demand-depressing effects of the inflation convergence process can be mitigated through union-wide fiscal redistribution policies (Denton, 1978). Transfers of tax revenues administered through a central fiscal authority will enable the region experiencing the wage emulation phenomenon to balance its current account by offsetting the trade deficit generated by the increased product costs (Allen, 1976).

THE EQUILIBRIUM LEVEL OF INDUSTRIAL OUTPUT IN A TWO-SECTOR CLOSED ECONOMY MODEL[6]

The Harrod trade multiplier also has application at the sectoral level in considering the process of industrialisation in a developing country in the early stages of development,[7] and in considering growth and fluctuations in industrial production in the world economy. Consider a closed economy with two sectors: agriculture and industry. The agricultural sector produces wage goods; the industrial sector produces investment goods, and trade takes place between the sectors at an equilibrium terms of trade. What determines the rate of growth of industrial output? Traditional development theory looks at this question purely from the supply side. If labour is in surplus on the land, however, and capital is a produced means of production, a supply-orientated approach to industrial growth is not satisfactory. Take, for example, the neoclassical two-sector development model of Jorgenson (1969). The answer to the question of what determines the rate of growth of industrial output lies in the allocation, or supply, of scarce factor endowments, technology and tastes – all exogenously determined. But neither labour nor capital is scarce in the manner envisaged by the model. It is very doubtful, particularly when considered in a growth context, whether less labour on the land means less agricultural output. All the evidence suggests an enormous 'dynamic' surplus of labour, with increasing production going hand in hand with a declining agricultural workforce. And as far as capital is concerned, it is not 'allocated'; it is accumulated. There is no way of withdrawing capital from one sector for use in another. The process of industrial production itself generates its own capital (see Young, 1928; Kaldor, 1979a). Another major objection to the neoclassical model is that there is no treatment of the complementarity between the output of one sector and the output of the other within the framework of reciprocal demand. The sectors are competitive. There is no recognition that the level of output in agriculture may itself determine the demand for the output of the industrial sector and vice versa, and there is no explicit role for the terms of trade as the mechanism for achieving balance between the supply of and demand for output in both sectors, so that growth is neither supply nor demand constrained below its potential.

Lewis's (1954) classical model is an improvement on neoclassical models in that labour is plentiful and capital is accumulated, but it is still basically a supply-orientated model, with the demand for the output of the industrial sector side-stepped. Lewis's discussion of the relationship between the two sectors focuses only on checks to the expansion of the capitalist surplus, and particularly on how a deterioration of the industrial terms of trade chokes the rate of capital accumulation. There is no recognition of the fact that a worsening terms of trade for industry may be associated with faster industrial growth because of higher rural incomes which accompany a faster growth of agriculture. There is no analysis of trade between the sectors. Johnston and Mellor (1961) recognised this worrying feature of the Lewis model many years ago when they perceptively remarked: 'one of the simplifying assumptions of the (Lewis) two sector model is that expansion of the capitalist sector is limited *only* by a shortage of capital. Given this assumption, an increase in rural net cash income is not a stimulus to industrialisation but an obstacle to the expansion of the capitalist sector.' Johnston and Mellor continue, 'there is clearly a conflict between emphasis on agriculture's essential contribution to the capital requirement for overall development and emphasis on increased farm purchasing power as a stimulus to industrialisation. Nor is there any easy reconciliation of the conflict.' There is a resolution to the conflict if the *complementarity* between industry and agriculture is recognised from the outset, and it is remembered that there must be an equilibrium terms of trade that balances the supply of and demand for output in both sectors.

Let us now model the interaction between the two sectors and derive the equilibrium level of industrial output.

Agriculture

In agriculture, disguised unemployment is assumed to exist, so that changes in output are assumed to be independent of the number of people employed, and the level of technology is assumed constant. Prices are assumed to be determined competitively in free markets. Capital is obtained from the industrial sector in exchange for the agricultural surplus or saving. The lower the price of industrial output in terms of agricultural output, the faster will be both the rate of increase in agricultural output and agriculture's purchasing power over industrial goods. This can be shown formally as follows:

Let a proportion of agricultural output ('corn') be consumed in agriculture itself and a constant proportion (s_a) saved to exchange for industrial goods ('steel', which may be invested or consumed). Agricultural saving may be expressed as:

$$S_a = s_a Q_a \tag{9.24}$$

where Q_a is agricultural output and S_a represents the agricultural surplus. The agricultural surplus may be used either for the purchase of investment goods (I_a) or consumption goods (C_{ia}) from industry. If p is the price of 'steel' in terms of 'corn' (or the industrial terms of trade), then the total amount of industrial goods obtained by the agricultural sector in exchange for the agricultural surplus is:

$$(I_a + C_{ia}) = S_a/p \tag{9.25}$$

Equation (9.25) is a market clearing equation.

Now the growth of agricultural output may be expressed as the product of the investment ratio in agriculture and the productivity of investment in agriculture $(\sigma = \Delta Q_a/I_a)$.[8]

$$\frac{\Delta Q_a}{Q_a} = \frac{\sigma I_a}{Q_a} \tag{9.26}$$

Substituting (9.24) into (9.25), and obtaining an expression for I_a for substitution in (9.26) gives:

$$\frac{\Delta Q_a}{Q_a} = \sigma \left(\frac{s_a}{p} - \frac{C_{ia}}{Q_a} \right) \tag{9.27}$$

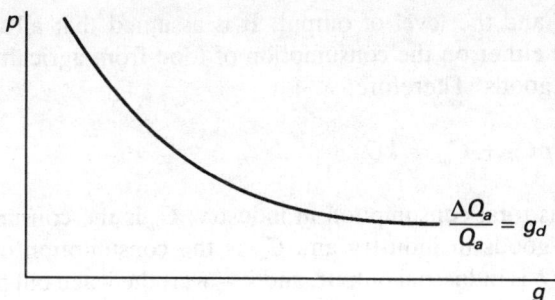

Figure 9.1

Equation (9.27) not only gives the rate of growth of agricultural output but also the rate of growth of purchasing power, or demand, over industrial goods (g_d). The equation traces out a hyperbola showing an inverse relation between the industrial terms of trade and the growth of agricultural demand for industrial goods. The more favourable the industrial terms of trade the lower the rate of growth of demand, and vice versa. The relation is shown in Figure 9.1 with the terms of trade between industry and agriculture (p) measured on the vertical axis and growth (g) measured on the horizontal axis. A rise in agricultural productivity will shift the curve outwards, as will a rise in the agricultural savings ratio. Notice that the higher the amount of agricultural saving devoted to consumption goods from industry, the lower the agricultural growth rate for any given terms of trade, and vice versa.

Industry

Industry produces 'steel' by means of inputs of labour and capital, and fixed coefficients of production are assumed. The productivity of labour can be improved by technical progress, but here the level of technology is held constant. Because of the existence of surplus labour in agriculture, the supply curve of labour to industry is infinitely elastic at some conventional real wage. All steel which is not sold to agriculture for food or consumed by industrial workers is invested. There are assumed to be profitable investment outlets for all saving.[9] The price of industrial goods is assumed to be determined by a markup on unit labour costs.

The consumption of workers in the industrial sector depends on the real wage and the level of output. It is assumed that all wages are consumed either on the consumption of food from agriculture or on industrial goods. Therefore:

$$C_i = pC_{ii} + C_{ai} = kQ_i \tag{9.28}$$

where C_i is total consumption in industry; C_{ii} is the consumption of industrial goods in industry and C_{ai} is the consumption of food in industry; Q_i is industrial output, and $k = wl$ is the wage bill per unit of steel output. w is the real wage measured in terms of food and l is labour input per unit of steel output (the reciprocal of labour productivity). For a given l, k is determined by the real wage, which is exogenous.

The growth of industrial output can be expressed as the product of the investment ratio in industry and the productivity of investment:

$$\frac{\Delta Q_i}{Q_i} = \frac{\xi I_i}{Q_i} \tag{9.29}$$

where $\xi = \Delta Q_i / I_i$ is the productivity of investment. Now I_i is equal to the total output of steel less the steel sold to agriculture and industrial workers:

$$I_i = Q_i - I_a - C_{ia} - C_{ii} \tag{9.30}$$

and from (9.25):

$$(I_a + C_{ia}) = S_a/p$$

Since the agricultural surplus is sold to industry for workers' consumption, $S_a = C_{ai} = \alpha k Q_i$, where α is the proportion of the wage bill spent on food (C_{ai}/kQ_i). Therefore $I_a = (\alpha k Q_i/p) - C_{ia}$. Substituting for I_a in equation (9.30) and the result into (9.29) gives:

$$\frac{\Delta Q_i}{Q_i} = \frac{\xi}{Q_i}\left(Q_i - \frac{\alpha k Q_I}{p} - C_{ii}\right) = \xi\left(1 - \frac{C_{ii}}{Q_i}\right) - \frac{\alpha \xi k}{p} \tag{9.31}$$

Since it is assumed that all industrial wages are consumed, it follows from equation (9.28) that $\alpha = 1 - (pC_{ii}/kQ_i)$, so that equation (9.31) may also be written as:

$$\frac{\Delta Q_i}{Q_i} = \xi \left(1 - \frac{k}{p} \right) \qquad (9.32)$$

In other words, the fact that workers consume only a portion of their wages on food, and the rest on industrial goods, makes no difference to the industrial growth rate. The surplus for reinvestment is the same however wages are disposed of. From (9.32) the positive non-linear relation between the industrial terms of trade and the growth of industrial output (g_s) is shown in Figure 9.2. The curve has an asymptote, ξ, and cuts the vertical axis at k, which gives the minimum price of steel (in terms of corn) below which no steel is reinvested in industry itself.

A rise in the productivity of investment in industry will shift the asymptote, ξ, outwards, and an improvement in labour productivity in industry, unmatched by an increase in the real wage, will shift the intercept (k) downwards. In discussing the equilibrium of the model, it will now be assumed for simplicity that all industrial goods are used for investment and $C_{ia} = 0$. This simplifies the algebra without affecting the insights of the model.

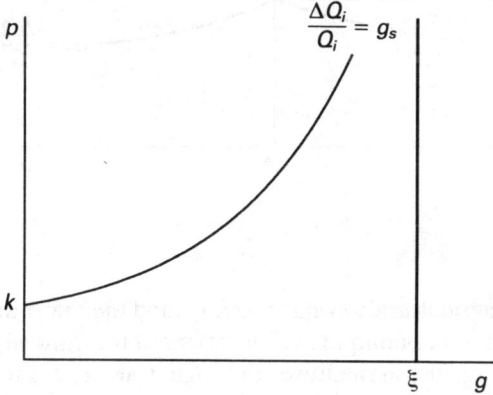

Figure 9.2

Equilibrium

The stationary equilibrium growth rate (g^*), and the equilibrium terms of trade (p^*), are found where the two curves (from Figures. 9.1 and 9.2) cross in Figure. 9.3.

Formally these equilibrium values are found by solving the pair of equations (9.27) and (9.32). This gives:

$$p^* = k + \frac{\sigma s_a}{\xi} \qquad (9.33)$$

and

$$g^* = \frac{1}{k/\sigma s_a + \dfrac{1}{\xi}} \qquad (9.34)$$

The equilibrium growth rate will be faster, the higher is the productivity of investment in industry and agriculture, ξ and σ; the

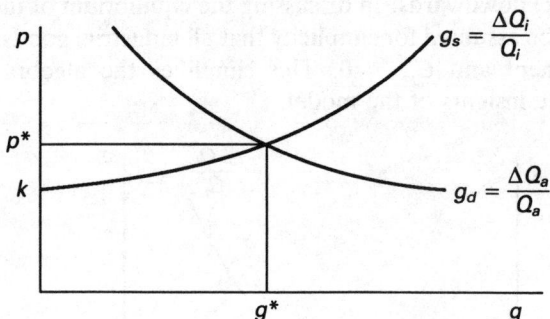

Figure 9.3

higher is the agricultural savings ratio, s_a, and the lower are industrial wage costs per unit of output, k. The terms of trade move in favour of industry and against agriculture, the higher are k, σ and s_a, and the lower is ξ.

This equilibrium solution implies that steel output and food output should be in a particular relationship to each other. If food demanded in exchange for steel is kQ_i[10] and food offered (the agricultural surplus) is $s_a Q_a$, then in equilibrium the ratio of steel output to food output must be:

$$\frac{Q_i}{Q_a} = \frac{s_a}{k} \qquad (9.35)$$

or:

$$Q_i = \frac{I_a}{k} \quad (\text{where } I_a = s_a Q_d / p) \tag{9.36}$$

This is the *Harrod trade multiplier result* that at a given terms of trade ($p = 1$) at which trade is balanced, industrial output is a linear multiple ($1/k$) of the 'export' of industrial goods (to agriculture), where k is the propensity of the industrial sector to import goods from agriculture.

In other words, the equilibrium level of industrial output is determined by the demand for industrial products coming from agriculture divided by the share of expenditure on agricultural products in total industrial income. By analogy with our previous dynamic version of the Harrod trade multiplier, the rate of growth of industrial output is determined by the rate of growth of demand for industrial products from agriculture divided by the income elasticity of demand for agricultural goods. In this simple model, the Harrod multiplier will always hold if there is a terms of trade which balances exports and imports between the two sectors. The growth of industrial exports to agriculture depends on the rate of growth of agricultural income times the income elasticity of demand for industrial products. Given that agricultural output is subject to diminishing returns, the major determinant of the rate of growth of agricultural income at a given terms of trade is the rate of land saving inventions.

As we said at the beginning, this simple model can be applied both to the world economy as a closed system, divided as it is between land-based and industrial activities, and to the industrial sector of an individual country in the earliest stage of development when its foreign trade sector is very small and the major source of autonomous demand for industrial output comes from agriculture. At the level of the world economy, therefore, the Harrod multiplier theory predicts that the rate of growth of world industrial production depends on the growth of income of primary producers, and at the individual country level the theory predicts that the speed of industrialisation will depend on the health of the agricultural sector – not an unfamiliar proposition but now with a stronger theoretical basis.

In the later stages of economic development, however, industrial exports will take over from agricultural demand as the major source of autonomous demand, and it will be the rate of growth of exports that determines the long-run rate of growth of industrial output and the growth of the economy as a whole.

USING THE MODEL FOR FORECASTING

Our basic expression for the balance-of-payments equilibrium growth rate, as outlined in Chapter 3, is:

$$y_B = \frac{(1 + \eta + \psi)(p_d - p_f - e) + \varepsilon z}{\pi} \tag{9.37}$$

where $(p_d - p_f - e)$ is the rate of change of relative prices measured in a common currency; z is the growth of 'world' income; η and ψ are the price elasticities of demand for exports and imports, respectively (η, $\psi < 0$), and ε and π are the income elasticities of demand for exports and imports, respectively (ε, $\pi > 0$).

This basic expression can be used for both policy analysis and forecasting purposes, given estimates of the parameters of the model and forecasts of the exogenous variables.

As far as policy analysis is concerned, if a country is interested in sustaining a particular target rate of growth consistent with balance-of-payments equilibrium, the implications for the parameters and variables it has under its control can be readily worked out. From the expression above, it is possible to solve for any of the variables consistent with a particular target for y_B. One important variable under a government's control is the exchange rate. In equation (9.37) above, e is the rate of change of the exchange rate measured as the domestic price of foreign currency. To raise or lower y_B requires a continuous depreciation ($e > 0$) or appreciation ($e < 0$) of the currency. If the target rate of growth is denoted as y_B^*, the rate of change of the exchange rate consistent with y_B^* is:

$$e = \frac{\varepsilon z - y_B^* \pi}{1 + \eta + \psi} + (p_d - p_f) \tag{9.38}$$

Let us give a simple numerical example. Suppose the target rate of growth is set at 3 per cent per annum (since all other countries are growing on average by 3 per cent per annum, i.e. $z = 0.03$), that $\varepsilon = 1.0$ and $\pi = 2.0$ (not dissimilar to the estimates for the UK), that the sum of the price elasticities of demand for exports and imports ($\eta + \psi$) is -1.5, so that the Marshall–Lerner condition is satisfied, and $(p_d - p_f)$ equals 0.04. Substituting these values into equation (9.38) gives:

$$e = \frac{1.0 \, (0.03) - (0.03)2}{1 - 1.5} + (0.04) = 0.1 \qquad (9.39)$$

In other words, to achieve a target rate of growth of 3 per cent, the currency would have to depreciate by 10 per cent per annum. This is necessary basically to offset the unfavourable discrepancy in the income elasticities of demand between exports and imports in the face of which imports would grow faster than exports if the country grew at the same rate as the rest of the world.

The model presented above has been used by Turner (1988) of the ESRC Macroeconomic Modelling Bureau at the University of Warwick for forecasting UK growth prospects. Using forecasts of the growth of world trade prepared by the National Institute of Economic and Social Research and the London Business School, Turner estimated a balance-of-payments equilibrium growth rate for the UK over the five years 1987 to 1992 of not more than 1 per cent per annum. On the assumption that the UK can sustain an average annual deficit of £5 billion for five years, the maximum growth rate sustainable (without a fall in the exchange rate) rises to between 1 and 1.5 per cent per annum. For the growth rate to average more than 2 per cent per annum with an annual deficit of £5 billion, a fall in the exchange rate of 20–30 per cent would be required, every five years. A nominal devaluation of 10 per cent is estimated to lead to a 4–6 per cent increase of total output over the five year period (with adjustment for fiscal policy to neutralise the output effect on imports and the balance-of-payments). We consider the simulations more fully in the next chapter.

If the exchange rate is ruled out as a policy instrument, and import controls are contemplated, the model can be solved for the income elasticity of demand for imports that would be required, namely:

$$\pi = \frac{(1 + \eta + \psi)(p_d - p_f - e) + \varepsilon z}{y_B^*} \qquad (9.40)$$

To give a numerical example, suppose that the exchange rate is fixed and domestic prices are rising by 8 per cent per annum while foreign prices are rising at only 4 per cent. Given the previous values for $\eta + \psi$, ε and z gives:

$$\pi = \frac{(1 - 1.5)(0.04) + 1(0.03)}{0.03} = 0.33 \qquad (9.41)$$

This represents a relatively low income elasticity of demand for imports, but nonetheless would be the value required to sustain 3 per cent growth in the face of growing price uncompetitiveness and a low income elasticity of demand for exports.

An alternative longer term strategy to achieve faster growth consistent with balance-of-payments equilibrium is to raise the income elasticity of demand for exports through policies to improve the various aspects of non-price competition discussed in Chapter 4. The required ε for 3 per cent growth, given the values of the variables and parameters assumed above, would be:

$$\varepsilon = \frac{y_B^* \pi - (1 + \eta + \psi)(p_d - p_f - e)}{z} \tag{9.42}$$

Therefore:

$$\varepsilon = \frac{(0.03)2 - (1 - 1.5)(0.04)}{0.03} = 2.67 \tag{9.43}$$

This is a relatively high income elasticity of demand for exports – at least by UK standards – although achieved by successful exporting countries such as Japan and Korea.

In a similar vein, it would clearly be possible to solve for other variables and parameters such as the rate of domestic price inflation (or disinflation) required, or the price elasticity of demand for exports if that was a feasible and practical policy option.

10 Two Case Studies of Balance-of-Payments Constrained Growth: The UK and Australia

INTRODUCTION

Up until now, the evidence for a country being balance-of-payments constrained has been obtained by examining the extent to which the balance-of-payments equilibrium growth rate approximates to the actual growth rate of that country. Using data from highly aggregated export and import demand functions, we concluded in Chapter 3 that for the vast majority of countries there was no significant difference between the two growth rates. From this we deduced that relative prices played an insignificant role in determining the growth of imports and exports (or, more implausibly, any effect was just compensated by offsetting capital flows). Additional support for our argument is provided by the fact that the relative price terms in the estimation of import and export demand functions are either small or statistically insignificant, or both (e.g. Houthakker and Magee, 1969). Nevertheless, while these results are instructive, the estimation of such highly aggregated export and import demand functions has been criticised because of, for example, the unreliability of the data and the problem of simultaneity (Morgan, 1970). Moreover, it is not possible to test directly the significance of the inflationary feedback from a currency depreciation to domestic costs (i.e. the real wage resistance hypothesis). The estimates of the price elasticities are also insufficiently precise to permit us to determine with any degree of confidence to what extent (if at all) the Marshall–Lerner conditions are satisfied. On the other hand, as we have seen, changes in relative prices are a relatively unimportant determinant of changes in export and import market shares, compared with disparities in non-price competitiveness.

In this chapter, the analysis is extended by a consideration of the extent to which three forecasting models support the contention that both the United Kingdom and Australia are balance-of-payments constrained. Two of the models are for the United Kingdom; namely, the National Institute for Economic and Social Research (NIESR) and the London Business School (LBS) macroeconomic models. (We also briefly consider Whitely *et al.*'s (1992) comparative study using four forecasting models, namely, those of the Treasury, the LBS, the NIESR and Oxford Economic Forecasting.) The third model is of the Australian economy and is that of the Melbourne-based National Institute for Social and Industrial Research (NIEIR). The advantage of using this approach is that the models are based on detailed estimations of the economic structure of the two economies with explicit allowances made for interlinkages and feedbacks through simulation exercises. The disadvantage is that the structure of the model has to be taken as given, although for the United Kingdom this is mitigated by considering two different models.

THE CASE OF THE UNITED KINGDOM

Turner (1988) has explicitly considered the NIESR and LBS models to determine how far our growth rule is appropriate for the United Kingdom, and we draw heavily on his research. Turner found, not surprisingly given the low income elasticity of demand for the United Kingdom's exports, that 'on plausible assumptions, principally concerning how fast world trade is likely to expand, and on the further critical assumption that there is no change in the competitiveness of exports and imports, the LBS and NIESR models both suggest that UK growth can average no more than 1% over the medium term if there is to be no further deterioration in the current account' (pp. 1–2) (see Table 10.1). This is reassuringly close to the prediction of our rule obtained using the aggregate elasticities, which was a value of 1.5 per cent per annum for the period 1970–83.

Turner next considers the effect of a depreciation of the exchange rate. He finds, and again not surprisingly, that a depreciation does relax the balance-of-payments constraint to some extent, but the quantitative effect is small.

In order for GDP growth to average more than 2% per annum [over a five year period] without the current account deficit exceeding £5 billion per annum (1987 prices), the exchange rate would need to fall by the order of magnitude of 20–30%. However even a fall in the exchange rate of this magnitude would not be sufficient to achieve a growth rate of 3% per annum [again over a five year period], which the Chancellor evidently believes is sustainable for the UK over the medium term (see evidence to the Treasury Select Committee on 'The 1987 Autumn Statement'), without the current account averaging more than £5 billion per annum. (p. 41)

The implications of this may be put thus. In order for the United Kingdom to raise its trend rate of growth by one percentage point per annum it would be necessary for there to be a *continuous* depreciation of sterling of between 5 and 12 per cent per annum, depending upon the assumptions made. Given the severe inflationary pressures that this would produce, it is most unlikely that such a rate could be maintained for very long. It would also be incompatible with any future membership of the Exchange Rate Mechanism (ERM). While the ERM does allow for the realignment of exchange rates, there is no provision for continuous depreciation. The latter is contrary to the whole *raison d'être* of the ERM. As the long-term growth potential of the United Kingdom is probably considerably in excess of 2 per cent per annum, we conclude that this provides further evidence that the United Kingdom is subject to a serious balance-of-payments constraint.

THE UK'S BALANCE-OF-PAYMENTS EQUILIBRIUM GROWTH RATE

Turner first calculated the balance-of-payments equilibrium growth rate for the United Kingdom using the relevant parameters and assumptions of the two forecasting models. The income elasticities are at a disaggregated level and consequently the aggregate values were calculated using the relevant sectoral shares in exports or imports as weights. (See Table 10.1.)

A further complication is that the disaggregated import and export demand functions sometimes include a time-trend. This captures directly the change in non-price competitiveness and therefore should be included in the calculation of the balance-of-payments equilibrium growth rate. For example, the aggregate import demand function in terms of growth rates, omitting the price term, is given by:

$$m = a_1 + \pi'tfe \qquad (10.1)$$

Table 10.1   Estimates of the parameters and variables used in the expression for the balance-of-payments equilibrium growth rate

		Model	
		NIESR	LBS
π'	Expenditure elasticity of demand for imports	1.18	1.77
a_1	Trend growth of imports	0.79% p.a.	0.46% p.a.
ε	World activity elasticity of demand for exports	0.65	0.64
z	Growth of world activity	3.59% p.a.	5.01% p.a.
εz	Export growth excluding effect of changes in relative prices	2.33% p.a.	3.21% p.a.
a_2	Trend growth of exports	–0.41% p.a.	–0.61% p.a.
k	See equation (10.2) for definition	0.95	0.77
y_B	Balance-of-payments equilibrium growth	0.9 % p.a.	0.9 % p.a.

Note: The growth of the sectoral world activity variables used to construct z are either the growth of world manufacturing trade, the growth of world trade or the growth of world industrial production.

Sources: Turner (1988, tables 2.3 and 2.4).

where m and *tfe* are the growth rates of imports and total final expenditure. a_1 is the growth of autonomous imports. π' is the final expenditure elasticity of the demand for imports. The NIESR values for a_1 and π' are 0.79 per cent per annum and 1.18 respectively, i.e. total imports are growing exogenously by 0.79 per cent per annum and the expenditure elasticity of demand for imports is 1.18. If the same data were to be used but with the time-trend omitted (as Houthakker and Magee, 1969, do with income elasticities), we should expect the value of the expenditure elasticity to be commensurately higher.

In order to calculate the balance-of-payments equilibrium growth rate, we need the relationship between the growth of imports and the growth of GDP, rather than the growth of total final expenditure. Since GDP is defined as total final expenditure less imports, and as imports account for 30 per cent of GDP, Turner shows that the growth of GDP is given by:

$$y = (1.30 - 0.30\pi')tfe = k\ tfe \qquad (10.2)$$

where k is a constant, equal here to $(1.30 - 0.30\pi')$.

We may thus express the growth of imports as a function of the growth of GDP by substituting equation (10.2) into equation (10.1) to obtain:

$$m = a_1 + \pi'tfe = a_1 + \pi'(1/k)y \tag{10.3}$$

The value of k in the NIESR model is 0.95 and in the LBS model it is 0.77.

The export demand function is given by:

$$x = a_2 + \varepsilon z \tag{10.4}$$

The balance-of-payments equilibrium growth rate is thus:

$$y_B = (\varepsilon z + a_2 - a_1)k/\pi' \tag{10.5}$$

Substituting the values for the various parameters of the two models (see Table 10.1) into equation (10.5) gives a value for the balance-of-payments equilibrium growth rate of 0.9 per cent per annum in both cases. It may be seen that the effect of the higher value of εz in the LBS model is exactly offset by the greater elasticity of demand for imports. The value of y_B is, of course, influenced by the assumption made about the growth of world activity, but for our purposes it is sufficient to note that on plausible assumptions of this value, the United Kingdom cannot grow at a rate faster than about 1 per cent per annum without the balance-of-payments deteriorating from initial equilibrium. Turner also made the assumption that world activity grew at the rate which it did over the period 1963–73, which, of course, is very much higher than in the period subsequent to 1973. The NIESR and LBS models gave a balance-of-payments equilibrium growth rate of 2.2 and 2.7 per cent per annum. This is very close to our estimate of between 2.7 and 2.9 per cent per annum reported in Chapter 3, based on Houthakker and Magee's (1969) estimates of the income elasticities. It suggests that there has been no radical change in the United Kingdom's non-price competitiveness, broadly defined, over the postwar period, although evidence is discussed below that indicates there may have been some slight improvement in the 1980s.

INTRODUCING THE EFFECTS OF A DEPRECIATION OF STERLING

The next question we shall examine is whether or not a depreciation of the exchange rate will improve the balance of payments, and if it does, to what extent. This depends upon the values of the various demand and supply elasticities of exports and imports.

Measuring the balance of payments in domestic currency, a devaluation will improve the balance, starting from equilibrium, if the following condition holds:

$$1 - \rho_X - \eta\rho_X - \rho_M - \psi\rho_M \qquad (10.6)$$

where:

ρ_X is the elasticity of the fall in the foreign price of exports with respect to a fall in the foreign price of domestic currency ($\rho_X > 0$);

ρ_M is the elasticity of the rise in the domestic price of imports with respect to a fall in the foreign price of domestic currency ($\rho_M > 0$);

η is the price elasticity of demand for exports ($\eta < 0$);

ψ is the price elasticity of demand for imports ($\psi < 0$).

If it is assumed that the volume of exports is demand constrained and there is excess capacity and so the elasticity of supply is infinite, ρ_X will take a value of unity. Likewise, if the elasticity of supply of imports is also infinite (the United Kingdom comprises only a small fraction of other countries' export markets), ρ_M will also take a value of unity. Under these circumstances, equation (10.6) reduces to the familiar Marshall–Lerner condition, *viz*, that a devaluation will improve the balance of payments provided that

$$-\eta - \psi > 1 \qquad (10.7)$$

that is, provided that the sum of the two (negative) price elasticities is greater than unity.

The two models do, in fact, assume that the domestic currency price of imports increases by the same proportion as the devaluation. In both models, however, the price of exports in foreign currency does not respond in full to the devaluation, and ρ_X takes a value of about 0.5

for the NIESR, and 0.3 for the LBS, model. Consequently the condition for a depreciation to improve the balance of payments is:

$$-\rho_x(1 + \eta) - \psi > 0 \qquad (10.8)$$

It can be seen that if $\rho_x < 1$, the Marshall–Lerner condition is not necessary for the above inequality to hold. In the NIESR model, the absolute value of the sum of the price elasticities of demand is 1.06 which suggests that the traditional Marshall–Lerner condition is only just satisfied. However, ρ_x takes a value of 0.51. If equation (10.8) is used instead, a greater improvement in the balance of payments may be shown, depending on the precise values of η and ψ. Likewise, although the Marshall–Lerner condition is not fulfilled for the LBS model, the inequality of equation (10.8) is satisfied and so again a devaluation will improve the balance of payments.

These calculations, however, are based on the assumption that there is no inflationary feedback into domestic costs and hence into the prices of exports. Once an allowance is made for this, the effectiveness of a given nominal devaluation is reduced by the extent of the induced domestic inflation.

In order to quantify the extent to which a devaluation relaxes the balance-of-payments constraint, Turner simulated the effect of an exogenous nominal 10 per cent devaluation over a five-year period using both forecasting models. The first simulation was carried out with no feedback effects from either domestic inflation or the increase in GDP, and then with an allowance for a feedback from domestic inflation. Under the assumption of no feedback effects, both models predicted an improvement in the balance of trade, although the improvement was greater in the LBS model. Allowing for the inflationary feedback reduces the trade balance, but by a greater margin in the LBS model than in the NIESR model so that the latter now shows the greater improvement. This leads Turner (1988, p. 24) to conclude that 'this result suggests that we are not justified in *entirely* excluding any consideration of changes in competitiveness when calculating a measure of equilibrium balance-of-payments growth rate, at least over the medium term horizon' (our emphasis). An important question is: to what extent does a devaluation quantitatively relax the balance-of-payments constraint? Fortunately, Turner undertakes some further simulations that shed light on this question. Once a feedback effect is also allowed from the increase in GDP, it is found that this dampens down the improvement in the trade balance, and in the NIESR simulation there is no significant improvement in the trade balance or current account on a *cumulative* basis.

Of particular interest are two further exercises Turner undertakes:

(i) The maximum additional increase in GDP permitted by the devaluation was estimated on the assumption that the fiscal stance was altered by appropriate changes to government spending to keep the current account in balance at the end of each year.
(ii) The procedure was the same as for (i) but changes in the rate of income tax were used as the regulator to ensure the current account was brought into balance.

These two simulations are of particular interest since they provide an indication of the extent to which the balance-of-payments equilibrium growth rate can be increased by a devaluation. The percentage point increase in the growth of GDP is shown in Table 10.2 for each of the five years after a 10 per cent devaluation. These figures may be interpreted as the percentage point increase each year (above or below the trend growth of 0.9 per cent per annum) which are caused by the devaluation and the associated government policies. It can be seen that in both scenarios (i) and (ii) the growth rate falls in the first year due to the J-curve effect. This is caused by an initial worsening of the current account which has to be offset by a contraction in the growth rate of GDP. The major benefit occurs in the second year and then the growth rate tends to oscillate as it approaches the trend growth rate.

The balance-of-payments equilibrium growth rate taking into account the effects of a continuous devaluation may be expressed as:

$$y_B' = y_B + he \qquad (10.9)$$

where y_B is the balance-of-payments equilibrium growth rate in the absence of any change in relative prices. h is the percentage point growth of GDP over the five year period induced by the 10 per cent devaluation, divided by a factor of ten. The variable e is the rate of depreciation of the nominal exchange rate expressed in percentage terms per annum. As may be seen from Table 10.2, the size of h ranges from 0.20 to 0.08. In the first case, an annual rate of depreciation of 1 per cent will raise the equilibrium balance-of-payments

Table 10.2   The effect of a 10 per cent nominal devaluation on the growth of GDP assuming the current account is constrained to be in balance

Percentage increase in GDP over previous year

Period	NIESR (i)	NIESR (ii)	LBS (i)	LBS (ii)
1	−1.09	−0.31	−0.71	−0.16
2	3.33	1.84	2.22	1.20
3	0.02	−0.24	0.29	0.37
4	−0.92	0.54	−0.22	−0.29
5	0.14	0.19	−0.48	−0.30

Increase in the balance-of-payments equilibrium growth rate induced by a one per cent continuous depreciation in the nominal exchange rate (= h)[a]

NIESR (i)	NIESR (ii)	LBS (i)	LBS (ii)
0.15	0.20	0.11	0.08

Notes: Columns (i) and (ii) are where the current account has been constrained to be in balance at the end of each year by government expenditure and income tax changes, respectively.

[a]Based on the assumption that the effect of a single devaluation has worked itself out after 5 years.

Source: Turner (1988, tables 3.3 and 3.4).

growth rate by 0.20 percentage points per annum. The values for h imply that a continuous depreciation of the nominal exchange rate of between 5 per cent and 12 per cent per annum is needed to raise the equilibrium growth rate by one percentage point to 2 per cent per annum. Given the substantial increase in the rate of inflation that this would quickly generate, together with the distinct possibility of a vicious inflation–depreciation circle developing, we are not sanguine that even this modest improvement could be sustained for very long.

Turner uses a slightly different procedure to that outlined above. From the reported increase in GDP given by the simulations, he calculates the 'smoothed growth rate' which, if maintained over a five-year period, would generate the predicted cumulated output that results from the 10 per cent devaluation.

The balance-of-payments equilibrium growth rate *over this five-year period* from a given *once-and-for-all* devaluation is given by:

$$y_B^* = y_B + 0.42 \, (d/10) \qquad \text{(NIESR)} \qquad (10.10)$$

and:

$$y_B^* = y_B + 0.28 \, (d/10) \qquad \text{(LBS)} \qquad (10.11)$$

where y_B takes a value of 0.9 per cent per annum in both equations and d is the percentage size of the nominal devaluation.[1] It is important to note that y_B^* is *not* the steady state growth rate, as this would require a continuous devaluation as in equation (10.9). This point may be made clearer with the help of an example. According to equation (10.10), a devaluation of 10 per cent will have an effect equivalent to raising the balance-of-payments equilibrium growth rate from 0.9 to 1.32 per cent per annum (i.e. by 0.42 percentage points) for five years before the growth rate reverts to 0.9 per cent per annum.

Turner uses equation (10.10) to predict the annual average current account balance over the medium (5 year) term on the assumption of a zero and a 10 per cent devaluation which he then compares with the NIESR published medium-term forecasts. The assumption of no devaluation implies, of course, a balance-of-payments equilibrium growth rate of 0.9 per cent per annum. The NIESR predicted a growth rate of 1.6 per cent per annum which suggests a worsening of the current balance. Turner calculates the expected deterioration in the current account given the amount by which this figure exceeds y_B^*; the elasticity of imports with respect to domestic demand; and the value of imports in the base year (1987). He finds that the change in the current account found from this admittedly rough and ready calculation 'corresponds reasonably closely to the NIESR main forecast' (p. 30). He also finds that the results of a 10 per cent devaluation by the NIESR also correspond closely to that predicted by equation (10.10), namely, output is predicted to grow at 1.4 per cent per annum over a five-year period and the current account shows little deterioration. Turner concludes that 'overall our expression for y_B^* seems to summarise reasonably well the balance-of-payments implications of the NIESR model for the November 1987 forecasts' (p. 30).

On the other hand, the LBS forecast, which was based on the assumption of little change in the exchange rate, predicted a growth rate of 2.9 per cent per annum over the period 1987–91, but surprisingly there was little deterioration predicted in the balance of payments. This is at variance with the result to be expected from equation (10.11). The reason is that the LBS chose to override the trade equations by substantially adjusting the residuals for reasons that were not entirely clear to Turner. When the model was re-run without this adjustment the growth rate fell to 1.7 per cent per annum and there is a very substantial deterioration in the current account of a magnitude 'which is reasonably close to that derived from our simple forecast rule based on y_B^*' (p. 32). This demonstrates that the rule was sufficiently precise to show that the divergence from it in the LBS forecast was due to substantial residual adjustments that had been made to the import and manufacturing export demand equations used in the LBS forecasting model. It was not due to the poor predictive ability of the rule! It may be noted that the growth rate from 1987 to 1990 was 2.4 per cent per annum and the current account deficit deteriorated from £4.2 billion (or 1.2 per cent of GDP at factor cost) in 1987 to £15.5 billion (3.2 per cent of GDP) in 1990, after peaking at £20.4 billion (4.7 per cent of GDP) in 1989. (The growth rate from 1987 to 1989 was 3.1 per cent per annum.)

HAS THERE BEEN A MARKED IMPROVEMENT IN THE UK'S EXPORT PERFORMANCE SINCE 1979?

The LBS consider that since 1980 there must have been a notable improvement in the United Kingdom's trade performance because the country has held on to its share of world trade, measured in volume terms, despite having an uncompetitive exchange rate for most of the period. The long-run LBS world activity elasticity of demand for manufacturing exports is 0.58, which implies that UK exports will take a *declining* share of world trade in manufactures. 'Thus evidence that the UK has been able to hold on to its share of world manufacturing trade might indeed be taken as providing a justification for adding positive residuals (which increase in magnitude over the forecast horizon) to the forecast of UK manufacturing exports' (Turner, 1988, p. 34). Turner re-estimated the LBS equation for manufacturing exports and did not find any evidence that the long-run elasticity had increased since 1980; in fact, the equation proved to be very stable. Turner found that the reason for the United Kingdom's improvement was the increase in cost competitiveness of 30 per cent that occurred from 1980 to the third quarter of 1986 and which was almost entirely due to a fall in the exchange rate. Hence, he concluded that the LBS were unwarranted in adjusting their forecast.

In contrast, Landesmann and Snell (1989) provide support for the procedure adopted by the LBS. They examined the impact that the 1979 recession had on the elasticity of demand for United Kingdom manufacturing exports with respect to world trade (ε'_{MF}).[2] They adopted the same interpretation of this parameter as do we, *viz* that it captures the effects of non-price competition (Landesmann and Snell, 1989, p. 1). Using quarterly time-series data, they estimated the LBS, NIESR and their own specifications of export demand functions for the periods 1972(1) to 1985(4) and found that the values of ε'_M were 0.64, 0.67 and 0.68, respectively. These are similar to the values reported in Table 10.1. When, however, the sample was restricted to the period from 1981(3) to 1986(2), the estimates were appreciably higher, being 0.98, 0.96 and 0.99, respectively. Tests indicated that there was structural instability in the post 1979(2) period. Subsequent estimations of Landesmann and Snell's export demand equation using spline functions and time-varying parameters over the whole sample period produced similar results; the world trade elasticity of demand for United Kingdom manufacturing exports had risen appreciably to about unity by 1986.

This finding was confirmed at a more disaggregated level when individual export demand functions were estimated for five manufacturing industries which together account for 80 per cent of the total value of manufacturing exports. These industries were chemicals, electrical engineering, mechanical engineering, transport equipment and textiles. The regression results showed a very dramatic fall in the values of the elasticities $(\varepsilon'_i s)$ immediately after 1979. This was attributed to the severe contraction that occurred in domestic output and hence export capacity. This *collapse* phase was followed by a period of *recovery* which lasted several quarters until the value of ε'_i regained its former peak. After this came the period of *consolidation* when the value of ε'_i continued to rise as exporters became more efficient and modernised. In all but one of the industries the value of ε'_i was higher at the end of the period, namely 1986, than it was at the beginning of the Thatcher period in 1979. This exception was chemicals, but even here there was a sharp continuing upward trend at the end of the estimation period.

Landesmann and Snell aggregated the individual results for the five industries and, not surprisingly, found a similar value for ε'_{MF} to that produced by the aggregated spline estimation. In the case of the summation of the five industries, the value of ε'_{MF} rose from 0.65 to 0.92 and this compares with the increase from 0.74 to 0.95 using aggregated data. The only difference was the absence of a *collapse* phase using aggregated data and this was attributed to aggregation errors.

Landesmann and Snell conclude that these results support their view that 'the shrunken remains of the U.K. manufacturing sector has a different nature to its predecessor and in particular has a stronger growth dynamic' (p. 23).

If we use the value of 0.95 for the manufacturing export elasticity in the calculation of y_B, we obtain values for the balance of payments equilibrium growth rate of 1.5 per cent per annum (NIESR) and 1.4 per cent per annum (LBS). These are substantial increases compared with the previous value of 0.9 per cent per annum and confirm our arguments about the importance of both non-price competition in international trade and export-led growth.[3]

A more recent study by Church (1991) also confirmed these results. The import and export demand functions of the main macroeconomic forecasting models are such that, in the absence of any improvement in price competitiveness, the maximum growth rate of GDP consistent with external balance is about one per cent per annum. However, if the improvement in export performance since about 1986 is assumed to persist, the balance of payments equilibrium growth rate rises to about 2 per cent per annum.

Whitley *et al.* (1992) addressed the question of whether or not the UK's macroeconomic policy regime in 1992 was compatible with the balance-of-payments by considering the predictions (made using common assumptions) of four forecasting models. These were the models of the Treasury, the NIESR, the LBS and Oxford Economic Forecasting. They also considered whether or not the forecasts for 1996 broadly met the targets for inflation, the PSBR and interest rates that were deemed to be necessary for the UK to adopt a single currency at the beginning of the third stage of the EMU.

Each model was run to give three forecasts based on different assumptions of export performance, with the central assumption being that the improved performance of exports in the latter half of the 1980s would be maintained. The sterling exchange rate was held constant over the forecast period at its level at the end of 1991. Government spending on current goods and services was kept constant at around 25 per cent of GDP and the basic rate of tax was held constant at 25p in the pound. The growth of world trade from 1992 to 1996 was assumed to be just under $4\frac{1}{2}$ per cent per annum. Unlike Turner's exercise, no attempt was made to ensure that the resulting outcome was compatible with a sustainable balance-of-payments position; indeed, the whole objective was to determine what the current account outcome was likely to be and whether or not a fixed exchange rate was feasible in these circumstances.

With the central assumption about the export growth rate, the growth of GDP was between $2\frac{1}{2}$ and 3 per cent per annum. Given that this is above the balance-of-payments equilibrium growth rate (calculated on the basis of the more favourable export growth rate since 1986) of about 2 per cent per annum, the current account deficit continues. The exact amount varies according to the precise model. The best outcome for 1996 is predicted by the LBS with a deficit of about £5 billion, whereas the worst is given by the Treasury model with a deficit of £16 billion (2.2 per cent of GDP). This performance can be regarded as reasonably satisfactory, but it depends crucially on the improvement in export performance being sustained. Under the low export growth scenario, the deficits range from £13.5 billion for the LBS in 1996 to £23.2 billion for the Treasury model. These deficits, in practice, would not be sustainable. The balance-of-payments equilibrium growth rate under the low export growth assumption is about one per cent per annum, about half the rate that has given rise to these large deficits. The general view of the modellers was that the increased export growth since the mid-1980s represents an improvement in non-price competitiveness, although they were uncertain whether this is likely to be sustained.

Bray is the most sceptical and argues that the improvement is merely a statistical illusion. Most of the increase in the growth of exports came from electrical and electronic goods, but these were accompanied by a large fall in relative prices. Adjusting for this, the growth of the volume of exports is 6 per cent per annum rather than 7 per cent per annum, 'effectively removing much of the relative improvement in the growth of the exports of manufactures' (Whitley *et al.*, 1992, p. A8). Bray concludes that 'this exercise on the Treasury model suggests that until firmer evidence of continuing improvement in non-price technological competitiveness is available, the present policy stance and priorities are if anything too loose, despite the slowness in recovering from the recession' (Whitley *et al.* 1992, p. A15).

The overall conclusion of the study is that

the main implications for policy are that the projections for the current account are based on some fairly fragile assumptions and that the down side risks for the current balance to the exchange rate during the transition to EMU could be considerable. The longer the delay in recognizing the problem of the deficit, the greater the risk that subsequent policy tightening may be so severe as to create another recession in the mid-1990s. If the problem is recognized early enough stronger supply-side measures could be taken to improve non-price competitiveness. Although these policies take time to work and are neither costless nor risk free, they do not have the disadvantage of restrictive demand policies which reduce growth and increase unemployment. (Whitley *et al.*, 1992, p. ii)

Moreover, before we conclude that there has, indeed, been a 'Thatcher economic miracle' it must be remembered that the balance-of-payments equilibrium growth rate is also a function of the income elasticity of demand for imports. There is evidence to suggest that the value of this parameter has also been rising over recent years and this would have the effect of reducing y_B.[4] Clearly, an important area for future research is to repeat the Landesmann and Snell exercise for imports. This merely provides further evidence of the importance for economic growth of the values taken by the import and export income elasticities.

DEINDUSTRIALISATION AND THE BALANCE OF PAYMENTS

Our discussion has an important bearing on the question of the causes of deindustrialisation in the UK. We mean by deindustrialisation the progressive loss of employment in manufacturing industry associated with the sluggish growth of manufacturing output. Some decline in the *share* of manufacturing employment in total employment is to be expected as countries get richer and the demand for services rises faster than the demand for manufactured goods, but an absolute decline in manufacturing employment is not inevitable, even in the most advanced countries, as the international evidence shows. Table 10.3 gives an international comparison of employment trends in manufacturing industry for 23 countries over two time periods, 1960–79 and 1960–89. It can be seen that the UK experienced the severest decline in manufacturing employment of all the industrialised countries, having lost nearly four million jobs since 1960 (and more since 1966 when manufacturing employment peaked). By contrast, the US, Canada, Japan and other countries have experienced an expansion in

Table 10.3   Manufacturing employment (thousands) in OECD countries 1960–89[a]

	1960	1979	Change 1960–79(%)	1989	Change 1960–89(%)
Canada	1,406[b]	2,047	+45.6	2,126	+51.2
USA	16,796	21,040	+25.3	21,652	+28.9
Japan	7,990	11,070	+38.5	14,840	+85.7
Australia	1,111	1,177	+5.9	1,236	+11.3
Austria	858	(850)	−1.0	910	+6.0
Belgium	1,043	888	−14.9	779	−25.3
Denmark[c]	741	793	+7.0	715	−3.5
Finland	431	582	+35.0	525	+21.8
France	6,322	5,291	−16.3	4,585	−27.5
Germany	9,433[d]	(8,370)	−11.3	8,582	−9.0
Greece[c]	598	994	+66.2	1,011	+69.1
Iceland[c]	24	38	+58.3	42	+75.0
Ireland	168[e]	(228)	+35.7	215	+28.0
Italy[e]	3,735	4,716	+26.3	4,729	+26.6
Luxembourg[e]	53	58	+9.4	37	−30.2
Netherlands	1,082	(1,037)	−4.2	1,152	+6.5
Norway	331	370	+11.8	308	−7.0
Portugal	571	(865)	+51.5	1,108	+94.1
Spain	2,009	2,742	+36.5	2,738	+36.3
Sweden[c]	1,499	1,359	−9.3	1,315	−12.3
Switzerland[c]	1,227	1,229	+0.1	1,234	+0.6
Turkey	885	1,572	+77.6	2,216	+150.4
UK	**8,996**	**7,253**	**−19.4**	**5,512**	**−38.7**

Notes: Figures in brackets are not strictly comparable with previous years.
[a]Wage and salary earners in the manufacturing sector unless otherwise specified.
[b]1961.
[c]Civilian employment in industry.
[d]1962.
[e]Wage and salary earners in industry.

manufacturing employment. Deindustrialisation has implications for unemployment, for growth and for the balance of payments.

The most convincing explanation of progressive deindustrialisation in the UK is the overall weakening of the foreign trade sector, with a slow growth of exports relative to other countries, and in relation to the income elasticity of demand for imports. We have seen that in the long run, the growth of a country cannot exceed its balance of payments equilibrium growth rate, $y_B = x/\pi$. Attempts to grow faster than this rate mean that exports cannot pay for imports, and the balance-of-payments constraint on demand affects the ability of the industrial sector to grow as fast as labour productivity. A decline in manufacturing employment is then inevitable.

The relation between the growth of manufacturing output (g_m) and the growth of total income (y) may be expressed as:

$$g_m = \zeta y \tag{10.12}$$

where ζ is the elasticity of manufacturing output with respect to total income, or a measure of the income elasticity of demand for manufactured goods. Given both ζ and the growth of total income consistent with balance-of-payments equilibrium, the rate of growth of manufacturing output consistent with balance-of-payments equilibrium (g_m^*) is also determined:

$$g_m^* = \zeta y_B \tag{10.13}$$

Since $y_B = x/\pi$, the maximum long-run growth of manufacturing output is:

$$g_m^* = \zeta x/\pi \tag{10.14}$$

The only ways to increase the long-run rate of growth of manufacturing output, given the overall constraint of the balance of payments, are to raise ζ by producing goods with a higher income elasticity of demand, to raise the rate of growth of total exports by making all goods more desirable abroad, and to lower π by making all foreign goods less desirable. If g_m^* is less than the rate of growth of labour productivity in manufacturing, less labour will be demanded. What are the facts?

For the period 1951 to 1966 we estimate the balance-of-payments constrained growth rate to have been about 2.4 per cent per annum. For the period since then our simple rule predicts an estimate of between 1.5 and 2.0 per cent depending on the assumed income elasticity of demand for imports and the growth of world income. From statistics on the share of manufacturing output (see Table 10.4), it would appear that ζ was virtually unity up to 1980, with the share of manufacturing output to total output remaining constant over time. This means that the growth of manufacturing output consistent with balance-of-payments equilibrium was exactly the

Table 10.4   Manufacturing employment and output in the
United Kingdom since 1950

	Share of manufacturing employment in total employment (%)	Share of manufacturing output in GDP at constant (1963) prices (%)	Level of manufacturing employment (000s)
1950	34.7	29.3	8519
1955	35.9	30.6	9222
1960	35.8	31.0	8850
1965	35.0	31.1	9028
1970	34.7	31.7	8910
1975	30.9	29.1	7488
1980	30.2	29.5	6807
1984	26.1	24.7	5517
1989	22.9	23.5	5167

Sources: Brown and Sheriff in Blackaby (1979) and *Monthly Digest of Statistics* (various months).

same as the overall balance-of-payments constrained growth rate. Now labour productivity growth in manufacturing industry over the period 1950 to 1964 was 2.7 per cent per annum which is approximately equal to the rate of growth of total output and manufacturing output, and thus is consistent with the economy retaining labour in the manufacturing sector over the period and the economy moving into payments deficit. From the mid-1960s to the early 1970s, however, productivity growth accelerated, but the growth of manufacturing output permitted by the overall balance-of-payments constraint did not rise commensurately and hence manufacturing employment declined. During the rest of the 1970s, productivity growth slowed but output growth slowed even more and was actually negative in 1980, causing further (sharp) falls in manufacturing employment, as shown in Table 10.4. In the 1980s a further wide discrepancy arose between the rate of productivity growth in manufacturing and the rate of growth of industrial output leading to a further shedding of labour. Such was the state of the economy that the level of manufacturing output effectively showed no increase at all between 1979 and 1987. Clearly, the explanation of the slow growth of manufacturing output over time cannot lie in the lack of factor supplies, but must be attributed to constraints on demand. As we argued in Chapter 4, the problem seems to lie in the characteristics of the goods that the UK produces and sells at home and abroad. The British treat them as 'inferior' goods and so does the rest of the world.

While a weak balance of payments has contributed to deindustrialisation, it is also the case that deindustrialisation has negative feedback effects on the trade balance. In 1983, the UK's balance of trade in manufactures went into deficit for the first time in British economic history, and since then the trend has continued to be adverse. If manufacturing output is stagnant this is hardly surprising since all increased demand for manufactured goods must then come from abroad. From 1979 to the time of writing there has been no net increase in manufacturing output at all, and yet expenditure on manufactured goods has risen by over 50 per cent. The gap between domestic demand and domestic output has been met from abroad.

It is conventional to attribute the decline in the UK's manufacturing trade balance to its poor industrial performance. This argument, however, has been challenged by Rowthorn and Wells (1987) who argue that the deteriorating balance of trade in manufactures and associated deindustrialisation has been the inevitable outcome of a growing improvement in the balance of trade in non-manufacturing, particularly food and raw materials. Because the balance-of-payments on current account must tend to zero in the long run, an improvement in one sector of the accounts must lead to deterioration elsewhere. To quote Rowthorn and Wells directly, 'this improvement [in the non-manufacturing trade balance] is mainly the result of autonomous factors such as greater domestic food production, economies in the use of materials, cheaper food and material imports, new service exports, North Sea Oil etc. . . . . our conclusion is that poor industrial performance is certainly one of the factors responsible for what has happened to the manufacturing balance. However, it is not the principal factor. The deterioration of the manufacturing balance is mainly a response to developments elsewhere in the balance-of-payments; it is mainly a counterpart to the autonomous improvements which have occurred in non-manufacturing trade' (p. 142).

The problem with this argument is that within the framework of a zero sum balance (on the current account), each of the two sectors has its dual. To lay all the stress on autonomous improvement in the non-manufacturing balance, leaving the manufacturing balance to adjust, must be seriously questioned. As we saw in Chapter 4, there are all sorts of autonomous factors that have weakened UK manufacturing industry and independently worsened the manufacturing trade balance. The position of manufacturing industry cannot simply be treated as passive or as an innocent victim of the system. Indeed, one question that immediately springs to mind is why did the emerging non-manufacturing sector not lead to a faster rate of economic growth if there was no serious (autonomous) industrial decline? The UK has had the lowest rate of economic growth, and of exports, of any industrialised country since 1950. This would indicate weakness right across the board. There are several autonomous forces that have been at work, associated with poor industrial performance, that have weakened the trade balance in manufacturing: for example, the inability to compete as tariffs have been removed; lack of innovation and technical dynamism; changes in tastes coupled with slow product development; switches in domestic demand associated with superior foreign marketing; and so on. Furthermore, if the major cause of deindustrialisation was the autonomous improvement in non-manufacturing trade, one might expect the effect on the trade balance to be fairly evenly spread across countries in relation to trade shares, but this is not so. The deficits are concentrated, particularly with Germany and Japan. This suggests (autonomous) industrial weakness relative to these countries.

If our own diagnosis of the cause of deindustrialisation is correct, it is difficult to see how the syndrome of slow growth leading to de-industrialisation, and deindustrialisation leading to balance-of-payments weakness and further slow growth, can be rectified without a combined industrial and trade strategy to revitalise the manufacturing sector of the economy. It must be remembered that still over 60 per cent of the UK's foreign exchange earnings come from manufactured exports, and that all manufactured goods are potentially tradeable whereas most service output is not. The shift of resources from manufacturing to non-tradeable services has profound implications for the balance of payments, and therefore profound implications for the ability of the country to achieve faster growth consistent with balance-of-payments equilibrium.

THE CASE OF AUSTRALIA

With a population of about sixteen million, Australia may be classed as a medium-sized advanced country. It has about the same population as the Netherlands and twice that of Sweden. In terms of per capita income, Australia, according to World Bank figures, now ranks 18th in the world, having declined from the leading position it held just prior to the First World War. The early high standard of living was the result of the exploitation of Australia's rich resource

Table 10.5   Percentage composition of Australian and world exports of
goods and services by sector of origin, 1972 and 1984

| | Australia | | World | |
	1972	1984[a]	1972	1984[a]
Agriculture	45.2	31.1	16.1	12.1
Minerals[b]	17.2	32.4	10.5	17.9
(Fuel)	(5.0)	(19.0)	(8.4)	(16.5)
(Other mining)	(12.3)	(13.3)	(2.1)	(1.5)
Primary products	62.4	63.5	26.6	30.0
Manufactures[c]	20.2	16.8	53.1	51.5
Services	14.3	14.0	18.6	17.0
Other	3.1	5.7	1.8	1.4
Secondary and Tertiary products	37.6	36.5	73.5	69.9
TOTAL	100.0	100.0	100.0	100.0

Notes: [a]Estimated.
   [b]Australian figures include alumina. For the world, alumina is included in manufactures.
   [c]Includes non-ferrous metals.
Sources: EPAC (1986b, p. 12).

base. This began with the gold boom of the 1850s which later gave
way to the rapid development of the pastoral industry. It was the
latter that was primarily responsible for Australia's rapid growth of
prosperity during the late nineteenth and early twentieth centuries.
This dependence was reflected in Australia's export structure which
was dominated by primary products. This composition has persisted
to the present, although the 'resources boom' of 1971 to 1973 saw the
dominance of wool challenged by mineral exports, especially those of
coal. As may be seen from Table 10.5, exports of primary products
accounted for over 60 per cent of Australia's total in 1984 and this is
double the figure for the world as a whole. The corollary is that
manufactures accounted for only 17 per cent of total exports in 1984,
while the comparable figure for the world was over 50 per cent. If the
comparison were to be made with the other advanced countries, the
contrast would be even more marked, as the figure for the latter is
nearer 80 per cent.
   The reason why the composition of Australia's exports gives cause
for concern is that the primary commodities have tended to be the
most slowly growing component of world trade and this is reflected in

their low income elasticity of demand. This is often of the order of 0.6 to 0.8 for individual commodities and implies that, *ceteris paribus*, the growth of such exports will only be 60 to 80 per cent as fast as world income. Moreover, the growth rate of primary commodities tends to be volatile with substantial swings leading periodically to a resources boom with a rapidly appreciating exchange rate. At other times, there can be a rapid fall in trade in primary commodities which leads to a balance-of-payments crisis, a rapidly depreciating exchange rate and the introduction of deflationary policies. Such severe swings can produce uncertainty over future growth rates and hence depress the level of investment in all sectors of the economy. These cyclical fluctuations have been superimposed on a general deterioration in Australia's terms of trade. If we exclude the period 1971–5 when a rapid improvement in the terms of trade from 1971–3 was followed in the subsequent two years by an equally rapid collapse, the secular rate of decline of the terms of trade has been over 3 per cent per annum. This has meant that each year Australia has had to export on average over 3 per cent more in volume terms just to maintain the same foreign earnings. The other advanced countries, apart from their rapid deterioration in the terms of trade over the years 1972–74, have generally experienced a small improvement, or at the very least, a small annual decline. (There was no corresponding substantial reversal of the change in the terms of trade for the other advanced countries immediately after the 1971 to 1973 boom.)

The problem has been compounded by the fact that much of Australia's limited exports of manufactured products consists of 'simply transformed manufactures'. These include such products as unworked iron, steel and other metals. The share of the 'elaborately transformed manufactures' (ETMs) such as machinery is only 55 per cent of Australia's manufactured products whereas the figure for the world is about 80 per cent. It is the ETMs which have proved to be the fastest growing sector of world trade and have the highest income elasticities of demand.

The result of this is that Australia has not shared fully in the rapid post-war expansion of world trade. The growth of the exports of the advanced countries has been generally about 50 to 60 per cent faster than the growth of GNP with the consequence that over the postwar period the ratio of exports (and imports) to total output has risen sharply. But in the case of Australia this has not occurred. While the share of exports of Western Europe as a whole has risen from 14 per cent of GNP in 1962 to 24 per cent in 1981, Australia's share over this period fell from 14 to 13 per cent. In terms of the proportion of GNP exported, Australia slipped from twelfth in the rankings in 1962 to twenty-third by 1983.

Another symptom of Australia's poor trade performance is that in spite of the small size of its GNP, the country remains a relatively closed economy. There is a well-defined propensity for the smaller countries to have a larger export/GNP ratio. (See, for example, Anderson and Garnaut, 1987, p. 15.) Australia has a considerably smaller ratio than would be predicted on the basis of its size of total output, with only the United States and Japan having a lesser value. The Netherlands, which is about the same size in terms of GNP as Australia, exports 45 per cent of its GNP (1986). EPAC (1986a, p. 12) calculates that about 60 per cent of the shortfall in Australia's export growth compared with the rest of the world can be attributed to an unfavourable commodity composition.

Many Australian economists consider that the country's trade problems have been exacerbated by the long history of manufacturing protectionism, which has its origins in the mid-nineteenth century. Not only is this length of time unusual for a now advanced country, but, with the exception of New Zealand, Australia has also had one of the most heavily protected manufacturing sectors. For much of this century, the desirability of protection was relatively uncontroversial, commanding wide support from within the Australian community. A notable exception to this consensus has been that most (though not all) Australian economists assume the benefits of free trade as virtually an article of faith.

What is remarkable has been the extent of the *volte face* on the part of governments of both political persuasions that occurred in the early 1970s with regard to the assumed advantages of protection. In 1973, the whole emphasis of policy switched with the introduction of an across-the-board cut in nominal tariffs of 25 per cent. Notwithstanding the subsequent introduction of quotas during the recession that commenced in the mid-1970s (especially for the troubled industries of textiles, clothing and footwear and motor vehicles), the general policy has been one of reducing tariffs in an attempt to compel domestic manufacturing industries to be more competitive internationally. The conventional wisdom now is that the 'made to measure' protectionism only succeeded in making Australian manufacturers inward-looking and inefficient.

AUSTRALIA'S BALANCE-OF-PAYMENTS CRISES

On coming to power in March 1983, the Australian Labor Party, under the leadership of Mr Hawke, found the economy in a state of recession. As may be seen from Table 10.6, GDP had fallen during the fiscal year 1982–3 by over one per cent and manufacturing had fared even worse, contracting by 8 per cent. Consequently, one of the first measures the incoming government undertook was to reflate the economy. For the next three years the rate of growth of GDP was just under 5 per cent per annum, and at that time, Australia was one of the fastest growing OECD countries. The result of this rapid growth, together with a collapse in the terms of trade that occurred, was a balance-of-payments deficit which in 1985/6 exceeded 6 per cent of GDP. This led to a substantial fall in the exchange rate in 1985, but did not markedly reduce the current account deficit for reasons that will be discussed below. Other measures, most notably cutting gov-

Table 10.6   Growth rates of selected economic indicators: Australia 1977/8 to 1987/8 (percentage change on previous period)

Year	GDP	Manufact-uring	Exports	Imports	Private GFCF	RULC	GDP Deflator	U
1977/78	0.9	−0.4	2.1	−4.8	−1.8	n.a.	7.8	6.0
1978/79	4.8	4.2	8.5	8.5	9.5	n.a.	7.9	6.3
1979/80	2.4	4.3	7.5	−0.3	1.4	n.a.	11.1	6.1
1980/81	3.4	2.0	−4.9	9.2	15.0	n.a.	10.3	5.8
1981/82	1.6	2.5	1.2	10.9	6.2	n.a.	10.2	6.1
1982/83	−1.4	−8.2	0.3	−8.5	−15.6	1.2	10.5	8.9
1983/84	5.5	1.5	8.5	5.2	3.1	−4.8	7.0	9.3
1984/85	5.4	5.2	13.6	15.5	13.1	−1.6	5.6	8.4
1985/86	4.5	2.4	5.9	1.5	2.9	−0.6	6.8	7.5
1986/87	2.5	1.3	8.9	−2.9	0.7	−0.6	7.4	7.9
1987/88	4.4	6.3	7.1	10.0	13.7	−1.7	8.0	7.3
1988/89	4.3	6.0	0.8	23.8	17.5	−3.7	9.4	6.2
1989/90	3.1	3.0	7.2	5.2	−3.9	−2.5	5.7	5.8
1990/91	−1.3	−5.2	12.8	−3.9	−11.2	−1.5	3.1	8.4*

Notes: GDP is the income measure.
GFCF is gross fixed capital formation (investment).
RULC is non-farm sector real unit labour costs.
U is the unemployment rate, percent.
* 11.0, April 1992.
n.a denotes not available.

Sources: The Treasury Round Up (various years), Australian Economic Indicators (1991, 1992).

Table 10.7   Australia's current account as a percentage of GDP and the trade weighted index of the A$ (TWI)

	Current account	Net transfers	Balance of trade	TWI
1959/60 to 1979/80 (average)	−2.4	−2.1	−0.3	n.a.
1980/81	−4.1	−2.1	−2.0	87.6
1981/82	−6.0	−2.2	−3.8	91.0
1982/83	−4.0	−2.0	−2.0	81.8
1983/84	−3.8	−2.5	−1.3	81.5
1984/85	−5.2	−3.0	−2.2	75.5
1985/86	−6.1	−2.8	−3.3	62.3
1986/87	−4.7	−2.6	−2.1	53.8
1987/88	−3.8	−2.8	−1.0	54.8
1988/89	−5.4	−2.6	−2.8	61.6
1989/90	−6.0	−3.1	−2.9	60.0
1990/91	−4.2	−4.1	−0.1	58.9

Notes: Net transfers comprises net income and unrequited net transfers.
n.a. denotes not available.

Sources: EPAC (1989), Norton and Aylmer (1988), Australian Economic Indicators (1991, 1992).

ernment expenditure and raising interest rates, had to be introduced to reduce the growth of output in order to correct the balance-of-payments deficit. This led to a severe recession in 1990. Unemployment, which had fallen from a high of 9.3 per cent in 1983/4 to a low of 5.8 per cent in 1989/90 almost doubled in the next eighteen months to reach a figure of 11 per cent. The Australian economy may thus be considered to have been unequivocally balance-of-payments constrained.

THE GROWTH OF THE FOREIGN DEBT

From Table 10.7 it may be seen that the deficit on goods and services (the balance of trade) deteriorated substantially during the 1980s compared with the average position over the previous two decades. But by 1987/8 there had been something of an improvement and by 1990/1 the balance of trade had was almost in equilibrium. Australia's

Table 10.8   Ratios of net foreign liabilities to GDP and ratios of net investment income to exports; Australia

| | Ratios of net foreign liabilities to GDP | | Ratios of net investment income to exports | |
	(a) Total	(b) Foreign debt[a]	(a) Total	(b) Foreign debt
1983/84	28.3	15.3	15.3	10.1
1984/85	36.0	23.7	17.4	12.6
1985/86	40.5	31.4	18.3	15.1
1986/87	44.4	32.6	18.4	16.2
1987/88	41.9	32.2	18.4	15.2
1988/89	43.8	34.3	23.3	17.4
1989/90	44.4	35.0	26.5	20.8
1990/91	46.8	36.3	25.9	19.6
1991/92	51.7	39.0	21.3	16.4

Note: [a] Average value from 1959/60 to 1979/89 is 5.6.

Sources: *International Investment Position, Australia* (June Quarter 1992).

current account deficit at this time stemmed from the large deficit in net income transfers, which is also classified as part of the current account.[5] The bulk of the net income transfers comprises the interest payments needed to service the borrowing from abroad and represents a legacy from the past balance-of-payments deficit. It is these transfers that have greatly contributed to the build up in the debt service ratio.

The size of Australia's external liabilities remained fairly stable in the 1960s and 1970s, and in 1980 the debt ratio was less than 6 per cent of GDP. By 1992 it had risen to over 39 per cent with a marked acceleration occurring after 1984/85 (Table 10.8). This deterioration would have been of less concern if it had resulted in increased investment that would have eventually led to an improvement in Australia's international competitiveness. But this did not prove to be the case. From 1975, through the 1980s, the share of investment in total output has been less than in any other comparable period and the foreign borrowing has been primarily for consumption purposes. Table 10.9 shows the rapid deterioration in Australia's net debt as a percentage of GDP compared with other advanced countries over the period from 1981 to 1987.

In spite of the increase in the debt to GDP ratio, the servicing cost as a proportion of exports fell from a high in 1990 of 20.8 per cent to 16.4 per cent in 1992. The major reason for this was the fall in world

Table 10.9 International comparisons.
Net debt as percentage of GDP: selected OECD countries

	1981		1987
Ireland	56	Ireland	87
Portugal[a]	32	New Zealand	66
Denmark	30	Iceland[b]	43
Iceland	28	Denmark[b]	41
Norway	27	**Australia[b]**	**30**
Canada	25	Norway[c]	28
New Zealand	22	Portugal	25
Finland	15	Canada	24
Sweden	15	Sweden	23
Australia	**6**	Finland	17

Notes: [a]1982; [b]1988; [c]1989.

Sources: EPAC (1989).

interest rates in 1991/92, which meant that Australia could roll over existing obligations at lower interest rates and new debts could also be negotiated at the lower rates. Nevertheless, the servicing costs are still large by the standards of the advanced countries (Table 10.10).

There has also been a change in the form taken by Australia's external liabilities. Prior to the early 1980s, borrowing primarily took the form of equity investment which meant part of the risk was born by foreigners. In a recession, the value of dividends and remitted profits fell as economic performance declined. In recent years, though, the majority of overseas borrowing has been in the form of debt, the cost being the prevailing interest rate. (The reason for this shift is that such interest payments were tax deductible whereas there was no comparable relief on dividend payments.) This form of income transfer abroad does not fall in a recession and is also dependent upon world interest rates.

A question that arises is why has the level of international debt risen so dramatically over the past few years? Dixon and McDonald (1986) have categorised the increase in the debt/GDP ratio into what they term the 'passive' and 'active' accumulation components. The increase in passive accumulation is that which is the direct result of the existing debt. It takes into account, for example, an increase in real interest rates, a real depreciation of the Australian dollar (which increases the debt when valued in domestic currency) and the growth of real GDP. Active accumulation represents new borrowings. Over

542   *Economic Growth and the Payments Constraint*

Table 10.10   External liabilities, servicing costs and current deficits: selected OECD countries; 1988–90 averages

Country	External liabilities (% of GNP/GDP)	Servicing costs (% of exports)	Current account (% of GNP/GDP)
UK	10	–3.2	–3.9
Japan	10	–7.6	2.1
West Germany	9	–2.3	4.6
US	1	–0.5	–2.1
France	–1	0.2	–0.5
Italy	–11	4.6	–1.1
Spain	–11	5.0	–2.4
Sweden	–12	3.3	–2.2
Portugal	–20	5.1	–0.7
Finland	–24	8.3	–4.1
Norway	–31	6.1	–0.4
Canada	–40	12.8	–2.9
Australia	**–43**	**22.0**	**–5.0**
Denmark	–53	11.4	–0.2
New Zealand	–59	17.1	–2.5
Ireland	–169	19.0	3.0

Source: EPAC (1992).

the period 1982 to 1985, one-third of the increase of 18 percentage points in the debt/GDP ratio was due to the passive factors, and in 1985, the last year covered by the study, the proportion was nearly 70 per cent. A significant contributory factor has been the substantial depreciation of the trade weighted index of the currencies of Australia's major trading partners. Between January 1985 and September 1986, this declined by about 40 per cent in nominal terms. This gives rise to the possibility of a vicious circle occurring where a depreciation increases the debt ratio through increasing the rate of passive accumulation, thereby setting up forces for a further fall in the exchange rate.

This would not be such a serious risk if the depreciation caused a marked long-term improvement of the balance of payments (as opposed to the severe recession of 1990), but this does not seem to have occurred for reasons we turn to next. (There was a rapid upturn in the world demand for Australia's exports in 1990–1, but for reasons outlined below, we are not sanguine about this persisting.)[6]

THE INEFFECTIVENESS OF EXCHANGE RATE ADJUSTMENT

The impact of the balance-of-payments constraint on Australian economic growth has been analysed by the (Melbourne) National Institute of Economic and Industrial Research (NIEIR) using their IMP model which may be best described as a neo-Keynesian forecasting model. The Institute's clearest summary of its prognosis for the Australian economy is to be found in Brain and Manning (1987) on whom we draw heavily. On the basis of simulations of the NIEIR's forecasting model, Brain and Manning (1987, p. 5) come to the following rather pessimistic conclusions.

> It is inevitable that Australia will enter the 1990s in poor economic shape. If the slide towards less-developed status is to be halted, drastic measures will be necessary.
>
> The present balance-of-payments problem is too deep-seated to be remedied by a floating exchange rate alone. The Marshall–Lerner conditions for an effective devaluation do not hold in the short run, and probably do not hold in the long run, and in any case debt servicing costs mean that the Marshall–Lerner conditions are not sufficient for success. This will require structural change, and in particular an increase in the proportion of Australian exports subject to high income elasticities of demand.[7]

A depreciation of the currency works most effectively if the price elasticities of export demand and supply are high. Similarly, the higher is both the price elasticity of substitution of domestic goods and services for imports and the elasticity of supply of import competing products, the more effective will be a depreciation. Furthermore, it is also necessary for real wages to fall so that there is no offsetting increase in domestic costs. Following Brain and Manning, let us consider these issues briefly in turn.

THE PRICE ELASTICITY OF DEMAND FOR AUSTRALIA'S EXPORTS

Given that Australia exports predominantly primary commodities which are relatively homogeneous, especially when compared with manufactured goods, and that Australia is a relatively small country compared with the rest of the world, it may be thought that the 'small country assumption' holds. This implies, *inter alia*, that Australia can sell as much on world markets at the world price as it wishes. The sales of exports are solely limited by profitability, and the price elasticity of demand for its exports is infinite. If this were the case Australia could clearly not be balance-of-payments constrained. Certainly, some estimates of the price elasticity of demand for Australian exports are indeed high. EPAC (1986b) cites the general equilibrium computable model ORANI as using an average estimate of around − 10 which would certainly meet the Marshall–Lerner conditions, and, more importantly, suggests that small changes in the exchange rate would have a quantitatively large impact on the balance of payments. On the other hand, the RBA82 (Reserve Bank of Australia's model) has the very much lower figure of − 0.3. The NIEIR argue that the correct figure is likely to be much nearer the Reserve Bank's projections.

The reason is that Australia is not a small supplier in terms of its individual exports of both rural and mineral products. The situation, the NIEIR argue, is more akin to oligopoly where Australia's competitors are likely to notice any change in Australia's competitiveness and to take measures to offset any possible loss of their own sales. Furthermore, competitors are likely to be affected by similar economic problems at the same time; for example, a marked deterioration in the terms of trade leading to balance-of-payments problems. They are thus likely to respond with competitive devaluations, as has happened in the past. Even though the elasticity of demand for the commodities of an individual producer may be very high (especially if they are primary commodities), the industry demand curve is likely to be very inelastic. Consequently, while competitive devaluations may drive the world price down, there is unlikely to be any substantial increase in total world sales. Mention must also be made of the fact that agriculture is often heavily subsidised in the industrialised countries and any attempt to increase the share of imports is frequently met with pressure for even greater subsidies – pressure that often achieves its aim. It is a fallacy to believe that primary commodity markets are competitive. For example, the market for coal is a near monopsony with Australian exporters heavily dependent on the Japanese steel industry, which has not been reluctant to use its market power to reap the benefits of devaluation for itself.[8] The implication of all this is that: 'In predicting the effect of a devaluation, perhaps the best rule of thumb is to assume that Australia will maintain market share, which means that the elasticity of demand for its exports should generally be taken as the world elasticity for the products concerned. This can be very low indeed: in the short run, if the market environment is subdued and stocks are high, the price elasticity of demand for wool over the price range involved in a devaluation may be as low as zero' (Brain and Manning, 1987, p. 16).

As a result of all these factors, the Melbourne Institute concludes that the short-run price elasticity of exports is approximately 0.5. The Institute is not confident that the position is much better in the long run and estimates that the value is only 0.7. The reason is that rapid improvements in agricultural technology and subsidisation and protection of the agricultural sector are allowing more countries to move towards self-sufficiency. As far as metals are concerned, the rapid rise in prices in the 1970s has led to countries adopting measures to economise on their use and 'these techniques are not going to be unlearnt' (Brain and Manning, 1987, p. 17.) The Institute expects coal prices to rise in the 1990s as a result of increases in the price of oil, largely justified (at least in the short term) by the 1990 Middle East conflict; but there will be no net saving on the balance of payments; the increased foreign exchange revenues from coal will be offset by the higher cost of oil imports.

In the long run, the solution lies in the development of manufacturing exports, and the Institute foresees the possibility of Australia replacing Japan as a supplier of manufactured goods to South East Asia and East Asia, especially if the yen appreciates against the Australian dollar. 'In such exports, with highly differentiated products, competitive advantage is found as much in product specification and back-up as in price, and analysis should take these into account in addition to the price elasticity (which for manufactured goods in general is reasonably high, say between 1 and 3) in the long run' (Brain and Manning, 1987, p. 17). This has been echoed in numerous other studies on the Australian balance-of-payments problem (see, for example, Bureau of Industry Economics, 1987). Unfortunately, Australia, like the United Kingdom, is very weak in the non-price aspects of competition; this is often attributed to the former high levels of protection and lack of competition in the domestic market.

The importance of non-price competitiveness for Australia has been confirmed by Lim and Shannon (1986) in their study of the effects of the 1985 devaluation. They found that 'non-price factors were frequently more important in determining the export demand for many ETMs [elaborately transformed manufactures] and PFs [processed foods]' (p. 14). It further transpired that

> the low price elasticities of many Australian manufactured goods can to a large extent be attributed to the relatively low degree of export orientation by the majority of Australian firms. A number of managers of major exporting firms indicated that, in general, Australian firms have neither the reputation for quality that firms in Japan and West Germany have, nor have they shown the same continuing high level of commitment to exporting. In the past many Australian firms have sold in export markets when they had excess capacity and then abandoned these markets when local demand increased. This practice has to some extent undermined our reputation as a reliable supplier in local markets. (Lim and Shannon, 1986)

A *Committee for the Economic Development of Australia* (CEDA) (1986) study on the opportunities open to Australian exporters in the Pacific Basin came to a similar conclusion. This area provides Australia with about 60 per cent of its exports and is likely to be even more important in the future, even though Australia has not always been able to hold its market share. CEDA found that many firms were spread very thinly over the Basin and had very little commitment to exporting. They were 'fringe exporters' with very little expertise in marketing overseas; with little knowledge of what sales opportunities there were; and with little idea of the local marketing requirements. The CEDA study further noted that 'While Australia is at or about the 50 per cent mark of countries [on a ranking of 28 countries] on product safety, marketing emphasis, design, styling, packaging, and after-sales service, it is in the bottom 50 per cent for product quality, on-time delivery and export flexibility (the willingness to modify products for local markets).'

Brain and Manning (1987 & 1989) have argued that Australian manufacturing industry is unlikely to benefit from the putative fall in the exchange rate because 'once more appropriate measures of the change in competitiveness are adopted, the 34 per cent improvement becomes a chimera' (1989, p. 2). The 34 per cent improvement from 1984 to 1987 was based on adjusting the nominal devaluation both for changes in the price level in the OECD economies and for changes in Australian tariff and subsidy levels. If the actual prices at which imports are available to Australia are used, the improvement in competitiveness 'disappears entirely' (1989, p. 2). Furthermore, if allowance is made for the developing countries' preference scheme, the overall effect was a *deterioration* in competitiveness of 4 per cent in 1987 compared with 1980. This will have further worsened because of the appreciation of the Australian dollar in 1988.

Brain and Manning identified several reasons for this lack of improvement in competitiveness. The first was that the Australian dollar had actually appreciated, not depreciated, against the currencies of many 'middle rank' economies with which Australia competes. There was a significant appreciation against the Chinese yuan which dramatically reduced the competitiveness of the textile, clothing and footwear industries. Secondly, although the dollar depreciated against the Japanese yen and the South Korean won, this was largely offset by those countries cutting their export prices and subsidising exports by their domestic market. Thirdly, devaluation increased the costs of the import content of Australian manufactured goods. Finally, as a result of biases in the tax system and high inflation in the past, many Australian firms substantially increased their gearing ratios. This raised their costs to the extent that they borrowed overseas and the depreciation aggravated their borrowings in domestic currency terms. The firms were further hit by the increase in real interest rates introduced in an attempt to slow down the growth of the Australian economy.

THE ELASTICITY OF SUPPLY OF EXPORTS

Since the price of Australian exports tends to fall in foreign currency terms, for export receipts to increase it is necessary for the volume of exports also to increase by enough to offset the lower prices. The Melbourne Institute considers – and we concur in their views – that in the short run there is little scope for switching agricultural products from the domestic to overseas market. There is also little opportunity for increasing output given the long production lags involved. The NIEIR also considers that both mining and manufacturing are operating near full capacity and hence the supply elasticity will be low. As we have noted above, exporting is only a marginal activity for Australian manufacturers. Consequently, the Institute estimates that the short-term price elasticity of supply is only 0.2. In the long run, for there to be a higher elasticity, there must be a marked increase in the capacity of the export industries. However, given the likely induced cost inflation and the possible appreciation of the Australian dollar (and the fact that for manufacturing industries there has been little or no improvement in competitiveness over the last few years), the Institute is not convinced that this will be forthcoming. This pessimism is also reinforced by the effect of the high interest rates necessary to finance the balance of payments deficit.

Moreover, in 1985/86, 90 per cent of private non-dwelling investment came in the form of imported capital goods and hence any increase in capacity is likely, at least in the short run, to place a further strain on the balance of payments.

THE PRICE ELASTICITY OF DEMAND AND SUPPLY FOR IMPORTS

It is plausible to assume that the elasticity of supply of imports is infinite given that Australia provides only a small fraction of other countries' exports markets. On the other hand, the price elasticity of demand for imports is very low – the Institute estimates it as around -0.4. This is because many types of imports, especially capital goods, are not manufactured in Australia. 'The result is that an increasing proportion of imports (including semi-finished components) is complementary to, rather than competitive with, Australian production. This has been particularly the case with investment goods, such as civil and military aircraft and the items required for the North West Shelf project' (Brain and Manning, 1989, p. 19).

AUSTRALIA'S BALANCE-OF-PAYMENTS CONSTRAINT

The above export elasticities suggest that a devaluation would reduce total export foreign currency revenues as the fall in the foreign currency price of exports would not be offset by an increase in export volumes. Any improvement in the current account would have to come from a reduction in expenditure on imports. While import volumes would fall, the amount would be reduced by the extent to which there is an increase in the costs of inputs into domestically produced import competing goods. Overall, Brain and Manning conclude that:

At best, a ten per cent devaluation might yield a 2 per cent reduction in foreign exchange earnings, and a 4 per cent reduction in foreign exchange purchases, so long as incomes remain constant both in Australia and the rest of the world.

Thus, a devaluation will have a small but beneficial effect on the balance of trade. The problem is that it will worsen the other component of the current account when expressed in domestic currency, namely, the debt service payments. This is because most net interest payments are denominated in foreign currency and so a devaluation means that correspondingly more domestic currency has to be found to meet these commitments. To the extent that such payments are denominated in Australian currency, this will not occur; but it is probable that higher interest charges will be required for new borrowings to cover the effects of the devaluation. Since the devaluation only brings such a small improvement in the balance of trade, there would be a consequential rise in the debt service ratio. 'It therefore offers no immediate solution to the balance-of-payments constraint. Short of imposing physical import restrictions, it becomes necessary to rely on changes in income levels to return the balance-of-payments to a satisfactory state' (Brain and Manning, 1987, p. 24).

In order to calculate the balance-of-payments equilibrium growth rate, it is plausible to assume that the growth of long-term capital flows is such as to offset the effect on the growth rate of the deterioration in the terms of trade. The latter, it will be recalled, were declining at a little over 3.5 per cent per annum. We further assume that a devaluation, because of the increase in net interest payments it causes, has no effect on the current account in the long run. The balance-of-payments equilibrium growth rate commencing from a balance-of-payments disequilibrium is given by:

$$y_B = (1 - \theta)(\varepsilon z/\pi) \tag{10.15}$$

with the same notation as before and where θ is the ratio of net financial flows (including changes in reserves) to total foreign exchange receipts. This takes a value of 0.28 in 1986. The Melbourne Institute estimates that in the long run the income elasticity of demand for Australian exports is 1.3 (1.0 in the short run) and for imports, 1.4. This implies that the equilibrium growth rate can only be 0.67 of the growth of world income if the present balance-of-payments deficit is not to worsen. If we assume, perhaps optimistically, that world income is likely to grow at 3.5 per cent per annum, this means that y_B will be only 2.3 per cent per annum (1.7 per cent per annum in the short run). If the balance-of-payments deficit is to be reduced, it will require the growth rate to be commensurately below this figure.

CONCLUSIONS

In this chapter we have considered the balance-of-payments equilibrium growth rate of two contrasting advanced countries. The United Kingdom is a major exporter of manufactured goods and despite the fall in its share of world manufactured exports, the country still accounts for 6 per cent of the world total. Australia, on the other hand, has an economy that has less than one-third of the United Kingdom's output and is heavily dependent on primary commodities for its exports. Yet, for both countries, exchange rate adjustments have at best a quantitatively small effect in improving the balance of payments. Consequently, the maximum growth rate consistent with either a balance-of-payments equilibrium (or, at least, no worsening in the current account) depends crucially upon the income elasticities of demand for exports and imports. Australia's income elasticity of demand for its exports is relatively low compared with the majority of the other developed countries. This is because of its dependence on primary commodities, the demand for which has traditionally grown very much more slowly than the demand for manufactured goods. Hence, the concern that is increasingly being voiced in Australia of the need to diversify into skill-intensive manufactured goods.

Yet, ironically, the long-run income elasticity of demand for Australia's exports is in excess of that for the United Kingdom's exports, because of the latter's poor non-price competitiveness. There may have been an improvement in this aspect of the United Kingdom's competitiveness in the 1980s; if so this may have raised the balance-of-payments equilibrium growth rate from the 0.9 per cent per annum that Turner (1988) estimates to about 1.5 per cent. (However, this is still below the growth rate of 2.5 per cent per annum experienced during the long boom.) Consequently, this demonstrates the importance of non-price competitiveness in determining growth rates, a factor which we have repeatedly emphasised in previous chapters.

Nevertheless, given plausible growth rates for the rest of the world, neither country can expect to emulate its pre-1973 economic performance without running an increasing balance-of-payments deficit. Both countries seem destined to grow at no more than approximately one-half the growth rate of the world economy as a whole.

We have tried in the preceeding pages to put forward a new and, we hope, convincing explanation of why the economic performance of regions and countries differs, as an alternative to the neoclassical supply orientated theories of growth which explain growth rate differences in terms of exogenously determined, and unexplained, differences in the growth of factor supplies and technical progress. We believe that factor supplies and technical progress should be regarded as largely endogenous to an economic system, determined by the strength of demand, and that the major determinant of demand pressure in the long run will be set by a country's or region's balance of payments position. We have shown how closely the growth experience of countries approximates to what we call a country's balance-of-payments equilibrium growth rate determined by the growth of exports, relative to the income elasticity of demand for imports, but there is still much work to be done in two major areas. Firstly, we still do not fully understand the causes of differential export performance, although we know that non-price competition is of vital importance. Second, there is still a great deal of scope for modelling the endogeneity of factor supplies and technical progress in relation to the pressure of demand and the growth of output itself. But we conclude, as we began, that (to paraphrase Alfred Marshall) 'the causes which determine the economic progress of nations belong to the study of international trade [and the balance of payments]'.

Notes

Chapter 1

1. Over the period 1979–88, the UK's relative economic performance improved in that its growth of GNP was faster than several other advanced countries. But the UK's growth rate of just over 2 per cent per annum was considerably below its trend growth rate of 2.7 per cent per annum obtained over 1951–73. Thus, the UK's comparative improvement was not due to any dramatic increase in its trend rate of growth, but rather to the slowdown in the growth of the other advanced countries. (If the period over which the UK's growth rate is calculated is taken as 1981–8 as it sometimes is, it improves to 3.2 per cent per annum. This is profoundly misleading, however, because in 1981 the economy was in the depths of its worst postwar recession, and this causes the growth rate to become artificially inflated over the subsequent years. Ideally, trend growth rates should be calculated between years which were peaks in the level of economic activity.)

2. The problem is that for much of the tertiary sector there is no market valuation for output and so the growth of the latter often cannot be measured independently of the growth of inputs (especially labour). This is particularly true of the output of public services (e.g. education and health), the financial sector, and community and personal services. Often the estimated growth of output is the growth of employment, with sometimes an imputed (and arbitrary) allowance for the increase in productivity. Alternatively, the proxy for the growth of output may be the growth of the deflated wage and salary bill. The difficulty is compounded by the fact that individual countries often adopt very different approaches for the same industry or sector. For example, the measurement of the growth of health services in some countries relies on the growth in the number of medical prescriptions; or the growth in the number of medical consultations; or the growth in the size of the health service staff; etc. The upshot is that we can have little confidence in measured productivity growth for between 40 per cent and 50 per cent of the economy. (For detailed discussions see Hill and McGibbon, 1966 and Hill, 1971.)

3. At the time of writing, 1992.

4. In the last few years there has developed a 'revisionist school' that argues that the postwar Japanese economic resurgence was *in spite of*, not because of, government intervention. Typical of this view is Trizise (1983, p. 18): 'To attribute to [Japanese] industrial policy a crucial role is an expression of faith, not an argument supported by discernible facts.' Boltho (1985), however, presents a convincing rebuttal to this reinterpretation of recent Japanese economic history.

5. The growth rates of net capital stock (not reported here) present the same picture. The only difference is that the growth of the net capital

stock is somewhat higher than the growth of the gross capital stock in the Long Boom and slower in the Climacteric.

6. Care must be taken in interpreting both the gross and net capital stock growth rates especially subsequent to 1973. It is likely that the rate of scrapping increased markedly during the slowdown, which means that the reported growth rates probably substantially overstate the actual growth of the capital input.

7. Canada, France, Germany, Italy, the UK, and the US.

8. In the earliest time-series studies undertaken by Cobb and Douglas no time trend was in fact included in the regressions which left them open to criticism from Mendershausen (1938) and Phelps Brown (1957).

9. The sources are OECD *National Accounts* (various years) and OECD *Stocks and Flows of Fixed Capital, 1950–1985*.

10. The data are taken from Denison and Chung (1976, table 4.8, pp. 42–3) where the growth rates of Net National Income over the period 1950–62, for some countries, have been further adjusted compared with the figures originally reported in Denison (1967). Denison (1967) calculated the sources of growth for two sub-periods, 1950–5 and 1955–62. In Denison and Chung (1976), he considers, for a few countries, that the residual for 1950–5 was either unduly large (Germany, Italy and the Netherlands) or unduly small (Denmark). He, therefore, somewhat arbitrarily assumed that the value of the residual in the first sub-period should be the same as that in the second (or, equivalently, that the residual for the whole period 1950–62 should be the same as that in 1955–62). This has the effect of altering the value of the growth of Net National Income for 1950–62 compared with Denison's (1967) earlier figures. Denison's justification for this procedure is that the residuals for Germany and Italy were exceptionally large for the first sub-period and this 'simply reflects the restoration of a functioning economy and balanced production during the period from 1950 to 1952 or 1953'. The residuals for the Netherlands and Denmark 'if not related to the war, probably result from imperfections in the data' (Denison and Chung, 1976, p. 41). This graphically illustrates just how subjective the growth accounting procedure can be.

11. Denison (1967, p. 36, footnote 5) argues that: 'For any reader who may be puzzled by my combination of assumptions that (1) there are returns to scale, some of which may be internal to the firm and (2) income shares can be used to measure relative marginal products, let me make it clear that I do *not* assume perfect competition in product markets. Its absence does not alter the combination of labor, capital, and land that produces a given amount of output at least cost, or factor prices at that level of output, and would cause no difficulty in the use of income shares as weights, which derives from the cost minimization principle, if returns to labor, capital and land could actually be isolated. Because profits arising from imperfect competition in product markets are counted statistically as returns to capital and land, I admit some probable overweighting of these factors, and corresponding underweighting of labor. If the last point is correct, it implies that since capital grows considerably faster than labor the use of income shares as weights will overstate the contribution that the growth of tangible factor inputs makes to the growth of

output. Consequently, the residual will be, in fact, larger than estimated.'

It should be noted that Denison has to assume perfect competition in the factor markets, which is highly debatable, to say the least.

Increasing returns provides a serious problem for the neoclassical marginal productivity theory of distribution since total factor payments will now more than exhaust the total product. Moreover, once we move into a world dominated by large corporations, there is no guarantee that cost minimisation will occur and, indeed, X-inefficiency is likely to be extremely important. Kaldor (1972) in his famous article on 'The Irrelevance of Equilibrium Economics' goes so far as to argue increasing returns to scale destroy the whole notion of 'the efficient allocation of resources'. This is considered in greater detail in Chapter 2.

12. Denison (1984, p. 1) considers that this early slowdown 'was small and easily explained'. It was the result of a fall in the intensity of use of the factors of production from a peak in 1965–6; a decline in the benefits of the inter-sectoral reallocation of labour; an increase in the proportion of inexperienced workers in the labour forces; and the costs of new social regulations.

13. Denison (1984 pp. 27–8 and 1985, p. 47) cites various studies that demonstrate the 'people don't want to work any more' hypothesis and its variant, 'young people don't work like we did at their age' as being untenable. The putative increasing importance of the 'black' or 'underground economy' is likewise dismissed. 'Advocates of the view that in the 1970s and 1980s the underground economy has introduced a new sharp downward bias in output measures have wholly failed to present a logical case that is consistent with procedures actually used to measure national income and product. Until they provide something serious to refute, there is no way to refute them seriously' (Denison, 1984, p. 36). Moreover, in order to explain the productivity slowdown, it would be necessary to show that the output of the black economy was excluded from the national income measures, whereas the corresponding labour input was actually included in the employment figures.

14. This is discussed in greater detail below.

15. We have already seen that some neoclassical studies assume, somewhat paradoxically, that while information is freely available to all firms within a country, there may be large disparities in the level of technology of the blueprints to which individual advanced countries have access (e.g. Gomulka, 1971).

16. This has led some authorities such as Kendrick (1981, p. 143) to conclude that, because of multicollinearity and specification problems in the econometric estimation of production functions, 'a growth-accounting approach, by which variables are weighted by their estimated marginal productivities, yields more reliable results'. But this, of course, merely assumes away the problems of interdependency. Griliches (1988b, p. 21), however, takes an opposite view to Kendrick. 'Production function estimation raises many problems of its own, including issues of aggregation, errors of measurement and simultaneity, but it is one of the few ways available to us for checking the validity of the attribution of produc-

various suggested "sources".' We are sceptical about both positions, as may be seen from the discussion of the Simon/Shaikh critique below.

17. It is, of course, possible that the actions of a special interest group may actually increase the efficiency of the economy or the rate of economic growth. However, if these actions are not costless, it may well not pay the group to undertake them unless it is able to reap more than a proportional share of the benefits. For example, patent protection, which allows rents to accrue temporarily to the patent holders, is necessary to promote R&D and hence to encourage technical progress. Clearly, not all 'restrictive practices' are harmful and some are distinctly beneficial. The same holds for the actions of special interest groups.

18. The following discussion draws heavily on McCombie and Dixon (1991).

19. A second more recent critique of the orthodox neoclassical approach is that of Scott (1989). Since this important criticism is somewhat technical, it is discussed in an appendix to this chapter.

20. For example, Intriligator (1978, p. 270) in discussing a virtually identical argument by Cramer (1969) only notes that it will lead to a bias in the estimates towards constant returns to scale and that factor shares will be approximately equal to the output elasticities. It is not mentioned that the problem removes entirely the possibility of interpreting the result of estimating a production function as a test of a technological relationship. To be fair, though, Cramer himself does not push his argument to its logical conclusion.

21. The total cost function could be defined alternatively as including the value of the material inputs used in the production process. This does not alter the substance of the argument because the corresponding production function should then be expressed in terms of gross output rather than value added. This means that materials should be included in the production function as an input in addition to capital and labour. (See, for example, Domar, 1961.) Since, however, most estimations of production functions are concerned with the specification in terms of value added, we have confined our discussion to this case.

22. The above argument follows Shaikh (1974). Simon (1979, pp. 467–9) develops a similar argument except that he shows how the identity will yield a Cobb–Douglas relationship provided there is a constant capital–output ratio and a constant rental price of capital. These two assumptions also imply that factor shares will be constant, although Simon's assumptions are more restrictive than Shaikh's.

23. See, for example, Nelson (1981) and above, for a discussion of the importance of organisational and institutional factors in determining productivity growth and which are neglected in conventional production function studies. Dixon (1986) also discusses the shortcomings of conventional production function analyses from a similar point of view.

24. The *Sunday Times*, 14 December 1975, cited by Hadjimatheou and Skouras (1979).

25. See Hadjimatheou and Skouras (1979).

26. This draws heavily on J.S.L. McCombie (1992) 'Is there a Residual in Economic Growth? An Assessment of Maurice Scott's *New View of Economic Growth*', Downing College, Cambridge, (mimeo).

27. This is not to say that the perpetual inventory method does not have its problems. Errors in the data (or in deciding which price index to use) 'reverberate throughout the time series' (Usher 1980b, p. 7). Furthermore, the 'perpetual inventory always works as long as there are data on gross investment, depreciation, and price indexes of capital goods. There is no red light that flashes, no internal check that tells us when the whole process becomes absurd' (Usher, 1980b, p. 7).

28. This approach is similar to Arrow's (1962) learning by doing growth model. The latter also contains a 'production function in a somewhat novel sense' as Arrow (1962, p.158) put it. Output is specified as a function of labour and cumulative gross investment, but in this case with the latter acting as an index of experience or learning.

29. We are grateful to Maurice Scott for elaborating on his argument in personal communication.

30. Scott (1989, pp. 84–6) argues that there are no diminishing returns to capital in the long run (although there may well be to the rate of investment).

31. Since $I/K = s(r - q)/(1 - a - s)$ (from Scott, 1989, p. 173, footnote 15, although note the different notation), it is a simple matter to prove that equations (A1.15) and (A1.20) are identical.

32. This is not a surprising result. It will be recalled that the accounting identity is given by:

$$q \equiv a_t \varphi_w + (1 - a_t)\varphi_r + a_t \ell + (1 - a_t)k \qquad \text{(i)}$$

Remembering that, empirically, the real rental price of capital and factor shares are roughly constant over time, equation (i) may be written as:

$$q \simeq a(q - \ell) + a\ell + (1 - a)k \qquad \text{(ii)}$$

and, given $q \simeq k$:

$$q \simeq 0\ell + 1k \simeq k \qquad \text{(iii)}$$

Chapter 2

1. Although admittedly the relationship is very much weaker for the period since 1973.

2. Kaldor reported neither the standard error of the intercept nor its t-value. Because these are of some interest, we recomputed the regression equation using his data. The result is very similar, but not identical, to that obtained by Kaldor.

3. Verdoorn, using the interwar data, reports the result: $\text{dlog}(Q/E) = 0.573 \, \text{dlog}Q + 0.00239$ (in our notation, where the upper cases denote levels of the variables). It is not clear how he derived these estimates.

4. Ironically, Black (1962) showed that the linear technical progress function may be derived from a traditional Cobb–Douglas production function. This has obvious implications for the Verdoorn Law and is dis-

cussed below in relation to the 'static-dynamic Verdoorn Law' paradox.
5. Recently published data for manufacturing gross capital stocks for a number of advanced countries makes it possible to test this assumption. k was regressed on q over the period 1955–65 (which roughly corresponds to Kaldor's sample period) for 8 countries. Because it takes about a year for new investment to come on stream, the growth of the capital stock was calculated with the initial and terminal years lagged one year behind those of output. Using pooled data for sub-periods over 1955–65 provides 8 observations for 5 countries and we obtain the following result:

$$k = \begin{array}{cc} -0.376 & + \quad 1.015 \quad q \\ (-0.21) & (3.05) \end{array} \qquad \begin{array}{l} \bar{r}^2 = 0.542 \\ SER = 1.396 \end{array}$$

(The countries in the sample are Canada, Germany, France, the US and the UK. The source for k is *Flows and Stocks of Fixed Capital, 1955–1980*, OECD, Paris (1982), and for q is *National Accounts*, OECD, Paris (various years).)

Because the degrees of freedom are so few, we also estimated the regression using the longer period of the Long Boom of 1955–73. This enables us to include data for Japan, Norway (using the growth of the net capital stock) and Sweden, and provides 25 observations. The regression result is:

$$k = \begin{array}{cc} 0.553 & + \quad 0.949q \\ (0.87) & (8.49) \end{array} \qquad \begin{array}{l} \bar{r}^2 = 0.747 \\ SER = 1.247 \end{array}$$

In both regression equations the regression coefficient does not differ significantly from unity at the 99 per cent confidence level. Thus, the assumption that the growth of the capital stock and of output are equal is reasonable, *pace* Michl (1985, p. 477) who argues to the contrary.
6. This result is very close to that obtained by Michl (1985), but differs because we have included an extra cycle, 1979–87, and the remainder of the sample differs in a number of small ways concerning choice of end years, etc.
7. In the acknowledgements of this study, it is stated that 'the investigations were started in 1968 under the direction of Professor N. Kaldor' (Cripps and Tarling, 1973).
8. Personal communication.
9. The two published papers of Chatterji and Wickens (1981) and (1982) are virtually identical in many respects. Both papers present the same regression results.
10. The direction of normalisation does not matter when the equation being estimated is exactly identified. For example, it would not make any difference if the same single instrument were used in both Rowthorn's Specification and the Verdoorn Law, but it would make a difference if either different instruments are used in the two formulations or there is more than one instrument.
11. The use of this variable to measure changes in capacity utilisation is somewhat curious. The growth of total hours worked is definitionally

equal to the growth in average hours worked plus the growth of employment. We argued above that it would be preferable to use the growth of total hours as a measure of the labour input and to adjust the growth of the capital stock by using some variable for the rate of change in capacity utilisation. Instead, Chatterji and Wickens prefer to use the growth of employment as the labour input with the growth of average hours worked as a proxy for changes in capacity utilisation.

12. Chatterji and Wickens (1981 and 1982) also specify a productivity relation for non-manufacturing as $p_n = \lambda e_n + \mu q_m$ to which they subsequently add the growth of average hours worked in the non-manufacturing sector and the growth of the non-manufacturing capital stock. They include q_m to test the 'externalities hypothesis'. They cite Kaldor's argument that 'the rate of growth of manufacturing production . . . will tend, indirectly, to raise the productivity growth in other sectors'. They continue: 'We shall call this proposition the Externalities Hypothesis as it suggests that the manufacturing sector generates external economies in which the growth of manufacturing output is positively related to productivity growth in non-manufacturing industries. Presumably part of these external economies is technical progress which is embodied in new machines' (Chatterji and Wickens, 1981, p. 406). In fact, Kaldor nowhere mentions embodied technical change as an important factor in accounting for disparities in economic growth except in Kaldor (1968) where he discounts its importance in explaining the Verdoorn Law in manufacturing. Kaldor's argument is that with surplus labour in agriculture, a faster growth of manufacturing output will *ceteris paribus* increase the rate of the intersectoral transfer of labour and thereby *indirectly* raise the productivity growth rate in the agricultural sector. It is difficult to see the rationale of including both e_n and q_m as exogenous variables and we shall not discuss the non-manufacturing sector further.

13. It will be recalled that the Verdoorn equation is given by:

$$e = -(\lambda/\alpha) + (1/\alpha)q - (\beta/\alpha)k$$

14. The static Verdoorn Law is akin to a conventional Cobb–Douglas production function except that output is deemed to be exogenous and productivity or employment is specified to be the dependent variable. Rowthorn's Specification in its static form is indistinguishable from an orthodox Cobb–Douglas production function.

15. This draws heavily on J.S.L. McCombie (1980), 'On the Quantitative Importance of Kaldor's Laws', *Bulletin of Economic Research*, November; and J.S.L. McCombie (1991), 'The Productivity Growth Slowdown of the Advanced Countries and the Intersectoral Transfer of Labour', *Australian Economic Papers*, March.

16. Ideally equation (2.43) should be expressed in terms of total factor productivity. Labour productivity growth and total factor productivity growth, however, tend to be highly correlated, mainly due to the relatively low weight assigned to the growth of capital in the calculation of total factor productivity growth. Hence, the use of the growth of labour

productivity rather than that of total factor productivity is unlikely to make any significant difference to the conclusions drawn.

17. McCombie (1980) considered the contribution to productivity growth of the transfer of labour under three additional sets of assumptions in addition to *Assumptions 1* and *2*: *viz* (3) surplus labour in agriculture, constant returns in the other two sectors; (4) constant returns in industry, surplus labour in the other two sectors; and (5) increasing returns in industry, surplus labour elsewhere. Somewhat paradoxically, under *Assumption 5* it is found that the assumption of surplus labour in the 'rest of the economy' considerably reduces the contribution of the structural component to overall productivity growth in both periods. This is because, unlike Agriculture, the growth of observed employment in the rest of the economy exceeded the growth of total employment, regardless of the period under consideration. Thus the standardised rate of growth of employment in the rest of the economy is less than that which actually occurred. Since the assumption of surplus labour means that actual and standardised output growth are identical, the standardised productivity growth in the rest of the economy actually exceeds the actual productivity growth (and the structural component for this sector is negative). This is opposite to the effect of the growth of structural productivity growth of Agriculture and Industry and so reduces the contribution that the overall structural component makes. Consequently, in the period 1951–65 the total structural component is not much greater than under *Assumption 1*. In the second period, it is often negative and smaller than under *Assumption 1*.

Chapter 3

1. This important point can be appreciated by specifying the national income equation first in units of domestic currency and then in real terms. Measured in domestic currency we have:

$$P_d Y = P_d C + P_d I + P_d X - P_f E M$$

where P_d is the domestic price of output; P_f is the foreign price of imports: E is the exchange rate measured as the domestic price of foreign currency: C is total domestic consumption and I is total domestic investment. Dividing through by P_d we have the equation for real income:

$$Y = C + I + X - (P_f E / P_d) M$$

An excess of real expenditure over real income implies $X < (P_f E / P_d) M$, which must be filled by real capital inflows (F_r or F / P_d). Thus:

$$X - (P_f E / P_d) M + F_r = 0$$

is the equilibrium condition. Letting $M = \mu Y$ we have:

$$Y = \left(\frac{X + F_r}{\mu} \right) (P_d/P_f E)$$

What happens to real income depends on exports, capital flows, and relative price movements measured in a common currency (the real terms of trade). If imports and exports are related to relative price movements, the price effect will consist of a pure terms of trade effect, and a volume effect on imports and exports if the price elasticities of demand differ from zero.

If accounting data are used to test the model, deviations from the trade multiplier result, due to a non-instantaneous multiplier process, are also ruled out.

The impact of capital flows is dealt with in greater detail later in the chapter.

2. The results of Bairam (1988), to be given later, cover the period 1970–85.
3. This section draws heavily on Thirlwall and Hussain (1982).
4. We made our own estimate for Brazil for a more recent time period.
5. The regression of y on y_B for the full sample gives: $y = 0.724y_B$ with a t-value of 13 and a coefficient of determination of 0.901. Excluding India, Japan and Greece gives $y = 0.892y_B$, with a t-value of 27 and a coefficient of determination of 0.983. However, it should be noted that there are problems in using y_B as the regressor (see Chapter 5).
6. For a survey of the evidence, see Thirlwall (1991).

Chapter 4

1. Recent years have seen the growing awareness in international trade theory of the importance of increasing returns to scale which has led to the development of 'strategic trade theory'. The result has been the construction of international trade models with differentiated products, based on the imperfect or monopolistic competition approach of Robinson and Chamberlin which were developed for a closed economy nearly fifty years ago (e.g. Helpman and Krugman, 1985).
2. For example, Winters (1980, p. 29) in his detailed econometric study of UK exports commented: 'None of these effects [of certain aspects of non-price competitiveness] can be explicitly modelled here although we believe that many of them will be adequately captured over the sample period by our various proxies: the time-trend, profitability and the pressure of demand. Nevertheless their absence limits our study.' Moreover, he further argues that the 'strongly negative trend found in all British export functions' is 'the most interesting and the most critical of the questions surrounding British trade performance' (Winters, 1980, p. 205). This undoubtedly largely reflects the decline in British non-price competitiveness.
3. The *Which? Guide to New and Used Cars 1990* reported that, out of 31 manufacturers, Lada acquired 1.22 per cent of the UK's market (in 14th place) and Skoda 0.59 per cent (in 18th place).
4. The relative price index of, for example, the US dollar is defined as

(P_iE/P_{US}) where P_i is the price in domestic currency of country i's export good, E is the exchange rate and P_{US} is the dollar price of the US product. The law of one price suggests that this ratio should be equal to a constant. Any change in either P_i or P_{US}, or in both, should be exactly compensated by changes in the exchange rate.

5. Another reason for a divergence is spatial price discrimination which would occur if a firm were in the position of being a monopolist faced with separate markets each with a different price elasticity. Tariffs will also cause prices to differ.
6. Mr J. Collyear, Letter to the *Financial Times*, 25 April 1989.
7. Although, as we shall see in Chapter 10, there is some econometric evidence of an improvement in the non-price competitiveness of UK manufactured exports since 1981.
8. *The Sunday Times*, 9 August 1978.
9. Reported in *Planning*, 19 February 1962.
10. SITC 2 is Crude Materials, Inedible, Except Fuels; SITC 5 is Chemicals; SITC 6 is Manufactures, Classified by Material; and SITC 7 is Machinery and Transport Equipment.
11. As the former German Finance Minister, Herr Hans Abel, once explained, 'obviously the variety and quality of German goods fits almost exactly what the customer wants. Also, customers can rely on the dates of delivery promised by German suppliers being met' (*The Banker*, April 1977).
12. High research intensive activities are where R&D is greater than 2.8 per cent of sales; medium research activities are where R&D is 1.1 per cent to 2.8 per cent of sales; and low research activities are where R&D is less than 1.1 per cent of sales.
13. The so-called Frascati definition.
14. Our discussion of Schott's model is purely diagrammatical; the interested reader is referred to Schott's paper for a mathematical presentation of the arguments.
15. The countries are the US, Japan, West Germany, France, the UK, Italy, Canada, Austria, Belgium, Denmark, the Netherlands, Norway, Sweden, Switzerland, and Finland. The data were supplied by Jan Fagerberg and a detailed discussion of the sources is contained in Fagerberg (1988).
16. These data were again supplied by Jan Fagerberg.
17. It is instructive to consider the results of the individual subperiods (pooling the two pre-1973 periods). The abbreviated results, which consist of the estimates of the coefficients of rp, their t-statistics (in parentheses) and the $\bar{r}^2$'s, are as follows.

1960–73: $-0.167\, rp$ (-0.49) $\bar{r}^2 = -0.029$
1973–79: $-0.403\, rp$ (-1.12) $\bar{r}^2 = -0.019$
1979–83: $-0.236\, rp$ (-1.01) $\bar{r}^2 = 0.002$

These results exclude Japan.
18. The suspicion that Fagerberg's own results may also be highly dependent

on the inclusion of Japan in his sample has been confirmed by Forbes (1991) who re-estimated Fagerberg's model excluding Japan.

Chapter 5

1. Taken from P.G. McGregor and J.K. Swales (1985), 'Professor Thirlwall and Balance of Payments Constrained Growth', *Applied Economics*, February.

2. See also Thirlwall (1982b) where this theory is not explicitly stated but is cited as an explanation of the extent of UK deindustrialisation.

3. It is argued in Thirlwall and Dixon (1979) that equation (5.1) can also be derived if $|\eta + \psi| = 1$. This is incorrect. If $|\eta + \psi| = 1$, then $y_B = \varepsilon z/\pi$ but, $\varepsilon z \neq x$, rather: $x = \eta(p_d - p_f - e) + \varepsilon z$.

4. Although it is the case that for manufactured goods, at least, there is a high degree of intra-industry trade between developed countries.

5. Changes in a country's share of world trade depend simply on the value of ε. If world income (z) is increasing, then the share will rise (fall) as ε is greater (less) than unity. But the value of ε depends solely on the product composition of a country's exports. If $\varepsilon > 1$, the country will be maintaining its share of markets which generally have a high income elasticity of demand and are therefore growing rapidly relative to other markets. That there is no link between a country's efficiency and its market share is curious given that this model was initially derived from an export led cumulative causation model of regional/national growth (Dixon and Thirlwall, 1975a; Thirlwall and Dixon, 1979). Supply side considerations can be added to a balance of payments constrained growth model. See, for example, Swales (1983).

6. Swales's (1983) analysis is conducted in a regional context where the potential for inter-regional transfer renders these extensions to the Thirlwall model particularly important. However, these modifications may also be important in an international context. Thus Johnson (1966) has suggested that international capital flows may be income sensitive and there is some empirical evidence in support of this hypothesis. See, for example, Miller and Whitman (1970).

7. The two overlapping time periods are 1953–76 and 1951–73. For both of these periods the values of π are taken from Houthakker and Magee (1969). For the earlier time period, the values of x are derived from Cornwall (1977); for the later time period these values are taken from Kern (1978).

8. Separate regressions were performed where data from Japan and the US were removed. Data from Japan were excluded on the grounds that Japan's growth is likely to have been supply constrained. Data on the US were excluded as the US had a persistent balance-of-payments deficit on current account in this period. These regressions do not substantially differ from those shown in Table 5.1.

9. The coefficient on y_B is not significantly different from 1: the constant is not significantly different from zero.

10. Here $\pi_r > \pi$ as long as $\pi > 1$. This is almost invariably the case.

11. The reason a term which includes changes in foreign tariffs does not appear in Equation (5.16) is that the effects of such tariff changes are reflected in the value of x. Without tariffs, $x = \varepsilon z$. With the introduction of tariffs, $x = \varepsilon z + \eta t_f$.

12. McCombie (1981) makes a similar point in arguing that the direction of causation might be other than that suggested by Thirlwall. However, he seems to be wrong in stating that Thirlwall's findings 'contradict the conclusions of the neoclassical equilibrium theory of international trade' (McCombie, 1981, p. 457): Thirlwall's findings are totally consistent with the more extreme versions of this theory.

13. The validity of the natural rate hypothesis in an open economy context requires purchasing power parity as well as the absence of money illusion.

14. Different assumptions concerning the fixity of the exchange rate and the rapidity with which trade flows and real wages adjust generate other short run adjustment paths, but the long-run equilibrium remains essentially the same.

15. Taken from A.P. Thirlwall (1986b), 'Balance of Payments Constrained Growth: A Reply to McGregor and Swales', *Applied Economics*, December.

16. See also Chapter 3 of this book.

17. Taken from P.G. McGregor and J.K. Swales (1986), 'Balance of Payments Constrained Growth: A Rejoinder to Professor Thirlwall', *Applied Economics*, December.

18. This would mean that equation (5.31) would be affected in the following way: s_i would depend on changes in nonprice competition and q_i would depend on changes in world income.

19. Taken from J.S.L. McCombie (1989), 'Thirlwall's Law and Balance of Payments Constrained Growth – A Comment on the Debate, *Applied Economics*, May.

20. This suggests that the omission of a term capturing the effect of changes in relative prices from the rule $y_B = x/\pi$ will lead to an under-estimate of the balance-of-payments equilibrium growth rate in the case of the US and an over-estimate for Japan and West Germany. It is instructive to note from Table 5.5 that for the US y_B is below y, the growth rates being 2.6 per cent and 3.7 per cent per annum, respectively. This is the expected result. In the case of Japan, the omission of the growth of relative prices, together with the omission of the growth of capital flows, explains why y_B exceeds y. (y_B and y are 12 per cent and 9.5 per cent per annum.) The case of West Germany is not so clear. The preferred estimate of y_B, calculated using the value of ε obtained from a regression analysis where there has been a correction for autocorrelation, is considerably below y (2 per cent as opposed to 5.7 per cent per annum). This is because the estimate of ε is surprisingly low, being less than the value for the UK. It also has a relatively large standard error (see Houthakker and Magee, 1969, table 8, p. 125) which suggests that perhaps not too much confidence should be placed in the case of West Germany on the value of ε and, hence, y_B.

21. The variable z in Thirlwall's law was defined earlier as the growth of the rest of the world's income rather than that of total world income. In

practice, however, these two variables are so highly correlated that they have been treated here as synonymous.

22. There is also evidence to suggest that even those small differences between countries in the value of ε that may be ascribed to disparities in the composition of exports are not independent of the effects of non-price competition. For example, the UK has been compelled to 'down-trade' into the slower growing markets for less-sophisticated products because of its inability to compete effectively in markets for technically sophisticated high quality goods, for which the world income elasticity of demand is high (Connell, 1979).

23. Taken from J.S.L. McCombie, (1992), 'Thirlwall's Law and Balance-of-Payments Constrained Growth – More on the Debate', *Applied Economics*, May.

24. McGregor and Swales (1985, p. 21) do mention, in passing, that 'when the law of one price is imposed, it is as though the whole world is producing the same good: the rationale for trade in these circumstances is unclear'. If, by this, McGregor and Swales mean that they do not believe in the extreme neoclassical model, then much of their discussion in McGregor and Swales (1985) reflects that curious hybrid creature – a cross between a red herring and a straw horse.

25. McGregor and Swales (1991) make two further points that are answered in McCombie (1992), but which are of little consequence and we do not include the full rejoinders here.

The first of these criticisms is that the distinction between the short-run and long-run import demand function is 'unnecessary and unwarranted'. (McGregor and Swales do not say how they reconcile this view with their subsequent statement that 'it clearly could be the case that there are empirical differences between short and long-run import functions'.) They suggest that the linear import demand function should be regarded as a linear approximation to the import demand function expressed as a power function. However, as the approximation becomes progressively more inaccurate as income grows, it is necessary to make repeated approximations evaluated at progressively higher values of income, to keep the accuracy of the approximation within reasonable bounds. Another way of looking at this is to consider the linear approximation as shifting as income increases, in a manner analogous to that set out by McCombie above. While the precise interpretations are different in the two cases, this is of no consequence in the interpretation of the law.

The second point is that McGregor and Swales consider Thirlwall's model to be 'naive', using the term, presumably, in a pejorative sense. If by this they mean that the model is highly aggregative, then it is also true of most, if not all, theoretical growth models and their view would seem to simply display a misunderstanding about the nature of theoretical modelling. The insights that this putative 'naive' Keynesian model gives into the present economic situation of the British economy are examined in Chapter 10.

26. The fact that the term 'law' has been used does not mean that it should be taken to apply universally, and indeed, as we have noted, it cannot be so interpreted. It is more a law in the sense of an 'empirical regularity' or a 'stylised fact', to use Kaldor's term. The term law is used here as in, for

example, the law of demand. The law of demand does not, of course, imply that that there are *no* exceptions to the rule that as price falls so, *ceteris paribus*, quantity demanded increases.

27. Outliers typically pose problems for statistical inference in regression analysis. For example, Maddala (1977) argues that 'if there are outliers, the usual procedure is to omit them and reestimate the regression equation'. He continues:

If we estimate a regression equation and look at the residuals, then decide some observations are outliers, and then estimate the equation omitting these observations, the standard errors and confidence intervals we report are no longer valid. On the other hand, if we do not discard these observations, even in view of some information we have on why they are out of the way, *the results we get are not meaningful*. (emphasis added)

Maddala quotes Fisher (1966) who, when considering this choice, prefers to omit the outliers. 'Faced with choosing between a procedure which yields, at best, precise results of little or no meaning and one which yields meaningful results of little or no precision, it seems clear that the latter alternative represents a more hopeful course' (Fisher, 1966, p. 13). In other words, to include the outliers as do McGregor and Swales yields results that 'are not meaningful'. As we have argued, Thirlwall's hypothesis is rejected by McGregor and Swales for all countries because of one or two outliers. (Even this is debatable, as will be shown below.)

As Maddala points out, there are some occasions where outliers convey useful information. This is especially true when there may be little variation over time between two variables until a large shock occurs. Maddala gives as an example the estimation of the price elasticity of demand for gasoline and the energy crisis. But this is clearly not relevant in the case under discussion here.

28. The countries are France, Italy, Japan, United Kingdom, United States and West Germany.

29. Nor can Thirlwall be accused of this: 'adverse relative price movements combined with various price elasticity conditions cannot be entirely ruled out as determinants of the balance of payments even though they may be of minor significance compared to income movements and income elasticities of demand for imports and exports' (Thirlwall, 1979). It is very surprising that McGregor and Swales should misinterpret Thirlwall on this point, as they actually cited the above quotation themselves (McGregor and Swales, 1985, p. 27). Prices are sticky in that, even though the Marshall–Lerner condition is satisfied, the growth in relative prices is insufficient to allow the trend rate of growth of income to be raised without incurring a growing balance-of-payments deficit. In other words, the neoclassical price auction model is inapplicable and we are in a Keynesian world.

30. McGregor and Swales (1991) state that 'we are surprised that an advocate of the law would not wish to suppress this term on the grounds that it is a statistically acceptable restriction which corresponds to the theory'.

One could equally put the point another way – it is surprising that critics of the theory should wish to suppress this variable.

31. McGregor and Swales (1991) argue that 'the fact that Thirlwall's Law is rejected in a cross-sectional regression, even where all the observations are for countries which are not rejected using McCombie's test, suggests that McCombie's test is not particularly demanding.' In fact, the result that a more correctly specified regression analysis does not refute Thirlwall's Law even when countries that are rejected by McCombie's test are included in the sample leads to precisely the opposite conclusion.

32. The estimate of the world income elasticity of demand for West Germany's exports from the Houthakker and Magee (1969) equation which had been corrected for autocorrelation is 0.91. This figure is implausibly low and is less than that for the UK. The estimate, where there was no correction for autocorrelation, is 2.08. However, using this value to calculate y_{B1} for West Germany does not alter the conclusions drawn. The intercept of the regression, with a t-statistic of -1.79, is not statistically significantly different from zero at the 95 per cent confidence level. The slope coefficient has a value of $|t'| = 2.18$ which implies that the slope is not statistically significantly different from unity at the 99 per cent confidence level and only just significantly different at the 95 per cent level (the critical value of $|t'|$ at the latter confidence level is 2.16).

33. Moreover, as pointed out in McCombie (1989), even if a low aggregate income elasticity of demand for a country's exports did reflect its exports being concentrated in the more slowly growing markets, this could itself mirror its poor non-price competitiveness. The country concerned may not be able to compete in the fast growing, generally high-technology, markets and is, therefore, forced 'down market'.

34. As Balassa points out, the calculation of the 'apparent' elasticities assumes that prices have no effect on the growth of exports or the commodity composition of trade. 'However, with fixed exchange rates applying in all countries other than Canada and very few changes in the rates taking place during the period covered, and with a considerable degree of absolute and relative price stability being maintained, the error possibilities due to the use of value instead of quantity data . . . are not likely to be large' (Balassa, 1979).

35. This excludes West Germany's implausibly low value of 0.91.

36. An alternative way of capturing the effect of changes in non-price competition is to include a time trend in the export and import demand functions, as McCombie (1989) noted. A negative time trend, as found in, for example, the UK export demand function, reflects the poor non-price competitiveness of UK exports (Winters, 1980).

Chapter 6

1. This is taken from J.S.L. McCombie (1985) 'Economic Growth, the Harrod Foreign Trade Multiplier and the Hicks Super-multiplier', *Applied Economics*, February, with corrections and revisions.

2. Harrod's formulation of the foreign trade multiplier actually predated the Keynesian investment multiplier by three years, although, of course,

it was subsequently overshadowed by the latter. The revival and reassessment of the foreign trade multiplier is largely due to Kaldor (1978a p. xxiv, 1979b) and Thirlwall (1979, 1982a).

3. These are very restrictive assumptions which will be relaxed later.

4. Kaldor uses the term 'region' to denote different countries, groups of countries and different areas within the same country.

5. The sample of advanced countries consists of 15 countries, namely: Australia, Austria, Belgium, Canada, Denmark, France, West Germany, Italy, Japan, the Netherlands, Norway, Sweden, Switzerland, the UK and the US. The less developed countries comprise the remaining 35 countries.

6. This criticism is based on the assumption that the relationship reflects only the direct impact of export growth on output growth through the foreign trade multiplier. It ignores the increase in output made possible through the relaxation of the balance-of-payments constraint. This point will be dealt with more fully below.

7. In order to avoid confusion between growth rates and the marginal propensities, for the remainder of this chapter we shall denote the growth of, for example, imports by M and the marginal propensity to import by the lower case letter m.

8. An interesting result from the New Cambridge School concerns the determinants of the balance-of-payments. Suppose there is a balance-of-payments deficit, equation (6.16) shows that, somewhat paradoxically, an increase in exports will not reduce it. This is because an increase of exports by a certain value will induce an equivalent increase in expenditure on imports. In other words, an increase in exports of ΔX induces an increase in income of $(1/m)\Delta Y$. This, in turn, increases imports by $\Delta M = \Delta X$. Any improvement in the balance of payments has to come through a reduction in the PSBR. This will reduce income and hence imports, while exports remain unaffected. It is, however, beyond the scope of this book to consider this proposition further.

9. The multiplier associated with the New Cambridge Model was also calculated, but as it is not clear how applicable this approach is to the other advanced countries we only report the results of the orthodox Keynesian multiplier. There is also evidence that the relationships of the New Cambridge model are not as robust as was once thought.

10. The CEPG multiplier, in this case, is defined as $1/(t + m)$.

11. Kaldor (1970) originally argued for the use of exchange rate policy to generate export-led growth. With the experience of floating exchange rates in the 1970s, however, he soon changed his mind. He subsequently argued that the putative efficacy of exchange rate adjustments in solving balance-of-payments problems had been grossly over-estimated (Kaldor, 1978c). It is difficult to alter the *real* exchange rate in the long term and the income elasticities of demand for exports and imports are much more important than price elasticities in determining trends in imports and exports.

12. It would be useful to estimate this relationship for each country separately using time-series data but this is outside the scope of the present study.

13. As we noted above, in our estimates of the marginal propensity to import we have made no allowance for changes in autonomous imports. In other words, we have attributed the whole change in imports to changes in income. Any increase in autonomous imports will therefore be reflected in a change in the marginal propensity to import. This is analogous to the procedure of estimating the income elasticity of demand using time series data and the logarithmic values of the various variables without including a time-trend (Houthakker and Magee, 1969). In the latter case, we have seen in Chapters 4 and 5 that differences between countries in the degree of non-price competition and in the commodity composition of imports will be reflected in differences in the income elasticities of demand.

14. Time series estimates of the income elasticity of demand for imports (and exports) often find this to be the case. See, for example, Houthakker and Magee (1969).

Chapter 7

1. Based on A.P. Thirlwall and R.J. Dixon, 'A Model of Export-Led Growth with a Balance-of-Payments Constraint' in J. Bowers (ed.), *Inflation Development and Integration: Essays in Honour of A.J. Brown*, University of Leeds Press, 1979.

2. Balance-of-payments equilibrium is defined here in terms of balance on the current account partly for simplicity but also in recognition that *net* long-term capital flows are likely to be relatively small in magnitude and that few countries are likely to be able to finance a growing current account deficit by continual short-term borrowing. There may, of course, be an asymmetry in the system. While it is assumed that a country's long-run growth rate cannot exceed that consistent with payments equilibrium, it can be lower.

3. Kaldor was once an advocate of exchange rate variations as a weapon of balance of payments adjustment, but then became disillusioned on account of their apparent ineffectiveness in correcting payments disequilibrium between countries.

4. This is possible in Beckerman's original specification of the model in which the export function is additive not multiplicative; but, as we argued in Chapter 3, if the *growth* of exports is a function of the rate at which relative prices are changing, a once-for-all devaluation cannot raise the rate of growth of exports *permanently*.

5. See Chapter 2.

6. In the short term, autonomous investment (e.g. originating from government) may compensate for poor export performance. As far as the model to be developed is concerned, however, the inclusion of two autonomous demand components would lead to complications in deriving the equilibrium solution to the model since the weights attached to the two components will vary with the growth rate. This, coupled with the fact that the export component will ultimately dominate the other component if export growth is faster than autonomous investment growth, leads Kaldor to ignore investment demand in the model. All investment is induced.

7. See Chapter 8.

8. This compares with the equilibrium growth rate derived from the Kaldor model without a balance-of-payments equilibrium condition, letting $y = \gamma x$, of:

$$y_B = \frac{\gamma[\eta(w - r_a + \tau - p_f - e) + \varepsilon z]}{1 + \gamma\eta\lambda} \tag{7.19a}$$

Notice that if the price and income elasticities of demand for imports are both unity (i.e. $\eta = 1$ and $\pi = 1$), and $\gamma = 1$, equation (7.19) collapses to (7.19a) because the balance of payments would always be in equilibrium whatever the rate of growth of income and foreign prices. In an export-led growth model without a balance-of-payments constraint, γ must take on that value which preserves balance of payments equilibrium as income and import prices change.

9. The parameter values and estimates of the variables (rates per annum) used were: $\eta + \psi = -1.5$; $w + \tau = 0.14$; $r_a = 0.01$; $p_f = 0.17$; $\varepsilon = 1$; $z = 0.03$; $\lambda = 0.5$; $\pi = 1.51$ and the exchange rate fell by about 4 per cent per annum over the period.

10. This is a revised version of J.S.L. McCombie (1985) 'The Balance of Payments as a Constraint on Economic Growth', Research Paper No.137, Department of Economics, The University of Melbourne, and is taken from J.S.L. McCombie (1993) 'Economic Growth, Trade Inter-linkages and the Balance-of-Payments Constraint', *Journal of Post Keynesian Economics* (Summer).

11. The ratio of the exports of goods and services to GDP at current prices in 1986.

12. This does not mean that the neoclassical approach comes into its own. Rather, demand was constrained by the, admittedly fast, rate at which labour could be transferred from the non-manufacturing to manufacturing sector and, in the case of West Germany, by the rate of growth of immigration. It was not the exogenous growth of the labour force that determined the growth of output.

13. Through the cumulative causation nature of growth (the Verdoorn effect), these resource constrained countries were also those whose competitiveness in overseas trade increased over the postwar period. They tended to run persistent balance of payments surpluses.

14. The slope of the line A_0 is less than that of the BP locus so $0 < \beta_1\pi_2 < \pi_2/\pi_1$. Consequently, $0 < \beta_1\pi_1 < 1$ and it may be similarly shown that $0 < \beta_2\pi_2 < 1$. Hence $(1 - \beta_1\beta_2\pi_1\pi_2) < 1$.

15. It should be noted that, for the growth of capital flows to be defined, there must be an initial balance-of-payments disequilibrium with $\varphi < 1$.

Chapter 8

1. Based on the articles by R. Dixon and A.P. Thirlwall (1975a) 'A Model of Regional Growth Rate Differences on Kaldorian Lines', *Oxford Economic Papers*, July; A.P. Thirlwall (1983) 'Foreign Trade Elasticities in

Centre–Periphery Models of Growth and Development', *Banca Nazionale del Lavoro Quarterly Review*, September; and J.S.L. McCombie (1988) 'A Synoptic View of Regional Growth and Unemployment: II – The Post-Keynesian Theory', *Urban Studies*, October.

2. Of course, even constant persistent growth-rate differences will be sufficient for regional per capita income levels to widen if population growth is the same in each region.

3. The time subscripts are now explicitly included because later we undertake dynamic analysis which requires the use of lagged variables.

4. Apart from the theoretical considerations underlying this specification there are a number of practical considerations that make export demand for highly specialised regions (or countries) extremely important. In most industries in a region, local demand is likely to be trivial compared with the optimum production capacity of the industries. The viability of regional enterprise must largely depend on the strength of demand from outside the region. There are also a number of important reasons why export demand may be a more potent growth-inducing force than other elements of demand, especially in open, backward areas – either regions or countries. The first is that exports allow regional specialisation which may bring dynamic as well as static gains. Secondly, exports permit imports and imports may be important in developing areas which lack the capacity to produce development goods themselves. Thirdly, if the exchange of information and technical knowledge is linked to trade, exporting facilitates the flow of technical knowledge which can improve the growth rate.

5. Kaldor, as Special Adviser to the Chancellor of the Exchequer from 1964 to 1968, was the inventor of the Regional Employment Premium in 1967 which gave a *flat-rate* subsidy per unit of labour employed to employers in manufacturing industry in Development Areas, as part of an active regional policy to achieve a greater degree of regional balance in the economy as a whole.

6. Since we specify (in keeping with Kaldor) the mark-up to be on unit labour costs and not on total prime costs (which include raw material costs), any change in imported raw material costs will be included in the last term of equation (8.3).

7. Relating productivity growth in the export sector to the rate of growth of total output, as opposed to the rate of growth of exports, is to treat the economy as if it were a single fully integrated firm in which it is impossible to distinguish between production runs for export and production runs for domestic consumption. On the assumption that $y = x$, however, the equilibrium growth rate is unaffected.

8. The effect of η is ambiguous since it appears in both the numerator and the denominator of the equation. Whether growth varies positively or negatively with the absolute size of η depends on the other variables and parameters. To determine the effect of variations in η numerical analysis would have to be resorted to.

9. A one-period lag in two of the equations, giving a second order system, yields two real roots $\pm (-\gamma\eta\lambda)$. The stability conditions are therefore the same as in the first-order system. This is true however many equations

are lagged. This fact considerably enhances the generality of our result.

10. Since the equations that constitute the model have omitted higher order terms containing y_t, the stability conditions of the model are necessarily an approximation.

11. Kaldor agreed in correspondence that implicit in his argument that regional growth rates may diverge is the assumption that $|\eta\lambda| > 1$ for one region, but did not regard $|\eta| > 2$ as an unrealistic assumption.

12. Ignoring time subscripts and assuming z and p_f do not differ between regions.

13. For evidence, see Thirlwall (1970).

14. And also higher price elasticities of demand if $\partial y/\partial p_d > 0$.

15. The Verdoorn effect is also an important determinant of the capacity (or natural) rate of growth, y_n. Let $y_n = r + n$ where r is the rate of growth of productivity and n is the rate of growth of the workforce. But $r = r_a + \lambda y$. Substituting, we have $y_n = r_a + \lambda y + n$. The higher is λ, the higher will be y_n. In the (implausible) case where $\lambda > 1$ there is no constraint on the growth rate. This is the situation of 'increasing returns for ever'.

16. However, regional devaluation could have a permanent effect on the percentage level of unemployment ($\%U$). The initial effect of devaluation will be to lower $\%U$. Since $\%U$ is the outcome of the difference between the growth of labour demand and supply, and the growth of demand is unaffected by devaluation, the lower level of $\%U$ can persist. Moreover, the cheapening of labour relative to capital could induce the use of more labour-intensive techniques. Interpreted as a weapon to combat unemployment, therefore, regional devaluation may have merit. As a means of stimulating regional growth, however, its value is doubtful.

17. In fact, if money wages are rising through time, a flat-rate wage subsidy per man will actually raise the rate of increase in money wage costs after the initial introduction of the subsidy since the percentage effect of the subsidy is smaller in the next period.

18. Beckerman (1962), who has used an additive function in a national context, is not clear on this point. See also the discussion in Chapter 7.

19. See Chapter 7.

20. This and the next section draw heavily on J.S.L. McCombie (1988) 'A Synoptic View of Regional Growth and Unemployment: II – The Post-Keynesian Theory, *Urban Studies*, October.

21. The periphery will, in fact, have to run a balance-of-trade surplus to the extent that it has to make net interest payments to the centre as a result of its past borrowings.

22. Based on the article by A.P. Thirlwall of the same title published in *Regional Studies*, 1980.

23. The work of Burridge and Gordon (1981) strongly suggests this type of function.

24. Starting with a positive level of unemployment the term $(1 - \rho)$ on the right-hand side of (8.37) should be $((L/N) - \rho)$, where L/N is the proportion of the workforce employed. For large absolute values of N, L and U, the approximation that $\Delta\%U = n - \ell$ is a very close one.

25. The rate of growth required to keep the unemployment rate steady

would, of course, define the natural rate of growth. The relationship between this growth rate, the actual growth rate and the balance-of-payments constrained growth rate will determine changes in the region's balance of payments and unemployment.

26. The effect of ρ depends on whether the term in square brackets in equation (8.37) is positive or negative.
27. This may involve the short-run sacrifice of comparative advantage but for the benefit of fuller utilisation of resources in the long run. Developing countries are confronted with a similar dilemma.
28. Myrdal (1957) stresses that the circular and cumulative causation mechanism can only operate efficiently in the absence of a balance-of-payments constraint.

Chapter 9

1. Based on G. Yannopoulos, 'The Spatial Distribution of the Effects of Economic Integration Schemes', and 'Towards a Dynamic Theory of Customs Unions', mimeo. The authors are very grateful to Dr Yannopoulos for allowing them to use these articles.
2. This approach has been taken by A.J. Marques Mendes in his pioneering study of economic integration and growth in Europe (see Mendes, 1987).
3. Flexible exchange rates may not be an optimal policy within the Union, or foreign exchange markets may not function perfectly.
4. First substituting equation (9.4).
5. For an empirical application on these lines, see Mendes (1990).
6. Based on A.P. Thirlwall, 'A General Model of Growth and Development on Kaldorian Lines', *Oxford Economic Papers*, July 1986.
7. See also Hicks's discussion of Cantillon's early model of Town and Country (Hicks, 1990).
8. Equation (9.26) is definitionally true, but does not imply that output depends *only* on capital. σ is the gross productivity of capital, not the net productivity holding other factors constant.
9. In other words, the natural growth rate is assumed to exceed the warranted rate, typical in developing countries.
10. Assuming $C_{ii} = 0$.

Chapter 10

1. The NIESR figure of 0.42 is the same regardless of which method is used to alter fiscal stance so as to ensure the current account is maintained in equilibrium. The LBS figure of 0.28 is that obtained when the rate of income tax is used as the regulator. When government expenditure is used to maintain balance-of-payments equilibrium the figure is 0.35. This is because of the lower import content of government expenditures so that for any given cost to the balance-of-payments a higher level of GDP can be obtained. Turner, however, prefers to use the lower figure because of the 'emphasis of current government fiscal policy towards income tax cuts and constraining government expenditure' (p. 28).

2. Note that the trade elasticities are always lower than income elasticities because world trade grows faster than world income.
3. Landesmann and Snell point out that part of this increase in the United Kingdom's export performance is due to the boom in the United States' growth rate since the United Kingdom does particularly well in the markets of the United States. Landesmann and Snell's 'provisional results on estimating [their] model excluding the United States as a market do show that this temporary compositional shift in export markets does not *fully* account for the improved performance' (p. 24, our emphasis). The balance-of-payments equilibrium growth rate will, however, be overstated to the extent that it does account for the improvement.
4. The income elasticity of demand for United Kingdom imports is by definition the same as the income elasticity of demand for the rest of the world's exports. An increase in the income elasticity of demand for the United Kingdom's exports does not imply any increase in non-price competitiveness if the income elasticity of demand for the rest of the world's exports (i.e. the United Kingdom's income elasticity of demand for imports) increases in equal proportion.
5. Of course, if the balance of trade had moved substantially into surplus, this would, *ceteris paribus*, have lessened the problem of the net income transfers.
6. The most recent data at the time of writing suggests that the rapid increase in exports may well be slowing. The index of exports of goods and services (1991(1) = 100 at 1984/5 constant prices) since the first quarter of 1991 is: 1991(1) 100; 1991(2) 107; 1991(3) 108; 1991(4) 109; 1992(1) 107. While exports grew at 7.1 per cent from 1991(1) to 1992(1), imports grew by 7.8 per cent.
7. As these conclusions are so similar to the main thesis of this book, we should perhaps hasten to reassure the reader that the NIEIR came to these conclusions independently of our research and vice versa!
8. Japan, in 1987, purchased coal from the United States in preference to the cheaper Australian coal. This was purely a result of political pressure brought about by a desire on the part of the Japanese government to reduce the substantial trading surplus Japan had with the United States.

References

Abramovitz, M. (1956) 'Resource and Output Trends in the United States since 1870', *American Economic Review*, (Supp) May.

Abramovitz, M. (1983) 'Notes on International Differences in Productivity Growth Rates', in D.C. Mueller (ed.), *The Political Economy of Growth*, New Haven: Yale University Press.

Allen, P. (1976) *Organisation and Administration of a Monetary Union*, Princeton Studies in International Finance, No. 38.

Anderson, F.J. (1976) 'The Effects of Remoteness and Size on Regional Real Wage Determination', *Regional Studies*, April.

Anderson, K. (1980) 'The Political Market for Government Assistance to Australian Manufacturing Industries', *Economic Record*, June.

Anderson, K. and Garnaut, K. (1987) *Australian Protectionism. Extent, Causes and Effects*, Sydney: Allen & Unwin.

Anderson, R. and Dunnett, A. (1987) 'Modelling the Behaviour of Export Volumes of Manufactures: An Evaluation of the Performance of Different Measures of International Competitiveness', *National Institute Economic Review*, August.

Anyadike-Danes, M. (1982) 'Chapter 4. The "New Cambridge" Hypothesis and Fiscal Planning', *Cambridge Economic Policy Review*, April.

Armington, P.S. (1977) 'The Role of "Non-Price Competitiveness" in Exporting', *The Banker*, August.

Arrow, K.J. (1962) 'The Economic Implications of Learning by Doing', *Review of Economic Studies*, June.

Bacon, R. and Eltis, W. (1975) 'Declining Britain', *Sunday Times*, 2, 9, 16 November.

Bacon, R. and Eltis, W. (1976) *Britain's Economic Problem: Too Few Producers* (2nd edn, 1978) London: Macmillan.

Bacon, R. and Eltis, W. (1979) 'The Measurement of the Growth of the Non-Market Sector and its Influence: A Reply to Hadjimatheou and Skouras', *Economic Journal*, June.

Bailey, M.N. (1981) 'Productivity and the Services of Capital and Labor', *Brookings Papers on Economic Activity*, vol. 1.

Bairam, E. (1987) 'The Verdoorn Law, Returns to Scale and Industrial Growth: A Review of the Literature', *Australian Economic Papers*, June.

Bairam, E. (1988) 'Balance of Payments, the Harrod Foreign Trade Multiplier and Economic Growth: The European and North American Experience, 1970–85', *Applied Economics*, December.

Bairam, E. (1990) 'The Harrod Foreign Trade Multiplier Revisited', *Applied Economics*, June.

Bairam, E. and Dempster, G. (1991) 'The Harrod Foreign Trade Multiplier and Economic Growth in Asian Countries', *Applied Economics*, November.

Balassa, B. (1963) 'Some Observations on Mr. Beckerman's "Export Propelled" Growth Model', *Economic Journal*, December.

Balassa, B. (1979) 'Export Composition and Export Performance in the Industrial Countries, 1953–71', *Review of Economics and Statistics*, November.

Ball, R.J., Burns, T. and Laury, J.S.E. (1977) 'The Role of Exchange Rate Changes in Balance of Payments Adjustment: The U.K. Case', *Economic Journal*, March.

Barker, T.S. (1977) 'International Trade and Economic Growth: An Alternative to the Neoclassical Approach', *Cambridge Journal of Economics*, June.

Barret Whale, P. (1937) 'The Working of the Pre-War Gold Standard', *Economica*, February.

Baumol, W.J. (1986) 'Productivity Growth, Convergence, and Welfare', *American Economic Review*, December.

Baumol, W.J. and Wolff, E.N. (1988) 'Productivity Growth, Convergence, and Welfare: Reply', *American Economic Review*, December.

Bazen, S. and Thirlwall, A.P. (1989) *Deindustrialization*, London: Heinemann.

Beckerman, W. (1962) 'Projecting Europe's Growth', *Economic Journal*, December.

Beckerman, W. (1963) 'A Reply to Balassa', *Economic Journal*, December.

Beckerman, W. (1965) *The British Economy in 1975*, Cambridge: Cambridge University Press.

Beckerman, W. (ed.) (1979) *Slow Growth in Britain. Causes and Consequences*, Oxford: Clarendon Press.

Beckerman, W. (1983) 'Review of *The Rise and Decline of Nations* by M. Olson', *Economic Journal*, December.

Black, J. (1962) 'The Technical Progress Function', *Economica*, May.

Blackaby, F. (ed.) (1979) *De-industrialisation*, National Institute of Economic and Social Research, Economic Policy Papers 2, London: Heinemann.

Blaug, M. (1974) *The Cambridge Revolution. Success or Failure?*, London: Institute of Economic Affairs.

Blaug, M. (1980) *The Methodology of Economics: Or How Economists Explain*, Cambridge: Cambridge University Press.

Boltho, A. (1985) 'Was Japan's Industrial Policy Successful?', *Cambridge Journal of Economics*, June.

Bosworth, B. and Lawrence, R.Z. (1982) *Commodity Prices and the New Inflation*, Washington, DC: The Brookings Institution.

Bowles, S. and Eatwell, J. (1983) 'Between Two Worlds: Interest Groups, Class Structure, and Capitalist Growth', in D.C. Mueller (ed.), *The Political Economy of Growth*, New Haven: Yale University Press.

Brain, P. and Manning, I. (1987) 'Australia's Economic Predicament; Chapter 1. The Balance of Payments Constraint', *National Economic Review*, June.

Brain, P. and Manning, I. (1989) 'A Role for the Tariff?', *National Economic Review*, March.

Brech, M.J. and Stout, D. (1981) 'The Rate of Exchange and Non-Price Competitiveness; A Provisional Study within UK Manufactured Exports', *Oxford Economic Papers*, (Supplement), July.

British Export Trade Research Organisation (1975) *Export Concentration*.

Brown, C.J.F. and Sheriff, T.D. (1978) 'Deindustrialisation in the U.K.: A Summary of Empirical Evidence and Alternative Explanations', in Blackaby (1979).

Brown, R.N., Enoch, C.A. and Mortimer-Lee, P.D. (1980) 'The Interrelationships Between Costs and Prices in the United Kingdom', *Bank of England Discussion Paper*, no. 8.

Bruno, M. (1984) 'Raw Materials, Profits, and the Productivity Slowdown', *Quarterly Journal of Economics*, February.

Bureau of Industry Economics (1987) *Productivity Growth: the Path to International Competitiveness*, (Canberra: AGPS).

Burridge, P. and Gordon, I. (1981) 'Unemployment in the British Metropolitan Labour Areas', *Oxford Economic Papers*, July.

Cable, V. (1983) *Protectionism and Industrial Decline*, London: Hodder & Stoughton.

Caldwell, B.J. (1982) *Beyond Positivism: Economic Methodology in the Twentieth Century*, London: George Allen & Unwin.

Cambridge Economic Policy Group (1981) 'A Formal Model of Fiscal Policy', *Cambridge Economic Policy Review*, April.

Caves, R.E. (1970) 'Export-Led Growth: The Post War Industrial Setting', in W. Eltis, M. Scott and J.N. Wolfe (eds) *Induction, Growth and Trade: Essays in Honour of Sir Roy Harrod*, Oxford.

Caves, R.E. (1976) 'Economic Models of Political Choice: Canada's Tariff Structure', *Canadian Journal of Economics*, May.

Chatterji, M. and Wickens, M.R. (1981) 'Verdoorn's Law – The Externalities Hypothesis and Economic Growth in the UK', in D. Currie, R. Nobay and D. Peel (eds), *Essays in Macroeconomics and Econometrics*, London: Croom Helm.

Chatterji, M. and Wickens, M.R. (1982) 'Productivity, Factor Transfers and Economic Growth in the U.K.', *Economica*, February.

Chatterji, M. and Wickens, M.R. (1983) 'Verdoorn's Law and Kaldor's Law: A Revisionist Interpretation?', *Journal of Post Keynesian Economics*, Spring.

Choi, K. (1983) 'A Statistical Test of Olson's Model', in D.C. Mueller (ed.), *The Political Economy of Growth*, New Haven: Yale University Press.

Church, K.B. (1991) 'Properties of the Fundamental Equilibrium Exchange Rate in Models of the UK Economy', *ESRC Macroeconomic Modelling Bureau*, Discussion Paper No. 26, University of Warwick.

Clark, C. (1940) *The Conditions of Economic Progress*, London: Macmillan.

Clark, G.L. (1981) 'The Regional Impact of Stagflation: A Conceptual Model and Empirical Evidence for Canada', in R.L. Martin (ed.) *Regional Wage Inflation and Unemployment*, London: Pion.

Committee for the Development of Australia (CEDA) (1986) *Exploiting Opportunities in the Pacific Basin*, mimeo, Strategic Issues Forum, Melbourne.

Connell, D. (1979) *The U.K.'s Performance in Export Markets – Some Evidence from International Trade Data*, National Economic Development Office, Discussion Paper 6.

Cooper, R.N. (1982) 'The Gold Standard: Historical Facts and Future Prospects', *Brookings Papers on Economic Activity*, no. 1.

Cornwall, J. (1976) 'Diffusion, Convergence and Kaldor's Laws', *Economic Journal*, June.

Cornwall, J. (1977) *Modern Capitalism: Its Growth and Transformation*, London: Martin Robertson.

Coutts, K., Godley, W. and Nordhaus, W. (1978) *Industrial Pricing in the United Kingdom*, Cambridge: Cambridge University Press.

Coutts, K., Godley, W., Rowthorn, R. and Zessa, G. (1990) *Britain's Economic Problems and Policies in the 1990s*, Institute for Public Policy Research, Economic Study no. 6.

Coutts, K., Tarling, R. and Wilkinson, F. (1976) 'Costs and Prices 1974–1976', *Economic Policy Review*, March.

Crafts, N.F.R. (1988) 'The Assessment: British Economic Growth Over the Long Run', *Oxford Review of Economic Policy*, Spring.

Crafts, N.F.R. (1990) 'Economic Growth', in N.F.R. Crafts and N.W.C. Woodward (eds) with the assistance of B.F.Duckham, *The British Economy Since 1945*, Oxford: Oxford University Press.

Cramer, J.S. (1969) *Empirical Economics*, Amsterdam: North Holland.

Creamer D. (1972) 'Measuring Capital Input for Total Factor Productivity Analysis: Comments by a Sometime Estimator', *Review of Income and Wealth*, March.

Cripps, T.F. (1978) 'Causes of Growth and Recession in World Trade', *Cambridge Economic Policy Review*, March.

Cripps, T.F. (1979) 'Comment', in Blackaby (1979).

Cripps, T.F. and Godley, W. (1978) 'Control of Imports as a Means to Full Employment and Expansion in World Trade: The UK's Case', *Cambridge Journal of Economics*, September.

Cripps, T.F. and Tarling, R.J. (1973) *Growth in Advanced Capitalist Economies: 1950–1970*, University of Cambridge, Department of Applied Economics, Occasional Paper 40. Cambridge: Cambridge University Press.

Cuthbertson, K. (1979) *Macroeconomic Policy: The New Cambridge, Keynesian and Monetarist Controversies*, London: Macmillan.

Daly, A., Hitchens, D.M.W.N. and Wagner, K. (1985) 'Productivity, Machinery and Skills in a Sample of British and German Manufacturing Plants. Results of a Pilot Study', *National Institute Economic Review*, February.

Davies, R. (1976) 'On the Relation Between Product Differentiation and International Trade Flows', University of Bath, Discussion Paper.

De Long, B. (1988) 'Productivity Growth, Convergence, and Welfare: Comment', *American Economic Review*, December.

Denison, E.F. (1957) 'Theoretical Aspects of Quality Change, Capital Consumption and Net Capital Formation', in *Problems in Capital Formation, Studies in Income and Wealth*, vol. 19, National Bureau of Economic Research, Princeton: Princeton University Press.

Denison, E.F. (1962) *The Sources of Economic Growth in the United States and the Alternatives Before Us*, New York: Committee for Economic Development.

Denison, E.F. (1964) 'The Unimportance of the Embodiment Question', *American Economic Review*, March.

Denison, E.F. assisted by Poullier, J-P. (1967) *Why Growth Rates Differ:*

Post-War Experience in Nine Western Countries, Washington DC: The Brookings Institution.

Denison, E.F. (1969) 'Some Major Issues in Productivity Analysis: An Examination of Estimates of Jorgenson and Griliches', *Survey of Current Business*, May.

Denison, E.F. (1972) 'Final Comments on Estimates by Jorgenson and Griliches', *Survey of Current Business*, May.

Denison, E.F. (1974) *Accounting For United States Economic Growth 1929–1969*, Washington, DC: The Brookings Institution.

Denison, E.F. (1979) *Accounting for Slower Economic Growth*, Washington, DC: The Brookings Institution.

Denison, E.F. (1984) 'Accounting for Slower Growth: An Update', in J.W. Kendrick (ed.), *International Comparisons of Productivity and Causes of the Slowdown*, Cambridge, Mass: Ballinger.

Denison, E.F. (1985) *Trends in American Economic Growth 1929–1982*, Washington, DC: The Brookings Institution.

Denison, E.F. (1991) 'Scott's *New View of Economic Growth*: A Review Article', *Oxford Economic Papers*, April.

Denison, E.F. and Chung, W.K. (1976) *How Japan's Economy Grew So Fast*, Washington DC: The Brookings Institution.

Denton, G.R. (1978) 'Reflections on Fiscal Federalism', *Journal of Common Market Studies*, June.

Department of Scientific and Industrial Research (1963) *Engineering Design*.

Design Council of Britain, *Three Year Corporate Plan*.

Dewhurst, J.F., Coppock, J.O. and Yates, P.L. (1961) *Europe's Needs and Resources*, London: Macmillan.

Dixon, R. J. (1986) 'Comments' (on C.M. Harris and R.W. Phillips, 'Productivity Trends in the Australian Manufacturing Sector'), in P. Scherer and T. Malone (eds), *The Measurement and Implications of Productivity Growth; Proceedings of a Workshop*, Bureau of Labour Market Research, Monograph Series No. 14, Canberra: Australian Government Printing Service.

Dixon, R.J. and Thirlwall, A.P. (1975a) 'A Model of Regional Growth Rate Differences on Kaldorian Lines', *Oxford Economic Papers*, July.

Dixon, R.J. and Thirlwall, A.P. (1975b) *Regional Growth and Unemployment in the United Kingdom*, London: Macmillan.

Dixon, P.B. and McDonald, D. (1986) 'Australia's Foreign Debt: 1975 to 1985', *Australian Economic Review*, 2nd Quarter.

Domar, E.D. (1961) 'On the Measurement of Technical Change', *Economic Journal*, December.

Dosi, G. and Soete, L. (1988) 'Technical Change and International Trade', in G. Dosi, C. Freeman, R. Nelson, G. Silverberg and L. Soete (eds), *Technical Change and Economic Theory*, London: Pinter Publishers.

Douglas, P.H. (1976) 'The Cobb–Douglas Production Function Once Again: Its History, Its Testing, and Some Empirical Values', *Journal of Political Economy*, October.

Dow, S.C. (1986) 'The Capital Account and Regional Balance of Payments Problems', *Urban Studies*, June.

Dowrick, S. and Nguyen, D-T. (1989) 'OECD Comparative Economic Growth 1950–1985', *American Economic Review*, December.

Dunning, J.H. (1981) *International Production and the Multinational Enterprise*, London: Allen & Unwin.

Dunning, J.H. and Pearce, R.D. (1985) *The World's Largest Industrial Enterprises 1962–1983*, London: Gower.

Economist, The (1987) 'Why Goliath Can't Export', July.

El-Agraa A.M. and Jones, A.J. (1981) *Theory of Customs Unions*, Oxford: Philip Allan.

Eltis, W. (1966) *Economic Growth*, London: Hutchinson.

Eltis, W. (1976) 'The Failure of the Keynesian Conventional Wisdom', *Lloyds Bank Review*, October.

Eltis, W. (1979) 'How Rapid Public Sector Growth Can Undermine the Growth of the National Product', in W. Beckerman (ed.), *Slow Growth in Britain: Causes and Consequences*, Oxford: Clarendon Press.

Emery, R.F. (1967) 'The Relation of Exports and Economic Growth', *Kyklos*, Fasc. 2.

Englander, S. and Mittelstädt, A. (1988) 'Total Factor Productivity: Macroeconomic and Structural Aspects of the Slowdown', *OECD Economic Studies*, Spring.

EPAC (Office of Economic Planning Advisory Council) (1986a), *International Trade Policy*, Council Paper No. 18, Canberra: AGPS.

EPAC (Office of Economic Planning Advisory Council) (1986b) *External Balance and Growth*, Council Paper No. 22, Canberra: AGPS.

EPAC (Office of Economic Planning Advisory Council) (1989) *External Debt: Trends and Issues*, Discussion Paper 89/06, (Canberra: AGPS).

EPAC (Office of Economic Planning Advisory Council) (1992) *Australia's External Constraint in the 1990s*, Canberra: AGPS.

Evenson, R.E. (1968) 'The Contribution of Agricultural Research and Extension to Agricultural Production', unpublished Ph.D. thesis, University of Chicago.

Fagerberg, J. (1988) 'International Competitiveness', *Economic Journal*, June.

Feder, G. (1983) 'On Exports and Economic Development', *Journal of Development Economics*, February/April.

Feinstein, C.H. (1982) 'Comment on Chapter 8', in Matthews (1982a).

Feinstein, C.H. and Matthews, R.C.O. (1990) 'The Growth of Output and Productivity in the UK: The 1980s as a Phase of the Post-War Period', *National Institute Economic Review*, August.

Feldstein, M. and Horioka, C. (1980) 'Domestic Saving and International Capital Flows', *Economic Journal*, June.

Fetherston, M., Moore, B. and Rhodes, J. (1977) 'Manufacturing Export Shares and Cost Competitiveness of Advanced Industrial Countries', *Economic Policy Review*, March.

Finger, J.M., Hall, H.K. and Nelson, D.R. (1982) 'The Political Economy of Administered Protection' *American Economic Review*, June.

Firn, J.R. (1975) 'External Control and Regional Development: The Case of Scotland', *Environment and Planning*, June.

Fischer, S. (1988) 'Symposium on the Slowdown in Productivity Growth', *Journal of Economic Perspectives*, Fall.

Fisher, F.M. (1966) *A Priori Information and Time-Series Analysis*, Amsterdam: North Holland.

Fisher, F.M. (1971) 'Aggregate Production Functions and the Explanation of Wages: A Simulation Experiment', *Review of Economics and Statistics*, November.

Forbes, A.J. (1991) 'How Useful is the Export-led Growth Hypothesis in Explaining the Differences in Post-War Economic Growth of the Advanced Countries?', unpublished BA dissertation, Faculty of Economics and Politics, University of Cambridge.

Freeman, C. (1965) 'Research and Development in Electronic Capital Goods', *National Institute Economic Review*, November.

Freeman, C. (1979) 'Technical Innovation and British Trade Performance', in Blackaby (1979).

Friedman, M. (1953) 'The Methodology of Positive Economics', in *Essays in Positive Economics*, Chicago: Chicago University Press.

Gabszewicz, J.J. and Thisse, J-F. (1979) 'Price Competition, Quality and Income Disparities', *Journal of Economic Theory*, June.

Giblin, L.F. (1930) *Australia 1930: An Inaugural Lecture*, Melbourne: Melbourne University Press.

Giersch, H. and Wolter, F. (1983) 'Towards an Explanation of the Productivity Slowdown: An Acceleration–Deceleration Hypothesis', *Economic Journal*, March.

Goldstein, M. and Khan, M.S. (1978) 'The Supply and Demand for Exports: A Simultaneous Approach', *Review of Economics and Statistics*, May.

Gomulka, S. (1971) *Inventive Activity, Diffusion, and Stages of Economic Growth*, Aarhus: Aarhus University.

Gomulka, S. (1979), 'Britain's Slow Economic Growth: Increasing Inefficiency Versus Low Rate of Technological Change', in W. Beckerman (ed.), *Slow Growth in Britain: Causes and Consequences*, Oxford: Clarendon Press.

Goodman, B. and Ceyhun, F. (1976) 'U.S. Export Performance in Manufacturing Industries: An Empirical Investigation', *Weltwirtschaftliches Archiv*, September.

Gordon, R.J. (1983) 'Energy Efficiency, User-Cost Change and the Measurement of Durable Goods' Prices', in M.F. Foss (ed), *National Income and Product Accounts*, Studies in Income and Wealth, Chicago: University of Chicago Press.

Greenhalgh, C. (1988) 'Innovation and the Structure of UK Trade 1951–81: An Exploration', *Applied Economics Discussion Paper, No. 63*, Institute of Economics and Statistics, University of Oxford.

Greenhalgh, C. (1990) 'Innovation and Trade Performance in the United Kingdom', *Economic Journal* (supplement).

Griliches, Z. (1973) 'Research Expenditures and Growth Accounting', in B.R. Williams (ed.), *Science and Technology in Economic Growth*, London: Macmillan.

Griliches, Z. (1979) 'Issues in Assessing the Contribution of Research and Development', *Bell Journal of Economics*, Spring.

Griliches, Z. (1988a) 'Productivity Puzzles and R&D: Another Non-Explanation', *Journal of Economic Perspectives*, Fall.

Griliches, Z. (1988b) *Technology, Education and Productivity*, Oxford: Basil Blackwell.

Griliches, Z. and Ringstad, V. (1971) *Economies of Scale and the Form of the Production Function*, Amsterdam: North-Holland.

Grubb, D. (1986) 'Raw Materials, Profits, and the Productivity Slowdown: Some Doubts', *Quarterly Journal of Economics*, February.

Grubel, H.G. and Lloyd, P.J. (1971) 'The Empirical Measurement of Intra-Industry Trade', *Economic Record*, December.

Hadjimatheou, G. and Skouras, A. (1979) 'Britain's Economic Problem: The Growth of the Non-Market Sector? An Interchange', *Economic Journal*, June.

Hall, R.L. and Hitch, C.I. (1939) 'Price Theory and Business Behaviour', *Oxford Economic Papers*, May.

Harcourt, G.C. (1972) *Some Cambridge Controversies in the Theory of Capital*, Cambridge: Cambridge University Press.

Harrod, R. (1933) *International Economics*, Cambridge: Cambridge University Press.

Harrod, R. (1939) 'An Essay in Dynamic Theory', *Economic Journal*, March.

Hart, R.A. and Mackay, O.I. (1977) 'Wage Inflation, Regional Policy and the Regional Earnings Structure', *Economica*, December.

Hazlewood, A. (1975) 'Benefits and Problems of Economic Integration', in A. Hazlewood (ed.), *Economic Integration: The East African Experience*, London: Heinemann.

Hegeland, H. (1954) *Multiplier Theory*, Lund: G.W.K. Gleerup.

Helpman, E. and Krugman, P. (1985) *Market Structure and Foreign Trade: Increasing Returns, Imperfect Competition and the International Economy*, Brighton: Wheatsheaf.

Hibberd, J. and Wren Lewis, S. (1978) *A Study of UK Imports of Manufactures*, Government Economic Service Working Paper No. 6.

Hicks, J. (1950) *The Trade Cycle*, Oxford: Clarendon Press.

Hicks, J. (1990) 'The Unification of Macroeconomics', *Economic Journal*, June.

Hill, T.P. (1971) *The Measurement of Real Product: A Theoretical and Empirical Analysis of the Growth Rates for Different Industries and Countries*, Paris: OECD.

Hill, T.P. and McGibbon, J. (1966) 'Growth of Real Product: Measure and Methods in Selected O.E.C.D. Countries', *Review of Income and Wealth*, March.

Hirsch, S. (1967) *Location of Industry and International Competitiveness*, Oxford: Clarendon Press.

Hirschman, A. (1958) *Strategy of Economic Development*, New Haven: Yale.

Holland, S. (1976) *Capital Versus the Regions*, London: Macmillan.

Houthakker, H. and Magee, S. (1969) 'Income and Price Elasticities in World Trade', *Review of Economics and Statistics*, May.

Hufbauer, G.C. (1970) 'The Impact of National Characteristics and Technology on the Commodity Composition of Trade in Manufactured Goods', in *The Technology Factor in International Trade*, Universities-National Bureau Conference Series, New York.

Hume, D. (1752) 'Of Money', in *Political Discourses*, Edinburgh: A. Kincaid and A. Donaldson.

Hyman, R. and Brough, I. (1975) *Social Values and Industrial Relations*, Oxford: Blackwell.

Ingram, J.C. (1959) 'State and Regional Payments Mechanisms', *Quarterly Journal of Economics*, November.

International Monetary Fund (1985) *International Financial Statistics Yearbook*.

Intriligator, M.D. (1978) *Econometric Models, Techniques and Applications*, Eaglewood Cliffs, NJ: Prentice Hall.

Isard, P. (1977) 'How Far Can We Push the "Law of One Price"?', *American Economic Review*, December.

Ishiyama, Y. (1975) 'The Theory of Optimum Currency Areas: A Survey', *IMF Staff Papers*, July.

Jarvis, V. and Prais, S.J. (1989) 'Two Nations of Shopkeepers: Training for Retailing in France and Britain', *National Institute Economic Review*, May.

Johnson, H.G. (1961) 'The General Theory After Twenty-Five Years', *American Economic Review*, May.

Johnson, H.G. (1966) 'Some Aspects of the Theory of Economic Policy in a World of Capital Mobility', in *Essays in Honour of Marco Fanno*, (ed.) T. Bagiotti, Cedam, Padua.

Johnston, B.F. and Mellor, J.W. (1961) 'The Role of Agriculture in Economic Development', *American Economic Review*, September.

Jones, H.G. (1975) *An Introduction to Modern Theories of Growth*, Sunbury-on-Thames: Nelson.

Jorgenson, D.W. (1969) 'The Role of Agriculture in Economic Development: Classical versus Neo-Classical Models of Growth', in C.R. Wharton (ed.), *Subsistence Agriculture and Economic Development*, Chicago: Aldane.

Jorgenson, D.W. (1981) 'Taxation and Technical Change', in *Technology in Society*, vol. 3, London: Pergamon Press.

Jorgenson, D.W., Gallop, F. and Fraumeni, B. (1987) *Productivity and US Growth*, Cambridge MA: Harvard University Press.

Jorgenson, D.W. and Griliches Z. (1967) 'The Explanation of Productivity Change', *Review of Economic Studies*, July.

Jorgenson, D.W and Griliches, Z. (1972) 'Issues in Growth Accounting: A Reply to Edward F. Denison', *Survey of Current Business*, May.

Junz, H. and Rhomberg, R. (1965) 'Prices and Export Performance of Industrial Countries 1953–1963', *IMF Staff Papers*, July.

Kaldor, N. (1957) 'A Model of Economic Growth', *Economic Journal*, December.

Kaldor, N. (1966a) 'Marginal Productivity and the Macro-Economic Theories of Distribution: Comment on Samuelson and Modigliani', *Review of Economic Studies*, October.

Kaldor, N. (1966b) *Causes of the Slow Rate of Economic Growth of the United Kingdom. An Inaugural Lecture*, Cambridge: Cambridge University Press.

Kaldor, N. (1967) *Strategic Factors in Economic Development*, New York: Ithaca.

Kaldor, N. (1968) 'Productivity and Growth in Manufacturing Industry: A Reply', *Economica*, November.

Kaldor, N. (1970) 'The Case for Regional Policies', *Scottish Journal of Political Economy*, November.

Kaldor, N. (1971) 'Conflicts in National Economic Objectives', *Economic Journal*, March.

Kaldor, N. (1972) 'The Irrelevance of Equilibrium Economics', *Economic Journal*, December.

Kaldor, N. (1974) 'The Road to Recovery', *New Statesman*, 1 March.

Kaldor, N. (1975a) 'What is Wrong with Economic Theory?', *Quarterly Journal of Economics*, August.

Kaldor, N. (1975b) 'Economic Growth and the Verdoorn Law – A Comment on Mr Rowthorn's Article', *Economic Journal*, December.

Kaldor, N. (1976) 'Inflation and Recession in the World Economy', *Economic Journal*, December.

Kaldor, N. (1978a), *Further Essays on Economic Theory*, London: Duckworth.

Kaldor, N. (1978b) *Further Essays on Applied Economics*, London: Duckworth.

Kaldor, N. (1978c) 'The Effects of Devaluation on Trade in Manufactures', in N. Kaldor, *Further Essays on Applied Economics*, London: Duckworth.

Kaldor, N. (1979a) 'Equilibrium Theory and Growth Theory', in M. Baskin (ed.), *Economic and Human Welfare: Essays in Honour of Tibor Skitovsky*, London: Academic Press.

Kaldor, N. (1979b) 'Comment', in Blackaby (1979).

Kaldor, N. (1981) 'Discussion' (of Chatterji and Wickens), in D. Currie, R. Nobay and D. Peel, (eds), *Macroeconomic Analysis: Essays in Macroeconomics and Econometrics*, London: Croom Helm.

Katz, J.M. (1969) *Production Functions, Foreign Investment and Growth*, Amsterdam: North Holland.

Kellman, M. (1983) 'Relative Prices and International Competitiveness: An Empirical Investigation', *Empirical Economics*, September/December.

Kendrick, J.W. (1981) 'International Comparisons of Recent Productivity Trends', in W. Fellner (ed.), *Essays in Contemporary Economic Problems: Demand, Productivity, and Population – 1981–82 Edition*, Washington DC: American Enterprise Institute.

Kendrick, J.W. (ed.) (1984) *International Comparisons of Productivity and Causes of the Slowdown*, Cambridge, MA: Ballinger.

Kennedy, C. and Thirlwall, A.P. (1979) 'Import Penetration, Export Performance and Harrod's Trade Multiplier', *Oxford Economic Papers*, July.

Kennedy, C. and Thirlwall, A.P. (1983) 'Import and Export Ratios and the Dynamic Harrod Trade Multiplier: A Reply to McGregor and Swales', *Oxford Economic Papers*, March.

Kennedy, K.A. (1971) *Productivity and Industrial Growth: The Irish Experience*, Oxford: Clarendon Press.

Kern, D. (1978) 'An International Comparison of Major Economic Trends 1953–76', *National Westminster Bank Quarterly Review*, May.

Keynes, J.M. (1936) *The General Theory of Employment, Interest and Money*, London: Macmillan.

Khan, M. (1974) 'Import and Export Demand in Developing Countries', *I.M.F. Staff Papers*, November.

Kilpatrick A. and Lawson, A. (1980) 'On the Nature of Industial Decline in the UK', *The Cambridge Journal of Economics*, March.

Kindleberger, C.P. (1967) *Europe's Postwar Growth. The Role of the Labor Supply*, Cambridge, Mass: Harvard University Press.

Koutsoyiannis, A. (1982) *Non-price Decisions. The Firm in a Modern Context*, London: Macmillan.

Kravis, I.B. and Lipsey, R.E. (1971) *Price Competitiveness in World Trade*, New York: National Bureau of Economic Research.

Kravis, I.B. and Lipsey, R.E. (1978) 'Price Behaviour in the Light of Balance of Payments Theories', *Journal of International Economics*, February.

Krugman, P (1989) 'Differences in Income Elasticities and Trends in Real Exchange Rates', *European Economic Review*, May.

Kuznets, S. (1951) Comment on 'A Perpetual Inventory of National Wealth since 1896', by R.W. Goldsmith in Conference on Research in Income and Wealth, *Studies in Income in Wealth*, New York: National Bureau of Income and Wealth.

Kuznets, S., assisted by Jenks, E (1961) *Capital in the American Economy*, Princeton University Press for the National Bureau of Economic Research.

Lakatos, I. (1970) 'Falsification and the Methodology of Scientific Research Programmes', in I. Lakatos and A. Musgrave (eds), *Criticism and the Growth of Knowledge*, Cambridge: Cambridge University Press.

Lamfalussy, A. (1961) *Investment and Growth in Mature Economies*, London: Macmillan.

Lamfalussy, A. (1963) *The United Kingdom and the Six: An Essay on Economic Growth in Western Europe*, London: Macmillan.

Lancaster, K.J. (1971) *Consumer Demand: A New Approach*, New York: Columbia University Press.

Lancaster, K.J. (1980) 'Intra-Industry Trade under Perfect Monopolistic Competition', *Journal of International Economics*, May.

Landesmann, M. and Snell, A. (1989) 'The Consequences of Mrs Thatcher for U.K. Manufacturing Exports', *Economic Journal*, March.

Larsen, F., Llewellyn, J. and Potter, S. (1983) 'International Economic Linkages', *OECD Economic Studies*, Autumn.

Lazonick, W. (1978) 'The Division of Labour and Machinery: The Development of British and U.S. Cotton Spinning', *Discussion Paper No. 620*, Cambridge MA: Harvard University.

Leibenstein, H. (1966) 'Allocative Efficiency vs. 'X-Efficiency', *American Economic Review*, June.

Lewis, W.A. (1954) 'Economic Development with Unlimited Supplies of Labour', *The Manchester School*, May.

Lim, G.C. and Shannon, J.H. (1986) *Manufactured Exports and the 1985 Devaluation: Survey Results*, Contributed Paper, Bureau of Industry Economics, Canberra: AGPS.

Lindbeck, A. (1983) 'The Recent Slowdown of Productivity Growth', *Economic Journal*, March.

Lindbeck, A. and Snower, D.J. (1986) 'Wage Setting, Unemployment, and Insider-Outsider Relations', *American Economic Review*, (Supplement), May.

Lindbeck, A. and Snower, D.J. (1987) 'Unemployment Activity, Unemployment Persistence and Wage-Employment Ratchets', *European Economic Review*, February/March.

Linder, S.B. (1961) *An Essay on Trade and Transformation*, New York: John Wiley.

Lipsey, R.G. (1970) *The Theory of Customs Unions: A General Equilibrium Analysis*, London: Weidenfeld & Nicolson.

Llewellyn, G.E.J. (1983) 'Resource Prices and Macroeconomic Policies: Lessons from Two Oil Price Shocks', *OECD Economic Studies*, Autumn.

Lucas, R.E. (1988) 'On the Mechanics of Economic Development', *Journal of Monetary Economics*, July.

McClosky, D. and Zecher, R. (1976) 'How the Gold Standard Worked: 1880–1913', in J.A. Frenkel and H.G. Johnson (eds), *The Monetary Approach to the Balance of Payments*, London: Allen & Unwin.

McCombie, J.S.L. (1980) 'On the Quantitative Importance of Kaldor's Laws', *Bulletin of Economic Research*, November.

McCombie, J.S.L. (1981a) 'What Still Remains of Kaldor's Laws?', *Economic Journal*, March.

McCombie, J.S.L. (1981b) 'Are International Growth Rates Constrained by the Balance of Payments? A Comment on Professor Thirlwall', *Banca Nazionale del Lavoro Quarterly Review*, December.

McCombie, J.S.L. (1982a) 'Economic Growth, Kaldor's Laws and the Static-Dynamic Verdoorn Law Paradox', *Applied Economics*, June.

McCombie, J.S.L. (1982b) 'How Important is the Spatial Diffusion of Innovations in Explaining Regional Growth Disparities?', *Urban Studies*, November.

McCombie, J.S.L. (1982c) 'Post-War Productivity and Output Growth of the Advanced Countries', Unpublished Ph.D. thesis, University of Cambridge.

McCombie, J.S.L. (1983) 'Kaldor's Laws in Retrospect', *Journal of Post Keynesian Economics*, Spring.

McCombie, J.S.L. (1985a) 'Economic Growth, the Harrod Foreign Trade Multiplier and the Hicks Super-Multiplier', *Applied Economics*, February.

McCombie, J.S.L. (1985b) 'Increasing Returns and the Manufacturing Industries: Some Empirical Issues', *The Manchester School*, March.

McCombie, J.S.L. (1985–6) 'Why Cutting Real Wages Will Not Neccesarily Reduce Unemployment – Keynes and the "Postulates of the Classical Economics"', *Journal of Post Keynesian Economics*, Winter.

McCombie, J.S.L., (1986) 'On Some Interpretations of the Relationship Between Productivity and Output Growth', *Applied Economics*, November.

McCombie, J.S.L. (1987) 'Does the Aggregate Production Function Imply Anything About the Laws of Production? A Note on the Simon and Shaikh Critiques', *Applied Economics*, August, [Errata (1988) *Applied Economics*, June].

McCombie, J.S.L. (1988) 'A Synoptic View of Regional Growth and Unemployment: II – The Post-Keynesian Theory', *Urban Studies*, October.

McCombie, J.S.L. (1989) '"Thirlwall's Law" and Balance of Payments Constrained Growth – A Comment on the Debate', *Applied Economics*, May.

McCombie. J.S.L. (1990) Review of M. FG. Scott, *A New View of Econ-*

omic Growth (Oxford: Clarendon Press, 1989), *Economic Journal*, March.

McCombie, J.S.L. (1991) 'The Productivity Growth Slowdown of the Advanced Countries and the Intersectoral Transfer of Labour', *Australian Economic Papers*, March.

McCombie, J.S.L. (1992) '"Thirlwall's Law" and Balance of Payments Constrained Growth: More on the Debate', *Applied Economics,* May.

McCombie, J.S.L. (1993) 'Economic Growth, Trade Interlinkages and the Balance of Payments Constraint', *Journal of Post Keynesian Economics*, (Summer).

McCombie, J.S.L. and de Ridder, J.R. (1983) 'Increasing Returns, Productivity and Output Growth: The Case of the United States', *Journal of Post Keynesian Economics*, Spring.

McCombie, J.S.L. and de Ridder, J.R. (1984) 'The Verdoorn Law Controversy: Some New Evidence Using US State Data', *Oxford Economic Papers*, June.

McCombie, J.S.L. and Dixon, R.J. (1991) 'Estimating Technical Change in Aggregate Production Functions: A Critique', *International Review of Applied Economics*, January.

McCraken, P., Carol, G., Giersch, H., Karaosmanoglu, A., Komiya, R., Lindbeck, A., Marjolin, R. and Matthews, R. (1977) *Towards Full Employment and Price Stability*, Paris: OECD.

McCrone, G. (1969a) *Regional Policy in Britain*, University of Glasgow Social and Economic Studies, London: George Allen & Unwin.

McCrone, G. (1969b) 'Regional Policy in the European Communities', in G.R. Denton (ed.), *Economic Integration in Europe*, London: Weidenfeld & Nicolson.

McGregor, P.G. and Swales, J.K. (1985) 'Professor Thirlwall and Balance of Payments Constrained Growth', *Applied Economics*, February.

McGregor, P.G. and Swales, J.K. (1986) 'Balance of Payments Constrained Growth: A Rejoinder to Professor Thirlwall', *Applied Economics*, December.

McGregor, P.G. and Swales, J.K. (1991) 'Thirlwall's Law and Balance of Payments Constrained Growth: Further Comment on the Debate', *Applied Economics*, February.

Machlup, F. (1967) 'Theories of the Firm: Marginalist, Behavioural, Managerial', *American Economic Review*, March.

McLachlan, H.V. and Swales, J.K. (1982) 'Friedman's Methodology: A Comment on Boland', *Journal of Economic Studies*, no. 1.

McPherson, C. (1972) *Tariff Structures and Political Exchanges*, Ph.D. Thesis, University of Chicago.

Maddala, G.S. (1977) *Econometrics*, Tokyo: McGraw Hill.

Maddison, A. (1970) *Economic Progress and Policy in Developing Countries*, London: Allen & Unwin.

Maddison, A. (1972) 'Explaining Economic Growth', *Banca Nazionale del Lavoro Quarterly Review*, September.

Maddison, A. (1982) *Phases of Capitalist Development*, Oxford: Oxford University Press.

Maddison, A. (1984) 'Comparative Analysis of the Productivity Situation in the Advanced Capitalist Countries', in J.W. Kendrick (ed.), *International Comparisons of Productivity and Causes of the Slowdown*, Cambridge, Mass: Ballinger.

Maddison, A. (1987) 'Growth and Slowdown in Advanced Capitalist Economies: Techniques of Quantitative Assessment', *Journal of Economic Literature*, June.

Marin, D. (1990) 'Is the Export-Led Growth Hypothesis Valid for Industrialised Countries?', *CEPR Discussion Paper Series, No. 362.*

Marris, R. (1982) 'How Much of the Slowdown was Catch-up?', in Matthews (1982a).

Matthews, R.C.O. (1968) 'Why has Britain had Full Employment since the War?', *Economic Journal*, September.

Matthews, R.C.O. (1973) 'The Contribution of Science and Technology to Economic Development', in B.R. Williams (ed.), *Science and Technology in Economic Growth*, London: Macmillan.

Matthews, R.C.O. (ed.) (1982a) *Slower Growth in the Western World*, London: Heinemann.

Matthews, R.C.O. (1982b) 'Introduction: A Summary View', in R.C.O. Matthews (ed.), *Slower Growth in the Western World*, London: Heinemann.

Matthews, R.C.O. and Bowen, A. (1988) 'Keynesian and Other Explanations of Post-War Macroeconomic Trends', in W. Eltis and P. Sinclair (eds), *Keynes and Economic Policy. The Relevance of The General Theory after Fifty Years*, London: Macmillan in association with the National Economic Development Office.

Matthews, R.C.O., Feinstein, C.H. and Odling-Smee, J.C. (1982) *British Economic Growth 1856–1973*, Oxford: Clarendon Press.

Mayes, D., Buxton, T. and Murfin, A. (1988) 'R&D Innovation and Trade Performance', NEDO, unpublished.

Meade, J.E. (1981) 'Note on the Inflationary Implications of the Wage-Fixing Assumption of the Cambridge Economic Policy Group', *Oxford Economic Papers*, March.

Mendershausen, H. (1938) 'On the Significance of Professor Douglas' Production Function', *Econometrica*, April.

Mendes, A.J. Marques (1987) *Economic Integration and Growth in Europe*, London: Croom Helm.

Mendes, A.J. Marques (1990) 'Economic Cohesion in Europe', *Journal of Common Market Studies*, September.

Michl, T.R. (1985) 'International Comparisons of Productivity Growth: Verdoorn's Law Revisited', *Journal of Post Keynesian Economics*, Summer.

Miller, E.M. (1983) 'Capital Aggregation in the Presence of Obsolescence-Inducing Technical Change', *Review of Income and Wealth*, September.

Miller, N.C. and Whitman, M.V.N. (1970) 'A Mean-Variance Analysis of United States Long-Term Portfolio Foreign Investment', *Quarterly Journal of Economics*, May.

Morgan, A. (1970) 'Income and Price Elasticities in World Trade: A Comment', *The Manchester School*, December.

Morgan, V.E. (1973) 'Regional Problems and Common Currencies', *Lloyds Bank Review*, October.

Moroney, J.R. (1975) 'Natural Resource Endowments and Comparative Labour Costs: A Hybrid Model of Comparative Advantage', *Journal of Regional Science*, August.

Moroney, J.R. and Walker, J.M. (1966) 'A Regional Test of the Heckscher-Ohlin Hypothesis', *Journal of Political Economy*, December.

Morris, D.J. (1983) 'Comment on the Paper by Professor Lindbeck', *Economic Journal*, March.

Myrdal, G. (1957) *Economic Theory and Underdeveloped Regions*, London: Duckworth.

NEDC (1965) *Imported Manufactures*, London: HMSO.

NEDC (1963) *Export Trends*, London: HMSO.

NEDO (1965) *Survey of Investment in Machine Tools*, London: HMSO.

Nelson, R.R. (1981) 'Research on Productivity Growth and Productivity Differences: Dead Ends and New Departures', *Journal of Economic Literature*, September.

Nevin, E. (1972) 'Europe and the Regions', *The Three Banks Review*, June.

Norcliffe, G.B. and Stevens, J.H. (1979) 'The Heckscher-Ohlin Hypothesis and Structural Divergence in Quebec and Ontario, 1961–65', *Canadian Geographer*, Fall.

Norsworthy, J.R. (1984) 'Growth Accounting and Productivity Measurement', *Review of Income and Wealth*, September.

Norton, W.E. and Aylmer, C.P. (1988) *Australian Economic Statistics. 1949–50 to 1986–87: 1 Tables*, Occasional Paper No. 8A. (Reserve Bank of Australia).

Oi, W.Y. (1962) 'Labor as a Quasi-Fixed Factor of Production', *Journal of Political Economy*, (Supplement), June.

Olson, M. (1965) *The Logic of Collective Action: Public Goods and the Theory of Groups*, Cambridge, Mass: Harvard University Press.

Olson, M. (1982) *The Rise and Decline of Nations: Economic Growth, Stagflation and Social Rigidities*, New Haven, CT: Yale University Press.

Olson, M. (1988) 'The Productivity Slowdown, the Oil Shocks, and the Real Cycle', *Journal of Economic Perspectives*, Fall.

Oulton, N. (1992) 'Depreciation, Obsolescence and the Role of Capital in Growth Accounting: A Comment on Scott's "Policy Implications of 'A New View of Economic Growth'"' , National Institute of Economic and Social Research, (mimeo).

Panić, M. (1975) 'Why the UK's Propensity to Import is so High', *Lloyds Bank Review,* January.

Parikh, A. (1978) 'Differences in Growth Rates and Kaldor's Laws', *Economica*, February.

Patel, P. and Pavitt, K. (1987) 'The Elements of British Technological Competitiveness', *National Institute Economic Review*, November.

Patel, P. and Pavitt, K. (1989) 'A Comparison of Technological Activities in West Germany and the United Kingdom', *National Westminster Bank Review*, May.

Pavitt, K. (ed.) (1980) *Technical Innovation and British Economic Performance*, London: Macmillan.

Pavitt, K. and Soete, L. (1980) 'Innovative Activities and Export Shares: Some Comparisons Between Industries and Countries', in Pavitt (1980).

Pearce, I.F. (1973) 'Some Aspect of European Monetary Integration', in H. Johnson and R. Nobay (eds), *Issues in Monetary Economics*, London: Croom Helm.

Perraton, J. (1990) 'The Harrod Trade Multiplier and the Developing Countries, 1970–1984: An Examination of the Thirlwall Hypothesis', *University of Nottingham* (mimeo.)

Phelps Brown, E.H. (1957) 'The Meaning of the Fitted Cobb–Douglas Function', *Quarterly Journal of Economics*, November.

Posner, M.V. (1961) 'International Trade and Technical Change', *Oxford Economic Papers*, October.

Posner, M.V. and Steer, A. (1979) 'Price Competitiveness and the Performance of Manufacturing Industry', in Blackaby (1979).

Prais, S.J. (1981) *Productivity and Industrial Structure*, Cambridge: Cambridge University Press.

Prais, S.J. (1983) 'Comment on the Paper by Professor Giersch and Dr Wolter', *Economic Journal*, March.

Prais S.J. and Steedman, H. (1986) 'Vocational Training in France and Britain: The Building Trades', *National Institute Economic Review*, May.

Prais S.J. and Steedman, H. (1987) 'Vocational Training in France and Britain: Office Work', *National Institute Economic Review*, May.

Prais S.J. and Steedman, H. (1988) 'Vocational Training in France and Britain: Mechanical and Electrical Craftsmen', *National Institute Economic Review*, November.

Prais, S.J and Wagner, K. (1983) 'Some Practical Aspects of Human Capital Investment: Training Standards in Five Occupations in Britain and Germany', *National Institute Economic Review*, August.

Prais, S.J. and Wagner, K. (1985) 'Schooling Standards in England and Germany: Some Summary Comparisons Bearing on Economic Performance', *National Institute Economic Review*, May.

Prebisch, R. (1950) *The Economic Development of Latin America and its Principal Problems*, New York: ECLA, UN.

Pryor, T.L. (1983) 'A Quasi-Test of Olson's Hypothesis', in D.C. Mueller, *The Political Economy of Growth*, New Haven: Yale University Press.

Quiggin, J. (1989) 'The Role and Consequences of Special Interest Groups and Political Factors', in B. Chapman (ed.), *Australian Economic Growth: Essays in Honour of Fred H. Gruen*, Melbourne: Macmillan.

Ram, R. (1986) 'Government Size and Economic Growth: A New Framework and Some Evidence from Cross-Section and Time-Series Data', *American Economic Review*, March.

Rao, V.V.B. (1989) 'Government Size and Economic Growth: A New Framework and Some Evidence from Cross-Section and Time-Series Data: Comment', *American Economic Review*, March.

Rees, A. (1980) 'Improving Productivity Measurement', *American Economic Review*, May.

Richardson, H. (1973) *Regional Growth Theory*, London: Macmillan.

Robson, R. (1980) *The Economics of International Integration*, London: Allen & Unwin.

Romer, P.M. (1986) 'Increasing Returns and Long-Run Growth', *Journal of Political Economy*, October.

Romer, P.M. (1987a) 'Growth Based on Increasing Returns due to Specialisation', *American Economic Review*, May.

590   *References*

Romer, P.M. (1987b) 'Crazy Explanations for the Productivity Slowdown',
NBER Macroeconomics Annual 1987, Cambridge, Mass: MIT Press.

Rowthorn, R.E. (1975a) 'What Remains of Kaldor's Law?', *Economic Journal*, March.

Rowthorn, R.E. (1975b) 'A Reply to Lord Kaldor's Comment', *Economic Journal*, December.

Rowthorn, R.E. (1979) 'A Note on Verdoorn's Law', *Economic Journal*, March.

Rowthorn, R.E. and Wells, J.R. (1987) *Deindustrialisation and Foreign Trade*, Cambridge: Cambridge University Press.

Salter, W.E.G. (1966) *Productivity and Technical Change* (2nd edition with addendum by W.B. Reddaway), Department of Applied Economics, University of Cambridge, Monograph 6, Cambridge University Press.

Sato, R. (1963) 'Fiscal Policy in a Neo-classical Growth Model: An Analysis of Time Required for Equilibrating Adjustment', *Review of Economic Studies*, February.

Saunders, P. (1985) 'Public Expenditure and Economic Performance in OECD Countries', *Journal of Public Policy*, February.

Sawyer, M.C. (1982) *Macroeconomics in Question, The Keynesian-Monetarist Orthodoxies and the Kaleckian Alternative*, Brighton: Wheatsheaf.

Schmookler, J. (1966) *Invention and Economic Growth*, Cambridge, MA: Harvard University Press.

Schott, K. (1984) 'The Simple Economics of Price and Quality Competition in International Trade', *Department of Political Economy, University College, London, Discussion Paper 1984–02*.

Schott, K. and Pick, K. (1984) 'The Effects of Price and Non-Price Factors on U.K. Export Performance and Import Penetration', *Department of Political Economy, University of London, Discussion Paper, 84–01*.

Schultz, T.W. (1961) 'Investment in Human Capital', *American Economic Review*, March.

Scott, M. FG. (1976) 'Investment and Growth', *Oxford Economic Papers*, November.

Scott, M. FG. (1981) 'The Contribution of Investment to Growth', *Scottish Journal of Political Economy*, November.

Scott, M. FG. (1986) 'Explaining Economic Growth', 1986 Keynes Lecture, *Proceedings of the British Academy*, vol. 72.

Scott, M. FG. (1989) *A New View of Economic Growth*, Oxford: Clarendon Press.

Scott, M. FG. (1990) 'Extended Accounts for National Income and Product: A Comment', *Journal of Economic Literature*, September.

Scott, M. FG. (1991a) *A New View of Economic Growth. Four Lectures*, World Bank Discussion Paper, No. 131.

Scott, M. FG. (1991b) 'A Reply to Denison', *Oxford Economic Papers*, April.

Scott, M. FG. (1991c) 'Obsolescence and the Analysis of Economic Growth', *Nuffield College, Oxford, Discussion Papers in Economics, No. 59*.

Scott, M. FG. (1992a) 'Policy Implications of "A New View of Economic Growth"', *Economic Journal*, May.

Scott, M. FG. (1992b) 'Depreciation, Obsolescence and the Role of Capital in Growth Accounting: A Reply to Oulton', *mimeo*, Nuffield College, Oxford.

Seers, D. (1962) 'A Model of Comparative Rates of Growth of the World Economy', *Economic Journal*, March.

Senghaas, D. (1985) *The European Experience. A Historical Critique of Development Theory*, Leamington Spa/Dover, New Hampshire: Berg Publishers.

Severn, A.K. (1968) 'Exports and Economic Growth: Comment', *Kyklos*, Fasc. 3.

Shackle, G.S.L. (1967) *The Years of High Theory*, Cambridge: Cambridge University Press.

Shaikh, A. (1974) 'Laws of Production and Laws of Algebra: The Humbug Production Function', *Review of Economics and Statistics*, February.

Shaikh, A. (1980) 'Laws of Production and Laws of Algebra: Humbug II', in E.J. Nell (ed.),*Growth, Profits and Property. Essays in the Revival of Political Economy*, Cambridge: Cambridge University Press.

Shaikh, A (1987) 'The Humbug Production Function', in J. Eatwell, M. Milgate and P. Newman (eds),*The New Palgrave: A Dictionary of Economics*, London: Macmillan.

Shaked, A. and Sutton, J. (1982) 'Relaxing Price Competition Through Product Differentiation', *Review of Economic Studies*, January.

Shann, E. (1982) 'Policy Issues in Mineral Sector Growth: A Keynesian Model', *Discussion Paper No. 60*, Centre for Economic Policy Research, Canberra: Australian National University.

Shaw, G.K. (1992) 'Policy Implications of Endogenous Growth Theory', *Economic Journal*, May.

Simon, H.A. (1979) 'On Parsimonious Explanations of Production Relations', *Scandinavian Journal of Economics*, December.

Simon, H.A. and Levy, F.K. (1963) 'A Note on the Cobb–Douglas Production Function', *Review of Economic Studies*, June.

Singer H.W. and Reynolds, L. (1975) 'Technological Backwardness and Productivity Growth', *Economic Journal*, December.

Singh, A. (1977) 'UK Industry and the World Economy: A Case of De-industrialisation?', *Cambridge Journal of Economics*, June.

Sleeper, R. (1970) 'Manpower Redeployment and the Selective Employment Tax', *Bulletin of the Oxford Institute of Economics and Statistics*, November.

Smith, A. (1776) *Inquiry into the Nature and Causes of the Wealth of Nations*, London: Strahan & Caddell.

Smith, B. (1975) 'Regional Specialisation and Trade in the United Kingdom', *Scottish Journal of Political Economy*, February.

Smith, D. (1975) 'Public Consumption and Economic Performance', *National Westminster Bank Review*, November.

Smith, M. (1986) 'U.K. Manufacturing: Output and Trade Performance', *Midland Bank Review*, Autumn.

Smith, R.P (1976) 'Demand Management and the "New School"', *Applied Economics*, September.

Soete, L. (1981) 'A General Test of Technological Gap Trade Theory', *Weltwirtschaftlichen Archiv*, December.

Solow, R. (1956) 'A Contribution to the Theory of Economic Growth', *Quarterly Journal of Economics*, February.

Solow, R.M. (1957) 'Technical Change and the Aggregate Production Function', *Review of Economics and Statistics*, August.

Solow, R.M. (1970) *Growth Theory: An Exposition*, Oxford: Clarendon Press.

Solow, R.M. (1974) 'Laws of Production and Laws of Algebra: The Humbug Production Function: A Comment', *Review of Economic Statistics*, February.

Solow, R.M. (1988) 'Growth Theory and After', *American Economic Review*, August.

Stafford, B. (1989) 'Deindustrialisation in Advanced Economies', *Cambridge Journal of Economics*, December.

Stern, N. (1991) 'The Determinants of Growth', *Economic Journal*, May.

Stern, R.M., Francis, J. and Schumacher, B. (1976) *Price Elasticities in International Trade*, London: Macmillan.

Stewart, M. (1983) *Controlling the Economic Future. Policy Dilemmas in a Shrinking World*, Brighton: Wheatsheaf.

Stigler, G.J. (1974) 'Free Riders and Collective Action: An Appendix to Theories of Economic Reputation', *Bell Journal of Economics and Management Science*, Autumn.

Stockwin, J.A.A. (1981) 'Comparative Politics' in P. Drysdale and H. Kitaoji (eds), *Japan and Australia: Two Societies and their Interaction*, Canberra: Australian National University Press.

Stoneman, P. (1979) 'Kaldor's Law and British Economic Growth, 1800–1972', *Applied Economics*, September.

Stout, D. (1977) *International Price Competitiveness, Non Price Factors and Export Performance*, London: National Economic Development Office.

Stout, D. (1979) 'De-industrialisation and Industrial Policy', in Blackaby (1979).

Swales, J.K. (1979) 'Relative Factor Prices and Regional Specialisation in the U.K.', *Scottish Journal of Political Economy*, June.

Swales, J.K. (1983) 'A Kaldorian Model of Cumulative Causation: Regional Growth with Induced Technical Change', in A. Gillespie (ed.), *Technical Change and Regional Development*, London: Pion Limited.

Swan, T. (1956) 'Economic Growth and Capital Accumulation', *Economic Record*, November.

Swords-Isherwood, N. (1980) 'British Management Compared', in K. Pavitt (ed.), *Technical Innovation and British Economic Performance*, London: Macmillan.

Syron, R.F. and Walsh, B.M. (1968) 'The Relation of Exports and Economic Growth: A Note', *Kyklos*, Fasc. 3.

Thirlwall, A.P. (1969) 'Okun's Law and the Natural Rate of Growth', *Southern Economic Journal*, July.

Thirlwall, A.P. (1970) 'Regional Phillips Curves', *Bulletin of the Oxford Institute of Economics and Statistics*, February.

Thirlwall, A.P. (1974) 'Regional Economic Disparities and Regional Policy in the Common Market', *Urban Studies*, February.

Thirlwall, A.P. (1978) 'The UK's Economic Problem: A Balance of Payments Constraint?', *National Westminster Bank Quarterly Review*, February.

Thirlwall, A.P. (1979) 'The Balance of Payments Constraint as an Explanation of International Growth Rate Differences', *Banca Nazionale del Lavoro Quarterly Review*, March.

Thirlwall, A.P. (1980a) 'Rowthorn's Interpretation of Verdoorn's Law', *Economic Journal*, June.

Thirlwall, A.P. (1980b) 'Regional Problems are "Balance-of-Payments" Problems', *Regional Studies*, 5.

Thirlwall, A.P. (1980c) *Balance-of-Payments Theory and the United Kingdom Experience* (first edition; fourth edition with H.D. Gibson (1992)),London: Macmillan.

Thirlwall, A.P. (1981) 'A Reply to Mr. McCombie', *Banca Nazionale del Lavoro Quarterly Review*, December.

Thirlwall, A.P. (1982a) 'The Harrod Trade Multiplier and the Importance of Export Led Growth', *Pakistan Journal of Applied Economics*, March.

Thirlwall, A.P. (1982b) 'Deindustrialisation in the U.K.', *Lloyds Bank Review*, April.

Thirlwall, A.P. (1983) 'Foreign Trade Elasticities in Centre-Periphery Models of Growth and Development', *Banca Nazionale del Lavoro Quarterly Review*, September.

Thirlwall, A.P. (1986a) 'A General Model of Growth and Development on Kaldorian Lines', *Oxford Economic Papers*, July.

Thirlwall, A.P. (1986b) 'Balance of Payments Constrained Growth: A Reply to McGregor and Swales', *Applied Economics*, December.

Thirlwall, A.P. (1987) *Nicholas Kaldor*, Brighton: Wheatsheaf Press.

Thirlwall, A.P. (1988) *Growth and Development: With Special Reference to Developing Economies*, 4th edn, London: Macmillan.

Thirlwall, A.P. (1991) 'The Terms of Trade of Primary Commodities, Debt, and Development', in P.A. Davidson and J. Kregel (eds), *Economic Problems of the 1990s*, Aldershot: Edward Elgar.

Thirlwall, A.P. and Dixon, R.J. (1979) 'A Model of Export-Led Growth with a Balance of Payments Constraint', in *Inflation, Development and Integration*, J.K. Bowers (ed.), Leeds: Leeds University Press.

Thirlwall, A.P. and Nureldin Hussain, M. (1982) 'The Balance of Payments Constraint, Capital Flows and Growth Rate Differences Between Developing Countries', *Oxford Economic Papers*, November.

Tovias, A. (1982) 'Testing Factor Price Equalisation in the EEC', *Journal of Common Market Studies*, June.

Treasury, The, *Economic Round-up* (monthly),Canberra: AGPS.

Triffin, R. (1964) *The Evaluation of the International Monetary System: Historical Reappraisal and Future Perspectives*, Princeton Studies in International Finance, No. 18, June.

Triffin, R. (1978) *Gold and Dollar Crisis: Yesterday and Tomorrow*, Essays in International Finance No. 132, Princeton University, December.

Trizise, P.H. (1983) 'Industrial Policy is Not the Major Reason for Japan's Success', *The Brookings Review*, Spring.

Turner, D. (1988) 'Does the U.K. Face a Balance of Payments Constraint on Growth? – A Quantitative Analysis Using the LBS and NIESR Models', *ESRC Macroeconomic Modelling Bureau*, University of Warwick, September.

Usher, D.(1980a) *The Measurement of Economic Growth*, Oxford: Basil Blackwell.

Usher, D. (ed.) (1980b) *The Measurement of Capital*, Studies in Income and Wealth, Vol 45, National Bureau of Economic Research, Conference on Research in Income and Wealth, Chicago: University of Chicago Press.

Van der Wee, H. (1987) *Prosperity and Upheaval. The World Economy, 1945–1980*, Middlesex: Penguin Books.

Vanderkamp, J. (1970) 'The Effect of Outmigration on Regional Employment', *Canadian Journal of Economics*, November.

Verdoorn, P.J. (1949) 'Fattori che Regolano lo Sviluppo della Produttivita del Lavoro', *L'Industria*. Translated by A.P. Thirlwall in D. Ironmonger, J. Perkins and T. Hoa (eds) (1988), *National Income and Economic Progress: Essays in Honour of Colin Clark*, London: Macmillan.

Verdoorn, P.J. (1980) 'Verdoorn's Law in Retrospect: A Comment', *Economic Journal*, June.

Vernon, R. (1966) 'International Investment and International Trade in the Product Cycle', *Quarterly Journal of Economics*, May.

Vernon, R. (ed.) (1970) *The Technology Factor in International Trade*, New York: Columbia University Press.

Walters, A.A. (1963) 'Production and Cost Functions: An Econometric Survey', *Econometrica*, January/April.

Ward, M. (1976) *The Measurement of Capital. The Methodology of Capital Stock Estimates in OECD Countries*, Paris: OECD.

Weddeburn, D. and Crompton, R. (1972) *Workers' Attitudes to Technology*, Cambridge: Cambridge University Press.

Wells, J.T. (1969) 'Test of a Product Cycle Model of International Trade: U.S. Exports of Consumer Durables', *Quarterly Journal of Economics*, February.

Wells, J.T. (1972) 'International Trade: The Product Life Cycle Approach', in *The Product Life Cycle and International Trade*, Cambridge, Mass: Harvard University Press.

Whitely, J. *et al.* (1992) 'UK Policies, Non-Price Competitiveness and Convergence to an EMU – An Inter-Model Comparison' *ESRC Macroeconomic Modelling Bureau*, University of Warwick, (mimeo), February.

Williamson, J. (1976) 'The Implications of European Monetary Integration for the Peripheral Areas', in J. Vaizey (ed.), *Economic Sovereignty and Regional Policy*, London: Macmillan.

Williamson, J. (1983) *The Open Economy and the World Economy: A Textbook in International Economics*, New York: Basic Books.

Williamson, J. (1984) 'Is There an External Constraint?', *National Institute Economic Review*, August.

Wilson, T. (1976) 'Effective Devaluation and Inflation', *Oxford Economic Papers*, March.

Winters, L.A. (1980) *An Econometric Model of the Export Sector. UK Visible Exports and Their Prices, 1955–1973*, Cambridge: Cambridge University Press.

Winters, L.A. (1985) *International Economics*, 3rd edn, London: George Allen & Unwin.

Wold, H. and Faxer, R. (1957) 'On the Specification Error in Regression Analysis', *Annals of Mathematical Statistics*, March.

Wolf, J. (1912) *Die Volkswirtschaft der Gegenwart und Zukunft*, Leipzig: Deichert.

Woolley, P. (1974) 'Integration of Capital Markets', in G.R. Denton (ed.), *Economic and Monetary Union in Europe*, London: Croom Helm.

Wrage, P. (1981) 'The Effects of Internal Migration on Regional Wage and Unemployment Disparities in Canada', *Journal of Regional Science*, February.

Yannopoulos, G. (1984) 'The Spatial Distribution of the Effects of Economic Integration Schemes', *University of Reading Discussion Papers in Economics, No. 156*.

Young, A. (1928) 'Increasing Returns and Economic Progress', *Economic Journal*, December.

Name Index

Abramovitz, M. xxviii, 24, 84, 86, 154
Allen, P. 492, 502
Anderson, F. 496
Anderson, K. 87, 537
Anderson, R. 349–50
Anyadike-Danes, M. 400
Armington, P.S. 266
Arrow, K.J. 39, 168, 556
Aylmer, C.P. 539

Bacon, R. xxviii, 3, 103–19
Bailey, M.N. 61
Bairam, E. 255–6, 390
  and balance-of-payments equilibrium
    growth 192, 232, 242, 243
  on Thirlwall's Law 363, 364, 365,
    368–70, 382
Balassa, B. 301
  export-led growth 195, 427
  income elasticity of demand for
    exports 373–4, 375, 377, 378–9,
    380, 385–7, 566
Ball, R.J. 236, 306
Barber, A. 109
Barker, T.S. 264, 284, 305
Barret Whale, P. xvii, 124
Baumol, W.J. 45, 46, 47
Beckerman, W. 37, 78, 195, 421,
  425–6, 427, 428, 568, 571
Black, J. 209, 211, 556
Blackaby, F. 278
Blaug, M. 20, 93, 381
Boltho, A. 84, 552
Bosworth, B. 17
Bowen, A. 14, 15
Bowles, S. 83–4
Brain, P. 543, 545, 546–7, 548–9
Bray, J. 528
Brech, M.J. 275, 276–7, 380
Brittan, S. xxv
Brough, I. 496
Brown, C.J.F. 532
Brown, R.N. 305–6
Bruno, M. 57
Burridge, P. 571
Buxton, T. 279

Cable, V. 499
Caldwell, B.J. 94, 383

Caves, R. 87, 426, 428
Ceyhun, F. 280
Chamberlin, E.H. 560
Chatterji, M. 192, 197, 198–9, 558
Choi, K. 85–6
Chung, W.K. 29, 553
Church, K.B. 527
Clark, C. 168
Clark, G.L. 497
Cobb, C.W. 20, 21–2, 45, 47, 553
Connell, D. 273–5, 350, 352, 564
Cooper, R.N. 123
Coppock, J.O. 9, 10
Cornwall, J. 45, 48, 50, 342, 350, 427
  demand constrained growth 195, 196
  differential growth 240, 241, 424
  on slow growth 428–9
  surplus labour hypothesis 36, 156,
    157, 158, 160, 162–3, 219, 337, 382
Coutts, K. 264, 306
Crafts, N.F.R. 301, 385–7
Cramer, J.S. 555
Creamer, D. 59–60
Cripps, T.F. 49, 187, 223, 338, 451
  agricultural output 36, 159, 219
  GDP growth 11, 14, 166
  productivity and output growth 7–8
  Verdoorn's Law 171, 172, 177,
    181–2
Crompton, R. 496
Cuthbertson, K. 400, 402

Daly, A. 74–7
Davies, R. 264, 284
De Long, B. 46
de Ridder, J.R. 175, 180, 197, 200,
  203, 207, 210
Dempster, G. 255–6, 363, 364
Denison, E.F. xxviii, 28–9, 32, 51,
  93–4
  differential growth 24–5, 232
  growth accounting approach 26–7,
    38, 72
  intersectoral transfer of labour 36–7
  labour input 27, 32, 382
  on R & D 39, 42, 44
  on residual 26, 553–4
  returns to scale 33–5, 554
  on Scott's *New View* 130, 131–2,

Subject Index

601